D0775479

# Windows PowerShell™ 3.0 Step by Step

Ed Wilson

Published with the authorization of Microsoft Corporation by:
O'Reilly Media, Inc.
1005 Gravenstein Highway North
Sebastopol, California 95472

Copyright © 2013 by Ed Wilson
All rights reserved. No part of the contents of this book may be reproduced or transmitted in any form or by any means without the written permission of the publisher.

ISBN: 978-0-735-66339-8

2 3 4 5 6 7 8 9 10  LSI  8 7 6 5 4 3

Printed and bound in the United States of America.

Microsoft Press books are available through booksellers and distributors worldwide. If you need support related to this book, email Microsoft Press Book Support at mspinput@microsoft.com. Please tell us what you think of this book at *http://www.microsoft.com/learning/booksurvey*.

Microsoft and the trademarks listed at *http://www.microsoft.com/about/legal/en/us/IntellectualProperty/ Trademarks/EN-US.aspx* are trademarks of the Microsoft group of companies.  All other marks are property of their respective owners.

The example companies, organizations, products, domain names, email addresses, logos, people, places, and events depicted herein are fictitious. No association with any real company, organization, product, domain name, email address, logo, person, place, or event is intended or should be inferred.

This book expresses the author's views and opinions. The information contained in this book is provided without any express, statutory, or implied warranties. Neither the author, O'Reilly Media, Inc., Microsoft Corporation, nor its resellers, or distributors will be held liable for any damages caused or alleged to be caused either directly or indirectly by this book.

**Acquisitions and Developmental Editor:** Michael Bolinger

**Production Editor:** Kristen Borg

**Editorial Production:** Zyg Group, LLC

**Technical Reviewer:** Thomas Lee

**Copyeditor:** Zyg Group, LLC

**Indexer:** Zyg Group, LLC

**Cover Design:** Twist Creative • Seattle

**Cover Composition:** Zyg Group, LLC

**Illustrators:** Rebecca Demarest and Robert Romano

[2013-04-19]

*To Teresa, who makes each day seem fresh with opportunity and new with excitement.*

# Contents at a Glance

# Contents

---

**What do you think of this book? We want to hear from you!**

Microsoft is interested in hearing your feedback so we can continually improve our
books and learning resources for you. To participate in a brief online survey, please visit:

**microsoft.com/learning/booksurvey**

## Chapter 17 Deploying Active Directory with Windows Server 2012    447

## Chapter 18 Debugging Scripts    461

## What do you think of this book? We want to hear from you!

Microsoft is interested in hearing your feedback so we can continually improve our
books and learning resources for you. To participate in a brief online survey, please visit:

### microsoft.com/learning/booksurvey

# Foreword

I've always known that automation was a critical IT Pro skill. Automation dramatically increases both productivity and quality of IT operations; it is a transformational skill that improves both the companies and the careers of the individuals that master it. Improving IT Pro automation was my top priority when I joined Microsoft in 1999 as the Architect for management products and technologies. That led to inventing Windows PowerShell and the long hard road to making it a centerpiece of the Microsoft management story. Along the way, the industry made some dramatic shifts. These shifts make it even more critical for IT Pros to become experts of automation.

During the development of PowerShell V1, the team developed a very strong partnership with Exchange. We thought Exchange would drive industry adoption of PowerShell. You can imagine our surprise (and delight) when we discovered that the most active PowerShell V1 community was VMWare customers. I reached out to the VMWare team to find out why it was so successful with their customers. They explained to me that their customers were IT Pros that were barely keeping up with the servers they had. When they adopted virtualization, they suddenly had 5-10 times the number of servers so it was either "automate or drown." Their hair was on fire and PowerShell was a bucket of water.

The move to the cloud is another shift that increases the importance of automation. The entire DevOps movement is all about making change safe through changes in culture and automation. When you run cloud scale applications, you can't afford to have it all depend upon a smart guy with a cup of coffee and a mouse—you need to automate operations with scripts and workflows. When you read the failure reports of the biggest cloud outages, you see that the root cause is often manual configuration. When you have automation and an error occurs, you review the scripts and modify them to it doesn't happen again. With automation, Nietzsche was right: that which does not kill you strengthens you. It is no surprise that Azure has supported PowerShell for some time, but I was delighted to see that Amazon just released 587 cmdlets to manage AWS.

Learning automation with PowerShell is a critical IT Pro skill and there are few people better qualified to help you do that than Ed Wilson. Ed Wilson is the husband of The Scripting Wife and the man behind the wildly popular blog The Scripting Guy. It is no exaggeration to say that Ed and his wife Teresa are two of the most active people in the PowerShell community. Ed is known for his practical "how to" approach to PowerShell. Having worked with so many customers and people learning PowerShell, Ed knows what questions you are going to have even before you have them and has taken the time to lay it all out for you in his new book: Windows PowerShell 3.0 Step by Step.

—*Jeffrey Snover, Distinguished Engineer and Lead Architect, Microsoft Windows*

# Introduction

Windows PowerShell 3.0 is an essential management and automation tool that brings the simplicity of the command line to next generation operating systems. Included in Windows 8 and Windows Server 2012, and portable to Windows 7 and Windows Server 2008 R2, Windows PowerShell 3.0 offers unprecedented power and flexibility to everyone from power users to enterprise network administrators and architects.

## Who should read this book

This book exists to help IT Pros come up to speed quickly on the exciting Windows PowerShell 3.0 technology. *Windows PowerShell 3.0 Step by Step* is specifically aimed at several audiences, including:

- **Windows networking consultants** Anyone desiring to standardize and to automate the installation and configuration of dot-net networking components.

- **Windows network administrators** Anyone desiring to automate the day-to-day management of Windows dot net networks.

- **Microsoft Certified Solutions Experts (MCSEs) and Microsoft Certified Trainers (MCTs)** Windows PowerShell is a key component of many Microsoft courses and certification exams.

- **General technical staff** Anyone desiring to collect information, configure settings on Windows machines.

- **Power users** Anyone wishing to obtain maximum power and configurability of their Windows machines either at home or in an unmanaged desktop workplace environment.

## Assumptions

This book expects that you are familiar with the Windows operating system, and therefore basic networking terms are not explained in detail. The book does not expect you to have any background in programming, development, or scripting. All elements related to these topics, as they arise, are fully explained.

## Who should not read this book

Not every book is aimed at every possible audience. This is not a Windows PowerShell 3.0 reference book, and therefore extremely deep, esoteric topics are not covered. While some advanced topics are covered, in general the discussion starts with beginner topics and proceeds through an intermediate depth. If you have never seen a computer, nor have any idea what a keyboard or a mouse are, then this book definitely is not for you.

## Organization of this book

This book is divided into three sections, each of which focuses on a different aspect or technology within the Windows PowerShell world. The first section provides a quick overview of Windows PowerShell and its fundamental role in Windows Management. It then delves into the details of Windows PowerShell remoting. The second section covers the basics of Windows PowerShell scripting. The last portion of the book covers different management technology and discusses specific applications such as Active Directory and Exchange.

### Finding your best starting point in this book

The different sections of *Windows PowerShell 3.0 Step by Step* cover a wide range of technologies associated with the data library. Depending on your needs and your existing understanding of Microsoft data tools, you may wish to focus on specific areas of the book. Use the following table to determine how best to proceed through the book.

| If you are | Follow these steps |
|---|---|
| New to Windows PowerShell | Focus on Chapters 1–3 and 5–9, or read through the entire book in order. |
| An IT pro who knows the basics of Windows PowerShell and only needs to learn how to manage network resources | Briefly skim Chapters 1–3 if you need a refresher on the core concepts. Read up on the new technologies in Chapters 4 and 10–14. |
| Interested in Active Directory and Exchange | Read Chapters 15–17 and 20. |
| Interested in Windows PowerShell Scripting | Read Chapters 5–8, 18, and 19. |

Most of the book's chapters include hands-on samples that let you try out the concepts just learned.

# Conventions and features in this book

This book presents information using conventions designed to make the information readable and easy to follow.

- Each chapter concludes with two exercises.

- Each exercise consists of a series of tasks, presented as numbered steps (1, 2, and so on) listing each action you must take to complete the exercise.

- Boxed elements with labels such as "Note" provide additional information or alternative methods for completing a step successfully.

- Text that you type (apart from code blocks) appears in bold.

- A plus sign (+) between two key names means that you must press those keys at the same time. For example, "Press Alt+Tab" means that you hold down the Alt key while you press the Tab key.

- A vertical bar between two or more menu items (e.g. File | Close), means that you should select the first menu or menu item, then the next, and so on.

# System requirements

You will need the following hardware and software to complete the practice exercises in this book:

- One of the following: Windows 7, Windows Server 2008 with Service Pack 2, Windows Server 2008 R2, Windows 8 or Windows Server 2012.

- Computer that has a 1.6GHz or faster processor (2GHz recommended)

- 1 GB (32 Bit) or 2 GB (64 Bit) RAM (Add 512 MB if running in a virtual machine or SQL Server Express Editions, more for advanced SQL Server editions)

- 3.5 GB of available hard disk space

- 5400 RPM hard disk drive

- DirectX 9 capable video card running at 1024 × 768 or higher-resolution display

- DVD-ROM drive (if installing Visual Studio from DVD)

- Internet connection to download software or chapter examples

Depending on your Windows configuration, you might require Local Administrator rights to install or configure Visual Studio 2010 and SQL Server 2008 products.

## Code samples

Most of the chapters in this book include exercises that let you interactively try out new material learned in the main text. All sample projects, in both their pre-exercise and post-exercise formats, can be downloaded from the following page:

*http://aka.ms/PowerShellSBS_book*

Follow the instructions to download the scripts.zip file.

> **Note** In addition to the code samples, your system should have Windows PowerShell 3.0 installed.

### Installing the code samples

Follow these steps to install the code samples on your computer so that you can use them with the exercises in this book.

1. After you download the scripts.zip file, make sure you unblock it by right-clicking on the scripts.zip file, and then clicking on the Unblock button on the property sheet.

2. Unzip the scripts.zip file that you downloaded from the book's website (name a specific directory along with directions to create it, if necessary).

## Acknowledgments

I'd like to thank the following people: my agent Claudette Moore, because without her this book would never have come to pass. My editors Devon Musgrave and Michael Bolinger for turning the book into something resembling English, and my technical reviewer Thomas Lee whose attention to detail definitely ensured a much better book. Lastly I want to acknowledge my wife Teresa (aka the Scripting Wife) who read every page and made numerous suggestions that will be of great benefit to beginning scripters.

## Errata and book support

We've made every effort to ensure the accuracy of this book and its companion content. Any errors that have been reported since this book was published are listed on our Microsoft Press site at *oreilly.com:*

> *http://go.microsoft.com/FWLink/?Linkid=275530*

If you find an error that is not already listed, you can report it to us through the same page.

If you need additional support, email Microsoft Press Book Support at *mspinput@microsoft.com.*

Please note that product support for Microsoft software is not offered through the addresses above.

## We want to hear from you

At Microsoft Press, your satisfaction is our top priority, and your feedback our most valuable asset. Please tell us what you think of this book at:

> *http://www.microsoft.com/learning/booksurvey*

The survey is short, and we read every one of your comments and ideas. Thanks in advance for your input!

## Stay in touch

Let's keep the conversation going! We're on Twitter: *http://twitter.com/MicrosoftPress*

# Overview of Windows PowerShell 3.0

**After completing this chapter, you will be able to:**

- Understand basic use and capabilities of Windows PowerShell.

- Install Windows PowerShell.

- Use basic command-line utilities inside Windows PowerShell.

- Use Windows PowerShell help.

- Run basic Windows PowerShell cmdlets.

- Get help on basic Windows PowerShell cmdlets.

- Configure Windows PowerShell to run scripts.

The release of Microsoft Windows PowerShell 3.0 marks a significant advance for the Windows network administrator. Combining the power of a full-fledged scripting language with access to command-line utilities, Windows Management Instrumentation (WMI), and even VBScript, Windows PowerShell provides the power and ease of use that have been missing from the Windows platform since the beginning of time. As part of the Microsoft Common Engineering Criteria, Windows PowerShell is quickly becoming the management solution for the Windows platform. IT professionals using the Windows Server 2012 core installation must come to grips with Windows PowerShell sooner rather than later.

## Understanding Windows PowerShell

Perhaps the biggest obstacle for a Windows network administrator in migrating to Windows PowerShell 3.0 is understanding what PowerShell actually is. In some respects, it is a replacement for the venerable CMD (command) shell. In fact, on Windows Server 2012 running in core mode, it is possible to replace the CMD shell with Windows PowerShell so that when the server boots up, it uses Windows PowerShell as the interface. As shown here, after Windows PowerShell launches, you can use *cd* to change the working directory, and then use *dir* to produce a directory listing in exactly the same way you would perform these tasks from the CMD shell.

```
Windows PowerShell
Copyright (C) 2012 Microsoft Corporation. All rights reserved.

PS C:\Users\administrator> cd c:\
PS C:\> dir


    Directory: C:\


Mode                LastWriteTime     Length Name
----                -------------     ------ ----
d----        3/22/2012    4:03 AM            PerfLogs
d-r--        3/22/2012    4:24 AM            Program Files
d-r--        3/23/2012    6:02 PM            Users
d----        3/23/2012    4:59 PM            Windows
-a---        3/22/2012    4:33 AM         24 autoexec.bat
-a---        3/22/2012    4:33 AM         10 config.sys


PS C:\>
```

You can also combine traditional CMD interpreter commands with some of the newer utilities, such as *fsutil*. This is shown here:

```
PS C:\> md c:\test


    Directory: C:\


Mode                LastWriteTime     Length Name
----                -------------     ------ ----
d----        4/22/2012    5:01 PM            test


PS C:\> fsutil file createnew C:\test\mynewfile.txt 1000
File C:\test\mynewfile.txt is created
PS C:\> cd c:\test
PS C:\test> dir


    Directory: C:\test


Mode                LastWriteTime     Length Name
----                -------------     ------ ----
-a---        4/22/2012    5:01 PM       1000 mynewfile.txt


PS C:\test>
```

The preceding two examples show Windows PowerShell being used in an interactive manner. Interactivity is one of the primary features of Windows PowerShell, and you can begin to use Windows PowerShell interactively by opening a Windows PowerShell prompt and typing commands. You can enter the commands one at a time, or you can group them together like a batch file. I will discuss this later because you will need more information to understand it.

## Using cmdlets

In addition to using Windows console applications and built-in commands, you can also use the *cmdlets* (pronounced *commandlets*) that are built into Windows PowerShell. Cmdlets can be created by anyone. The Windows PowerShell team creates the core cmdlets, but many other teams at Microsoft were involved in creating the hundreds of cmdlets shipping with Windows 8. They are like executable programs, but they take advantage of the facilities built into Windows PowerShell, and therefore are easy to write. They are not scripts, which are uncompiled code, because they are built using the services of a special .NET Framework namespace. Windows PowerShell 3.0 comes with about 1,000 cmdlets on Windows 8, and as additional features and roles are added, so are additional cmdlets. These cmdlets are designed to assist the network administrator or consultant to leverage the power of Windows PowerShell without having to learn a scripting language. One of the strengths of Windows PowerShell is that cmdlets use a standard naming convention that follows a verb-noun pattern, such as *Get-Help*, *Get-EventLog*, or *Get-Process*. The cmdlets using the *get* verb display information about the item on the right side of the dash. The cmdlets that use the *set* verb modify or set information about the item on the right side of the dash. An example of a cmdlet that uses the *set* verb is *Set-Service*, which can be used to change the start mode of a service. All cmdlets use one of the standard verbs. To find all of the standard verbs, you can use the *Get-Verb* cmdlet. In Windows PowerShell 3.0, there are nearly 100 approved verbs.

## Installing Windows PowerShell

Windows PowerShell 3.0 comes with Windows 8 Client and Windows Server 2012. You can download the Windows Management Framework 3.0 package containing updated versions of Windows Remote Management (WinRM), WMI, and Windows PowerShell 3.0 from the Microsoft Download center. Because Windows 8 and Windows Server 2012 come with Windows PowerShell 3.0, there is no Windows Management Framework 3.0 package available for download—it is not needed. In order to install Windows Management Framework 3.0 on Windows 7, Windows Server 2008 R2, and Windows Server 2008, they all must be running at least Service Pack (SP) 1 and the Microsoft .NET Framework 4.0. There is no package for Windows Vista, Windows Server 2003, or earlier versions of the operating system. You can run both Windows PowerShell 3.0 and Windows PowerShell 2.0 on the same system, but this requires both the .NET Framework 3.5 and 4.0.

To prevent frustration during the installation, it makes sense to use a script that checks for the operating system, service pack level, and .NET Framework 4.0. A sample script that will check for the prerequisites is Get-PowerShellRequirements.ps1, which follows.

```
Get-PowerShellRequirements.ps1
Param([string[]]$computer = @($env:computername, "LocalHost"))
 foreach ($c in $computer)
   {
     $o = Get-WmiObject win32_operatingsystem -cn $c
     switch ($o.version)
     {
         {$o.version -gt 6.2} {"$c is Windows 8 or greater"; break}
         {$o.version -gt 6.1}
           {
            If($o.ServicePackMajorVersion -gt 0){$sp = $true}
            If(Get-WmiObject Win32_Product -cn $c |
               where { $_.name -match '.NET Framework 4'}) {$net = $true }
            If($sp -AND $net) { "$c meets the requirements for PowerShell 3" ; break}
            ElseIF (!$sp) {"$c needs a service pack"; break}
            ELSEIF (!$net) {"$c needs a .NET Framework upgrade"} ; break}
         {$o.version -lt 6.1} {"$c does not meet standards for PowerShell 3.0"; break}
         Default {"Unable to tell if $c meets the standards for PowerShell 3.0"}
     }

   }
```

# Deploying Windows PowerShell to down-level operating systems

After Windows PowerShell is downloaded from *http://www.microsoft.com/downloads*, you can deploy it to your enterprise by using any of the standard methods. Here are few of the methods that you can use to accomplish Windows PowerShell deployment:

- Create a Microsoft Systems Center Configuration Manager package and advertise it to the appropriate organizational unit (OU) or collection.

- Create a Group Policy Object (GPO) in Active Directory Domain Services (AD DS) and link it to the appropriate OU.

- Approve the update in Software Update Services (SUS) when available.

- Add the Windows Management Framework 3.0 packages to a central file share or webpage for self service.

If you are not deploying to an entire enterprise, perhaps the easiest way to install Windows PowerShell is to download the package and step through the wizard.

> **Note** To use a command-line utility in Windows PowerShell, launch Windows PowerShell by choosing Start | Run | PowerShell. At the PowerShell prompt, type in the command to run.

# Using command-line utilities

As mentioned earlier, command-line utilities can be used directly within Windows PowerShell. The advantages of using command-line utilities in Windows PowerShell, as opposed to simply running them in the CMD interpreter, are the Windows PowerShell pipelining and formatting features. Additionally, if you have batch files or CMD files that already use existing command-line utilities, you can easily modify them to run within the Windows PowerShell environment. The following procedure illustrates adding *ipconfig* commands to a text file.

## Running *ipconfig* commands

1. Start Windows PowerShell by choosing Start | Run | Windows PowerShell. The PowerShell prompt will open by default at the root of your Documents folder.

2. Enter the command **ipconfig /all**. This is shown here:

   ```
   PS C:\> ipconfig /all
   ```

3. Pipe the result of *ipconfig /all* to a text file. This is illustrated here:

   ```
   PS C:\> ipconfig /all >ipconfig.txt
   ```

4. Open Notepad to view the contents of the text file, as follows:

   ```
   PS C:\> notepad ipconfig.txt
   ```

Typing a single command into Windows PowerShell is useful, but at times you may need more than one command to provide troubleshooting information or configuration details to assist with setup issues or performance problems. This is where Windows PowerShell really shines. In the past, you would have either had to write a batch file or type the commands manually. This is shown in the TroubleShoot.bat script that follows.

**TroubleShoot.bat**

```
ipconfig /all >C:\tshoot.txt
route print >>C:\tshoot.txt
hostname >>C:\tshoot.txt
net statistics workstation >>C:\tshoot.txt
```

Of course, if you typed the commands manually, then you had to wait for each command to complete before entering the subsequent command. In that case, it was always possible to lose your place in the command sequence, or to have to wait for the result of each command. Windows PowerShell eliminates this problem. You can now enter multiple commands on a single line, and then leave the computer or perform other tasks while the computer produces the output. No batch file needs to be written to achieve this capability.

> **Tip** Use multiple commands on a single Windows PowerShell line. Type each complete command, and then use a semicolon to separate each command.

The following exercise describes how to run multiple commands. The commands used in the procedure are in the RunningMultipleCommands.txt file.

### Running multiple commands

1. Open Windows PowerShell by choosing Start | Run | Windows PowerShell. The PowerShell prompt will open by default at the root of your Documents And Settings folder.

2. Enter the **ipconfig /all** command. Pipe the output to a text file called Tshoot.txt by using the redirection arrow (>). This is the result:

   ```
   ipconfig /all >tshoot.txt
   ```

3. On the same line, use a semicolon to separate the *ipconfig /all* command from the *route print* command. Append the output from the command to a text file called Tshoot.txt by using the redirect-and-append arrow (>>). Here is the command so far:

   ```
   ipconfig /all >tshoot.txt; route print >>tshoot.txt
   ```

4. On the same line, use a semicolon to separate the *route print* command from the *hostname* command. Append the output from the command to a text file called Tshoot.txt by using the redirect-and-append arrow. The command up to this point is shown here:

   ```
   ipconfig /all >tshoot.txt; route print >>tshoot.txt; hostname >>tshoot
   .txt
   ```

5. On the same line, use a semicolon to separate the *hostname* command from the *net statistics workstation* command. Append the output from the command to a text file called Tshoot.txt by using the redirect-and-append arrow. The completed command looks like the following:

   ```
   ipconfig /all >tshoot.txt; route print >>tshoot.txt; netdiag /q >>tshoot
   .txt; net statistics workstation >>tshoot.txt
   ```

# Security issues with Windows PowerShell

As with any tool as versatile as Windows PowerShell, there are bound to be some security concerns. Security, however, was one of the design goals in the development of Windows PowerShell.

When you launch Windows PowerShell, it opens in your Documents folder; this ensures you are in a directory where you will have permission to perform certain actions and activities. This is far safer than opening at the root of the drive, or even opening in system root.

To change to a directory in the Windows PowerShell console, you cannot automatically go up to the next level; you must explicitly name the destination of the change-directory operation (although you can use the *cd ..* command to move up one level).

The running of scripts is disabled by default and can be easily managed through group policy. It can also be managed on a per-user or per-session basis.

# Controlling execution of PowerShell cmdlets

Have you ever opened a CMD interpreter prompt, typed in a command, and pressed Enter so that you could see what it does? What if that command happened to be *Format C:\*? Are you sure you want to format your C drive? This section will cover some arguments that can be supplied to cmdlets that allow you to control the way they execute. Although not all cmdlets support these arguments, most of those included with Windows PowerShell do. The three arguments you can use to control execution are *-whatif*, *-confirm*, and suspend. *Suspend* is not really an argument that is supplied to a cmdlet, but rather is an action you can take at a confirmation prompt, and is therefore another method of controlling execution.

> **Note** To use *-whatif* at a Windows PowerShell prompt, enter the cmdlet. Type the **-whatif** parameter after the cmdlet. This only works for cmdlets that change system state. Therefore, there is no *-whatif* parameter for cmdlets like *Get-Process* that only display information.

Windows PowerShell cmdlets that change system state (such as *Set-Service*) support a *prototype mode* that you can enter by using the *-whatif* parameter. The developer decides to implement *-whatif* when developing the cmdlet; however, the Windows PowerShell team recommends that developers implement *-whatif*. The use of the *-whatif* argument is shown in the following procedure. The commands used in the procedure are in the UsingWhatif.txt file.

### Using *-whatif* to prototype a command

1. Open Windows PowerShell by choosing Start | Run | Windows PowerShell. The PowerShell prompt will open by default at the root of your Documents And Settings folder.

2. Start an instance of Notepad.exe. Do this by typing **notepad** and pressing the Enter key. This is shown here:

   ```
   notepad
   ```

3. Identify the Notepad process you just started by using the *Get-Process* cmdlet. Type enough of the process name to identify it, and then use a wildcard asterisk (*) to avoid typing the entire name of the process, as follows:

   ```
   Get-Process note*
   ```

4. Examine the output from the *Get-Process* cmdlet and identify the process ID. The output on my machine is shown here. Please note that in all likelihood, the process ID used by your instance of Notepad.exe will be different from the one on my machine.

```
Handles  NPM(K)    PM(K)     WS(K) VM(M)   CPU(s)     Id ProcessName
-------  ------    -----     ----- -----   ------     -- -----------
     39       2      944       400    29     0.05   1056 notepad
```

5. Use *-whatif* to see what would happen if you used *Stop-Process* to stop the process ID you obtained in step 4. This process ID will be found under the Id column in your output. Use the *-id* parameter to identify the Notepad.exe process. The command is as follows:

```
Stop-Process -id 1056 -whatif
```

6. Examine the output from the command. It tells you that the command will stop the Notepad process with the process ID that you used in your command.

```
What if: Performing operation "Stop-Process" on Target "notepad (1056)"
```

## Confirming actions

As described in the previous section, you can use *-whatif* to prototype a cmdlet in Windows PowerShell. This is useful for seeing what a cmdlet would do; however, if you want to be prompted before the execution of the cmdlet, you can use the *-confirm* argument. The cmdlets used in the "Confirming the execution of cmdlets" procedure are listed in the ConfirmingExecutionOfCmdlets.txt file.

### Confirming the execution of cmdlets

1. Open Windows PowerShell, start an instance of Notepad.exe, identify the process, and examine the output, just as in steps 1 through 4 in the previous exercise.

2. Use the *-confirm* argument to force a prompt when using the *Stop-Process* cmdlet to stop the Notepad process identified by the *Get-Process note** command. This is shown here:

```
Stop-Process -id 1768 -confirm
```

The *Stop-Process* cmdlet, when used with the *-confirm* argument, displays the following confirmation prompt:

```
Confirm
Are you sure you want to perform this action?
Performing operation "Stop-Process" on Target "notepad (1768)".
[Y] Yes  [A] Yes to All  [N] No  [L] No to All  [S] Suspend  [?] Help
(default is "Y"):
```

3. Type **y** and press Enter. The Notepad.exe process ends. The Windows PowerShell prompt returns to the default, ready for new commands, as shown here:

```
PS C:\>
```

> **Tip** To suspend cmdlet confirmation, at the confirmation prompt from the cmdlet, type **s** and press Enter.

## Suspending confirmation of cmdlets

The ability to prompt for confirmation of the execution of a cmdlet is extremely useful and at times may be vital to assisting in maintaining a high level of system uptime. There may be times when you type in a long command and then remember that you need to check on something else first. For example, you may be in the middle of stopping a number of processes, but you need to view details on the processes to ensure you do not stop the wrong one. For such eventualities, you can tell the confirmation you would like to suspend execution of the command. The commands used for suspending execution of a cmdlet are in the SuspendConfirmationOfCmdlets.txt file.

### Suspending execution of a cmdlet

1. Open Windows PowerShell, start an instance of Notepad.exe, identify the process, and examine the output, just as in steps 1 through 4 in the previous exercise. The output on my machine is shown following. Please note that in all likelihood, the process ID used by your instance of Notepad.exe will be different from the one on my machine.

```
Handles  NPM(K)    PM(K)      WS(K) VM(M)   CPU(s)    Id ProcessName
-------  ------    -----      ----- -----   ------    -- -----------
     39       2      944        400    29     0.05  3576 notepad
```

2. Use the *-confirm* argument to force a prompt when using the *Stop-Process* cmdlet to stop the Notepad process identified by the *Get-Process note** command. This is illustrated here:

```
Stop-Process -id 3576 -confirm
```

The *Stop-Process* cmdlet, when used with the *-confirm* argument, displays the following confirmation prompt:

```
Confirm
Are you sure you want to perform this action?
Performing operation "Stop-Process" on Target "notepad (3576)".
[Y] Yes  [A] Yes to All  [N] No  [L] No to All  [S] Suspend  [?] Help
(default is "Y"):
```

3. To suspend execution of the *Stop-Process* cmdlet, enter **s**. A triple-arrow prompt will appear, as follows:

```
PS C:\>>>
```

4. Use the *Get-Process* cmdlet to obtain a list of all the running processes that begin with the letter *n*. The syntax is as follows:

**Get-Process** n*

On my machine, two processes appear. The Notepad process I launched earlier and another process. This is shown here:

```
Handles  NPM(K)    PM(K)     WS(K) VM(M)   CPU(s)     Id ProcessName
-------  ------    -----     ----- -----   ------     -- -----------
     39       2      944       400    29     0.05   3576 notepad
     75       2     1776      2708    23     0.09    632 nvsvc32
```

5. Return to the previous confirmation prompt by typing **exit**.

Once again, the confirmation prompt appears as follows:

```
Confirm
Are you sure you want to perform this action?
Performing operation "Stop-Process" on Target "notepad (3576)".
[Y] Yes  [A] Yes to All  [N] No  [L] No to All  [S] Suspend  [?] Help
(default is "Y"):
```

6. Type **y** and press Enter to stop the Notepad process. There is no further confirmation. The prompt now displays the default Windows PowerShell prompt, as shown here:

```
PS C:\>
```

# Working with Windows PowerShell

This section will go into detail about how to access Windows PowerShell and configure the Windows PowerShell console.

## Accessing Windows PowerShell

After Windows PowerShell is installed on a down-level system, it becomes available for immediate use. However, using the Windows flag key on the keyboard and pressing R to bring up a *run* command prompt—or mousing around and choosing Start | Run | Windows PowerShell all the time—will become time-consuming and tedious. (This is not quite as big a problem on Windows 8, where you can just type **PowerShell** on the Start screen). On Windows 8, I pin both Windows PowerShell and the PowerShell ISE to both the Start screen and the taskbar. On Windows Server 2012 in core mode, I replace the CMD prompt with the Windows PowerShell console. For me and the way I work, this is ideal, so I wrote a script to do it. This script can be called through a log-on script to automatically deploy the shortcut on the desktop. On Windows 8, the script adds both the Windows PowerShell ISE and the Windows PowerShell console to both the Start screen and the taskbar. On Windows 7, it adds both to the taskbar and to the Start menu. The script only works for U.S. English–language operating systems. To make it work in other languages, change the value of *$pinToStart* or *$pinToTaskBar* to the equivalent values in the target language.

> **Note** Using Windows PowerShell scripts is covered in Chapter 5, "Using PowerShell Scripts." See that chapter for information about how the script works and how to actually run the script.

The script is called PinToStartAndTaskBar.ps1, and is as follows:

**PinToStartAndTaskBar.ps1**

```
$pinToStart = "Pin to Start"
$pinToTaskBar = "Pin to Taskbar"
$file = @((Join-Path -Path $PSHOME  -childpath "PowerShell.exe"),
          (Join-Path -Path $PSHOME  -childpath "powershell_ise.exe") )
Foreach($f in $file)
 {$path = Split-Path $f
  $shell=New-Object -com "Shell.Application"
  $folder=$shell.Namespace($path)
  $item = $folder.parsename((Split-Path $f -leaf))
  $verbs = $item.verbs()
  foreach($v in $verbs)
    {if($v.Name.Replace("&","") -match $pinToStart){$v.DoIt()}}
  foreach($v in $verbs)
    {if($v.Name.Replace("&","") -match $pinToTaskBar){$v.DoIt()}} }
```

# Configuring the Windows PowerShell console

Many items can be configured for Windows PowerShell. These items can be stored in a Psconsole file. To export the console configuration file, use the *Export-Console* cmdlet, as shown here:

```
PS C:\> Export-Console myconsole
```

The Psconsole file is saved in the current directory by default and has an extension of .psc1. The Psconsole file is saved in XML format. A generic console file is shown here:

```
<?xml version="1.0" encoding="utf-8"?>
<PSConsoleFile ConsoleSchemaVersion="1.0">
  <PSVersion>3.0</PSVersion>
  <PSSnapIns />
</PSConsoleFile>
```

## Controlling PowerShell launch options

1. Launch Windows PowerShell without the banner by using the *-nologo* argument. This is shown here:

   ```
   PowerShell -nologo
   ```

2. Launch a specific version of Windows PowerShell by using the *-version* argument. (To launch Windows PowerShell 2.0, you must install the .NET Framework 3.5). This is shown here:

```
PowerShell -version 2
```

3. Launch Windows PowerShell using a specific configuration file by specifying the *-psconsolefile* argument, as follows:

```
PowerShell -psconsolefile myconsole.psc1
```

4. Launch Windows PowerShell, execute a specific command, and then exit by using the *-command* argument. The command itself must be prefixed by an ampersand (&) and enclosed in curly brackets. This is shown here:

```
Powershell -command "& {Get-Process}"
```

# Supplying options for cmdlets

One of the useful features of Windows PowerShell is the standardization of the syntax in working with cmdlets. This vastly simplifies the learning of the new shell and language. Table 1-1 lists the common parameters. Keep in mind that some cmdlets cannot implement some of these parameters. However, if these parameters are used, they will be interpreted in the same manner for all cmdlets, because the Windows PowerShell engine itself interprets the parameters.

**TABLE 1-1** Common parameters

| Parameter | Meaning |
| --- | --- |
| *-whatif* | Tells the cmdlet to not execute, but to tell you what would happen if the cmdlet were to run. |
| *-confirm* | Tells the cmdlet to prompt before executing the command. |
| *-verbose* | Instructs the cmdlet to provide a higher level of detail than a cmdlet not using the verbose parameter. |
| *-debug* | Instructs the cmdlet to provide debugging information. |
| *-ErrorAction* | Instructs the cmdlet to perform a certain action when an error occurs. Allowed actions are *continue*, *stop*, *silently-Continue*, and *inquire*. |
| *-ErrorVariable* | Instructs the cmdlet to use a specific variable to hold error information. This is in addition to the standard $error variable. |
| *-OutVariable* | Instructs the cmdlet to use a specific variable to hold the output information. |
| *-OutBuffer* | Instructs the cmdlet to hold a certain number of objects before calling the next cmdlet in the pipeline. |

> **Note** To get help on any cmdlet, use the *Get-Help <cmdletname>* cmdlet. For example, use *Get-Help Get-Process* to obtain help with using the *Get-Process* cmdlet.

## Working with the help options

One of the first commands to run when opening Windows PowerShell for the first time is the *Update-Help* cmdlet. This is because Windows PowerShell does not ship help files with the product. This does not mean that no help presents itself—it does mean that help beyond simple syntax display requires an additional download.

A default installation of Windows PowerShell 3.0 contains numerous modules that vary from installation to installation depending upon the operating system features and roles selected. In fact, Windows PowerShell 3.0 installed on Windows 7 workstations contains far fewer modules and cmdlets than are available on a similar Windows 8 workstation. This does not mean all is chaos, however, because the essential Windows PowerShell cmdlets—the *core* cmdlets—remain unchanged from installation to installation. The difference between installations is because additional features and roles often install additional Windows PowerShell modules and cmdlets.

The modular nature of Windows PowerShell requires additional consideration when updating help. Simply running *Update-Help* does not update all of the modules loaded on a particular system. In fact, some modules may not support updatable help at all—these generate an error when you attempt to update help. The easiest way to ensure you update all possible help is to use both the *module* parameter and the *force* switched parameter. The command to update help for all installed modules (that support updatable help) is shown here:

```
Update-Help -Module * -Force
```

The result of running the *Update-Help* cmdlet on a typical Windows 8 client system is shown in Figure 1-1.

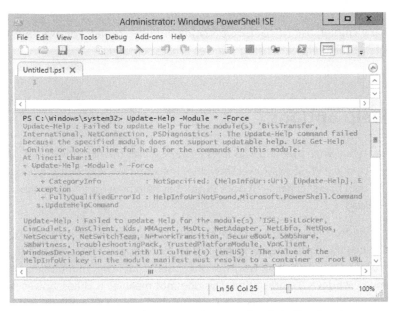

**FIGURE 1-1** Errors appear when attempting to update help files that do not support updatable help.

One way to update help and not to receive a screen full of error messages is to run the *Update-Help* cmdlet and suppress the errors all together. This technique appears here:

```
Update-Help -Module * -Force -ea 0
```

The problem with this approach is that you can never be certain that you have actually received updated help for everything you wanted to update. A better approach is to hide the errors during the update process, but also to display errors after the update completes. The advantage to this approach is the ability to display cleaner errors. The UpdateHelpTrackErrors.ps1 script illustrates this technique. The first thing the UpdateHelpTrackErrors.ps1 script does is to empty the error stack by calling the *clear* method. Next, it calls the *Update-Help* module with both the *module* parameter and the *force* switched parameter. In addition, it uses the *ErrorAction* parameter (*ea* is an alias for this parameter) with a value of 0. A 0 value means that errors will not be displayed when the command runs. The script concludes by using a *For* loop to walk through the errors and displays the error exceptions. The complete UpdateHelpTrackErrors.ps1 script appears here.

> **Note** For information about writing Windows PowerShell scripts and about using the *For* loop, see Chapter 5.

```
UpdateHelpTrackErrors.ps1
$error.Clear()
Update-Help -Module * -Force -ea 0
For ($i = 0 ; $i -lt $error.Count ; $i ++)
  { "`nerror $i" ; $error[$i].exception }
```

Once the UpdateHelpTrackErrors script runs, a progress bar displays indicating the progress as the updatable help files update. Once the script completes, any errors appear in order. The script and associated errors appear in Figure 1-2.

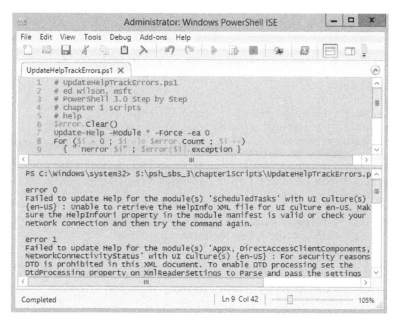

**FIGURE 1-2** Cleaner error output from updatable help generated by the UpdateHelpTrackErrors script.

You can also determine which modules receive updated help by running the *Update-Help* cmdlet with the *-verbose* parameter. Unfortunately, when you do this, the output scrolls by so fast that it is hard to see what has actually updated. To solve this problem, redirect the verbose output to a text file. In the command that follows, all modules attempt to update *help*. The verbose messages redirect to a text file named updatedhelp.txt in a folder named fso off the root.

```
Update-Help -module * -force -verbose 4>>c:\fso\updatedhelp.txt
```

Windows PowerShell has a high level of discoverability; that is, to learn how to use PowerShell, you can simply use PowerShell. Online help serves an important role in assisting in this discoverability. The help system in Windows PowerShell can be entered by several methods. To learn about using Windows PowerShell, use the *Get-Help* cmdlet as follows:

```
Get-Help Get-Help
```

This command prints out help about the *Get-Help* cmdlet. The output from this cmdlet is illustrated here:

NAME
    **Get-Help**

SYNOPSIS
    Displays information about Windows PowerShell commands and concepts.


SYNTAX
    **Get-Help** [[-Name] <String>] [-Category <String>] [-Component <String>] [-Full
    [<SwitchParameter>]] [-Functionality <String>] [-Path <String>] [-Role
    <String>] [<CommonParameters>]

    **Get-Help** [[-Name] <String>] [-Category <String>] [-Component <String>]
    [-Functionality <String>] [-Path <String>] [-Role <String>] -Detailed
    [<SwitchParameter>] [<CommonParameters>]

    **Get-Help** [[-Name] <String>] [-Category <String>] [-Component <String>]
    [-Functionality <String>] [-Path <String>] [-Role <String>] -Examples
    [<SwitchParameter>] [<CommonParameters>]

    **Get-Help** [[-Name] <String>] [-Category <String>] [-Component <String>]
    [-Functionality <String>] [-Path <String>] [-Role <String>] -Online
    [<SwitchParameter>] [<CommonParameters>]

    **Get-Help** [[-Name] <String>] [-Category <String>] [-Component <String>]
    [-Functionality <String>] [-Path <String>] [-Role <String>] -Parameter <String>
    [<CommonParameters>]

    **Get-Help** [[-Name] <String>] [-Category <String>] [-Component <String>]
    [-Functionality <String>] [-Path <String>] [-Role <String>] -ShowWindow
    [<SwitchParameter>] [<CommonParameters>]


DESCRIPTION
    The **Get-Help** cmdlet displays information about Windows PowerShell concepts and
    commands, including cmdlets, providers, functions, aliases and scripts.

    **Get-Help** gets the **help** content that it displays from **help** files on your
    computer. Without the **help** files, **Get-Help** displays only basic information
    about commands. Some Windows PowerShell modules come with **help** files. However,
    beginning in Windows PowerShell 3.0, the modules that come with Windows
    PowerShell do not include **help** files. To download or update the **help** files for
    a module in Windows PowerShell 3.0, use the **Update-Help** cmdlet. You can also
    view the **help** topics for Windows PowerShell online in the TechNet Library at http:
    //go.microsoft.com/fwlink/?LinkID=107116

    To get **help** for a Windows PowerShell command, type "**Get-Help**" followed by the
    command name. To get a list of all **help** topics on your system, type "**Get-Help**
    *".

    Conceptual **help** topics in Windows PowerShell begin with "about_", such as
    "about_Comparison_Operators". To see all "about_" topics, type "**Get-Help**
    about_*". To see a particular topic, type "**Get-Help** about_<topic-name>", such
    as "**Get-Help** about_Comparison_Operators".

You can display the entire **help** topic or use the parameters of the **Get-Help** cmdlet to get selected parts of the topic, such as the syntax, parameters, or examples. You can also use the Online parameter to display an online version of a **help** topic for a command in your Internet browser.

If you type "**Get-Help**" followed by the exact name of a **help** topic, or by a word unique to a **help** topic, **Get-Help** displays the topic contents. If you enter a word or word pattern that appears in several **help** topic titles, **Get-Help** displays a list of the matching titles. If you enter a word that does not appear in any **help** topic titles, **Get-Help** displays a list of topics that include that word in their contents.

In addition to "**Get-Help**", you can also type "**help**" or "man", which displays one screen of text at a time, or "<cmdlet-name> -?", which is identical to **Get-Help** but works only for cmdlets.

For information about the symbols that **Get-Help** displays in the command syntax diagram, see about_Command_Syntax http://go.microsoft.com/fwlink/?LinkID=113215. For information about parameter attributes, such as Required and Position, see about_Parameters http://go.microsoft.com/fwlink/?LinkID=113243.


RELATED LINKS
    Online Version: http://go.microsoft.com/fwlink/?LinkID=113316
    **Get-Command**
    **Get-Member**
    **Get-PSDrive**
    about_Command_Syntax
    about_Comment_Based_**Help**
    about_Parameters

REMARKS
    To see the examples, type: "**Get-Help Get-Help** -examples".
    For more information, type: "**Get-Help Get-Help** -detailed".
    For technical information, type: "**Get-Help Get-Help** -full".
    For online **help**, type: "**Get-Help Get-Help** -online"

The good thing about help with the Windows PowerShell is that it not only displays help about cmdlets, which you would expect, but it also has three levels of display: normal, detailed, and full. Additionally, you can obtain help about concepts in Windows PowerShell. This last feature is equivalent to having an online instruction manual. To retrieve a listing of all the conceptual help articles, use the *Get-Help about** command, as follows:

**Get-Help** about*

Suppose you do not remember the exact name of the cmdlet you wish to use, but you remember it was a *get* cmdlet? You can use a wildcard, such as an  asterisk (*), to obtain the name of the cmdlet. This is shown here:

**Get-Help** get*

This technique of using a wildcard operator can be extended further. If you remember that the cmdlet was a *get* cmdlet, and that it started with the letter *p*, you can use the following syntax to retrieve the desired cmdlet:

```
Get-Help get-p*
```

Suppose, however, that you know the exact name of the cmdlet, but you cannot exactly remember the syntax. For this scenario, you can use the *-examples* argument. For example, for the *Get-PSDrive* cmdlet, you would use *Get-Help* with the *-examples* argument, as follows:

```
Get-Help Get-PSDrive -examples
```

To see help displayed one page at a time, you can use the *Help* function. The *Help* function passes your input to the *Get-Help* cmdlet, and pipelines the resulting information to the *more.com* utility. This causes output to display one page at a time in the Windows PowerShell console. This is useful if you want to avoid scrolling up and down to see the help output.

> **Note** Keep in mind that in the Windows PowerShell ISE, the pager does not work, and therefore you will see no difference in output between *Get-Help* and *Help*. In the ISE, both *Get-Help* and *Help* behave the same way. However, it is likely that if you are using the Windows PowerShell ISE, you will use *Show-Command* for your help instead of relying on *Get-Help*.

This formatted output is shown in Figure 1-3.

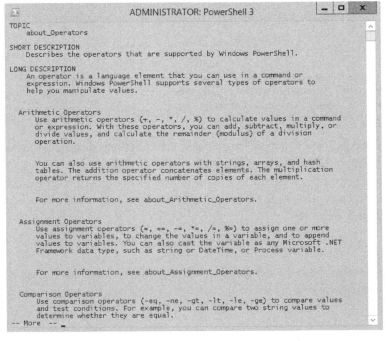

**FIGURE 1-3** Using *Help* to display information one page at a time.

Getting tired of typing *Get-Help* all the time? After all, it is eight characters long. The solution is to create an alias to the *Get-Help* cmdlet. An alias is a shortcut keystroke combination that will launch a program or cmdlet when typed. In the "Creating an alias for the *Get-Help* cmdlet" procedure, you will assign the *Get-Help* cmdlet to the G+H key combination.

> **Note** When creating an alias for a cmdlet, confirm it does not already have an alias by using *Get-Alias*. Use *New-Alias* to assign the cmdlet to a unique keystroke combination.

### Creating an alias for the *Get-Help* cmdlet

1.  Open Windows PowerShell by choosing Start | Run | Windows PowerShell. The PowerShell prompt will open by default at the root of your Documents folder.

2.  Retrieve an alphabetic listing of all currently defined aliases, and inspect the list for one assigned to either the *Get-Help* cmdlet or the keystroke combination G+H. The command to do this is as follows:

    ```
    Get-Alias sort
    ```

3.  After you have determined that there is no alias for the *Get-Help* cmdlet and that none is assigned to the G+H keystroke combination, review the syntax for the *New-Alias* cmdlet. Use the *-full* argument to the *Get-Help* cmdlet. This is shown here:

    ```
    Get-Help New-Alias -full
    ```

4.  Use the *New-Alias* cmdlet to assign the G+H keystroke combination to the *Get-Help* cmdlet. To do this, use the following command:

    ```
    New-Alias gh Get-Help
    ```

## Exploring commands: step-by-step exercises

In the following exercises, you'll explore the use of command-line utilities in Windows PowerShell. You will see that it is as easy to use command-line utilities in Windows PowerShell as in the CMD interpreter; however, by using such commands in Windows PowerShell, you gain access to new levels of functionality.

## Using command-line utilities

1. Open Windows PowerShell by choosing Start | Run | Windows PowerShell. The PowerShell prompt will open by default at the root of your Documents folder.

2. Change to the C:\root directory by typing **cd c:\** inside the PowerShell prompt:

   ```
   cd c:\
   ```

3. Obtain a listing of all the files in the C:\root directory by using the *dir* command:

   ```
   dir
   ```

4. Create a directory off the C:\root directory by using the *md* command:

   ```
   md mytest
   ```

5. Obtain a listing of all files and folders off the root that begin with the letter *m*:

   ```
   dir m*
   ```

6. Change the working directory to the PowerShell working directory. You can do this by using the *Set-Location* command as follows:

   ```
   Set-Location $pshome
   ```

7. Obtain a listing of memory counters related to the available bytes by using the *typeperf* command. This command is shown here:

   ```
   typeperf "\memory\available bytes"
   ```

8. After a few counters have been displayed in the PowerShell window, press Ctrl+C to break the listing.

9. Display the current boot configuration by using the *bootcfg* command (note that you must run this command with admin rights):

   ```
   bootcfg
   ```

10. Change the working directory back to the C:\Mytest directory you created earlier:

    ```
    Set-Location c:\mytest
    ```

11. Create a file named mytestfile.txt in the C:\Mytest directory. Use the *fsutil* utility, and make the file 1,000 bytes in size. To do this, use the following command:

    ```
    fsutil file createnew mytestfile.txt 1000
    ```

12. Obtain a directory listing of all the files in the C:\Mytest directory by using the *Get-ChildItem* cmdlet.

13. Print out the current date by using the *Get-Date* cmdlet.

**14.** Clear the screen by using the *cls* command.

**15.** Print out a listing of all the cmdlets built into Windows PowerShell. To do this, use the *Get-Command* cmdlet.

**16.** Use the *Get-Command* cmdlet to get the *Get-Alias* cmdlet. To do this, use the *-name* argument while supplying *Get-Alias* as the value for the argument. This is shown here:

```
Get-Command -name Get-Alias
```

This concludes the step-by-step exercise. Exit Windows PowerShell by typing **exit** and pressing Enter.

In the following exercise, you'll use various help options to obtain assistance with various cmdlets.

## Obtaining help

**1.** Open Windows PowerShell by choosing Start | Run | Windows PowerShell. The PowerShell prompt will open by default at the root of your Documents folder.

**2.** Use the *Get-Help* cmdlet to obtain help about the *Get-Help* cmdlet. Use the command *Get-Help Get-Help* as follows:

```
Get-Help Get-Help
```

**3.** To obtain detailed help about the *Get-Help* cmdlet, use the *-detailed* argument as follows:

```
Get-Help Get-Help -detailed
```

**4.** To retrieve technical information about the *Get-Help* cmdlet, use the *-full* argument. This is shown here:

```
Get-Help Get-Help -full
```

**5.** If you only want to obtain a listing of examples of command usage, use the *-examples* argument as follows:

```
Get-Help Get-Help -examples
```

**6.** Obtain a listing of all the informational help topics by using the *Get-Help* cmdlet and the *about* noun with the asterisk (*) wildcard operator. The code to do this is shown here:

```
Get-Help about*
```

**7.** Obtain a listing of all the help topics related to *get* cmdlets. To do this, use the *Get-Help* cmdlet, and specify the word *get* followed by the wildcard operator as follows:

```
Get-Help get*
```

8. Obtain a listing of all the help topics related to *set* cmdlets. To do this, use the *Get-Help* cmdlet, followed by the *set* verb, followed by the asterisk wildcard. This is shown here:

```
Get-Help set*
```

This concludes this exercise. Exit Windows PowerShell by typing **exit** and pressing Enter.

# Chapter 1 quick reference

| To | Do This |
|---|---|
| Use an external command-line utility | Type the name of the command-line utility while inside Windows PowerShell. |
| Use multiple external command-line utilities sequentially | Separate each command-line utility with a semicolon on a single Windows PowerShell line. |
| Obtain a list of running processes | Use the *Get-Process* cmdlet. |
| Stop a process | Use the *Stop-Process* cmdlet and specify either the name or the process ID as an argument. |
| Model the effect of a cmdlet before actually performing the requested action | Use the *-whatif* argument. |
| Instruct Windows PowerShell to start up, run a cmdlet, and then exit | Use the *PowerShell* command while prefixing the cmdlet with & and enclosing the name of the cmdlet in curly brackets. |
| Prompt for confirmation before stopping a process | Use the *Stop-Process* cmdlet while specifying the *-confirm* argument. |

# CHAPTER 2

# Using Windows PowerShell Cmdlets

**After completing this chapter, you will be able to:**

- Understand the basic use of Windows PowerShell cmdlets.

- Use *Get-Command* to retrieve a listing of cmdlets.

- Configure cmdlet search options.

- Configure output display.

- Use *Get-Member*.

- Use *Show-Command*.

- Use *New-Object*.

The inclusion of a large amount of cmdlets in Microsoft Windows PowerShell makes it immediately useful to network administrators and others who need to perform various maintenance and administrative tasks on their Windows servers and desktop systems. In this chapter, you'll review several of the more useful cmdlets as a means of highlighting the power and flexibility of Windows PowerShell. However, the real benefit of this chapter is the methodology you'll use to discover the use of the various cmdlets. All the scripts mentioned in this chapter are located in the download package from the Microsoft TechNet Script Center Script Repository (*http://aka.ms/PowerShellSBS_book*).

## Understanding the basics of cmdlets

In Chapter 1, "Overview of Windows PowerShell 3.0," you learned about using the various help utilities available that demonstrate how to use cmdlets. You looked at a couple of cmdlets that are helpful in finding out what commands are available and how to obtain information about them. In this section, you will learn some additional ways to use cmdlets in Windows PowerShell.

**Tip** Typing long cmdlet names can be somewhat tedious. To simplify this process, type enough of the cmdlet name to uniquely distinguish it, and then press the Tab key on the keyboard. What is the result? *Tab completion* completes the cmdlet name for you. This also works with parameter names and other things you are entering (such as .NET objects, directories, registry keys, and so on). Feel free to experiment with this great time-saving technique. You may never have to type *Get-Command* again!

Because the cmdlets return objects instead of string values, you can obtain additional information about the returned objects. The additional information would not be available if you were working with just string data. To take information from one cmdlet and feed it to another cmdlet, you can use the pipe character (|). This may seem complicated, but it is actually quite simple and, by the end of this chapter, will seem quite natural. At the most basic level, consider obtaining a directory listing; after you have the directory listing, perhaps you would like to format the way it is displayed—as a table or a list. As you can see, obtaining the directory information and formatting the list are two separate operations. The second task takes place on the right side of the pipe.

## Using the *Get-ChildItem* cmdlet

In Chapter 1, you used the *dir* command to obtain a listing of all the files and folders in a directory. This works because there is an alias built into Windows PowerShell that assigns the *Get-ChildItem* cmdlet to the letter combination *dir*.

### Obtaining a directory listing

In a Windows PowerShell console, enter the *Get-ChildItem* cmdlet followed by the directory to list. (Remember that you can use tab completion to compete the command. Type **get-ch** and press Tab to complete the command name.) Here is the command:

```
Get-ChildItem C:\
```

**Note** Windows PowerShell is not case sensitive, therefore *get-Childitem, Get-childitem,* and *Get-ChildItem* all work the same way, because Windows PowerShell views all three as the same command.

In Windows PowerShell, there actually is no cmdlet called *dir*, nor does Windows PowerShell actually use the *dir* command from the DOS days. The alias *dir* is associated with the *Get-ChildItem* cmdlet. This is why the output from *dir* is different in Windows PowerShell from output appearing in the CMD.exe interpreter. The Windows PowerShell cmdlet *Get-Alias* resolves the association between *dir* and the *Get-ChildItem* cmdlet as follows:

```
PS C:\> Get-Alias dir

CommandType     Name                                               ModuleName
-----------     ----                                               ----------
Alias           dir -> Get-ChildItem
```

If you use the *Get-ChildItem* cmdlet to obtain the directory listing, the output appears exactly the same as output produced in Windows PowerShell by using *dir* because *dir* is simply an alias for the *Get-ChildItem* cmdlet. This is shown here:

```
PS C:\> dir c:\


    Directory: C:\


Mode                LastWriteTime     Length Name
----                -------------     ------ ----
d----         3/22/2012   4:03 AM            PerfLogs
d-r--         3/22/2012   4:24 AM            Program Files
d----         4/22/2012   7:14 PM            test
d-r--         3/23/2012   6:02 PM            Users
d----         3/23/2012   4:59 PM            Windows
-a---         3/22/2012   4:33 AM         24 autoexec.bat
-a---         3/22/2012   4:33 AM         10 config.sys


PS C:\> Get-ChildItem c:\


    Directory: C:\


Mode                LastWriteTime     Length Name
----                -------------     ------ ----
d----         3/22/2012   4:03 AM            PerfLogs
d-r--         3/22/2012   4:24 AM            Program Files
d----         4/22/2012   7:14 PM            test
d-r--         3/23/2012   6:02 PM            Users
d----         3/23/2012   4:59 PM            Windows
-a---         3/22/2012   4:33 AM         24 autoexec.bat
-a---         3/22/2012   4:33 AM         10 config.sys


PS C:\>
```

If you were to use *Get-Help* and then *dir*, you would receive the same output as if you were to use *Get-Help Get-ChildItem*. This is shown following, where only the name and the synopsis of the cmdlets are displayed in the output:

```
PS C:\> Get-Help dir | select name, synopsis | Format-Table -AutoSize

Name          Synopsis
----          --------
Get-ChildItem Gets the files and folders in a file system drive.

PS C:\> Get-Help Get-ChildItem | select name, synopsis | Format-Table -AutoSize

Name          Synopsis
----          --------
Get-ChildItem Gets the files and folders in a file system drive.

PS C:\>
```

In Windows PowerShell, an alias and a full cmdlet name perform in exactly the same manner. You do not use an alias to modify the behavior of a cmdlet. (To do that, create a function or a proxy function.)

## Formatting a directory listing using the *Format-List* cmdlet

In a Windows PowerShell console, enter the *Get-ChildItem* cmdlet, followed by the directory to list, followed by the pipe character and the *Format-List* cmdlet. Here's an example:

```
Get-ChildItem C:\ | Format-List
```

### Formatting output with the *Format-List* cmdlet

1.  Open the Windows PowerShell console.

2.  Use the *Get-ChildItem* cmdlet to obtain a directory listing of the C:\ directory.

    ```
    Get-ChildItem C:\
    ```

3.  Use the *Format-List* cmdlet to arrange the output of *Get-ChildItem*:

    ```
    Get-ChildItem | Format-List
    ```

4.  Use the *-property* argument of the *Format-List* cmdlet to retrieve only a listing of the name of each file in the root.

    ```
    Get-ChildItem C:\ | Format-List -property name
    ```

5.  Use the *-property* argument of the *Format-List* cmdlet to retrieve only a listing of the name and length of each file in the root.

    ```
    Get-ChildItem C:\ | Format-List -property name, length
    ```

# Using the *Format-Wide* cmdlet

In the same way that you use the *Format-List* cmdlet to produce output in a list, you can use the *Format-Wide* cmdlet to produce output that's more compact. The difference is that *Format-Wide* permits the selection of only a single property; however, you can choose how many columns you will use to display the information. By default, the *Format-Wide* cmdlet uses two columns.

## Formatting a directory listing using *Format-Wide*

1. In a Windows PowerShell prompt, enter the *Get-ChildItem* cmdlet, followed by the directory to list, followed by the pipe character and the *Format-Wide* cmdlet. Here's an example:

   ```
   Get-ChildItem C:\ | Format-Wide
   ```

2. Change to a three-column display and specifically select the *name* property.

   ```
   Get-ChildItem | Format-Wide -Column 3 -Property name
   ```

3. Allow Windows PowerShell to maximize the amount of space between columns and display as many columns as possible. Use the *-AutoSize* switched parameter to do this:

   ```
   Get-ChildItem | Format-Wide -Property name –AutoSize
   ```

4. Force Windows PowerShell to truncate the columns by choosing a number of columns greater than can be displayed on the screen:

   ```
   Get-ChildItem | Format-Wide -Property name -Column 8
   ```

## Formatting output with the *Format-Wide* cmdlet

1. Open the Windows PowerShell console.

2. Use the *Get-ChildItem* cmdlet to obtain a directory listing of the C:\Windows directory.

   ```
   Get-ChildItem C:\Windows
   ```

3. Use the *-recursive* argument to cause the *Get-ChildItem* cmdlet to walk through a nested directory structure, including only .txt files in the output. Hide errors by using the *-ea* parameter (*ea* is an alias for *ErrorAction*) and assign a value of 0 (which means that errors will be ignored):

   ```
   Get-ChildItem C:\Windows -recurse -include *.txt -ea 0
   ```

Partial output from the command is shown here:

```
PS C:\> Get-ChildItem C:\Windows -recurse -include *.txt -ea 0
    Directory: C:\Windows\ehome\en-US


Mode                LastWriteTime       Length Name
----                -------------       ------ ----
-a---          3/22/2012   4:17 AM       15826 epgtos.txt
-a---          3/22/2012   4:17 AM       14642 playready_eula.txt
-a---          3/22/2012   4:17 AM       36672 playReady_eula_oem.txt
PS C:\>
```

4. Use the *Format-Wide* cmdlet to adjust the output from the *Get-ChildItem* cmdlet. Use the -*columns* argument and supply a parameter of *3* to it. This is shown here:

```
Get-ChildItem C:\Windows -recurse -include *.txt -ea 0| Format-Wide -column 3
```

Once this command is run, you will see output similar to this:

```
PS C:\> Get-ChildItem C:\Windows -recurse -include *.txt -ea 0 | Format-Wide -Column
3

    Directory: C:\Windows\ehome\en-US


epgtos.txt                      playready_eula.txt              playReady_eula_oem.txt

    Directory: C:\Windows\SoftwareDistribution\SelfUpdate

wuident.txt
```

5. Use the *Format-Wide* cmdlet to adjust the output from the *Get-ChildItem* cmdlet. Use the -*property* argument to specify the *name* property, and group the outputs by size. The command shown here appears on two lines; however, when typed into Windows PowerShell, it is a single command and can be on one line. In addition, when typed into the Windows PowerShell console, if you continue typing when approaching the end of a line, Windows PowerShell will automatically wrap the command to the next line; therefore, you do not need to press the Enter key.

```
Get-ChildItem C:\Windows -recurse -include *.txt |
Format-Wide -property name -groupby length -column 3
```

Partial output is shown here. Note that although three columns were specified, if there are not three files of the same length, only one column will be used:

```
PS C:\> Get-ChildItem C:\Windows -recurse -include *.txt -ea 0 |
Format-Wide -Column3 -GroupBy length

    Directory: C:\Windows\ehome\en-US


epgtos.txt

    Directory: C:\Windows\ehome\en-US


playready_eula.txt

    Directory: C:\Windows\ehome\en-US
```

## Formatting a directory listing using *Format-Table*

In a Windows PowerShell console, enter the *Get-ChildItem* cmdlet, followed by the directory to list, followed by the pipe character and the *Format-Table* cmdlet. Here's an example:

```
Get-ChildItem C:\ | Format-Table
```

### Formatting output with the *Format-Table* cmdlet

1.  Open Windows PowerShell by choosing Start | Run | Windows PowerShell. The PowerShell prompt will open by default at the root of your Documents And Settings folder.

2.  Use the *Get-ChildItem* cmdlet to obtain a directory listing of the C:\Windows directory:

    ```
    Get-ChildItem C:\Windows -ea 0
    ```

3.  Use the *-recursive* argument to cause the *Get-ChildItem* cmdlet to walk through a nested directory structure. Include only .txt files in the output.

    ```
    Get-ChildItem C:\Windows -recurse -include *.txt -ea 0
    ```

4.  Use the *Format-Table* cmdlet to adjust the output from the *Get-ChildItem* cmdlet. This is shown here:

    ```
    Get-ChildItem C:\Windows -recurse -include *.txt -ea 0 | Format-Table
    ```

The command results in the creation of a table, as follows:

```
PS C:\> Get-ChildItem C:\Windows -recurse -include *.txt -ea 0 | Format-Table


    Directory: C:\Windows\ehome\en-US


Mode                LastWriteTime     Length Name
----                -------------     ------ ----
-a---         3/22/2012    4:17 AM     15826 epgtos.txt
-a---         3/22/2012    4:17 AM     14642 playready_eula.txt
-a---         3/22/2012    4:17 AM     36672 playReady_eula_oem.txt


    Directory: C:\Windows\SoftwareDistribution\SelfUpdate


Mode                LastWriteTime     Length Name
----                -------------     ------ ----
-----         3/13/2012    5:51 PM       275 wuident.txt
```

5. Use the *-property* argument of the *Format-Table* cmdlet and choose the *name, length,* and *last-write-time* properties. This is shown here:

```
Get-ChildItem C:\Windows -recurse -include *.txt -ea 0 |Format-Table -property
name, length, lastwritetime
```

This command results in producing a table with the name, length, and last write time as column headers. A sample of this output is shown here:

```
PS C:\> Get-ChildItem C:\Windows -recurse -include *.txt -ea 0 |Format-Table -property
  name, length, lastwritetime

Name                                    Length LastWriteTime
----                                    ------ -------------
epgtos.txt                               15826 3/22/2012 4:17:20 AM
playready_eula.txt                       14642 3/22/2012 4:17:20 AM
playReady_eula_oem.txt                   36672 3/22/2012 4:17:20 AM
wuident.txt                                275 3/13/2012 5:51:28 PM
dberr.txt                               177095 3/23/2012 4:55:52 PM
gmreadme.txt                               646 11/27/2010 6:57:47 PM
erofflps.txt                              9183 3/22/2012 4:17:06 AM
about_Aliases.help.txt                    6551 2/28/2012 4:48:38 AM
about_Arithmetic_Operator...             14241 2/28/2012 4:48:38 AM
```

# Formatting output with *Out-GridView*

The *Out-GridView* cmdlet is different from the other formatting cmdlets explored thus far in this chapter. *Out-GridView* is an interactive cmdlet—that is, it does not format output for display on the Windows PowerShell console, or for sending to a printer. Instead, *Out-GridView* provides a control permitting exploration of the pipelined data. It does this by adding the data to a table in a floating window. For example, the following command pipelines the results of the *Get-Process* cmdlet to the *Out-GridView* cmdlet (*gps* is an alias for the *Get-Process* cmdlet):

```
gps | Out-GridView
```

When the *Get-Process* cmdlet completes, a grid appears containing process information arranged in columns and in rows. Figure 2-1 shows the new window displaying the process information in a grid. One useful feature of the *Out-GridView* cmdlet is that the returned control contains the command producing the control in the title bar. Figure 2-1 lists the command *gps | Out-GridView* in the title bar (the command that is run to produce the grid control).

| Handles | NPM(K) | PM(K) | WS(K) | VM(M) | CPU(s) | Id | ProcessName |
|---|---|---|---|---|---|---|---|
| 48 | 4 | 1792 | 6944 | 47 | 20.83 | 2,780 | conhost |
| 189 | 6 | 1008 | 1548 | 34 | 0.69 | 368 | csrss |
| 195 | 7 | 1260 | 2020 | 42 | 4.38 | 440 | csrss |
| 83 | 5 | 892 | 860 | 31 | 0.11 | 3,268 | csrss |
| 192 | 11 | 12356 | 29136 | 99 | 5.30 | 772 | dwm |
| 182 | 8 | 16388 | 16204 | 76 | 0.17 | 3,244 | dwm |
| 1,370 | 55 | 32476 | 58200 | 343 | 20.00 | 3,688 | explorer |
| 0 | 0 | 0 | 28 | 0 | | 0 | Idle |
| 345 | 15 | 8360 | 11136 | 167 | 0.53 | 1,180 | LogonUI |
| 947 | 17 | 3332 | 7256 | 35 | 3.98 | 540 | lsass |
| 440 | 17 | 50712 | 28376 | 172 | 92.78 | 1,464 | MsMpEng |
| 660 | 35 | 410748 | 438340 | 691 | 301.98 | 1,036 | powershell |
| 215 | 6 | 1580 | 4800 | 64 | 1.52 | 3,672 | rdpclip |
| 38 | 3 | 624 | 2600 | 32 | 0.03 | 2,580 | rdrleakdiag |
| 72 | 3 | 672 | 1832 | 31 | 0.08 | 996 | RDVGHelper |
| 82 | 4 | 680 | 700 | 32 | 0.08 | 1,820 | RDVGHelper |
| 562 | 18 | 16148 | 9168 | 102 | 1.66 | 3,060 | SearchIndex... |
| 242 | 7 | 3724 | 6732 | 40 | 4.23 | 532 | services |
| 39 | 1 | 180 | 472 | 3 | 0.05 | 280 | smss |
| 380 | 10 | 2972 | 5596 | 42 | 1.08 | 1,236 | spoolsv |
| 264 | 7 | 2144 | 3052 | 20 | 1.11 | 624 | svchost |

**FIGURE 2-1** The *Out-GridView* cmdlet accepts pipelined input and displays a control that permits further exploration.

You can click the column headings to sort the output in descending order. Clicking the same column again changes the sort to ascending order. Figure 2-2 sorts the processes by the number of handles used by each process. The sort is ordered from largest number of handles to smallest.

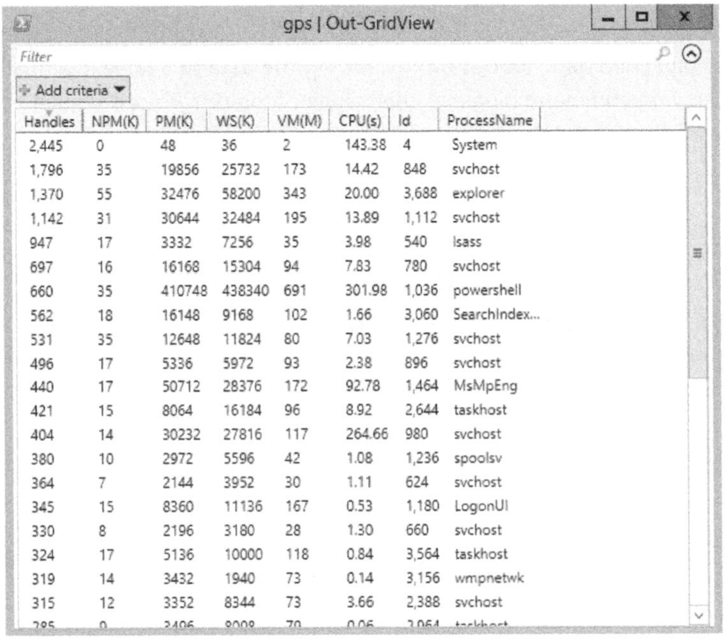

| Handles | NPM(K) | PM(K) | WS(K) | VM(M) | CPU(s) | Id | ProcessName |
|---|---|---|---|---|---|---|---|
| 2,445 | 0 | 48 | 36 | 2 | 143.38 | 4 | System |
| 1,796 | 35 | 19856 | 25732 | 173 | 14.42 | 848 | svchost |
| 1,370 | 55 | 32476 | 58200 | 343 | 20.00 | 3,688 | explorer |
| 1,142 | 31 | 30644 | 32484 | 195 | 13.89 | 1,112 | svchost |
| 947 | 17 | 3332 | 7256 | 35 | 3.98 | 540 | lsass |
| 697 | 16 | 16168 | 15304 | 94 | 7.83 | 780 | svchost |
| 660 | 35 | 410748 | 438340 | 691 | 301.98 | 1,036 | powershell |
| 562 | 18 | 16148 | 9168 | 102 | 1.66 | 3,060 | SearchIndex... |
| 531 | 35 | 12648 | 11824 | 80 | 7.03 | 1,276 | svchost |
| 496 | 17 | 5336 | 5972 | 93 | 2.38 | 896 | svchost |
| 440 | 17 | 50712 | 28376 | 172 | 92.78 | 1,464 | MsMpEng |
| 421 | 15 | 8064 | 16184 | 96 | 8.92 | 2,644 | taskhost |
| 404 | 14 | 30232 | 27816 | 117 | 264.66 | 980 | svchost |
| 380 | 10 | 2972 | 5596 | 42 | 1.08 | 1,236 | spoolsv |
| 364 | 7 | 2144 | 3952 | 30 | 1.11 | 624 | svchost |
| 345 | 15 | 8360 | 11136 | 167 | 0.53 | 1,180 | LogonUI |
| 330 | 8 | 2196 | 3180 | 28 | 1.30 | 660 | svchost |
| 324 | 17 | 5136 | 10000 | 118 | 0.84 | 3,564 | taskhost |
| 319 | 14 | 3432 | 1940 | 73 | 0.14 | 3,156 | wmpnetwk |
| 315 | 12 | 3352 | 8344 | 73 | 3.66 | 2,388 | svchost |
| 285 | 0 | 2406 | 8008 | 70 | 0.06 | 3,064 | taskhost |

**FIGURE 2-2** Clicking the column heading buttons permits sorting in either descending or ascending order.

*Out-GridView* accepts input from other cmdlets, as well as from the *Get-Process* cmdlet. For example, you can pipeline the output from the *Get-Service* cmdlet to *Out-GridView* by using the syntax that appears here (*gsv* is an alias for the *Get-Service* cmdlet, and *ogv* is an alias for the *Out-GridView* cmdlet):

```
gsv | ogv
```

Figure 2-3 shows the resulting grid view.

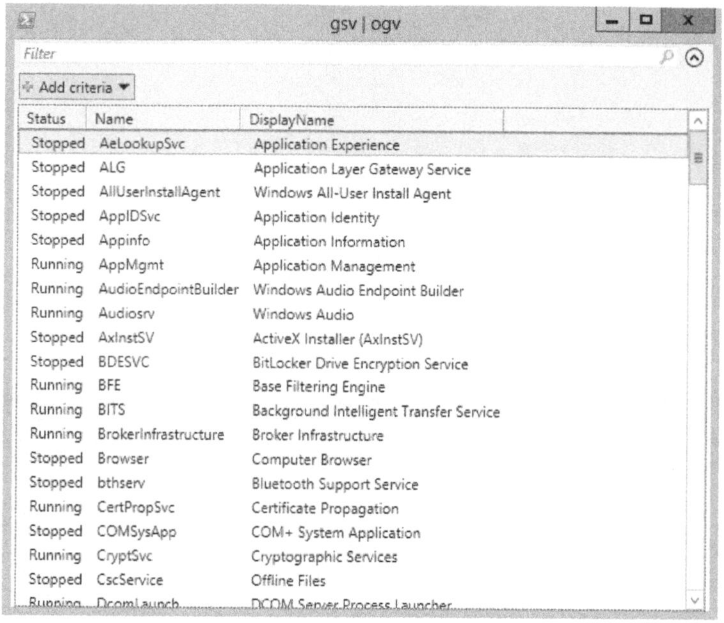

**FIGURE 2-3** *Out-GridView* displays service controller information, such as the current status of all defined services.

The *Out-GridView* cmdlet automatically detects the data type of the incoming properties. It uses this data type to determine how to present the filtered and the sorted information to you. For example, the data type of the *Status* property is a string. Clicking the Add Criteria button, choosing the *status* property, and selecting Add adds a filter that permits choosing various ways of interacting with the text stored in the *status* property. The available options include the following: *contains, does not contain, equals, does not equal, ends with, is empty,* and *is not empty.* The options change depending upon the perceived data type of the incoming property.

To filter only running services, you can change the filter to *equals* and the value to *running.* Keep in mind that if you choose an equality operator, your filtered string must match exactly. Therefore, *equals run* will not return any matches. Only *equals running* works. On the other hand, if you choose a *starts with* operator, you will find all the running services with the first letter. For instance, *starts with r* returns everything. As you continue to type, matches continue to be refined in the output.

> **Note** Keep in the mind the difference in the behavior of the various filters. Depending on the operator you select, the self-updating output is extremely useful. This works especially well when attempting to filter out numerical data if you are not very familiar with the data ranges and what a typical value looks like. This technique appears in Figure 2-4.

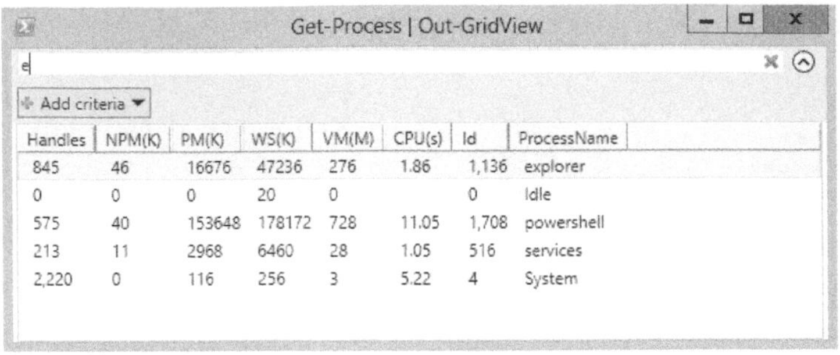

**FIGURE 2-4** The *Out-GridView* self-updates when you type in the filter box.

By the time you type the first two letters of the *explorer* process name in the filter box, the resultant process information changes to display the single matching process name. The output appears in Figure 2-5.

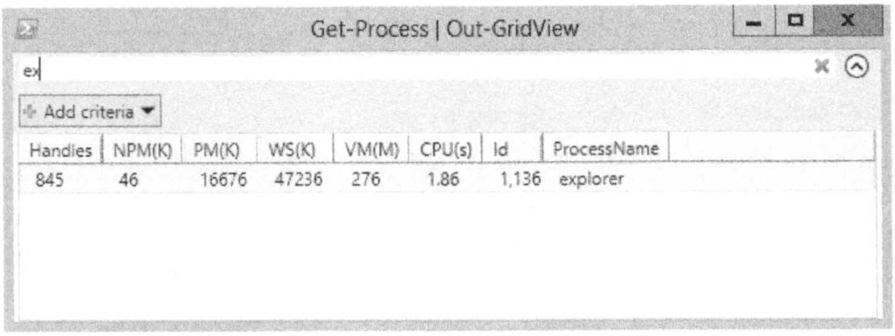

**FIGURE 2-5** Clicking the red *X* at the right of the filter box clears the *explorer* filter you added.

### Filtering processes using CPU time with a memory working set greater than 20,000

1. First use the Add Criteria button to choose CPU(s).

2. Click the blue plus symbol on the Add Criteria button beneath the Filter dialog box.

3. In the Add Criteria selection menu that appears, place a check beside CPU(s) and press the Add button.

4. Click the underlined word *contains* and select Is Not Empty from the selection menu.

5. Click the blue plus symbol on the Add Criteria button.

6. Places a check next to the WS(K) item.

7. Click the Add button to add the working set memory to the criteria.

8. Click the blue underlined "is less than or equal to" criterion to change it to "is greater than or equal to."

9. Add the number 20000 to the box beside the "is greater than or equal to" criterion.

## Creating a sorted process list

1. Type the following command into the Windows PowerShell console:

   ```
   Get-Process
   ```

2. Send the output of the *Get-Process* cmdlet to the *Get-Member* cmdlet:

   ```
   Get-Process | Get-Member
   ```

3. Examine the property section. Note that CPU is a *script* property.

4. Pipeline the results from the *Get-Process* cmdlet to the *Sort-Object* cmdlet and use the *cpu* property:

   ```
   Get-Process | Sort-Object cpu
   ```

5. Retrieve the previous command and add the *-Descending* switched parameter:

   ```
   Get-Process | Sort-Object cpu -Descending
   ```

6. Send the whole thing to the *Out-GridView* cmdlet. The command appears here:

   ```
   Get-Process | Sort-Object cpu -Descending | Out-GridView
   ```

7. Remove columns from the grid view. Right-click the column process names and select the columns.

8. When the select-column prompt appears, click it to bring up the Select Columns dialog box. Click to add or remove the columns individually.

   The Select Columns dialog box appears in Figure 2-6.

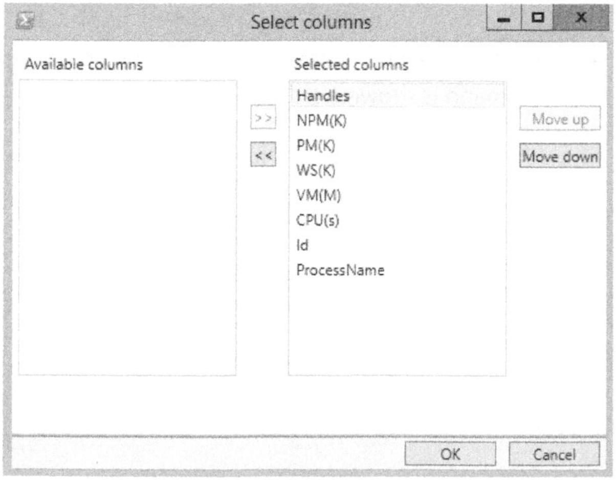

**FIGURE 2-6** Use the Select Columns dialog box to control columns appearing in the *gridview* control.

> **Note** Because the process of selecting columns is a bit slow, if you only want to see a few columns, it is best to filter the columns by using the *Select-Object* cmdlet before you send it to the *Out-GridView* cmdlet.

## Leveraging the power of *Get-Command*

The *Get-Command* cmdlet gets details of every command available to you. These commands include cmdlets, functions, workflows, aliases, and executable commands. Using the *Get-Command* cmdlet, you can obtain a listing of all the cmdlets installed on Windows PowerShell, but there is much more that can be done using this extremely versatile cmdlet. For example, you can use wildcard characters to search for cmdlets using *Get-Command*. This is shown in the following procedure.

### Searching for cmdlets using wildcard characters

In a Windows PowerShell prompt, enter the *Get-Command* cmdlet followed by a wildcard character:

```
Get-Command *
```

#### Finding commands by using the *Get-Command* cmdlet

1. Open Windows PowerShell.

2. Use an alias to refer to the *Get-Command* cmdlet. To find the correct alias, use the *Get-Alias* cmdlet as follows:

   ```
   Get-Alias g*
   ```

   This command produces a listing of all the aliases defined that begin with the letter *g*. An example of the output of this command is shown here:

   ```
   CommandType     Name                         ModuleName
   -----------     ----                         ----------
   Alias           gal -> Get-Alias
   Alias           gbp -> Get-PSBreakpoint
   Alias           gc -> Get-Content
   Alias           gci -> Get-ChildItem
   Alias           gcm -> Get-Command
   Alias           gcs -> Get-PSCallStack
   Alias           gdr -> Get-PSDrive
   Alias           ghy -> Get-History
   Alias           gi -> Get-Item
   Alias           gjb -> Get-Job
   Alias           gl -> Get-Location
   ```

```
Alias          gm -> Get-Member
Alias          gmo -> Get-Module
Alias          gp -> Get-ItemProperty
Alias          gps -> Get-Process
Alias          group -> Group-Object
Alias          gsn -> Get-PSSession
Alias          gsnp -> Get-PSSnapin
Alias          gsv -> Get-Service
Alias          gu -> Get-Unique
Alias          gv -> Get-Variable
Alias          gwck -> Get-WmiKey                              HSGWMImoduleV6
Alias          gwcm -> Get-WmiClassMethods                     HSGWMImoduleV6
Alias          gwcp -> Get-WmiClassProperties                  HSGWMImoduleV6
Alias          gwcq -> Get-WMIClassesWithQualifiers            HSGWMImoduleV6
Alias          gwkv -> Get-WmiKeyvalue                         HSGWMImoduleV6
Alias          gwmi -> Get-WmiObject
Alias          gwq -> Get-WmiClassesAndQuery                   HSGWMImoduleV6
```

**3.** Using the *gcm* alias, use the *Get-Command* cmdlet to return the *Get-Command* cmdlet. This is shown here:

```
gcm Get-Command
```

This command returns the *Get-Command* cmdlet. The output is shown here:

```
CommandType    Name                                           ModuleName
-----------    ----                                           ----------
Cmdlet         Get-Command                                    Microsoft.Powe...
```

**4.** Using the *gcm* alias to get the *Get-Command* cmdlet, pipe the output to the *Format-List* cmdlet. Use the wildcard asterisk (*) to obtain a listing of all the properties of the *Get-Command* cmdlet. This is shown here:

```
gcm Get-Command |Format-List *
```

This command will return all the properties from the *Get-Command* cmdlet. The output is shown here:

```
HelpUri            : http://go.microsoft.com/fwlink/?LinkID=113309
DLL                : C:\WINDOWS\Microsoft.Net\assembly\GAC_MSIL\System.Management
                     .Automation\v4.0_3.0.0.0__31bf3856ad364e35\System.Management
                     .Automation.dll
Verb               : Get
Noun               : Command
HelpFile           : System.Management.Automation.dll-Help.xml
PSSnapIn           : Microsoft.PowerShell.Core
ImplementingType   : Microsoft.PowerShell.Commands.GetCommandCommand
Definition         :
                     Get-Command [[-ArgumentList] <Object[]>] [-Verb <string[]>]
                     [-Noun <string[]>] [-Module <string[]>] [-TotalCount <int>]
                     [-Syntax] [-All] [-ListImported] [-ParameterName <string[]>]
                     [-ParameterType <PSTypeName[]>] [<CommonParameters>]
```

```
                       Get-Command [[-Name] <string[]>] [[-ArgumentList] <Object[]>]
                       [-Module <string[]>] [-CommandType <CommandTypes>]
                       [-TotalCount <int>] [-Syntax] [-All] [-ListImported]
                       [-ParameterName <string[]>] [-ParameterType <PSTypeName[]>]
                       [<CommonParameters>]

DefaultParameterSet : CmdletSet
OutputType          : {System.Management.Automation.AliasInfo,
                       System.Management.Automation.ApplicationInfo,
                       System.Management.Automation.FunctionInfo,
                       System.Management.Automation.CmdletInfo...}
Options             : ReadOnly
Name                : Get-Command
CommandType         : Cmdlet
Visibility          : Public
ModuleName          : Microsoft.PowerShell.Core
Module              :
RemotingCapability  : PowerShell
Parameters          : {[Name, System.Management.Automation.ParameterMetadata],
                       [Verb, System.Management.Automation.ParameterMetadata],
                       [Noun, System.Management.Automation.ParameterMetadata],
                       [Module, System.Management.Automation.ParameterMetadata]...}
ParameterSets       : {[[-ArgumentList] <Object[]>] [-Verb <string[]>] [-Noun
                       <string[]>] [-Module <string[]>] [-TotalCount <int>]
                       [-Syntax] [-All] [-ListImported] [-ParameterName <string[]>]
                       [-ParameterType <PSTypeName[]>] [<CommonParameters>],
                       [[-Name] <string[]>] [[-ArgumentList] <Object[]>] [-Module
                       <string[]>] [-CommandType <CommandTypes>] [-TotalCount <int>]
                       [-Syntax] [-All] [-ListImported] [-ParameterName <string[]>]
                       [-ParameterType <PSTypeName[]>] [<CommonParameters>]}
```

5. Using the *gcm* alias and the *Get-Command* cmdlet, pipe the output to the *Format-List* cmdlet. Use the *-property* argument and specify the *definition* property of the *Get-Command* cmdlet. Rather than retyping the entire command, use the up arrow on your keyboard to retrieve the previous *gcm Get-Command | Format-List * * command. Use the Backspace key to remove the asterisk, and then simply add *-property definition* to your command. This is shown here:

```
gcm Get-Command | Format-List -property definition
```

This command only returns the property definition for the *Get-Command* cmdlet. The returned definition is shown here:

```
Definition :
            Get-Command [[-ArgumentList] <Object[]>] [-Verb <string[]>] [-Noun
            <string[]>] [-Module <string[]>] [-TotalCount <int>] [-Syntax] [-All]
            [-ListImported] [-ParameterName <string[]>] [-ParameterType
            <PSTypeName[]>] [<CommonParameters>]

            Get-Command [[-Name] <string[]>] [[-ArgumentList] <Object[]>] [-Module
            <string[]>] [-CommandType <CommandTypes>] [-TotalCount <int>]
            [-Syntax] [-All] [-ListImported] [-ParameterName <string[]>]
            [-ParameterType <PSTypeName[]>] [<CommonParameters>]
```

**6.** Because objects are returned from cmdlets instead of simply string data, you can also retrieve the definition of the *Get-Command* cmdlet by directly using the *definition* property. This is done by putting the expression inside parentheses and using *dotted notation*, as shown here:

```
(gcm Get-Command).definition
```

The definition returned from the previous command is virtually identical to the one returned by using the *Format-List* cmdlet.

**7.** Use the *gcm* alias and specify the *-verb* argument. Use *se\** for the verb. This is shown here:

```
gcm -verb se*
```

The previous command returns a listing of all the cmdlets that contain a verb beginning with *se*. The result is as follows:

```
CommandType     Name                                    ModuleName
-----------     ----                                    ----------
Function        Set-BCAuthentication                    BranchCache
Function        Set-BCCache                             BranchCache
Function        Set-BCDataCacheEntryMaxAge              BranchCache
Function        Set-BCMinSMBLatency                     BranchCache
Function        Set-BCSecretKey                         BranchCache
Function        Set-ClusteredScheduledTask              ScheduledTasks
Function        Set-CmdLetBoldFace                      DocModule
Function        Set-DAClientExperienceConfiguration     DirectAccessCl...
Function        Set-DAEntryPointTableItem               DirectAccessCl...
Function        Set-Disk                                Storage
Function        Set-DnsClient                           DnsClient
Function        Set-DnsClientGlobalSetting              DnsClient
Function        Set-DnsClientNrptGlobal                 DnsClient
Function        Set-DnsClientNrptRule                   DnsClient
Function        Set-DnsClientServerAddress              DnsClient
Function        Set-DtcAdvancedHostSetting              MsDtc
Function        Set-DtcAdvancedSetting                  MsDtc
Function        Set-DtcClusterDefault                   MsDtc
Function        Set-DtcClusterTMMapping                 MsDtc
Function        Set-DtcDefault                          MsDtc
Function        Set-DtcLog                              MsDtc
Function        Set-DtcNetworkSetting                   MsDtc
Function        Set-DtcTransaction                      MsDtc
Function        Set-DtcTransactionsTraceSession         MsDtc
Function        Set-DtcTransactionsTraceSetting         MsDtc
Function        Set-FileIntegrity                       Storage
Function        Set-InitiatorPort                       Storage
Function        Set-IscsiChapSecret                     iSCSI
Function        Set-LocalGroup                          LocalUserManag...
Function        Set-LocalUser                           LocalUserManag...
Function        Set-LocalUserPassword                   LocalUserManag...
Function        Set-LogProperties                       PSDiagnostics
Function        Set-MMAgent                             MMAgent
Function        Set-NCSIPolicyConfiguration             NetworkConnect...
Function        Set-Net6to4Configuration                NetworkTransition
Function        Set-NetAdapter                          NetAdapter
```

| | | |
|---|---|---|
| Function | Set-NetAdapterAdvancedProperty | NetAdapter |
| Function | Set-NetAdapterBinding | NetAdapter |
| Function | Set-NetAdapterChecksumOffload | NetAdapter |
| Function | Set-NetAdapterEncapsulatedPacketTaskOffload | NetAdapter |
| Function | Set-NetAdapterIPsecOffload | NetAdapter |
| Function | Set-NetAdapterLso | NetAdapter |
| Function | Set-NetAdapterPowerManagement | NetAdapter |
| Function | Set-NetAdapterQos | NetAdapter |
| Function | Set-NetAdapterRdma | NetAdapter |
| Function | Set-NetAdapterRsc | NetAdapter |
| Function | Set-NetAdapterRss | NetAdapter |
| Function | Set-NetAdapterSriov | NetAdapter |
| Function | Set-NetAdapterVmq | NetAdapter |
| Function | Set-NetConnectionProfile | NetConnection |
| Function | Set-NetDnsTransitionConfiguration | NetworkTransition |
| Function | Set-NetFirewallAddressFilter | NetSecurity |
| Function | Set-NetFirewallApplicationFilter | NetSecurity |
| Function | Set-NetFirewallInterfaceFilter | NetSecurity |
| Function | Set-NetFirewallInterfaceTypeFilter | NetSecurity |
| Function | Set-NetFirewallPortFilter | NetSecurity |
| Function | Set-NetFirewallProfile | NetSecurity |
| Function | Set-NetFirewallRule | NetSecurity |
| Function | Set-NetFirewallSecurityFilter | NetSecurity |
| Function | Set-NetFirewallServiceFilter | NetSecurity |
| Function | Set-NetFirewallSetting | NetSecurity |
| Function | Set-NetIPAddress | NetTCPIP |
| Function | Set-NetIPHttpsConfiguration | NetworkTransition |
| Function | Set-NetIPInterface | NetTCPIP |
| Function | Set-NetIPsecDospSetting | NetSecurity |
| Function | Set-NetIPsecMainModeCryptoSet | NetSecurity |
| Function | Set-NetIPsecMainModeRule | NetSecurity |
| Function | Set-NetIPsecPhase1AuthSet | NetSecurity |
| Function | Set-NetIPsecPhase2AuthSet | NetSecurity |
| Function | Set-NetIPsecQuickModeCryptoSet | NetSecurity |
| Function | Set-NetIPsecRule | NetSecurity |
| Function | Set-NetIPv4Protocol | NetTCPIP |
| Function | Set-NetIPv6Protocol | NetTCPIP |
| Function | Set-NetIsatapConfiguration | NetworkTransition |
| Function | Set-NetLbfoTeam | NetLbfo |
| Function | Set-NetLbfoTeamMember | NetLbfo |
| Function | Set-NetLbfoTeamNic | NetLbfo |
| Function | Set-NetNatTransitionConfiguration | NetworkTransition |
| Function | Set-NetNeighbor | NetTCPIP |
| Function | Set-NetOffloadGlobalSetting | NetTCPIP |
| Function | Set-NetQosPolicy | NetQos |
| Function | Set-NetRoute | NetTCPIP |
| Function | Set-NetTCPSetting | NetTCPIP |
| Function | Set-NetTeredoConfiguration | NetworkTransition |
| Function | Set-NetUDPSetting | NetTCPIP |
| Function | Set-NetVirtualizationCustomerRoute | NetWNV |
| Function | Set-NetVirtualizationGlobal | NetWNV |
| Function | Set-NetVirtualizationLookupRecord | NetWNV |
| Function | Set-NetVirtualizationProviderAddress | NetWNV |
| Function | Set-NetVirtualizationProviderRoute | NetWNV |
| Function | Set-OdbcDriver | Wdac |
| Function | Set-OdbcDsn | Wdac |

| | | |
|---|---|---|
| Function | Set-Partition | Storage |
| Function | Set-PhysicalDisk | Storage |
| Function | Set-PrintConfiguration | PrintManagement |
| Function | Set-Printer | PrintManagement |
| Function | Set-PrinterProperty | PrintManagement |
| Function | Set-Profile | |
| Function | Set-Profile | PowerShellISEM... |
| Function | Set-PsConsole | |
| Function | Set-PSConsoleFont | |
| Function | Set-PsISE | MenuModule |
| Function | Set-ResiliencySetting | Storage |
| Function | Set-ScheduledTask | ScheduledTasks |
| Function | Set-SmbClientConfiguration | SmbShare |
| Function | Set-SmbServerConfiguration | SmbShare |
| Function | Set-SmbShare | SmbShare |
| Function | Set-StoragePool | Storage |
| Function | Set-StorageSetting | Storage |
| Function | Set-StorageSubSystem | Storage |
| Function | Set-VirtualDisk | Storage |
| Function | Set-Volume | Storage |
| Function | Set-VolumeScrubPolicy | Storage |
| Function | Set-VpnConnection | VpnClient |
| Function | Set-VpnConnectionProxy | VpnClient |
| Cmdlet | Select-Object | Microsoft.Powe... |
| Cmdlet | Select-String | Microsoft.Powe... |
| Cmdlet | Select-Xml | Microsoft.Powe... |
| Cmdlet | Send-DtcDiagnosticTransaction | MsDtc |
| Cmdlet | Send-MailMessage | Microsoft.Powe... |
| Cmdlet | Set-Acl | Microsoft.Powe... |
| Cmdlet | Set-Alias | Microsoft.Powe... |
| Cmdlet | Set-AppLockerPolicy | AppLocker |
| Cmdlet | Set-AuthenticodeSignature | Microsoft.Powe... |
| Cmdlet | Set-BitsTransfer | BitsTransfer |
| Cmdlet | Set-CertificateAutoEnrollmentPolicy | PKI |
| Cmdlet | Set-CimInstance | CimCmdlets |
| Cmdlet | Set-Content | Microsoft.Powe... |
| Cmdlet | Set-Culture | International |
| Cmdlet | Set-Date | Microsoft.Powe... |
| Cmdlet | Set-ExecutionPolicy | Microsoft.Powe... |
| Cmdlet | Set-Item | Microsoft.Powe... |
| Cmdlet | Set-ItemProperty | Microsoft.Powe... |
| Cmdlet | Set-JobTrigger | PSScheduledJob |
| Cmdlet | Set-KdsConfiguration | Kds |
| Cmdlet | Set-Location | Microsoft.Powe... |
| Cmdlet | Set-PSBreakpoint | Microsoft.Powe... |
| Cmdlet | Set-PSDebug | Microsoft.Powe... |
| Cmdlet | Set-PSSessionConfiguration | Microsoft.Powe... |
| Cmdlet | Set-ScheduledJob | PSScheduledJob |
| Cmdlet | Set-ScheduledJobOption | PSScheduledJob |
| Cmdlet | Set-SecureBootUEFI | SecureBoot |
| Cmdlet | Set-Service | Microsoft.Powe... |
| Cmdlet | Set-StrictMode | Microsoft.Powe... |
| Cmdlet | Set-TpmOwnerAuth | TrustedPlatfor... |
| Cmdlet | Set-TraceSource | Microsoft.Powe... |
| Cmdlet | Set-Variable | Microsoft.Powe... |
| Cmdlet | Set-VHD | Hyper-V |

| | | |
|---|---|---|
| Cmdlet | Set-VM | Hyper-V |
| Cmdlet | Set-VMBios | Hyper-V |
| Cmdlet | Set-VMComPort | Hyper-V |
| Cmdlet | Set-VMDvdDrive | Hyper-V |
| Cmdlet | Set-VMFibreChannelHba | Hyper-V |
| Cmdlet | Set-VMFloppyDiskDrive | Hyper-V |
| Cmdlet | Set-VMHardDiskDrive | Hyper-V |
| Cmdlet | Set-VMHost | Hyper-V |
| Cmdlet | Set-VMMemory | Hyper-V |
| Cmdlet | Set-VMMigrationNetwork | Hyper-V |
| Cmdlet | Set-VMNetworkAdapter | Hyper-V |
| Cmdlet | Set-VMNetworkAdapterFailoverConfiguration | Hyper-V |
| Cmdlet | Set-VMNetworkAdapterVlan | Hyper-V |
| Cmdlet | Set-VMProcessor | Hyper-V |
| Cmdlet | Set-VMRemoteFx3dVideoAdapter | Hyper-V |
| Cmdlet | Set-VMReplication | Hyper-V |
| Cmdlet | Set-VMReplicationAuthorizationEntry | Hyper-V |
| Cmdlet | Set-VMReplicationServer | Hyper-V |
| Cmdlet | Set-VMResourcePool | Hyper-V |
| Cmdlet | Set-VMSan | Hyper-V |
| Cmdlet | Set-VMSwitch | Hyper-V |
| Cmdlet | Set-VMSwitchExtensionPortFeature | Hyper-V |
| Cmdlet | Set-VMSwitchExtensionSwitchFeature | Hyper-V |
| Cmdlet | Set-WinAcceptLanguageFromLanguageListOptOut | International |
| Cmdlet | Set-WinCultureFromLanguageListOptOut | International |
| Cmdlet | Set-WinDefaultInputMethodOverride | International |
| Cmdlet | Set-WindowsEdition | Dism |
| Cmdlet | Set-WindowsProductKey | Dism |
| Cmdlet | Set-WinHomeLocation | International |
| Cmdlet | Set-WinLanguageBarOption | International |
| Cmdlet | Set-WinSystemLocale | International |
| Cmdlet | Set-WinUILanguageOverride | International |
| Cmdlet | Set-WinUserLanguageList | International |
| Cmdlet | Set-WmiInstance | Microsoft.Powe... |
| Cmdlet | Set-WSManInstance | Microsoft.WSMa... |
| Cmdlet | Set-WSManQuickConfig | Microsoft.WSMa... |

**8.** Use the *gcm* alias and specify the *-noun* argument. Use *o\** for the noun. This is shown here:

```
gcm -noun o*
```

The previous command will return all the cmdlets that contain a noun that begins with the letter *o*. This result is as follows:

| CommandType | Name | ModuleName |
|---|---|---|
| Function | Add-OdbcDsn | Wdac |
| Function | Disable-OdbcPerfCounter | Wdac |
| Function | Enable-OdbcPerfCounter | Wdac |
| Function | Get-OdbcDriver | Wdac |
| Function | Get-OdbcDsn | Wdac |
| Function | Get-OdbcPerfCounter | Wdac |
| Function | Get-OffloadDataTransferSetting | Storage |
| Function | Get-OptimalSize | BasicFunctions |
| Function | Remove-OdbcDsn | Wdac |
| Function | Set-OdbcDriver | Wdac |

```
Function        Set-OdbcDsn                     Wdac
Cmdlet          Compare-Object                  Microsoft.Powe...
Cmdlet          ForEach-Object                  Microsoft.Powe...
Cmdlet          Group-Object                    Microsoft.Powe...
Cmdlet          Measure-Object                  Microsoft.Powe...
Cmdlet          New-Object                      Microsoft.Powe...
Cmdlet          Register-ObjectEvent            Microsoft.Powe...
Cmdlet          Select-Object                   Microsoft.Powe...
Cmdlet          Sort-Object                     Microsoft.Powe...
Cmdlet          Tee-Object                      Microsoft.Powe...
Cmdlet          Where-Object                    Microsoft.Powe...
Cmdlet          Write-Output                    Microsoft.Powe...
```

**9.** Retrieve only the syntax of the *Get-Command* cmdlet by specifying the *-syntax* argument. Use the *gcm* alias to do this, as shown here:

```
gcm -syntax Get-Command
```

The syntax of the *Get-Command* cmdlet is returned by the previous command. The output is as follows:

```
Get-Command [[-ArgumentList] <Object[]>] [-Verb <String[]>] [-Noun <String[]>]
[-PSSnapin <String[]>] [-TotalCount <Int32>] [-Syntax] [-Verbose] [-Debug]
 [-ErrorAction <ActionPreference>] [-ErrorVariable <String>] [-OutVariable <String>]
[-OutBuffer <Int32>]
Get-Command [[-Name] <String[]>] [[-ArgumentList] <Object[]>] [-CommandType
<CommandTypes>]
 [-TotalCount <Int32>] [-Syntax] [-Verbose] [-Debug] [-ErrorAction
<ActionPreference>] [-ErrorVariable <String>] [-OutVariable <String>] [-OutBuffer
<Int32>]
```

**10.** Try to use only aliases to repeat the *Get-Command* syntax command to retrieve the syntax of the *Get-Command* cmdlet. This is shown here:

```
gcm -syntax gcm
```

The result of this command is not the nice syntax description of the previous command. The rather disappointing result is as follows:

```
Get-Command
```

This concludes the procedure for finding commands by using the *Get-Command* cmdlet.

---

## Quick Check

**Q.** To retrieve a definition of the *Get-Command* cmdlet, using the dotted notation, what command would you use?

**A.** *(gcm Get-Command).definition*

---

# Using the *Get-Member* cmdlet

The *Get-Member* cmdlet retrieves information about the members of objects. Although this may not seem very exciting, remember that because everything returned from a cmdlet is an object, you can use the *Get-Member* cmdlet to examine the methods and properties of objects. When the *Get-Member* cmdlet is used with *Get-ChildItem* on the file system, it returns a listing of all the methods and properties available to work with the *DirectoryInfo* and *FileInfo* objects.

### Objects, properties, and methods

One of the fundamental features of Windows PowerShell is that cmdlets return objects. An object is a thing that gives us the ability to either describe something or do something. If you are not going to describe or do something, then there is no reason to create the object. Depending on the circumstances, you may be more interested in the methods or the properties. As an example, let's consider rental cars. I used to travel a great deal when I was a consultant at Microsoft, and I often needed to obtain a rental car.

To put this into programming terms, when I got to the airport, I would go to the rental car counter, and I would use the *New-Object* cmdlet to create a *rentalCAR* object. When I used this cmdlet, I was only interested in the methods available from the *rentalCAR* object. I needed to use the *DriveDowntheRoad* method, the *StopAtaRedLight* method, and perhaps the *PlayNiceMusic* method. I was not, however, interested in the properties of the *rentalCAR* object.

At home, I have a cute little sports car. It has exactly the same methods as the *rentalCAR* object, but I created the *sportsCAR* object primarily because of its properties. It is green and has alloy rims, a convertible top, and a 3.5-liter engine. Interestingly enough, it has exactly the same methods as the *rentalCAR* object. It also has the *DriveDowntheRoad* method, the *StopAtaRedLight* method, and the *PlayNiceMusic* method, but the deciding factor in creating the *sportsCAR* object was the properties, not the methods.

## Using the *Get-Member* cmdlet to examine properties and methods

In a Windows PowerShell prompt, enter the *Get-ChildItem* cmdlet followed by the path to a folder, and pipe it to the *Get-Member* cmdlet. Here's an example:

```
Get-ChildItem C:\ | Get-Member
```

## Using the *Get-Member* cmdlet

1.  Open Windows PowerShell by choosing Start | Run | Windows PowerShell. The PowerShell prompt will open by default at the root of your Documents And Settings folder.

2.  Use an alias to refer to the *Get-Alias* cmdlet. To find the correct alias, use the *Get-Alias* cmdlet as follows:

```
Get-Alias g*
```

3.  After you have retrieved the alias for the *Get-Alias* cmdlet, use it to find the alias for the *Get-Member* cmdlet. One way to do this is to use the following command, simply using *gal* in place of the *Get-Alias* name you used in the previous command:

```
gal g*
```

The listing of aliases defined that begin with the letter *g* appears as a result of the previous command. The output is shown here:

```
CommandType     Name                                       ModuleName
-----------     ----                                       ----------
Alias           gal -> Get-Alias
Alias           gbp -> Get-PSBreakpoint
Alias           gc -> Get-Content
Alias           gci -> Get-ChildItem
Alias           gcm -> Get-Command
Alias           gcs -> Get-PSCallStack
Alias           gdr -> Get-PSDrive
Alias           ghy -> Get-History
Alias           gi -> Get-Item
Alias           gjb -> Get-Job
Alias           gl -> Get-Location
Alias           gm -> Get-Member
Alias           gmo -> Get-Module
Alias           gp -> Get-ItemProperty
Alias           gps -> Get-Process
Alias           group -> Group-Object
Alias           gsn -> Get-PSSession
Alias           gsnp -> Get-PSSnapin
Alias           gsv -> Get-Service
Alias           gu -> Get-Unique
Alias           gv -> Get-Variable
Alias           gwck -> Get-WmiKey                          HSGWMImoduleV6
Alias           gwcm -> Get-WmiClassMethods                 HSGWMImoduleV6
Alias           gwcp -> Get-WmiClassProperties              HSGWMImoduleV6
Alias           gwcq -> Get-WMIClassesWithQualifiers        HSGWMImoduleV6
Alias           gwkv -> Get-WmiKeyvalue                     HSGWMImoduleV6
Alias           gwmi -> Get-WmiObject
Alias           gwq -> Get-WmiClassesAndQuery               HSGWMImoduleV6
```

4. Use the *gal* alias to obtain a listing of all aliases that begin with the letter *g*. Pipe the results to the *Sort-Object* cmdlet and sort on the property attribute called *definition*. This is shown here:

```
gal g* |Sort-Object -property definition
```

The listings of cmdlets that begin with the letter *g* are now sorted, and the results of the command are as follows:

```
CommandType      Name                                    ModuleName
-----------      ----                                    ----------
Alias            gal -> Get-Alias
Alias            gci -> Get-ChildItem
Alias            gcm -> Get-Command
Alias            gc -> Get-Content
Alias            ghy -> Get-History
Alias            gi -> Get-Item
Alias            gp -> Get-ItemProperty
Alias            gjb -> Get-Job
Alias            gl -> Get-Location
Alias            gm -> Get-Member
Alias            gmo -> Get-Module
Alias            gps -> Get-Process
Alias            gbp -> Get-PSBreakpoint
Alias            gcs -> Get-PSCallStack
Alias            gdr -> Get-PSDrive
Alias            gsn -> Get-PSSession
Alias            gsnp -> Get-PSSnapin
Alias            gsv -> Get-Service
Alias            gu -> Get-Unique
Alias            gv -> Get-Variable
Alias            gwq -> Get-WmiClassesAndQuery           HSGWMImoduleV6
Alias            gwcq -> Get-WMIClassesWithQualifiers    HSGWMImoduleV6
Alias            gwcm -> Get-WmiClassMethods             HSGWMImoduleV6
Alias            gwcp -> Get-WmiClassProperties          HSGWMImoduleV6
Alias            gwck -> Get-WmiKey                       HSGWMImoduleV6
Alias            gwkv -> Get-WmiKeyvalue                  HSGWMImoduleV6
Alias            gwmi -> Get-WmiObject
Alias            group -> Group-Object
```

5. Use the alias for the *Get-ChildItem* cmdlet and pipe the output to the alias for the *Get-Member* cmdlet. This is shown here:

```
gci | gm
```

6. To only see properties available for the *Get-ChildItem* cmdlet, use the *-membertype* argument and supply a value of *property*. Use tab completion this time, rather than the *gci | gm* alias. This is shown here:

```
Get-ChildItem -Force | Get-Member -membertype property
```

The output from this command is shown here:

```
   TypeName: System.IO.DirectoryInfo

Name                   MemberType Definition
----                   ---------- ----------
Attributes             Property   System.IO.FileAttributes Attributes {get;set;}
CreationTime           Property   datetime CreationTime {get;set;}
CreationTimeUtc        Property   datetime CreationTimeUtc {get;set;}
Exists                 Property   bool Exists {get;}
Extension              Property   string Extension {get;}
FullName               Property   string FullName {get;}
LastAccessTime         Property   datetime LastAccessTime {get;set;}
LastAccessTimeUtc      Property   datetime LastAccessTimeUtc {get;set;}
LastWriteTime          Property   datetime LastWriteTime {get;set;}
LastWriteTimeUtc       Property   datetime LastWriteTimeUtc {get;set;}
Name                   Property   string Name {get;}
Parent                 Property   System.IO.DirectoryInfo Parent {get;}
Root                   Property   System.IO.DirectoryInfo Root {get;}


   TypeName: System.IO.FileInfo

Name                   MemberType Definition
----                   ---------- ----------
Attributes             Property   System.IO.FileAttributes Attributes {get;set;}
CreationTime           Property   datetime CreationTime {get;set;}
CreationTimeUtc        Property   datetime CreationTimeUtc {get;set;}
Directory              Property   System.IO.DirectoryInfo Directory {get;}
DirectoryName          Property   string DirectoryName {get;}
Exists                 Property   bool Exists {get;}
Extension              Property   string Extension {get;}
FullName               Property   string FullName {get;}
IsReadOnly             Property   bool IsReadOnly {get;set;}
LastAccessTime         Property   datetime LastAccessTime {get;set;}
LastAccessTimeUtc      Property   datetime LastAccessTimeUtc {get;set;}
LastWriteTime          Property   datetime LastWriteTime {get;set;}
LastWriteTimeUtc       Property   datetime LastWriteTimeUtc {get;set;}
Length                 Property   long Length {get;}
Name                   Property   string Name {get;}
```

7. Use the *-membertype* parameter of the *Get-Member* cmdlet to view the methods available from the object returned by the *Get-ChildItem* cmdlet. To do this, supply a value of method to the *-membertype* parameter, as follows:

```
Get-ChildItem | Get-Member -membertype method
```

**8.** The output from the previous list returns all the methods defined for the *Get-ChildItem* cmdlet. This output is shown here:

```
TypeName: System.IO.DirectoryInfo

Name                        MemberType Definition
----                        ---------- ----------
Create                      Method     void Create(), void Create(System.Security.A...
CreateObjRef                Method     System.Runtime.Remoting.ObjRef CreateObjRef(...
CreateSubdirectory          Method     System.IO.DirectoryInfo CreateSubdirectory(s...
Delete                      Method     void Delete(), void Delete(bool recursive)
EnumerateDirectories        Method     System.Collections.Generic.IEnumerable[Syste...
EnumerateFiles              Method     System.Collections.Generic.IEnumerable[Syste...
EnumerateFileSystemInfos    Method     System.Collections.Generic.IEnumerable[Syste...
Equals                      Method     bool Equals(System.Object obj)
GetAccessControl            Method     System.Security.AccessControl.DirectorySecur...
GetDirectories              Method     System.IO.DirectoryInfo[] GetDirectories(), ...
GetFiles                    Method     System.IO.FileInfo[] GetFiles(string searchP...
GetFileSystemInfos          Method     System.IO.FileSystemInfo[] GetFileSystemInfo...
GetHashCode                 Method     int GetHashCode()
GetLifetimeService          Method     System.Object GetLifetimeService()
GetObjectData               Method     void GetObjectData(System.Runtime.Serializat...
GetType                     Method     type GetType()
InitializeLifetimeService   Method     System.Object InitializeLifetimeService()
MoveTo                      Method     void MoveTo(string destDirName)
Refresh                     Method     void Refresh()
SetAccessControl            Method     void SetAccessControl(System.Security.Access...
ToString                    Method     string ToString()
```

**9.** Use the up arrow key in the Windows PowerShell console to retrieve the previous *Get-ChildItem* | *Get-Member -MemberType* method command, and change the value method to *m\** to use a wildcard to retrieve the methods. The output will be exactly the same as the previous listing of members because the only member type beginning with the letter *m* on the *Get-ChildItem* cmdlet is the *MemberType* method. The command is as follows:

```
Get-ChildItem | Get-Member -membertype m*
```

**10.** Use the *-inputobject* argument to the *Get-Member* cmdlet to retrieve member definitions of each property or method in the list. The command to do this is as follows:

```
Get-Member -inputobject Get-ChildItem
```

The output from the previous command is shown here:

```
PS C:\> Get-Member -inputobject Get-ChildItem

   TypeName: System.String
```

```
Name                 MemberType            Definition
----                 ----------            ----------
Clone                Method                System.Object Clone()
CompareTo            Method                System.Int32 CompareTo(Object value),...
Contains             Method                System.Boolean Contains(String value)
CopyTo               Method                System.Void CopyTo(Int32 sourceIndex,...
EndsWith             Method                System.Boolean EndsWith(String value)...
Equals               Method                System.Boolean Equals(Object obj), Sy...
GetEnumerator        Method                System.CharEnumerator GetEnumerator()
GetHashCode          Method                System.Int32 GetHashCode()
GetType              Method                System.Type GetType()
GetTypeCode          Method                System.TypeCode GetTypeCode()
get_Chars            Method                System.Char get_Chars(Int32 index)
get_Length           Method                System.Int32 get_Length()
IndexOf              Method                System.Int32 IndexOf(Char value, Int3...
IndexOfAny           Method                System.Int32 IndexOfAny(Char[] anyOf,...
Insert               Method                System.String Insert(Int32 startIndex...
IsNormalized         Method                System.Boolean IsNormalized(), System...
LastIndexOf          Method                System.Int32 LastIndexOf(Char value, ...
LastIndexOfAny       Method                System.Int32 LastIndexOfAny(Char[] an...
Normalize            Method                System.String Normalize(), System.Str...
PadLeft              Method                System.String PadLeft(Int32 totalWidt...
PadRight             Method                System.String PadRight(Int32 totalWid...
Remove               Method                System.String Remove(Int32 startIndex...
Replace              Method                System.String Replace(Char oldChar, C...
Split                Method                System.String[] Split(Params Char[] s...
StartsWith           Method                System.Boolean StartsWith(String valu...
Substring            Method                System.String Substring(Int32 startIn...
ToCharArray          Method                System.Char[] ToCharArray(), System.C...
ToLower              Method                System.String ToLower(), System.Strin...
ToLowerInvariant     Method                System.String ToLowerInvariant()
ToString             Method                System.String ToString(), System.Stri...
ToUpper              Method                System.String ToUpper(), System.Strin...
ToUpperInvariant     Method                System.String ToUpperInvariant()
Trim                 Method                System.String Trim(Params Char[] trim...
TrimEnd              Method                System.String TrimEnd(Params Char[] t...
TrimStart            Method                System.String TrimStart(Params Char[]...
Chars                ParameterizedProperty System.Char Chars(Int32 index) {get;}
Length               Property              System.Int32 Length {get;}
```

This concludes the procedure for using the *Get-Member* cmdlet.

## Quick Check

**Q.** To retrieve a listing of aliases beginning with the letter *g* that is sorted on the *-definition* property, what command would you use?

**A.** *gal g\* | Sort-Object -property definition*

# Using the *New-Object* cmdlet

The use of objects in Windows PowerShell provides many exciting opportunities to do things that are not built into the PowerShell. You may recall from using VBScript that there is an object called the *wshShell* object. If you are not familiar with this object, see Figure 2-7, which shows a drawing of the object model.

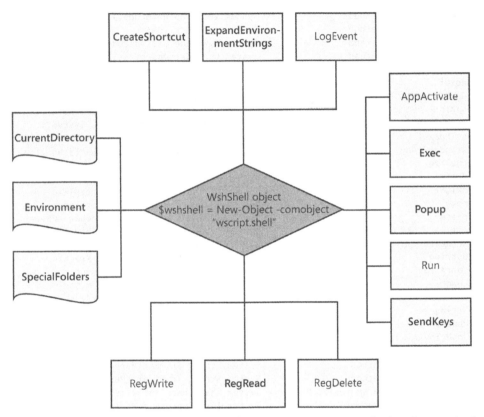

**FIGURE 2-7** The VBScript *wshShell* object contributes many easy-to-use methods and properties for the network administrator.

## Creating and Using the *wshShell* Object

To create a new instance of the *wshShell* object, use the *New-Object* cmdlet while specifying the *-comobject* argument and supplying the program ID of *wscript.shell*. Hold the object created in a variable. Here's an example:

```
$wshShell = New-Object -comobject "wscript.shell":
```

After the object has been created and stored in a variable, you can directly use any of the methods that are provided by the object. This is shown in the two lines of code that follow:

```
$wshShell = New-Object -comobject "wscript.shell"
$wshShell.run("calc.exe")
```

In this code, you use the *New-Object* cmdlet to create an instance of the *wshShell* object. You then use the *run* method to launch Calculator. After the object is created and stored in the variable, you can use tab completion to suggest the names of the methods contained in the object. This is shown in Figure 2-8.

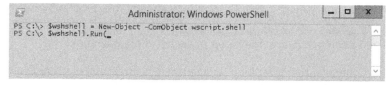

**FIGURE 2-8** Tab completion enumerates methods provided by the object.

### Creating the *wshShell* object

1.  Open Windows PowerShell by choosing Start | Run | Windows PowerShell. The PowerShell prompt will open by default at the root of your Documents And Settings folder.

2.  Create an instance of the *wshShell* object by using the *New-Object* cmdlet. Supply the -comobject argument to the cmdlet and specify the program ID for the *wshShell* object, which is *wscript.shell*. Assign the result of the *New-Object* cmdlet to the variable *$wshShell*. The code to do this is as follows:

    ```
    $wshShell = New-Object -comobject "wscript.shell"
    ```

3.  Launch an instance of Calculator by using the *run* method from the *wshShell* object. Use tab completion to avoid having to type the entire name of the method. To use the method, begin the line with the variable you used to hold the *wshShell* object, followed by a period and the name of the method. Then supply the name of the program to run inside parentheses and quotes, as shown here:

    ```
    $wshShell.run("Calc.exe")
    ```

4.  Use the *ExpandEnvironmentStrings* method to print out the path to the Windows directory. It is stored in an environment variable called *%windir%*. The tab-completion feature of Windows PowerShell is useful for this method name. The environment variable must be enclosed in quotation marks, as shown here:

    ```
    $wshShell.ExpandEnvironmentStrings("%windir%")
    ```

5. This command reveals the full path to the Windows directory on your machine. On my computer, the output looks like the following:

```
C:\WINDOWS
```

## Using the *Show-Command* cmdlet

The *Show-Command* cmdlet displays a graphical command picker that enables you to select cmdlets from a list. At first glance, the *Show-Command* cmdlet might appear to be a graphical version of the *Get-Command* cmdlet, but it is actually much more. The first indication of this is that it blocks the Windows PowerShell console—that is, control to the Windows PowerShell console does not return until you have either selected a command from the picker or canceled the operation.

When you run the *Show-Command* cmdlet with no parameters, a window 600 pixels high and 300 pixels wide appears. You can control the size of the window by using the *-Height* and *-Width* parameters. The following command creates a command window 500 pixels high and 350 pixels wide.

**Show-Command** -Height 500 -Width 350

The command window created by the this command appears in Figure 2-9.

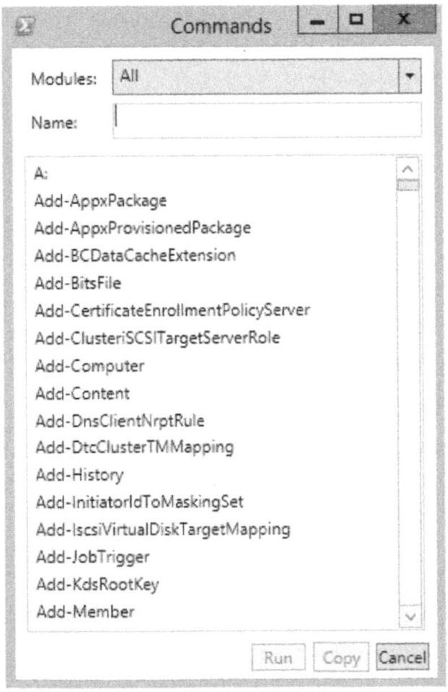

**FIGURE 2-9** The *Show-Command* cmdlet displays all commands from all modules by default.

To retrieve a specific command, supply the name of a specific cmdlet when calling the *Show-Command* cmdlet. This technique appears here:

**Show-Command** -Height 500 -Name **Get-Process**

When the command dialog box appears, use the check boxes to enable switched parameters, and the rectangular boxes to supply values for other parameters. This technique appears in Figure 2-10.

**FIGURE 2-10** Use the check boxes to add switched parameters to a command and the rectangular boxes to add values for parameters in the command dialog box.

Once you have the created the command you wish to use, you can either copy the command to the clipboard or run the command. If you choose to run it, the Windows PowerShell console displays both the created command and the output from the command. This appears in Figure 2-11.

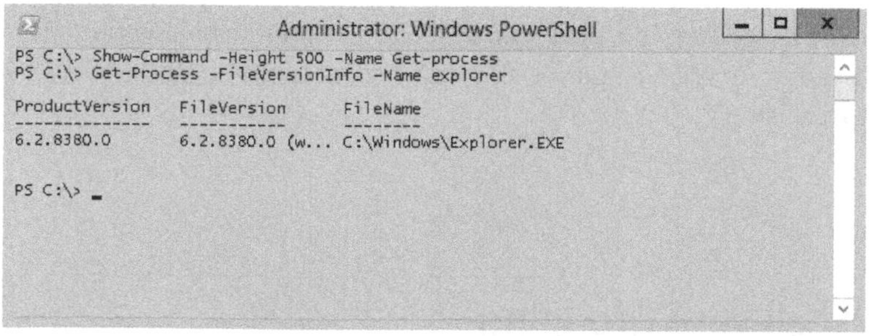

**FIGURE 2-11** Both the created command and the output from that command return to the Windows PowerShell console when using the *Show-Command* cmdlet.

# Windows PowerShell cmdlet naming helps you learn

One of the great things about Windows PowerShell is the verb-noun naming convention. In Windows PowerShell, the verbs indicate an action to perform, such as *set* to make a change or *get* to retrieve a value. The noun indicates the item with which to work, such as a process or a service. By mastering the verb-noun naming convention, you can quickly hypothesize what a prospective command might be called. For example, if you need to obtain information about a process, and you know that Windows PowerShell uses the verb *get* to retrieve information, you can surmise that the command might be called *Get-Process*. To obtain information about services, you could try *Get-Service*, and once again you would be correct.

> **Note** When guessing Windows PowerShell cmdlet names, always try the singular form first. Windows PowerShell convention uses the singular form of nouns. It is not a design requirement, but it is a strong preference. For example, the cmdlets are named *Get-Service* and *Get-Process*, not *Get-Services* and *Get-Processes*.

To see the list of approved verbs, use the *Get-Verb* cmdlet:

```
Get-Verb
```

There are 98 approved verbs in Windows PowerShell 3.0. This number increases the 96 approved verbs from Windows PowerShell 2.0 by only 2 new verbs. The new verbs are *use* and *unprotect*. This appears in the command that follows, where the *Measure-Object* cmdlet returns the count of the different verbs.

```
PS C:\> (Get-Verb | Measure-Object).count
98
```

But you do not need to add the *Measure-Object* cmdlet to the previous command because the *Get-Verb* cmdlet returns an array. Array objects always contain a *count* property. Therefore, an easier form of the command appears here:

```
PS C:\> (Get-verb).count
98
```

## Windows PowerShell verb grouping

While learning 100 different verbs might be difficult, the Windows PowerShell team grouped the verbs together to make them easier to learn. For example, analyzing the common verbs reveals a pattern. The common verbs appear here:

```
PS C:\> Get-Verb | where group -match 'common' | Format-Wide verb -auto
Add      Clear    Close    Copy     Enter    Exit     Find      Format   Get
Hide     Join     Lock     Move     New      Open     Optimize  Pop      Push
Redo     Remove   Rename   Reset    Resize   Search   Select    Set      Show
Skip     Split    Step     Switch   Undo     Unlock   Watch
```

The pattern to the verbs emerges when you analyze them: *Add/Remove, Enter/Exit, Get/Set, Select/Skip, Lock/Unlock, Push/Pop*, and so on. By learning the pattern of opposite verbs, you quickly gain a handle on the Windows PowerShell naming convention. Not every verb has an opposite partner, but there are enough that it makes sense to look for them.

By using the Windows PowerShell verb grouping, you can determine where to focus your efforts. The PowerShell team separated the verbs into seven different groups based on common IT tasks, such as working with data and performing diagnostics. The following command lists the Windows PowerShell verb grouping:

```
PS C:\> Get-Verb | select group -Unique
Group
-----
Common
Data
Lifecycle
Diagnostic
Communications
Security
Other
```

## Windows PowerShell verb distribution

Another way to get a better handle on the Windows PowerShell cmdlets is to analyze the verb distribution. While there are nearly 100 different approved verbs (as well as a variety of unapproved ones), you'll typically only use a fraction of them often in a standard Windows PowerShell installation, and some not at all. If you use the *Group-Object* cmdlet (which has an alias of *group*) and the *Sort-Object* cmdlet (which has an alias of *sort*), the distribution of the cmdlets quickly becomes evident. The following command shows the verb distribution:

```
Get-Command -CommandType cmdlet | group verb | sort count -Descending
```

**Note** The exact number of Windows PowerShell cmdlets and the exact distribution of Windows PowerShell cmdlet verbs and nouns depend on the version of the operating system used, as well as which features are enabled on the operating system. In addition, the installation of certain programs and applications adds additional Windows PowerShell cmdlets. Therefore, when following along with this section, your numbers probably will not exactly match what appears here. This is fine, and does not indicate a problem with the command or your installation.

Figure 2-12 shows the command and the associated output.

```
Administrator: Windows PowerShell                          _ □ X

PS C:\> Get-Command -CommandType cmdlet | group verb | sort count -Descending

Count Name                Group
----- ----                -----
   94 Get                 {Get-Acl, Get-Alias, Get-AppLockerFileInformation...
   48 Set                 {Set-Acl, Set-Alias, Set-AppLockerPolicy, Set-Aut...
   38 New                 {New-Alias, New-AppLockerPolicy, New-CertificateN...
   30 Remove              {Remove-AppxProvisionedPackage, Remove-BitsTransf...
   15 Add                 {Add-AppxProvisionedPackage, Add-BitsFile, Add-Ce...
   11 Invoke              {Invoke-BpaModel, Invoke-CimMethod, Invoke-Comman...
   11 Import              {Import-Alias, Import-Certificate, Import-Clixml,...
   11 Export              {Export-Alias, Export-Certificate, Export-Clixml,...
   10 Test                {Test-AppLockerPolicy, Test-Certificate, Test-Com...
   10 Enable              {Enable-ComputerRestore, Enable-JobTrigger, Enabl...
   10 Disable             {Disable-ComputerRestore, Disable-JobTrigger, Dis...
    9 Clear               {Clear-Content, Clear-EventLog, Clear-History, Cl...
    8 Start               {Start-BitsTransfer, Start-DtcDiagnosticResourceM...
    8 Write               {Write-Debug, Write-Error, Write-EventLog, Write-...
    7 Out                 {Out-Default, Out-File, Out-GridView, Out-Host...}
    6 Stop                {Stop-Computer, Stop-DtcDiagnosticResourceManager...
    6 ConvertTo           {ConvertTo-Csv, ConvertTo-Html, ConvertTo-Json, C...
    6 Register            {Register-CimIndicationEvent, Register-EngineEven...
    5 Format              {Format-Custom, Format-List, Format-SecureBootUEF...
    4 Update              {Update-FormatData, Update-Help, Update-List, Upd...
    4 ConvertFrom         {ConvertFrom-Csv, ConvertFrom-Json, ConvertFrom-S...
    3 Wait                {Wait-Event, Wait-Job, Wait-Process}
    3 Unregister          {Unregister-Event, Unregister-PSSessionConfigurat...
    3 Suspend             {Suspend-BitsTransfer, Suspend-Job, Suspend-Service}
    3 Show                {Show-Command, Show-ControlPanelItem, Show-EventLog}
    3 Complete            {Complete-BitsTransfer, Complete-DtcDiagnosticTra...
    3 Select              {Select-Object, Select-String, Select-Xml}
    3 Resume              {Resume-BitsTransfer, Resume-Job, Resume-Service}
    3 Receive             {Receive-DtcDiagnosticTransaction, Receive-Job, R...
    3 Rename              {Rename-Computer, Rename-Item, Rename-ItemProperty}
    2 Measure             {Measure-Command, Measure-Object}
    2 Use                 {Use-Transaction, Use-WindowsUnattend}
    2 Undo                {Undo-DtcDiagnosticTransaction, Undo-Transaction}
    2 Unblock             {Unblock-File, Unblock-Tpm}
    2 Checkpoint          {Checkpoint-Computer, Checkpoint-IscsiVirtualDisk}
```

**FIGURE 2-12** Using *Get-Command* to display the Windows PowerShell verbs.

The output shown in Figure 2-12 makes it clear that most cmdlets only use a few of the verbs. For instance, of 436 cmdlets on my particular machines, 278 of the cmdlets use 1 of only 10 different verbs. This appears here:

```
PS C:\> (Get-Command -CommandType cmdlet | measure).count
436
PS C:\> $count = 0 ; Get-Command -CommandType cmdlet | group verb | sort count -Descending
 | select -First 10 | % { $count += $_.count ; $count }
94
142
180
210
225
236
247
258
268
278
```

Therefore, all you need to do is master the 10 different verbs listed earlier and you will have a good handle on more than one-half of the cmdlets that ship with Windows PowerShell 3.0.

# Creating a Windows PowerShell profile

As you create various aliases and functions, you may decide you like a particular keystroke combination and wish you could use your definition without always having to create it each time you run Windows PowerShell.

**Tip** I recommend reviewing the listing of all the aliases defined within Windows PowerShell before creating very many new aliases. The reason is that it will be easy, early on, to create duplicate settings (with slight variations).

Of course, you could create your own script that would perform your configuration if you remember to run it; however, what if you wish to have a more standardized method of working with your profile? To do this, you need to create a custom profile that will hold your settings. The really useful feature of creating a Windows PowerShell profile is that after the profile is created, it loads automatically when PowerShell is launched.

**Note** A Windows PowerShell profile is a Windows PowerShell script that runs each time Windows PowerShell starts. Windows PowerShell does not enable script support by default. In a network situation, the Windows PowerShell script execution policy may be determined by your network administrator via group policy. In a workgroup, or at home, the execution policy is not determined via group policy. For information about enabling Windows PowerShell script execution, see Chapter 5, "Using PowerShell Scripts."

The steps for creating a Windows PowerShell profile appear next.

## Creating a personal Windows PowerShell profile

1. In a Windows PowerShell console, check your script execution policy:

   ```
   Get-ExecutionPolicy
   ```

2. If the script execution policy is *restricted*, change it to *remotesigned*, but only for the current user:

   ```
   Set-ExecutionPolicy -Scope currentuser -ExecutionPolicy remotesigned
   ```

3. Review the description about Windows PowerShell execution policies, and enter **Y** to agree to make the change.

4. In a Windows PowerShell prompt, determine whether a profile exists by using the following command (by default, the Windows PowerShell profile does not exist):

   ```
   Test-Path $profile
   ```

5. If *tests-profile* returns *false*, create a new profile file by using the following command:

   ```
   New-Item -path $profile -itemtype file -force
   ```

6. Open the profile file in the Windows PowerShell ISE by using the following command:

   ```
   ise $profile
   ```

7. Create an alias in the profile named *gh* that resolves to the *Get-Help* cmdlet. This command appears here:

   ```
   Set-Alias gh Get-Help
   ```

8. Create a function that edits your Windows PowerShell console profile. This function appears here:

   ```
   Function Set-Profile
   {
    Ise $profile
   }
   ```

9. Start the Windows PowerShell *Transcript* command via the Windows PowerShell profile. To do this, add the *Start-Transcript* cmdlet as it appears here (the *Start-Transcript* cmdlet creates a record of all Windows PowerShell commands, as well as the output from those commands).

   ```
   Start-Transcript
   ```

10. Save the modifications to the Windows PowerShell console profile by pressing the Save icon in the tool bar, or by choosing Save from the File menu.

11. Close the Windows PowerShell ISE and close the Windows PowerShell console.

12. Open the Windows PowerShell console. You should now see the output in the console from starting the Windows PowerShell transcript utility.

13. Test the newly created *gh* alias.

14. Open the profile in the Windows PowerShell ISE by using the newly created *Set-Profile* function.

15. Review the Windows PowerShell profile and close the Windows PowerShell ISE.

    This concludes the exercise on creating a Windows PowerShell profile.

## Finding all aliases for a particular object

If you know the name of an object and you would like to retrieve all aliases for that object, you can use the *Get-Alias* cmdlet to retrieve the list of all aliases. Then you need to pipe the results to the *Where-Object* cmdlet and specify the value for the *definition* property. An example of doing this for the *Get-ChildItem* cmdlet is as follows:

```
gal | Where definition -match "Get-ChildItem"
```

# Working with cmdlets: step-by-step exercises

In the following exercise, you'll explore the use of the *Get-ChildItem* and *Get-Member* cmdlets in Windows PowerShell. You'll see that it is easy to use these cmdlets to automate routine administrative tasks. You'll also continue to experiment with the pipelining feature of Windows PowerShell.

### Working with the *Get-ChildItem* and *Get-Member* cmdlets

1. Open the Windows PowerShell console.

2. Use the *Get-Alias* cmdlet to retrieve a listing of all the aliases defined on the computer. Pipe this output to a *Where-Object* cmdlet. Specify a *-match* argument against the *definition* property that matches the name of the *Get-ChildItem* cmdlet. The code is as follows:

   ```
   gal | Where definition -match "Get-ChildItem"
   ```

   The results from the previous command show three aliases defined for the *Get-ChildItem* cmdlet:

   ```
   CommandType     Name                              ModuleName
   -----------     ----                              ----------
   Alias           dir -> Get-ChildItem
   Alias           gci -> Get-ChildItem
   Alias           ls -> Get-ChildItem
   ```

3. Using the *gci* alias for the *Get-ChildItem* cmdlet, obtain a listing of files and folders contained in the root directory. Type *gci* at the prompt.

4. To identify large files more quickly, pipe the output to a *Where-Object* cmdlet, and specify the *-gt* argument with a value of 1000 to evaluate the *length* property. This is shown here:

   ```
   gci | Where length -gt 1000
   ```

5. To remove the data cluttering your Windows PowerShell window, use *cls* to clear the screen.

6. Use the *Get-Alias* cmdlet to resolve the cmdlet to which the *cls* alias points. You can use the *gal* alias to avoid typing *Get-Alias* if you wish. This is shown here:

   ```
   gal cls
   ```

7. Use the *Get-Alias* cmdlet to resolve the cmdlet to which the *mred* alias points. This is shown here:

```
gal mred
```

8. It is likely that no *mred* alias is defined on your machine. In this case, you will see the following error message:

```
gal : This command cannot find a matching alias because an alias with the name
'mred' does not exist.
At line:1 char:1
+ gal mred
+ ~~~~~~~~
    + CategoryInfo          : ObjectNotFound: (mred:String) [Get-Alias],
    ItemNotFoundException
    + FullyQualifiedErrorId : ItemNotFoundException,Microsoft.PowerShell.Commands.
GetAliasCommand
```

9. Use the *Clear-Host* cmdlet to clear the screen. This is shown here:

```
clear-host
```

10. Use the *Get-Member* cmdlet to retrieve a list of properties and methods from the *Get-ChildItem* cmdlet. This is shown here:

```
Get-ChildItem | Get-Member -membertype property
```

11. The output from the preceding command is shown following. Examine the output, and identify a property that could be used with a *Where-Object* cmdlet to find the date when files were modified.

```
   TypeName: System.IO.DirectoryInfo

Name              MemberType Definition
----              ---------- ----------
Attributes        Property   System.IO.FileAttributes Attributes {get;set;}
CreationTime      Property   datetime CreationTime {get;set;}
CreationTimeUtc   Property   datetime CreationTimeUtc {get;set;}
Exists            Property   bool Exists {get;}
Extension         Property   string Extension {get;}
FullName          Property   string FullName {get;}
LastAccessTime    Property   datetime LastAccessTime {get;set;}
LastAccessTimeUtc Property   datetime LastAccessTimeUtc {get;set;}
LastWriteTime     Property   datetime LastWriteTime {get;set;}
LastWriteTimeUtc  Property   datetime LastWriteTimeUtc {get;set;}
Name              Property   string Name {get;}
Parent            Property   System.IO.DirectoryInfo Parent {get;}
Root              Property   System.IO.DirectoryInfo Root {get;}
```

12. Use the *Where-Object* cmdlet and include the *LastWriteTime* property, as follows:

```
Get-ChildItem | Where LastWriteTime
```

13. Use the up arrow in the Windows PowerShell console and bring the previous command back up on the command line. Now specify the *-gt* argument and choose a recent date from your previous list of files, so you can ensure the query will return a result. My command looks like the following:

```
Get-ChildItem | Where LastWriteTime -gt "12/25/2011"
```

14. Use the up arrow and retrieve the previous command. Now direct the *Get-ChildItem* cmdlet to a specific folder on your hard drive, such as C:\fso, which may have been created in the step-by-step exercise in Chapter 1. You can, of course, use any folder that exists on your machine. This command will look like the following:

```
Get-ChildItem "C:\fso"| Where LastWriteTime -gt "12/25/2011"
```

15. Once again, use the up arrow and retrieve the previous command. Add the *-recurse* argument to the *Get-ChildItem* cmdlet. If your previous folder was not nested, then you may want to change to a different folder. You can, of course, use your Windows folder, which is rather deeply nested. I used my VBScript workshop folder, and the command is shown here:

```
Get-ChildItem -Recurse C:\Windows | where lastwritetime -gt "12/12/11"
```

This concludes this step-by-step exercise.

In the following exercise, you'll create a couple of COM-based objects.

## One step further: working with *New-Object*

1. Open the Windows PowerShell console.

2. Create an instance of the *wshNetwork* object by using the *New-Object* cmdlet. Use the *-comobject* parameter and give it the program ID for the *wshNetwork* object, which is *wscript. network*. Store the results in a variable called *$wshnetwork*. The code looks like the following:

```
$wshnetwork = New-Object -comobject "wscript.network"
```

3. Use the *EnumPrinterConnections* method from the *wshNetwork* object to print out a list of printer connections that are defined on your local computer. To do this, use the *wshNetwork* object that is contained in the *$wshnetwork* variable. The command for this is as follows:

```
$wshnetwork.EnumPrinterConnections()
```

4. Use the *EnumNetworkDrives* method from the *wshNetwork* object to print out a list of network connections that are defined on your local computer. To do this, use the *wshNetwork* object that is contained in the *$wshnetwork* variable. The command for this is as follows:

```
$wshnetwork.EnumNetworkDrives()
```

5. Press the up arrow twice and retrieve the *$wshnetwork.EnumPrinterConnections()* command. Use the *$colPrinters* variable to hold the collection of printers that is returned by the command. The code looks as follows:

```
$colPrinters = $wshnetwork.EnumPrinterConnections()
```

6. Use the up arrow and retrieve the *$wshnetwork.EnumNetworkDrives()* command. Use the Home key to move the insertion point to the beginning of the line. Modify the command so that it holds the collection of drives returned by the command in a variable called *$colDrives*. This is shown here:

```
$colDrives = $wshnetwork.EnumNetworkDrives()
```

7. Use the *$userName* variable to hold the name that is returned by querying the *username* property from the *wshNetwork* object. This is shown here:

```
$userName = $wshnetwork.UserName
```

8. Use the *$userDomain* variable to hold the name that is returned by querying the *UserDomain* property from the *wshNetwork* object. This is shown here:

```
$userDomain = $wshnetwork.UserDomain
```

9. Use the *$computerName* variable to hold the name that is returned by querying the *ComputerName* property from the *wshNetwork* object. This is shown here:

```
$computerName = $wshnetwork.ComputerName
```

10. Create an instance of the *wshShell* object by using the *New-Object* cmdlet. Use the *-comobject* argument and give it the program ID for the *wshShell* object, which is *wscript.shell*. Store the results in a variable called *$wshShell*. The code for this follows:

```
$wshShell = New-Object -comobject "wscript.shell"
```

11. Use the *Popup* method from the *wshShell* object to produce a pop-up box that displays the domain name, user name, and computer name. The code for this follows:

```
$wshShell.Popup($userDomain+"\$userName on $computerName")
```

12. Use the *Popup* method from the *wshShell* object to produce a pop-up box that displays the collection of printers held in the *$colPrinters* variable. The code is as follows:

```
$wshShell.Popup($colPrinters)
```

13. Use the *Popup* method from the *wshShell* object to produce a pop-up box that displays the collection of drives held in the *$colDrives* variable. The code is as follows:

```
$wshShell.Popup($colDrives)
```

This concludes this exercise.

# Chapter 2 quick reference

| To | Do This |
| --- | --- |
| Produce a list of all the files in a folder | Use the *Get-ChildItem* cmdlet and supply a value for the folder. |
| Produce a list of all the files in a folder and in the subfolders | Use the *Get-ChildItem* cmdlet, supply a value for the folder, and specify the *-recurse* argument. |
| Produce a wide output of the results of a previous cmdlet | Use the appropriate cmdlet and pipe the resulting object to the *Format-Wide* cmdlet. |
| Produce a listing of all the methods available from the *Get-ChildItem* cmdlet | Use the cmdlet and pipe the results into the *Get-Member* cmdlet. Use the *-membertype* argument and supply the Noun method. |
| Produce a pop-up box | Create an instance of the *wshShell* object by using the *New-Object* cmdlet. Use the Popup method. |
| Retrieve the name of the currently logged-on user | Create an instance of the *wshNetwork* object by using the *New-Object* cmdlet. Query the *username* property. |
| Retrieve a listing of all currently mapped drives | Create an instance of the *wshNetwork* object by using the *New-Object* cmdlet. Use the EnumNetworkDrives method. |

# CHAPTER 3

# Understanding and Using PowerShell Providers

**After completing this chapter, you will be able to:**

- Understand the role of providers in Windows PowerShell.

- Use the *Get-PSProvider* cmdlet.

- Use the *Get-PSDrive* cmdlet.

- Use the *New-PSDrive* cmdlet.

- Use the *Get-Item* cmdlet.

- Use the *Set-Location* cmdlet.

- Use the file system model to access data from each of the built-in providers.

Microsoft Windows PowerShell provides a consistent way to access information external to the shell environment. To do this, it uses *providers*. These providers are actually .NET programs that hide all the ugly details to provide an easy way to access information. The beautiful thing about the way the provider model works is that all the different sources of information are accessed in exactly the same manner using a common set of cmdlets—*Get-ChildItem*, for example—to work with different types of data. This chapter demonstrates how to leverage the PowerShell providers.

**Note** All scripts and files mentioned in this chapter are available via the Microsoft TechNet Script Center (*http://aka.ms/powershellsbs_book*).

## Understanding PowerShell providers

By identifying the providers installed with Windows PowerShell, you can begin to understand the capabilities intrinsic to a default installation. Providers expose information contained in different data stores by using a drive-and-file-system analogy. An example of this is obtaining a listing of registry keys—to do this, you would connect to the registry "drive" and use the *Get-ChildItem* cmdlet, which is exactly the same method you would use to obtain a listing of files on the hard drive. The only difference is the specific name associated with each drive. Developers familiar with Windows .NET programming can create new providers, but writing a provider can be complex. (See *http://msdn.microsoft.com/en-us/library/windows/desktop/ee126192(v=vs.85).aspx* for more information.) When a new provider is created, it might ship in a snap-in. A *snap-in* is a *dynamic-link library (DLL)* file that must be installed into Windows PowerShell. After a snap-in has been installed, it cannot be uninstalled unless the developer provides removal logic—however, the snap-in can be removed from the current Windows PowerShell console. The preferred way to ship a provider is via a Windows PowerShell module. Modules are installable via an Xcopy deployment, and therefore do not necessarily require admin rights.

To obtain a listing of all the providers, use the *Get-PSProvider* cmdlet. This command produces the following list on a default installation of Windows PowerShell (Windows 8 does not include the *WSMan* provider):

```
Name            Capabilities                   Drives
----            ------------                   ------
Alias           ShouldProcess                  {Alias}
Environment     ShouldProcess                  {Env}
FileSystem      Filter, ShouldProcess, Crede... {C, A, D}
Function        ShouldProcess                  {Function}
Registry        ShouldProcess, Transactions    {HKLM, HKCU}
Variable        ShouldProcess                  {Variable}
Certificate     ShouldProcess                  {Cert}
WSMan           Credentials                    {WSMan}
```

## Understanding the alias provider

In Chapter 1, "Overview of Windows PowerShell 3.0," I presented the various help utilities available that show how to use cmdlets. The alias provider provides easy-to-use access to all aliases defined in Windows PowerShell. To work with the aliases on your machine, use the *Set-Location* cmdlet and specify the Alias:\ drive. You can then use the same cmdlets you would use to work with the file system.

> **Tip** With the alias provider, you can use a *Where-Object* cmdlet and filter to search for an alias by name or description.

### Working with the alias provider

1. Open the Windows PowerShell console.

2. Obtain a listing of all the providers by using the *Get-PSProvider* cmdlet.

**3.** The PowerShell drive (PS drive) associated with the alias provider is called Alias. This is shown in the listing produced by the *Get-PSProvider* cmdlet. Use the *Set-Location* cmdlet to change to the Alias drive. Use the *sl* alias to reduce typing. This command is shown here:

```
sl alias:\
```

**4.** Use the *Get-ChildItem* cmdlet to produce a listing of all the aliases that are defined on the system. To reduce typing, use the alias *gci* in place of *Get-ChildItem*. This is shown here:

```
gci
```

**5.** Use a *Where-Object* cmdlet filter to reduce the amount of information that is returned by using the *Get-ChildItem* cmdlet. Produce a listing of all the aliases that begin with the letter s. This is shown here:

```
gci | Where name -like "s*"
```

**6.** To identify other properties that could be used in the filter, pipeline the results of the *Get-ChildItem* cmdlet into the *Get-Member* cmdlet. This is shown here (keep in mind that different providers expose different objects that will have different properties):

```
Get-ChildItem | Get-Member
```

**7.** Press the up arrow key twice, and edit the previous filter to include only definitions that contain the word *set*. The modified filter is shown here:

```
gci | Where definition -like "set*"
```

**8.** The results of this command are shown here:

```
CommandType     Name                                          ModuleName
-----------     ----                                          ----------
Alias           cd -> Set-Location
Alias           chdir -> Set-Location
Alias           sal -> Set-Alias
Alias           sbp -> Set-PSBreakpoint
Alias           sc -> Set-Content
Alias           set -> Set-Variable
Alias           si -> Set-Item
Alias           sl -> Set-Location
Alias           sp -> Set-ItemProperty
Alias           sv -> Set-Variable
Alias           swmi -> Set-WmiInstance
```

**9.** Press the up arrow key three times, and edit the previous filter to include only names of aliases that are like the letter *w*. This revised command is shown here:

```
gci | Where name -like "*w*"
```

The results from this command will be similar to those shown here:

```
CommandType        Name                                           ModuleName
-----------        ----                                           ----------
Alias              fw -> Format-Wide
Alias              gwmi -> Get-WmiObject
Alias              iwmi -> Invoke-WmiMethod
Alias              iwr -> Invoke-WebRequest
Alias              pwd -> Get-Location
Alias              rwmi -> Remove-WmiObject
Alias              swmi -> Set-WmiInstance
Alias              where -> Where-Object
Alias              wjb -> Wait-Job
Alias              write -> Write-Output
```

**10.** In the preceding list, note that *where* is an alias for the *Where-Object* cmdlet. Press the up arrow key one time to retrieve the previous command. Edit it to use the *where* alias instead of spelling out the entire *Where-Object* cmdlet name. This revised command is shown here:

```
gci | where name -like "*w*"
```

**Caution** When using the *Set-Location* cmdlet to switch to a different PS drive, you must follow the name of the PS drive with a colon. A trailing forward slash or backward slash is optional. An error will be generated if the colon is left out, as shown in Figure 3-1. I prefer to use the backward slash (\) because it is consistent with normal Windows file system operations.

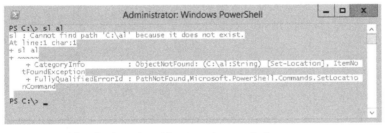

**FIGURE 3-1** Using *Set-Location* without a colon results in an error.

# Understanding the certificate provider

The preceding section explored working with the alias provider. Because the file system model applies to the certificate provider in much the same way as it does the alias provider, many of the same cmdlets can be used. To find information about the certificate provider, use the *Get-Help* cmdlet and search for *about_Providers*. If you are unsure what articles in help may be related to certificates, you can use the wildcard asterisk (*) parameter. This command is shown here:

```
Get-Help *cer*
```

In addition to allowing you to use the certificate provider, Windows PowerShell gives you the ability to sign scripts; Windows PowerShell can work with signed and unsigned scripts as well. The certificate provider gives you the ability search for, copy, move, and delete certificates. Using the certificate provider, you can open the Certificates Microsoft Management Console (MMC). The commands used in the following procedure use the certificate provider to obtain a listing of the certificates installed on the local computer.

### Obtaining a listing of certificates

1. Open the Windows PowerShell console.

2. Set your location to the cert PS drive. To do this, use the *Set-Location* cmdlet, as shown here:

   ```
   Set-Location cert:\
   ```

3. Use the *Get-ChildItem* cmdlet to produce a list of the certificates, as shown here:

   ```
   Get-ChildItem
   ```

   The list produced is shown here:

   ```
   Location   : CurrentUser
   StoreNames : {?, UserDS, AuthRoot, CA...}

   Location   : LocalMachine
   StoreNames : {?, AuthRoot, CA, AddressBook...}
   ```

4. Use the *-recurse* argument to cause the *Get-ChildItem* cmdlet to produce a list of all the certificate stores and the certificates in those stores. To do this, press the up arrow key one time and add the *-recurse* argument to the previous command. This is shown here:

   ```
   Get-ChildItem -recurse
   ```

5. Use the *-path* argument for *Get-ChildItem* to produce a listing of certificates in another store, without using the *Set-Location* cmdlet to change your current location. Use the *gci* alias, as shown here:

   ```
   GCI -path currentUser
   ```

   Your listing of certificate stores will look similar to the one shown here:

   ```
   Name : ?

   Name : UserDS

   Name : AuthRoot

   Name : CA

   Name : AddressBook
   ```

```
Name : ?

Name : Trust

Name : Disallowed

Name : _NMSTR

Name : ?????k

Name : My

Name : Root

Name : TrustedPeople

Name : ACRS

Name : TrustedPublisher

Name : REQUEST
```

**6.** Change your working location to the currentuser\authroot certificate store. To do this, use the *sl* alias followed by the path to the certificate store (*sl* is an alias for the *Set-Location* cmdlet). This command is shown here:

```
sl currentuser\authroot
```

**7.** Use the *Get-ChildItem* cmdlet to produce a listing of certificates in the currentuser\authroot certificate store that contain the name *C&W* in the subject field. Use the *gci* alias to reduce the amount of typing. Pipeline the resulting object to a *Where-Object* cmdlet, but use the *where* alias instead of typing *Where-Object*. The code to do this is shown here:

```
gci | where subject -like "*c&w*"
```

On my machine, there are four certificates listed. These are shown here:

```
Thumbprint                                Subject
----------                                -------
F88015D3F98479E1DA553D24FD42BA3F43886AEF  O=C&W HKT SecureNet CA SGC Root, C=hk
9BACF3B664EAC5A17BED08437C72E4ACDA12F7E7  O=C&W HKT SecureNet CA Class A, C=hk
4BA7B9DDD68788E12FF852E1A024204BF286A8F6  O=C&W HKT SecureNet CA Root, C=hk
47AFB915CDA26D82467B97FA42914468726138DD  O=C&W HKT SecureNet CA Class B, C=hk
```

8. Use the up arrow key, and edit the previous command so that it will return only certificates that contain the phrase *SGC Root* in the subject property. The revised command is shown here:

```
gci | where subject -like "*SGC Root*"
```

9. The resulting output on my machine contains an additional certificate. This is shown here:

```
Thumbprint                                Subject
----------                                -------
F88015D3F98479E1DA553D24FD42BA3F43886AEF  O=C&W HKT SecureNet CA SGC Root, C=hk
687EC17E0602E3CD3F7DFBD7E28D57A0199A3F44  O=SecureNet CA SGC Root, C=au
```

10. Use the up arrow key and edit the previous command. This time, change the *Where-Object* cmdlet so that it filters on the thumbprint attribute that is equal to *F88015D3F98479E1DA553D24FD42BA3F43886AEF*. You do not have to type that, however; to copy the thumbprint, you can highlight it and press Enter in Windows PowerShell, as shown in Figure 3-2. The revised command is shown here:

```
gci | where thumbprint -eq "F88015D3F98479E1DA553D24FD42BA3F43886AEF"
```

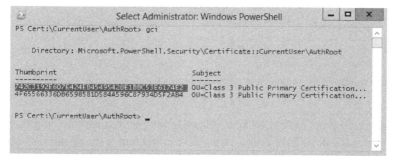

**FIGURE 3-2** Highlight items to copy using the mouse.

**Troubleshooting** If copying from inside the Windows PowerShell console window does not work, then you may need to enable QuickEdit mode. To do this, right-click the PowerShell icon in the upper-left corner of the Windows PowerShell window. Choose Properties, click the Options tab, and then select QuickEdit Mode. This is shown in Figure 3-3.

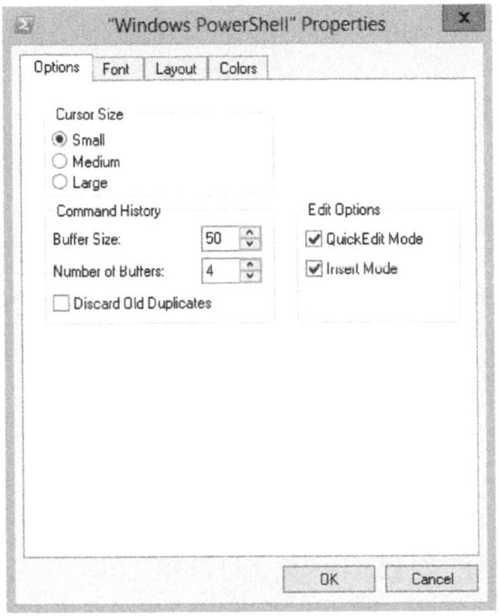

**FIGURE 3-3** Enable QuickEdit mode to enable clipboard support.

11. To see all the properties of the certificate, pipeline the certificate object to a *Format-List* cmdlet and choose all the properties. The revised command is shown here:

```
gci | where thumbprint -eq " E0AB0594207254930560620236670F7CD2EFC6666" |
Format-List *
```

The output contains all the properties of the certificate object and is shown here:

```
PSPath                  : Microsoft.PowerShell.Security\Certificate::currentuser\
                          authroot\E0AB0594207254930560620236670F7CD2EFC6666
PSParentPath            : Microsoft.PowerShell.Security\Certificate::currentuser\
                          authroot
PSChildName             : E0AB0594207254930560620236670F7CD2EFC6666
PSDrive                 : Cert
PSProvider              : Microsoft.PowerShell.Security\Certificate
PSIsContainer           : False
EnhancedKeyUsageList    : {Server Authentication (1.3.6.1.5.5.7.3.1), Code Signing
                          (1.3.6.1.5.5.7.3.3), Time Stamping (1.3.6.1.5.5.7.3.8)}
DnsNameList             : {Thawte Premium Server CA}
```

```
SendAsTrustedIssuer        : False
EnrollmentPolicyEndPoint : Microsoft.CertificateServices.Commands.EnrollmentEndPoint
                           Property
EnrollmentServerEndPoint : Microsoft.CertificateServices.Commands.EnrollmentEndPoint
                           Property
PolicyId                   :
Archived                   : False
Extensions                 : {System.Security.Cryptography.Oid}
FriendlyName               : Thawte Premium Server CA (SHA1)
IssuerName                 : System.Security.Cryptography.X509Certificates.X500
                             DistinguishedName
NotAfter                   : 1/1/2021 6:59:59 PM
NotBefore                  : 7/31/1996 8:00:00 PM
HasPrivateKey              : False
PrivateKey                 :
PublicKey                  : System.Security.Cryptography.X509Certificates.PublicKey
RawData                    : {48, 130, 3, 54...}
SerialNumber               : 36122296C5E338A520A1D25F4CD70954
SubjectName                : System.Security.Cryptography.X509Certificates.X500
                             DistinguishedName
SignatureAlgorithm         : System.Security.Cryptography.Oid
Thumbprint                 : E0AB0594207254930560620236 70F7CD2EFC6666
Version                    : 3
Handle                     : 647835770000
Issuer                     : E=premium-server@thawte.com, CN=Thawte Premium Server
                             CA, OU=Certification Services Division, O=Thawte
                             Consulting cc, L=Cape Town, S=Western Cape, C=ZA
Subject                    : E=premium-server@thawte.com, CN=Thawte Premium Server
                             CA, OU=Certification Services Division, O=Thawte
                             Consulting cc, L=Cape Town, S=Western Cape, C=ZA
```

**12.** Open the Certificates MMC file. This MMC file is called Certmgr.msc; you can launch it by simply typing the name inside Windows PowerShell, as shown here:

```
Certmgr.msc
```

**13.** But it is more fun to use the *Invoke-Item* cmdlet to launch the Certificates MMC. To do this, supply the PS drive name of cert:\ to the *Invoke-Item* cmdlet. This is shown here:

```
Invoke-Item cert:\
```

**14.** Compare the information obtained from Windows PowerShell with the information displayed in the Certificates MMC. It should be the same. The certificate is shown in Figure 3-4.

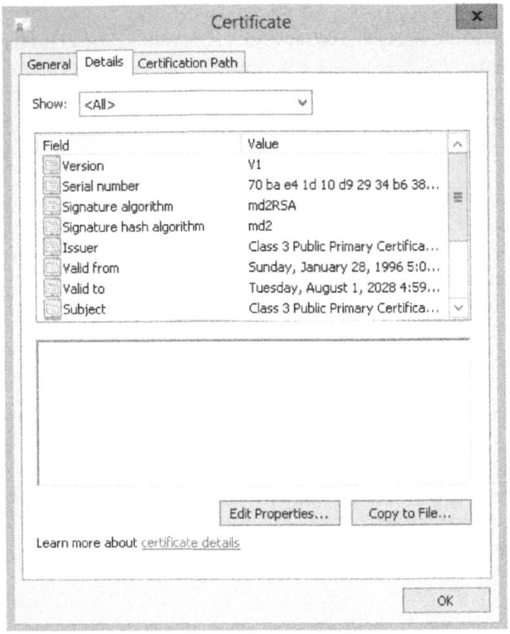

**FIGURE 3-4** Certmgr.msc can be used to examine certificate properties.

This concludes this procedure.

## Searching for specific certificates

To search for specific certificates, you may want to examine the *subject* property. For example, the following code examines the *subject* property of every certificate in the currentuser store beginning at the root level. It does a recursive search, and returns only the certificates that contain the word *test* in some form in the *subject* property. This command and associated output appear here:

```
PS C:\Users\administrator.IAMMRED> dir Cert:\CurrentUser -Recurse | ? subject -match
'test'


    Directory: Microsoft.PowerShell.Security\Certificate::CurrentUser\Root


Thumbprint                                Subject
----------                                -------
8A334AA8052DD244A647306A76B8178FA215F344  CN=Microsoft Testing Root Certificate A...
2BD63D28D7BCD0E251195AEB519243C13142EBC3  CN=Microsoft Test Root Authority, OU=Mi...
```

To delete these *test* certificates simply requires pipelining the results of the previous command to the *Remove-Item* cmdlet.

> **Note** When performing any operation that may alter system state, it is a good idea to use the *-whatif* parameter to prototype the command prior to actually executing it.

The following command uses the *-whatif* parameter from *Remove-Item* to prototype the command to remove all of the certificates from the currentuser store that contain the word *test* in the *subject* property. Once completed, retrieve the command via the up arrow key and remove the *-whatif* switched parameter from the command prior to actual execution. This technique appears here:

```
PS C:\Users\administrator.IAMMRED> dir Cert:\CurrentUser -Recurse | ? subject -match
'test' | Remove-Item -WhatIf
What if: Performing operation "Remove certificate" on Target "Item: CurrentUser\Root\
8A334AA8052DD244A647306A76B8178FA215F344 ".
What if: Performing operation "Remove certificate" on Target "Item: CurrentUser\Root\
2BD63D28D7BCD0E251195AEB519243C13142EBC3 ".
PS C:\Users\administrator.IAMMRED> dir Cert:\CurrentUser -Recurse | ? subject -match
'test' | Remove-Item
```

## Finding expiring certificates

A common task in companies using certificates is to identify certificates that either have expired or are about to expire. Using the certificate provider, it is simple to identify expired certificates. To do this, use the *notafter* property from the certificate objects returned from the certificate drives. One approach is to look for certificates that expire prior to a specific date. This technique appears here:

```
PS Cert:\> dir .\\CurrentUser -Recurse | where notafter -lt "5/1/2012"
```

A more flexible approach is to use the current date—therefore, each time the command runs, it retrieves expired certificates. This technique appears here:

```
PS Cert:\> dir .\\CurrentUser -Recurse | where notafter -lt (Get-Date)
```

One problem with simply using the *Get-ChildItem* cmdlet on the currentuser store is that it returns certificate stores as well as certificates. To obtain only certificates, you must filter out the *psiscontainer* property. Because you will also need to filter based upon date, you can no longer use the simple *Where-Object* syntax. The *$_* character represents the current certificate as it comes across the pipeline. Because you're comparing two properties, you must repeat the *$_* character for each property. The following command retrieves the expiration dates, thumbprints, and subjects of all expired certificates. It also creates a table displaying the information. (The command is a single logical command, but it is broken at the pipe character to permit better display in the book.)

```
PS Cert:\> dir .\\CurrentUser -Recurse |
where { !$_.psiscontainer -AND $_.notafter -lt (Get-Date)} |
ft notafter, thumbprint, subject -AutoSize -Wrap
```

> **Caution** All versions of Microsoft Windows ship with expired certificates to permit verification of old executables that were signed with those certificates. Do not arbitrarily delete an expired certificate—if you do, you could cause serious damage to your system.

If you want to identify certificates that will expire in the next 30 days, you use the same technique involving a compound *Where-Object* command. The command appearing here identifies certificates expiring in the next 30 days:

```
PS Cert:\> dir .\\CurrentUser -Recurse |
where { $_.NotAfter -gt (Get-Date) -AND $_.NotAfter -le (Get-Date).Add(30) }
```

# Understanding the environment provider

The environment provider in Windows PowerShell is used to provide access to the system environment variables. If you open a CMD (command) shell and type **set**, you will obtain a listing of all the environment variables defined on the system. (You can run the old-fashioned command prompt inside Windows PowerShell.)

> **Note** It is easy to forget you are running the CMD prompt when you are inside of the Windows PowerShell console. Typing **exit** returns you to Windows PowerShell. The best way to determine whether you are running the command shell or Windows PowerShell is to examine the prompt. The default Windows PowerShell prompt is PS C:\>, assuming that you are working on drive C.

If you use the *echo* command in the CMD interpreter to print out the value of *%windir%*, you will obtain the results shown in Figure 3-5.

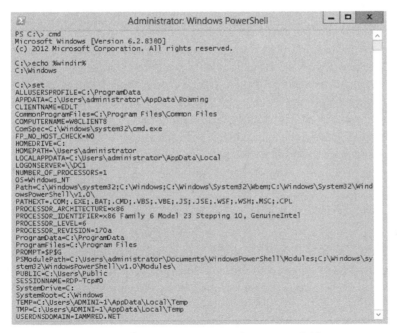

**FIGURE 3-5** Use *set* at a CMD prompt to see environment variables.

Various applications and other utilities use environment variables as a shortcut to provide easy access to specific files, folders, and configuration data. By using the environment provider in Windows PowerShell, you can obtain a listing of the environment variables. You can also add, change, clear, and delete these variables.

## Obtaining a listing of environment variables

1. Open the Windows PowerShell console.

2. Obtain a listing of the PS drives by using the *Get-PSDrive* cmdlet. This is shown here:

   ```
   Get-PSDrive
   ```

3. Note that the Environment PS drive is called *Env.* Use the *Env* name with the *Set-Location* cmdlet and change to the Environment PS drive. This is shown here:

   ```
   Set-Location Env:\
   ```

4. Use the *Get-Item* cmdlet to obtain a listing of all the environment variables on the system. This is shown here:

   ```
   Get-Item *
   ```

5. Use the *Sort-Object* cmdlet to produce an alphabetical listing of all the environment variables by name. Use the up arrow key to retrieve the previous command, and pipeline the returned object into the *Sort-Object* cmdlet. Use the *-property* argument, and supply *name* as the value. This command is shown here:

   ```
   Get-Item * | Sort-Object  -property value
   ```

6. Use the *Get-Item* cmdlet to retrieve the value associated with the environment variable *windir.* This is shown here:

   ```
   Get-Item windir
   ```

7. Use the up arrow key and retrieve the previous command. Pipeline the object returned to the *Format-List* cmdlet and use the wildcard character to print out all the properties of the object. The modified command is shown here:

   ```
   Get-Item windir | Format-List *
   ```

8. The properties and their associated values are shown here:

```
PSPath        : Microsoft.PowerShell.Core\Environment::windir
PSDrive       : Env
PSProvider    : Microsoft.PowerShell.Core\Environment
PSIsContainer : False
Name          : windir
Key           : windir
Value         : C:\WINDOWS
```

This concludes this procedure. Do not close Windows PowerShell. Leave it open for the next procedure.

### Creating a temporary new environment variable

1. You should still be in the Environment PS drive from the previous procedure. If not, use the *Set-Location env:\* command).

2. Use the *Get-Item* cmdlet to produce a listing of all the environment variables. Pipeline the returned object to the *Sort-Object* cmdlet using the property *name*. To reduce typing, use the *gi* alias and the *sort* alias. This is shown here:

```
gi * | sort -property name
```

3. Use the *New-Item* cmdlet to create a new environment variable. The *-path* argument will be dot (.) because you are already on the env:\ PS drive. The *-Name* argument will be *admin*, and the *-value* argument will be your given name. The completed command is shown here:

```
New-Item -Path . -Name admin -Value mred
```

4. Use the *Get-Item* cmdlet to ensure the *admin* environment variable was properly created. This command is shown here:

```
Get-Item admin
```

The results of the previous command are shown here:

```
Name                           Value
----                           -----
admin                          mred
```

5. Use the up arrow key to retrieve the previous command. Pipeline the results to the *Format-List* cmdlet and choose All Properties. This command is shown here:

```
Get-Item admin | Format-List *
```

The results of the previous command include the PS path, PS drive, and additional information about the newly created environment variable. These results are shown here:

```
PSPath        : Microsoft.PowerShell.Core\Environment::admin
PSDrive       : Env
PSProvider    : Microsoft.PowerShell.Core\Environment
PSIsContainer : False
Name          : admin
Key           : admin
Value         : mred
```

The new environment variable exists until you close the Windows PowerShell console.

This concludes this procedure. Leave PowerShell open for the next procedure.

## Renaming an environment variable

1. Use the *Get-ChildItem* cmdlet to obtain a listing of all the environment variables. Pipeline the returned object to the *Sort-Object* cmdlet and sort the list on the *name* property. Use the *gci* and *sort* aliases to reduce typing. The code to do this is shown here:

   ```
   gci | sort -property name
   ```

2. The *admin* environment variable should be near the top of the list of system variables. If it is not, then create it by using the *New-Item* cmdlet. The *-path* argument has a value of dot (.); the *-name* argument has the value of *admin*, and the *-value* argument should be the user's given name. If this environment variable was created in the previous exercise, then PowerShell will report that it already exists. The command appearing here allows you to re-create the *admin* environment variable:

   ```
   New-Item -Path . -Name admin -Value mred
   ```

3. Use the *Rename-Item* cmdlet to rename the *admin* environment variable to *super*. The *-path* argument combines the PS drive name with the environment variable name. The *-NewName* argument is the desired new name without the PS drive specification. This command is shown here:

   ```
   Rename-Item -Path env:admin -NewName super
   ```

4. To verify that the old environment variable *admin* has been renamed *super*, press the up arrow key two or three times to retrieve the *gci | sort -property name* command. This command is shown here:

   ```
   gci | sort -property name
   ```

This concludes this procedure. Do not close Windows PowerShell. Leave it open for the next procedure.

1. Use the *Get-ChildItem* cmdlet to obtain a listing of all the environment variables. Pipeline the returned object to the *Sort-Object* cmdlet and sort the list on the *name* property. Use the *gci* and *sort* aliases to reduce typing. The code to do this is shown here:

```
gci | sort -property name
```

2. The *super* environment variable should be in the list of system variables. If it is not, then create it by using the *New-Item* cmdlet. The *-path* argument has a value of dot (.), the *-name* argument has a value of *super*, and the *-value* argument should be the user's given name. If this environment variable was created in the previous exercise, then PowerShell will report that it already exists. If you have deleted the *admin* environment variable, the command appearing here creates it:

```
New-Item -Path . -Name super -Value mred
```

3. Use the *Remove-Item* cmdlet to remove the *super* environment variable. The name of the item to be removed is typed following the name of the cmdlet. If you are still in the env:\ PS drive, you will not need to supply a *-path* argument. The command is shown here:

```
Remove-Item env:super
```

4. Use the *Get-ChildItem* cmdlet to verify that the environment variable *super* has been removed. To do this, press the up arrow key two or three times to retrieve the *gci | sort -property name* command. This command is shown here:

```
gci | sort -property name
```

This concludes this procedure.

# Understanding the filesystem provider

The filesystem provider is the easiest Windows PowerShell provider to understand—it provides access to the file system. When Windows PowerShell is launched, it automatically opens on the user documents folder. Using the Windows PowerShell filesystem provider, you can create both directories and files. You can retrieve properties of files and directories, and you can delete them as well. In addition, you can open files and append or overwrite data to the files. This can be done with inline code, or by using the pipelining feature of Windows PowerShell. The commands used in the procedure are in the IdentifyingPropertiesOfDirectories.txt, CreatingFoldersAndFiles.txt, and ReadingAndWritingForFiles.txt files and are available from the Technet Script Repository, at *http://aka.ms/powershellSBS_book.*

## Working with directory listings

1.  Open the Windows PowerShell console.

2.  Use the *Get-ChildItem* cmdlet to obtain a directory listing of drive C. Use the *gci* alias to reduce typing. This is shown here:

    ```
    GCI C:\
    ```

3.  Use the up arrow key to retrieve the *gci C:\* command. Pipeline the object created into a *Where-Object* cmdlet and look for containers. This will reduce the output to only directories. The modified command is shown here:

    ```
    GCI C:\ | where psiscontainer
    ```

4.  Use the up arrow key to retrieve the *gci C:\ | where psiscontainer* command, and use the exclamation point (!) (meaning *not*) to retrieve only items in the PS drive that are not directories. The modified command is shown here. (The simplified *Where-Object* syntax does not support using the *not* operator directly on the input property.)

    ```
    gci | ? {!($psitem.psiscontainer)}
    ```

    This concludes this procedure. Do not close Windows PowerShell. Leave it open for the next procedure.

## Identifying properties of directories

1.  Use the *Get-ChildItem* cmdlet and supply a value of *C:\* for the *-path* argument. Pipeline the resulting object into the *Get-Member* cmdlet. Use the *gci* and *gm* aliases to reduce typing. This command is shown here:

    ```
    gci  -path C:\ | gm
    ```

2.  The resulting output contains methods, properties, and more. Filter the output by pipelining it into a *Where-Object* cmdlet and specifying the *membertype* attribute as equal to *property*. To do this, use the up arrow key to retrieve the previous *gci -path C:\ | gm* command. Pipeline the resulting object into the *Where-Object* cmdlet and filter on the *membertype* attribute. The resulting command is shown here:

    ```
    gci  -path C:\ | gm | Where {$_.membertype -eq "property"}
    ```

3.  On Windows 8, you need to use the *-force* parameter to see hidden files. Here is the command:

    ```
    gci  -path C:\ -force | gm | Where {$_.membertype -eq "property"}
    ```

4. The preceding *gci -path C:\ | gm | where {$_.membertype -eq "property"}* command returns information on both the *System.IO.DirectoryInfo* and *System.IO.FileInfo* objects (on Windows 8, you need to use the *-force* switch to see hidden files). To reduce the output to only the properties associated with the *System.IO.FileInfo* object, you need to use a compound *Where-Object* cmdlet. Use the up arrow key to retrieve the *gci -path C:\ | gm | where {$_.membertype -eq "property"}* command. Add the *And* conjunction and retrieve objects that have a type name that is like *\*file\**. The modified command is shown here:

```
gci  -path C:\ | gm |
where {$_.membertype -eq "property" -AND $_.typename -like  "*file*"}
```

5. On Windows 8, you need to use the *-force* parameter. Here is the command to do that:

```
gci  -path C:\ -force | gm |
where {$_.membertype -eq "property" -AND $_.typename -like  "*file*"}
```

6. The resulting output contains only the properties for a *System.IO.FileInfo* object. These properties are shown here:

```
TypeName: System.IO.FileInfo

Name                  MemberType Definition
----                  ---------- ----------
Attributes            Property   System.IO.FileAttributes Attributes {get;set;}
CreationTime          Property   System.DateTime CreationTime {get;set;}
CreationTimeUtc       Property   System.DateTime CreationTimeUtc {get;set;}
Directory             Property   System.IO.DirectoryInfo Directory {get;}
DirectoryName         Property   System.String DirectoryName {get;}
Exists                Property   System.Boolean Exists {get;}
Extension             Property   System.String Extension {get;}
FullName              Property   System.String FullName {get;}
IsReadOnly            Property   System.Boolean IsReadOnly {get;set;}
LastAccessTime        Property   System.DateTime LastAccessTime {get;set;}
LastAccessTimeUtc     Property   System.DateTime LastAccessTimeUtc {get;set;}
LastWriteTime         Property   System.DateTime LastWriteTime {get;set;}
LastWriteTimeUtc      Property   System.DateTime LastWriteTimeUtc {get;set;}
Length                Property   System.Int64 Length {get;}
Name                  Property   System.String Name {get;}
```

This concludes this procedure. Do not close Windows PowerShell. Leave it open for the next procedure.

## Creating folders and files

1. Use the *Get-Item* cmdlet to obtain a listing of files and folders. Pipeline the resulting object into the *Where-Object* cmdlet and use the *PsisContainer* property to look for folders. Use the name property to find names that contain the word *my* in them. Use the *gi* alias and the *where* alias to reduce typing. The command is shown here:

```
Set-Location c:\Mytest
GI * | Where {$_.PsisContainer -AND $_.name -Like "*my*"}
```

2. If you were following along in the previous chapters, you will have a folder called Mytest off the root of drive C. Use the *Remove-Item* cmdlet to remove the Mytest folder. Specify the *-recurse* argument to also delete files contained in the C:\Mytest folder. If your location is still set to Env, then change it to C or search for C:\Mytest. The command is shown here:

```
RI mytest -recurse
```

3. Press the up arrow key twice and retrieve the *gi \* | where {$_.PsisContainer -AND $_.name -Like "\*my\*"}* command to confirm the folder was actually deleted. This command is shown here:

```
gi * | where {$_.PsisContainer -AND $_.name -Like "*my*"}
```

4. Use the *New-Item* cmdlet to create a folder named Mytest. Use the *-path* argument to specify the path of C:\. Use the *-name* argument to specify the name of Mytest, and use the *-type argument* to tell Windows PowerShell the new item will be a directory. This command is shown here:

```
New-Item -Path C:\ -name mytest -type directory
```

The resulting output, shown here, confirms the operation:

```
Directory: Microsoft.PowerShell.Core\FileSystem::C:\

Mode                LastWriteTime     Length Name
----                -------------     ------ ----
d----         5/4/2012    2:43 AM            mytest
```

5. Use the *New-Item* cmdlet to create an empty text file. To do this, use the up arrow key and retrieve the previous *New-Item -path C:\ -name Mytest -type directory* command. Edit the *-path* argument so that it is pointing to the C:\Mytest directory. Edit the *-name* argument to specify a text file named Myfile, and specify the *-type* argument as *file*. The resulting command is shown here:

```
New-Item -path C:\mytest -name myfile.txt -type file
```

The resulting message, shown here, confirms the creation of the file:

```
Directory: Microsoft.PowerShell.Core\FileSystem::C:\mytest

Mode                LastWriteTime     Length Name
----                -------------     ------ ----
-a---         5/4/2012    3:12 AM          0 myfile.txt
```

This concludes this procedure. Do not close Windows PowerShell. Leave it open for the next procedure.

## Reading and writing for files

1. Delete Myfile.txt (created in the previous procedure). To do this, use the *Remove-Item* cmdlet and specify the *-path* argument as C:\Mytest\Myfile.txt. This command is shown here:

```
RI -Path C:\mytest\myfile.txt
```

2. Use the up arrow key twice to retrieve the *New-Item -path C:\Mytest -name Myfile.txt -type* command. Add the *-value* argument to the end of the command line and supply a value of *My file*. This command is shown here:

```
New-Item -Path C:\mytest -Name myfile.txt -Type file -Value "My file"
```

3. Use the *Get-Content* cmdlet to read the contents of myfile.txt. This command is shown here:

```
Get-Content C:\mytest\myfile.txt
```

4. Use the *Add-Content* cmdlet to add additional information to the myfile.txt file. This command is shown here:

```
Add-Content C:\mytest\myfile.txt -Value "ADDITIONAL INFORMATION"
```

5. Press the up arrow key twice and retrieve the *Get-Content C:\mytest\myfile.txt* command, which is shown here:

```
Get-Content C:\mytest\myfile.txt
```

6. The output from the *Get-Content C:\mytest\myfile.txt* command is shown here:

```
My fileADDITIONAL INFORMATION
```

7. Press the up arrow key twice, and retrieve the *Add-Content C:\mytest\myfile.txt -value "ADDITIONAL INFORMATION"* command to add additional information to the file. This command is shown here:

```
Add-Content C:\mytest\myfile.txt -Value "ADDITIONAL INFORMATION"
```

8. Use the up arrow key to retrieve the *Get-Content C:\mytest\myfile.txt* command, which is shown here:

```
Get-Content C:\mytest\myfile.txt
```

9. The output produced is shown here. Notice that the second time the command runs, the *"ADDITIONAL INFORMATION"* string is added to a new line in the original file.

```
My fileADDITIONAL INFORMATION
ADDITIONAL INFORMATION
```

**10.** Use the *Set-Content* cmdlet to overwrite the contents of the Myfile.txt file. Specify the *-value* argument as *Setting information*. This command is shown here:

```
Set-Content C:\mytest\myfile.txt -value "Setting information"
```

**11.** Use the up arrow key to retrieve the *Get-Content C:\Mytest\Myfile.txt* command, which is shown here:

```
Get-Content C:\mytest\myfile.txt
```

The output from the *Get-Content* command is shown here:

```
Setting information
```

This concludes this procedure.

## Understanding the function provider

The function provider provides access to the functions defined in Windows PowerShell. By using the function provider, you can obtain a listing of all the functions on your system. You can also add, modify, and delete functions. The function provider uses a file system–based model, and the cmdlets described earlier apply to working with functions. The commands used in the following procedure are in the ListingAllFunctionsOnTheSystem.txt file.

### Listing all functions on the system

**1.** Open the Windows PowerShell console.

**2.** Use the *Set-Location* cmdlet to change the working location to the Function PS drive. This command is shown here:

```
Set-Location function:\
```

**3.** Use the *Get-ChildItem* cmdlet to enumerate all the functions. Do this by using the *gci* alias, as shown here:

```
gci
```

**4.** The resulting list contains many functions that use *Set-Location* to change the current location to different drive letters. A partial view of this output is shown here:

```
CommandType      Name                              ModuleName
-----------      ----                              ----------
Function         A:
Function         B:
Function         C:
Function         cd..
Function         cd\
Function         Clear-Host
<truncated...>
```

```
Function        Get-Verb
Function        H:
Function        help
Function        I:
Function        ImportSystemModules
<truncated...>
Function        mkdir
Function        more
Function        N:
Function        O:
Function        oss
Function        P:
Function        Pause
Function        prompt
<truncated ...>
Function        TabExpansion2
<truncated ...>
```

5. To return only the functions that are used for drives, use the *Get-ChildItem* cmdlet and pipe the object returned into a *Where-Object* cmdlet. Use the default *$_* variable to filter on the *definition* attribute. Use the *-like* argument to search for definitions that contain the word *set*. The resulting command is shown here:

```
gci | Where definition -like "set*"
```

6. If you are more interested in functions that are not related to drive mappings, then you can use the *-notlike* argument instead of *-like*. The easiest way to make this change is to use the up arrow key and retrieve the *gci | where {$_.definition -like "set*"}* command, and then change the filter from *-like* to *-notlike*. The resulting command is shown here:

```
gci | Where definition -notlike "set*"
```

The resulting listing of functions is shown here:

```
CommandType     Name                            ModuleName
-----------     ----                            ----------
Function        Clear-Host
Function        Get-Verb
Function        help
Function        ImportSystemModules
Function        mkdir
Function        more
Function        oss
Function        Pause
Function        prompt
Function        TabExpansion2
```

**7.** Use the *Get-Content* cmdlet to retrieve the text of the *pause* function. This is shown here (*gc* is an alias for the *Get-Content* cmdlet):

```
gc pause
```

The content of the *pause* function is shown here:

```
Read-Host 'Press Enter to continue...' | Out-Null
```

This concludes this procedure.

# Using the registry provider to manage the Windows registry

In Windows PowerShell 1.0, the registry provider made it easy to work with the registry on the local system. Unfortunately, without remoting, you were limited to working with the local computer or using some other remoting mechanism (perhaps a log-on script) to make changes on remote systems. Beginning with Windows PowerShell 2.0, the inclusion of remoting makes it possible to make remote registry changes as easily as changing the local registry.

The registry provider permits access to the registry in the same manner that the filesystem provider permits access to a local disk drive. The same cmdlets used to access the file system—*New-Item*, *Get-ChildItem*, *Set-Item*, *Remove-Item*, and so on—also work with the registry.

## The two registry drives

By default, the registry provider creates two registry drives. To find all of the drives exposed by the registry provider, use the *Get-PSDrive* cmdlet. These drives appear here:

```
PS C:\> Get-PSDrive -PSProvider registry | select name, root

Name                                      Root
----                                      ----
HKCU                                      HKEY_CURRENT_USER
HKLM                                      HKEY_LOCAL_MACHINE
```

You can create additional registry drives by using the *New-PSDrive* cmdlet. For example, it is common to create a registry drive for the HKEY_CLASSES_ROOT registry hive. The code to do this appears here:

```
PS C:\> New-PSDrive -PSProvider registry -Root HKEY_CLASSES_ROOT -Name HKCR

WARNING: column "CurrentLocation" does not fit into the display and was removed.

Name            Used (GB)     Free (GB) Provider      Root
----            ---------     --------- --------      ----
HKCR                                    Registry      HKEY_CLASSES_ROOT
```

Once created, the new HKCR drive is accessible in the same way as any other drive. For example, to change the working location to the HKCR drive, use either the *Set-Location* cmdlet or one of its aliases (such as *cd*). This technique appears here:

```
PS C:\> Set-Location HKCR:
```

To determine the current location, use the *Get-Location* cmdlet. This technique appears here:

```
PS HKCR:\> Get-Location

Path
----
HKCR:\
```

Once you've set the new working location, explore it by using the *Get-ChildItem* cmdlet (or one of the aliases for that cmdlet, such as *dir*). This technique appears in Figure 3-6.

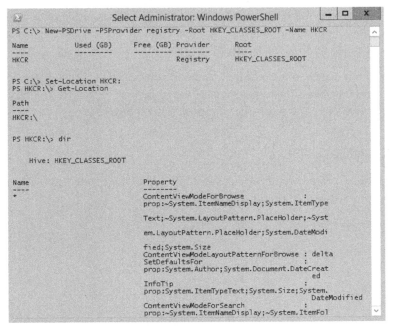

**FIGURE 3-6** Creating a new registry drive for the HKEY_CLASSES_ROOT registry hive enables easy access to class registration information.

## Retrieving registry values

To view the values stored in a registry key, use either the *Get-Item* or the *Get-ItemProperty* cmdlet. Using the *Get-Item* cmdlet reveals there is one property (named *default*). This appears here:

```
PS HKCR:\> Get-Item .\.ps1 | fl *


PSPath          : Microsoft.PowerShell.Core\Registry::HKEY_CLASSES_ROOT\.ps1
PSParentPath    : Microsoft.PowerShell.Core\Registry::HKEY_CLASSES_ROOT
PSChildName     : .ps1
PSDrive         : HKCR
PSProvider      : Microsoft.PowerShell.Core\Registry
PSIsContainer   : True
Property        : {(default)}
SubKeyCount     : 1
ValueCount      : 1
Name            : HKEY_CLASSES_ROOT\.ps1
```

To access the value of the *default* property, you must use the *Get-ItemProperty* cmdlet, as shown here:

```
PS HKCR:\> Get-ItemProperty .\.ps1 | fl *

PSPath       : Microsoft.PowerShell.Core\Registry::HKEY_CLASSES_ROOT\.ps1
PSParentPath : Microsoft.PowerShell.Core\Registry::HKEY_CLASSES_ROOT
PSChildName  : .ps1
PSDrive      : HKCR
PSProvider   : Microsoft.PowerShell.Core\Registry
(default)    : Microsoft.PowerShellScript.1
```

The technique for accessing registry keys and the values associated with them appears in Figure 3-7.

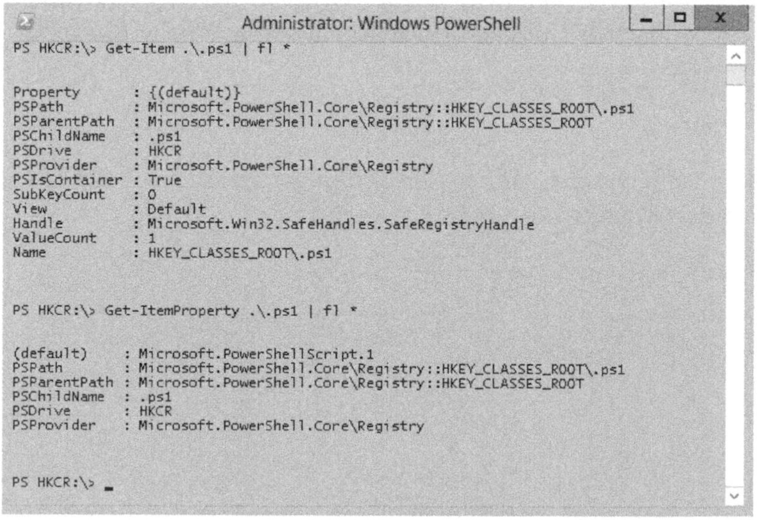

**FIGURE 3-7** Use the *Get-ItemProperty* cmdlet to access registry property values.

Returning only the value of the *default* property requires a bit of manipulation. The *default* property requires using literal quotation marks to force the evaluation of the parentheses in the name. This appears here:

```
PS HKCR:\> (Get-ItemProperty .\.ps1 -Name '(default)').'(default)'
Microsoft.PowerShellScript.1
```

The registry provider provides a consistent and easy way to work with the registry from within Windows PowerShell. Using the registry provider, you can search the registry, create new registry keys, delete existing registry keys, and modify values and access control lists (ACLs) from within Windows PowerShell.

The commands used in the following procedure are in the UnderstandingTheRegistryProvider.txt file. Two PS drives are created by default. To identify the PS drives that are supplied by the registry provider, you can use the *Get-PSDrive* cmdlet, pipeline the resulting objects into the *Where-Object* cmdlet, and filter on the *provider* property while supplying a value that is like the word *registry*. This command is shown here:

```
PS C:\> Get-PSDrive | ? provider -match registry

Name            Used (GB)   Free (GB) Provider    Root
----            ---------   --------- --------    ----
HKCR                                  Registry    HKEY_CLASSES_ROOT
HKCU                                  Registry    HKEY_CURRENT_USER
HKLM                                  Registry    HKEY_LOCAL_MACHINE
```

### Obtaining a listing of registry keys

1. Open the Windows PowerShell console.

2. Use the *Get-ChildItem* cmdlet and supply *HKLM:\ PSDrive* as the value for the *-path* argument. Specify the software key to retrieve a listing of software applications on the local machine. The resulting command is shown here:

```
GCI -path HKLM:\software
```

A partial listing of similar output is shown here. The corresponding keys, as displayed in Regedit.exe, are shown in Figure 3-8.

```
    Hive: HKEY_LOCAL_MACHINE\SOFTWARE


Name                         Property
----                         --------
ATI Technologies
Classes
Clients
Intel
Microsoft
ODBC
Policies
```

```
RegisteredApplications          Paint                    : SOFTWARE\Microsoft\
                                Windows\CurrentVersion\Applets\Paint\Capabilities
                                Windows Search           :
                                Software\Microsoft\Windows Search\Capabilities
                                Windows Disc Image Burner :
                                Software\Microsoft\IsoBurn\Capabilities
                                Windows File Explorer    : SOFTWARE\Microsoft\
                                Windows\CurrentVersion\Explorer\Capabilities
                                Windows Photo Viewer     :
                                Software\Microsoft\Windows Photo Viewer\Capabilities
                                Wordpad                  : Software\Microsoft\
                                Windows\CurrentVersion\Applets\Wordpad\Capabilities
                                Windows Media Player     :
                                Software\Clients\Media\Windows Media
                                Player\Capabilities
                                Internet Explorer        :
                                SOFTWARE\Microsoft\Internet Explorer\Capabilities
                                Windows Address Book     :
                                Software\Clients\Contacts\Address Book\Capabilities
```

This concludes this procedure. Do not close Windows PowerShell. Leave it open for the next procedure.

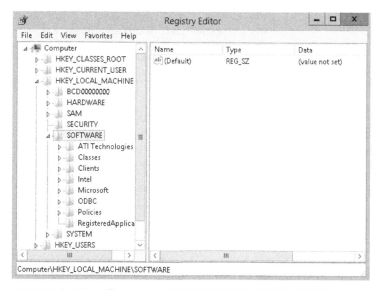

**FIGURE 3-8** A Regedit.exe view of HKEY_LOCAL_MACHINE\SOFTWARE.

## Searching for software

1. Use the *Get-ChildItem* cmdlet and supply a value for the *-path* argument. Use the HKLM:\ PS drive and supply a path of *SOFTWARE\Microsoft\Windows\CurrentVersion\Uninstall*. To make the command easier to read, use a single quote (') to encase the string. You can use tab completion to assist with the typing. The completed command is shown here:

```
gci -path 'HKLM:SOFTWARE\Microsoft\Windows\CurrentVersion\Uninstall'
```

The resulting listing of software is shown in the output here, in abbreviated fashion:

```
    Hive: HKEY_LOCAL_MACHINE\SOFTWARE\Microsoft\Windows\CurrentVersion\Uninstall


Name                          Property
----                          --------
AddressBook
CNXT_AUDIO_HDA                DisplayName    : Conexant 20672 SmartAudio HD
                              DisplayVersion : 8.32.23.2
                              VersionMajor   : 8
                              VersionMinor   : 0
                              Publisher      : Conexant
                              DisplayIcon    : C:\Program
                              Files\CONEXANT\CNXT_AUDIO_HDA\UIU64a.exe
                              UninstallString : C:\Program
                              Files\CONEXANT\CNXT_AUDIO_HDA\UIU64a.exe -U -G
                                              -Ichdrt.inf
Connection Manager            SystemComponent : 1
DirectDrawEx
DXM_Runtime
Fontcore
IE40
IE4Data
IE5BAKEX
IEData
MobileOptionPack
MPlayer2
Office15.PROPLUS              Publisher                : Microsoft Corporation
                             CacheLocation             : C:\MSOCache\All Users
                             DisplayIcon               : C:\Program Files\Common
```

2. To retrieve information on a single software package, you will need to add a *Where-Object* cmdlet. You can do this by using the up arrow key to retrieve the previous *gci -path 'HKLM:SOFTWARE\Microsoft\Windows\CurrentVersion\Uninstall'* command and pipelining the resulting object into the *Where-Object* cmdlet. Supply a value for the *name* property, as shown in the code listed here. Alternatively, supply a name from the previous output.

```
PS C:\> gci -path 'HKLM:SOFTWARE\Microsoft\Windows\CurrentVersion\Uninstall' | where
name -match 'office'
```

This concludes this procedure.

## Creating new registry keys

Creating a new registry key by using Windows PowerShell is the same as creating a new file or a new folder—all three processes use the *New-Item* cmdlet. In addition to using the *New-Item* cmdlet, you might use the *Test-Path* cmdlet to determine if the registry key already exists. You may also wish to change your working location to one of the registry drives. If you do this, you might use the *Push-Location* cmdlet, *Set-Location* and the *Pop-Location* cmdlets. This is, of course, the long way of doing things. These steps appear next.

> **Note** The registry contains information vital to the operation and configuration of your computer. Serious problems could arise if you edit the registry incorrectly. Therefore, it is important to back up your system prior to attempting to make any changes. For information about backing up your registry, see Microsoft TechNet article KB322756. For general information about working with the registry, see Microsoft TechNet article KB310516.

1. Store the current working location by using the *Push-Location* cmdlet.

2. Change the current working location to the appropriate registry drive by using the *Set-Location* cmdlet.

3. Use the *Test-Path* cmdlet to determine if the registry key already exists.

4. Use the *New-Item* cmdlet to create the new registry key.

5. Use the *Pop-Location* cmdlet to return to the starting working location.

The following example creates a new registry key named HSG off the HKEY_CURRENT_USERS software registry hive. It illustrates each of the five steps detailed previously.

```
Push-Location
Set-Location HKCU:
Test-Path .\Software\test
New-Item -Path .\Software -Name test
Pop-Location
```

The commands and the associated output from the commands appear in Figure 3-9.

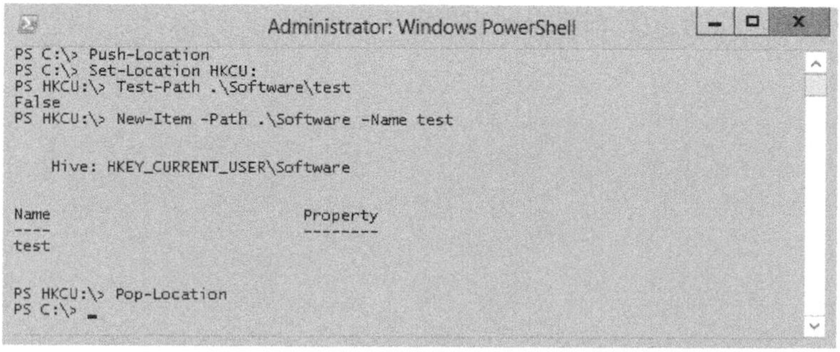

**FIGURE 3-9** Creating a new registry key by using the *New-Item* cmdlet.

## The short way to create a new registry key

It is not always necessary to change the working location to a registry drive when creating a new registry key. In fact, it is not even necessary to use the *Test-Path* cmdlet to determine if the registry key exists. If the registry key already exists, an error is generated. If you want to overwrite the registry key, use the *-force* parameter. This technique works for all the Windows PowerShell providers, not just for the registry provider.

> **Note** How to deal with an already existing registry key is one of those *design decisions* that confront IT professionals who venture far into the world of scripting. Software developers are very familiar with these types of decisions and usually deal with them in the analyzing-requirements portion of the development life cycle. IT professionals who open the Windows PowerShell ISE first and think about the design requirements second can become easily stymied, and possibly write in problems. For more information about this, see my book *Windows PowerShell 2.0 Best Practices* (Microsoft Press, 2010).

The following example creates a new registry key named *test* in the HKCU:\SOFTWARE location. Because the command includes the full path, it does not need to execute from the HKCU drive. Because the command uses the *-force* switched parameter, the command overwrites the HKCU:\SOFTWARE\TEST registry key if it already exists.

```
New-Item -Path HKCU:\Software -Name test -Force
```

> **Note** To see the *New-Item* cmdlet in action when using the *-force switched* parameter, use the *-verbose* switched parameter. The command appears here:
>
> ```
> New-Item -Path HKCU:\Software -Name test -Force -Verbose
> ```

1. Include the full path to the registry key to create.

2. Use the *-force* parameter to overwrite any existing registry key of the same name.

In Figure 3-10, the first attempt to create a test registry key fails because the key already exists. The second command uses the *-force* parameter, causing the command to overwrite the existing registry key, and therefore it succeeds without creating an error.

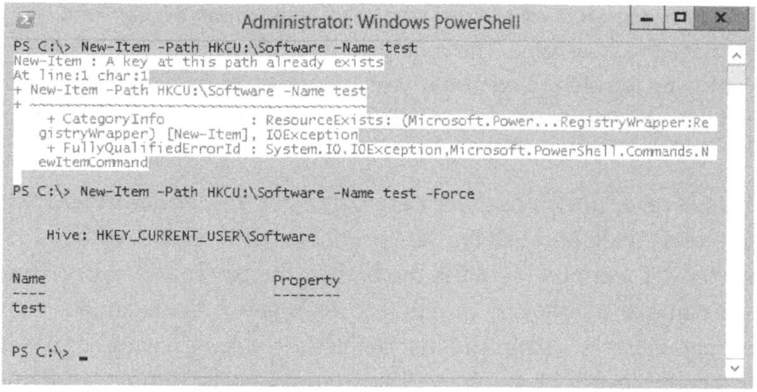

**FIGURE 3-10** Use the *-force* parameter when creating a new registry key to overwrite the key if it already exists.

## Setting the default value for the key

The previous examples do not set the default value for the newly created registry key. If the registry key already exists (as it does in this specific case), you can use the *Set-Item* cmdlet to assign a default value to the registry key. The steps to accomplish this appear here:

1.  Use the *Set-Item* cmdlet and supply the complete path to the existing registry key.

2.  Supply the default value in the *value* parameter of the *Set-Item* cmdlet.

    The following command assigns the value *test key* to the default property value of the HSG registry key contained in the HKCU:\SOFTWARE location:

    **Set-Item** -Path HKCU:\Software\test -Value "test key"

## Using *New-Item* to create and assign a value

It is not necessary to use the *New-Item* cmdlet to create a registry key and then to use the *Set-Item* cmdlet to assign a default value. You can combine these steps into a single command. The following command creates a new registry key with the name of HSG1 and assigns a default value of *default value* to the registry key:

**New-Item** -Path HKCU:\Software\hsg1 -Value "default value"

## Modifying the value of a registry property value

Modifying the value of a registry property value requires using the *Set-PropertyItem* cmdlet.

1.  Use the *Push-Location* cmdlet to save the current working location.

2.  Use the *Set-Location* cmdlet to change to the appropriate registry drive.

3.  Use the *Set-ItemProperty* cmdlet to assign a new value to the registry property.

4.  Use the *Pop-Location* cmdlet to return to the original working location.

When you know that a registry property value exists, the solution is simple: you use the *Set-ItemProperty* cmdlet and assign a new value. The code that follows saves the current working location, changes the new working location to the registry key, uses the *Set-ItemProperty* cmdlet to assign new values, and then uses the *Pop-Location* cmdlet to return to the original working location.

> **Note** The code that follows relies upon positional parameters for the *Set-ItemProperty* cmdlet. The first parameter is *-path*. Because the *Set-Location* cmdlet set the working location to the registry key, a period identifies the path as the current directory. The second parameter is the name of the registry property to change—in this example, it is *newproperty*. The last parameter is *-value*, and that defines the value to assign to the *registry* property. In this example, it is *mynewvalue*. The command with complete parameter names would thus be *Set-ItemProperty -Path . -name newproperty -value mynewvalue*. The quotation marks in the following code are not required, but do not harm anything either.

```
PS C:\> Push-Location
PS C:\> Set-Location HKCU:\Software\test
PS HKCU:\Software\test> Set-ItemProperty . newproperty "mynewvalue"
PS HKCU:\Software\test> Pop-Location
PS C:\>
```

Of course, all the pushing, popping, and setting of locations is not really required. It is entirely possible to change the registry property value from any location within the Windows PowerShell provider subsystem.

## The short way to change a registry property value

To change a registry property value simply, use the *Set-ItemProperty* cmdlet to assign a new value. Ensure you specify the complete path to the registry key. Here is an example of using the *Set-ItemProperty* cmdlet to change a registry property value without first navigating to the registry drive.

```
PS C:\> Set-ItemProperty -Path HKCU:\Software\test -Name newproperty -Value anewvalue
```

## Dealing with a missing registry property

If you need to set a registry property value, you can set the value of that property easily by using the *Set-ItemProperty* cmdlet. But what if the registry property does not exist? How do you set the property value then? You can still use the *Set-ItemProperty* cmdlet to set a registry property value, even if the registry property does not exist, as follows:

```
Set-ItemProperty -Path HKCU:\Software\test -Name missingproperty -Value avalue
```

To determine if a registry key exists, you can simply use the *Test-Path* cmdlet. It returns *true* if the key exists and *false* if it does not exist. This technique appears here:

```
PS C:\> Test-Path HKCU:\Software\test
True
PS C:\> Test-Path HKCU:\Software\test\newproperty
False
```

Unfortunately, this technique does not work for a registry key property. It always returns *false*—
even if the registry property exists. This appears here:

```
PS C:\> Test-Path HKCU:\Software\test\newproperty
False
PS C:\> Test-Path HKCU:\Software\test\bogus
False
```

Therefore, if you do not want to overwrite a registry key property if it already exists, you need a
way to determine if the registry key property exists—and using the *Test-Path* cmdlet does not work.
The following procedure shows how to handle this.

### Testing for a registry key property prior to writing a new value

1.  Use the *if* statement and the *Get-ItemProperty* cmdlet to retrieve the value of the registry key
    property. Specify the *erroraction* (*ea* is an alias) of *silentlycontinue* (0 is the enumeration value
    associated with *silentlycontinue*).

2.  In the script block for the *if* statement, display a message that the registry property exists, or
    simply exit.

3.  In the *else* statement, call *Set-ItemProperty* to create and set the value of the registry key
    property.

    This technique appears here:

    ```
    if((Get-ItemProperty -Path HKCU:\Software\test -Name bogus -ea 0).bogus)
    {'Propertyalready exists'}
     ELSE { Set-ItemProperty -Path HKCU:\Software\test -Name bogus -Value 'initial value'}
    ```

# Understanding the variable provider

The variable provider provides access to the variables that are defined within Windows PowerShell.
These variables include both user-defined variables, such as *$mred*, and system-defined variables,
such as *$host*. You can obtain a listing of the cmdlets designed to work specifically with variables by
using the *Get-Help* cmdlet and specifying the asterisk (*) variable. The commands used in the procedure are in the UnderstandingTheVariableProvider.txt and WorkingWithVariables.txt files. To return
only cmdlets, you use the *Where-Object* cmdlet and filter on the category that is equal to cmdlet. This
command is shown here:

```
Get-Help *variable | Where-Object category -eq "cmdlet"
```

The resulting list contains five cmdlets, but is a little jumbled and difficult to read. So let's modify the preceding command and specify the properties to return. To do this, use the up arrow key and pipeline the returned object into the *Format-List* cmdlet. Add the three properties you are interested in: *name*, *category*, and *synopsis*. The revised command is shown here:

```
Get-Help *variable | Where-Object {$_.category -eq "cmdlet"} |
Format-List name, category, synopsis
```

**Note** You will not get this output from Windows PowerShell 3.0 if you have not run the *Update-Help* cmdlet.

The resulting output is much easier to read and understand; it is shown here:

```
Name     : Get-Variable
Category : Cmdlet
Synopsis : Gets the variables in the current console.

Name     : New-Variable
Category : Cmdlet
Synopsis : Creates a new variable.

Name     : Set-Variable
Category : Cmdlet
Synopsis : Sets the value of a variable. Creates the variable if one with the requested
name does not exist.

Name     : Remove-Variable
Category : Cmdlet
Synopsis : Deletes a variable and its value.

Name     : Clear-Variable
Category : Cmdlet
Synopsis : Deletes the value of a variable.
```

### Working with variables

1. Open the Windows PowerShell console.

2. Use the *Set-Location* cmdlet to set the working location to the Variable PS drive. Use the *sl* alias to reduce typing needs. This command is shown here:

   ```
   SL variable:\
   ```

3. Produce a complete listing of all the variables currently defined in Windows PowerShell. To do this, use the *Get-ChildItem* cmdlet. You can use the alias *gci* to produce this list. The command is shown here:

   ```
   Get-ChildItem
   ```

4. The resulting list is jumbled. Press the up arrow key to retrieve the *Get-ChildItem* command, and pipeline the resulting object into the *Sort-Object* cmdlet. Sort on the *name* property. This command is shown here:

```
Get-ChildItem | Sort Name
```

The output from the previous command is shown here:

```
Name                           Value
----                           -----
$                              variable:
?                              True
^                              sl
args                           {}
ConfirmPreference              High
ConsoleFileName
DebugPreference                SilentlyContinue
Error                          {Failed to update Help for the module(s) 'Schedule...
ErrorActionPreference          Continue
ErrorView                      NormalView
ExecutionContext               System.Management.Automation.EngineIntrinsics
false                          False
FormatEnumerationLimit         4
HOME                           C:\Users\administrator
Host                           System.Management.Automation.Internal.Host.Interna...
input                          System.Collections.ArrayList+ArrayListEnumeratorSi...
MaximumAliasCount              4096
MaximumDriveCount              4096
MaximumErrorCount              256
MaximumFunctionCount           4096
MaximumHistoryCount            4096
MaximumVariableCount           4096
MyInvocation                   System.Management.Automation.InvocationInfo
NestedPromptLevel              0
null
OutputEncoding                 System.Text.ASCIIEncoding
PID                            3308
PROFILE                        C:\Users\administrator\Documents\WindowsPowerShell...
ProgressPreference             Continue
PSBoundParameters              {}
PSCommandPath
PSCulture                      en-US
PSDefaultParameterValues       {}
PSEmailServer
PSHOME                         C:\Windows\System32\WindowsPowerShell\v1.0
PSScriptRoot
PSSessionApplicationName       wsman
PSSessionConfigurationName     http://schemas.microsoft.com/powershell/Microsoft...
PSSessionOption                System.Management.Automation.Remoting.PSSessionOption
PSUICulture                    en-US
PSVersionTable                 {PSVersion, WSManStackVersion, SerializationVersio...
PWD                            Variable:\
```

```
ShellId                    Microsoft.PowerShell
StackTrace                 at System.Management.Automation.CommandDiscover...
true                       True
VerbosePreference          SilentlyContinue
WarningPreference          Continue
WhatIfPreference           False
```

5. Use the *Get-Variable* cmdlet to retrieve a specific variable. Use the *ShellId* variable. You can use tab completion to speed up typing. The command is shown here:

**Get-Variable** ShellId

6. Press the up arrow key to retrieve the previous *Get-Variable ShellId* command. Pipeline the object returned into a *Format-List* cmdlet and return all properties. This is shown here:

**Get-Variable** ShellId | **Format-List** *

The resulting output includes the description of the variable, value, and other information shown here:

```
PSPath        : Microsoft.PowerShell.Core\Variable::shellid
PSDrive       : Variable
PSProvider    : Microsoft.PowerShell.Core\Variable
PSIsContainer : False
Name          : ShellId
Description   : The ShellID identifies the current shell.  This is used by
                #Requires.
Value         : Microsoft.PowerShell
Visibility    : Public
Module        :
ModuleName    :
Options       : Constant, AllScope
Attributes    : {}
```

7. Create a new variable called *administrator*. To do this, use the *New-Variable* cmdlet. This command is shown here:

**New-Variable** administrator

8. Use the *Get-Variable* cmdlet to retrieve the new *administrator* variable. This command is shown here:

**Get-Variable** administrator

The resulting output is shown here. Notice that there is no value for the variable.

```
Name                       Value
----                       -----
administrator
```

9. Assign a value to the new administrator variable. To do this, use the *Set-Variable* cmdlet. Specify the *administrator* variable name, and supply your given name as the value for the variable. This command is shown here:

```
Set-Variable administrator -value mred
```

10. Press the up arrow key one time to retrieve the previous *Get-Variable administrator* command. This command is shown here:

```
Get-Variable administrator
```

The output displays both the variable name and the value associated with the variable. This is shown here:

```
Name                          Value
----                          -----
administrator                 mred
```

11. Use the *Remove-Variable* cmdlet to remove the administrator variable you previously created. This command is shown here:

```
Remove-Variable administrator
```

You could also use the *Del* alias, as follows:

```
Del variable:administrator
```

12. Press the up arrow key one time to retrieve the previous *Get-Variable administrator* command. This command is shown here:

```
Get-Variable administrator
```

The variable is deleted. The resulting output is shown here:

```
Get-Variable : Cannot find a variable with name 'administrator'.
At line:1 char:13
+ Get-Variable <<<< administrator
```

This concludes this procedure.

# Exploring PowerShell providers: step-by-step exercises

In this exercise, you'll explore the use of the certificate provider in Windows PowerShell. You will navigate the certificate provider by using the same types of commands used with the file system. You will then explore the environment provider by using the same methodology.

## Exploring the certificate provider

1. Open the Windows PowerShell console.

2. Obtain a listing of all the properties available for use with the *Get-ChildItem* cmdlet by piping the results into the *Get-Member* cmdlet. To filter out only the properties, pipeline the results into a *Where-Object* cmdlet and specify the *membertype* to be equal to *property*. This command is shown here:

```
Get-ChildItem |Get-Member | Where-Object {$_.membertype -eq "property"}
```

3. Set your location to the Certificate drive. To identify the Certificate drive, use the *Get-PSDrive* cmdlet. Use the *Where-Object* cmdlet and filter on names that begin with the letter c. This is shown here:

```
Get-PSDrive |where name -like "c*"
```

The results of this command are shown here:

```
Name            Used (GB)      Free (GB) Provider       Root

----            ---------      --------- --------       ----

C                 110.38          38.33 FileSystem      C:\

Cert                                    Certificate     \
```

4. Use the *Set-Location* cmdlet to change to the Certificate drive:

```
SL cert:\
```

5. Use the *Get-ChildItem* cmdlet to produce a listing of all the certificates on the machine:

```
GCI
```

The output from the previous command is shown here:

```
Location   : CurrentUser
StoreNames : {?, UserDS, AuthRoot, CA...}

Location   : LocalMachine
StoreNames : {?, AuthRoot, CA, AddressBook...}
```

6. The listing seems somewhat incomplete. To determine whether there are additional certificates installed on the machine, use the *Get-ChildItem* cmdlet again, but this time specify the *-recurse* argument. Modify the previous command by using the up arrow key. The command is shown here:

```
GCI -recurse
```

7. The output from the previous command seems to take a long time to run and produces hundreds of lines of output. To make the listing more readable, pipe the output to a text file, and then open the file in Notepad. The command to do this is shown here:

```
GCI -recurse >C:\a.txt;notepad.exe a.txt
```

This concludes this step-by-step exercise.

In the following exercise, you'll work with the Windows PowerShell environment provider.

## Examining the environment provider

1. Open the Windows PowerShell console.

2. Use the *New-PSDrive* cmdlet to create a drive mapping to the alias provider. The name of the new PS drive will be *al*. The *-PSProvider* parameter is *alias*, and the root will be dot (.). This command is shown here:

```
New-PSDrive -name al -PSProvider alias -Root .
```

3. Change your working location to the new PS drive you called *al*. To do this, use the *sl* alias for the *Set-Location* cmdlet. This is shown here:

```
SL al:\
```

4. Use the *gci* alias for the *Get-ChildItem* cmdlet, and pipeline the resulting object into the *Sort-Object* cmdlet by using the *sort* alias. Supply *name* as the property to sort on. This command is shown here:

```
GCI | Sort -property name
```

5. Press the up arrow key to retrieve the previous *gci | sort -property name* command, and modify it to use a *Where-Object* cmdlet to return aliases only when the name begins with a letter after *t* in the alphabet. Use the *where* alias to avoid typing the entire name of the cmdlet. The resulting command is shown here:

```
GCI | sort -property name | Where Name -gt "t"
```

6. Change your location back to drive C. To do this, use the *sl* alias and supply the C:\ argument. This is shown here:

```
SL C:\
```

7. Remove the PS drive mapping for al. To do this, use the *Remove-PSDrive* cmdlet and supply the name of the PS drive to remove. Note that this command does not take a trailing colon (:) or colon with backslash (:\). The command is shown here:

```
Remove-PSDrive al
```

**8.** Use the *Get-PSDrive* cmdlet to ensure the al drive has been removed. This is shown here:

```
Get-PSDrive
```

**9.** Use the *Get-Item* cmdlet to obtain a listing of all the environment variables. Use the *-path* argument and supply *env:\* as the value. This is shown here:

```
Get-Item -path env:\
```

**10.** Press the up arrow key to retrieve the previous command and pipeline the resulting object into the *Get-Member* cmdlet. This is shown here:

```
Get-Item -path env:\ | Get-Member
```

The results from the previous command are shown here:

```
TypeName: System.Collections.Generic.Dictionary'2+ValueCollection[[System.
String, mscorlib, Version=2.0.0.0, Culture=neutral, PublicKeyToken=b77a5c561934e0
89],[System.Collections.DictionaryEntry, mscorlib, Version=2.0.0.0, Culture=
neutral, PublicKeyToken=b77a5c561934e089]]

Name            MemberType   Definition
----            ----------   ----------
CopyTo          Method       System.Void CopyTo(DictionaryEntry[] array, Int32...
Equals          Method       System.Boolean Equals(Object obj)
GetEnumerator   Method       System.Collections.Generic.Dictionary'2+ValueColl...
GetHashCode     Method       System.Int32 GetHashCode()
GetType         Method       System.Type GetType()
get_Count       Method       System.Int32 get_Count()
ToString        Method       System.String ToString()
PSDrive         NoteProperty System.Management.Automation.PSDriveInfo PSDrive=Env
PSIsContainer   NoteProperty System.Boolean PSIsContainer=True
PSPath          NoteProperty System.String PSPath=Microsoft.PowerShell.Core\En...
PSProvider      NoteProperty System.Management.Automation.ProviderInfo PSProvi...
Count           Property     System.Int32 Count {get;}
```

**11.** Press the up arrow key twice to return to the *Get-Item -path env:\* command. Use the Home key to move your insertion point to the beginning of the line. Add a variable called *$objEnv* and use it to hold the object returned by the *Get-Item -path env:\* command. The completed command is shown here:

```
$objEnv=Get-Item -path env:\
```

**12.** From the listing of members of the environment object, find the count property. Use this property to print out the total number of environment variables. As you type **$o**, try to use tab completion to avoid typing. Also try to use tab completion as you type the *c* in *count*. The completed command is shown here:

```
$objEnv.Count
```

**13.** Examine the methods of the object returned by *Get-Item -path env:\*. Notice there is a *Get_Count* method. Let's use that method. The code is shown here:

```
$objEnv.Get_count
```

When this code is executed, however, the results define the method rather than execute the *Get_Count* method. These results are shown here:

```
MemberType          : Method
OverloadDefinitions : {System.Int32 get_Count()}
TypeNameOfValue     : System.Management.Automation.PSMethod
Value               : System.Int32 get_Count()
Name                : get_Count
IsInstance          : True
```

**14.** To retrieve the actual number of environment variables, you need to use empty parentheses at the end of the method. This is shown here:

```
$objEnv.Get_count()
```

**15.** If you want to know exactly what type of object is contained in the *$objEnv* variable, you can use the *GetType* method, as shown here:

```
$objEnv.GetType()
```

This command returns the results shown here:

```
IsPublic IsSerial Name                             BaseType
-------- -------- ----                             --------
False    True     ValueCollection                  System.Object
```

This concludes this exercise.

# Chapter 3 quick reference

| To | Do this |
|---|---|
| Produce a listing of all variables defined in a Windows PowerShell session | Use the *Set-Location* cmdlet to change location to the Variable PS drive, and then use the *Get-ChildItem* cmdlet. |
| Obtain a listing of all the aliases | Use the *Set-Location* cmdlet to change location to the Alias PS drive, and then use the *Get-ChildItem* cmdlet to produce a listing of aliases. Pipeline the resulting object into the *Where-Object* cmdlet and filter on the *name* property for the appropriate value. |
| Delete a directory that is empty | Use the *Remove-Item* cmdlet and supply the name of the directory. |
| Delete a directory that contains other items | Use the *Remove-Item* cmdlet and supply the name of the directory and specify the *-recurse* argument. |
| Create a new text file | Use the *New-Item* cmdlet and specify the *-path* argument for the directory location. Supply the *-name* argument and specify the *-type* argument as *file*.<br>Example: *New-Item -path C:\Mytest -name Myfile.txt -type file.* |
| Obtain a listing of registry keys from a registry hive | Use the *Get-ChildItem* cmdlet and specify the appropriate PS drive name for the *-path* argument. Complete the path with the appropriate registry path.<br>Example: *gci -path HKLM:\software* |
| Obtain a listing of all functions on the system | Use the *Get-ChildItem* cmdlet and supply the PS drive name of *function:\ * to the *-path* argument.<br>Example: *gci -path function:\ * |

# CHAPTER 4

# Using PowerShell Remoting and Jobs

**After completing this chapter, you will be able to:**

- Use Windows PowerShell remoting to connect to a remote system.

- Use Windows PowerShell remoting to run commands on a remote system.

- Use Windows PowerShell jobs to run commands in the background.

- Receive the results of background jobs.

- Keep the results from background jobs.

## Understanding Windows PowerShell remoting

One of the great improvements in Microsoft Windows PowerShell 3.0 is the change surrounding remoting. The configuration is easier than it was in Windows PowerShell 2.0, and in most cases, Windows PowerShell remoting just works. When talking about Windows PowerShell remoting, a bit of confusion can arise because there are several different ways of running commands against remote servers. Depending on your particular network configuration and security needs, one or more methods of remoting may not be appropriate.

## Classic remoting

Classic remoting in Windows PowerShell relies on protocols such as DCOM and RPC to make connections to remote machines. Traditionally, these protocols require opening many ports in the firewall and starting various services that the different cmdlets utilize. To find the Windows PowerShell cmdlets that natively support remoting, use the *Get-Help* cmdlet. Specify a value of *computername* for the *-parameter* parameter of the *Get-Help* cmdlet. This command produces a nice list of all cmdlets that have native support for remoting. The command and associated output appear here:

```
PS C:\> get-help * -Parameter computername | sort name | ft name, synopsis -auto -wrap
```

Name                              Synopsis
----                              --------
Add-Computer                      Add the local computer to a domain or workgroup.
Add-Printer                       Adds a printer to the specified computer.
Add-PrinterDriver                 Installs a printer driver on the specified
                                  computer.
Add-PrinterPort                   Installs a printer port on the specified computer.
Clear-EventLog                    Deletes all entries from specified event logs on
                                  the local or remote computers.
Connect-PSSession                 Reconnects to disconnected sessions.
Connect-WSMan                     Connects to the WinRM service on a remote
                                  computer.
Disconnect-PSSession              Disconnects from a session.
Disconnect-WSMan                  Disconnects the client from the WinRM service on
                                  a remote computer.
Enter-PSSession                   Starts an interactive session with a remote
                                  computer.
Get-CimAssociatedInstance

                                  Get-CimAssociatedInstance [-InputObject]
                                  <ciminstance> [[-Association] <string>]
                                  [-ResultClassName <string>] [-Namespace <string>]
                                  [-OperationTimeoutSec <uint32>] [-ResourceUri
                                  <uri>] [-ComputerName <string[]>] [-KeyOnly]
                                  [<CommonParameters>]

                                  Get-CimAssociatedInstance [-InputObject]
                                  <ciminstance> [[-Association] <string>]
                                  -CimSession <CimSession[]> [-ResultClassName
                                  <string>] [-Namespace <string>]
                                  [-OperationTimeoutSec <uint32>] [-ResourceUri
                                  <uri>] [-KeyOnly] [<CommonParameters>]

Get-CimClass

                                  Get-CimClass [[-ClassName] <string>]
                                  [[-Namespace] <string>] [-OperationTimeoutSec
                                  <uint32>] [-ComputerName <string[]>] [-MethodName
                                  <string>] [-PropertyName <string>]
                                  [-QualifierName <string>] [<CommonParameters>]

                                  Get-CimClass [[-ClassName] <string>]
                                  [[-Namespace] <string>] -CimSession
                                  <CimSession[]> [-OperationTimeoutSec <uint32>]
                                  [-MethodName <string>] [-PropertyName <string>]
                                  [-QualifierName <string>] [<CommonParameters>]

Write-EventLog                    Writes an event to an event log.

As you can see, many of the Windows PowerShell cmdlets that have the *-computername* parameter relate to Web Services Management (WSMAN), Common Information Model (CIM), or sessions. To remove these cmdlets from the list, modify the command a bit to use *Where-Object* (*?* Is an alias for *Where-Object*). The revised command and associated output appear here:

```
PS C:\> Get-Help * -Parameter computername -Category cmdlet | ? modulename -match
'PowerShell.Management' | sort name | ft name, synopsis -AutoSize -Wrap
```

| Name | Synopsis |
| ---- | -------- |
| Add-Computer | Add the local computer to a domain or workgroup. |
| Clear-EventLog | Deletes all entries from specified event logs on the local or remote computers. |
| Get-EventLog | Gets the events in an event log, or a list of the event logs, on the local or remote computers. |
| Get-HotFix | Gets the hotfixes that have been applied to the local and remote computers. |
| Get-Process | Gets the processes that are running on the local computer or a remote computer. |
| Get-Service | Gets the services on a local or remote computer. |
| Get-WmiObject | Gets instances of Windows Management Instrumentation (WMI) classes or information about the available classes. |
| Invoke-WmiMethod | Calls Windows Management Instrumentation (WMI) methods. |
| Limit-EventLog | Sets the event log properties that limit the size of the event log and the age of its entries. |
| New-EventLog | Creates a new event log and a new event source on a local or remote computer. |
| Register-WmiEvent | Subscribes to a Windows Management Instrumentation (WMI) event. |
| Remove-Computer | Removes the local computer from its domain. |
| Remove-EventLog | Deletes an event log or unregisters an event source. |
| Remove-WmiObject | Deletes an instance of an existing Windows Management Instrumentation (WMI) class. |
| Rename-Computer | Renames a computer. |
| Restart-Computer | Restarts ("reboots") the operating system on local and remote computers. |
| Set-Service | Starts, stops, and suspends a service, and changes its properties. |
| Set-WmiInstance | Creates or updates an instance of an existing Windows Management Instrumentation (WMI) class. |
| Show-EventLog | Displays the event logs of the local or a remote computer in Event Viewer. |
| Stop-Computer | Stops (shuts down) local and remote computers. |
| Test-Connection | Sends ICMP echo request packets ("pings") to one or more computers. |

```
<-- output truncated -->
```

Some of the cmdlets provide the ability to specify credentials. This allows you to use a different user account to make the connection and to retrieve the data. Figure 4-1 displays the credential dialog box that appears when the cmdlet runs.

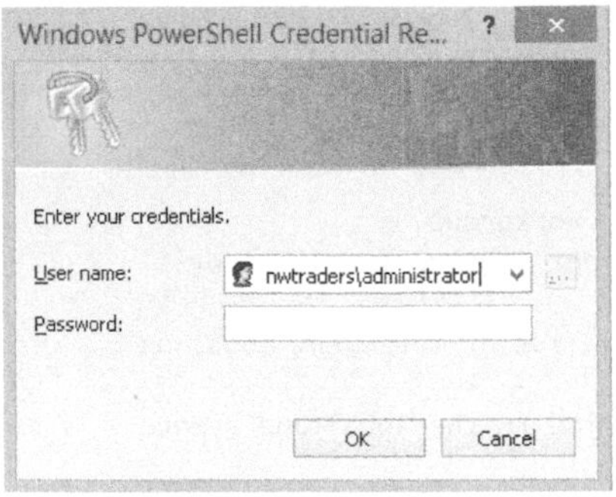

**FIGURE 4-1** Cmdlets that support the *-credential* parameter prompt for credentials when supplied with a user name.

This technique of using the *-computername* and *-credential* parameters in a cmdlet appears here:

```
PS C:\> Get-WinEvent -LogName application -MaxEvents 1 -ComputerName ex1 -Credential
nwtraders\administrator

TimeCreated              ProviderName                    Id Message
-----------              ------------                    -- -------
7/1/2012 11:54:14 AM MSExchange ADAccess               2080 Process MAD.EXE (...
```

However, as mentioned earlier, use of these cmdlets often requires opening holes in the firewall or starting specific services. By default, these types of cmdlets fail when run against remote machines that don't have relaxed access rules. An example of this type of error appears here:

```
PS C:\> Get-WinEvent -LogName application -MaxEvents 1 -ComputerName dc1 -Credential
nwtraders\administrator
Get-WinEvent : The RPC server is unavailable
At line:1 char:1
+ Get-WinEvent -LogName application -MaxEvents 1 -ComputerName dc1 -Credential iam
...
+ ~~~~~~~~~~~~~~~~~~~~~~~~~~~~~~~~~~~~~~~~~~~~~~~~~~~~~~~~~~~~~~~~~~~~~~~~~~~~~~~~~~~~
    + CategoryInfo          : NotSpecified: (:) [Get-WinEvent], EventLogException
    + FullyQualifiedErrorId : System.Diagnostics.Eventing.Reader.EventLogException,
   Microsoft.PowerShell.Commands.GetWinEventCommand
```

Other cmdlets, such as *Get-Service* and *Get-Process*, do not have a *-credential* parameter, and therefore the commands associated with cmdlets such as *Get-Service* or *Get-Process* impersonate the logged-on user. Such a command appears here:

```
PS C:\> Get-Service -ComputerName hyperv -Name bits

Status   Name       DisplayName
------   ----       -----------
Running  bits       Background Intelligent Transfer Ser...


PS C:\>
```

Just because the cmdlet does not support alternate credentials does not mean that the cmdlet must impersonate the logged-on user. Holding down the Shift key and right-clicking the Windows PowerShell icon from the taskbar brings up an action menu that allows you to run the program as a different user. This menu appears in Figure 4-2.

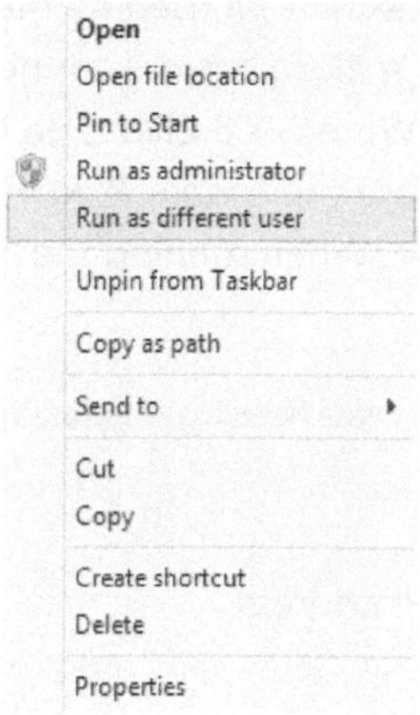

**FIGURE 4-2** The menu from the Windows PowerShell console permits running with different security credentials.

The Run As Different User dialog box appears in Figure 4-3.

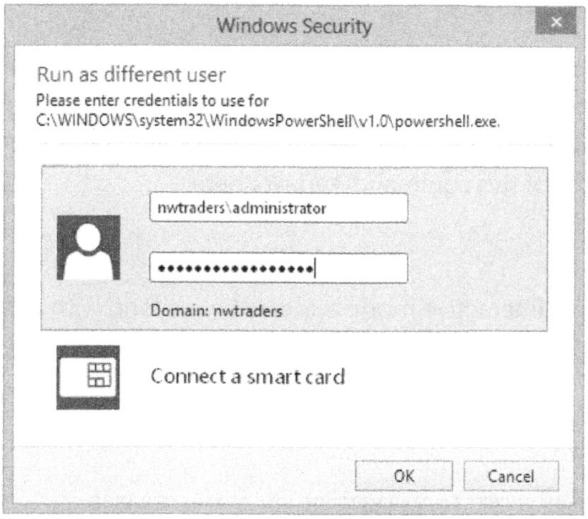

**FIGURE 4-3** The Run As Different User dialog box permits entering a different user context.

Using the Run As Different User dialog box makes alternative credentials available for Windows PowerShell cmdlets that do not support the -*credential* parameter.

# WinRM

Windows Server 2012 installs with Windows Remote Management (WinRM) configured and running to support remote Windows PowerShell commands. WinRM is Microsoft's implementation of the industry standard WS-Management protocol. As such, WinRM provides a firewall-friendly method of accessing remote systems in an interoperable manner. It is the remoting mechanism used by the new CIM cmdlets. As soon as Windows Server 2012 is up and running, you can make a remote connection and run commands, or open an interactive Windows PowerShell console. Windows 8 Client, on the other hand, ships with WinRM locked down. Therefore, the first step is to use the *Enable-PSRemoting* function to configure Windows PowerShell remoting on the client machine. When running the *Enable-PSRemoting* function, the function performs the following steps:

1. Starts or restarts the WinRM service

2. Sets the WinRM service startup type to Automatic

3. Creates a listener to accept requests from any Internet Protocol (IP) address

4. Enables inbound firewall exceptions for WSMAN traffic

5. Sets a target listener named *Microsoft.powershell*

6. Sets a target listener named *Microsoft.powershell.workflow*

7. Sets a target listener named *Microsoft.powershell32*

During each step of this process, the function prompts you to agree to performing the specified action. If you are familiar with the steps the function performs and you do not make any changes from the defaults, you can run the command with the *-force* switched parameter, and it will not prompt prior to making the changes. The syntax of this command appears here:

```
Enable-PSRemoting -force
```

The use of the *Enable-PSRemoting* function in interactive mode appears here, along with all associated output from the command:

```
PS C:\> Enable-PSRemoting

WinRM Quick Configuration
Running command "Set-WSManQuickConfig" to enable remote management of this computer
by using the Windows Remote Management (WinRM) service.
 This includes:
    1. Starting or restarting (if already started) the WinRM service
    2. Setting the WinRM service startup type to Automatic
    3. Creating a listener to accept requests on any IP address
    4. Enabling Windows Firewall inbound rule exceptions for WS-Management traffic
(for http only).
```

```
Do you want to continue?
[Y] Yes  [A] Yes to All  [N] No  [L] No to All  [S] Suspend  [?] Help
(default is "Y"):y
WinRM has been updated to receive requests.
WinRM service type changed successfully.
WinRM service started.

WinRM has been updated for remote management.
Created a WinRM listener on HTTP://* to accept WS-Man requests to any IP on this machine.
WinRM firewall exception enabled.


Confirm
Are you sure you want to perform this action?
Performing operation "Set-PSSessionConfiguration" on Target "Name:
microsoft.powershell SDDL:
O:NSG:BAD:P(A;;GA;;;BA)(A;;GA;;;RM)S:P(AU;FA;GA;;;WD)(AU;SA;GXGW;;;WD). This will
allow selected users to remotely run Windows PowerShell commands on this computer".
[Y] Yes  [A] Yes to All  [N] No  [L] No to All  [S] Suspend  [?] Help
(default is "Y"):y

Confirm
Are you sure you want to perform this action?
Performing operation "Set-PSSessionConfiguration" on Target "Name:
microsoft.powershell.workflow SDDL:
O:NSG:BAD:P(A;;GA;;;BA)(A;;GA;;;RM)S:P(AU;FA;GA;;;WD)(AU;SA;GXGW;;;WD). This will
allow selected users to remotely run Windows PowerShell commands on this computer".
[Y] Yes  [A] Yes to All  [N] No  [L] No to All  [S] Suspend  [?] Help
(default is "Y"):y

Confirm
Are you sure you want to perform this action?
Performing operation "Set-PSSessionConfiguration" on Target "Name:
microsoft.powershell32 SDDL:
O:NSG:BAD:P(A;;GA;;;BA)(A;;GA;;;RM)S:P(AU;FA;GA;;;WD)(AU;SA;GXGW;;;WD). This will
allow selected users to remotely run Windows PowerShell commands on this computer".
[Y] Yes  [A] Yes to All  [N] No  [L] No to All  [S] Suspend  [?] Help
(default is "Y"):y
PS C:\>
```

Once Windows PowerShell remoting is configured, use the *Test-WSMan* cmdlet to ensure that the WinRM remoting is properly configured and is accepting requests. A properly configured system replies with the information appearing here:

```
PS C:\> Test-WSMan -ComputerName w8c504


wsmid           : http://schemas.dmtf.org/wbem/wsman/identity/1/wsmanidentity.xsd
ProtocolVersion : http://schemas.dmtf.org/wbem/wsman/1/wsman.xsd
ProductVendor   : Microsoft Corporation
ProductVersion  : OS: 0.0.0 SP: 0.0 Stack: 3.0
```

This cmdlet works with Windows PowerShell 2.0 remoting as well. The output appearing here is from a domain controller running Windows 2008 with Windows PowerShell 2.0 installed and WinRM configured for remote access:

```
PS C:\> Test-WSMan -ComputerName dc1}
wsmid            : http://schemas.dmtf.org/wbem/wsman/identity/1/wsmanidentity.xsd
ProtocolVersion : http://schemas.dmtf.org/wbem/wsman/1/wsman.xsd
ProductVendor   : Microsoft Corporation
ProductVersion  : OS: 0.0.0 SP: 0.0 Stack: 2.0
```

If WinRM is not configured, an error returns from the system. Such an error from a Windows 8 client appears here:

```
PS C:\> Test-WSMan -ComputerName w8c10
Test-WSMan : <f:WSManFault
xmlns:f="http://schemas.microsoft.com/wbem/wsman/1/wsmanfault" Code="2150859046"
Machine="w8c504.iammred.net"><f:Message>WinRM cannot complete the operation. Verify
that the specified computer name is valid, that the computer is accessible over the
network, and that a firewall exception for the WinRM service is enabled and allows
access from this computer. By default, the WinRM firewall exception for public
profiles limits access to remote computers within the same local subnet.
</f:Message></f:WSManFault>
At line:1 char:1
+ Test-WSMan -ComputerName w8c10
+ ~~~~~~~~~~~~~~~~~~~~~~~~~~~~~~~
    + CategoryInfo          : InvalidOperation: (w8c10:String) [Test-WSMan], Invalid
    OperationException
    + FullyQualifiedErrorId : WsManError,Microsoft.WSMan.Management.TestWSManCommand
```

Keep in mind that configuring WinRM via the *Enable-PSRemoting* function does not enable the *Remote Management* firewall exception, and therefore *PING* commands will not work by default when pinging to a Windows 8 client system. This appears here:

```
PS C:\> ping w8c504

Pinging w8c504.iammred.net [192.168.0.56] with 32 bytes of data:
Request timed out.
Request timed out.
Request timed out.
Request timed out.

Ping statistics for 192.168.0.56:
    Packets: Sent = 4, Received = 0, Lost = 4 (100% loss).
```

Pings to a Windows 2012 server, do however, work. This appears here:

```
PS C:\> ping w8s504

Pinging w8s504.iammred.net [192.168.0.57] with 32 bytes of data:
Reply from 192.168.0.57: bytes=32 time<1ms TTL=128
Reply from 192.168.0.57: bytes=32 time<1ms TTL=128
Reply from 192.168.0.57: bytes=32 time<1ms TTL=128
Reply from 192.168.0.57: bytes=32 time<1ms TTL=128
```

```
Ping statistics for 192.168.0.57:
    Packets: Sent = 4, Received = 4, Lost = 0 (0% loss),
Approximate round trip times in milli-seconds:
    Minimum = 0ms, Maximum = 0ms, Average = 0ms
```

## Creating a remote Windows PowerShell session

For simple configuration on a single remote machine, entering a remote Windows PowerShell session is the answer. To enter a remote Windows PowerShell session, use the *Enter-PSSession* cmdlet. This creates an interactive remote Windows PowerShell session on a target machine and uses the default remote endpoint. If you do not supply credentials, the remote session impersonates the currently logged on user The output appearing here illustrates connecting to a remote computer named dc1. Once the connection is established, the Windows PowerShell prompt changes to include the name of the remote system. *Set-Location* (which has an alias of *sl*) changes the working directory on the remote system to C:\. Next, the *Get-WmiObject* cmdlet retrieves the BIOS information on the remote system. The *exit* command exits the remote session, and the Windows PowerShell prompt returns to the prompt configured previously.

```
PS C:\> Enter-PSSession -ComputerName dc1
[dc1]: PS C:\Users\Administrator\Documents> sl c:\
[dc1]: PS C:\> gwmi win32_bios


SMBIOSBIOSVersion : A01
Manufacturer      : Dell Computer Corporation
Name              : Default System BIOS
SerialNumber      : 9HQ1S21
Version           : DELL   - 6



[dc1]: PS C:\> exit
PS C:\>
```

The good thing is that when using the Windows PowerShell transcript tool via *Start-Transcript*, the transcript tool captures output from the remote Windows PowerShell session, as well as output from the local session. Indeed, all commands typed appear in the transcript. The following commands illustrate beginning a transcript, entering a remote Windows PowerShell session, typing a command, exiting the session, and stopping the transcript:

```
PS C:\> Start-Transcript
Transcript started, output file is C:\Users\administrator.IAMMRED\Documents\PowerShell_
transcript.20120701124414.txt
PS C:\> Enter-PSSession -ComputerName dc1
[dc1]: PS C:\Users\Administrator\Documents> gwmi win32_bios


SMBIOSBIOSVersion : A01
Manufacturer      : Dell Computer Corporation
Name              : Default System BIOS
SerialNumber      : 9HQ1S21
Version           : DELL   - 6
```

```
[dc1]: PS C:\Users\Administrator\Documents> exit
PS C:\> Stop-Transcript
Transcript stopped, output file is C:\Users\administrator.IAMMRED\Documents\PowerShell_
transcript.20120701124414.txt
PS C:\>
```

Figure 4-4 displays a copy of the transcript from the previous session.

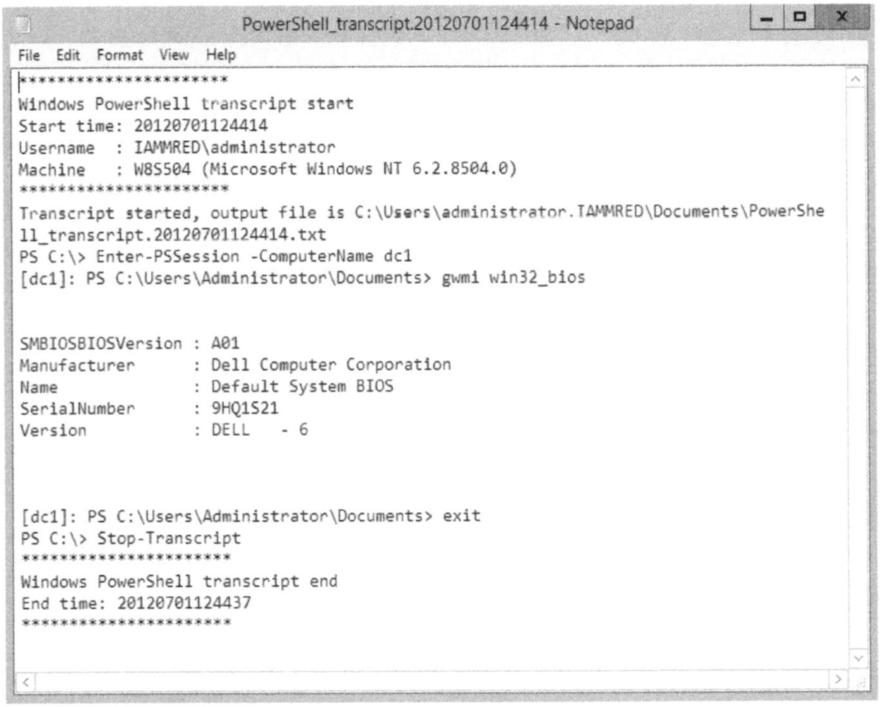

**FIGURE 4-4** The Windows PowerShell transcript tool records commands and output received from a remote Windows PowerShell session.

If you anticipate making multiple connections to a remote system, use the *New-PSSession* cmdlet to create a remote Windows PowerShell session. *New-PSSession* permits you to store the remote session in a variable and provides you with the ability to enter and to leave the remote session as often as required—without the additional overhead of creating and destroying remote sessions. In the commands that follow, a new Windows PowerShell session is created via the *New-PSSession* cmdlet. The newly created session is stored in the *$dc1* variable. Next, the *Enter-PSSession* cmdlet is used to enter the remote session by using the stored session. A command retrieves the remote hostname, and the remote session is exited via the *exit* command. Next, the session is reentered, and the last process is retrieved. The session is exited once again. Finally, the *Get-PSSession* cmdlet retrieves Windows PowerShell sessions on the system, and all sessions are removed via the *Remove-PSSession* cmdlet.

```
PS C:\> $dc1 = New-PSSession -ComputerName dc1 -Credential iammred\administrator
PS C:\> Enter-PSSession $dc1
[dc1]: PS C:\Users\Administrator\Documents> hostname
dc1
[dc1]: PS C:\Users\Administrator\Documents> exit
PS C:\> Enter-PSSession $dc1
[dc1]: PS C:\Users\Administrator\Documents> gps | select -Last 1

Handles  NPM(K)    PM(K)      WS(K) VM(M)   CPU(s)     Id ProcessName
-------  ------    -----      ----- -----   ------     -- -----------
    292       9    39536      50412   158     1.97   2332 wsmprovhost


[dc1]: PS C:\Users\Administrator\Documents> exit
PS C:\> Get-PSSession

 Id Name            ComputerName   State        ConfigurationName    Availability
 -- ----            ------------   -----        -----------------    ------------
  8 Session8        dc1            Opened       Microsoft.PowerShell    Available


PS C:\> Get-PSSession | Remove-PSSession
PS C:\>
```

## Running a single Windows PowerShell command

If you have a single command to run, it does not make sense to go through all the trouble of building and entering an interactive remote Windows PowerShell session. Instead of creating a remote
Windows PowerShell console session, you can run a single command by using the *Invoke-Command*
cmdlet. If you have a single command to run, use the cmdlet directly and specify the computer name
as well as any credentials required for the connection. You are still creating a remote session, but you
are also removing the session. Therefore, if you have a lot of commands to run against the remote
machine, a performance problem could arise. But for single commands, this technique works well. The
technique is shown here, where the last process running on the Ex1 remote server appears:

```
PS C:\> Invoke-Command -ComputerName ex1 -ScriptBlock {gps | select -Last 1}

Handles  NPM(K)    PM(K)      WS(K) VM(M)   CPU(s)     Id ProcessName   PSComputerNa
                                                                        me
-------  ------    -----      ----- -----   ------     -- -----------   ------------
    224      34    47164      51080   532     0.58  10164 wsmprovhost   ex1
```

If you have several commands, or if you anticipate making multiple connections, the *Invoke-
Command* cmdlet accepts a session name or a session object in the same manner as the *Enter-
PSSession* cmdlet. In the output appearing here, a new PSSession is created to a remote computer
named dc1. The remote session is used to retrieve two different pieces of information. Once the
Windows PowerShell remote session is completed, the session stored in the *$dc1* variable is explicitly
removed.

```
PS C:\> $dc1 = New-PSSession -ComputerName dc1 -Credential iammred\administrator
PS C:\> Invoke-Command -Session $dc1 -ScriptBlock {hostname}
dc1
PS C:\> Invoke-Command -Session $dc1 -ScriptBlock {Get-EventLog application -Newest 1}


   Index Time            EntryType   Source              InstanceID Message PSCompu
                                                                            terName

   ----- ----            ---------   ------              ---------- ------- -------
   17702 Jul 01 12:59    Information ESENT                      701 DFSR... dc1


PS C:\> Remove-PSSession $dc1
```

Using *Invoke-Command*, you can run the same command against a large number of remote systems. The secret behind this power is that the *-computername* parameter from the *Invoke-Command* cmdlet accepts an array of computer names. In the output appearing here, an array of computer names is stored in the variable *$cn*. Next, the *$cred* variable holds the *PSCredential* object for the remote connections. Finally, the *Invoke-Command* cmdlet is used to make connections to all of the remote machines and to return the BIOS information from the systems. The nice thing about this technique is that an additional parameter, *PSComputerName*, is added to the returning object, permitting easy identification of which BIOS is associated with which computer system. The commands and associated output appear here:

```
PS C:\> $cn = "dc1","dc3","ex1","sql1","wsus1","wds1","hyperv1","hyperv2","hyperv3"
PS C:\> $cred = get-credential iammred\administrator
PS C:\> Invoke-Command -cn $cn -cred $cred -ScriptBlock {gwmi win32_bios}


SMBIOSBIOSVersion : BAP6710H.86A.0072.2011.0927.1425
Manufacturer      : Intel Corp.
Name              : BIOS Date: 09/27/11 14:25:42 Ver: 04.06.04
SerialNumber      :
Version           : INTEL  - 1072009
PSComputerName    : hyperv3

SMBIOSBIOSVersion : A11
Manufacturer      : Dell Inc.
Name              : Phoenix ROM BIOS PLUS Version 1.10 A11
SerialNumber      : BDY91L1
Version           : DELL   - 15
PSComputerName    : hyperv2

SMBIOSBIOSVersion : A01
Manufacturer      : Dell Computer Corporation
Name              : Default System BIOS
SerialNumber      : 9HQ1S21
Version           : DELL   - 6
PSComputerName    : dc1
```

```
SMBIOSBIOSVersion : 090004
Manufacturer      : American Megatrends Inc.
Name              : BIOS Date: 03/19/09 22:51:32  Ver: 09.00.04
SerialNumber      : 3692-0963-1044-7503-9631-2546-83
Version           : VRTUAL - 3000919
PSComputerName    : wsus1

SMBIOSBIOSVersion : V1.6
Manufacturer      : American Megatrends Inc.
Name              : Default System BIOS
SerialNumber      : To Be Filled By O.E.M.
Version           : 7583MS - 20091228
PSComputerName    : hyperv1

SMBIOSBIOSVersion : 080015
Manufacturer      : American Megatrends Inc.
Name              : Default System BIOS
SerialNumber      : None
Version           : 091709 - 20090917
PSComputerName    : sql1

SMBIOSBIOSVersion : 080015
Manufacturer      : American Megatrends Inc.
Name              : Default System BIOS
SerialNumber      : None
Version           : 091709 - 20090917
PSComputerName    : wds1

SMBIOSBIOSVersion : 090004
Manufacturer      : American Megatrends Inc.
Name              : BIOS Date: 03/19/09 22:51:32  Ver: 09.00.04
SerialNumber      : 8994-9999-0865-2542-2186-8044-69
Version           : VRTUAL - 3000919
PSComputerName    : dc3

SMBIOSBIOSVersion : 090004
Manufacturer      : American Megatrends Inc.
Name              : BIOS Date: 03/19/09 22:51:32  Ver: 09.00.04
SerialNumber      : 2301-9053-4386-9162-8072-5664-16
Version           : VRTUAL - 3000919
PSComputerName    : ex1


PS C:\>
```

# Using Windows PowerShell jobs

Windows PowerShell jobs permit you to run one or more commands in the background. Once you start the Windows PowerShell job, the Windows PowerShell console returns immediately for further use. This permits you to accomplish multiple tasks at the same time. You can begin a new Windows

PowerShell job by using the *Start-Job* cmdlet. The command to run as a job is placed in a script block, and the jobs are sequentially named *Job1*, *Job2*, and so on. This is shown here:

```
PS C:\> Start-Job -ScriptBlock {get-process}

Id    Name      PSJobTypeName   State     HasMoreData   Location
--    ----      -------------   -----     -----------   --------
10    Job10     BackgroundJob   Running   True          localhost


PS C:\>
```

The jobs receive job IDs that are also sequentially numbered. The first job created in a Windows PowerShell console always has a job ID of 1. You can use either the job ID or the job name to obtain information about the job. This is shown here:

```
PS C:\> Get-Job -Name job10

Id    Name      PSJobTypeName   State       HasMoreData   Location
--    ----      -------------   -----       -----------   --------
10    Job10     BackgroundJob   Completed   True          localhost

PS C:\> Get-Job -Id 10

Id    Name      PSJobTypeName   State       HasMoreData   Location
--    ----      -------------   -----       -----------   --------
10    Job10     BackgroundJob   Completed   True          localhost


PS C:\>
```

Once you see that the job has completed, you can receive the job. The *Receive-Job* cmdlet returns the same information that returns if a job is not used. The Job1 output is shown here (truncated to save space):

```
PS C:\> Receive-Job -Name job10

Handles  NPM(K)   PM(K)    WS(K)  VM(M)   CPU(s)     Id ProcessName
-------  ------   -----    -----  -----   ------     -- -----------
     62       9    1672     6032     80     0.00   1408 apdproxy
    132       9    2316     5632     62            1364 atieclxx
    122       7    1716     4232     32             948 atiesrxx
    114       9   14664    15372     48            1492 audiodg
    556      62   53928     5368    616     3.17   3408 CCC
     58       8    2960     7068     70     0.19    928 conhost
     32       5    1468     3468     52     0.00   5068 conhost
    784      14    3284     5092     56             416 csrss
    529      27    2928    17260    145             496 csrss
    182      13    8184    11152     96     0.50   2956 DCPSysMgr
    135      11    2880     7552     56            2056 DCPSysMgrSvc
... (truncated output)
```

Once a job has been received, that is it—the data is gone, unless you saved it to a variable or you call the *Receive-Job* cmdlet with the *-keep* switched parameter. The following code attempts to retrieve the information stored from job10, but as appears here, no data returns:

```
PS C:\> Receive-Job -Name job10
PS C:\>
```

What can be confusing about this is that the job still exists, and the *Get-Job* cmdlet continues to retrieve information about the job. This is shown here:

```
PS C:\> Get-Job -Id 10
```

| Id | Name | PSJobTypeName | State | HasMoreData | Location |
|----|------|---------------|-------|-------------|----------|
| -- | ---- | ------------- | ----- | ----------- | -------- |
| 10 | Job10 | BackgroundJob | Completed | False | localhost |

As a best practice, use the *Remove-Job* cmdlet to delete remnants of completed jobs when you are finished using the job object. This will avoid confusion regarding active jobs, completed jobs, and jobs waiting to be processed. Once a job has been removed, the *Get-Job* cmdlet returns an error if you attempt to retrieve information about the job—because it no longer exists. This is illustrated here:

```
PS C:\> Remove-Job -Name job10
PS C:\> Get-Job -Id 10
Get-Job : The command cannot find a job with the job ID 10. Verify the value of the
Id parameter and then try the command again.
At line:1 char:1
+ Get-Job -Id 10
+ ~~~~~~~~~~~~~~~
    + CategoryInfo          : ObjectNotFound: (10:Int32) [Get-Job], PSArgumentException
    + FullyQualifiedErrorId : JobWithSpecifiedSessionNotFound,Microsoft.PowerShell.
Commands.GetJobCommand
```

When working with the job cmdlets, I like to give the jobs their own name. A job that returns process objects via the *Get-Process* cmdlet might be called *getProc*. A contextual naming scheme works better than trying to keep track of names such as *Job1* and *Job2*. Do not worry about making your job names too long, because you can use wildcard characters to simplify the typing requirement. When you receive a job, make sure you store the returned objects in a variable. This is shown here:

```
PS C:\> Start-Job -Name getProc -ScriptBlock {get-process}
```

| Id | Name | PSJobTypeName | State | HasMoreData | Location |
|----|------|---------------|-------|-------------|----------|
| -- | ---- | ------------- | ----- | ----------- | -------- |
| 12 | getProc | BackgroundJob | Running | True | localhost |

```
PS C:\> Get-Job -Name get*
```

| Id | Name | PSJobTypeName | State | HasMoreData | Location |
|----|------|---------------|-------|-------------|----------|
| -- | ---- | ------------- | ----- | ----------- | -------- |
| 12 | getProc | BackgroundJob | Completed | True | localhost |

```
PS C:\> $procObj = Receive-Job -Name get*
PS C:\>
```

Once you have the returned objects in a variable, you can use the objects with other Windows PowerShell cmdlets. One thing to keep in mind is that the object is deserialized. This is shown here, where I use *gm* as an alias for the *Get-Member* cmdlet:

```
PS C:\> $procObj | gm
```

```
TypeName: Deserialized.System.Diagnostics.Process
```

This means that not all the standard members from the *System.Diagnostics.Process* .NET Framework object are available. The default methods are shown here (*gps* is an alias for the *Get-Process* cmdlet, *gm* is an alias for *Get-Member*, and *-m* is enough of the *-membertype* parameter to distinguish it on the Windows PowerShell console line):

```
PS C:\> gps | gm -m method
```

```
   TypeName: System.Diagnostics.Process

Name                     MemberType Definition
----                     ---------- ----------
BeginErrorReadLine       Method     System.Void BeginErrorReadLine()
BeginOutputReadLine      Method     System.Void BeginOutputReadLine()
CancelErrorRead          Method     System.Void CancelErrorRead()
CancelOutputRead         Method     System.Void CancelOutputRead()
Close                    Method     System.Void Close()
CloseMainWindow          Method     bool CloseMainWindow()
CreateObjRef             Method     System.Runtime.Remoting.ObjRef CreateObjRef(type
                                    requestedType)
Dispose                  Method     System.Void Dispose()
Equals                   Method     bool Equals(System.Object obj)
GetHashCode              Method     int GetHashCode()
GetLifetimeService       Method     System.Object GetLifetimeService()
GetType                  Method     type GetType()
InitializeLifetimeService Method    System.Object InitializeLifetimeService()
Kill                     Method     System.Void Kill()
Refresh                  Method     System.Void Refresh()
Start                    Method     bool Start()
ToString                 Method     string ToString()
WaitForExit              Method     bool WaitForExit(int milliseconds), System.Void
                                    WaitForExit()
WaitForInputIdle         Method     bool WaitForInputIdle(int milliseconds), bool
                                    WaitForInputIdle()
```

Methods from the deserialized object are shown here, where I use the same command I used previously:

```
PS C:\> $procObj | gm -m method


    TypeName: Deserialized.System.Diagnostics.Process

Name        MemberType Definition
----        ---------- ----------
ToString Method        string ToString(), string ToString(string format, System.IFormatProvider
formatProvider)


PS C:\>
```

A listing of the cmdlets that use the noun *job* is shown here:

```
PS C:\> Get-Command -Noun job | select name

Name
----
Get-Job
Receive-Job
Remove-Job
Resume-Job
Start-Job
Stop-Job
Suspend-Job
Wait-Job
```

When starting a Windows PowerShell job via the *Start-Job* cmdlet, you can specify a name to hold the returned job object. You can also assign the returned job object in a variable by using a straight-forward value assignment. If you do both, you end up with two copies of the returned job object. This is shown here:

```
PS C:\> $rtn = Start-Job -Name net -ScriptBlock {Get-Net6to4Configuration}
PS C:\> Get-Job -Name net

Id     Name        PSJobTypeName State     HasMoreData  Location
--     ----        ------------- -----     -----------  --------
18     net         BackgroundJob Completed True         localhost

PS C:\> $rtn

Id     Name        PSJobTypeName State     HasMoreData  Location
--     ----        ------------- -----     -----------  --------
18     net         BackgroundJob Completed True         localhost
```

Retrieving the job via the *Receive-Job* cmdlet consumes the data. You cannot come back and retrieve the returned data again. This code shown here illustrates this concept:

```
PS C:\> Receive-Job $rtn
```

```
RunspaceId          : e8ed4ab6-eb88-478c-b2de-5991b5636ef1
Caption             :
Description         : 6to4 Configuration
ElementName         :
InstanceID          : ActiveStore
AutoSharing         : 0
PolicyStore         : ActiveStore
RelayName           : 6to4.ipv6.microsoft.com.
RelayState          : 0
ResolutionInterval  : 1440
State               : 0
```

```
PS C:\> Receive-Job $rtn
PS C:\>
```

The next example illustrates examining the command and cleaning up the job. When you use *Receive-Job*, an error message is displayed. To find additional information about the code that triggered the error, use the job object stored in the *$rtn* variable or the *Get-Net6to4Configuration* job. You may prefer using the job object stored in the *$rtn* variable, as shown here:

```
PS C:\> $rtn.Command
Get-Net6to4Configuration
```

To clean up first, remove the leftover job objects by getting the jobs and removing the jobs. This is shown here:

```
PS C:\> Get-Job | Remove-Job
PS C:\> Get-Job
PS C:\>
```

When you create a new Windows PowerShell job, it runs in the background. There is no indication as the job runs whether it ends in an error or it's successful. Indeed, you do not have any way to tell when the job even completes, other than to use the *Get-Job* cmdlet several times to see when the job state changes from *running* to *completed*. For many jobs, this may be perfectly acceptable. In fact, it may even be preferable, if you wish to regain control of the Windows PowerShell console as soon as the job begins executing. On other occasions, you may wish to be notified when the Windows PowerShell job completes. To accomplish this, you can use the *Wait-Job* cmdlet. You need to give the *Wait-Job* cmdlet either a job name or a job ID. Once you have done this, the Windows PowerShell console will pause until the job completes. The job, with its *completed* status, displays on the console. You can then use the *Receive-Job* cmdlet to receive the deserialized objects and store them in a variable (*cn* is a parameter alias for the *-computername* parameter used in the *Get-WmiObject* command). The command appearing here starts a job to receive software products installed on a remote server named hyperv1. It impersonates the currently logged-on user and stores the returned object in a variable named *$rtn*.

```
PS C:\> $rtn = Start-Job -ScriptBlock {gwmi win32_product -cn hyperv1}
PS C:\> $rtn

Id    Name      PSJobTypeName   State     HasMoreData   Location
--    ----      -------------   -----     -----------   --------
22    Job22     BackgroundJob   Running   True          localhost

PS C:\> Wait-Job -id 22

Id    Name      PSJobTypeName   State       HasMoreData   Location
--    ----      -------------   -----       -----------   --------
22    Job22     BackgroundJob   Completed   True          localhost

PS C:\> $prod = Receive-Job -id 22
PS C:\> $prod.Count
2
```

In a newly open Windows PowerShell console, the *Start-Job* cmdlet is used to start a new job. The returned job object is stored in the *$rtn* variable. You can pipeline the job object contained in the *$rtn* variable to the *Stop-Job* cmdlet to stop the execution of the job. If you try to use the job object in the *$rtn* variable directly to get job information, an error will be generated. This is shown here:

```
PS C:\> $rtn = Start-Job -ScriptBlock {gwmi win32_product -cn hyperv1}
PS C:\> $rtn | Stop-Job
PS C:\> Get-Job $rtn
Get-Job : The command cannot find the job because the job name
System.Management.Automation.PSRemotingJob was not found. Verify the value of the
Name parameter, and then try the command again.
At line:1 char:1
+ Get-Job $rtn
+ ~~~~~~~~~~~~
    + CategoryInfo        : ObjectNotFound: (System.Manageme...n.PSRemotingJob:
    String) [Get-Job], PSArgumentException
    + FullyQualifiedErrorId : JobWithSpecifiedNameNotFound,Microsoft.PowerShell.
Commands.GetJobCommand
```

You can pipeline the job object to the *Get-Job* cmdlet and see that the job is in a stopped state. Use the *Receive-Job* cmdlet to receive the job information and the *count* property to see how many software products are included in the variable, as shown here:

```
PS C:\> $rtn | Get-Job

Id    Name      PSJobTypeName   State     HasMoreData   Location
--    ----      -------------   -----     -----------   --------
2     Job2      BackgroundJob   Stopped   False         localhost

PS C:\> $products = Receive-Job -Id 2
PS C:\> $products.count
0
```

In the preceding list you can see that no software packages were enumerated. This is because the *Get-WmiObject* command to retrieve information from the *Win32_Product* class did not have time to finish.

If you want to keep the data from your job so that you can use it again later, and you do not want to bother storing it in an intermediate variable, use the *-keep* parameter. In the command that follows, the *Get-NetAdapter* cmdlet is used to return network adapter information.

```
PS C:\> Start-Job -ScriptBlock {Get-NetAdapter}
```

| Id | Name | PSJobTypeName | State | HasMoreData | Location |
|----|------|---------------|-------|-------------|----------|
| 4 | Job4 | BackgroundJob | Running | True | localhost |

When checking on the status of a background job, and you are monitoring a job you just created, use the *-newest* parameter instead of typing a job number, as it is easier to remember. This technique appears here:

```
PS C:\> Get-Job -Newest 1
```

| Id | Name | PSJobTypeName | State | HasMoreData | Location |
|----|------|---------------|-------|-------------|----------|
| 4 | Job4 | BackgroundJob | Completed | True | localhost |

Now, to retrieve the information from the job and to keep the information available, use the *-keep* switched parameter as illustrated here:

```
PS C:\> Receive-Job -Id 4 -Keep

ifAlias                          : Ethernet
InterfaceAlias                   : Ethernet
ifIndex                          : 12
ifDesc                           : Microsoft Hyper-V Network Adapter
ifName                           : Ethernet_7
DriverVersion                    : 6.2.8504.0
LinkLayerAddress                 : 00-15-5D-00-2D-07
MacAddress                       : 00-15-5D-00-2D-07
LinkSpeed                        : 10 Gbps
MediaType                        : 802.3
PhysicalMediaType                : Unspecified
AdminStatus                      : Up
MediaConnectionState             : Connected
DriverInformation                : Driver Date 2006-06-21 Version
                                   6.2.8504.0 NDIS 6.30
DriverFileName                   : netvsc63.sys
NdisVersion                      : 6.30
ifOperStatus                     : Up
RunspaceId                       : 9ce8f8e6-1a09-4103-a508-c60398527
<output truncated>
```

You can continue to work directly with the output in a normal Windows PowerShell fashion, like so:

```
PS C:\> Receive-Job -Id 4 -Keep | select name

name
----
Ethernet


PS C:\> Receive-Job -Id 4 -Keep | select transmitlinksp*


                                              TransmitLinkSpeed
                                              -----------------
                                                    10000000000
```

# Using Windows PowerShell remoting: step-by-step exercises

In this exercise, you will practice using Windows PowerShell remoting to run remote commands. For the purpose of this exercise, you can use your local computer. First, you will open the Windows PowerShell console, supply alternate credentials, create a Windows PowerShell remote session, and run various commands. Next, you will create and receive Windows PowerShell jobs.

### Supplying alternate credentials for remote Windows PowerShell sessions

1. Log on to your computer with a user account that does not have administrator rights.

2. Open the Windows PowerShell console.

3. Notice the Windows PowerShell console prompt. An example of such a prompt appears here:

   ```
   PS C:\Users\ed.IAMMRED>
   ```

4. Use a variable named *$cred* to store the results of using the *Get-Credential* cmdlet. Specify administrator credentials to store in the *$cred* variable. An example of such a command appears here:

   ```
   $cred = Get-Credential iammred\administrator
   ```

5. Use the *Enter-PSSession* cmdlet to open a remote Windows PowerShell console session. Use the credentials stored in the *$cred* variable, and use *localhost* as the name of the remote computer. Such a command appears here:

   ```
   Enter-PSSession -ComputerName localhost -Credential $cred
   ```

6. Notice how the Windows PowerShell console prompt changes to include the name of the remote computer, and also changes the working directory. Such a changed prompt appears here:

   ```
   [localhost]: PS C:\Users\administrator\Documents>
   ```

7. Use the *whoami* command to verify the current context. The results of the command appear here:

```
[localhost]: PS C:\Users\administrator\Documents> whoami

iammred\administrator
```

8. Use the *exit* command to exit the remote session. Use the *whoami* command to verify that the user context has changed.

9. Use WMI to retrieve the BIOS information on the local computer. Use the alternate credentials stored in the *$cred* variable. This command appears here:

```
gwmi -Class win32_bios -cn localhost -Credential $cred
```

The previous command fails and produces the following error. This error comes from WMI and states that you are not permitted to use alternate credentials for a local WMI connection.

```
gwmi : User credentials cannot be used for local connections
At line:1 char:1
+ gwmi -Class win32_bios -cn localhost -Credential $cred
+ ~~~~~~~~~~~~~~~~~~~~~~~~~~~~~~~~~~~~~~~~~~~~~~~~~~~~~~~~
    + CategoryInfo          : InvalidOperation: (:) [Get-WmiObject], ManagementException
    + FullyQualifiedErrorId : GetWMIManagementException,Microsoft.PowerShell.Commands.
GetWmiObjectCommand
```

10. Put the WMI command into the *-scriptblock* parameter for *Invoke-Command*. Specify the local computer as the value for *computername* and use the credentials stored in the *$cred* variable. The command appears here (using *-script* as a shortened version of *-scriptblock*):

```
Invoke-Command -cn localhost -script {gwmi -Class win32_bios} -cred $cred
```

11. Press the up arrow key to retrieve the previous command and erase the *credential* parameter. The revised command appears here:

```
Invoke-Command -cn localhost -script {gwmi -Class win32_bios}
```

When you run the command, it generates the error appearing here because a normal user does not have remote access by default (if you have admin rights, then the command works):

```
[localhost] Connecting to remote server localhost failed with the following error

message : Access is denied. For more information, see the about_Remote_Troubleshooting

Help topic.

    + CategoryInfo          : OpenError: (localhost:String) [], PSRemotingTransport

Exception

    + FullyQualifiedErrorId : AccessDenied,PSSessionStateBroken
```

**12.** Create an array of computer names. Store the computer names in a variable named *$cn*. Use the array appearing here:

```
$cn = $env:COMPUTERNAME,"localhost","127.0.0.1"
```

**13.** Use *Invoke-Command* to run the WMI command against all three computers at once. The command appears here:

```
Invoke-Command -cn $cn -script {gwmi -Class win32_bios}
```

This concludes this step-by-step exercise.

In the following exercise, you will create and receive Windows PowerShell jobs.

### Creating and receiving jobs

**1.** Open the Windows PowerShell console as a non-elevated user.

**2.** Start a job named *Get-Process* that uses a *-scriptblock* parameter that calls the *Get-Process* cmdlet (*gps* is an alias for *Get-Process*). The command appears here:

```
Start-Job -Name gps -ScriptBlock {gps}
```

**3.** Examine the output from starting the job. It lists the name, state, and other information about the job. Sample output appears here:

```
Id     Name          PSJobTypeName  State     HasMoreData   Location
--     ----          -------------  -----     -----------   --------
9      gps           BackgroundJob  Running   True          localhost
```

**4.** Use the *Get-Process* cmdlet to determine if the job has completed. The command appears here:

```
Get-Job gps
```

**5.** Examine the output from the previous command. The *state* reports *completed* when the job has completed. If data is available, the *hasmoredata* property reports *true*. Sample output appears here:

```
Id     Name          PSJobTypeName  State      HasMoreData   Location
--     ----          -------------  -----      -----------   --------
9      gps           BackgroundJob  Completed  True          localhost
```

**6.** Receive the results from the job. To do this, use the *Receive-Job* cmdlet as shown here:

```
Receive-Job gps
```

7. Press the up arrow key to retrieve the *Get-Job* command. Run it. Note that the *hasmoredata* property now reports *false*, as shown here:

```
Id   Name      PSJobTypeName   State       HasMoreData   Location
--   ----      -------------   -----       -----------   --------
9    gps       BackgroundJob   Completed   False         localhost
```

8. Create a new job with the same name as the previous job: *gps*. This time, change the *-script-block* parameter value to *gsv* (the alias for *Get-Service*). The command appears here:

```
Start-Job -Name gps -ScriptBlock {gsv}
```

9. Now use the *Get-Job* cmdlet to retrieve the job with the name *gps*. Note that the command retrieves both jobs, as shown here:

```
Get-Job -name gps
```

```
Id   Name      PSJobTypeName   State       HasMoreData   Location
--   ----      -------------   -----       -----------   --------
9    gps       BackgroundJob   Completed   False         localhost
11   gps       BackgroundJob   Completed   True          localhost
```

10. Use the *Receive-Job* cmdlet to retrieve the job ID associated with your new job. This time, use the *-keep* switch, as shown here:

```
Receive-Job -Id 11 -keep
```

11. Use the *Get-Job* cmdlet to retrieve your job. Note that the *hasmoredata* property still reports *true* because you're using the *-keep* switch.

This concludes this exercise.

# Chapter 4 quick reference

| To | Do this |
|---|---|
| Work interactively on a remote system | Use the *Enter-PSSession* cmdlet to create a remote session. |
| Configure Windows PowerShell remoting | Use the *Enable-PSRemoting* function. |
| Run a command on a remote system | Use the *Invoke-Command* cmdlet and specify the command in a *-scriptblock* parameter. |
| Run a command as a job | Use the *Start-Job* cmdlet to execute the command. |
| Check on the progress of a job | Use the *Get-Job* cmdlet and specify either the job ID or the job name. |
| Check on the progress of the newest job | Use the *Get-Job* cmdlet and specify the *-newest* parameter, and supply the number of new jobs to monitor. |
| Retrieve the results from a job | Use the *Receive-Job* cmdlet and specify the job ID. |

# CHAPTER 5

# Using PowerShell Scripts

**After completing this chapter, you will be able to:**

- Understand the reasons for writing Windows PowerShell scripts.

- Make the configuration changes required to run Windows PowerShell scripts.

- Understand how to run Windows PowerShell scripts.

- Understand how to break lines in a script.

- Understand the use of variables and constants in a script.

- Create objects in a Windows PowerShell script.

- Call methods in a Windows PowerShell script.

With the ability to perform so many actions from inside Microsoft Windows PowerShell in an interactive fashion, you may wonder, "Why do I need to write scripts?" For many network administrators, one-line PowerShell commands will indeed solve many routine problems. This can become extremely powerful when the commands are combined into batch files and perhaps called from a login script. However, there are some very good reasons to write Windows PowerShell scripts. We will examine them as we move into this chapter.

## Why write Windows PowerShell scripts?

Perhaps the number-one reason to write a Windows PowerShell script is to address recurring needs. As an example, consider the activity of producing a directory listing. The simple *Get-ChildItem* cmdlet does a good job, but after you decide to sort the listing and filter out only files of a certain size, you end up with the command shown here:

```
Get-ChildItem c:\fso | Where-Object Length -gt 1000 | Sort-Object -Property name
```

Even using tab completion, the previous command requires a bit of typing. One way to shorten it would be to create a user-defined function (a technique that I'll discuss later). For now, the easiest solution is to write a Windows PowerShell script. The DirectoryListWithArguments.ps1 script is shown here:

```
# DirectoryListWithArguments.ps1
foreach ($i in $args)
   {Get-ChildItem $i | Where-Object length -gt 1000 |
    Sort-Object -property name}
```

The DirectoryListWithArguments.ps1 script takes a single, unnamed argument that allows the script to be modified when it is run. This makes the script much easier to work with and adds flexibility.

An additional reason that network administrators write Windows PowerShell scripts is to run the scripts as scheduled tasks. In the Windows world, there are multiple task-scheduler engines. Using the *WIN32_ScheduledJob* Windows Management Instrumentation (WMI) class, you can create, monitor, and delete scheduled jobs. This WMI class has been available since the Windows NT 4 days.

The ListProcessesSortResults.ps1 script, shown following, is a script that a network administrator may want to schedule to run several times a day. It produces a list of currently running processes and writes the results out to a text file as a formatted and sorted table.

```
# ListProcessesSortResults.ps1
$args = "localhost","loopback","127.0.0.1"

foreach ($i in $args)
   {$strFile = "c:\mytest\"+ $i +"Processes.txt"
    Write-Host "Testing" $i "please wait ...";
    Get-WmiObject -computername $i -class win32_process |
    Select-Object name, processID, Priority, ThreadCount, PageFaults, PageFileUsage |
    Where-Object {!$_.processID -eq 0} | Sort-Object -property name |
    Format-Table | Out-File $strFile}
```

One other reason for writing Windows PowerShell scripts is that it makes it easy to store and share both the "secret commands" and the ideas behind the scripts. For example, suppose you develop a script that will connect remotely to workstations on your network and search for user accounts that do not require a password. Obviously, an account without a password is a security risk! After some searching around, you discover the *WIN32_UserAccount* WMI class and develop a script that performs to your expectation. Because this is likely a script you would want to use on a regular basis, and perhaps share with other network administrators in your company, it makes sense to save it as a script. A sample of such a script is AccountsWithNoRequiredPassword.ps1, which is shown here:

```
# AccountsWithNoRequiredPassword.ps1
$args = "localhost"

foreach ($i in $args)
   {Write-Host "Connecting to" $i "please wait ...";
    Get-WmiObject -computername $i -class win32_UserAccount |
    Select-Object Name, Disabled, PasswordRequired, SID, SIDType |
    Where-Object {$_.PasswordRequired -eq 0} |
    Sort-Object -property name | Write-Host}
```

# Scripting fundamentals

In its most basic form, a Windows PowerShell script is a collection of PowerShell commands. Here's an example:

**Get-Process** notepad | **Stop-Process**

You can put a command into a Windows PowerShell script and run it directly as it written.

To create a Windows PowerShell script, you simply have to copy the command in a text file and save the file by using a .ps1 extension. If you create the file in the Windows PowerShell ISE and save the file, the .ps1 extension will be added automatically. If you double-click the file, it will open in Notepad by default.

## Running Windows PowerShell scripts

To run the script, you can open the Windows PowerShell console and drag the file to the console. If you first copy the path of the script, and later right-click inside the Windows PowerShell console to paste the path of your script there, and then press Enter, you will print out a string that represents the path of the script, as shown here:

```
PS C:\> "C:\fso\test.ps1"
C:\fso\test.ps1
```

In Windows PowerShell, when you want to print a string in the console, you put it inside quotation marks. You do not have to use *Wscript.Echo* or similar commands such as those used in VBScript. This method is easier and simpler, but takes some getting used to. For example, say you figure out that your previous attempts to run a Windows PowerShell script just displayed a string—the path to the script—instead of running the script. Therefore, you remove the quotation marks and press Enter, and this time, you receive a real error message. "What now?" you may ask. The error message shown in Figure 5-1 relates to the script execution policy that disallows the running of scripts.

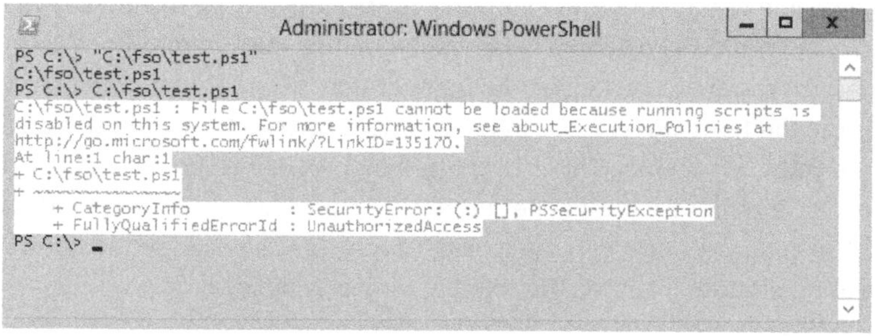

**FIGURE 5-1** By default, an attempt to run a Windows PowerShell script generates an error message.

# Enabling Windows PowerShell scripting support

By default, Windows PowerShell disallows the execution of scripts. Script support can be controlled by using group policy, but if it is not, and if you have administrator rights on your computer, you can use the *Set-ExecutionPolicy* Windows PowerShell cmdlet to turn on script support. There are six levels that can be enabled by using the *Set-ExecutionPolicy* cmdlet. These options are displayed here:

- **Restricted**   Does not load configuration files such as the Windows PowerShell profile or run other scripts. *Restricted* is the default.

- **AllSigned**   Requires that all scripts and configuration files be signed by a trusted publisher, including scripts that you write on the local computer.

- **RemoteSigned**   Requires that all scripts and configuration files downloaded from the Internet zone be signed by a trusted publisher.

- **Unrestricted**   Loads all configuration files and runs all scripts. If you run an unsigned script that was downloaded from the Internet, you are prompted for permission before it runs.

- **Bypass**   Blocks nothing and issues no warnings or prompts.

- **Undefined**   Removes the currently assigned execution policy from the current scope. This parameter will not remove an execution policy that is set in a group policy scope.

In addition to six levels of execution policy, there are three different scopes:

- **Process**   The execution policy affects only the current Windows PowerShell process.

- **CurrentUser**   The execution policy affects only the current user.

- **LocalMachine**   The execution policy affects all users of the computer. Setting the *LocalMachine* execution policy requires administrator rights on the local computer. By default, a non-elevated user has rights to set the script execution policy for the *CurrentUser* user scope that affects their own execution policy.

With so many choices available to you for script execution policy, you may be wondering which one is appropriate for you. The Windows PowerShell team recommends the *RemoteSigned* setting, stating that it is "appropriate for most circumstances." Remember that, even though descriptions of the various policy settings use the term *Internet*, this may not always refer to the World Wide Web, or even to locations outside your own firewall. This is because Windows PowerShell obtains its script origin information by using the Internet Explorer zone settings. This basically means anything that comes from a computer other than your own is in the Internet zone. You can change the Internet Explorer zone settings by using Internet Explorer, the registry, or group policy.

If you do not want to see the confirmation message when you change the script execution policy on Windows PowerShell 3.0, use the *-force* parameter.

To view the execution policy for all scopes, use the *-list* parameter when calling the *Get-ExecutionPolicy* cmdlet. This technique appears here:

```
PS C:\> Get-ExecutionPolicy -List

                    Scope                    ExecutionPolicy
                    -----                    ---------------
            MachinePolicy                          Undefined
               UserPolicy                          Undefined
                  Process                          Undefined
              CurrentUser                       RemoteSigned
             LocalMachine                         Restricted
```

### Retrieving script execution policy

1. Open Windows PowerShell.

2. Use the *Get-ExecutionPolicy* cmdlet to retrieve the effective script execution policy. This is shown here:

   ```
   Get-ExecutionPolicy
   ```

This concludes this procedure. Leave Windows PowerShell open for the next procedure.

---

## Quick check

**Q.** Do Windows PowerShell scripts work by default?

**A.** No. Windows PowerShell scripts must be explicitly enabled.

**Q.** What cmdlet can be used to retrieve the resultant execution policy?

**A.** The *Get-ExecutionPolicy* cmdlet can retrieve the resultant execution policy.

**Q.** What cmdlet can be used to set the script execution policy?

**A.** The *Set-ExecutionPolicy* cmdlet can be used to set the script execution policy.

---

### Setting script execution policy

1. Use the *Set-ExecutionPolicy* cmdlet to change the script execution policy to *unrestricted*. This command is shown here:

   ```
   Set-ExecutionPolicy unrestricted
   ```

**2.** Use the *Get-ExecutionPolicy* cmdlet to retrieve the current effective script execution policy. This command is shown here:

```
Get-ExecutionPolicy
```

**3.** The result prints out to the Windows PowerShell console, as shown here:

```
Unrestricted
```

This concludes this procedure.

> **Tip** If the execution policy on Windows PowerShell is set to *restricted*, how can you use a script to determine the execution policy? One method is to use the *bypass* parameter when calling Windows PowerShell to run the script. The *bypass* parameter bypasses the script execution policy for the duration of the script when it is called.

## Transitioning from command line to script

Now that you have everything set up to enable script execution, you can run your StopNotepad.ps1 script. This is shown here:

```
# StopNotepad.ps1
Get-Process Notepad | Stop-Process
```

If an instance of the Notepad process is running, everything is successful. However, if there is no instance of Notepad running, the error shown here is generated:

```
Get-Process : Cannot find a process with the name 'Notepad'. Verify the process
 name and call the cmdlet again.
At C:\Documents and Settings\ed\Local Settings\Temp\tmp1DB.tmp.ps1:14 char:12
+ Get-Process  <<<< Notepad | Stop-Process
```

It is important to get into the habit of reading the error messages. The first part of the error message gives a description of the problem. In this example, it could not find a process with the name of *Notepad*. The second part of the error message shows the position in the code where the error occurred. This is known as the *position message*. The first line of the position message states the error occurred on line 14. The second portion has a series of arrows that point to the command that failed. The *Get-Process* cmdlet command is the one that failed. This is shown here:

```
At C:\Documents and Settings\ed\Local Settings\Temp\tmp1DB.tmp.ps1:14 char:12
+ Get-Process  <<<< Notepad | Stop-Process
```

The easiest way to eliminate this error message is to use the *-erroraction* parameter and specify the *silentlycontinue* value. You can also use the *-ea* alias and avoid having to type out *-erroraction*. This is basically the same as using the *On Error Resume Next* command from VBScript (but not exactly the same, as it only handles nonterminating errors). The really useful feature of the *-erroraction* parameter is that it can be specified on a cmdlet-by-cmdlet basis. In addition, there are five enumeration names or values that can be used. The allowed names and values for the -*erroraction* parameter are shown in Table 5-1.

**TABLE 5-1** Names and values for -*erroraction*

| Enumeration | Value |
|---|---|
| Ignore | 4 |
| Inquire | 3 |
| Continue | 2 |
| Stop | 1 |
| SilentlyContinue | 0 |

In the StopNotepadSilentlyContinue.ps1 script, you add the -*erroraction* parameter to the *Get-Process* cmdlet to skip past any error that may arise if the Notepad process does not exist. To make the script easier to read, you break the code at the pipe character. The pipe character is not the line-continuation character. The backtick (`) character, also known as the grave character, is used when a line of code is too long and must be broken into two physical lines of code. The key thing to be aware of is that the two physical lines form a single logical line of code. An example of how to use line continuation is shown here:

```
Write-Host -foregroundcolor green "This is a demo " `
          "of the line continuation character"
```

The StopNotepadSilentlyContinue.ps1 script is shown here:

StopNotepadSilentlyContinue.ps1

```
Get-Process -name Notepad -erroraction silentlycontinue |
Stop-Process
```

Because you are writing a script, you can take advantage of some features of a script. One of the first things you can do is use a variable to hold the name of the process to be stopped. This has the advantage of enabling you to easily change the script to allow for stopping of processes other than Notepad. All variables begin with the dollar sign. The line that holds the name of the process in a variable is shown here:

```
$process= "notepad"
```

Another improvement to the script is one that provides information about the process that is stopped. The *Stop-Process* cmdlet returns no information when it is used. But by using the -*passthru* parameter of the *Stop-Process* cmdlet, the process object is passed along in the pipeline. You use this parameter and pipeline the process object to the *ForEach-Object* cmdlet. You use the *$_* automatic variable to refer to the current object on the pipeline and select the name and the process ID of the process that is stopped. The concatenation operator in Windows PowerShell is the plus sign (+), and you use it to display the values of the selected properties in addition to the strings completing you sentence. This line of code is shown here:

```
ForEach-Object { $_.name + ' with process ID: ' + $_.ID + ' was stopped.'}
```

The complete StopNotepadSilentlyContinuePassThru.ps1 script is shown here:

StopNotepadSilentlyContinuePassThru.ps1

```
$process = "notepad"
Get-Process -name $Process -erroraction silentlycontinue |
Stop-Process -passthru |
ForEach-Object { $_.name + ' with process ID: ' + $_.ID + ' was stopped.'}
```

When you run the script with two instances of Notepad running, the following output is shown:

```
notepad with process ID: 2088 was stopped.
notepad with process ID: 2568 was stopped.
```

An additional advantage of the StopNotepadSilentlyContinuePassThru.ps1 script is that you can use it to stop different processes. You can assign multiple process names (an array) to the *$process* variable, and when you run the script, each process will be stopped. In this example, you assign the Notepad the Calc processes to the *$process* variable. This is shown here:

```
$process= "notepad", "calc"
```

When you run the script, both processes are stopped, as shown here:

```
calc with process ID: 3428 was stopped.
notepad with process ID: 488 was stopped.
```

You could continue changing your script. You could put the code in a function, write command-line help, and change the script so that it accepts command-line input or even reads a list of processes from a text file. As soon as you move from the command line to script, such options suddenly become possible. These topics are covered in Chapter 6, "Working with Functions," and Chapter 7, "Creating Advanced Functions and Modules."

## Running Windows PowerShell scripts

You cannot simply double-click a Windows PowerShell script and have it run (unless you change the file association, but that is not supported or recommended). You cannot type the name in the *Run* dialog box either. If you are inside Windows PowerShell, you can run scripts if you have enabled the execution policy, but you need to type the entire path to the script you wish to run and make sure you include the ps1 extension.

To run a Windows PowerShell script from inside the Windows PowerShell console, type the full path to the script. Include the name of the script. Ensure you include the ps1 extension.

If you need to run a script from outside Windows PowerShell, you need to type the full path to the script, but you must feed it as an argument to the PowerShell.exe program. In addition, you probably want to specify the *-noexit* argument so that you can read the output from the script. This is shown in Figure 5-2.

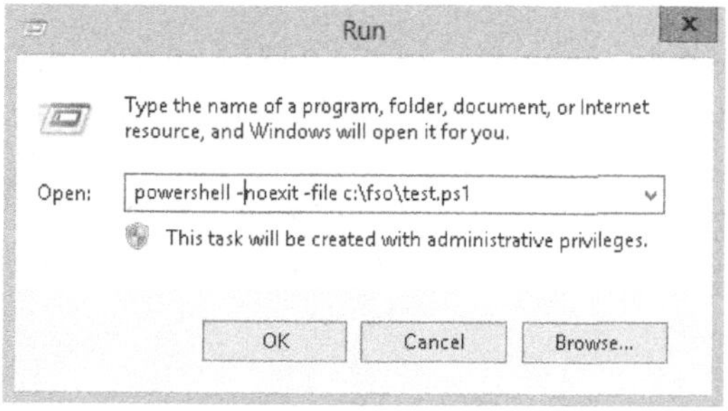

**FIGURE 5-2** Use the *-noexit* argument for the PowerShell.exe program to keep the console open after a script runs.

To run a Windows PowerShell script from outside PowerShell, type the full path to the script. Include the name of the script. Ensure you include the ps1 extension. Feed this to the PowerShell.exe program. Use the *-noexit* argument to keep the PowerShell console after script execution.

The RetrieveAndSortServiceState.ps1 script uses the *Get-WmiObject* cmdlet to make a connection and retrieve service information. Chapter 10, "Using WMI," and Chapter 11, "Querying WMI," examine WMI as it relates to Windows PowerShell, but because of the way Windows PowerShell uses cmdlets, you do not need to know everything about the technology to use it in your script. The RetrieveAndSortServiceState.ps1 script creates a list of all the services that are defined on a machine. It then checks to see if they are running, stopped, or disabled, and reports the status of the service. The script also collects the service account that the service is running under.

In this script, the *Sort-Object* cmdlet is used to perform three sorts on the data: it sorts first by the start mode of the service (that is, automatic, manual, disabled); it sorts next by the state of the service (that is, running, stopped, and so forth); and it then alphabetizes the list by the name of each service in the two previous categories. After the sorting process, the script uses a *Format-Table* cmdlet and produces table output in the console window. The RetrieveAndSortServiceState.ps1 script is shown following, and the "Running scripts inside Windows PowerShell" procedure, which examines running this script, follows that.

The script is designed to run against multiple remote machines, and it holds the names of the destination machines in the system variable *$args*. As written, it uses two computer names that always refer to the local machine: *localhost* and *loopback*. By using these two names, you can simulate the behavior of connecting to networked computers.

RetrieveAndSortServiceState.ps1

```
$args = "localhost","loopback"

    foreach ($i in $args)
        {Write-Host "Testing" $i "..."
            Get-WmiObject -computer $args -class win32_service |
            Select-Object -property name, state, startmode, startname |
            Sort-Object -property startmode, state, name |
            Format-Table *}
```

**Note** For the following procedure, I copied the RetrieveAndSortServiceState.ps1 script to the C:\Mytest directory created in Chapter 3, "Understanding and Using PowerShell Providers." This makes it much easier to type the path and has the additional benefit of making the examples clearer. To follow the procedures, you will need to either modify the path to the script or copy the RetrieveAndSortServiceState.ps1 script to the C:\Mytest directory.

### Running scripts inside Windows PowerShell

1. Open the Windows PowerShell console.

2. Type the full path to the script you wish to run (for example, C:\Mytest). You can use tab completion. On my system, I only had to type C:\My and then press Tab. Add a backslash (\), and type the script name. You can use tab completion for this as well. If you copied the RetrieveAndSortServiceState.ps1 into the C:\Mytest directory, then simply typing *r* and pressing Tab should retrieve the script name. The completed command is shown here:

   ```
   C:\mytest\RetrieveAndSortServiceState.ps1
   ```

   Partial output from the script is shown here:

   ```
   Testing loopback ...

   name           state       startmode    startname
   ----           -----       ---------    ---------
   Alerter        Running     Auto         NT AUTHORITY\Loc...
   Alerter        Running     Auto         NT AUTHORITY\Loc...
   AudioSrv       Running     Auto         LocalSystem
   AudioSrv       Running     Auto         LocalSystem
   ```

   This concludes this procedure. Please close Windows PowerShell.

**Tip** Add a shortcut to Windows PowerShell in your SendTo folder. This folder is located in the Documents and Settings\\*username*% folder. When you create the shortcut, make sure you specify the *-noexit* switch for PowerShell.exe, or else the output will scroll by so fast that you will not be able to read it. You can do this by hand, or modify the CreateShortCutToPowerShell.vbs script from Chapter 1, "Overview of Windows PowerShell 3.0."

1. Open the Run dialog box (Choose Start | Run, or press the Windows flag key + R, or press Ctrl+Esc and then R).

2. Type **PowerShell** and use the *-noexit* switch. Type the full path to the script. The command for this is shown here:

```
Powershell  -noexit C:\mytest\RetrieveAndSortServiceState.ps1
```

This concludes this procedure.

---

## Quick check

**Q.** Which command can you use to sort a list?

**A.** The *Sort-Object* cmdlet can be used to sort a list.

**Q.** How do you use the *Sort-Object* cmdlet to sort a list?

**A.** To use the *Sort-Object* cmdlet to sort a list, specify the property to sort on in the *-property* argument.

---

# Understanding variables and constants

Understanding the use of variables and constants in Windows PowerShell is fundamental to much of the flexibility of the PowerShell scripting language. Variables are used to hold information for use later in the script. Variables can hold any type of data, including text, numbers, and even objects.

## Use of variables

By default, when working with Windows PowerShell, you do not need to declare variables before use. When you use a variable to hold data, it is declared. All variable names must be preceded with a dollar sign ($) when they are referenced. There are a number of special variables in Windows PowerShell. These variables are created automatically and have a special meaning. A listing of the special variables and their associated meaning appears in Table 5-2.

**TABLE 5-2** Use of special variables

| Name | Use |
|------|-----|
| $^ | This contains the first token of the last line input into the shell. |
| $$ | This contains the last token of the last line input into the shell. |
| $_ | This is the current pipeline object; it's used in script blocks, filters, *Where-Object*, *ForEach-Object*, and *Switch*. |
| $? | This contains the success/fail status of the last statement. |
| $Args | This is used with functions or scripts requiring parameters that do not have a *param* block. |
| $Error | This saves the error object in the *$error* variable if an error occurs. |
| $ExecutionContext | This contains the execution objects available to cmdlets. |
| $foreach | This refers to the enumerator in a *foreach* loop. |
| $HOME | This is the user's home directory (set to %HOMEDRIVE%\%HOMEPATH%). |
| $Input | This is input that is piped to a function or code block. |
| $Match | This is a hash table consisting of items found by the *-match* operator. |
| $MyInvocation | This contains information about the currently executing script or command line. |
| $PSHome | This is the directory where PowerShell is installed. |
| $Host | This contains information about the currently executing host. |
| $LastExitCode | This contains the exit code of the last native application to run. |
| $true | This is used for Boolean *TRUE*. |
| $false | This is used for Boolean *FALSE*. |
| $null | This represents a null object. |
| $this | In the Types.ps1xml file and some script block instances, this represents the current object. |
| $OFS | This is the output field separator used when converting an array to a string. |
| $ShellID | This is the identifier for the shell; this value is used by the shell to determine the execution policy and what profiles are run at startup. |
| $StackTrace | This contains detailed stack trace information about the last error. |

In the ReadUserInfoFromReg.ps1 script that follows, there are five variables used. These are listed in Table 5-3.

**TABLE 5-3** ReadUserInfoFromReg.ps1 variables

| Name | Use |
|------|-----|
| $strUserPath | This is for the path to registry subkey SOFTWARE\MICROSOFT\WINDOWS\CURRENTVERSION\EXPLORER. |
| $strUserName | This is for the registry value Logon User Name. |
| $strPath | This is for the path to registry subkey VOLATILE ENVIRONMENT. |
| $strName | This contains an array of registry values: LOGONSERVER, HOMEPATH, APPDATA, HOMEDRIVE. |
| $i | This holds a single registry value name from the *$strName* array of registry values; *$i* gets assigned the value by using the *ForEach* alias. |

The ReadUserInfoFromReg.ps1 script uses the *Set-Location* cmdlet to change to the HKCU PS drive. This makes it easier to work with the registry. After the location has been set to the HKCU drive, the script uses the *Get-ItemProperty* cmdlet to retrieve the data stored in the specified registry key. The *Get-ItemProperty* cmdlet needs two arguments to be supplied: *-path* and *-name*. The *-path* argument receives the registry path that is stored in the *$strUserPath* variable, whereas the *-name* argument receives the string stored in the *$strUserName* variable.

> **Tip** Because the *$strUserPath* registry subkey was rather long, I used the grave accent (`` ` ``) to continue the subkey on the next line. In addition, because I had to close out the string with quotation marks, I used the plus symbol (+) to concatenate (glue) the two pieces of the string back together.

After the value is retrieved from the registry, the object is pipelined to the *Format-List* cmdlet, which once again uses the string contained in the *$strUserName* variable as the property to display.

> **Note** The *Format-List* cmdlet is required in the ReadUserInfoFromReg.ps1 script because of the way the *Get-ItemProperty* cmdlet displays the results of its operation—it returns information about the object as well as the value contained in the registry key. The use of *Format-List* mitigates this behavior.

The really powerful aspect of the ReadUserInfoFromReg.ps1 script is that it uses the array of strings contained in the *$strName* variable. To read the values out of the registry, you need to *singularize* the strings contained within the *$strName* variable. To do this, you use the *ForEach-Object* cmdlet (however, you reference it by the alias *foreach*). After you have an individual value from the *$strName* array, you store the string in a variable called *$i*. The *Get-ItemProperty* cmdlet is used in exactly the same manner as it was used earlier. However, this time, you use the string contained in the *$strPath* variable, and the name of the registry key to read is contained in the *$i* variable, whose value will change four times with the execution of each pass through the array.

When the ReadUserInfoFromReg.ps1 script is run, it reads five pieces of information from the registry: the logon user name, the logon server name, the user's home path location, the user's application data store, and the user's home drive mapping. The ReadUserInfoFromReg.ps1 script is shown here:

```
# ReadUserInfoFromReg.ps1
$strUserPath = "\Software\Microsoft\Windows\CurrentVersion\" `
               + "Explorer"
$strUserName = "Logon User Name"
$strPath = "\Volatile Environment"
$strName = "LOGONSERVER","HOMEPATH", "APPDATA","HOMEDRIVE"
```

```
Set-Location HKCU:\
    Get-ItemProperty -path $strUserPath -name $strUserName |
        Format-List $strUserName
foreach ($i in $strName)
    {Get-ItemProperty -path $strPath -name $i |
        Format-List $i}
```

## Quick check

**Q.** To read a value from the registry, which provider is used?

**A.** The registry provider is used to read from the registry.

**Q.** Which cmdlet is used to retrieve a registry key value from the registry?

**A.** The *Get-ItemProperty* cmdlet is used to retrieve a registry key value from the registry.

**Q.** How do you concatenate two string values?

**A.** You can use the plus symbol (+) to concatenate two string values.

### Exploring strings

1.  Open Windows PowerShell.

2.  Create a variable called *$a* and assign the value *this is the beginning* to it. The code for this is shown here:

    ```
    $a = "this is the beginning"
    ```

3.  Create a variable called *$b* and assign the number 22 to it. The code for this is shown here:

    ```
    $b = 22
    ```

4.  Create a variable called *$c* and make it equal to *$a + $b*. The code for this is shown here:

    ```
    $c = $a + $b
    ```

5.  Print out the value of *$c*. The code for this is shown here:

    ```
    $c
    ```

6.  The results of printing out *c$* are shown here:

    ```
    this is the beginning22
    ```

7. Modify the value of $a. Assign the string *this is a string* to the variable $a. This is shown here:

```
$a = "this is a string"
```

8. Press the up arrow key and retrieve the $c = $a + $b command:

```
$c = $a + $b
```

9. Now print out the value of $c. The command to do this is shown here:

```
$c
```

10. Assign the string *this is a number* to the variable $b. The code to do this is shown here:

```
$b = "this is a number"
```

11. Press the up arrow key to retrieve the $c = $a + $b command. This will cause Windows PowerShell to reevaluate the value of $c. This command is shown here:

```
$c = $a + $b
```

12. Print out the value of $c. This command is shown here:

```
$c
```

13. Change the $b variable so that it can only contain an integer. (Data type aliases are shown in Table 5-4.) Use the $b variable to hold the number 5. This command is shown here:

```
[int]$b = 5
```

14. Print out the value contained in the $c variable, as shown here:

```
$c
```

15. Assign the string *this is a string* to the $b variable. This command is shown here:

```
$b = "this is a string"
```

Attempting to assign a string to a variable that has an *[int]* constraint placed on it results in the error shown here (these results are wrapped for readability):

```
Cannot convert value "this is a number" to type "System.Int32".
Error: "Input string was not in a correct format."
At line:1 char:3
+ $b  <<<< = "this is a string"
```

This concludes this procedure.

**TABLE 5-4** Data type aliases

| Alias | Type |
|---|---|
| [int] | A 32-bit signed integer |
| [long] | A 64-bit signed integer |
| [string] | A fixed-length string of Unicode characters |
| [char] | A Unicode 16-bit character, UTF-16 |
| [bool] | A *true/false* value |
| [byte] | An 8-bit unsigned integer |
| [double] | A double-precision 64-bit floating-point number |
| [decimal] | An 128-bit decimal value |
| [single] | A single-precision 32-bit floating-point number |
| [array] | An array of values |
| [xml] | An XML document |
| [hashtable] | A *hashtable* object (similar to a *dictionary* object) |

## Use of constants

Constants in Windows PowerShell are like variables, with two important exceptions: their value never changes, and they cannot be deleted. Constants are created by using the *Set-Variable* cmdlet and specifying the *-option* argument to be equal to *constant*.

> **Note** When referring to a constant in the body of the script, you must prefix it with the dollar sign ($), just like any other variable. However, when creating the constant (or variable for that matter) by using the *Set-Variable* cmdlet, when you specify the *-name* argument, you do not use the dollar sign.

In the GetHardDiskDetails.ps1 script, you create a constant called *$intDriveType* and assign the value of 3 to it because the *WIN32_LogicalDisk* WMI class uses a value of 3 in the *disktype* property to describe a local fixed disk. Because you are not interested in network drives, removable drives, or RAM drives, you use the *Where-Object* to return only items that have a drive type of 3.

## Quick check

**Q.** How do you create a constant in a script?

**A.** You create a constant in a script by using *Set-Variable* and specifying a value of *constant* for the *-option* argument.

**Q.** How do you indicate that a variable will only hold integers?

**A.** To indicate that a variable will only contain integers, use *[int]* in front of the variable name when assigning a value to the variable.

In looking at the GetHardDiskDetails.ps1 script, the value of *$intDriveType* is never changed. It is assigned the value of 3 on the *Set-Variable* line. The *$intDriveType* constant is only used with the *Where* filter line. The value of *$strComputer*, however, will change once for each computer name that is specified in the array *$aryComputers*. In this script, it will change twice. The first time through the loop, it will be equal to *loopback*, and the second time through the loop, it will be equal to *localhost*. However, if you added 250 different computer names, the effect would be the same—the value of *$strComputer* would change each time through the loop.

```
GetHardDiskDetails.ps1
$aryComputers = "loopback", "localhost"
Set-Variable -name intDriveType -value 3 -option constant

foreach ($strComputer in $aryComputers)

    {"Hard drives on: " + $strComputer
    Get-WmiObject -class win32_logicaldisk -computername $strComputer|
        Where {$_.drivetype -eq $intDriveType}}
```

## Using the *While* statement

In VBScript, you had the *While...Wend* loop. An example of using the *While...Wend* loop is the WhileReadLineWend.vbs script that follows. The first thing you do in the script is create an instance of the *FileSystemObject* and store it in the *objFSO* variable. You then use the *OpenTextFile* method to open a test file, and store that object in the *objFile* variable. You then use the *While...Not...Wend* construction to read one line at a time from the text stream and display it on the screen. You continue to do this until you are at the end of the text stream object. A *While...Wend* loop continues to operate as long as a condition is evaluated as *true*. In this example, as long as you are not at the end of the stream, you will continue to read the line from the text file. The WhileReadLineWend.vbs script is shown here:

```
# WhileReadLineWend.vbs
Set objFSO = CreateObject("Scripting.FileSystemObject")
Set objFile = objFSO.OpenTextFile("C:\fso\testfile.txt")

While Not objFile.AtEndOfStream
 WScript.Echo objFile.ReadLine
Wend
```

# Constructing the *While* statement in PowerShell

As you probably have already guessed, you have the same kind of construction available to you in Windows PowerShell. The *While* statement in Windows PowerShell is used in the same way that the *While...Wend* statement is used in VBScript. In the DemoWhileLessThan.ps1 script that follows, you first initialize the variable *$i* to be equal to 0. You then use the *while* keyword to begin the *while* loop. In Windows PowerShell, you must include the condition that will be evaluated inside a set of parentheses. For this example, you determine the value of the *$i* variable with each pass through the loop. If the value of *$i* is less than the number 5, you will perform the action that is specified inside the braces (curly brackets) to delimit the script block. In VBScript, the condition that is evaluated is positioned on the same line with the *While* statement, but no parentheses are required. Although this is convenient from a typing perspective, it actually makes the code a bit confusing to read. In Windows PowerShell, the statement is outside the parentheses and the condition is clearly delimited by the parentheses. In VBScript, the action that is performed is added between two words: *While* and *Wend*. In Windows PowerShell, there is no *Wend* statement, and the action to be performed is positioned inside a pair of braces. Although shocking at first to users coming from a VBScript background, the braces are always used to contain code. This is what is called a *script block*, and it is used everywhere. As soon as you are used to seeing script blocks here, you will find them with other language statements also. The good thing is that you do not have to look for items such as the keyword *Wend* or the keyword *Loop* (of *Do...Loop* fame).

## Understanding expanding strings

In Windows PowerShell, there are two kinds of strings: literal strings and expanding strings. In the DemoWhileLessThan.ps1 script, you use the *expanding string*, signified when you use the double quotation mark, " (the literal string uses the single quotation mark, '). You want to display the name of the variable, and you want to display the value that is contained in the variable. This is a perfect place to showcase the expanding string. In an expanding string, the value that is contained in a variable is displayed to the screen when a line is evaluated. As an example, consider the following code. You assign the value 12 to the variable *$i*. You then put *$i* inside a pair of double quotation marks, making an expanding string. When the line "*$i* is equal to *$i*" is evaluated, you obtain "12 is equal to 12," which while true is barely illuminating. This is shown here:

```
PS C:\> $i = 12
PS C:\> "$i is equal to $i"
12 is equal to 12
PS C:\>
```

## Understanding literal strings

What you probably want to do is display both the name of the variable and the value that is contained inside it. In VBScript, you would have to use concatenation. For this example to work, you have to use the literal string as shown here:

```
PS C:\> $i = 12
PS C:\> '$i is equal to ' + $i
$i is equal to 12
PS C:\>
```

If you want to use the advantage of the expanding string, you have to suppress the expanding nature of the expanding string for the first variable (*escape* the variable). To do this, you use the escape character, which is the backtick (or grave character). This is shown here:

```
PS C:\> $i = 12
PS C:\> "`$i is equal to $i"
$i is equal to 12
PS C:\>
```

In the DemoWhileLessThan.ps1 script, you use the expanding string to print the status message of the value of the *$i* variable during each trip through the *While* loop. You suppress the expanding nature of the expanding string for the first *$i* variable so you can see which variable you are talking about. As soon as you have done this, you increment the value of the *$i* variable by one. To do this, you use the *$i++* syntax. This is identical to saying the following:

```
$i = $i + 1
```

The advantage is that the *$i++* syntax requires less typing. The DemoWhileLessThan.ps1 script is shown here:

**DemoWhileLessThan.ps1**

```
$i = 0
While ($i -lt 5)
 {
   "`$i equals $i. This is less than  5"
   $i++
 } #end while $i lt 5
```

When you run the DemoWhileLessThan.ps1 script, you receive the following output:

```
$i equals 0. This is less than  5
$i equals 1. This is less than  5
$i equals 2. This is less than  5
$i equals 3. This is less than  5
$i equals 4. This is less than  5
PS C:\>
```

# A practical example of using the *While* statement

Now that you know how to use the *While* loop, let's examine the WhileReadLine.ps1 script. The first thing you do is initialize the *$i* variable and set it equal to 0. You then use the *Get-Content* cmdlet to read the contents of testfile.txt and to store the contents into the *$fileContents* variable.

Use the *While* statement to loop through the contents of the text file. You do this as long as the value of the *$i* variable is less than or equal to the number of lines in the text file. The number of lines in the text file is represented by the *length* property. Inside the script block, you treat the contents of the *$fileContents* variable like it is an array (which it is), and you use the *$i* variable to index into the array to print the value of each line in the *$fileContents* variable. You then increment the value of the *$i* variable by one. The WhileReadLine.ps1 script is shown here:

**WhileReadLine.ps1**

```
$i = 0
$fileContents = Get-Content -path C:\fso\testfile.txt
While ( $i -le $fileContents.length )
 {
  $fileContents[$i]
  $i++
 }
```

# Using special features of Windows PowerShell

If you are thinking the WriteReadLine.ps1 script is a bit difficult, note that it is not really any more difficult than the VBScript version. The difference is you resorted to using arrays to work with the content you received from the *Get-Content* cmdlet. The VBScript version uses a *FileSystemObject* and a *TextStreamObject* to work with the data. In reality, you would not have to use a script exactly like the WhileReadLine.ps1 script to read the contents of the text file. This is because the *Get-Content* cmdlet does this for you automatically. All you really have to do to display the contents of TestFile.txt is use *Get-Content*. This command is shown here:

```
Get-Content -path c:\fso\TestFile.txt
```

Because the results of the command are not stored in a variable, the contents are automatically emitted to the screen. You can further shorten the *Get-Content* command by using the *gc* alias and by omitting the name of the *-path* parameter (which is the default parameter). When you do this, you create a command that resembles the following:

```
gc c:\fso\TestFile.txt
```

To find the available aliases for the *Get-Content* cmdlet, you use the *Get-Alias* cmdlet with the *-definition* parameter. The *Get-Alias* cmdlet searches for aliases that have a definition that matches *Get-Content*. Here is the command, including the output you receive:

```
PS C:\> Get-Alias -Definition Get-Content

CommandType     Name                    Definition
-----------     ----                    ----------
Alias           cat                     Get-Content
Alias           gc                      Get-Content
Alias           type                    Get-Content
```

This section showed that you can use the *While* statement in Windows PowerShell to perform looping. It also showed that activities in VBScript that require looping do not always require you to use the looping behavior in Windows PowerShell because some cmdlets automatically display information. Finally, it discussed how to find aliases for cmdlets you frequently use.

## Using the *Do...While* statement

The *Do While...Loop* statement was often used when working with VBScript. This section covers some of the advantages of the similar *Do...While* statement in Windows PowerShell.

The DemoDoWhile.vbs script illustrates using the *Do...While* statement in VBScript. The first thing you do is assign a value of 0 to the variable *i*. You then create an array. To do this, you use the *Array* function, and assign the numbers 1 through 5 to the variable *ary*. You then use the *Do While...Loop* construction to walk through the array of numbers. As long as the value of the variable *i* is less than the number 5, you display the value of the variable *i*. You then increment the value of the variable and loop back around. The DemoDoWhile.vbs script is shown here:

**DemoDoWhile.vbs**
```
i = 0
ary = Array(1,2,3,4,5)
Do While i < 5
 WScript.Echo ary(i)
 i = i + 1
Loop
```

When you run the DemoDoWhile.vbs script in Cscript at the command prompt, you see the numbers 1 through 5 displayed at the command prompt.

You can achieve the same thing by using Windows PowerShell. The DemoDoWhile.ps1 and DemoDoWhile.vbs scripts are essentially the same. The differences between the two scripts are due to syntax differences between Windows PowerShell and VBScript. With the Windows PowerShell script, the first thing you do is assign a value of 1 to the variable $i. You then create an array of the numbers 1 through 5 and store that array in the $ary variable. You use a shortcut in Windows PowerShell to make this a bit easier. Actually, arrays in Windows PowerShell are fairly easy anyway. If you want to create an array, you just have to assign multiple pieces of data to the variable. To do this, you separate each piece of data by a comma. This is shown here:

```
$ary = 1,2,3,4,5
```

## Using the range operator

If you needed to create an array with 32,000 numbers in it, it would be impractical to type each number and separate it with a comma. In VBScript, you would have to use a *For...Next* loop to add the numbers to the array. You can write a loop in Windows PowerShell as well, but it is easier to use the range operator. To do this, you use a variable to hold the array of numbers that is created, and type the beginning and the ending number separated by two periods. This is shown here:

```
$ary = 1..5
```

Unfortunately, the range operator does not work for letters. But there is nothing to prevent you from creating a range of numbers that represent the ASCII value of each letter, and then casting it to a string later.

## Operating over an array

You are now ready for the *Do...While* loop in Windows PowerShell. You use the *Do* statement and open a set of braces (curly brackets). Inside these curly brackets you have a script block. The first thing you do is index into the array. On your first pass through the array, the value of *$i* is equal to 0. You therefore display the first element in the *$ary* array. You next increment the value of the *$i* variable by one. You are now done with the script block, so you look at the *While* statement. The condition you are examining is the value of the *$i* variable. As long as it is less than 5, you will continue to loop around. As soon as the value of *$i* is no longer less than 5, you stop looping. This is shown here:

**DemoDoWhile.ps1**

```
$i = 0
$ary = 1..5
do
{
 $ary[$i]
 $i++
} while ($i -lt 5)
```

One thing to be aware of, because it can be a bit confusing, is that you are evaluating the value of *$i*. You initialized *$i* at 0. The first number in your array was 1. But the first element number in the array is always 0 in Windows PowerShell (unlike VBScript, in which arrays can start with 0 or 1). The *While* statement evaluates the value contained in the *$i* variable, not the value that is contained in the array. That is why you see the number 5 displayed.

## Casting to ASCII values

You can change the DemoDoWhile.ps1 script to display uppercase letters from *A* to *Z*. To do this, you first initialize the *$i* variable and set it to 0. You then create a range of numbers from 65 through 91. These are the ASCII values for the capital letter *A* through the capital letter *Z*. Then you begin the *Do* statement and open your script block. To this point, the script is identical to the previous one. To obtain letters from numbers, cast the integer to a char. To do this, you use the *char* data type and put it inside square brackets. You then use this to convert an integer to an uppercase letter. The code to display the uppercase letter *B* from the ASCII value 66 would resemble the following:

```
PS C:\> [char]66
B
```

Because you know that the *$caps* variable contains an array of numbers from 65 through 91, and that the variable *$i* will hold numbers from 0 through 26, you index into the *$caps* array, cast the integer to a char, and display the results, as follows:

```
[char]$caps[$i]
```

You then increment the value of *$i* by one, close the script block, and enter the *While* statement, where you check the value of *$i* to make sure it is less than 26. As long as *$i* is less than 26, you continue to loop around. The complete DisplayCapitalLetters.ps1 script is shown here:

**DisplayCapitalLetters.ps1**
```
$i = 0
$caps = 65..91
do
{
 [char]$caps[$i]
 $i++
} while ($i -lt 26)
```

This section explored the *Do...While* construction from Windows PowerShell by comparing it to the similar construction from VBScript. In addition, the use of the range operator and casting was also examined.

## Using the *Do...Until* statement

Looping technology is something that is essential to master. It occurs everywhere, and should be a tool that you can use without thought. When you are confronted with a collection of items, an array, or another bundle of items, you have to know how to easily walk through the mess without resorting to research, panic, or hours searching the Internet. This section examines the *Do...Until* construction. Most of the scripts that do looping at the Microsoft Technet Script Center seem to use *Do...While*. The scripts that use *Do...Until...Loop* are typically used to read through a text file (do something until the end of the stream) or to read through an ActiveX Data Object (ADO) recordset (do something until the end of the file). As you will see here, these are not required coding conventions and are not meant to be limitations. You can frequently perform the same thing by using any of the different looping constructions.

# Comparing the PowerShell *Do...Until* statement with VBScript

Before you get too far into this topic, consider the DemoDoUntil.vbs script. In this script, you first assign a value of 0 to the variable *i*. You then create an array with the numbers 1 through 5 contained in it. You use the *Do...Until* construction to walk through the array until the value of the variable *i* is equal to 5. The script will continue to run until the value of the variable *i* is equal to 5. This is what a *Do...Until* construction does—it runs until a condition is met. The difference between *Do...Until* and *Do...While*, examined in the previous section, is that *Do...While* runs while a condition is true and *Do...Until* runs until a condition becomes true. In VBScript, this means that *Do...Until* will always run at least once, because the condition is evaluated at the bottom of the loop, whereas *Do...While* is evaluated at the top of the loop, and therefore will never run if the condition is not true. This is not true for Windows PowerShell, however, as will be shown later in this section.

Inside the loop, you first display the value that is contained in the array element 0 on the first pass through the loop. This is because you first set the value of the variable *i* equal to 0. You next increment the value of the variable *i* by one and loop around until the value of *i* is equal to 5. The DemoDoUntil.vbs script is shown here:

**DemoDoUntil.vbs**

```
i = 0
ary = array(1,2,3,4,5)
Do Until i = 5
 wscript.Echo ary(i)
 i = i+1
Loop
```

# Using the Windows PowerShell *Do* statement

You can write the same script using Windows PowerShell. In the DemoDoUntil.ps1 script, you first set the value of the *$i* variable to 0. You then create an array with the numbers 1 through 5 in it. You store that array in the *$ary* variable. You then arrive at the *Do* (do-until) construction. After the *Do* keyword, you open a set of curly brackets. Inside the curly brackets, you use the *$i* variable to index into the *$ary* array and to retrieve the value that is stored in the first element (element 0) of the array. You then increment the value of the *$i* variable by one. You continue to loop through the elements in the array until the value of the *$i* variable is equal to 5. At that time, you end the script. This script resembles the DemoDoWhile.ps1 script examined in the previous section.

**DemoDoUntil.ps1**

```
$i = 0
$ary = 1..5

Do
{
 $ary[$i]
 $i ++
} Until ($i -eq 5)
```

## The *Do...While* and *Do...Until* statements always run once

In VBScript, if a *Do...While...Loop* condition was never true, the code inside the loop would never execute. In Windows PowerShell, the *Do...While* and *Do...Until* constructions always run at least once. This can be unexpected behavior, and is something that you should focus on. This is illustrated in the DoWhileAlwaysRuns.ps1 script. The script assigns a value of 1 to the variable *$i*. Inside the script block for the *Do...While* loop, you print out a message that states you are inside the *Do* loop. The loop condition is "while the variable *$i* is equal to 5." As you can see, the value of the *$i* variable is 1. Therefore, the value of the *$i* variable will never reach 5, because you are not incrementing it. The DoWhileAlwaysRuns.ps1 script is shown here:

**DoWhileAlwaysRuns.ps1**

```
$i = 1

Do
{
 "inside the do loop"
} While ($i -eq 5)
```

When you run the script, the text "inside the do loop" is printed out once.

What about a similar script that uses the *Do...Until* construction? The EndlessDoUntil.ps1 script is the same as the DoWhileAlwaysRuns.ps1 script, except for one small detail. Instead of using *Do...While*, you are using *Do...Until*. The rest of the script is the same. The value of the *$i* variable is equal to 1, and in the script block for the *Do...Until* loop, you print the string *inside the do loop*. This line of code should execute once for each *Do* loop until the value of *$i* is equal to 5. Because the value of *$i* is never increased to 5, the script will continue to run. The EndlessDoUntil.ps1 script is shown here:

**EndlessDoUntil.ps1**

```
$i = 1

Do
{
 "inside the do loop"
} Until ($i -eq 5)
```

Before you run the EndlessDoUntil.ps1 script, you should know how to interrupt the running of the script. You hold down the Ctrl key and press C (Ctrl+C). This is the same keystroke sequence that would break a runaway VBScript that was run in Cscript.

## The *While* statement is used to prevent unwanted execution

If you have a situation where the script block must not execute if the condition is not true, you should use the *While* statement. The use of the *While* statement was examined in an earlier section. Again, you have the same kind of script. You assign the value of 0 to the variable *$i*, and instead of using a *Do...* kind of construction, you use the *While* statement. The condition you are looking at is the same condition you used for the other scripts (do something *while* the value of $i is equal to 5). Inside the script block, you display a string that states you are inside the *While* loop. The WhileDoesNotRun.ps1 script is shown here:

**WhileDoesNotRun.ps1**

```
$i = 0

While ($i -eq 5)
{
 "Inside the While Loop"
}
```

It is perhaps a bit anticlimactic, but go ahead and run the WhileDoesNotRun.ps1 script. There should be no output displayed to the console.

# The *For* statement

In VBScript, a *For...Next* loop was somewhat easy to create. An example of a simple *For...Next* loop is shown in DemoForLoop.vbs. You use the *For* keyword, define a variable to keep track of the count, indicate how far you will go, define your action, and ensure that you specify the *Next* keyword. That is about all there is to it. The DemoForLoop.vbs is shown here:

**DemoForLoop.vbs**

```
For i = 1 To 5
 WScript.Echo i
Next
```

## Using the *For* statement

You can achieve the same thing in Windows PowerShell. The structure of the *For* loop in Windows PowerShell resembles the structure for VBScript. They both begin with the keyword *For*, they both initialize the variable, and they both specify how far the loop will progress. One thing that is different is that a *For...Next* loop in VBScript automatically increments the counter variable. In Windows PowerShell, the variable is not automatically incremented; instead, you add $i++ to increment the $i variable by one. Inside the script block (curly brackets), you display the value of the $i variable. The DemoForLoop.ps1 script is shown here:

**DemoForLoop.ps1**

```
For($i = 0; $i -le 5; $i++)
{
 '$i equals ' + $i
}
```

The Windows PowerShell *For* statement is very flexible, and you can leave one or more elements of it out. In the DemoForWithoutInitOrRepeat.ps1 script, you exclude the first and the last sections of the *For* statement. You set the $i variable equal to 0 on the first line of the script. You next come to the *For* statement. In the DemoForLoop.ps1 script, the *$i = 0* was moved from inside the *For* statement to the first line of the script. The semicolon is still required because it is used to separate the three sections of the statement. The condition portion, *$i -le 5*, is the same as in the previous script. The repeat section, *$i ++*, is not used.

In the script section of the *For* statement, you display the value of the *$i* variable, and you also increment the value of *$i* by one. There are two kinds of Windows PowerShell strings: expanding and literal. These two types of strings were examined earlier in this chapter. The DemoForLoop.ps1 script demonstrates an example of a literal string—what is entered is what is displayed. This is shown here:

```
'$i equals ' + $i
```

In the DemoForWithoutInitOrRepeat.ps1 script is an example of an expanding string. The value of the variable is displayed—not the variable name itself. To suppress the expanding nature of the expanding string, escape the variable by using the backtick character. When you use the expanding string in this manner, it enables you to avoid concatenating the string and the variable, as you did in the DemoForLoop.ps1 script. This is shown here:

```
"`$i is equal to $i"
```

The value of *$i* must be incremented somewhere. Because it was not incremented in the repeat section of the *For* statement, you have to be able to increment it inside the script block. The DemoForWithoutInitOrRepeat.ps1 script is shown here:

**DemoForWithoutInitOrRepeat.ps1**
```
$i = 0
For(;$i -le 5; )
{
 "`$i is equal to $i"
 $i++
}
```

When you run the DemoForWithoutInitOrRepeat.ps1 script, the output that is displayed resembles the output produced by DemoForLoop.ps1. You would never be able to tell it was missing two-thirds of the parameters.

You can make your *For* statement into an infinite loop by omitting all three sections of the *For* statement. You must leave the semicolons as position holders. When you omit the three parts of the *For* statement, it will resemble the following:

```
for(;;)
```

While you can create an endless loop with the ForEndlessLoop.ps1 script, you do not have to do this if this is not your desire. You could use an *If* statement to evaluate a condition and take action when the condition is met. *If* statements will be covered in the section "The *If* statement" later in this chapter. In the ForEndlessLoop.ps1 script, you display the value of the *$i* variable and increment it by one. The semicolon is used to represent a new line. You could therefore write the *For* statement on three lines if you wanted to. This would be useful if you had a very complex *For* statement, as it would make the code easier to read. The script block for the ForEndlessLoop.ps1 script could be written on different lines and exclude the semicolon. This is shown here:

```
{
 $i
 $i++
}
# ForEndlessLoop.ps1
for(;;)
{
 $i ; $i++
}
```

When you run the ForEndlessLoop.ps1 script, you are greeted with a long line of numbers. To break out of the endless loop, press Ctrl+C inside the Windows PowerShell prompt.

You can see that working with Windows PowerShell is all about choices: how you want to work and the things that you want to try to achieve. The *For* statement in Windows PowerShell is very flexible, and maybe one day, you will find just the problem waiting for the solution that you have.

## Using the *Foreach* statement

The *Foreach* statement resembles the *For…Each…Next* construction from VBScript. In the DemoForEachNext.vbs script you create an array of five numbers, 1 through 5. You then use the *For…Each…Next* statement to walk your way through the array that is contained in the variable *ary*. The variable *i* is used iterate through the elements of the array. The *For…Each* block is entered as long as there is at least one item in the collection or array. When the loop is entered, all statements inside the loop are executed for the first element. In the DemoForEachNext.vbs script, this means that the following command is executed for each element in the array:

```
Wscript.Echo i
```

As long as there are more elements in the collection or array, the statements inside the loop continue to execute for each element. When there are no more elements in the collection or array, the loop is exited, and execution continues with the statement following the *Next* statement. This is shown in DemoForEachNext.vbs:

**DemoForEachNext.vbs**

```
ary = Array(1,2,3,4,5)
For Each i In ary
  WScript.Echo i
Next
Wscript.echo "All done"
```

The DemoForEachNext.vbs script works exactly like the DemoForEach.ps1 script. In the DemoForEach.ps1 PowerShell script, you first create an array that contains the numbers 1 through 5, and then store that array in the *$ary* variable. This is shown here:

```
$ary = 1..5
```

Then you use the *Foreach* statement to walk through the array contained in the *$ary* variable. Use the *$i* variable to keep track of your progress through the array. Inside the script block, you display the value of each variable. The DemoForEach.ps1 script is shown here:

DemoForEach.ps1

```
$ary = 1..5
Foreach ($i in $ary)
{
 $i
}
```

### Using the *Foreach* statement from the Windows PowerShell console

The great thing about Windows PowerShell is that you can also use the *Foreach* statement from inside the Windows PowerShell console. This is shown here:

```
PS C:\> $ary = 1..5
PS C:\> foreach($i in $ary) { $i }
1
2
3
4
5
```

The ability to use the *Foreach* statement from inside the Windows PowerShell console can give you excellent flexibility when you are working interactively. However, much of the work done at the Windows PowerShell console consists of using pipelining. When you are working with the pipeline, you can use the *ForEach-Object* cmdlet. This cmdlet behaves in a similar manner to the *Foreach* statement but is designed to handle pipelined input. The difference is that you do not have to use an intermediate variable to hold the contents of the array. You can create the array and send it across the pipeline. The other difference is that you do not have to create a variable to use for the enumerator. You use the *$_* automatic variable (which represents the current item on the pipeline) instead. This is shown here:

```
PS C:\> 1..5 | ForEach-Object { $_ }
1
2
3
4
5
```

## Exiting the *Foreach* statement early

Suppose that you do not want to work with all the numbers in the array. In VBScript terms, leaving a *For...Each...Loop* early is done with an *Exit For* statement. You have to use an *If* statement to perform the evaluation of the condition. When the condition is met, you call *Exit For*. In the DemoExitFor.vbs script, you use an inline *If* statement to make this determination. The inline syntax is more efficient for these kinds of things than spreading the statement across three different lines. The key thing to remember about the inline *If* statement is it does not conclude with the final *End If* statement. The DemoExitFor.vbs script is shown here:

**DemoExitFor.vbs**

```
ary = Array(1,2,3,4,5)
For Each i In ary
 If i = 3 Then Exit For
 WScript.Echo i
Next
WScript.Echo "Statement following Next"
```

## Using the *Break* statement

In Windows PowerShell terms, you use the *Break* statement to leave the loop early. Inside the script block, you use an *If* statement to evaluate the value of the $i variable. If it is equal to 3, you call the *Break* statement and leave the loop. This line of code is shown here:

```
if($i -eq 3) { break }
```

The complete DemoBreakFor.ps1 script is shown here:

**DemoBreakFor.ps1**

```
$ary = 1..5
ForEach($i in $ary)
{
 if($i -eq 3) { break }
 $i
}
"Statement following foreach loop"
```

When the DemoBreakFor.ps1 script runs, it displays the numbers 1 and 2. Then it leaves the *Foreach* loop and runs the line of code following the *Foreach* loop. This is shown here:

```
1
2
Statement following foreach loop
```

## Using the *Exit* statement

If you did not want to run the line of code after the loop statement, you would use the *exit* statement instead of the *Break* statement. This is shown in the DemoExitFor.ps1 script.

**DemoExitFor.ps1**

```
$ary = 1..5
ForEach($i in $ary)
{
 if($i -eq 3) { exit }
 $i
}
"Statement following foreach loop"
```

When the DemoExitFor.ps1 script runs, the line of code following the *Foreach* loop never executes. This is because the *exit* statement ends the script (In the Windows PowerShell ISE, discussed in Chapter 8, "Using the Windows PowerShell ISE," the *exit* command attempts to close the ISE). The results of running the DemoExitF0r.ps1 script are shown here:

```
1
2
```

You could achieve the same thing in VBScript by using the *Wscript.Quit* statement instead of *Exit For*. As with the DemoExitFor.ps1 script, the DemoQuitFor.vbs script never comes to the line of code following the *For...Each* loop. This is shown in DemoQuitFor.vbs here:

**DemoQuitFor.vbs**

```
ary = Array(1,2,3,4,5)
For Each i In ary
 If i = 3 Then WScript.Quit
 WScript.Echo i
Next
WScript.Echo "Statement following Next"
```

In this section, the use of the *Foreach* statement was examined. It is used when you do not know how many items are contained within a collection. It allows you to walk through the collection and to work with items from that collection on an individual basis. In addition, two techniques for exiting a *Foreach* statement were also examined.

# The *If* statement

In VBScript, the *If...Then...End If* statement was somewhat straightforward. There were several things to be aware of:

- The *If* and the *Then* statements must be on the same line.

- The *If...Then...End If* statement must conclude with *End If*.

- *End If* is two words, not one.

The VBScript *If...Then...End If* statement is shown in the DemoIf.vbs script:

**DemoIf.vbs**

```
a = 5
If a = 5 Then
 WScript.Echo "a equals 5"
End If
```

In the Windows PowerShell version of the *If...Then...End If* statement, there is no *Then* keyword, nor is there an *End If* statement. The PowerShell *If* statement is easier to type. This simplicity, however, comes with a bit of complexity. The condition that is evaluated in the *If* statement is positioned between a set of parentheses. In the DemoIf.ps1 script, you are checking whether the variable *$a* is equal to 5. This is shown here:

```
If ($a -eq 5)
```

The code that is executed when the condition is *true* is positioned inside a script block. The script block for the DemoIf.ps1 script is shown here:

```
{
    '$a equals 5'
}
```

The Windows PowerShell version of the DemoIf.vbs script is the DemoIf.ps1 script:

```
# DemoIf.ps1
$a = 5
If($a -eq 5)
 {
    '$a equals 5'
 }
```

The one thing that is different about the Windows PowerShell *If* statement is the comparison operators. In VBScript, the equal sign (=) is used as an assignment operator. It is also used as an equality operator for comparison. On the first line of code, the variable *$a* is assigned the value 5. This uses the equal sign as an assignment. On the next line of code, the *If* statement is used to see whether the value of *a* is equal to 5. On this line of code, the equal sign is used as the equality operator. This is shown here:

```
a = 5
If a = 5 Then
```

In simple examples such as this, it is fairly easy to tell the difference between an equality operator and an assignment operator. In more complex scripts, however, things could be confusing. Windows PowerShell removes that confusion by having special comparison operators. One thing that might help is to realize that the main operators are two letters long. Common comparison operators are shown in Table 5-5.

**TABLE 5-5** Common comparison operators

| Operator | Description | Example | Result |
|----------|-------------|---------|--------|
| -eq | Equals | $a = 5 ; $a -eq 4 | False |
| -ne | Not equal | $a = 5 ; $a -ne 4 | True |
| -gt | Greater than | $a = 5 ; $a -gt 4 | True |
| -ge | Greater than or equal to | $a = 5 ; $a -ge 5 | True |
| -lt | Less than | $a = 5 ; $a -lt 5 | False |
| -le | Less than or equal to | $a = 5 ; $a -le 5 | True |
| -like | Wildcard comparison | $a = "This is Text" ; $a -like "Text" | False |
| -notlike | Wildcard comparison | $a = "This is Text" ; $a -notlike "Text" | True |
| -match | Regular expression comparison | $a = "Text is Text" ; $a -match "Text" | True |
| -notmatch | Regular expression comparison | $a = "This is Text" ; $a -notmatch "Text$" | False |

# Using assignment and comparison operators

Any value assignment in a condition block will evaluate to *true*, and therefore the script block is executed. In this example, you assign the value 1 to the variable *$a*. In the condition for the *If* statement, you assign the value of 12 to the variable *$a*. Any assignment evaluates to *true*, and the script block executes.

```
PS C:\> $a = 1 ; If ($a = 12) { "its true" }
its true
```

Rarely do you test a condition and perform an action. Sometimes, you have to perform one action if the condition is *true* and another action if the condition is *false*. In VBScript, you used the *If...Else...End If* construction. The *Else* clause went immediately after the first action to be performed if the condition was *true*. This is shown in the DemoIfElse.vbs script.

**DemoIfElse.vbs**
```
a = 4
If a = 5 Then
 WScript.Echo "a equals 5"
Else
 WScript.Echo "a is not equal to 5"
End If
```

In Windows PowerShell, the syntax is not surprising. Following the closing curly bracket from the *If* statement script block, you add the *Else* keyword and open a new script block to hold the alternative outcome. This is shown here:

**DemoIfElse.ps1**
```
$a = 4
If ($a -eq 5)
{
 '$a equals 5'
}
Else
{
 '$a is not equal to 5'
}
```

Things become confusing with VBScript when you want to evaluate multiple conditions and have multiple outcomes. The *Else If* clause provides for the second outcome. You have to evaluate the second condition. The *Else If* clause receives its own condition, which is followed by the *Then* keyword. Following the *Then* keyword, you list the code that you want to execute. This is followed by the *Else* keyword and a pair of *End If* statements. This is shown in the DemoIfElseIfElse.vbs script:

DemoIfElseIfElse.vbs

```
a = 4
If a = 5 Then
 WScript.Echo "a equals 5"
Else If a = 3 Then
 WScript.Echo "a equals 3"
Else
 WScript.Echo "a does not equal 3 or 5"
End If
End If
```

## Evaluating multiple conditions

The Windows PowerShell demoIfElseIfElse.ps1 script is a bit easier to understand because it avoids the double–*End If* kind of scenario. For each condition that you want to evaluate, you use *ElseIf* (be aware that it is a single word). You put the condition inside a pair of parentheses and open your script block. Here is the demoIfElseIfElse.ps1 script:

demoIfElseIfElse.ps1

```
$a = 4
If ($a -eq 5)
{
 '$a equals 5'
}
ElseIf ($a -eq 3)
{
 '$a is equal to 3'
}
Else
{
 '$a does not equal 3 or 5'
}
```

In this section, the use of the *If* statement was examined. Comparison operators and assignment operators were also covered.

# The *Switch* statement

As a best practice, you generally avoid using the *ElseIf* type of construction from either VBScript or Windows PowerShell because there is a better way to write the same code.

In VBScript, you would use the *Select Case* statement to evaluate a condition and select one outcome from a group of potential statements. In the DemoSelectCase.vbs script, the value of the variable *a* is assigned the value of 2. The *Select Case* statement is used to evaluate the value of the variable *a*. The syntax is shown here:

```
Select Case testexpression
```

The test expression that is evaluated is the variable *a*. Each of the different cases contains potential values for the test expression. If the value of the variable *a* is equal to 1, the code *Wscript.Echo "a = 1"* is executed. This is shown here:

```
Case 1
   WScript.Echo "a = 1"
```

Each of the different cases is evaluated in the same manner. The *Case Else* expression is run if none of the previous expressions evaluate to *true*. The complete DemoSelectCase.vbs script is shown here:

**DemoSelectCase.vbs**

```
a = 2
Select Case a
 Case 1
   WScript.Echo "a = 1"
 Case 2
   WScript.Echo "a = 2"
 Case 3
   WScript.Echo "a = 3"
 Case Else
   WScript.Echo "unable to determine value of a"
End Select
WScript.Echo "statement after select case"
```

# Using the *Switch* statement

In Windows PowerShell, there is no *Select Case* statement. There is, however, the *Switch* statement. The *Switch* statement is the most powerful statement in the Windows PowerShell language. The basic *Switch* statement begins with the *Switch* keyword, followed by the condition to be evaluated positioned inside a pair of parentheses. This is shown here:

```
Switch ($a)
```

Next, a script block is used to mark off the script block for the *Switch* statement. Inside this outer script block, you will find an inner script block to be executed. Each condition to be evaluated begins with a value, followed by the script block to be executed in the event the value matches the condition. This is shown here:

```
1 { '$a = 1' }
2 { '$a = 2' }
3 { '$a = 3' }
```

## Defining the *default* condition

If no match is found in the script block and the *Default* statement is not used, the *Switch* statement exits and the line of code that follows the *Switch* statement is executed. The *Default* statement performs a function similar to the *Case Else* statement from the *Select Case* statement. The *Default* statement is shown here:

```
Default { 'unable to determine value of $a' }
```

The complete DemoSwitchCase.ps1 script is shown here:

**DemoSwitchCase.ps1**

```
$a = 2
Switch ($a)
{
 1 { '$a = 1' }
 2 { '$a = 2' }
 3 { '$a = 3' }
 Default { 'unable to determine value of $a' }
}
"Statement after switch"
```

## Understanding matching with the *Switch* statement

With the *Select Case* statement, the first matching case is the one that is executed. As soon as that code executes, the line following the *Select Case* statement is executed. If the condition matches multiple cases in the *Select Case* statement, only the first match in the list is executed. Matches from lower in the list are not executed. Therefore, make sure that the most desirable code to execute is positioned highest in the *Select Case* order.

With the *Switch* statement in Windows PowerShell, order is not a major design concern. This is because every match from inside the *Switch* statement will be executed by default. An example of this is shown in the DemoSwitchMultiMatch.ps1 script.

**DemoSwitchMultiMatch.ps1**

```
$a = 2
Switch ($a)
{
 1 { '$a = 1' }
 2 { '$a = 2' }
 2 { 'Second match of the $a variable' }
 3 { '$a = 3' }
 Default { 'unable to determine value of $a' }
}
"Statement after switch"
```

When the DemoSwitchMultiMatch.ps1 script runs, the second and third conditions will both be matched, and therefore their associated script blocks will be executed. The DemoSwitchMultiMatch.ps1 script produces the output shown here:

```
$a = 2
Second match of the $a variable
Statement after switch
```

## Evaluating an array

If an array is stored in the variable *a* in the DemoSelectCase.vbs script, a type-mismatch error will be produced. This error is shown here:

```
Microsoft VBScript runtime error: Type mismatch
```

The Windows PowerShell *Switch* statement can handle an array in the variable $a without any modification. The array is shown here:

```
$a = 2,3,5,1,77
```

The complete DemoSwitchArray.ps1 script is shown here:

**DemoSwitchArray.ps1**

```
$a = 2,3,5,1,77
Switch ($a)
{
 1 { '$a = 1' }
 2 { '$a = 2' }
 3 { '$a = 3' }
 Default { 'unable to determine value of $a' }
}
"Statement after switch"
```

## Controlling matching behavior

If you do not want the multimatch behavior of the *Switch* statement, you can use the *Break* statement to change the behavior. In the DemoSwitchArrayBreak.ps1 script, the *Switch* statement will be exited when the first match occurs because each of the match condition script blocks contains the *Break* statement. This is shown here:

```
 1 { '$a = 1' ; break }
 2 { '$a = 2' ; break }
 3 { '$a = 3' ; break }
```

You are not required to include the *Break* statement with each condition; instead, you could use it to exit the switch only after a particular condition is matched. The complete DemoSwitchArrayBreak.ps1 script is shown here:

**DemoSwitchArrayBreak.ps1**

```
$a = 2,3,5,1,77
Switch ($a)
{
 1 { '$a = 1' ; break }
 2 { '$a = 2' ; break }
 3 { '$a = 3' ; break }
 Default { 'unable to determine value of $a' }
}
"Statement after switch"
```

In this section, the use of Windows PowerShell *Switch* statement was examined. The matching behavior of the *Switch* statement and the use of *Break* was also discussed.

# Creating multiple folders: step-by-step exercises

In this exercise, you'll explore the use of constants, variables, concatenation, decision-making, and looping as you create 10 folders in the C:\Mytest directory. This directory was created earlier. If you do not have this folder on your machine, you can either create it manually or modify the following two exercises to use a folder that exists on your machine. In the second exercise in this section, you will modify the script to delete the 10 folders.

## Creating multiple folders via PowerShell scripting

1. Open the Windows PowerShell ISE.

2. Create a variable called *$intFolders* and have it hold the value 10. The code to do this is shown here:

   ```
   $intFolders = 10
   ```

3. Create a variable called *$intPad*. Do not put anything in the variable yet. This code is shown here:

   ```
   $intPad
   ```

4. Create a variable called *$i* and put the value 1 in it. The code to do this is shown here:

   ```
   $i = 1
   ```

5. Use the *New-Variable* cmdlet to create a variable named *strPrefix*. Use the *-value* argument of the cmdlet to assign a value of *testFolder* to the variable. Use the *-option* argument to make *$strPrefix* into a constant. The code to do this is shown here:

   ```
   New-Variable -Name strPrefix -Value "testFolder" -Option constant
   ```

6. Begin a *Do...Until* statement. Include the opening curly bracket for the script block. This code is shown here:

   ```
   do {
   ```

7. Begin an *If...Else* statement. The condition to be evaluated is if the variable *$i* is less than 10. The code that does this is shown here:

   ```
   if ($i -lt 10)
   ```

8. Open the script block for the *If* statement. Assign the value 0 to the variable *$intPad*. This is shown here:

   ```
   {$intPad=0
   ```

9. Use the *New-Item* cmdlet to create a new folder. The new folder will be created in the C:\Mytest directory. The name of the new folder will comprise the *$strPrefix* constant *test-Folder*, the number 0 from the *$intPad* variable, and the number contained in the *$i* variable. The code that does this is shown here:

```
New-Item -path c:\mytest -name $strPrefix$intPad$i -type directory}
```

10. Add the *Else* clause. This code is shown here:

```
else
```

11. The *Else* script block is the same as the *If* script block, except it does not include the 0 in the name that comes from the *$intPad* variable. Copy the *New-Item* line of code from the *If* statement and delete the *$intPad* variable from the *-name* argument. The revised line of code is shown here:

```
{New-Item -path c:\mytest -name $strPrefix$i -type directory}
```

12. Increment the value of the *$i* variable by one. To do this, use the double–plus symbol operator (++) . The code that does this is shown here:

```
$i++
```

13. Close the script block for the *Else* clause and add the *Until* statement. The condition that *Until* will evaluate is if the *$i* variable is equal to the value contained in the *$intFolders* variable + 1. The reason for adding 1 to *$intFolders* is so the script will actually create the same number of folders as are contained in the *$intFolders* variable. Because this script uses a *Do...Until* loop and the value of *$i* is incremented before entering the *Until* evaluation, the value of *$i* is always 1 more than the number of folders created. This code is shown here:

```
}until ($i -eq $intFolders+1)
```

14. Save your script as *<yourname>*CreateMultipleFolders.ps1. Run your script. You should see 10 folders created in the C:\Mytest directory. This concludes this step-by-step exercise.

The next exercise will show you how to delete multiple folders.

## Deleting multiple folders

1. Open the *<yourname>*CreateMultipleFolders.ps1 script created in the previous exercise in the Windows PowerShell ISE.

2. In the *If...Else* statement, the *New-Item* cmdlet is used twice to create folders in the C:\Mytest directory. You want to delete these folders. To do this, you need to change the *New-Item* cmdlet to the *Remove-Item* cmdlet. The two edited script blocks are shown here:

```
{$intPad=0
        Remove-Item -path c:\mytest -name $strPrefix$intPad$i -type directory}
    else
        {Remove-Item -path c:\mytest -name $strPrefix$i -type directory}
```

3. The *Remove-Item* cmdlet does not have a *-name* argument. Therefore, you need to remove this argument but keep the code that creates the folder name. You can basically replace *-name* with a backslash, as shown here:

```
{$intPad=0
        Remove-Item -path c:\mytest\$strPrefix$intPad$i -type directory}
    else
        {Remove-Item -path c:\mytest\$strPrefix$i -type directory}
```

4. The *Remove-Item* cmdlet does not take a *-type* argument. Because this argument is not needed, it can also be removed from both *Remove-Item* statements. The revised script block is shown here:

```
{$intPad=0
      Remove-Item -path c:\mytest\$strPrefix$intPad$i}
    else
      {Remove-Item -path c:\mytest\$strPrefix$i}
```

5. This concludes this exercise. Save your script as *<yourname>*DeleteMultipleFolders.ps1. Run your script. You should see the 10 previously created folders deleted.

## Chapter 5 quick reference

| To | Do this |
|----|---------|
| Retrieve the script execution policy | Use the *Get-ExecutionPolicy* cmdlet. |
| Set the script execution policy | Use the *Set-ExecutionPolicy* cmdlet. |
| Create a variable | Type the variable name in the script. |
| Create a constant | Use the *New-Variable* cmdlet and specify *constant* for the *-option* argument. |
| Loop through a collection when you do not know how many items are in the collection | Use the *ForEach-Object* cmdlet. |
| Read the contents of a text file | Use the *Get-Content* cmdlet and supply the path to the file as the value for the *-path* argument. |
| Delete a folder | Use the *Remove-Item* cmdlet and supply the path to the folder as the value for the *-path* argument. |

# Working with Functions

**After completing this chapter, you will be able to:**

- Understand functions.

- Use functions to encapsulate logic.

- Use functions to provide ease of modification.

- Use functions to provide ease of reuse.

There are clear-cut guidelines that can be used to design functions. These guidelines can be used to ensure that functions are easy to understand, easy to maintain, and easy to troubleshoot. This chapter will examine the reasons for the scripting guidelines and provide examples of both good and bad code design.

## Understanding functions

In Microsoft Windows PowerShell, functions have moved to the forefront as the primary programming element used when writing Windows PowerShell scripts. This is not necessarily due to improvements in functions per se, but rather a combination of factors, including the maturity of Windows PowerShell script writers. In Windows PowerShell 1.0, functions were not well understood, perhaps due to the lack of clear documentation as to their use, purpose, and application.

VBScript included both subroutines and functions. According to the classic definitions, a subroutine was used to encapsulate code that would do things like write to a database or create a Microsoft Word document. Functions, on the other hand, were used to return a value. An example of a classic VBScript function is one that converts a temperature from Fahrenheit to Celsius. The function receives the value in Fahrenheit and returns the value in Celsius. The classic function always returns a value—if it does not, a subroutine should be used instead.

> **Note** Needless to say, the concepts of functions and subroutines were a bit confusing
> for many VBScript writers. A common question I used to receive when teaching VBScript
> classes was, "When do I use a subroutine and when do I use a function?" After expounding
> the classic definition, I would then show them that you could actually write a subroutine
> that would behave like a function. Next, I would write a function that acted like a subrou-
> tine. It was great fun, and the class loved it. The Windows PowerShell team has essentially
> done the same thing. There is no confusion over when to use a subroutine and when to use
> a function, because there are no subroutines in Windows PowerShell—only functions.

To create a function in Windows PowerShell, you begin with the *Function* keyword, followed by the name of the function. As a best practice, use the Windows PowerShell verb-noun combination when creating functions. Pick the verb from the standard list of PowerShell verbs to make your functions easier to remember. It is a best practice to avoid creating new verbs when there is an existing verb that can easily do the job.

An idea of the verb coverage can be obtained by using the *Get-Command* cmdlet and piping the results to the *Group-Object* cmdlet. This is shown here:

```
Get-Command -CommandType cmdlet | Group-Object -Property Verb |
Sort-Object -Property count -Descending
```

When the preceding command is run, the resulting output is shown. This command was run on Windows Server 2012 and includes cmdlets from the default modules. As shown in the listing, *Get* is used the most by the default cmdlets, followed distantly by *Set*, *New*, and *Remove*.

```
Count Name                 Group
----- ----                 -----
   98 Get                  {Get-Acl, Get-Alias, Get-AppLockerFileInformation...
   48 Set                  {Set-Acl, Set-Alias, Set-AppLockerPolicy, Set-Aut...
   38 New                  {New-Alias, New-AppLockerPolicy, New-CertificateN...
   31 Remove               {Remove-AppxPackage, Remove-AppxProvisionedPackag...
   15 Add                  {Add-AppxPackage, Add-AppxProvisionedPackage, Add...
   11 Invoke               {Invoke-BpaModel, Invoke-CimMethod, Invoke-Comman...
   11 Import               {Import-Alias, Import-Certificate, Import-Clixml,...
   11 Export               {Export-Alias, Export-Certificate, Export-Clixml,...
   10 Test                 {Test-AppLockerPolicy, Test-Certificate, Test-Com...
   10 Enable               {Enable-ComputerRestore, Enable-JobTrigger, Enabl...
   10 Disable              {Disable-ComputerRestore, Disable-JobTrigger, Dis...
    9 Clear                {Clear-Content, Clear-EventLog, Clear-History, Cl...
    8 Start                {Start-BitsTransfer, Start-DtcDiagnosticResourceM...
    8 Write                {Write-Debug, Write-Error, Write-EventLog, Write-...
    7 Out                  {Out-Default, Out-File, Out-GridView, Out-Host...}
    6 ConvertTo            {ConvertTo-Csv, ConvertTo-Html, ConvertTo-Json, C...
    6 Register             {Register-CimIndicationEvent, Register-EngineEven...
    6 Stop                 {Stop-Computer, Stop-DtcDiagnosticResourceManager...
    5 Format               {Format-Custom, Format-List, Format-SecureBootUEF...
    4 Update               {Update-FormatData, Update-Help, Update-List, Upd...
    4 Unregister           {Unregister-Event, Unregister-PSSessionConfigurat...
    4 Show                 {Show-Command, Show-ControlPanelItem, Show-EventL...
```

```
4 ConvertFrom            {ConvertFrom-Csv, ConvertFrom-Json, ConvertFrom-S...
3 Receive                {Receive-DtcDiagnosticTransaction, Receive-Job, R...
3 Wait                   {Wait-Event, Wait-Job, Wait-Process}
3 Complete               {Complete-BitsTransfer, Complete-DtcDiagnosticTra...
3 Select                 {Select-Object, Select-String, Select-Xml}
3 Resume                 {Resume-BitsTransfer, Resume-Job, Resume-Service}
3 Suspend                {Suspend-BitsTransfer, Suspend-Job, Suspend-Service}
3 Rename                 {Rename-Computer, Rename-Item, Rename-ItemProperty}
2 Restore                {Restore-Computer, Restore-IscsiVirtualDisk}
2 Resolve                {Resolve-DnsName, Resolve-Path}
2 Restart                {Restart-Computer, ReStart-Service}
2 Save                   {Save-Help, Save-WindowsImage}
2 Send                   {Send-DtcDiagnosticTransaction, Send-MailMessage}
2 Disconnect             {Disconnect-PSSession, Disconnect-WSMan}
2 Dismount               {Dismount-IscsiVirtualDiskSnapshot, Dismount-Wind...
2 Connect                {Connect-PSSession, Connect-WSMan}
2 Checkpoint             {Checkpoint-Computer, Checkpoint-IscsiVirtualDisk}
2 Move                   {Move-Item, Move-ItemProperty}
2 Mount                  {Mount-IscsiVirtualDiskSnapshot, Mount-WindowsImage}
2 Measure                {Measure-Command, Measure-Object}
2 Join                   {Join-DtcDiagnosticResourceManager, Join-Path}
2 Install                {Install-NfsMappingStore, Install-WindowsFeature}
2 Unblock                {Unblock-File, Unblock-Tpm}
2 Convert                {Convert-IscsiVirtualDisk, Convert-Path}
2 Undo                   {Undo-DtcDiagnosticTransaction, Undo-Transaction}
2 Copy                   {Copy-Item, Copy-ItemProperty}
2 Use                    {Use-Transaction, Use-WindowsUnattend}
1 Tee                    {Tee-Object}
1 Trace                  {Trace-Command}
1 Uninstall              {Uninstall-WindowsFeature}
1 Switch                 {Switch-Certificate}
1 Compare                {Compare-Object}
1 Repair                 {Repair-WindowsImage}
1 Sort                   {Sort-Object}
1 Reset                  {Reset-ComputerMachinePassword}
1 Confirm                {Confirm-SecureBootUEFI}
1 Read                   {Read-Host}
1 Push                   {Push-Location}
1 Where                  {Where-Object}
1 Limit                  {Limit-EventLog}
1 Initialize             {Initialize-Tpm}
1 Group                  {Group-Object}
1 ForEach                {ForEach-Object}
1 Expand                 {Expand-IscsiVirtualDisk}
1 Exit                   {Exit-PSSession}
1 Enter                  {Enter-PSSession}
1 Debug                  {Debug-Process}
1 Split                  {Split-Path}
1 Pop                    {Pop-Location}
```

A function is not required to accept any parameters. In fact, many functions do not require input to perform their job in the script. Let's use an example to illustrate this point. A common task for network administrators is obtaining the operating system version. Script writers often need to do this to ensure their script uses the correct interface or exits gracefully. It is also quite common that one set of files would be copied to a desktop running one version of the operating system, and a different set of files would be copied for another version of the operating system. The first step in creating a function is to come up with a name. Since the function is going to retrieve information, in the listing of cmdlet verbs shown earlier, the best verb to use is *Get*. For the noun portion of the name, it is best to use something that describes the information that will be obtained. In this example, a noun of *OperatingSystemVersion* makes sense. An example of such a function is shown in the Get-OperatingSystemVersion.ps1 script. The *Get-OperatingSystemVersion* function uses Windows Management Instrumentation (WMI) to obtain the version of the operating system. In this basic form of the function, you have the function keyword followed by the name of the function, and a script block with code in it, which is delimited by curly brackets. This pattern is shown here:

```
Function Function-Name
{
 #insert code here
}
```

In the Get-OperatingSystemVersion.ps1 script, the *Get-OperatingSystemVersion* function is at the top of the script. It uses the *Function* keyword to define the function, followed by the name, *Get-OperatingSystemVersion*. The script block opens, followed by the code, and then the script block closes. The function uses the *Get-WmiObject* cmdlet to retrieve an instance of the *Win32_OperatingSystem* WMI class. Since this WMI class only returns a single instance, the properties of the class are directly accessible. The *version* property is the one you'll work with, so use parentheses to force the evaluation of the code inside. The returned management object is used to emit the version value. The braces are used to close the script block. The operating system version is returned to the code that calls the function. In this example, a string that writes "This OS is Version" is used. A subexpression is used to force evaluation of the function. The version of the operating system is returned to the place where the function was called. This is shown here:

Get-OperatingSystemVersion.ps1

```
Function Get-OperatingSystemVersion
{
 (Get-WmiObject -Class Win32_OperatingSystem).Version
} #end Get-OperatingSystemVersion

"This OS is version $(Get-OperatingSystemVersion)"
```

Now let's look at choosing the cmdlet verb. In the earlier listing of cmdlet verbs, there is one cmdlet that uses the verb *Read*. It is the *Read-Host* cmdlet, which is used to obtain information from the command line. This would indicate that the verb *Read* is not used to describe reading a file. There is no verb called "Display," and the *Write* verb is used in cmdlet names such as *Write-Error* and *Write-Debug*, both of which do not really seem to have the concept of displaying information. If you were writing a function that would read the content of a text file and display statistics about that file, you might call the function *Get-TextStatistics*. This is in keeping with cmdlet names such as *Get-Process* and *Get-Service*, which include the concept of emitting their retrieved content within their essential functionality. The *Get-TextStatistics* function accepts a single parameter called *path*. The interesting thing about parameters for functions is that when you pass a value to the parameter, you use a hyphen. When you refer to the value inside the function, it is a variable such as *$path*. To call the

*Get-TextStatistics* function, you have a couple of options. The first is to use the name of the function and put the value inside parentheses. This is shown here:

```
Get-TextStatistics("C:\fso\mytext.txt")
```

This is a natural way to call the function, and it works when there is a single parameter. It does not work when there are two or more parameters. Another way to pass a value to the function is to use the hyphen and the parameter name. This is shown here:

```
Get-TextStatistics -path "C:\fso\mytext.txt"
```

Note from the previous example that no parentheses are required. You can also use positional arguments when passing a value. In this usage, you omit the name of the parameter entirely and simply place the value for the parameter following the call to the function. This is illustrated here:

```
Get-TextStatistics "C:\fso\mytext.txt"
```

> **Note** The use of positional arguments works well when you are working from the command line and want to speed things along by reducing the typing load. However, it can be a bit confusing to rely on positional arguments, and in general I tend to avoid it—even when working at the command line. This is because I often copy my working code from the console directly into a script, and as a result, would need to retype the command a second time to get rid of aliases and unnamed arguments. With the improvements in tab expansion, I feel that the time saved by using positional arguments or partial arguments does not sufficiently warrant the time involved in retyping commands when they need to be transferred to scripts. The other reason for always using named arguments is that it helps you to be aware of the exact command syntax.

One additional way to pass a value to a function is to use partial parameter names. All that is required is enough of the parameter name to disambiguate it from other parameters. This is illustrated here:

```
Get-TextStatistics -p "C:\fso\mytext.txt"
```

The complete text of the *Get-TextStatistics* function is shown here:

**Get-TextStatistics Function**

```
Function Get-TextStatistics($path)
{
 Get-Content -path $path |
 Measure-Object -line -character -word
}
```

Between PowerShell 1.0 and PowerShell 2.0, the number of verbs grew from 40 to 60. In Windows PowerShell 3.0, the number of verbs grew from 60 to 98. The list of approved verbs appears here:

| | | | | | | |
|---|---|---|---|---|---|---|
| Add | Clear | Close | Copy | Enter | Exit | Find |
| Format | Get | Hide | Join | Lock | Move | New |
| Open | Optimize | Pop | Push | Redo | Remove | Rename |
| Reset | Resize | Search | Select | Set | Show | Skip |
| Split | Step | Switch | Undo | Unlock | Watch | Backup |
| Checkpoint | Compare | Compress | Convert | ConvertFrom | ConvertTo | Dismount |
| Edit | Expand | Export | Group | Import | Initialize | Limit |
| Merge | Mount | Out | Publish | Restore | Save | Sync |
| Unpublish | Update | Approve | Assert | Complete | Confirm | Deny |
| Disable | Enable | Install | Invoke | Register | Request | Restart |
| Resume | Start | Stop | Submit | Suspend | Uninstall | Unregister |
| Wait | Debug | Measure | Ping | Repair | Resolve | Test |
| Trace | Connect | Disconnect | Read | Receive | Send | Write |
| Block | Grant | Protect | Revoke | Unblock | Unprotect | Use |

Once the function has been named, you should specify any parameters the function may require. The parameters are contained within parentheses. In the *Get-TextStatistics* function, the function accepts a single parameter: *-path*. When you have a function that accepts a single parameter, you can pass the value to the function by placing the value for the parameter inside parentheses. This is known as calling a function like a method, and is disallowed when you use *Set-StrictMode* with the *-latest* switch. The following command generates an error when the latest strict mode is in effect—otherwise, it is a permissible way to call a function.

```
Get-TextLength("C:\fso\test.txt")
```

The path C:\fso\test.txt is passed to the *Get-TextStatistics* function via the *-path* parameter. Inside the function, the string C:\fso\text.txt is contained in the *$path* variable. The *$path* variable only lives within the confines of the *Get-TextStatistics* function. It is not available outside the scope of the function. It is available from within child scopes of the *Get-TextStatistics* function. A *child scope* of *Get-TextStatistics* is one that is created from within the *Get-TextStatistics* function. In the Get-TextStatisticsCallChildFunction.ps1 script, the *Write-Path* function is called from within the *Get-TextStatistics* function. This means the *Write-Path* function will have access to variables that are created within the *Get-TextStatistics* function. This is the concept of *variable scope*, which is extremely important when working with functions. As you use functions to separate the creation of objects, you must always be aware of where the objects get created, and where you intend to use them. In the *Get-TextStatisticsCallChildFunction*, the *$path* variable does not obtain its value until it is passed to the function. It therefore lives within the *Get-TextStatistics* function. But since the *Write-Path* function is called from within the *Get-TextStatistics* function, it inherits the variables from that scope. When you call a function from within another function, variables created within the parent function are available to the child function. This is shown in the Get-TextStatisticsCallChildFunction.ps1 script, which follows:

**Get-TextStatisticsCallChildFunction.ps1**

```
Function Get-TextStatistics($path)
{
 Get-Content -path $path |
 Measure-Object -line -character -word
 Write-Path
}
```

```
Function Write-Path()
{
 "Inside Write-Path the `$path variable is equal to $path"
}

Get-TextStatistics("C:\fso\test.txt")
"Outside the Get-TextStatistics function `$path is equal to $path"
```

Inside the *Get-TextStatistics* function, the *$path* variable is used to provide the path to the *Get-Content* cmdlet. When the *Write-Path* function is called, nothing is passed to it. But inside the *Write-Path* function, the value of *$path* is maintained. Outside both of the functions, however, *$path* does not have any value. The output from running the script is shown here:

```
          Lines               Words          Characters Property
          -----               -----          ---------- --------
            3                   41               210
Inside Write-Path the $path variable is equal to C:\fso\test.txt
Outside the Get-TextStatistics function $path is equal to
```

You will then need to open and to close a script block. A pair of opening and closing braces is used to delimit the script block on a function. As a best practice, when writing a function, I will always use the *Function* keyword, and type in the name, the input parameters, and the curly brackets for the script block at the same time. This is shown here:

```
Function My-Function

{
 #insert code here
}
```

In this manner, I do not forget to close the curly brackets. Trying to identify a missing curly bracket within a long script can be somewhat problematic, as the error that is presented does not always correspond to the line that is missing the curly bracket. For example, suppose the closing curly bracket is left off of the *Get-TextStatistics* function, as shown in the Get-TextStatisticsCallChildFunction-DoesNOTWork-MissingClosingBracket.ps1 script. An error will be generated, as shown here:

```
Missing closing '}' in statement block.
At C:\Scripts\Get-TextStatisticsCallChildFunction-DoesNOTWork-MissingClosingBracket.ps1:28
char:1
```

The problem is that the position indicator of the error message points to the first character on line 28. Line 28 happens to be the first blank line after the end of the script. This means that Windows PowerShell scanned the entire script looking for the closing curly bracket. Since it did not find it, it states that the error is the end of the script. If you were to place a closing curly bracket on line 28, the error in this example would go away, but the script would not work either. The Get-TextStatisticsCallChildFunction-DoesNOTWork-MissingClosingBracket.ps1 script is shown here, with a comment that indicates where the missing closing curly bracket should be placed:

```
Get-TextStatisticsCallChildFunction-DoesNOTWork-MissingClosingBracket.ps1
Function Get-TextStatistics($path)
{
 Get-Content -path $path |
 Measure-Object -line -character -word
 Write-Path
# Here is where the missing bracket goes

Function Write-Path()
{
 "Inside Write-Path the `$path variable is equal to $path"
}
Get-TextStatistics("C:\fso\test.txt")
Write-Host "Outside the Get-TextStatistics function `$path is equal to $path"
```

One other technique to guard against the problem of the missing curly bracket is to add a comment to the closing curly bracket of each function.

# Using functions to provide ease of code reuse

When scripts are written using well-designed functions, it makes it easier to reuse them in other scripts, and to provide access to these functions from within the Windows PowerShell console. To get access to these functions, you will need to *dot-source* the containing script by placing a dot in front of the path to the script when you call it, and put the functions in a module or load them via the profile. An issue with dot-sourcing scripts to bring in functions is that often the scripts may contain global variables or other items you do not want to bring into your current environment.

An example of a useful function is the ConvertToMeters.ps1 script because it converts feet to meters. There are no variables defined outside the function, and the function itself does not use the *Write-Host* cmdlet to break up the pipeline. The results of the conversion will be returned directly to the calling code. The only problem with the ConvertToMeters.ps1 script is that when it is dot-sourced into the Windows PowerShell console, it runs, and returns the data because all executable code in the script is executed. The ConvertToMeters.ps1 script is shown here:

ConvertToMeters.ps1

```
Function Script:ConvertToMeters($feet)
{
   "$feet feet equals $($feet*.31) meters"
} #end ConvertToMeters
$feet = 5
ConvertToMeters -Feet $feet
```

With well-written functions, it is trivial to collect them into a single script—you just cut and paste. When you are done, you have created a function library.

When pasting your functions into the function library script, pay attention to the comments at the end of the function. The comments at the closing curly bracket for each function not only point to the end of the script block, but also provide a nice visual indicator for the end of each function. This can be helpful when you need to troubleshoot a script. An example of such a function library is the ConversionFunctions.ps1 script, which is shown here:

**ConversionFunctions.ps1**

```
Function Script:ConvertToMeters($feet)
{
  "$feet feet equals $($feet*.31) meters"
} #end ConvertToMeters

Function Script:ConvertToFeet($meters)
{
 "$meters meters equals $($meters * 3.28) feet"
} #end ConvertToFeet

Function Script:ConvertToFahrenheit($celsius)
{
 "$celsius celsius equals $((1.8 * $celsius) + 32 ) fahrenheit"
} #end ConvertToFahrenheit

Function Script:ConvertTocelsius($fahrenheit)
{
 "$fahrenheit fahrenheit equals $( (($fahrenheit - 32)/9)*5 ) celsius"
} #end ConvertTocelsius

Function Script:ConvertToMiles($kilometer)
{
  "$kilometer kilometers equals $( ($kilometer *.6211) ) miles"
} #end convertToMiles

Function Script:ConvertToKilometers($miles)
{
  "$miles miles equals $( ($miles * 1.61) ) kilometers"
} #end convertToKilometers
```

One way to use the functions from the ConversionFunctions.ps1 script is to use the dot-sourcing operator to run the script so that the functions from the script are part of the calling scope. To dot-source the script, you use the dot-source operator (the period, or dot symbol), followed by a space, followed by the path to the script containing the functions you wish to include in your current scope. Once you do this, you can call the function directly, as shown here:

```
PS C:\> . C:\scripts\ConversionFunctions.ps1
PS C:\> convertToMiles 6
6 kilometers equals 3.7266 miles
```

All of the functions from the dot-sourced script are available to the current session. This can be demonstrated by creating a listing of the function drive, as shown here:

```
PS C:\> dir function: | Where { $_.name -like 'co*'} |
Format-Table -Property name, definition -AutoSize

Name              Definition
----              ----------
ConvertToMeters   param($feet) "$feet feet equals $($feet*.31) meters"...
ConvertToFeet     param($meters) "$meters meters equals $($meters * 3.28) feet"...
ConvertToFahrenheit param($celsius) "$celsius celsius equals $((1.8 * $celsius) + 32 )
fahrenheit"...
ConvertTocelsius  param($fahrenheit) "$fahrenheit fahrenheit equals $( (($fahrenheit -
32)/9)*5 ) celsius...
ConvertToMiles    param($kilometer) "$kilometer kilometers equals $( ($kilometer *.6211) )
miles"...
ConvertToKilometers param($miles) "$miles miles equals $( ($miles * 1.61) ) kilometers"...
```

# Including functions in the Windows PowerShell environment

In PowerShell 1.0, you could include functions from previously written scripts by dot-sourcing the script. The use of a module offers greater flexibility than dot-sourcing due to the ability to create a *module manifest*, which specifies exactly which functions and programming elements will be imported into the current session.

## Using dot-sourcing

This technique of dot-sourcing still works in Windows PowerShell 3.0, and it offers the advantage of simplicity and familiarity. In the TextFunctions.ps1 script shown following, two functions are created. The first function is called *New-Line*, and the second is called *Get-TextStats*. The TextFunctions.ps1 script is shown here:

**TextFunctions.ps1**

```
Function New-Line([string]$stringIn)
{
 "-" * $stringIn.length
} #end New-Line

Function Get-TextStats([string[]]$textIn)
{
 $textIn | Measure-Object -Line -word -char
} #end Get-TextStats
```

The *New-Line* function will create a string of hyphen characters as long as the length of the input text. This is helpful when you want an underline for text separation purposes that is sized to the text. Traditional VBScript users copy the function they need to use into a separate file and run the newly produced script. An example of using the *New-Line* text function in this manner is shown here:

**CallNew-LineTextFunction.ps1**

```
Function New-Line([string]$stringIn)
{
 "-" * $stringIn.length
} #end New-Line

Function Get-TextStats([string[]]$textIn)
{
 $textIn | Measure-Object -Line -word -char
} #end Get-TextStats

# *** Entry Point to script ***
"This is a string" | ForEach-Object  {$_ ; New-Line $_}
```

When the script runs, it returns the following output:

```
This is a string

----------------
```

Of course, this is a bit inefficient and limits your ability to use the functions. If you have to copy the entire text of a function into each new script you wish to produce, or edit a script each time you wish to use a function in a different manner, you dramatically increase your workload. If the functions were available all the time, you might be inclined to utilize them more often. To make the text functions available in your current Windows PowerShell console, you need to dot-source the script containing the functions into your console, put it in a module, or load it via your profile. You will need to use the entire path to the script unless the folder that contains the script is in your search path. The syntax to dot-source a script is so easy that it actually becomes a stumbling block for some people who are expecting some complex formula or cmdlet with obscure parameters. It is none of that—just a period (dot), followed by a space, followed by the path to the script that contains the function. This is why it is called dot-sourcing: you have a dot and the source (path) to the functions you wish to include. This is shown here:

```
PS C:\> . C:\fso\TextFunctions.ps1
```

Once you have included the functions in your current console, all the functions in the source script are added to the Function drive. This is shown in Figure 6-1.

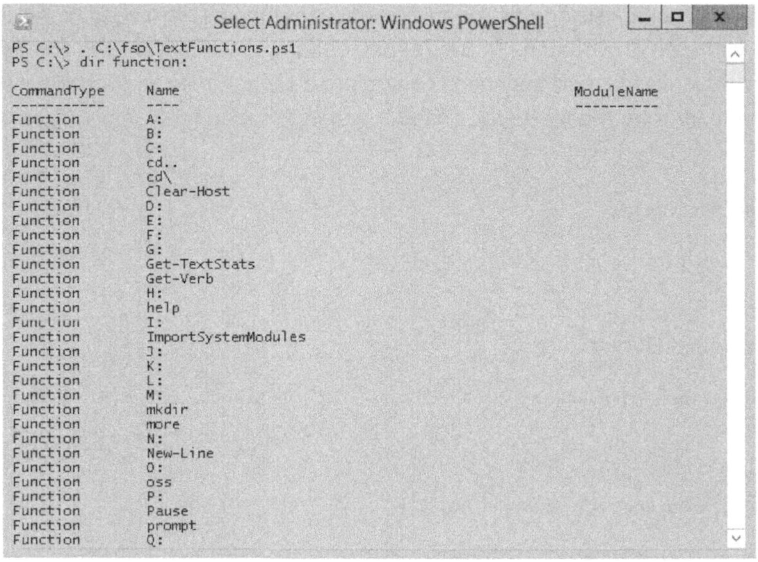

**FIGURE 6-1** Functions from a dot-sourced script are available via the Function drive.

## Using dot-sourced functions

Once the functions have been introduced to the current console, you can incorporate them into your normal commands. This flexibility should also influence the way you write the function. If the functions are written so they will accept pipelined input and do not change the system environment, by adding global variables, for example, you will be much more likely to use the functions, and they will be less likely to conflict with either functions or cmdlets that are present in the current console.

As an example of using the *New-Line* function, consider the fact that the *Get-CimInstance* cmdlet allows the use of an array of computer names for the *-computername* parameter. In this example, BIOS information is obtained from two separate workstations. This is shown here:

```
PS C:\> Get-CimInstance win32_bios -ComputerName w8server8, w8client8

SMBIOSBIOSVersion : 090004
Manufacturer      : American Megatrends Inc.
Name              : BIOS Date: 03/19/09 22:51:32  Ver: 09.00.04
SerialNumber      : 6516-4289-5671-5458-4791-0966-09
Version           : VRTUAL - 3000919
PSComputerName    : w8server8

SMBIOSBIOSVersion : 090004
Manufacturer      : American Megatrends Inc.
Name              : BIOS Date: 03/19/09 22:51:32  Ver: 09.00.04
SerialNumber      : 9454-6382-0248-8429-3463-9488-79
Version           : VRTUAL - 3000919
PSComputerName    : w8client8
```

You can improve the display of the information returned by the *Get-CimInstance* by pipelining the output to the *New-Line* function so that you can underline each computer name as it comes across the pipeline. You do not need to write a script to produce this kind of display. You can type the command directly into the Windows PowerShell console. The first thing you need to do is to dot-source the TextFunctions.ps1 script. This makes the functions directly available in the current Windows PowerShell console session. You then use the same *Get-CimInstance* query you used earlier to obtain BIOS information via WMI from two computers. Pipeline the resulting management objects to the *ForEach-Object* cmdlet. Inside the script block section, you use the *$_* automatic variable to reference the current object on the pipeline and retrieve the *pscomputername* property. You send this information to the *New-Line* function so the server name is underlined, and you display the BIOS information that is contained in the *$_* variable.

The command to import the *New-Line* function into the current Windows PowerShell session and use it to underline the server names is shown here:

```
Get-CimInstance win32_bios -ComputerName w8server8, w8client8 |
ForEach-Object { $_.pscomputername ; New-Line $_.pscomputername ; $_ }
```

The results of using the *New-Line* function are shown in Figure 6-2.

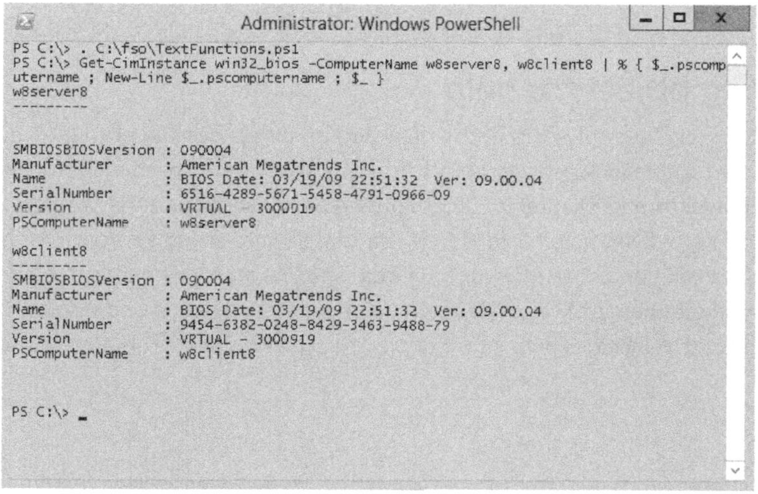

**FIGURE 6-2** Functions that are written to accept pipelined input find an immediate use in your daily work routine.

The *Get-TextStats* function from the TextFunctions.ps1 script provides statistics based upon an input text file or text string. Once the TextFunctions.ps1 script is dot-sourced into the current console, the statistics it returns when the function is called are word count, number of lines in the file, and number of characters. An example of using this function is shown here:

```
Get-TextStats "This is a string"
```

When the *Get-TextStats* function is used, the following output is produced:

```
   Lines              Words          Characters Property
   -----              -----          ---------- --------
       1                  4                  16
```

In this section, the use of functions was discussed. The reuse of functions could be as simple as copying the text of the function from one script into another script. It is easier, however, to dot-source the function than to reuse it. This can be done from within the Windows PowerShell console or from within a script.

# Adding help for functions

When you dot-source functions into the current Windows PowerShell console, one problem is introduced. Because you are not required to open the file that contains the function to use it, you may be unaware of everything the file contains within it. In addition to functions, the file could contain variables, aliases, PowerShell drives, or any number of other things. Depending on what you are actually trying to accomplish, this may or may not be an issue. The need sometimes arises, however, to have access to help information about the features provided by the Windows PowerShell script.

## Using a *here-string* object for help

In Windows PowerShell 1.0, you could solve this problem by adding a *help* parameter to the function and storing the help text within a *here-string* object. You can use this approach in Windows PowerShell 3.0 as well, but as shown in Chapter 7, "Creating Advanced Functions and Modules," there is a better approach to providing help for functions. The classic *here-string* approach for help is shown in the GetWmiClassesFunction.ps1 script, which follows. The first step that needs to be done is to define a switched parameter named *$help*. The second step involves creating and displaying the results of a *here-string* object that includes help information. The GetWmiClassesFunction.ps1 script is shown here:

```
# GetWmiClassesFunction.ps1
Function Get-WmiClasses(
                $class=($paramMissing=$true),
                $ns="root\cimv2",
                [switch]$help
               )
{
  If($help)
   {
    $helpstring = @"
    NAME
      Get-WmiClasses
    SYNOPSIS
      Displays a list of WMI Classes based upon a search criteria
```

```
  SYNTAX
   Get-WmiClasses [[-class] [string]] [[-ns] [string]] [-help]
  EXAMPLE
   Get-WmiClasses -class disk -ns root\cimv2"
   This command finds wmi classes that contain the word disk. The
   classes returned are from the root\cimv2 namespace.
"@
  $helpString
   break #exits the function early
 }
 If($local:paramMissing)
  {
    throw "USAGE: getwmi2 -class <class type> -ns <wmi namespace>"
  } #$local:paramMissing
"`nClasses in $ns namespace ...."
Get-WmiObject -namespace $ns -list |
Where-Object {
              $_.name -match $class -and `
              $_.name -notlike 'cim*'
           }
 #
} #end get-wmiclasses
```

The *here-string* technique works pretty well for providing function help if you follow the cmdlet help pattern. This is shown in Figure 6-3.

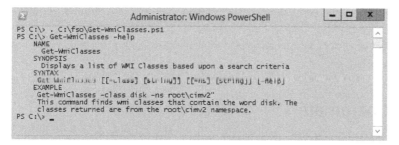

**FIGURE 6-3** Manually created help can mimic the look of core cmdlet help.

The drawback with manually creating help for a function is that it is tedious, and as a result, only the most important functions receive help information when you use this methodology. This is unfortunate, as it then requires the user to memorize the details of the function contract. One way to work around this is to use the *Get-Content* cmdlet to retrieve the code that was used to create the function. This is much easier to do than searching for the script that was used to create the function and opening it up in Notepad. To use the *Get-Content* cmdlet to display the contents of a function, you type *Get-Content* and supply the path to the function. All functions available to the current Windows PowerShell environment are available via the Function PowerShell drive. You can therefore use the following syntax to obtain the content of a function:

```
PowerShell C:\> Get-Content Function:\Get-WmiClasses
```

The technique of using *Get-Content* to read the text of the function is shown in Figure 6-4.

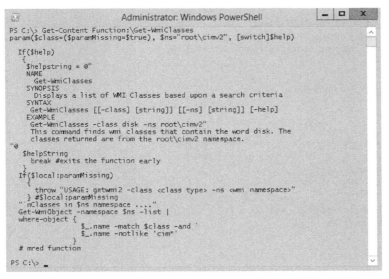

**FIGURE 6-4** The *Get-Content* cmdlet can retrieve the contents of a function.

An easier way to add help, by using comment-based help, is discussed in Chapter 7. Comment-based help, although more complex than the method discussed here, offers a number of advantages—primarily due to the integration with the Windows PowerShell help subsystem. When you add comment-based help, users of your function can access your help in exactly the same manner as any of the core Windows PowerShell cmdlets.

## Using two input parameters

To create a function that uses multiple input parameters, you use the *Function* keyword, specify the name of the function, use variables for each input parameter, and then define the script block within the curly brackets. The pattern is shown here:

```
Function My-Function($Input1,$Input2)
{
 #Insert Code Here
}
```

An example of a function that takes multiple parameters is the *Get-FreeDiskSpace* function, which is shown in the Get-FreeDiskSpace.ps1 script from the "Obtaining specific WMI data" section sidebar, which follows.

The Get-FreeDiskSpace.ps1 script begins with the *Function* keyword and is followed by the name of the function and the two input parameters. The input parameters are placed inside parentheses, as shown here:

```
Function Get-FreeDiskSpace($drive,$computer)
```

Inside the function's script block, the *Get-FreeDiskSpace* function uses the *Get-WmiObject* cmdlet to query the *Win32_LogicalDisk* WMI class. It connects to the computer specified in the *$computer* parameter, and it filters out only the drive that is specified in the *$drive* parameter. When the function is called, each parameter is specified as *-drive* and *-computer*. In the function definition, the variables *$drive* and *$computer* are used to hold the values supplied to the parameters.

Once the data from WMI is retrieved, it is stored in the *$driveData* variable. The data that is stored in the *$driveData* variable is an instance of the *Win32_LogicalDisk* class. This variable contains a complete instance of the class. The members of this class are shown in Table 6-1.

**TABLE 6-1** Members of the *Win32_LogicalDisk* class

| Name | Member type | Definition |
| --- | --- | --- |
| Chkdsk | Method | System.Management.ManagementBaseObject Chkdsk(System.Boolean FixErrors, System. Boolean VigorousIndexCheck, System.Boolean SkipFolderCycle, System.Boolean ForceDismount, System.Boolean RecoverBadSectors, System.Boolean OkToRunAtBootUp) |
| Reset | Method | System.Management.ManagementBaseObject Reset() |
| SetPowerState | Method | System.Management.ManagementBaseObject SetPowerState(System.UInt16 PowerState, System. String Time) |
| Access | Property | System.UInt16 Access {get;set;} |
| Availability | Property | System.UInt16 Availability {get;set;} |
| BlockSize | Property | System.UInt64 BlockSize {get;set;} |
| Caption | Property | System.String Caption {get;set;} |
| Compressed | Property | System.Boolean Compressed {get;set;} |
| ConfigManagerErrorCode | Property | System.UInt32 ConfigManagerErrorCode {get;set;} |
| ConfigManagerUserConfig | Property | System.Boolean ConfigManagerUserConfig {get;set;} |
| CreationClassName | Property | System.String CreationClassName {get;set;} |
| Description | Property | System.String Description {get;set;} |
| DeviceID | Property | System.String DeviceID {get;set;} |
| DriveType | Property | System.UInt32 DriveType {get;set;} |
| ErrorCleared | Property | System.Boolean ErrorCleared {get;set;} |
| ErrorDescription | Property | System.String ErrorDescription {get;set;} |
| ErrorMethodology | Property | System.String ErrorMethodology {get;set;} |
| FileSystem | Property | System.String FileSystem {get;set;} |
| FreeSpace | Property | System.UInt64 FreeSpace {get;set;} |
| InstallDate | Property | System.String InstallDate {get;set;} |
| LastErrorCode | Property | System.UInt32 LastErrorCode {get;set;} |
| MaximumComponentLength | Property | System.UInt32 MaximumComponentLength {get;set;} |
| MediaType | Property | System.UInt32 MediaType {get;set;} |
| Name | Property | System.String Name {get;set;} |

| Name | Member type | Definition |
|------|-------------|------------|
| NumberOfBlocks | Property | System.UInt64 NumberOfBlocks {get;set;} |
| PNPDeviceID | Property | System.String PNPDeviceID {get;set;} |
| PowerManagementCapabilities | Property | System.UInt16[] PowerManagementCapabilities {get;set;} |
| PowerManagementSupported | Property | System.Boolean PowerManagementSupported {get;set;} |
| ProviderName | Property | System.String ProviderName {get;set;} |
| Purpose | Property | System.String Purpose {get;set;} |
| QuotasDisabled | Property | System.Boolean QuotasDisabled {get;set;} |
| QuotasIncomplete | Property | System.Boolean QuotasIncomplete {get;set;} |
| QuotasRebuilding | Property | System.Boolean QuotasRebuilding {get;set;} |
| Size | Property | System.UInt64 Size {get;set;} |
| Status | Property | System.String Status {get;set;} |
| StatusInfo | Property | System.UInt16 StatusInfo {get;set;} |
| SupportsDiskQuotas | Property | System.Boolean SupportsDiskQuotas {get;set;} |
| SupportsFileBasedCompression | Property | System.Boolean SupportsFileBasedCompression {get;set;} |
| SystemCreationClassName | Property | System.String SystemCreationClassName {get;set;} |
| SystemName | Property | System.String SystemName {get;set;} |
| VolumeDirty | Property | System.Boolean VolumeDirty {get;set;} |
| VolumeName | Property | System.String VolumeName {get;set;} |
| VolumeSerialNumber | Property | System.String VolumeSerialNumber {get;set;} |
| __CLASS | Property | System.String __CLASS {get;set;} |
| __DERIVATION | Property | System.String[] __DERIVATION {get;set;} |
| __DYNASTY | Property | System.String __DYNASTY {get;set;} |
| __GENUS | Property | System.Int32 __GENUS {get;set;} |
| __NAMESPACE | Property | System.String __NAMESPACE {get;set;} |
| __PATH | Property | System.String __PATH {get;set;} |
| __PROPERTY_COUNT | Property | System.Int32 __PROPERTY_COUNT {get;set;} |
| __RELPATH | Property | System.String __RELPATH {get;set;} |
| __SERVER | Property | System.String __SERVER {get;set;} |
| __SUPERCLASS | Property | System.String __SUPERCLASS {get;set;} |
| PSStatus | Property set | PSStatus {Status, Availability, DeviceID, StatusInfo} |
| ConvertFromDateTime | Script method | System.Object ConvertFromDateTime(); |
| ConvertToDateTime | Script method | System.Object ConvertToDateTime(); |

## Obtaining specific WMI data

While storing the complete instance of the object in the *$driveData* variable is a bit inefficient due to the amount of data it contains, in reality the class is rather small, and the ease of using the *Get-WmiObject* cmdlet is usually worth the wasteful methodology. If performance is a primary consideration, the use of the *[wmi]* type accelerator would be a better solution. To obtain the free disk space using this method, you would use the following syntax:

```
([wmi]"Win32_logicalDisk.DeviceID='c:'").FreeSpace
```

To put the preceding command into a usable function, you would need to substitute the hard-coded drive letter for a variable. In addition, you would want to modify the class constructor to receive a path to a remote computer as well. The newly created function is contained in the Get-DiskSpace.ps1 script, shown here:

```
# Get-DiskSpace.ps1
Function Get-DiskSpace($drive,$computer)
{
  ([wmi]"\\$computer\root\cimv2:Win32_logicalDisk.DeviceID='$drive'").FreeSpace
}
Get-DiskSpace -drive "C:" -computer "Office"
```

Once you have made the preceding changes, the code only returns the value of the *FreeSpace* property from the specific drive. If you were to send the output to *Get-Member,* you would see you have an integer. This technique is more efficient than storing an entire instance of the *WIN32_LogicalDisk* class and then selecting a single value.

Once you have the data stored in the *$driveData* variable, you will want to print out some information to the user of the script. The first thing to do is print out the name of the computer and the name of the drive. To do this, you can place the variables inside double quotation marks. Double quotes are expanding strings, and variables placed inside double quotes emit their value, not their name. This is shown here:

```
"$computer free disk space on drive $drive"
```

The next thing you will want to do is to format the data that is returned. To do this, use the .NET Framework format strings to specify two decimal places. You will need to use a subexpression to prevent unraveling of the WMI object inside the expanding-string double quotation marks. The subexpression uses the dollar sign and a pair of parentheses to force the evaluation of the expression before returning the data to the string. This is shown here:

Get-FreeDiskSpace.ps1

```
Function Get-FreeDiskSpace($drive,$computer)
{
 $driveData = Get-WmiObject -class win32_LogicalDisk `
 -computername $computer -filter "Name = '$drive'"
```

```
"
$computer free disk space on drive $drive
    $("{0:n2}" -f ($driveData.FreeSpace/1MB)) MegaBytes
"
}

Get-FreeDiskSpace -drive "C:" -computer "w8client1"
```

## Using a type constraint in a function

When accepting parameters for a function, it may be important to use a type constraint to ensure the function receives the correct type of data. To do this, you place the desired type name inside square brackets in front of the input parameter. This constrains the data type and prevents the entry of an incorrect type of data. Allowable type accelerators appear in Table 6-2.

**TABLE 6-2**   Data type aliases

| Alias | Type |
| --- | --- |
| *[int]* | 32-bit signed integer |
| *[long]* | 64-bit signed integer |
| *[string]* | Fixed-length string of Unicode characters |
| *[char]* | Unicode 16-bit character |
| *[bool]* | True/false value |
| *[byte]* | 8-bit unsigned integer |
| *[double]* | Double-precision 64-bit floating-point number |
| *[decimal]* | 128-bit decimal value |
| *[single]* | Single-precision 32-bit floating-point number |
| *[array]* | Array of values |
| *[xml]* | XML object |
| *[hashtable]* | Hashtable object (similar to a dictionary object) |

In the *Resolve-ZipCode* function, which is shown in the following Resolve-ZipCode.ps1 script, the *$zip* input parameter is constrained to only allow a 32-bit signed integer for input. (Obviously, the *[int]* type constraint would eliminate most of the world's postal codes, but the web service the script uses only resolves US-based postal codes, so it is a good addition to the function.)

In the *Resolve-ZipCode* function, the first thing that is done is to use a string that points to the WSDL (Web Services Description Language) for the web service. Next, the *New-WebServiceProxy* cmdlet is used to create a new web service proxy for the ZipCode service. The WSDL for the ZipCode service defines a method called the *GetInfoByZip* method. It will accept a standard U.S.-based postal code. The results are displayed as a table. The Resolve-ZipCode.ps1 script is shown here:

**Resolve-ZipCode.ps1**

```
#Requires -Version 2.0
Function Resolve-ZipCode([int]$zip)
{
 $URI = "http://www.webservicex.net/uszip.asmx?WSDL"
 $zipProxy = New-WebServiceProxy -uri $URI -namespace WebServiceProxy -class ZipClass
 $zipProxy.getinfobyzip($zip).table
} #end Get-ZipCode
```

```
Resolve-ZipCode 28273
```

When using a type constraint on an input parameter, any deviation from the expected data type will generate an error similar to the one shown here:

```
Resolve-ZipCode : Cannot process argument transformation on parameter 'zip'. Cannot convert
value "COW" to type "System
.Int32". Error: "Input string was not in a correct format."
At C:\Users\edwils.NORTHAMERICA\AppData\Local\Temp\tmp3351.tmp.ps1:22 char:16
+ Resolve-ZipCode <<<< "COW"
    + CategoryInfo          : InvalidData: (:) [Resolve-ZipCode], ParameterBindin...
mationException
    + FullyQualifiedErrorId : ParameterArgumentTransformationError,Resolve-ZipCode
```

Needless to say, such an error could be distracting to the users of the function. One way to handle the problem of confusing error messages is to use the *Trap* keyword. In the DemoTrapSystemException.ps1 script, the My-Test function uses *[int]* to constrain the *$myinput* variable to only accept a 32-bit unsigned integer for input. If such an integer is received by the function when it is called, the function will return the string *It worked*. If the function receives a string for input, an error will be raised, similar to the one shown previously.

Rather than display a raw error message, which most users and many IT professionals find confusing, it is a best practice to suppress the display of the error message, and perhaps inform the user an error condition has occurred and provide more meaningful and direct information that the user can then relay to the help desk. Many times, IT departments will display such an error message, complete with either a local telephone number for the appropriate help desk, or even a link to an internal web page that provides detailed troubleshooting and corrective steps the user can perform. You could even provide a web page that hosted a script that the user could run to fix the problem. This is similar to the "Fix it for me" web pages Microsoft introduced.

When creating an instance of a *System.SystemException* class (when a system exception occurs), the *Trap* statement will trap the error, rather than allowing it to display the error information on the screen. If you were to query the *$error* variable, you would see that the error had in fact occurred and was actually received by the error record. You would also have access to the *ErrorRecord* class via the *$_* automatic variable, which means the error record has been passed along the pipeline. This gives you the ability to build a rich error-handling solution. In this example, the string *error trapped* is displayed, and the *Continue* statement is used to continue the script execution on the next line of code. In this example, the next line of code that is executed is the *After the error* string. When the DemoTrapSystemException.ps1 script is run, the following output is shown:

```
error trapped
After the error
```

The complete DemoTrapSystemException.ps1 script is shown here:

**DemoTrapSystemException.ps1**

```
Function My-Test([int]$myinput)
{

 "It worked"
} #End my-test function
# *** Entry Point to Script ***

Trap [SystemException] { "error trapped" ; continue }
My-Test -myinput "string"
"After the error"
```

# Using more than two input parameters

When using more than two input parameters, I consider it a best practice to modify the way the function is structured. This not only makes the function easier to read, but it also permits cmdlet binding. In the basic function pattern shown here, the function accepts three input parameters. When considering the default values and the type constraints, the parameters begin to become long. Moving them to the inside of the function body highlights the fact that they are input parameters, and it makes them easier to read, understand, and maintain. It also permits decorating the parameters with attributes.

```
Function Function-Name
{
  Param(
        [int]$Parameter1,
        [String]$Parameter2 = "DefaultValue",
        $Parameter3
        )
#Function code goes here
} #end Function-Name
```

An example of a function that uses three input parameters is the *Get-DirectoryListing* function. With the type constraints, default values, and parameter names, the function signature would be rather cumbersome to include on a single line. This is shown here:

```
Function Get-DirectoryListing (String]$Path,[String]$Extension = "txt",[Switch]$Today)
```

If the number of parameters were increased to four, or if a default value for the *-path* parameter were desired, the signature would easily scroll to two lines. The use of the *Param* statement inside the function body also provides the ability to specify input parameters to a function.

**Note** The use of the *Param* statement inside the function body is often regarded as a personal preference. It requires additional work, and often leaves the reader of the script wondering why this was done. When there are more than two parameters, visually the *Param* statement stands out, and it is obvious why it was done in this particular manner. But, as will be shown in Chapter 7, using the *Param* statement is the only way to gain access to advanced function features such as cmdlet binding, parameter attributes, and other powerful features of Windows PowerShell.

Following the *Function* keyword, the name of the function, and the opening script block, the *Param* keyword is used to identify the parameters for the function. Each parameter must be separated by a comma. All the parameters must be surrounded with a set of parentheses. If you want to assign a default value for a parameter, such as the extension .txt for the *Extension* parameter in the *Get-DirectoryListing* function, you perform a straight value assignment followed by a comma.

In the *Get-DirectoryListing* function, the *Today* parameter is a switched parameter. When it is supplied to the function, only files written to since midnight on the day the script is run will be displayed. If it is not supplied, all files matching the extension in the folder will be displayed. The Get-DirectoryListingToday.ps1 script is shown here:

**Get-DirectoryListingToday.ps1**

```
Function Get-DirectoryListing
{
 Param(
        [String]$Path,
        [String]$Extension = "txt",
        [Switch]$Today
        )
 If($Today)
    {
     Get-ChildItem -Path $path\* -include *.$Extension |
     Where-Object { $_.LastWriteTime -ge (Get-Date).Date }
    }
 ELSE
   {
     Get-ChildItem -Path $path\* -include *.$Extension
   }
} #end Get-DirectoryListing

# *** Entry to script ***
Get-DirectoryListing -p c:\fso -t
```

> **Note** As a best practice, you should avoid creating functions that have a large number of input parameters. It is very confusing. When you find yourself creating a large number of input parameters, you should ask if there is a better way to do things. It may be an indicator that you do not have a single-purpose function. In the *Get-DirectoryListing* function, I have a switched parameter that will filter the files returned by the ones written to today. If I were writing the script for production use, instead of just to demonstrate multiple function parameters, I would have created another function called something like *Get-FilesByDate.* In that function, I would have a *Today* switch, and a *Date* parameter to allow a selectable date for the filter. This separates the data-gathering function from the filter/presentation function. See the "Use of functions to provide ease of modification" section later in the chapter for more discussion of this technique.

## Use of functions to encapsulate business logic

There are two kinds of logic with which scriptwriters need to be concerned. The first is program logic, and the second is business logic. *Program logic* includes the way the script works, the order in which things need to be done, and the requirements of code used in the script. An example of program logic is the requirement to open a connection to a database before querying the database.

*Business logic* is something that is a requirement of the business, but not necessarily a requirement of the program or script. The script can often operate just fine regardless of the particulars of the business rule. If the script is designed properly, it should operate perfectly fine no matter what gets supplied for the business rules.

In the BusinessLogicDemo.ps1 script, a function called *Get-Discount* is used to calculate the discount to be granted to the total amount. One good thing about encapsulating the business rules for the discount into a function is that as long as the contract between the function and the calling code does not change, you can drop any kind of convoluted discount schedule into the script block of the *Get-Discount* function that the business decides to come up with—including database calls to determine on-hand inventory, time of day, day of week, total sales volume for the month, the buyer's loyalty level, and the square root of some random number that is used to determine instant discount rate.

So, what is the contract with the function? The contract with the *Get-Discount* function says, "If you give me a rate number as a type of *system.double* and a total as an integer, I will return to you a number that represents the total discount to be applied to the sale." As long as you adhere to that contract, you never need to modify the code.

The *Get-Discount* function begins with the *Function* keyword and is followed by the name of the function and the definition for two input parameters. The first input parameter is the *$rate* parameter, which is constrained to be of type *system.double* (which will permit you to supply decimal numbers).

The second input parameter is the *$total* parameter, which is constrained to be of type *system.integer*, and therefore will not allow decimal numbers. In the script block, the value of the *-total* parameter is multiplied by the value of the *-rate* parameter. The result of this calculation is returned to the pipeline.

The *Get-Discount* function is shown here:

```
Function Get-Discount([double]$rate,[int]$total)
{
  $rate * $total
} #end Get-Discount
```

The entry point to the script assigns values to both the *$total* and *$rate* variables, as shown here:

```
$rate = .05
$total = 100
```

The variable *$discount* is used to hold the result of the calculation from the *Get-Discount* function. When calling the function, it is a best practice to use the full parameter names. It makes the code easier to read, and will help make it immune to unintended problems if the function signature ever changes.

```
$discount = Get-Discount -rate $rate -total $total
```

**Note** The signature of a function is the order and names of the input parameters. If you typically supply values to the signature via positional parameters, and the order of the input parameters changes, the code will fail, or worse yet, produce inconsistent results. If you typically call functions via partial parameter names, and an additional parameter is added, the script will fail due to difficulty with the disambiguation process. Obviously, you take this into account when first writing the script and the function, but months or years later, when making modifications to the script or calling the function via another script, the problem can arise.

The remainder of the script produces output for the screen. The results of running the script are shown here:

```
Total: 100
Discount: 5
Your Total: 95
```

The complete text of the BusinessLogicDemo.ps1 script is shown here:

**BusinessLogicDemo.ps1**

```
Function Get-Discount([double]$rate,[int]$total)
{
  $rate * $total
} #end Get-Discount
```

```
$rate = .05
$total = 100
$discount = Get-Discount -rate $rate -total $total
"Total: $total"
"Discount: $discount"
"Your Total: $($total-$discount)"
```

Business logic does not have to be related to business purposes. Business logic is anything that is arbitrary that does not affect the running of the code. In the FindLargeDocs.ps1 script, there are two functions. The first function, *Get-Doc*, is used to find document files (files with an extension of .doc, .docx, or .dot) in a folder that is passed to the function when it is called. The *-recurse* switch, when used with the *Get-ChildItem* cmdlet, causes the function to look in the present folder, as well as within child folders. This function is stand-alone and has no dependency on any other functions.

The *LargeFiles* piece of code is a filter. A filter is kind of special-purpose function that uses the *Filter* keyword rather than using the *Function* keyword when it is created.

```
FindLargeDocs.ps1
Function Get-Doc($path)
{
 Get-ChildItem -Path $path -include *.doc,*.docx,*.dot -recurse
} #end Get-Doc

Filter LargeFiles($size)
{
  $_ |
  Where-Object { $_.length -ge $size }
} #end LargeFiles

Get-Doc("C:\FSO") | LargeFiles 1000
```

# Use of functions to provide ease of modification

It is a truism that a script is never completed. There is always something else to add to a script—a change that will improve it, or additional functionality someone requests. When a script is written as one long piece of inline code, without recourse to functions, it can be rather tedious and error prone to modify.

An example of an inline script is the InLineGetIPDemo.ps1 script, which follows. The first line of code uses the *Get-WmiObject* cmdlet to retrieve the instances of the *Win32_NetworkAdapterConfiguration* WMI class that Internet Protocol (IP) enabled. The results of this WMI query are stored in the *$IP* variable. This line of code is shown here:

```
$IP = Get-WmiObject -class Win32_NetworkAdapterConfiguration -Filter "IPEnabled = $true"
```

Once the WMI information has been obtained and stored, the remainder of the script prints out information to the screen. The *IPAddress*, *IPSubNet*, and *DNSServerSearchOrder* properties are all stored in an array. For this example, you are only interested in the first IP address, and you therefore print out element 0, which will always exist if the network adapter has an IP address. This section of the script is shown here:

```
"IP Address: " + $IP.IPAddress[0]
"Subnet: " + $IP.IPSubNet[0]
"GateWay: " + $IP.DefaultIPGateway
"DNS Server: " + $IP.DNSServerSearchOrder[0]
"FQDN: " + $IP.DNSHostName + "." + $IP.DNSDomain
```

When the script is run, it produces output similar to the following:

```
IP Address: 192.168.2.5
Subnet: 255.255.255.0
GateWay: 192.168.2.1
DNS Server: 192.168.2.1
FQDN: w8client1.nwtraders.com
```

The complete InLineGetIPDemo.ps1 script is shown here:

**InLineGetIPDemo.ps1**
```
$IP = Get-WmiObject -class Win32_NetworkAdapterConfiguration -Filter "IPEnabled = $true"
"IP Address: " + $IP.IPAddress[0]
"Subnet: " + $IP.IPSubNet[0]
"GateWay: " + $IP.DefaultIPGateway
"DNS Server: " + $IP.DNSServerSearchOrder[0]
"FQDN: " + $IP.DNSHostName + "." + $IP.DNSDomain
```

With just a few modifications to the script, a great deal of flexibility can be obtained. The modifications, of course, involve moving the inline code into functions. As a best practice, a function should be narrowly defined and should encapsulate a single thought. While it would be possible to move the entire previous script into a function, you would not have as much flexibility. There are two thoughts or ideas that are expressed in the script. The first is obtaining the IP information from WMI, and the second is formatting and displaying the IP information. It would be best to separate the gathering and the displaying processes from one another, because they are logically two different activities.

To convert the InLineGetIPDemo.ps1 script into a script that uses a function, you only need to add the *Function* keyword, give the function a name, and surround the original code with a pair of curly brackets. The transformed script is now named GetIPDemoSingleFunction.ps1 and is shown here:

**GetIPDemoSingleFunction.ps1**
```
Function Get-IPDemo
{
 $IP = Get-WmiObject -class Win32_NetworkAdapterConfiguration -Filter "IPEnabled = $true"
 "IP Address: " + $IP.IPAddress[0]
 "Subnet: " + $IP.IPSubNet[0]
 "GateWay: " + $IP.DefaultIPGateway
 "DNS Server: " + $IP.DNSServerSearchOrder[0]
 "FQDN: " + $IP.DNSHostName + "." + $IP.DNSDomain
} #end Get-IPDemo

# *** Entry Point To Script ***

Get-IPDemo
```

If you go to all the trouble to transform the inline code into a function, what benefit do you derive? By making this single change, your code will become

- Easier to read

- Easier to understand

- Easier to reuse

- Easier to troubleshoot

The script is easier to read because you do not really need to read each line of code to see what it does. You see that there is a function that obtains the IP address, and it is called from outside the function. That is all the script does.

The script is easier to understand because you see there is a function that obtains the IP address. If you want to know the details of that operation, you read that function. If you are not interested in the details, you can skip that portion of the code.

The script is easier to reuse because you can dot-source the script, as shown here. When the script is dot-sourced, all the executable code in the script is run. As a result, because each of the scripts prints information, the following is displayed:

```
IP Address: 192.168.2.5
Subnet: 255.255.255.0
GateWay: 192.168.2.1
DNS Server: 192.168.2.1
FQDN: w8client1.nwtraders.com


 w8client1 free disk space on drive C:
    48,767.16 MegaBytes


This OS is version 6.2
```

The DotSourceScripts.ps1 script is shown following. As you can see, it provides a certain level of flexibility to choose the information required, and it also makes it easy to mix and match the required information. If each of the scripts had been written in a more standard fashion, and the output had been more standardized, the results would have been more impressive. As it is, three lines of code produce an exceptional amount of useful output that could be acceptable in a variety of situations.

```
# DotSourceScripts.ps1

. C:\Scripts\GetIPDemoSingleFunction.ps1
. C:\Scripts\Get-FreeDiskSpace.ps1
. C:\Scripts\Get-OperatingSystemVersion.ps1
```

A better way to work with the function is to think about the things the function is actually doing. In the FunctionGetIPDemo.ps1 script, there are two functions. The first connects to WMI, which returns a management object. The second function formats the output. These are two completely unrelated tasks. The first task is data gathering, and the second task is the presentation of the information. The FunctionGetIPDemo.ps1 script is shown here:

**FunctionGetIPDemo.ps1**

```
Function Get-IPObject
{
 Get-WmiObject -class Win32_NetworkAdapterConfiguration -Filter "IPEnabled = $true"
} #end Get-IPObject

Function Format-IPOutput($IP)
{
 "IP Address: " + $IP.IPAddress[0]
 "Subnet: " + $IP.IPSubNet[0]
 "GateWay: " + $IP.DefaultIPGateway
 "DNS Server: " + $IP.DNSServerSearchOrder[0]
 "FQDN: " + $IP.DNSHostName + "." + $IP.DNSDomain
} #end Format-IPOutput

# *** Entry Point To Script

$ip = Get-IPObject
Format-IPOutput -ip $ip
```

By separating the data-gathering and the presentation activities into different functions, you gain additional flexibility. You could easily modify the *Get-IPObject* function to look for network adapters that were not IP enabled. To do this, you would need to modify the *-filter* parameter of the *Get-WmiObject* cmdlet. Since most of the time you would actually be interested only in network adapters that are IP enabled, it would make sense to set the default value of the input parameter to *$true*. By default, the behavior of the revised function is exactly as it was prior to modification. The advantage is that you can now use the function and modify the objects returned by it. To do this, you supply *$false* when calling the function. This is illustrated in the Get-IPObjectDefaultEnabled.ps1 script.

**Get-IPObjectDefaultEnabled.ps1**

```
Function Get-IPObject([bool]$IPEnabled = $true)
{
 Get-WmiObject -class Win32_NetworkAdapterConfiguration -Filter "IPEnabled = $IPEnabled"
} #end Get-IPObject

Get-IPObject -IPEnabled $False
```

By separating the gathering of the information from the presentation of the information, you gain flexibility not only in the type of information that is garnered, but also in the way the information is displayed. When gathering network adapter configuration information from a network adapter that is not enabled for IP, the results are not as impressive as for one that is enabled for IP. You might therefore decide to create a different display to list only the pertinent information. As the function that displays the information is different from the one that gathers the information, a change can easily be made that customizes the information that is most germane. The *Begin* section of the function is run once during the execution of the function. This is the perfect place to create a header for the output data. The *Process* section executes once for each item on the pipeline, which in this example will be each of the non-IP-enabled network adapters. The *Write-Host* cmdlet is used to easily write the data out to the Windows PowerShell console. The backtick-*t* character combination (`t) is used to produce a tab.

> **Note** The `t character is a string character, and as such works with cmdlets that accept string input.

The Get-IPObjectDefaultEnabledFormatNonIPOutput.ps1 script is shown here:

**Get-IPObjectDefaultEnabledFormatNonIPOutput.ps1**

```
Function Get-IPObject([bool]$IPEnabled = $true)
{
 Get-WmiObject -class Win32_NetworkAdapterConfiguration -Filter "IPEnabled = $IPEnabled"
} #end Get-IPObject

Function Format-NonIPOutput($IP)
{
  Begin { "Index #  Description" }
 Process {
  ForEach ($i in $ip)
  {
   Write-Host $i.Index `t $i.Description
  } #end ForEach
 } #end Process
} #end Format-NonIPOutPut

$ip = Get-IPObject -IPEnabled $False
Format-NonIPOutput($ip)
```

You can use the *Get-IPObject* function to retrieve the network adapter configuration, and you can use the *Format-NonIPOutput* and *Format-IPOutput* functions in a script to display the IP information as specifically formatted output.

**CombinationFormatGetIPDemo.ps1**

```
Function Get-IPObject([bool]$IPEnabled = $true)
{
 Get-WmiObject -class Win32_NetworkAdapterConfiguration -Filter "IPEnabled = $IPEnabled"
} #end Get-IPObject

Function Format-IPOutput($IP)
{
 "IP Address: " + $IP.IPAddress[0]
 "Subnet: " + $IP.IPSubNet[0]
 "GateWay: " + $IP.DefaultIPGateway
 "DNS Server: " + $IP.DNSServerSearchOrder[0]
 "FQDN: " + $IP.DNSHostName + "." + $IP.DNSDomain
} #end Format-IPOutput
```

```
Function Format-NonIPOutput($IP)
{
  Begin { "Index #  Description" }
 Process {
  ForEach ($i in $ip)
  {
   Write-Host $i.Index `t $i.Description
  } #end ForEach
 } #end Process
} #end Format-NonIPOutPut

# *** Entry Point ***
$IPEnabled = $false
$ip = Get-IPObject -IPEnabled $IPEnabled
If($IPEnabled) { Format-IPOutput($ip) }
ELSE { Format-NonIPOutput($ip) }
```

## Understanding filters

A filter is a special-purpose function. It is used to operate on each object in a pipeline and is often used to reduce the number of objects that are passed along the pipeline. Typically, a filter does not use the *Begin* or the *End* parameters that a function might need to use. So, a filter is often thought of as a function that only has a *Process* block. But then, many functions are written without using the *Begin* or *End* parameters, while filters are never written in such a way that they use the *Begin* or the *End* parameters. The biggest difference between a function and a filter is a bit subtler, however. When a function is used inside a pipeline, it actually halts the processing of the pipeline until the first element in the pipeline has run to completion. The function then accepts the input from the first element in the pipeline and begins its processing. When the processing in the function is completed, it then passes the results along to the next element in the script block. A function runs once for the pipelined data. A filter, on the other hand, runs once for each piece of data passed over the pipeline. In short, a filter will stream the data when in a pipeline, and a function will not. This can make a big difference in the performance. To illustrate this point, let's examine a function and a filter that accomplish the same things.

In the MeasureAddOneFilter.ps1 script, which follows, an array of 50,000 elements is created by using the *1..50000* syntax. (In Windows PowerShell 1.0, 50,000 was the maximum size of an array created in this manner. In Windows PowerShell 2.0 and 3.0, this ceiling is raised to the maximum size of an *[Int32]* (2,146,483,647). The use of this size is dependent upon memory. This is shown here:

```
PS C:\ > 1..[Int32]::MaxValue
The '..' operator failed: Exception of type 'System.OutOfMemoryException' was thrown..
At line:1 char:4
+ 1.. <<<< 2147483647
    + CategoryInfo          : InvalidOperation: (:) [], RuntimeException
    + FullyQualifiedErrorId : OperatorFailed
```

The array is then pipelined into the *AddOne* filter. The filter prints out the string *add one filter* and then adds the number 1 to the current number on the pipeline. The length of time it takes to run the command is then displayed. On my computer, it takes about 2.6 seconds to run the MeasureAddOneFilter.ps1 script.

**MeasureAddOneFilter.ps1**

```
Filter AddOne
{
 "add one filter"
  $_ + 1
}
```

**Measure-Command** { 1..50000 | addOne }

The function version is shown following. In a similar fashion to the MeasureAddOneFllter.ps1 script, it creates an array of 50,000 numbers and pipelines the results to the *AddOne* function. The string *Add One Function* is displayed. An automatic variable is created when pipelining input to a function. It is called *$input*. The *$input* variable is an enumerator, not just a plain array. It has a *moveNext* method, which can be used to move to the next item in the collection. Since *$input* is not a plain array, you cannot index directly into it—*$input[0]* would fail. To retrieve a specific element, you use the *$input.current* property. When I run the script below, it takes 4.3 seconds on my computer (that is almost twice as long as the filter).

**MeasureAddOneFunction.ps1**

```
Function AddOne
{
  "Add One Function"
  While ($input.moveNext())
   {
     $input.current + 1
   }
}
```

**Measure-Command** { 1..50000 | addOne }

What was happening that made the filter so much faster than the function in this example? The filter runs once for each item on the pipeline. This is shown here:

```
add one filter
2
add one filter
3
add one filter
4
add one filter
5
add one filter
6
```

The DemoAddOneFilter.ps1 script is shown here:

**DemoAddOneFilter.ps1**

```
Filter AddOne
{
 "add one filter"
  $_ + 1
}

1..5 | addOne
```

The *AddOne* function runs to completion once for all the items in the pipeline. This effectively stops the processing in the middle of the pipeline until all the elements of the array are created. Then all the data is passed to the function via the *$input* variable at one time. This type of approach does not take advantage of the streaming nature of the pipeline, which in many instances is more memory-efficient.

```
Add One Function
2
3
4
5
6
```

The DemoAddOneFunction.ps1 script is shown here:

**DemoAddOneFunction.ps1**

```
Function AddOne
{
  "Add One Function"
  while ($input.movenext())
   {
     $input.current + 1
   }
}

1..5 | addOne
```

To close this performance issue between functions and filters when used in a pipeline, you can write your function in such a manner that it behaves like a filter. To do this, you must explicitly call out the *Process* block. When you use the *Process* block, you are also able to use the *$_* automatic variable instead of being restricted to using *$input*. When you do this, the script will look like DemoAddOneR2Function.ps1, the results of which are shown here:

```
add one function r2
2
add one function r2
3
add one function r2
4
add one function r2
5
add one function r2
6
```

The complete DemoAddOneR2Function.ps1 script is shown here:

**DemoAddOneR2Function.ps1**

```
Function AddOneR2
{
    Process {
    "add one function r2"
    $_ + 1
    }
} #end AddOneR2

1..5 | addOneR2
```

What does using an explicit *Process* block do to the performance? When run on my computer, the function takes about 2.6 seconds, which is virtually the same amount of time taken by the filter. The MeasureAddOneR2Function.ps1 script is shown here:

**MeasureAddOneR2Function.ps1**

```
Function AddOneR2
{
    Process {
    "add one function r2"
    $_ + 1
    }
} #end AddOneR2

Measure-Command {1..50000 | addOneR2 }
```

Another reason for using filters is that they visually stand out, and therefore improve readability of the script. The typical pattern for a filter is shown here:

```
Filter FilterName
{
 #insert code here
}
```

The *HasMessage* filter, found in the FilterHasMessage.ps1 script, begins with the *Filter* keyword, and is followed by the name of the filter, which is *HasMessage*. Inside the script block (the curly brackets), the *$_* automatic variable is used to provide access to the pipeline. It is sent to the *Where-Object* cmdlet, which performs the filter. In the calling script, the results of the *HasMessage* filter is sent to the *Measure-Object* cmdlet, which tells the user how many events in the application log have a message attached to them. The FilterHasMessage.ps1 script is shown here:

**FilterHasMessage.ps1**

```
Filter HasMessage
{
 $_ |
 Where-Object { $_.message }
} #end HasMessage

Get-WinEvent -LogName Application | HasMessage | Measure-Object
```

Although the filter has an implicit *Process* block, this does not prevent you from using the *Begin*, *Process*, and *End* script blocks explicitly. In the FilterToday.ps1 script, a filter named *IsToday* is created. To make the filter a stand-alone entity with no external dependencies required (such as the passing of a *DateTime* object to it), you need the filter to obtain the current date. However, if the call to the *Get-Date* cmdlet was done inside the *Process* block, the filter would continue to work, but the call to *Get-Date* would be made once for each object found in the input folder. So, if there were 25 items in the folder, the *Get-Date* cmdlet would be called 25 times. When you have something that you want to occur only once in the processing of the filter, you can place it in a *Begin* block. The *Begin* block is called only once, while the *Process* block is called once for each item in the pipeline. If you wanted any post-processing to take place (such as printing out a message stating how many files were found today), you would place the relevant code in the *End* block of the filter. The FilterToday.ps1 script is shown here:

**FilterToday.ps1**

```
Filter IsToday
{
 Begin {$dte = (Get-Date).Date}
 Process { $_ |
          Where-Object { $_.LastWriteTime -ge $dte }
        }
}

Get-ChildItem -Path C:\fso | IsToday
```

# Creating a function: step-by-step exercises

In this exercise, you'll explore the use of the *Get-Verb* cmdlet to find permissible Windows PowerShell verbs. You will also use *Function* keyword and create a function. Once you have created the basic function, you'll add additional functionality to the function in the next exercise.

## Creating a basic function

1. Start Windows PowerShell ISE.

2. Use the *Get-Verb* cmdlet to obtain a listing of approved verbs.

3. Select a verb that would be appropriate for a function that obtains a listing of files by date last modified. In this case, the appropriate verb is *Get*.

4. Create a new function named *Get-FilesByDate*. The code to do this appears here:

```
Function Get-FilesByDate
{

}
```

5. Add four command-line parameters to the function. The first parameter is an array of file types, the second is for the month, the third parameter is for the year, and the last parameter is an array of file paths. This portion of the function appears here:

```
Param(
  [string[]]$fileTypes,
  [int]$month,
  [int]$year,
  [string[]]$path)
```

6. Following the *Param* portion of the function, add the code to perform a recursive search of paths supplied via the *$path* variable. Limit the search to include only file types supplied via the *$filetypes* variable. This portion of the code appears here:

```
Get-ChildItem -Path $path -Include $filetypes -Recurse |
```

7. Add a *Where-Object* clause to limit the files returned to the month of the *lastwritetime* property that equals the month supplied via the command line, and the year supplied via the command line. This portion of the function appears here:

```
Where-Object {
  $_.lastwritetime.month -eq $month -AND $_.lastwritetime.year -eq $year }
```

8. Save the function in a .ps1 file named Get-FilesByDate.ps1.

9. Run the script containing the function inside the Windows PowerShell ISE.

10. In the command pane, call the function and supply appropriate parameters for the function. One such example of a command line appears here:

```
Get-FilesByDate -fileTypes *.docx -month 5 -year 2012 -path c:\data
```

The completed function appears here:

```
Function Get-FilesByDate
{
 Param(
  [string[]]$fileTypes,
  [int]$month,
  [int]$year,
  [string[]]$path)
  Get-ChildItem -Path $path -Include $filetypes -Recurse |
  Where-Object {
  $_.lastwritetime.month -eq $month -AND $_.lastwritetime.year -eq $year }
 } #end function Get-FilesByDate
```

This concludes this step-by-step exercise.

In the following exercise, you will add additional functionality to your Windows PowerShell function. The functionality will include a default value for the file types and making the *$month*, *$year*, and *$path* parameters mandatory.

## Adding additional functionality to an existing function

1. Start the Windows PowerShell ISE.

2. Open the Get-FilesByDate.ps1 script (created in the previous exercise) and use the Save As feature of the Windows PowerShell ISE to save the file with a new name of Get-FilesByDateV2.ps1.

3. Create an array of default file types for the *$filetypes* input variable. Assign the array of file types to the *$filetypes* input variable. Use array notation when creating the array of file types. For this exercise use *.doc* and *.docx*. The command to do this appears here:

```
[string[]]$fileTypes = @(".doc","*.docx")
```

4. Use the *[Parameter(Mandatory=$true)]* parameter tag to make the *$month* parameter mandatory. The tag appears just above the input parameter in the *param* portion of the script. Do the same thing for the *$year* and *$path* parameters as well. The revised portion of the *param* section of the script appears here:

```
[Parameter(Mandatory=$true)]
  [int]$month,
  [Parameter(Mandatory=$true)]
  [int]$year,
  [Parameter(Mandatory=$true)]
  [string[]]$path)
```

5. Save and run the function. Call the function without assigning a value for the path. An input box should appear permitting you to type in a path. Type in a single path residing on your system and press Enter. A second prompt appears (because the *$path* parameter accepts an array). Simply press Enter a second time. An appropriate command line appears here:

```
Get-FilesByDate -month 10 -year 2011
```

6. Now run the function and assign a path value. An appropriate command line appears here:

```
Get-FilesByDate -month 10 -year 2011 -path c:\data
```

7. Now run the function and look for a different file type. In the example appearing here, I look for Excel documents.

```
Get-FilesByDate -month 10 -year 2011 -path c:\data -fileTypes *.xlsx,*.xls
```

The revised function appears here:

```
Function Get-FilesByDate
{
 Param(
  [string[]]$fileTypes = @(".DOC","*.DOCX"),
  [Parameter(Mandatory=$true)]
  [int]$month,
  [Parameter(Mandatory=$true)]
  [int]$year,
  [Parameter(Mandatory=$true)]
  [string[]]$path)
  Get-ChildItem -Path $path -Include $filetypes -Recurse |
  Where-Object {
  $_.lastwritetime.month -eq $month -AND $_.lastwritetime.year -eq $year }
 } #end function Get-FilesByDate
```

This concludes the exercise.

# Chapter 6 quick reference

| To | Do this |
|---|---|
| Create a function | Use the *Function* keyword, and provide a name and a script block. |
| Reuse a Windows PowerShell function | Dot-source the file containing the function. |
| Constrain a data type | Use a type constraint in square brackets and place it in front of the variable or data to be constrained. |
| Provide input to a function | Use the *Param* keyword and supply variables to hold the input. |
| To use a function | Load the function into memory. |
| To store a function | Place the function in a script file. |
| To name a function | Use *Get-Verb* to identify an appropriate verb and use the verb-noun naming convention. |

# Creating Advanced Functions and Modules

**After completing this chapter, you will be able to:**

- Understand the use of the *[cmdletbinding]* attribute.

- Use parameter validation attributes to prevent errors.

- Configure *shouldprocess* to permit the use of *-whatif.*

- Configure *Write-Verbose* to provide additional information.

- Create a module.

- Install a module.

Advanced functions incorporate advanced Microsoft Windows PowerShell features and can therefore behave like cmdlets. They do not have to be complicated. In fact, advanced functions do not even have to be difficult to write or to use. What makes a function advanced is the capabilities it possesses that enable it to behave in a similar manner to a cmdlet. Back during the beta of Windows PowerShell 2.0, the name for the advanced function was *script cmdlet*, and while the name change is perhaps understandable because script cmdlets really are just advanced functions, in reality, the name was very descriptive. This is because an advanced function mimics the behavior of a regular Windows PowerShell cmdlet. In fact, the best advanced functions behave exactly like a Windows PowerShell cmdlet and implement the same capabilities.

## The *[cmdletbinding]* attribute

The first step in creating an advanced function is to add the *[cmdletbinding]* attribute to modify the way the function works. This single addition adds several capabilities, such as additional parameter checking and the ability to use easily the *Write-Verbose* cmdlet. To use the *[cmdletbinding]* attribute, you place the attribute in a square-bracket attribute tag and include it in the first noncommented line in the function. In addition, the *[cmdletbinding]* attribute requires the use of the *Param* keyword. If your advanced function requires no parameters, you can use the *Param* keyword without specifying any parameters. This technique appears here:

```
function my-function
{
 [cmdletbinding()]
 Param()

}
```

Once you have the basic outline of the advanced function, you can begin to fill in the blanks. For example, using the *Write-Verbose* cmdlet only requires adding the command. Without the use of the *[cmdletbinding]* attribute, you would need to manually change the value of the *$VerbosePreference* automatic variable from *silentlycontinue* to *continue* (and presumably later change it back to the default value). The use of the *[cmdletbinding]* attribute and *Write-Verbose* appear here:

```
function my-function
{
 [cmdletbinding()]
 Param()
 Write-Verbose "verbose stream"
}
```

### Enabling cmdlet binding for a function

1. Begin a function by using the *Function* keyword and supplying the name of the function.

2. Open a script block.

3. Type the *[cmdletbinding()]* attribute.

4. Add the *Param* statement.

5. Close the script block.

## Easy verbose messages

Once loaded, the function permits the use of the *-verbose* switched parameter. Use of this parameter causes each *Write-Verbose* statement to write to the Windows PowerShell console output. When the function runs without the *-verbose* switch, no output displays from the verbose stream. Use of this technique appears in Figure 7-1.

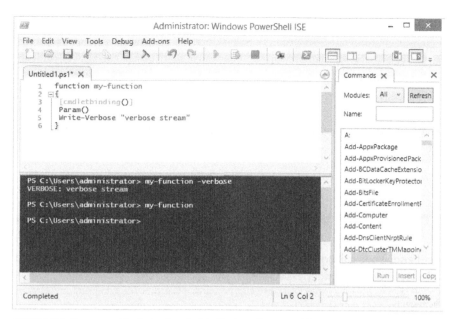

**FIGURE 7-1** Once specified, the *[cmdletbinding]* attribute enables easy access to the verbose stream.

The great thing about using the *-verbose* switch is that detailed information (such as the progress in making remote connections, loading modules, and other operations that could cause a script to fail) is output as events happen. This provides a built-in diagnostic mode for the advanced function—with virtually no additional programming required.

### Providing verbose output

1. Inside a function, add the *[cmdletbinding()]* attribute.

2. Add a *Param* statement.

3. Use the *Write-Verbose* cmdlet for each status message to display.

4. When calling the function, use the *-verbose* switched parameter.

## Automatic parameter checks

The default behavior for a Windows PowerShell function is that any additional values beyond the defined number of arguments are supplied to an unnamed argument and are therefore available in the automatic *$args* variable. This behavior, while potentially useful, easily becomes a source of errors for a script. The following function illustrates this behavior:

```
function my-function
{
 #[cmdletbinding()]
 Param($a)
 $a
 #$args
}
```

When the preceding function runs, any value supplied to the *-a* parameter appears in the output. This appears here:

```
PS C:\Users\ed.IAMMRED> my-function -a 1,2,3,4
1
2
3
4
```

If, on the other hand, when calling the function you omit the first comma, no error is generated—but the output displayed does not meet expectations. This appears here:

```
PS C:\Users\ed.IAMMRED> my-function -a 1 2,3,4
1
```

The remaining parameters appear in the automatic *$args* variable. Placing the *$args* variable in the function illustrates this. First add the *$args* automatic variable as appears here:

```
function my-function
{
 #[cmdletbinding()]
 Param($a)
 $a
 $args
}
```

Now, when calling the function, while omitting the first comma, the following output appears.

```
PS C:\Users\ed.IAMMRED> my-function -a 1 2,3,4
1
2
3
4
```

While interesting, you may not want this supplying of additional values to an unnamed argument behavior. One way to correct it is to check the number of arguments supplied to the function. You can do this by monitoring the count property of the *$args* variable. This appears here:

```
function my-function
{
 #[cmdletbinding()]
 Param($a)
 $a
 $args.count
}
```

When passing multiple arguments to the function, the value of *count* increments. In the output appearing here, the first number, 1, returns from the *-a* position. The number 3 is the count of extra arguments (those not supplied for the named argument).

```
PS C:\Users\ed.IAMMRED> my-function 1 2 3 4
1
3
```

By using this feature and checking the *count* property of *$args*, you can detect extra arguments coming to the function with one line of code. This change appears here:

```
function my-function
{
 #[cmdletbinding()]
 Param($a,$b)
 $a
 $b
 if($args.count -gt 0) {Write-Error "unhandled arguments supplied"}
}
```

When the code is run, as shown following, the first two parameters supplied are accepted for the *-a* and the *-b* parameters. The two remaining parameters go into the *$args* automatic variable. This increases the *count* property of *$args* to a value greater than 0, and therefore an error occurs.

```
PS C:\Users\ed.IAMMRED> my-function 1 2 3 4
1
2
my-function : unhandled arguments supplied
At line:1 char:12
+ my-function <<<<  1 2 3 4
    + CategoryInfo          : NotSpecified: (:) [Write-Error], WriteErrorException
    + FullyQualifiedErrorId : Microsoft.PowerShell.Commands.WriteErrorException,my-
    function
```

The easiest way to identify unhandled parameters supplied to a Windows PowerShell function is to use the *[cmdletbinding]* attribute. One of the features of the *[cmdletbinding]* attribute is that it generates an error when unhandled parameter values appear on the command line. The following function illustrates the *[cmdletbinding]* attribute:

```
function my-function
{
 [cmdletbinding()]
 Param($a,$b)
 $a
 $b
}
```

When you call the preceding function with too many arguments, the following error appears:

```
PS C:\Users\ed.IAMMRED> my-function 1 2 3 4
my-function : A positional parameter cannot be found that accepts argument '3'.
At line:1 char:12
+ my-function <<<< 1 2 3 4
    + CategoryInfo          : InvalidArgument: (:) [my-function], ParameterBindingException
    + FullyQualifiedErrorId : PositionalParameterNotFound,my-function
```

## Adding support for the *-whatif* parameter

One of the great features of Windows PowerShell is the use of the *-whatif* parameter on cmdlets that change system state, such as the *Stop-Service* and *Stop-Process* cmdlets. If you consistently use the *-whatif* switched parameter, you can avoid many inadvertent system outages or potential data loss. As a Windows PowerShell best practice, you should also implement the *-whatif* parameter in advanced functions that potentially change system state. In the past, this meant creating special parameters and adding lots of extra code to handle the output. Now it requires a single line of code.

> **Note** *[cmdletbinding()]* appears with empty parentheses because there are other things, such as *SupportsShouldProcess*, that can appear between the parentheses.

Inside the parentheses of the *[cmdletbinding]* attribute, set *SupportsShouldProcess* to *true*. The following function illustrates this technique:

```
function my-function
{
 [cmdletbinding(SupportsShouldProcess=$True)]
 Param($path)
 md $path
}
```

Now when you call the function with the *-whatif* switched parameter, a message appears in the output detailing the exact behavior the cmdlet takes when run without the *-whatif* parameter. This appears in Figure 7-2.

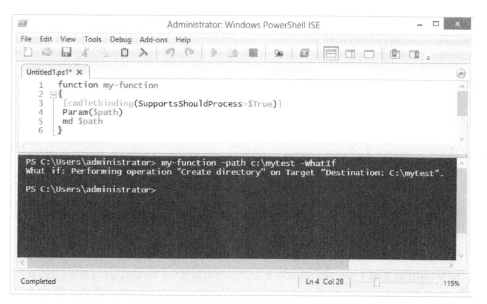

**FIGURE 7-2** Using *-whatif* when running a function with *SupportsShouldProcess* informs you what the function will do when run.

### Adding *-whatif* support

1. Inside a function, add the *[cmdletbinding()]* attribute.

? Inside the parentheses of the *[cmdletbinding]* attribute, add *SupportsShouldProcess = $true*.

3. Add a *Param* statement.

4. When calling the function, use the *-whatif* switched parameter.

## Adding support for the *-confirm* parameter

If all you want to do is to enable users of your function to use the *-confirm* switched parameter when calling the function, the command is exactly the same as the one to enable *-whatif*. The *SupportsShouldProcess* attribute turns on both *-whatif* and *-confirm*. Therefore, when you run the function that follows with the *-confirm* switch, it prompts you prior to executing the specific action.

```
function my-function
{
 [cmdletbinding(SupportsShouldProcess=$True)]
 Param($path)
 md $path
}
```

The following command illustrates calling the function with the *-confirm* parameter:

```
my-function -path c:\mytest -confirm
```

The dialog box in Figure 7-3 displays as a result of the previous command line when the code runs from within the Windows PowerShell ISE.

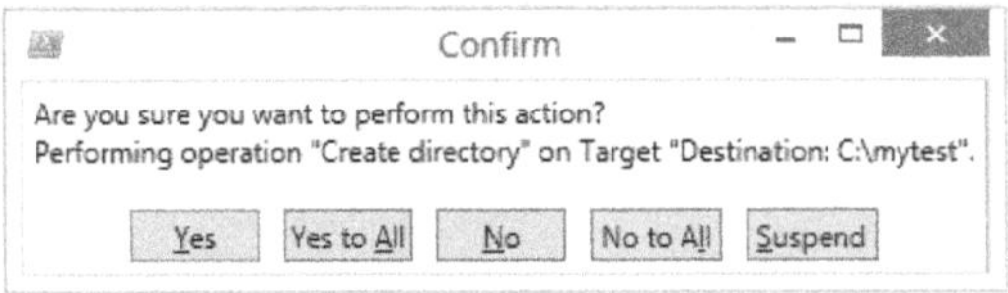

**FIGURE 7-3** Use of *SupportsShouldProcess* also enables the *-confirm* switch.

Most of the time, when you do something in Windows PowerShell, it executes the command instead of prompting. For example, the following command stops all processes on the computer.

```
Get-Process | Stop-Process
```

> **Note** On Windows 8, the preceding command prompts prior to stopping the CRSS process that will cause the computer to shut down. On operating systems prior to Windows 8, the command executes without prompting.

If you do not want a cmdlet to execute by default—that is, you wish for it to prompt by default—you add an additional property to the *[cmdletbinding]* attribute: the *confirmimpact* property. This technique appears here:

```
[cmdletbinding(SupportsShouldProcess=$True, confirmimpact="high")]
```

There values for the *confirmimpact* property are *High*, *Medium*, *Low*, and *None*. They correspond to the values for the automatic *$confirmpreference* variable.

## Specifying the default parameter set

Properties specified for the *[cmdletbinding]* attribute impact the entire function. Therefore, when an advanced function contains multiple parameter sets (or different groupings of parameters for the same cmdlet), the function needs to know which one of several potential possibilities is the default. The following command illustrates finding the default Windows PowerShell parameter set for a cmdlet:

```
PS C:\> (Get-Command Stop-Process).parametersets | Format-Table name, isdefault -AutoSize

Name        IsDefault
----        ---------
Id            True
Name          False
InputObject   False
```

To specify a default parameter set for an advanced function, use the *DefaultParameterSetName* property of the *[cmdletbinding]* attribute. When doing this, you tell Windows PowerShell that if a particular parameter set is not specified and not resolved by its data type, then the parameter set with the *DefaultParameterSetName* attribute is to be used. Here is the code to specify the *DefaultParameterSetName* property of the *[cmdletbinding]* attribute:

```
[cmdletbinding(DefaultParameterSetName="name")]
```

More information about creating parameter sets appears in the following section.

## The *parameter* attribute

The *parameter* attribute accepts a number of properties that add power and flexibility to your advanced Windows PowerShell function. The *parameter* attribute properties are shown in Table 7-1.

**TABLE 7-1** Advanced function parameter attribute properties and meanings

| Parameter attribute property | Example | Meaning |
|---|---|---|
| *Mandatory* | *Mandatory=$true* | The parameter must be specified. |
| *Position* | *Position=0* | The parameter occupies the first position when calling the function. |
| *ParameterSetName* | *ParameterSetName="name"* | The parameter belongs to the specified parameter set. |
| *ValueFromPipeline* | *ValueFromPipeline=$true* | The parameter accepts pipelined input. |
| *ValueFromPipelineByPropertyName* | *ValueFromPipelineByPropertyName =$true* | The parameter uses a property on the object instead of the entire object. |
| *ValueFromRemainingArguments* | *ValueFromRemainingArguments=$ true* | The parameter collects unassigned arguments. |
| *HelpMessage* | *HelpMessage="parameter help info"* | A short help message for the parameter is displayed. |

## The *mandatory* parameter property

The *mandatory* parameter attribute property turns a function's parameter from optional to mandatory. By default, all parameters to an advanced function are optional; by using the *mandatory* property, you can change that behavior on a parameter-by-parameter basis. When a function runs with missing mandatory parameters, Windows PowerShell prompts for the missing parameter.

Use of the *mandatory* parameter appears here:

```
Function Test-Mandatory
{
 Param(
 [Parameter(mandatory=$true)]
 $name)
 "hello $name"
}
```

When you run the *Test-Mandatory* function without supplying a value for the *name* parameter, Windows PowerShell prompts for the missing value. This appears in the output that follows:

```
PS C:\> Test-Mandatory
cmdlet Test-Mandatory at command pipeline position 1
Supply values for the following parameters:
name: Ed Wilson
hello Ed Wilson
```

If, the user does not supply a value for the missing parameter, but instead skips past the prompt, no error occurs, and the function continues to run, because the user is really assigning something (*$null*) to the parameter.

> **Note** If the code itself generates errors when run with no parameter values, these errors are displayed. In this way, the *mandatory* parameter property causes a prompt, but it is not an error-handling technique.

The output appears in Figure 7-4.

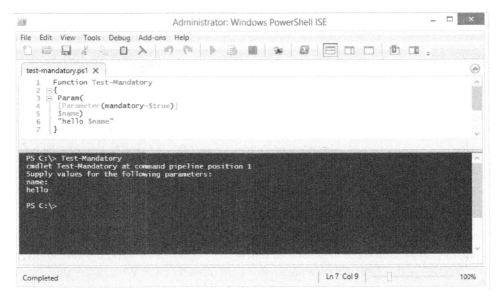

**FIGURE 7-4** No error appears when skipping past a mandatory parameter.

# The *position* parameter property

The *position* parameter property tells Windows PowerShell that the specific parameter receives values when it occupies a specific position. Position numbers are zero based, and therefore the first position is parameter position 0. By default, Windows PowerShell parameters are positional—that is, you can supply values for them in the order in which they appear in the parameter set. However, once you use the *position* parameter property for any single parameter, the parameters default to being nonpositional—that is, you will now need to use the parameter names to supply values.

> **Note** When supplying values for named parameters, you only need to type enough of the parameter name to distinguish it from other parameter names (including the default parameters).

The code that appears here illustrates using the *position* parameter property:

```
Function Test-Positional
{
 Param(
 [Parameter(Position=0)]
 $greeting,
 $name)
 "$greeting $name"
}
```

## The *ParameterSetName* parameter property

The *ParameterSetName* property identifies groups of parameters that taken together create a specific command set. It is quite common for cmdlets and advanced functions to expose multiple ways of calling the code. One thing to keep in mind when creating different parameter sets is that the same parameter cannot appear in more than one parameter set. Therefore, only the parameters that are unique to each parameter set appear.

> **Note** When creating a parameter set, it is a best practice always to include one mandatory parameter in each set.

If your parameter set uses more than a single parameter, use the *ParameterSetName* property from the automatic *$PSCmdlet* variable in a *switch* statement to evaluate actions to take place. This technique appears in the *Test-ParameterSet* function that follows.

```
Function Test-ParameterSet
{
 Param(
  [Parameter(ParameterSetName="City",Mandatory=$true)]
  $city,
  [Parameter(ParameterSetName="City")]
  $state,
  [Parameter(ParameterSetName="phone",Mandatory=$true)]
  $phone,
  [Parameter(ParameterSetName="phone")]
  $ext,
  [Parameter(Mandatory=$true)]
  $name)
  Switch ($PSCmdlet.ParameterSetName)
```

```
    {
     "city" {"$name from $city in $state"}
     "phone" {"$name phone is $Phone extension $ext"}
    }
}
```

## The *ValueFromPipeline* property

The *ValueFromPipeline* property causes Windows PowerShell to accept objects from the pipeline. The entire object passes into the function's *Process* block when you use the *ValueFromPipeline* parameter property. Because the entire object passes to the function, you can access specific properties from the pipeline with dotted notation. An example of this technique appears here:

```
Function Test-PipedValue
{
 Param(
   [Parameter(ValueFromPipeline=$true)]
   $process)
   Process {Write-Host $process.name  $process.id}
}
```

Instead of receiving an entire object from the pipeline, the *ValueFromPipelineByPropertyName* property can often simplify code by allowing your function to pick properties from the input object directly from the pipeline. The *Test-PipedValueByPropertyName* function illustrates this technique:

```
Function Test-PipedValueByPropertyName
{
 Param(
   [Parameter(ValueFromPipelineByPropertyName=$true)]
   $processname,
   [Parameter(ValueFromPipelineByPropertyName=$true)]
   $id)
   Process {Write-Host $processname  $id}
}
```

When you need to accept arbitrary information that may or may not align with specific parameters, the *ValueFromRemainingArguments* parameter property provides the answer. Such a technique permits flexibility in the use of the parameters, and the remaining items in the arguments comprise an array and are therefore accessible via standard array notation. The *Test-ValueFromRemainingArguments* function illustrates using the *ValueFromRemainingArguments* parameter property in a function:

```
Function Test-ValueFromRemainingArguments
{
 Param(
   $Name,
   [Parameter(ValueFromRemainingArguments=$true)]
   $otherInfo)
   Process { "Name: $name `r`nOther info: $otherinfo" }
}
```

Figure 7-5 illustrates calling the *Test-ValueFromRemainingArguments* function and providing additional arguments to the function.

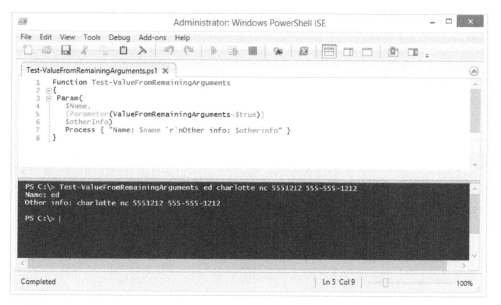

**FIGURE 7-5** The *ValueFromRemainingArguments* parameter property permits access to extra arguments.

## The *HelpMessage* property

The *HelpMessage* property provides a small amount of help related to a specific parameter. This information becomes accessible when Windows PowerShell prompts for a missing parameter. This means that it only makes sense to use the *HelpMessage* parameter property when it is coupled with the *Mandatory* parameter property.

> **Note** It is a Windows PowerShell best practice to use the *HelpMessage* parameter property when using the *Mandatory* parameter property.

When Windows PowerShell prompts for a missing parameter, and when the *HelpMessage* parameter property exists, an additional line appears in the output. This line appears here:

```
(Type !? for Help.)
```

To view the help, type **!?** and press Enter, and the string value for the *HelpMessage* parameter property will be displayed.

```
Function Test-HelpMessage
{
 Param(
    [Parameter(Mandatory=$true, HelpMessage="Enter your name please")]
    $name)
    "Good to meet you $name"
}
```

# Understanding modules

Windows PowerShell 2.0 introduced the concept of modules. A module is a package that can contain Windows PowerShell cmdlets, aliases, functions, variables, type/format XML, help files, other scripts, and even providers. In short, a Windows PowerShell module can contain the kinds of things that you might put into your profile, but it can also contain things that Windows PowerShell 1.0 required a developer to incorporate into a PowerShell snap-in. There are several advantages of modules over snap-ins:

- Anyone who can write a Windows PowerShell script can create a module.

- To install a module, you do not need to write a Windows Installer package.

- To install a module, you do not have to have administrator rights.

These advantages should be of great interest to the IT professional.

# Locating and loading modules

There are two default locations for Windows PowerShell modules. The first location is in the user's home directory, and the second is in the Windows PowerShell home directory. These locations are defined in *$env:psmodulepath*, a default environmental variable. You can add additional default module path locations by editing this variable. The modules directory in the Windows PowerShell home directory always exists. However, the modules directory in the user's home directory is not present by default. The modules directory will only exist in the user's home directory if it has been created. The creation of the modules directory in the user's home directory does not normally happen until someone has decided to create and to store modules there. A nice feature of the modules directory is that when it exists, it is the first place Windows PowerShell uses when it searches for a module. If the user's module directory does not exist, the modules directory within the Windows PowerShell home directory is used.

# Listing available modules

Windows PowerShell modules exist in two states: loaded and unloaded. To display a list of all loaded modules, use the *Get-Module* cmdlet without any parameters. This is shown here:

```
PS C:\> Get-Module

ModuleType Name                                ExportedCommands
---------- ----                                ----------------
Script     ISE                                 {Get-IseSnippet, Import-IseSnippet, New-
IseSnip...
Manifest   Microsoft.PowerShell.Management     {Add-Computer, Add-Content, Checkpoint-
Computer...
Manifest   Microsoft.PowerShell.Utility        {Add-Member, Add-Type, Clear-Variable,
Compare-...
```

If there are multiple modules loaded when the *Get-Module* cmdlet runs, each module will appear along with its accompanying exported commands on their own individual lines. This is shown here:

```
PS C:\> Get-Module

ModuleType Name                ExportedCommands
---------- ----                ----------------
Script     GetFreeDiskSpace    Get-FreeDiskSpace
Script     HelloWorld          {Hello-World, Hello-User}
Script     TextFunctions       {New-Line, Get-TextStats}
Manifest   BitsTransfer        {Start-BitsTransfer, Remove-BitsTransfe...
Script     PSDiagnostics       {Enable-PSTrace, Enable-WSManTrace, Sta...


PS C:\>
```

If no modules are loaded, nothing displays to the Windows PowerShell console. No errors appear, nor is there any confirmation that the command has actually run. This situation never occurs on Windows 8 because Windows PowerShell core cmdlets reside in two basic modules: the *Microsoft.PowerShell.Management* and *Microsoft.PowerShell.Utility* modules. These two modules always load unless Windows PowerShell launches with the *-noprofile* switch. But even then, the *Microsoft.PowerShell.Management* module loads due to autoload.

To obtain a listing of all modules that are available on the system, you use the *Get-Module* cmdlet with the *-ListAvailable* parameter. The *Get-Module* cmdlet with the *-ListAvailable* parameter lists all modules that are available whether or not the modules are loaded into the Windows PowerShell console. The output appearing here illustrates the default installation of a Windows 8 client system:

```
PS C:\> Get-Module -ListAvailable

    Directory: C:\Windows\system32\WindowsPowerShell\v1.0\Modules


ModuleType  Name                                  ExportedCommands
----------  ----                                  ----------------
Manifest    AppLocker                             {Get-AppLockerFileInformation, Get...
Manifest    Appx                                  {Add-AppxPackage, Get-AppxPackage,...
Manifest    BitLocker                             {Unlock-BitLocker, Suspend-BitLock...
Manifest    BitsTransfer                          {Add-BitsFile, Complete-BitsTransf...
Manifest    BranchCache                           {Add-BCDataCacheExtension, Clear-B...
Manifest    CimCmdlets                            {Get-CimAssociatedInstance, Get-Ci...
Manifest    DirectAccessClientComponents          {Disable-DAManualEntryPointSelecti...
Script      Dism                                  {Add-AppxProvisionedPackage, Add-W...
Manifest    DnsClient                             {Resolve-DnsName, Clear-DnsClientC...
Manifest    International                         {Get-WinDefaultInputMethodOverride...
Manifest    iSCSI                                 {Get-IscsiTargetPortal, New-IscsiT...
Script      ISE                                   {New-IseSnippet, Import-IseSnippet...
Manifest    Kds                                   {Add-KdsRootKey, Get-KdsRootKey, T...
Manifest    Microsoft.PowerShell.Diagnostics      {Get-WinEvent, Get-Counter, Import...
Manifest    Microsoft.PowerShell.Host             {Start-Transcript, Stop-Transcript}
Manifest    Microsoft.PowerShell.Management        {Add-Content, Clear-Content, Clear...
Manifest    Microsoft.PowerShell.Security         {Get-Acl, Set-Acl, Get-PfxCertific...
Manifest    Microsoft.PowerShell.Utility          {Format-List, Format-Custom, Forma...
Manifest    Microsoft.WSMan.Management             {Disable-WSManCredSSP, Enable-WSMa...
Manifest    MMAgent                               {Disable-MMAgent, Enable-MMAgent, ...
Manifest    MsDtc                                 {New-DtcDiagnosticTransaction, Com...
Manifest    NetAdapter                            {Disable-NetAdapter, Disable-NetAd...
Manifest    NetConnection                         {Get-NetConnectionProfile, Set-Net...
Manifest    NetLbfo                               {Add-NetLbfoTeamMember, Add-NetLbf...
Manifest    NetQos                                {Get-NetQosPolicy, Set-NetQosPolic...
Manifest    NetSecurity                           {Get-DAPolicyChange, New-NetIPsecA...
Manifest    NetSwitchTeam                         {New-NetSwitchTeam, Remove-NetSwit...
Manifest    NetTCPIP                              {Get-NetIPAddress, Get-NetIPInterf...
Manifest    NetworkConnectivityStatus             {Get-DAConnectionStatus, Get-NCSIP...
Manifest    NetworkTransition                     {Add-NetIPHttpsCertBinding, Disabl...
Manifest    PKI                                   {Add-CertificateEnrollmentPolicySe...
Manifest    PrintManagement                       {Add-Printer, Add-PrinterDriver, A...
Script      PSDiagnostics                         {Disable-PSTrace, Disable-PSWSManC...
Binary      PSScheduledJob                        {New-JobTrigger, Add-JobTrigger, R...
Manifest    PSWorkflow                            {New-PSWorkflowExecutionOption, Ne...
Manifest    PSWorkflowUtility                     Invoke-AsWorkflow
Manifest    ScheduledTasks                        {Get-ScheduledTask, Set-ScheduledT...
Manifest    SecureBoot                            {Confirm-SecureBootUEFI, Set-Secur...
Manifest    SmbShare                              {Get-SmbShare, Remove-SmbShare, Se...
Manifest    SmbWitness                            {Get-SmbWitnessClient, Move-SmbWit...
Manifest    Storage                               {Add-InitiatorIdToMaskingSet, Add-...
Manifest    TroubleshootingPack                   {Get-TroubleshootingPack, Invoke-T...
Manifest    TrustedPlatformModule                 {Get-Tpm, Initialize-Tpm, Clear-Tp...
Manifest    VpnClient                             {Add-VpnConnection, Set-VpnConnect...
Manifest    Wdac                                  {Get-OdbcDriver, Set-OdbcDriver, G...
Manifest    WindowsDeveloperLicense               {Get-WindowsDeveloperLicense, Show...
Script      WindowsErrorReporting                 {Enable-WindowsErrorReporting, Dis....
```

**Note** Windows PowerShell 3.0 still installs into the \\windows\system32\WindowsPowerShell\ v1.0 directory (even on Windows 8). The reason for adherence to this location is for compatibility with applications that expect this location. A common question I receive via the Hey Scripting Guy! blog (*http://www.scriptingguys.com/blog*) is related to this folder name. To determine the version of Windows PowerShell you are running, use the *$PSVersionTable* automatic variable.

## Loading modules

Once you have identified a module you wish to load, you use the *Import-Module* cmdlet to load the module into the current Windows PowerShell session. This appears here:

```
PS C:\> Import-Module -Name NetConnection
PS C:\>
```

If the module exists, the *Import-Module* cmdlet completes without displaying any information. If the module is already loaded, no error message displays. This behavior appears as follows, where you press the up arrow key to retrieve the previous command and press Enter to execute the command. The *Import-Module* command runs three times but no errors appear.

```
PS C:\> Import-Module -Name NetConnection
PS C:\> Import-Module -Name NetConnection
PS C:\> Import-Module -Name NetConnection
PS C:\>
```

Once you import the module, you may want to use the *Get-Module* cmdlet to quickly see the functions exposed by the module. (You can also use the *Get-Command -module <modulename>* command as well.) It is not necessary to type the complete module name. You can use wildcards, and you can even use tab expansion to expand the module name. The wildcard technique appears here:

```
PS C:\> Get-Module net*

ModuleType Name                           ExportedCommands
---------- ----                           ----------------
Manifest   netconnection                  {Get-NetConnectionProfile, Set-Net...
```

As shown previously, the *netconnection* module exports two commands: the *Get-NetConnectionProfile* function, and some other command that is probably *Set-NetConnectionProfile* (the guess is due to the fact that the *Get* and the *Set* Windows PowerShell verbs often go together. Because the first three letters of the noun for the second function is *net,* I am assuming the command name). The one problem with using the *Get-Module* cmdlet is that it truncates the *exportedcommands* property (the truncate behavior is controlled by the value assigned to the *$formatEnumeration* automatic variable). The easy solution to this problem is to pipeline the resulting *psmoduleinfo* object to the *Select-Object* cmdlet and expand the *exportedcommands* property. This technique appears here:

```
PS C:\> Get-Module net* | select -expand *comm*

Key                                    Value
---                                    -----
Get-NetConnectionProfile               Get-NetConnectionProfile
Set-NetConnectionProfile               Set-NetConnectionProfile
```

When loading modules that have long names, you are not limited to typing the entire module name. You can use wildcards or tab expansion to complete the module name. When using wildcards to load modules, it is a best practice to type a significant portion of the module name so that you only match a single module from the list of modules that are available to you. If you do not match a single module, an error is generated. The following error appears because *net\** matches multiple modules.

```
PS C:\> Import-Module net*
Import-Module : The specified module 'net*' was not loaded because no valid module
file was found in any module directory.
At line:1 char:1
+ Import-Module net*
+ ~~~~~~~~~~~~~~~~~~
    . + CategoryInfo          : ResourceUnavailable: (net*:String) [Import-Module],
    FileNotFoundException
    + FullyQualifiedErrorId : Modules_ModuleNotFound,Microsoft.PowerShell.Commands.
    ImportModuleCommand
```

> **Important** In Windows PowerShell 2.0, if a wildcard pattern matches more than one module name, the first matched module loads and the remaining matches are ignored. This leads to inconsistent and unpredictable results. Therefore, Windows PowerShell 3.0 changes this behavior to generate an error when a wildcard pattern matches more than one module name.

If you want to load all of the modules that are available on your system, you can use the *Get-Module* cmdlet with the *-ListAvailable* parameter and pipeline the resulting *PSModuleInfo* objects to the *Import-Module* cmdlet. This is shown here:

```
PS C:\> Get-Module -ListAvailable | Import-Module
PS C:\>
```

If you have a module that contains a function, cmdlet, or workflow that uses a verb that is not on the allowed verb list, a warning message displays when you import the module. The functions in the module still work, and the module will work, but the warning displays to remind you to check the authorized verb list. This behavior appears here:

```
PS C:\> Import-Module HelloUser
WARNING: The names of some imported commands from the module 'HelloUser' include
unapproved verbs that might make them less discoverable. To find the commands with
unapproved verbs, run the Import-Module command again with the Verbose parameter.
For a list of approved verbs, type Get-Verb.
PS C:\> hello-user
hello administrator
```

To obtain more information about which unapproved verbs are being used, you use the *-Verbose* parameter of *Import-Module*. This command is shown here:

```
PS C:\> Import-Module HelloUser -Verbose
```

The results of the *Import-Module -Verbose* command are shown in Figure 7-6.

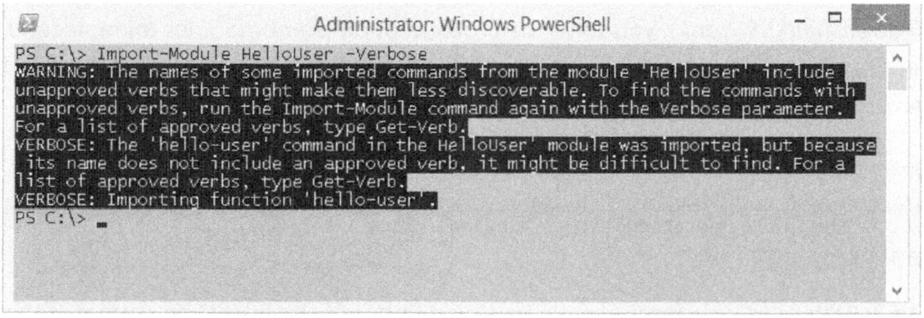

**FIGURE 7-6** The *-Verbose* parameter of *Import-Module* displays information about each function exported, as well as illegal verb names. The *hello* verb used in *Hello-User* is not an approved verb.

In this section, the concept of locating and loading modules was discussed. You can list modules by using the *-ListAvailable* switched parameter with the *Get-Module* cmdlet. Modules are loaded via the *Import-Module* cmdlet.

# Installing modules

One of the features of modules is that they can be installed without elevated rights. Because each user has a modules folder in the %userprofile% directory that the user has rights to use, the installation of a module does not require administrator rights to install into the personal module store. An additional feature of modules is that they do not require a specialized installer (of course, some complex modules do use specialized installers to make it easier for users to deploy). The files associated with a module can be copied by using the Xcopy utility, or they can be copied by using Windows PowerShell cmdlets.

## Creating a per-user Modules folder

The users' modules folder does not exist by default. To avoid confusion, you may decide to create the modules directory in the user's profile prior to deploying modules, or you may simply create a module-installer script (or even a logon script) that checks for the existence of the user's modules folder, creates the folder if it does not exist, and then copies the modules. One thing to remember when directly accessing the user's modules directory is that the modules folder is in a different location depending on the version of the operating system. On Windows XP and Windows Server 2003, the user's modules folder is in the My Documents folder, and on Windows Vista and above, the user's modules folder is in the Documents folder.

**Note** Windows PowerShell 3.0 does not install on Windows Vista or below. So, in a pure Windows PowerShell 3.0 environment, you can skip the operating system check and simply create the folder in the Documents folder.

In the Copy-Modules.ps1 script (available with the scripts for this chapter from *http://aka.ms/PowerShellSBS_book*), you solve the problem of different modules folder locations by using the *Get-OperatingSystemVersion* function, which retrieves the major version number of the operating system. The *Get-OperatingSystemVersion* function appears here:

```
Function Get-OperatingSystemVersion
{
 (Get-WmiObject -Class Win32_OperatingSystem).Version
} #end Get-OperatingSystemVersion
```

The *Test-ModulePath* function uses the major version number of the operating system. If the major version number of the operating system is greater than 6, it means the operating system is at least Windows Vista and will therefore use the Documents folder in the path to the modules. If the major version number of the operating system is not greater than 6, the script will use the *My Documents* folder for the module location. Once the version of the operating system is determined and the path to the module location is ascertained, it is time to determine if the modules folders exist or not. The best tool for the job of checking for the existence of folders is the *Test-Path* cmdlet. The *Test-Path* cmdlet returns a Boolean value. As you are only interested in the absence of the folder, you can use the *-not* operator in the completed *Test-ModulePath* function, as shown here:

```
Function Test-ModulePath
{
 $VistaPath = "$env:userProfile\documents\WindowsPowerShell\Modules"
 $XPPath =  "$env:Userprofile\my documents\WindowsPowerShell\Modules"
 if ([int](Get-OperatingSystemVersion).substring(0,1) -ge 6)
   {
     if(-not(Test-Path -path $VistaPath))
       {
         New-Item -Path $VistaPath -itemtype directory | Out-Null
       } #end if
   } #end if
 Else
   {
     if(-not(Test-Path -path $XPPath))
       {
         New-Item -path $XPPath -itemtype directory | Out-Null
       } #end if
   } #end else
} #end Test-ModulePath
```

Upon creating the user's Modules folder, it is time to create a child folder to hold the new module. A module installs into a folder that has the same name as the module itself. The name of the module is the name of the folder. For the module to be valid, it needs a file of the same name with either a .psm1 or .psd1 extension. The location is shown in Figure 7-7.

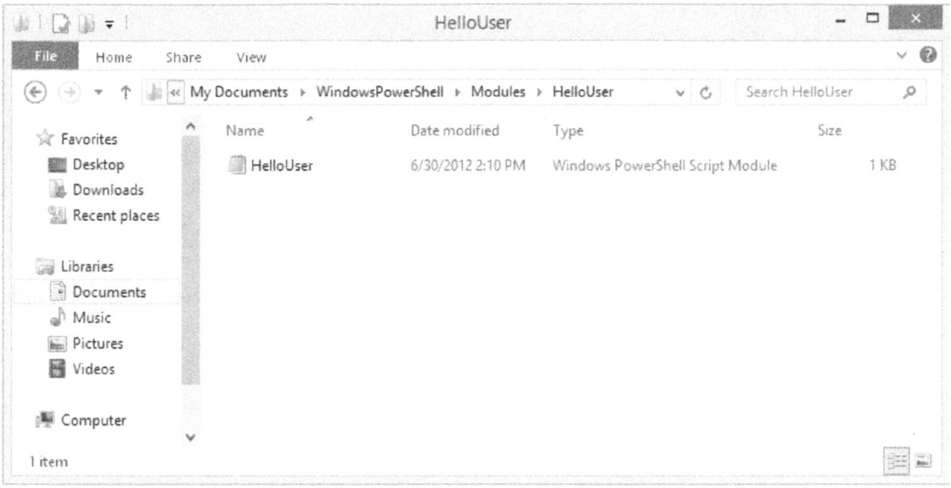

**FIGURE 7-7** Modules are placed in the user's Modules directory.

In the *Copy-Module* function from the Copy-Modules.ps1 script, the first action retrieves the value of the *PSModulePath* environmental variable. Because there are two default locations in which modules can be stored, the *PSModulePath* environmental variable contains the path to both locations. *PSModulePath* is not stored as an array; it is stored as a string. The value contained in *PSModulePath* appears here:

```
PS C:\> $env:PSModulePath
C:\Users\administrator\Documents\WindowsPowerShell\Modules;C:\Windows\system32\
WindowsPowerShell\v1.0\Modules\
```

If you attempt to index into the data stored in the *PSModulePath* environmental variable, you will retrieve one letter at a time. This is shown here:

```
PS C:\> $env:psmodulePath[0]
C
PS C:\> $env:psmodulePath[1]
:
PS C:\> $env:psmodulePath[2]
\
PS C:\> $env:psmodulePath[3]
U
```

Attempting to retrieve the path to the user's module location one letter at a time would be problematic at best and error prone at worst. Because the data is a string, you can use string methods to manipulate the two paths. To break a string into an usable array, you use the *split* method from the *System.String* class. You only need to pass a single value to the *split* method: the character upon which to split. Because the value stored in the *PSModulePath* variable is a set of strings separated by semicolons, you can access the *split* method directly. This technique appears here:

```
PS C:\> $env:PSModulePath.Split(";")
C:\Users\administrator\Documents\WindowsPowerShell\Modules
C:\Windows\system32\WindowsPowerShell\v1.0\Modules\
```

You can see from the preceding output that the first string displayed is the path to the user's modules folder, and the second string is the path to the system modules folder. Because the *split* method turns a string into an array, you can now index into the array and retrieve the path to the user's modules folder by using the *[0]* syntax. You do not need to use an intermediate variable to store the returned array of paths if you do not wish to. You can index into the returned array directly. If you were to use the intermediate variable to hold the returned array, and then index into the array, the code would resemble the following:

```
PS C:\> $aryPaths = $env:PSModulePath.Split(";")
PS C:\> $aryPaths[0]
C:\Users\administrator\Documents\WindowsPowerShell\Modules
```

Because the array is immediately available once the *split* method has been called, you directly retrieve the user's modules path. This is shown here:

```
PS C:\> $env:PSModulePath.Split(";")[0]
C:\Users\administrator\Documents\WindowsPowerShell\Modules
```

## Working with the *$modulePath* variable

The path that will be used to store the module is stored in the *$modulepath* variable. This path includes the path to the user's modules folder plus a child folder that has the same name as the module itself. To create the new path, it is a best practice to use the *Join-Path* cmdlet instead of doing string concatenation and attempting to manually build the path to the new folder. The *Join-Path* cmdlet will put together a parent path and a child path to create a new path. This is shown here:

```
$ModulePath = Join-Path -path $userPath `
              -childpath (Get-Item -path $name).basename
```

Windows PowerShell adds a script property called *basename* to the *System.Io.FileInfo* class. This makes it easy to retrieve the name of a file without the file extension. Prior to Windows PowerShell 2.0, it was common to use the *split* method or some other string-manipulation technique to remove the extension from the file name. Use of the *basename* property appears here:

```
PS C:\> (Get-Item -Path C:\fso\HelloWorld.psm1).basename
HelloWorld
```

Finally, you need to create the subdirectory that will hold the module and copy the module files into the directory. To avoid cluttering the display with the returned information from the *New-Item* and *Copy-Item* cmdlets, the results are pipelined to the *Out-Null* cmdlet. This is shown here:

```
New-Item -path $modulePath -itemtype directory | Out-Null
Copy-Item -path $name -destination $ModulePath | Out-Null
```

The entry point to the Copy-Modules.ps1 script calls the *Test-ModulePath* function to determine if the user's modules folder exists. It then uses the *Get-ChildItem* cmdlet to retrieve a listing of all the module files in a particular folder. The *-Recurse* parameter is used to retrieve all the module files in the path. The resulting *FileInfo* objects are pipelined to the *ForEach-Object* cmdlet. The *fullname* property of each *FileInfo* object is passed to the *Copy-Module* function. This is shown here:

```
Test-ModulePath
Get-ChildItem -Path C:\fso -Include *.psm1,*.psd1 -Recurse |
ForEach-Object { Copy-Module -name $_.fullname }
```

The complete Copy-Modules.ps1 script is shown here:

**Copy-Modules.ps1**
```
Function Get-OperatingSystemVersion
{
 (Get-WmiObject -Class Win32_OperatingSystem).Version
} #end Get-OperatingSystemVersion

Function Test-ModulePath
{
 $VistaPath = "$env:userProfile\documents\WindowsPowerShell\Modules"
 $XPPath =  "$env:Userprofile\my documents\WindowsPowerShell\Modules"
 if ([int](Get-OperatingSystemVersion).substring(0,1) -ge 6)
   {
     if(-not(Test-Path -path $VistaPath))
       {
          New-Item -Path $VistaPath -itemtype directory | Out-Null
       } #end if
   } #end if
 Else
   {
     if(-not(Test-Path -path $XPPath))
       {
          New-Item -path $XPPath -itemtype directory | Out-Null
       } #end if
   } #end else
} #end Test-ModulePath

Function Copy-Module([string]$name)
{
 $UserPath = $env:PSModulePath.split(";")[0]
 $ModulePath = Join-Path -path $userPath `
               -childpath (Get-Item -path $name).basename
 New-Item -path $modulePath -itemtype directory | Out-Null
 Copy-Item -path $name -destination $ModulePath | Out-Null
}

# *** Entry Point to Script ***
Test-ModulePath
Get-ChildItem -Path C:\fso -Include *.psm1,*.psd1 -Recurse |
ForEach-Object { Copy-Module -name $_.fullname }
```

**Note** You must set the script execution policy to permit running of scripts to use user-created script modules. Script support does not need to be enabled in Windows PowerShell to use the system modules. However, to run Copy-Modules.ps1 to install modules to the user's profile, you would need scripting support. To enable scripting support in Windows PowerShell, you use the *Set-ExecutionPolicy* cmdlet.

## Creating a module drive

An easy way to work with modules is to create a couple of Windows PowerShell drives using the filesystem provider. Since the modules live in a location that is not easily navigated to from the command line, and since *$PSModulePath* returns a string that contains the path to both the user's and system modules folders, it makes sense to provide an easier way to work with the modules' locations. To create a Windows PowerShell drive for the user module location, you use the *New-PSDrive* cmdlet, specify a name, such as mymods, use the filesystem provider, and obtain the root location from the *$PSModulePath* environmental variable by using the *split* method from the .NET Framework *String* class. For the user's modules folder, you use first element from the returned array. This is shown here:

```
PS C:\> New-PSDrive -Name mymods -PSProvider filesystem -Root ($env:PSModulePath.Split(";")[0])

Name            Used (GB)    Free (GB) Provider      Root
----            ---------    --------- --------      ----
mymods                         116.50 FileSystem    C:\Users\administrator\Docum...
```

The command to create a Windows PowerShell drive for the system module location is similar to the one used to create a Windows PowerShell drive for the user module location. The exceptions are specifying a different name, such as sysmods, and choosing the second element from the array obtained via the *split* method call on the *$PSModulePath* variable. This command appears here:

```
PS C:\> New-PSDrive -Name sysmods -PSProvider filesystem -Root ($env:PSModulePath.Split(";")[1])

Name            Used (GB)    Free (GB) Provider      Root
----            ---------    --------- --------      ----
sysmods                        116.50 FileSystem    C:\Windows\system32\WindowsP...
```

You can also write a script that creates Windows PowerShell drives for each of the two module locations. To do this, you first create an array of names for the Windows PowerShell drives. You then use a *For* statement to walk through the array of PowerShell drive names and call the *New-PSDrive* cmdlet. Because you are running the commands inside a script, the new PowerShell drives by default will live within the script scope. Once the script ends, the script scope goes away. This means the Windows PowerShell drives will not be available once the script ended—which would defeat your purposes in creating them in the first place. To combat this scoping issue, you need to create the PowerShell drives within the global scope, which means they will be available in the Windows PowerShell console once the script has completed running. To avoid displaying confirmation messages when creating the PowerShell drives, you pipe the results to the *Out-Null* cmdlet.

In the New-ModulesDrive.ps1 script, create another function. This function displays global file system PowerShell drives. When the script runs, call the *New-ModuleDrive* function. Then call the *Get-FileSystemDrives* function. The complete *New-ModuleDrive* function appears here:

**New-ModuleDrive function**

```
Function New-ModuleDrive
{
<#
    .SYNOPSIS
    Creates two PS drives: myMods and sysMods
    .EXAMPLE
    New-ModuleDrive
    Creates two PS drives: myMods and sysMods. These correspond
    to the users' modules folder and the system modules folder respectively.
#>
 $driveNames = "myMods","sysMods"

 For($i = 0 ; $i -le 1 ; $i++)
 {
  New-PSDrive -name $driveNames[$i] -PSProvider filesystem `
  -Root ($env:PSModulePath.split(";")[$i]) -scope Global |
  Out-Null
 } #end For
} #end New-ModuleDrive

Function Get-FileSystemDrives
{
<#
    .SYNOPSIS
    Displays global PS drives that use the filesystem provider
    .EXAMPLE
    Get-FileSystemDrives
    Displays global PS drives that use the filesystem provider
#>
 Get-PSDrive -PSProvider FileSystem -scope Global
} #end Get-FileSystemDrives

# *** EntryPoint to Script ***
New-ModuleDrive
Get-FileSystemDrives
```

This section covered the concept of installing modules. Before installing modules, create a special modules folder in the user's profile. A script was developed that will perform this action. The use of a *$modulepath* variable was examined. The section concluded with a script that creates a PowerShell drive to provide easy access to installed modules.

# Checking for module dependencies

One problem with using modules is you now have a dependency to external code, and this means that a script that uses the module must have the module installed, or else the script will fail. If you control the environment, taking an external dependency is not a bad thing; if you do not control the environment, an external dependency can be a disaster.

Because of the potential for problems, Windows PowerShell 3.0 adds additional capabilities to the *#requires* statement. The *#requires* statement can check for Windows PowerShell version, modules, snap-ins, and even module and snap-in version numbers. Unfortunately, use of *#requires* only works in a script, not in a function, cmdlet, or snap-in. Figure 7-8 illustrates using the *#requires* statement to ensure the presence of a specific module prior to script execution. The script requires a module named *bogus* that does not exist. Because the *bogus* module does not exist, an error occurs.

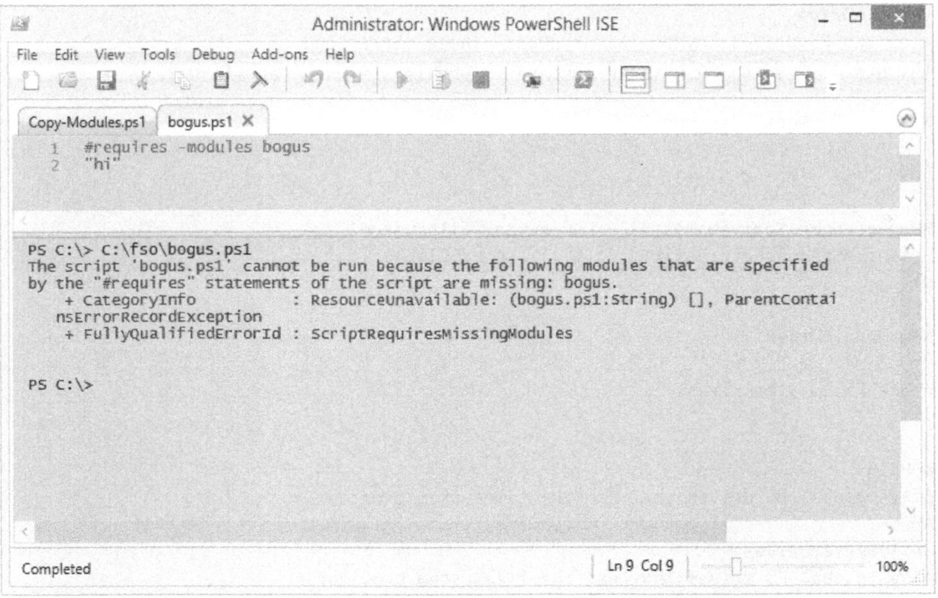

**FIGURE 7-8** Use the *#requires* statement to prevent execution of a script when a required module does not exist.

Because you cannot use the *#requires* statement inside a function, you may want to use the *Get-MyModule* function to determine if a module exists or is already loaded (the other way to do this is to use a manifest). The complete *Get-MyModule* function appears here:

```
Get-MyModule.ps1
Function Get-MyModule
{
 Param([string]$name)
 if(-not(Get-Module -name $name))
   {
    if(Get-Module -ListAvailable |
       Where-Object { $_.name -eq $name })
      {
       Import-Module -Name $name
       $true
      } #end if module available then import
    else { $false } #module not available
   } # end if not module
  else { $true } #module already loaded

} #end function get-MyModule

get-mymodule -name "bitsTransfer"
```

The *Get-MyModule* function accepts a single string: the name of the module to check. The *if* statement is used to see if the module is currently loaded. If it is not loaded, the *Get-Module* cmdlet is used to see if the module exists on the system. If it does exist, the module is loaded.

If the module is already loaded into the current Windows PowerShell session, the *Get-MyModule* function returns *$true* to the calling code. Let's dig into the function a bit further to see how it works.

The first thing you do is use the *if* statement to see if the module is not loaded into the current session. To do this, use the *-not* operator to see if the module is not loaded. Use the *Get-Module* cmdlet to search for the required module by name. This section of the script appears here:

```
Function Get-MyModule
{
 Param([string]$name)
 if(-not(Get-Module -name $name))
   {
```

To obtain a list of modules that are installed on a system, use the *Get-Module* cmdlet with the *-ListAvailable* switch. Unfortunately, there is no way to filter the results, and this necessitates pipelining the results to the *Where-Object* cmdlet to see if the required cmdlet is installed on the system. If the module exists on the system, the function uses the *Import-Module* cmdlet to import the module, and it returns *$true* to the calling code. This section of the script is shown here:

```
if(Get-Module -ListAvailable |
      Where-Object { $_.name -eq $name })
     {
      Import-Module -Name $name
      $true
     } #end if module available then import
```

Finally, you need to handle the two other cases. If the module is not available, the *Where-Object* cmdlet will not find anything. This triggers the first *else* clause, where *$false* is returned to the calling code. If the module is already loaded, the second *else* clause returns *$true* to the script. This section of the script is shown here:

```
  else { $false } #module not available
  } # end if not module
else { $true } #module already loaded

} #end function get-MyModule
```

A simple use of the *Get-MyModule* function is to call the function and pass the name of a module to it. This example is actually shown in the last line of the Get-MyModule.ps1 script:

```
get-mymodule -name "bitsTransfer"
```

When called in this manner, the *Get-MyModule* function will load the bitsTransfer module if it exists on your system and if it is not already loaded. If the module is already loaded, or if it is loaded by the function, *$true* is returned to the script. If the module does not exist, *$false* is returned. The use of the *Get-MyModule* function appears in Figure 7-9.

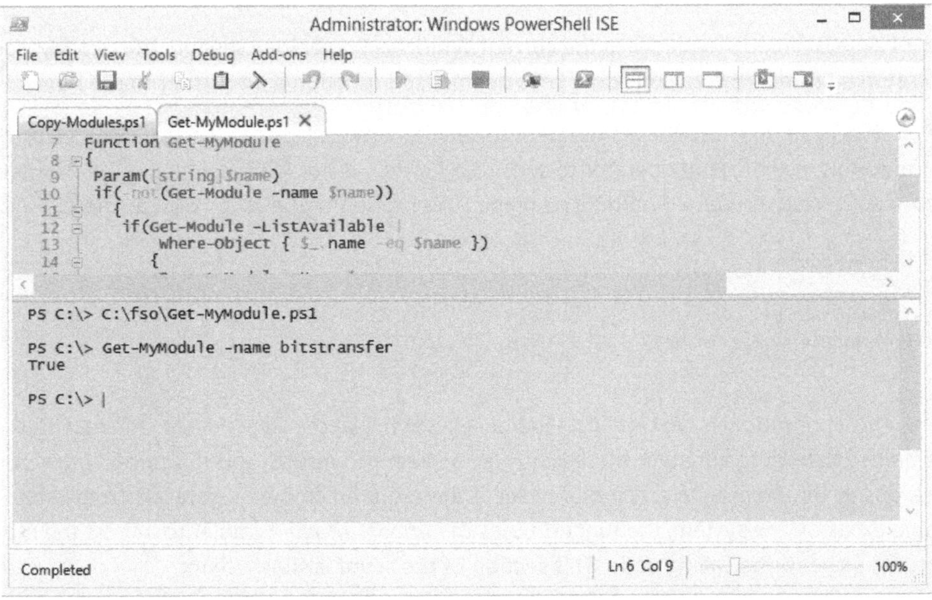

**FIGURE 7-9** Use the *Get-MyModule* function to ensure a module exists prior to attempting to load it.

A better use of the *Get-MyModule* function is as a prerequisite check for a function that uses a particular module. Your syntax might look something like this:

```
If(Get-MyModule -name "bitsTransfer") { call your bits code here }
ELSE { "Bits module is not installed on this system." ; exit }
```

# Using a module from a share

Using a module from a central file share is no different from using a module from one of the two default locations. When a module is placed in the %windir%\System32\WindowsPowerShell\v1.0\Modules folder, it is available to all users. If a module is placed in the %UserProfile%\My documents\WindowsPowerShell\Modules folder, it is only available to the specific user. The advantage of placing modules in the %UserProfile% location is that the user automatically has permission to perform the installation; modules in the system location, on the other hand, require administrator rights.

Speaking of installation of Windows PowerShell modules, in many cases the installation of a Windows PowerShell module is no more complicated than placing the *.psm1 file in a folder in the default user location. The key point is that the folder created under the \Modules folder must have the same name as the module itself. When you install a module on a local computer, use the Copy-Modules.ps1 script to simplify the process of creating and naming the folders.

When copying a Windows PowerShell module to a network-shared location, follow the same rules: make sure that the folder that contains the module has the same name as the module. In the following procedure, you'll copy the ConversionModuleV6 module to a network share.

### Using a network-shared module

1. Create a share on a networked server and assign appropriate permissions.

2. Use the *Get-ChildItem* cmdlet (for which *dir* is the alias) to view the share and the associated modules. Here's an example:

```
PS C:\> dir '\\w8s504\shared'


    Directory: \\w8s504\shared


Mode                LastWriteTime     Length Name
----                -------------     ------ ----
d----         6/30/2012   1:00 PM            ConversionModuleV6
```

3. Import the module by using the *Import-Module* cmdlet and the UNC (Universal Naming Convention) path to the folder containing the module. The following command imports the module from the W8s504 server:

```
PS C:\> Import-Module \\w8s504\shared\Conv*
```

4.  Verify that the module has loaded properly by using the *Get-Module* cmdlet. This command appears here:

```
PS C:\> Get-Module

ModuleType Name                                    ExportedCommands
---------- ----                                    ----------------
Script     ConversionModuleV6                      {ConvertTo-celsius, ConvertTo-Fahr...
Manifest   Microsoft.PowerShell.Management         {Add-Computer, Add-Content, Checkp...
Manifest   Microsoft.PowerShell.Security           {ConvertFrom-SecureString, Convert...
Manifest   Microsoft.PowerShell.Utility            {Add-Member, Add-Type, Clear-Varia...
```

5.  Use the *Get-Command* cmdlet to see the commands exported by the module. This technique appears here (*gcm* is an alias for the *Get-Command* cmdlet):

```
PS C:\> gcm -Module conv*

CommandType     Name                        ModuleName
-----------     ----                        ----------
Function        ConvertTo-celsius           ConversionModu...
Function        ConvertTo-Fahrenheit        ConversionModu...
Function        ConvertTo-Feet              ConversionModu...
Function        ConvertTo-Kilometers        ConversionModu...
Function        ConvertTo-Liters            ConversionModu...
Function        ConvertTo-Meters            ConversionModu...
Function        ConvertTo-MetersPerSecond   ConversionModu...
Function        ConvertTo-Miles             ConversionModu...
Function        ConvertTo-Pounds            ConversionModu...
```

You need to keep in mind a couple of things. The first is that a Windows PowerShell module is basically a script—in our particular application. If the script execution policy is set to the default level of *Restricted*, an error will be generated—even if the logged-on user is an administrator. Fortunately, the error that is returned informs you of that fact. Even if the execution policy is set to *Restricted* on a particular machine, you can always run a Windows PowerShell script (or module) if you start Windows PowerShell with the *bypass* option. The command to do this is shown here:

```
powershell -executionpolicy bypass
```

One of the really cool uses of a shared module is to permit centralization of Windows PowerShell profiles for networked users. To do this, the profile on the local computer would simply import the shared module. In this way, you only need to modify one module in one location to permit updates for all the users on the network.

# Creating a module

The first thing you will probably want to do is to create a module. You can create a module in the Windows PowerShell ISE. The easiest way to create a module is to use functions you have previously written. One of the first things to do is to locate the functions you wish to store in the module. You can copy them directly into the Windows PowerShell ISE. This technique appears in Figure 7-10.

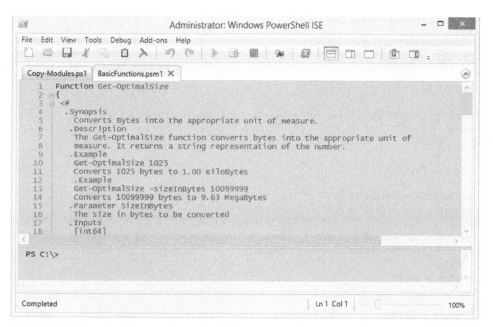

**FIGURE 7-10** Using the Windows PowerShell ISE makes creating a new module as easy as copying and pasting existing functions into a new file.

Once you have copied your functions into the new module, save it with the .psm1 extension. The basicFunctions.psm1 module appears here:

**BasicFunctions.psm1**

```
Function Get-OptimalSize
{
 <#
  .Synopsis
    Converts Bytes into the appropriate unit of measure.
  .Description
    The Get-OptimalSize function converts bytes into the appropriate unit of
    measure. It returns a string representation of the number.
  .Example
    Get-OptimalSize 1025
    Converts 1025 bytes to 1.00 KiloBytes
  .Example
    Get-OptimalSize -sizeInBytes 10099999
    Converts 10099999 bytes to 9.63 MegaBytes
  .Parameter SizeInBytes
    The size in bytes to be converted
  .Inputs
    [int64]
  .OutPuts
    [string]
  .Notes
    NAME:  Get-OptimalSize
    AUTHOR: Ed Wilson
    LASTEDIT: 6/30/2012
```

```
    KEYWORDS: Scripting Techniques, Modules
   .Link
     Http://www.ScriptingGuys.com
 #Requires -Version 2.0
 #>
[CmdletBinding()]
param(
     [Parameter(Mandatory = $true,Position = 0,valueFromPipeline=$true)]
     [int64]
     $sizeInBytes
) #end param
 Switch ($sizeInBytes)
  {
  {$sizeInBytes -ge 1TB} {"{0:n2}" -f  ($sizeInBytes/1TB) + " TeraBytes";break}
  {$sizeInBytes -ge 1GB} {"{0:n2}" -f  ($sizeInBytes/1GB) + " GigaBytes";break}
  {$sizeInBytes -ge 1MB} {"{0:n2}" -f  ($sizeInBytes/1MB) + " MegaBytes";break}
  {$sizeInBytes -ge 1KB} {"{0:n2}" -f  ($sizeInBytes/1KB) + " KiloBytes";break}
  Default { "{0:n2}" -f $sizeInBytes + " Bytes" }
  } #end switch
  $sizeInBytes = $null
} #end Function Get-OptimalSize

Function Get-ComputerInfo
{
 <#
  .Synopsis
   Retrieves basic information about a computer.
  .Description
   The Get-ComputerInfo cmdlet retrieves basic information such as
   computer name, domain name, and currently logged on user from
   a local or remote computer.
  .Example
   Get-ComputerInfo
   Returns computer name, domain name and currently logged on user
   from local computer.
  .Example
   Get-ComputerInfo -computer berlin
   Returns computer name, domain name and currently logged on user
   from remote computer named berlin.
  .Parameter Computer
   Name of remote computer to retrieve information from
  .Inputs
   [string]
  .OutPuts
   [object]
  .Notes
   NAME:  Get-ComputerInfo
   AUTHOR: Ed Wilson
   LASTEDIT: 6/30/2012
   KEYWORDS: Desktop mgmt, basic information
  .Link
     Http://www.ScriptingGuys.com
 #Requires -Version 2.0
 #>
```

```
    Param([string]$computer=$env:COMPUTERNAME)
    $wmi = Get-WmiObject -Class win32_computersystem -ComputerName $computer
    $pcinfo = New-Object psobject -Property @{"host" = $wmi.DNSHostname
            "domain" = $wmi.Domain
            "user" = $wmi.Username}
    $pcInfo
} #end function Get-ComputerInfo
```

You can control what is exported from the module by creating a manifest (or you can control what the module exports by using the *Export-ModuleMember* cmdlet). If you place together related functions that you will more than likely want to use in a single session, you can avoid creating a manifest (although you may still wish to create a manifest for documentation and for management purposes). In the BasicFunctions.psm1 module, there are two functions: one that convert numbers from bytes to a more easily understood numeric unit, and another function that returns basic computer information.

The *Get-ComputerInfo* function returns a custom object that contains information about the user, computer name, and computer domain. Once you have created and saved the module, you will need to install the module by copying it to your module store. You can do this manually by navigating to the module directory, creating a folder for the module, and placing a copy of the module in the folder. I prefer to use the Copy-Modules.ps1 script discussed earlier in this chapter.

Once the module has been copied to its own directory (installed), you can use the *Import-Module* cmdlet to import it into the current Windows PowerShell session. If you are not sure of the name of the module, you can use the *Get-Module* cmdlet with the *-ListAvailable* switch, as shown here:

```
PS C:\> Get-Module -ListAvailable


    Directory: C:\Users\administrator\Documents\WindowsPowerShell\Modules


ModuleType Name                              ExportedCommands
---------- ----                              ----------------
Script     BasicFunctions                    {Get-OptimalSize, Get-ComputerInfo}
Script     ConversionModuleV6                {ConvertTo-MetersPerSecond, Conver...
Script     HelloUser                         hello-user


    Directory: C:\Windows\system32\WindowsPowerShell\v1.0\Modules


ModuleType Name                              ExportedCommands
---------- ----                              ----------------
Manifest   AppLocker                         {Get-AppLockerFileInformation, Get...
Manifest   Appx                              {Add-AppxPackage, Get-AppxPackage,...
Manifest   BitLocker                         {Unlock-BitLocker, Suspend-BitLock...
Manifest   BitsTransfer                      {Add-BitsFile, Complete-BitsTransf...
Manifest   BranchCache                       {Add-BCDataCacheExtension, Clear-B...
Manifest   CimCmdlets                        {Get-CimAssociatedInstance, Get-Ci...
Manifest   DirectAccessClientComponents      {Disable-DAManualEntryPointSelecti...
Script     Dism                              {Add-AppxProvisionedPackage, Add-W...
Manifest   DnsClient                         {Resolve-DnsName, Clear-DnsClientC...
Manifest   International                     {Get-WinDefaultInputMethodOverride...
Manifest   iSCSI                             {Get-IscsiTargetPortal, New-IscsiT...
```

```
Script      ISE                                   {New-IseSnippet, Import-IseSnippet...
Manifest    Kds                                   {Add-KdsRootKey, Get-KdsRootKey, T...
Manifest    Microsoft.PowerShell.Diagnostics      {Get-WinEvent, Get-Counter, Import...
Manifest    Microsoft.PowerShell.Host             {Start-Transcript, Stop-Transcript}
Manifest    Microsoft.PowerShell.Management        {Add-Content, Clear-Content, Clear...
Manifest    Microsoft.PowerShell.Security         {Get-Acl, Set-Acl, Get-PfxCertific...
Manifest    Microsoft.PowerShell.Utility          {Format-List, Format-Custom, Forma...
Manifest    Microsoft.WSMan.Management             {Disable-WSManCredSSP, Enable-WSMa...
Manifest    MMAgent                               {Disable-MMAgent, Enable-MMAgent, ...
Manifest    MsDtc                                 {New-DtcDiagnosticTransaction, Com...
Manifest    NetAdapter                            {Disable-NetAdapter, Disable-NetAd...
Manifest    NetConnection                         {Get-NetConnectionProfile, Set-Net...
Manifest    NetLbfo                               {Add-NetLbfoTeamMember, Add-NetLbf...
Manifest    NetQos                                {Get-NetQosPolicy, Set-NetQosPolic...
Manifest    NetSecurity                           {Get-DAPolicyChange, New-NetIPsecA...
Manifest    NetSwitchTeam                         {New-NetSwitchTeam, Remove-NetSwit...
Manifest    NetTCPIP                              {Get-NetIPAddress, Get-NetIPInterf...
Manifest    NetworkConnectivityStatus             {Get-DAConnectionStatus, Get-NCSIP...
Manifest    NetworkTransition                     {Add-NetIPHttpsCertBinding, Disabl...
Manifest    PKI                                   {Add-CertificateEnrollmentPolicySe...
Manifest    PrintManagement                       {Add-Printer, Add-PrinterDriver, A...
Script      PSDiagnostics                         {Disable-PSTrace, Disable-PSWSManC...
Binary      PSScheduledJob                        {New-JobTrigger, Add-JobTrigger, R...
Manifest    PSWorkflow                            {New-PSWorkflowExecutionOption, Ne...
Manifest    PSWorkflowUtility                     Invoke-AsWorkflow
Manifest    ScheduledTasks                        {Get-ScheduledTask, Set-ScheduledT...
Manifest    SecureBoot                            {Confirm-SecureBootUEFI, Set-Secur...
Manifest    SmbShare                              {Get-SmbShare, Remove-SmbShare, Se...
Manifest    SmbWitness                            {Get-SmbWitnessClient, Move-SmbWit...
Manifest    Storage                               {Add-InitiatorIdToMaskingSet, Add-...
Manifest    TroubleshootingPack                   {Get-TroubleshootingPack, Invoke-T...
Manifest    TrustedPlatformModule                 {Get-Tpm, Initialize-Tpm, Clear-Tp...
Manifest    VpnClient                             {Add-VpnConnection, Set-VpnConnect...
Manifest    Wdac                                  {Get-OdbcDriver, Set-OdbcDriver, G...
Manifest    WindowsDeveloperLicense               {Get-WindowsDeveloperLicense, Show...
Script      WindowsErrorReporting                 {Enable-WindowsErrorReporting, Dis...
```

Once you have imported the module, you can use the *Get-Command* cmdlet with the *-module* parameter to see what commands are exported by the module.

```
PS C:\> Import-Module basicfunctions
PS C:\> Get-Command -Module basic*

CommandType     Name                                               ModuleName
-----------     ----                                               ----------
Function        Get-ComputerInfo                                   basicfunctions
Function        Get-OptimalSize                                    basicfunctions
```

Once you have added the functions from the module, you can use them directly from the Windows PowerShell prompt. Using the *Get-ComputerInfo* function is illustrated here:

```
PS C:\> Get-ComputerInfo

host                              domain                      user
----                              ------                      ----
mred1                             NWTraders.Com               NWTRADERS\ed


PS C:\> (Get-ComputerInfo).user
NWTRADERS\ed
PS C:\> (Get-ComputerInfo).host
mred1
PS C:\> Get-ComputerInfo -computer win8-pc | Format-Table -AutoSize

host    domain          user
----    ------          ----
win8-PC NWTraders.Com NWTRADERS\Administrator


PS C:\>
```

Because the help tags were used when creating the functions, you can use the *Get-Help* cmdlet to obtain information about using the function. In this manner, the function that was created in the module behaves exactly like a regular Windows PowerShell cmdlet. This includes tab expansion.

```
PS C:\> Get-Help Get-ComputerInfo

NAME
    Get-ComputerInfo

SYNOPSIS
    Retrieves basic information about a computer.


SYNTAX
    Get-ComputerInfo [[-computer] <String>] [<CommonParameters>]


DESCRIPTION
    The Get-ComputerInfo cmdlet retrieves basic information such as
    computer name, domain name, and currently logged on user from
    a local or remote computer.


RELATED LINKS
    Http://www.ScriptingGuys.com
    #Requires -Version 2.0

REMARKS
    To see the examples, type: "Get-Help Get-ComputerInfo -examples".
    For more information, type: "Get-Help Get-ComputerInfo -detailed".
    For technical information, type: "Get-Help Get-ComputerInfo -full".
```

```
PS C:\> Get-Help Get-ComputerInfo -Examples
```

NAME
    Get-ComputerInfo

SYNOPSIS
    Retrieves basic information about a computer.

    ------------------------ EXAMPLE 1 ------------------------

    C:\PS>Get-ComputerInfo


    Returns computer name, domain name and currently logged on user
    from local computer.




    ------------------------ EXAMPLE 2 ------------------------

    C:\PS>Get-ComputerInfo -computer berlin


    Returns computer name, domain name and currently logged on user
    from remote computer named berlin.



```
PS C:\>
```

The *Get-OptimalSize* function can even receive input from the pipeline, as shown here:

```
PS C:\> (Get-WmiObject win32_volume -Filter "driveletter = 'c:'").freespace
26513960960
PS C:\> (Get-WmiObject win32_volume -Filter "driveletter = 'c:'").freespace | Get-OptimalSize
24.69 GigaBytes
PS C:\>
```


## Creating, installing, and importing a module

1. Place functions into a text file and save the file with a .psm1 extension.

2. Copy the newly created module containing the functions to the modules directory. Use the Copy-Modules.ps1 script to do this.

3. Obtain a listing of available modules by using the *Get-Modules* cmdlet with the *-ListAvailable* switched parameter.

4. Optionally, import modules into your current Windows PowerShell session by using the *Import-Module* cmdlet.

5. See what commands are available from the newly created module by using the *Get-Command* cmdlet with the *-module* parameter.

6. Use *Get-Help* to obtain information about the imported functions.

7. Use the functions like you would use any other cmdlet.

# Creating an advanced function: step-by-step exercises

In this exercise, you'll explore creating an advanced function. You will use a template from the Windows PowerShell ISE to create the basic framework. Next, you will add help and functionality to the advanced function. Following this exercise, you will add the advanced function to a module and install the module on your system.

### Creating an advanced function

1. Start the Windows PowerShell ISE.

2. Use the *cmdlet (advanced function)* snippet from the Windows PowerShell ISE to create the basic framework for an advanced function.

3. Move the comment-based help from outside the function body to inside the function body. The moved comment-based help appears here:

```
function Verb-Noun
{
 <#
.Synopsis
    Short description
.DESCRIPTION
    Long description
.EXAMPLE
    Example of how to use this cmdlet
.EXAMPLE
    Another example of how to use this cmdlet
#>
```

4. Change the name of the function from *Verb-Noun* to *Get-MyBios*. This change appears here:

```
function Get-MyBios
```

5. Modify the comment-based help. Fill in the synopsis, description, and example parameters. Add a comment for *parameter*. This revised comment-based help appears here:

```
<#
.Synopsis
    Gets bios information from local or remote computer
.DESCRIPTION
    This function gets bios information from local or remote computer
.Parameter computername
 The name of the remote computer
.EXAMPLE
    Get-MyBios
    Gets bios information from local computer
.EXAMPLE
    Get-MyBios -cn remoteComputer
    Gets bios information from remote computer named remotecomputer
#>
```

6. Add the #*requires* statement and require Windows PowerShell version 3.0. This command appears here:

```
#requires -version 3.0
```

7. Modify the parameter name to *computername*. Add an *alias* attribute with a value of *cn*. Configure parameter properties for *ValueFromPipeline* and *ParameterSetName*. Constrain the *computername* parameter to be a string. The code to do this appears here:

```
Param
    (
        # name of remote computer
        [Alias("cn")]
        [Parameter(ValueFromPipeline=$true,
                    Position=0,
                    ParametersetName="remote")]
        [string]
        $ComputerName)
```

8. Remove the *begin* and *end* statements from the snippet.

9. Add a *Switch* statement that evaluates *$PSCmdlet.ParameterSetName*. If *ParameterSetName* equals *remote*, use the -*classname* and -*computername* parameters from the *Get-CimInstance* cmdlet. Default to querying the *Get-CimInstance* cmdlet without using the -*computername* parameter. The *Switch* statement appears here:

```
Switch ($PSCmdlet.ParameterSetName)
    {
      "remote" { Get-CimInstance -ClassName win32_bios -cn $ComputerName }
      DEFAULT { Get-CimInstance -ClassName Win32_BIOS }
    } #end switch
```

10. Save the advanced function as Get-MyBios.ps1 in an easily accessible folder, because you'll turn this into a module in the next exercise.

11. Inside the Windows PowerShell ISE, run the function.

12. In the command pane, call the *Get-MyBios* function with no parameters. You should receive back BIOS information from your local computer.

13. Now call the *Get-MyBios* function with the *-cn* alias and the name of a remote computer. You should receive BIOS information from the remote computer.

14. Use *help* and view the full help from the advanced function. Sample output appears here:

```
PS C:\> help Get-MyBios -Full

NAME
    Get-MyBios

SYNOPSIS
    Gets bios information from local or remote computer

SYNTAX
    Get-MyBios [[-ComputerName] <String>] [<CommonParameters>]

DESCRIPTION
    This function gets bios information from local or remote computer

PARAMETERS
    -ComputerName <String>
        The name of the remote computer

        Required?                    false
        Position?                    1
        Default value
        Accept pipeline input?       true (ByValue)
        Accept wildcard characters?  false

    <CommonParameters>
        This cmdlet supports the common parameters: Verbose, Debug,
        ErrorAction, ErrorVariable, WarningAction, WarningVariable,
        OutBuffer and OutVariable. For more information, see
        about_CommonParameters (http://go.microsoft.com/fwlink/?LinkID=113216).

INPUTS

OUTPUTS

    ------------------------- EXAMPLE 1 -------------------------

    C:\PS>Get-MyBios


    Gets bios information from local computer
```

```
----------------------- EXAMPLE 2 -----------------------

C:\PS>Get-MyBios -cn remoteComputer


Gets bios information from remote computer named remotecomputer

requires -version 3.0
```

RELATED LINKS

This concludes this step-by-step exercise.

In the following exercise, you'll explore creating a module.

## Creating and installing a module

1. Start the Windows PowerShell ISE.

2. Open the Get-MyBios.ps1 file you created in the previous exercise and copy the contents into an empty Windows PowerShell ISE script pane.

3. Save the newly copied code as a module by specifying the .psm1 file extension. Call your file mybios.psm1. Choose the Save As option from the File menu, and save the file in a convenient location.

4. In your *mybios.psm1* file, just after the end of the script block for the *Get-MyBios* function, use the *New-Alias* cmdlet to create a new alias named *gmb*. Set the value of this alias to *Get-MyBios*. This command appears here:

   ```
   New-Alias -Name gmb -Value Get-MyBios
   ```

5. Add the *Export-ModuleMember* cmdlet to the script to export all aliases and functions from the mybios module. This command appears here:

   ```
   Export-ModuleMember -Function * -Alias *
   ```

6. Save your changes and close the module file.

7. Use the *Copy-Modules* script to create a modules folder named mybios in your current user's directory and copy the module to that location.

8. Open the Windows PowerShell console and use the *Import-Module* cmdlet to import the *mybios* module. This command appears here:

   ```
   Import-Module mybios
   ```

9. Use the *Get-MyBios* advanced function to return the BIOS information from the current computer.

**10.** Use the *Help* function to retrieve complete help information from the advanced function. This command appears here:

```
help Get-MyBios -full
```

**11.** Pipeline the name of a remote computer to the *Get-MyBios* advanced function. This command appears here:

```
"w8s504" | Get-MyBios
```

This concludes the exercise.

# Chapter 7 quick reference

| To | Do this |
|---|---|
| Display help for a command that is missing a parameter | Use the *HelpMessage* parameter property. |
| Make a parameter mandatory | Use the *Mandatory* parameter property in the *param* section of the function. |
| Implement -*verbose* in a function | Use the *[cmdletbinding]* attribute and write the messages via the *Write-Verbose* cmdlet. |
| Implement the -*whatif* switched parameter in a function | Use the *[cmdletbinding()]* attribute with the *SupportsShouldProcess* property. |
| Ensure that only defined parameters pass values to the function | Use the *[cmdletbinding()]* attribute. |
| Group sets of parameters for ease of use and checking | Create a parameter set via the *ParameterSetName* parameter property. |
| Assign a specific position to a parameter | Use the *Position* parameter property and assign a specific zero-based numeric position. |

# CHAPTER 8

# Using the Windows PowerShell ISE

**After completing this chapter, you will be able to:**

■ Understand the use of tab completion to complete cmdlet names, types, and paths.

■ Use code snippets to simplify programming.

■ Use the command pane to run or insert commands.

■ Use the Windows PowerShell ISE to connect to a remote system and run commands.

■ Run script commands without saving the script.

■ Write, save, and load a Windows PowerShell script.

## Running the Windows PowerShell ISE

On Microsoft Windows 8, the Windows PowerShell ISE appears to be a bit hidden. In fact, on Windows Server 2012, it also is a bit hidden. However, on Windows Server 2012, a Windows PowerShell shortcut automatically appears on the desktop taskbar. Likewise, pinning Windows PowerShell to the Windows 8 desktop taskbar is a Windows PowerShell best practice. To start the Windows PowerShell ISE, you have a couple of choices. On the Start page of Windows Server 2012, you can type **PowerShell**, and both Windows PowerShell and the Windows PowerShell ISE appear as search results. However, on Windows 8 this is not the case. You must type **PowerShell_ISE** to find the Windows PowerShell ISE. You can also launch the Windows PowerShell ISE by right-clicking the Windows PowerShell icon and choosing either Windows PowerShell ISE or Run ISE As Administrator from the Tasks menu that appears. This Tasks menu appears in Figure 8-1.

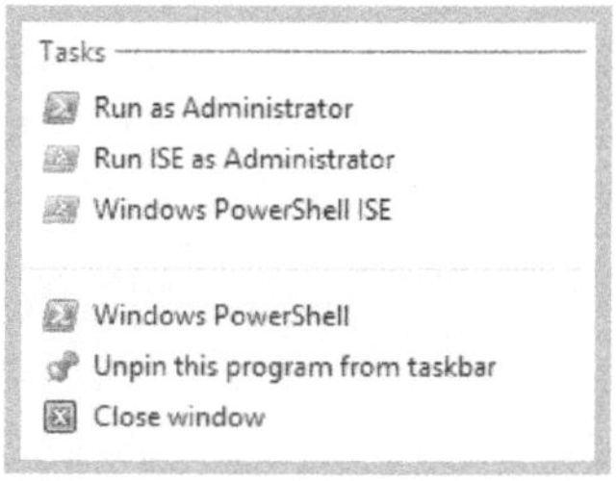

**FIGURE 8-1** Right-clicking the Windows PowerShell icon on the desktop taskbar brings up the Tasks menu, from which you can launch the Windows PowerShell ISE.

Inside the Windows PowerShell console, you only need to type **ise** to launch the Windows PowerShell ISE. This shortcut permits quick access to the Windows PowerShell ISE when you need to type more than a few interactive commands.

## Navigating the Windows PowerShell ISE

Once the Windows PowerShell ISE launches, two panes appear. On the left side of the screen is an interactive Windows PowerShell console. On the right side of the screen is the Commands add-on. The Commands add-on is really a Windows PowerShell command explorer window. When using the Windows PowerShell ISE in an interactive fashion, the Commands add-on provides you the ability to build a command by using the mouse. Once you have built the command, click the Run button to copy the command to the console window and execute the command. This view of the Windows PowerShell ISE appears in Figure 8-2.

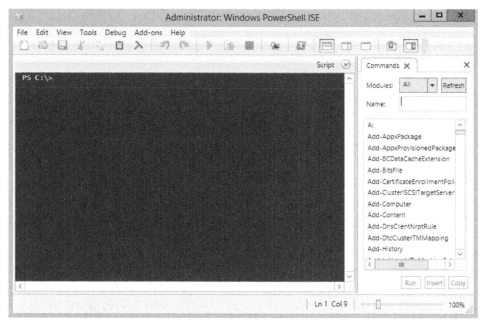

**FIGURE 8-2** The Windows PowerShell ISE presents a Windows PowerShell console on the left and a Commands add-on on the right side of the screen.

Typing into the Name input box causes the Commands add-on to search through all Windows PowerShell modules to retrieve a matching command. This is a great way to discover and locate commands. By default, the Commands add-on uses a wildcard search pattern. Therefore, typing **wmi** returns five cmdlets that include that letter pattern. This appears in Figure 8-3.

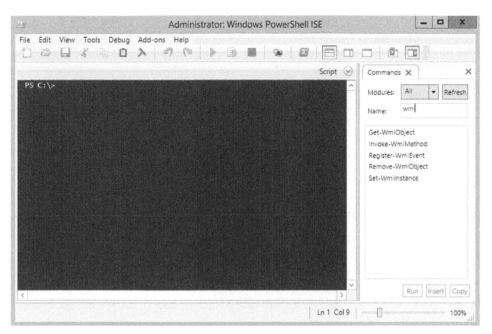

**FIGURE 8-3** The Commands add-on uses a wildcard search pattern to find matching cmdlets.

Once you find the cmdlet that interests you, select it from the filtered list of cmdlet names. Upon selection, the Commands pane changes to display the parameters for the selected cmdlet. Each parameter set appears on a different tab. Screen resolution really affects the usability of this feature. The greater the screen resolution, the more usable this feature becomes. With a small resolution, you have to scroll back and forth to see the parameter sets, and you have to scroll up and down to see the available parameters for a particular parameter set. In this view, it is easy to miss important parameters. In Figure 8-4, the *Get-WmiObject* cmdlet queries the *Win32_Bios* Windows Management Instrumentation (WMI) class. Upon entering the WMI class name in the Class box, click the Run button to execute the command. The console pane displays first the command, and then the output from running the command.

> **Note** Using the Insert button inserts the command to the console, but does not execute the command. This is great for occasions when you want to look over the command prior to actually executing it. It also provides you with the chance to edit the command prior to execution.

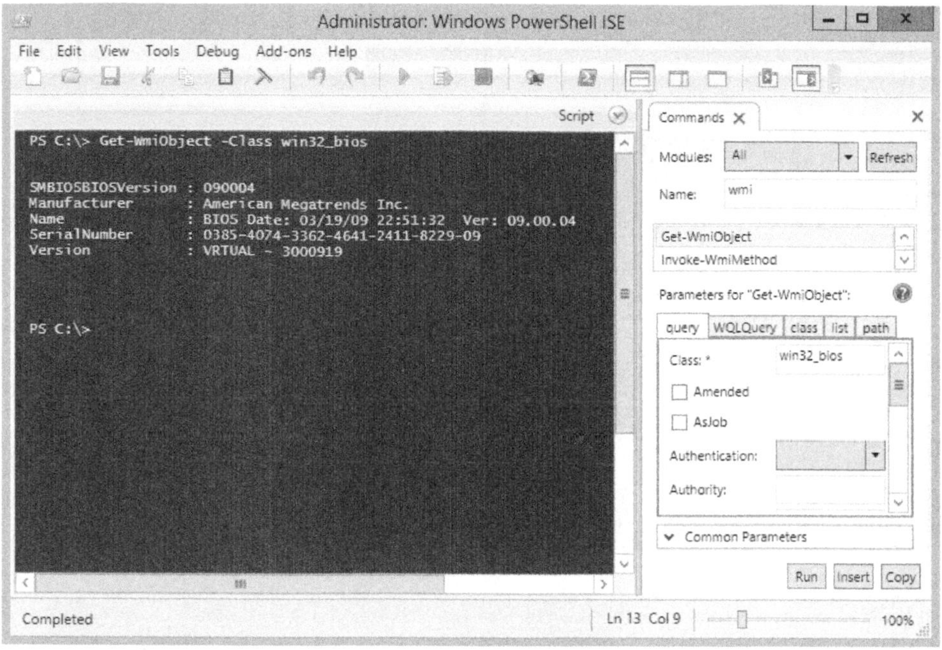

**FIGURE 8-4** Select the command to run from the Commands add-on, fill out the required parameters, and click Run to execute Windows PowerShell cmdlets inside the Windows PowerShell ISE.

### Finding and running commands via the Commands add-on

1. In the Name box of the Commands add-on, enter the command you are interested in running.

2. Select the command from the filtered list.

3. Enter the parameters in the *Parameters For...* parameter box.

4. Click the Run button when finished.

## Working with the script pane

Pressing the down arrow beside the word *script* in the upper-right corner of the console pane reveals a new script pane into which you can start entering a script. You can also obtain a new script pane by selecting New from the File menu, or clicking the small white piece-of-paper icon in the upper-left corner of the Windows PowerShell ISE. You can also use the keyboard shortcut Ctrl+N.

Just because it is called the *script pane* does not mean that it requires you to enable script support to use it. As long as the file is not saved, you can enter commands that are as complex as you wish into the script pane, with script support restricted, and the code will run when you execute the script. Once the file is saved, however, it becomes a script, and you will need to deal with the script execution policy at that point.

You can still use the Commands add-on with the script pane, but it requires an extra step. Use the Commands add-on as described in the previous section, but instead of using the Run or the Insert buttons, use the Copy button. Navigate to the appropriate section in the script pane, and then use the Paste command (which you can access from the shortcut menu, from the Edit menu, by clicking the Paste icon on the toolbar, or by simply pressing Ctrl+V).

> **Note** If you click the Insert button while the script pane is maximized, the command is inserted into the hidden console pane. Clicking Insert a second time inserts the command a second time on the same command line in the hidden console pane. No notification that this occurs is presented.

To run commands present in the script pane, click the Run Script button (the green triangle in the middle of the toolbar), press F5, or choose Run from the File menu. The commands from the script pane transfer to the console pane and then execute. Any output associated with the commands appears under the transferred commands. Once saved as a script, the commands no longer transfer to the command pane. Rather, the path to the script appears in the console pane along with any associated output.

You can continue to use the Commands add-on to build your commands as you pipeline the output from one cmdlet to another one. In Figure 8-5, the output from the *Get-WmiObject* cmdlet pipes to the *Format-Table* cmdlet. The properties chosen in the *Format-Table* cmdlet as well as the implementation of the *-Wrap* switch are configured via the Commands add-on.

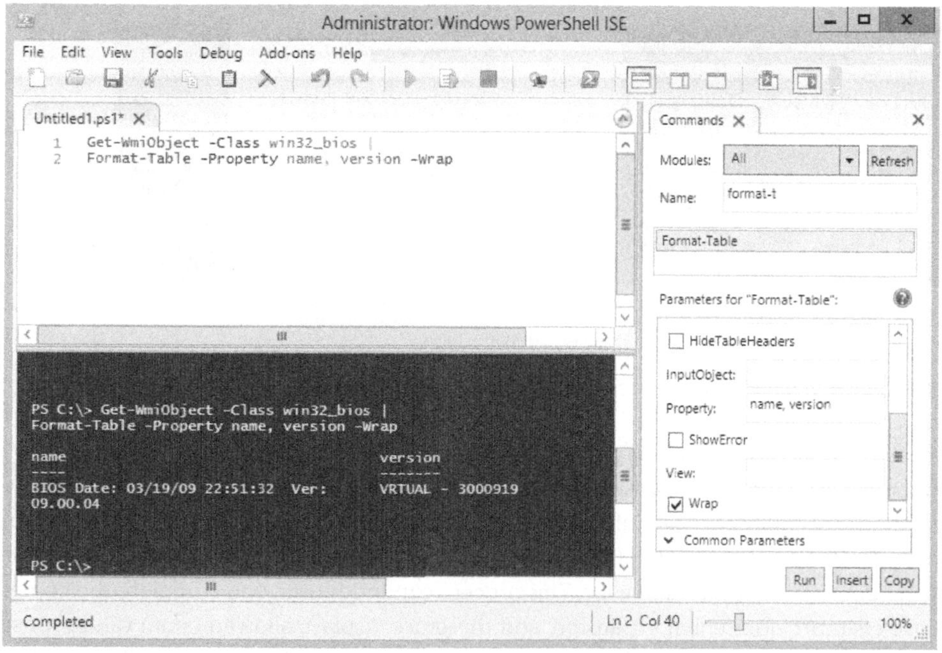

**FIGURE 8-5** Use of the Commands add-on permits easy building of commands.

# Tab expansion and IntelliSense

Novice scripters will find the Commands add-on very useful, but it does consume valuable screen real estate, and it requires the use of the mouse to find and create commands. For advanced scripters, tab expansion and IntelliSense are the keys to productivity. To turn off the Commands add-on, either click the *X* in the upper-right corner of the Commands add-on or deselect Show Commands Add-On from the View menu. Once you've deselected this, the Windows PowerShell ISE remembers your preference, and will not display the Commands add-on again until you reselect this option.

IntelliSense provides pop-up help and options while you type, permitting rapid command development without requiring complete syntax knowledge. As you are typing a cmdlet name, IntelliSense supplies possible matches. Once you select the cmdlet, IntelliSense displays the complete syntax of the cmdlet. This appears in Figure 8-6.

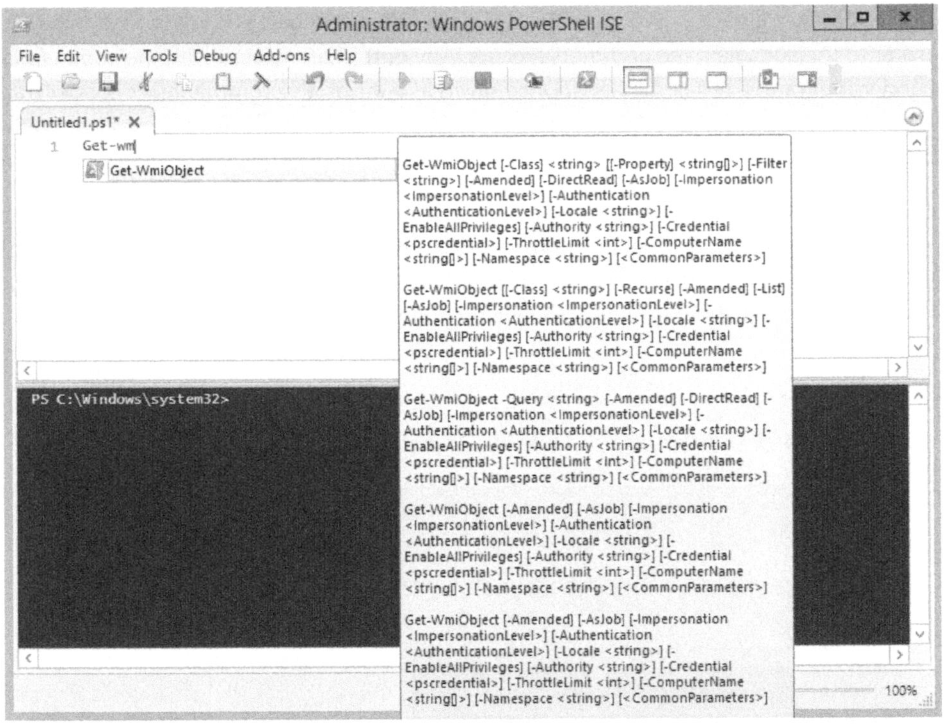

**FIGURE 8-6** Once you select a particular cmdlet from the list, IntelliSense displays the complete syntax.

After selecting a cmdlet, if you type parameter names, IntelliSense displays the applicable parameters in a list. Once IntelliSense appears, use the up and down arrow keys to navigate within the list. Press Enter to accept the highlighted option. You can then fill in required values for parameters and go to the next parameter. Once again, as you approach a parameter position, IntelliSense displays the appropriate options in a list. This process continues until you complete the command. IntelliSense even provides enum expansion, and therefore displays allowed enum values for specific parameters. Figure 8-7 illustrates selecting the *Property* parameter from the IntelliSense list of optional parameters.

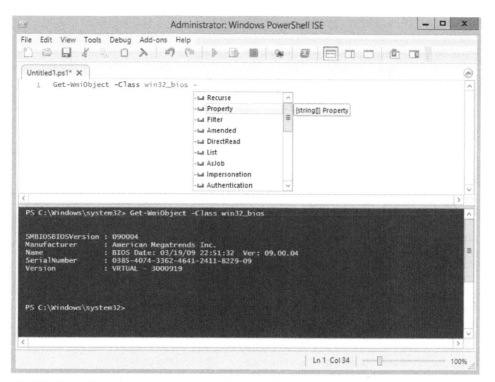

**FIGURE 8-7** IntelliSense displays parameters in a drop-down list. When you select a particular parameter, the data type of the property appears.

## Working with Windows PowerShell ISE snippets

Snippets are pieces of code, or code fragments. They are designed to simplify routine coding tasks by permitting the insertion of boilerplate code directly into the script. Even experienced scripters love to use the Windows PowerShell ISE snippets because they are great time-savers. It takes just a little bit of familiarity with the snippets themselves, along with a bit of experience with the Windows PowerShell syntax. Once you have the requirements under your belt, you will be able to use the Windows PowerShell ISE snippets and create code faster than you previously believed was possible. The great thing is you can create your own snippets, and even share them with others via the TechNet wiki.

### Using Windows PowerShell ISE snippets to create code

To start the Windows PowerShell ISE snippets, use the Ctrl+J keystroke combination (you can also use the mouse to choose Start Snippets from the Edit menu). Once the snippets appear, type the first letter of the snippet name to quickly jump to the appropriate portion of the snippets (you can also use the mouse to navigate up and down the snippet list). Once you have identified the snippet you wish to use, press Enter to place the snippet at the current insertion point in your Windows PowerShell script pane.

The following two exercises go into greater depth about working with snippets.

## Creating a new function via Windows PowerShell ISE snippets

1.  Press Ctrl+J to start the Windows PowerShell ISE snippets.

2.  Type **f** to move to the "F" section of the Windows PowerShell ISE snippets.

3.  Use the down arrow until you arrive at the simple *function* snippet.

4.  Press Enter to enter the simple *function* snippet into your code.

## Using Windows PowerShell ISE snippets to create a simple function

1.  Start the Windows PowerShell ISE.

2.  Add a new script pane. To do this, press Ctrl+N.

3.  Start the Windows PowerShell ISE snippets by pressing Ctrl+J.

4.  Select the simple *function* snippet and add it to your script pane. Use the down arrow to select the snippet, and press Enter to insert it into your script.

5.  Move your insertion point to inside the script block for the function.

6.  Start the Windows PowerShell ISE snippets again by pressing Ctrl+J.

7.  Select the *switch* statement by typing **s** to move to the "Switch" section of the snippet list. Press Enter to insert the snippet into your script block.

8.  Double-click $param1 and press Ctrl+C to copy the parameter name. Double-click value1 and press Ctrl+V to paste it.

9.  Double-click $param2 to select it and press Ctrl+C to copy the parameter name. Double-click value3 to select it and press Ctrl+V to paste param2.

10. Check your work; at this point, your code should appear as shown here:

```
function MyFunction ($param1, $param2)
{
    switch ($x)
    {
        'param1' {}
        {$_ -in 'A','B','C'} {}
        'param2' {}
        Default {}
    }
}
```

11. Delete the line that appears here, because it will not be used:

```
{$_ -in 'A','B','C'} {}
```

12. Delete the line for the default parameter:

```
Default {}
```

13. Replace the $x condition with the code to display the keys of the bound parameters collection. This line of code appears here:

```
$MyInvocation.BoundParameters.Keys
```

14. In the script block for *param1*, add a line of code that describes the parameter and displays the value. The code appears here:

```
"param1" {"param1 is $param1" }
```

15. In the script block for *param2*, add a line of code that describes the parameter and displays the value. The code appears here:

```
"param2" {"param2 is $param2" }
```

The completed function appears here:

```
function MyFunction ($param1, $param2)
{
    switch ($MyInvocation.BoundParameters.Keys)
    {
     "param1" {"param1 is $param1" }
     "param2" {"param2 is $param2" }
     }
}
```

This concludes the procedure.

## Creating new Windows PowerShell ISE snippets

After you spend a bit of time using Windows PowerShell ISE snippets, you will wonder how you ever existed previously. In that same instant, you will also begin to think in terms of new snippets. Luckily, it is very easy to create a new Windows PowerShell ISE snippet. In fact, there is even a cmdlet to do this: the *New-IseSnippet* cmdlet.

> **Note** To create or use a user-defined Windows PowerShell ISE snippet, you must change the script execution policy to permit the execution of scripts. This is because user-defined snippets load from XML files. Reading and loading files (of any type) requires the script execution policy to permit running scripts. To verify your script execution policy, use the *Get-ExecutionPolicy* cmdlet. To set the script execution policy, use the *Set-ExecutionPolicy* cmdlet.

You can use the *New-IseSnippet* cmdlet to create a new Windows PowerShell ISE snippet. Once you create the snippet, it becomes immediately available in the Windows PowerShell ISE once you start the Windows PowerShell ISE snippets. The command syntax is simple, but the command takes a decent amount of space to complete. Only three parameters are required: *Description*, *Text*, and *Title*. The name of the snippet is specified via the *Title* parameter. The snippet itself is typed into the *Text* parameter. A great way to simplify snippet creation is to place the snippet into a *here-string* object, and then pass that value to the *New-IseSnippet* cmdlet. When you want your code to appear on multiple lines, use the *`r* special character. Of course, doing this means your *Text* parameter must appear inside double quotation marks, not single quotes. The following code creates a new Windows PowerShell ISE snippet that has a simplified *switch* syntax. It is a single logical line of code.

```
New-IseSnippet -Title SimpleSwitch -Description "A simple switch statement"
-Author "ed wilson" -Text "Switch () `r{'param1' {  }`r}" -CaretOffset 9
```

Once you execute the *New-IseSnippet* command, it creates a new snippets.xml file in the Snippets directory within your WindowsPowerShell folder in your Documents folder. The simple *switch* snippet XML file is shown in Figure 8-8.

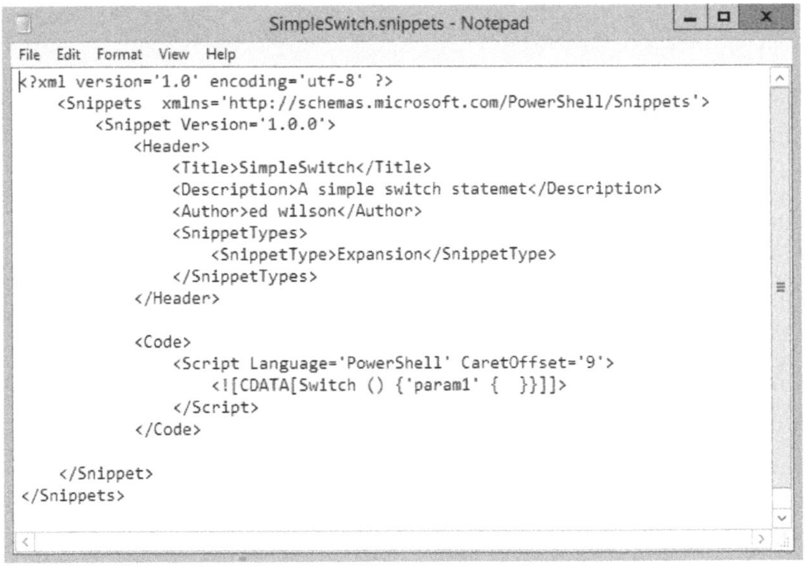


```
<?xml version='1.0' encoding='utf-8' ?>
    <Snippets  xmlns='http://schemas.microsoft.com/PowerShell/Snippets'>
        <Snippet Version='1.0.0'>
            <Header>
                <Title>SimpleSwitch</Title>
                <Description>A simple switch statemet</Description>
                <Author>ed wilson</Author>
                <SnippetTypes>
                    <SnippetType>Expansion</SnippetType>
                </SnippetTypes>
            </Header>

            <Code>
                <Script Language='PowerShell' CaretOffset='9'>
                    <![CDATA[Switch () {'param1' {  }}]]>
                </Script>
            </Code>

    </Snippet>
</Snippets>
```

**FIGURE 8-8** Windows PowerShell snippets are stored in a *snippets.xml* file in your Windows PowerShell folder.

User-defined snippets are permanent—that is, they survive closing and reopening the Windows PowerShell ISE. They also survive reboots because they reside as XML files in your WindowsPowerShell folder.

# Removing user-defined Windows PowerShell ISE snippets

While there is a *New-IseSnippet* cmdlet and a *Get-IseSnippet* cmdlet, there is no *Remove-IseSnippet* cmdlet. There is no need for one, really, because you can use *Remove-Item* instead. To delete all of your custom Windows PowerShell ISE snippets, use the *Get-IseSnippet* cmdlet to retrieve the snippets and the *Remove-Item* cmdlet to delete them. The command appears here:

```
Get-IseSnippet | Remove-Item
```

If you do not want to delete all of your custom Windows PowerShell ISE snippets, use the *Where-Object* cmdlet to filter only the ones you do wish to delete. The following uses the *Get-IseSnippet* cmdlet to list all the user-defined Windows PowerShell ISE snippets on the system:

```
PS C:\Windows\system32> Get-IseSnippet


    Directory: C:\Users\administrator.IAMMRED\Documents\WindowsPowerShell\Snippets


Mode                LastWriteTime     Length Name
----                -------------     ------ ----
-a---         7/1/2012   1:03 AM         653 bogus.snippets.ps1xml
-a---         7/1/2012   1:02 AM         653 mysnip.snippets.ps1xml
-a---         7/1/2012   1:02 AM         671 simpleswitch.snippets.ps1xml
```

Next, use the *Where-Object* cmdlet (*?* is an alias for the *Where-Object*) to return all of the user-defined Windows PowerShell ISE snippets except the ones that contain the word *switch* within the name. The snippets that make it through the filter are pipelined to the *Remove-Item* cmdlet. In the code that follows, the *-whatif* switch shows which snippets would be removed by the command

```
PS C:\Windows\system32> Get-IseSnippet | ? name -NotMatch 'switch' | Remove-Item -WhatIf
What if: Performing operation "Remove file" on Target "C:\Users\administrator.IAMMRED\Documents\
WindowsPowerShell\Snippets\bogus.snippets.ps1xml".
What if: Performing operation "Remove file" on Target "C:\Users\administrator.IAMMRED\Documents\
WindowsPowerShell\Snippets\mysnip.snippets.ps1xml".
```

Once you have confirmed that only the snippets you do not want keep will be deleted, remove the *-whatif* switch from the *Remove-Item* cmdlet and run the command a second time. To confirm which snippets remain, use the *Get-IseSnippet* cmdlet to see which Windows PowerShell ISE snippets are left on the system.

```
PS C:\Windows\system32> Get-IseSnippet | ? name -NotMatch 'switch' | Remove-Item

PS C:\Windows\system32> Get-IseSnippet


    Directory: C:\Users\administrator.IAMMRED\Documents\WindowsPowerShell\Snippets


Mode                LastWriteTime     Length Name
----                -------------     ------ ----
-a---          7/1/2012   1:02 AM        671 simpleswitch.snippets.ps1xml
```

# Using the Commands add-on: step-by-step exercises

In this exercise, you will explore using the Commands add-on by looking for cmdlets related to WMI. You will then select the *Invoke-WmiMethod* cmdlet from the list and create new processes. Following this exercise, you will use Windows PowerShell ISE snippets to create a WMI script.

### Using the Commands add-on to use WMI methods

1.  Start the Windows PowerShell ISE.

2.  Use the Commands add-on to search for cmdlets related to WMI.

3.  Select the *Invoke-WmiMethod* cmdlet from the list.

4.  In the *class* block, add the WMI class name *Win32_Process*.

5.  In the *name* block, enter the method name *create*.

6.  In the argument list, enter **notepad**.

7.  Click the Run button. In the output console, you should see the following command, and on the next line the output from the command. Sample output appears here:

    ```
    PS C:\Windows\system32> Invoke-WmiMethod -Class win32_process -Name create -ArgumentList
    notepad (note: your processID will more than likely be different than mine).


    __GENUS          : 2
    __CLASS          : __PARAMETERS
    __SUPERCLASS     :
    __DYNASTY        : __PARAMETERS
    __RELPATH        :
    __PROPERTY_COUNT : 2
    __DERIVATION     : {}
    __SERVER         :
    __NAMESPACE      :
    __PATH           :
    ProcessId        : 2960
    ReturnValue      : 0
    PSComputerName   :
    ```

**8.** Modify the *ArgumentList* block by adding *calc* to the argument list. Use a semicolon to separate the arguments, as shown here:

```
Notepad; calc
```

**9.** Click the Run button a second time to execute the revised command.

**10.** In the Commands add-on, look for cmdlets with the word *process* in the name. Select the *Stop-Process* cmdlet from the list of cmdlets.

**11.** Choose the *name* parameter set in the *parameters for Stop-Process* block.

**12.** In the Name box, type **notepad** and **calc**. The command appears here:

```
notepad, calc
```

**13.** Click the Run button to execute the command.

**14.** Under the *name* block showing the process-related cmdlets, choose the *Get-Process* cmdlet.

**15.** In the *name* parameter set, enter **calc, notepad**.

**16.** Click the Run button to execute the command.

Two errors should appear, stating that the *calc* and *notepad* processes aren't running. The errors appear here:

```
PS C:\Windows\system32> Get-Process -Name calc, notepad
Get-Process : Cannot find a process with the name "calc". Verify the process
name and call the cmdlet again.
At line:1 char:1
+ Get-Process -Name calc, notepad
+ ~~~~~~~~~~~~~~~~~~~~~~~~~~~~~~~~
    + CategoryInfo          : ObjectNotFound: (calc:String) [Get-Process],
    ProcessCommandException
    + FullyQualifiedErrorId : NoProcessFoundForGivenName,Microsoft.PowerShell.
    Commands.GetProcessCommand

Get-Process : Cannot find a process with the name "notepad". Verify the
process name and call the cmdlet again.
At line:1 char:1
+ Get-Process -Name calc, notepad
+ ~~~~~~~~~~~~~~~~~~~~~~~~~~~~~~~~
    + CategoryInfo          : ObjectNotFound: (notepad:String) [Get-Process],
    ProcessCommandException
    + FullyQualifiedErrorId : NoProcessFoundForGivenName,Microsoft.PowerShell.
    Commands.GetProcessCommand
```

This concludes the exercise. Leave the Windows PowerShell ISE console open for the next exercise.

In the following exercise, you will explore using Windows PowerShell ISE snippets to simplify script creation.

## Using Windows PowerShell ISE snippets

1. Start the Windows PowerShell ISE.

2. Close the Commands add-on.

3. Display the script pane.

4. Use the *Get-WmiObject* cmdlet to retrieve a listing of process objects from the local host. Store the returned process objects in a variable named *$process*. As you type the command, ensure you use IntelliSense to reduce typing. You should be able to type **Get-Wm** and press Enter to select the *Get-WmiObject* cmdlet from the IntelliSense list. You should also be able to type **-c** and then press Enter to choose the *-class* parameter from the IntelliSense list. The complete command appears here:

   ```
   $process = Get-WmiObject -Class win32_process
   ```

5. Use the *foreach* code snippet to walk through the collection of process objects stored in the *$process* variable. To do this, type Ctrl+J to start the code snippets. Once the snippet list appears, type **f** to quickly move to the "F" section of the snippets. To choose the *foreach* snippet, you can continue to type **fore** and then press Enter to add the *foreach* snippet to your code. It is easier, however, to use the down arrow once you are in the "F" section of the snippets. The complete *foreach* snippet appears here:

   ```
   foreach ($item in $collection)
   {

   }
   ```

6. Change the *$collection* variable in the *foreach* snippet to *$process* because that variable holds your collection of process objects. The easiest way to do this is to use the mouse and double-click the *$process* variable on line 1 of your code. Doing this only selects the noun portion of variable name, not the dollar sign. So, the process is to double-click *$process*, press Ctrl+C, double-click *$collection*, and press Ctrl+V. The *foreach* snippet now appears as shown here:

   ```
   foreach ($item in $process)
   {

   }
   ```

7. Inside the script block portion of the *foreach* snippet, use the *$item* variable to display the name of each process object. The code to do this appears here:

   ```
   $item.name
   ```

8. Run the code by either clicking the green triangle on the toolbar or pressing F5. The output should list the name of each process on your system. The completed code appears here:

```
$process = Get-WmiObject -Class win32_process
foreach ($item in $process)
{
    $item.name
}
```

This concludes the exercise.

# Chapter 8 quick reference

| To | Do this |
|---|---|
| Create a Windows PowerShell command without typing | Use the Commands add-on. |
| Find a specific Windows PowerShell command | Use the Commands add-on and type a search term in the *Name* box. |
| Quickly type a command in either the script pane or the console pane | Use IntelliSense and press Enter to use the selected command or parameter. |
| Run a script from the Windows PowerShell ISE | Press F5 to run the entire script. |
| Run only a specific selection of the script | Select the applicable portion of the script and press F8 to run the selection. |
| Create a user-defined Windows PowerShell ISE snippet | Use the *New-IseSnippet* cmdlet and enter the *Title*, *Description*, and *Text* parameters. |
| Remove all user-defined Windows PowerShell ISE snippets | Use the *Get-ISESnippet* cmdlet and pipeline the results to the *Remove-Item* cmdlet. |

# CHAPTER 9

# Working with Windows PowerShell Profiles

**After completing this chapter, you will be able to:**

- Understand the different Windows PowerShell profiles.

- Use *New-Item* to create a new Windows PowerShell profile.

- Use the *$profile* automatic variable.

- Describe the best profile to provide specific functionality.

## Six Different PowerShell profiles

A Microsoft Windows PowerShell profile creates a standardized environment by creating custom functions, aliases, PS drives, and variables upon startup. Windows PowerShell profiles are a bit confusing—there are, in fact, six different ones. Both the Windows PowerShell console and the Windows PowerShell ISE have their own profiles. In addition, there are profiles for the current user, as well as profiles for all users. Table 9-1 lists the six different profiles and their associated locations. In the table, the automatic variable *$home* points to the users\username directory on the system. The *$pshome* automatic variable points to the Windows PowerShell installation folder. This location typically is C:\Windows\System32\WindowsPowerShell\v1.0 (for compatibility reasons, the Windows PowerShell installation folder is in the v1.0 folder—even on Windows PowerShell 3.0).

**TABLE 9-1** The six different Windows PowerShell profiles and their paths

| Description | Path |
| --- | --- |
| Current User, Current Host (console) | $Home\[My ]Documents\WindowsPowerShell\Profile.ps1 |
| Current User, All Hosts | $Home\[My ]Documents\Profile.ps1 |
| All Users, Current Host (console) | $PsHome\Microsoft.PowerShell_profile.ps1 |
| All Users, All Hosts | $PsHome\Profile.ps1 |
| Current User, Current Host (ISE) | $Home\[My ]Documents\WindowsPowerShell\Microsoft.PowerShellISE_profile.ps1 |
| All Users, Current Host (ISE) | $PsHome\Microsoft.PowerShellISE_profile.ps1 |

# Understanding the six different Windows PowerShell profiles

The first thing to do in understanding the six different Windows PowerShell profiles is to keep in mind that the value of *$profile* changes depending on which Windows PowerShell host you use. As long as you realize it is a moving target, you will be fine. In most cases, when talking about the Windows PowerShell profile, people are referring to the Current User, Current Host profile. In fact, if there is no qualifier for the Windows PowerShell profile with its associated scope or description, it is safe to assume the reference is to the Current User, Current Host profile.

> **Note** The Windows PowerShell profile (any one of the six) is simply a Windows PowerShell script. It has a special name, and it resides in a special place, but it is simply a script. In this regard, it is sort of like the old-fashioned autoexec.bat batch file. Because the Windows PowerShell profile is a Windows PowerShell script, you must enable the script execution policy prior to configuring and using a Windows PowerShell profile.

# Examining the *$profile* variable

In Windows PowerShell, the *$profile* automatic variable contains the path to the Current User, Current Host profile. This makes sense, and is a great way to easily access the path to the profile. The following illustrates this technique from within the Windows PowerShell console:

```
PS C:\> $profile
C:\Users\ed.IAMMRED\Documents\WindowsPowerShell\Microsoft.PowerShell_profile.ps1
```

Inside the Windows PowerShell ISE, when I query the *$profile* automatic variable, I receive the output appearing here:

```
PS C:\Users\ed.IAMMRED> $profile
C:\Users\ed.IAMMRED\Documents\WindowsPowerShell\Microsoft.PowerShellISE_profile.ps1
```

To save you a bit of analyzing, the difference between the Windows PowerShell console Current User, Current Host profile path and the Windows PowerShell ISE Current User, Current Host profile path is three letters: *ISE*.

> **Note** These three letters, *ISE*, often cause you problems. When modifying your profile, you may be setting something in your Windows PowerShell console profile, and it is not available inside the Windows PowerShell ISE.

# Unraveling the different profiles

You can pipeline the *$profile* variable to the *Get-Member* cmdlet and see additional properties that exist on the *$profile* variable. This technique appears here:

```
PS C:\>
Name
----
AllUsersAllHosts
AllUsersCurrentHost
CurrentUserAllHosts
CurrentUserCurrentHost
```

If accessing the *$profile* variable from within the Windows PowerShell console, the *AllUsersCurrentHost* and *CurrentUserCurrentHost* note properties refer to the Windows PowerShell console. If you access the *$profile* variable from within the Windows PowerShell ISE, the *AllUsersCurrentHost* and *CurrentUserCurrentHost* note properties refer to the Windows PowerShell ISE profiles.

## Using the *$profile* variable to refer to more than the current host

When you reference the *$profile* variable, by default it refers to the Current User, Current Host profile. If you pipeline the variable to the *Format-List* cmdlet, it still refers to the Current User, Current Host profile. This technique appears here:

```
PS C:\> $PROFILE | Format-List *
C:\Users\ed.IAMMRED\Documents\WindowsPowerShell\Microsoft.PowerShell_profile.ps1
```

This can lead to a bit of confusion, especially because the *Get-Member* cmdlet reveals the existence of multiple profiles and multiple note properties. The way to see all of the profiles for the current host is to use the *-force* parameter—it reveals the hidden properties. The command illustrating this technique appears here:

```
$PROFILE | Format-List * -Force
```

The command to display the various profiles and the associated output from the command appear in Figure 9-1.

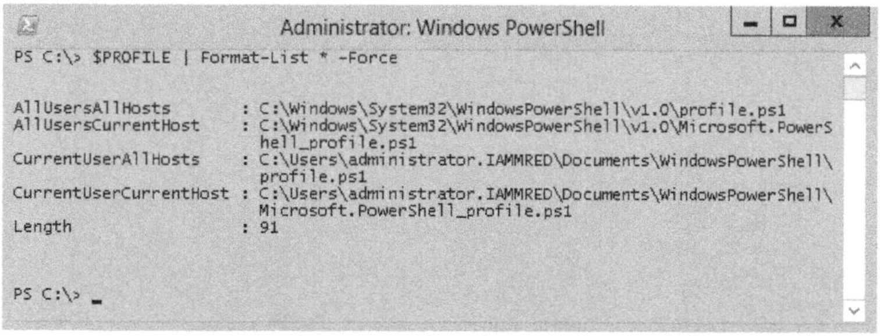

**FIGURE 9-1** The *$profile* variable contains the path to several different Windows PowerShell profiles.

It is possible to directly access each of these specific properties—just like you would access any other property—via dotted notation. This technique appears here:

```
$PROFILE.CurrentUserAllHosts
```

The path to each of the four different profiles for the Windows PowerShell console appears in Figure 9-2.

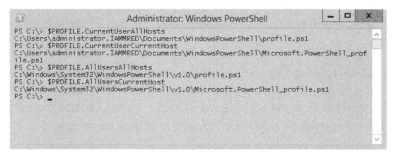

**FIGURE 9-2** Use dotted notation to access the various properties of the *$profile* variable.

## Determining whether a specific profile exists

To determine if a specific profile exists, use the *Test-Path* cmdlet and the appropriate note property of the *$profile* variable. For example, to determine if a Current User, Current Host profile exists, you can use the *$profile* variable with no modifier, or you can use the *CurrentUserCurrentHost* note property. The following example illustrates both of these:

```
PS C:\> test-path $PROFILE
True
PS C:\> test-path $PROFILE.CurrentUserCurrentHost
True
PS C:\>
```

In the same manner, the other three profiles that apply to the current host (in this example, I am using the Windows PowerShell console) are determined not to exist. This appears in the code that follows:

```
PS C:\> test-path $PROFILE.AllUsersAllHosts
False
PS C:\> test-path $PROFILE.AllUsersCurrentHost
False
PS C:\> test-path $PROFILE.CurrentUserAllHosts
False
PS C:\>
```

## Creating a new profile

To create a new profile for the Current User, All Hosts profile, use the *CurrentUserAllHosts* property of the *$profile* automatic variable and the *New-Item* cmdlet. This technique appears here:

```
PS C:\> new-item $PROFILE.CurrentUserAllHosts -ItemType file -Force


    Directory: C:\Users\ed.IAMMRED\Documents\WindowsPowerShell


Mode                LastWriteTime     Length Name
----                -------------     ------ ----
-a---        5/17/2012   2:59 PM          0 profile.ps1
```

To open the profile for editing, use the *ise* alias, as appears here:

```
ise $PROFILE.CurrentUserAllHosts
```

Once you are finished editing the profile, save it, close the Windows PowerShell console, reopen the Windows PowerShell console, and test that your changes work properly.

# Design considerations for profiles

The first thing to do when deciding how to implement your Windows PowerShell profile is to analyze the way in which you use Windows PowerShell. For example, if you confine yourself to running a few Windows PowerShell scripts from within the Windows PowerShell ISE, there is little reason to worry about a Windows PowerShell console profile. If you use a different Windows PowerShell scripting environment than the Windows PowerShell ISE, but you also work interactively from the Windows PowerShell console, you may need to add stuff to the other scripting environment's profile (assuming it has one), as well as the Windows PowerShell console profile, to enable you to maintain a consistent environment. If you work extensively in both the scripting environment and the Windows PowerShell console, and you find yourself desiring certain modifications to both environments, then that leads to a different scenario.

There are three different names used for the Windows PowerShell profiles. The names appear in Table 9-2 along with the profile usage.

**TABLE 9-2** Windows PowerShell profile names and name usage

| Profile Name | Name Usage |
| --- | --- |
| Microsoft.PowerShell_profile.ps1 | Refers to profiles (either current user or all users) for the Windows PowerShell console |
| profile.ps1 | Refers to profiles (either current user or all users) for all Windows PowerShell hosts |
| Microsoft.PowerShellISE_profile.ps1 | Refers to profiles (either current user or all users) for the Windows PowerShell ISE |

The distinction between the Windows PowerShell ISE profiles and the Windows PowerShell console profiles is the *ISE* in the name of the Windows PowerShell ISE profiles. The location of the Windows PowerShell profile determines the scoping (whether the profile applies to either the current user or to all users. All user profiles (any one of the three profiles detailed in Table 9-2) appear in the

Windows\system32\WindowsPowerShell\v1.0 directory, a location referenced by the *$pshome* variable. The following illustrates using the *$pshome* variable to obtain this folder:

```
PS C:\Users\ed.IAMMRED> $PSHOME
C:\Windows\System32\WindowsPowerShell\v1.0
```

The folder containing the three different *current user* Windows PowerShell profiles is the WindowsPowerShell folder in the user's mydocuments special folder. The location of the user's mydocuments special folder is obtained by using the *GetFolderPath* method from the *System.Environment* .NET Framework class. This technique appears here:

```
PS C:\> [environment]::getfolderpath("mydocuments")
C:\Users\ed.IAMMRED\Documents
```

Table 9-3 details a variety of use-case scenarios, and points to the profile to use for specific purposes.

**TABLE 9-3** Windows PowerShell usage patterns, profile names, and locations

| Windows PowerShell use | Location and profile name |
|---|---|
| Near-exclusive Windows PowerShell console work as a non-admin user | MyDocuments Microsoft.PowerShell_profile.ps1 |
| Near-exclusive Windows PowerShell console work as an administrative user | $PSHome Microsoft.PowerShell_profile.ps1 |
| Near-exclusive Windows PowerShell ISE work as a non-admin user | MyDocuments Microsoft.PowerShellISE_profile.ps1 |
| Near-exclusive Windows PowerShell ISE work as an administrative user | $PSHome Microsoft.PowerShellISE_profile.ps1 |
| Balanced Windows PowerShell work as a non-admin user | MyDocuments profile.ps1 |
| Balanced Windows PowerShell work as an administrative user | $psHome profile.ps1 |

**Note** Depending on how you perform administrative work, you may decide that you wish to use a Current User type of profile. This would be because you log on with a specific account to perform administrative work. If your work requires that you log on with a number of different user accounts, it makes sense to use an All Users type of profile.

# Using one or more profiles

Many Windows PowerShell users end up using more than one Windows PowerShell profile—it may not be intentional, but that is how it winds up. What happens is that they begin by creating a Current User, Current Host profile via the Windows PowerShell $profile variable. After adding a number of items in the Windows PowerShell profile, the user decides that they would like the same features in the Windows PowerShell console or the Windows PowerShell ISE—whichever one they did not use in the beginning. Then, after creating an additional profile, they soon realize they are duplicating their work. In addition, various packages, such as the Script Explorer, add commands to the Windows PowerShell profile.

Depending on how much you add to your Windows PowerShell profile, you may be perfectly fine with having multiple Windows PowerShell profiles. If your profile does not have very many items in it, using one Windows PowerShell profile for the Windows PowerShell console and another profile for the Windows PowerShell ISE may be a perfectly acceptable solution. Simplicity makes this approach work. For example, certain commands, such as the *Start-Transcript* cmdlet, do not work in the Windows PowerShell ISE. In addition, certain commands, such as those requiring Single-Threaded Apartment model (STA), do not work by default in the Windows PowerShell console. By creating multiple *$profile* profiles (Current User, Current Host) and only editing them from the appropriate environment, you can greatly reduce the complexity of the profile-creation process.

However, it will not be long before duplication leads to inconsistency, which leads to frustration, and finally a desire for correction and solution. A better approach is to plan for multiple environments from the beginning. The following list describes the advantages and disadvantages to using more than one profile, along with the scenarios in which you'd most likely do this:

- Advantages of using more than one profile:

  - It's simple and hassle free

  - *$profile* always refers to the correct profile.

  - It removes concern about incompatible commands.

- Disadvantages:

  - It often means you're duplicating effort.

  - It can cause inconsistencies between profiles (for variables, functions, PS drives, and aliases)

  - Maintenance may increase due to the number of potential profiles.

- Uses:

  - Use with a simple profile.

  - Use when you do not have administrator or non-elevated user requirements.

## Using modules

If you need to customize both the Windows PowerShell console and the Windows PowerShell ISE (or other Windows PowerShell host), and you need to log on with multiple credentials, your need for Windows PowerShell profiles increases exponentially. Attempting to keep a number of different Windows PowerShell profiles in sync quickly becomes a maintenance nightmare. This is especially true if you are prone to making quick additions to your Windows PowerShell profile as you see a particular need.

In addition to having a large number of different profiles, it is also possible for a Windows PowerShell profile to grow to inordinate proportions—especially when you begin to add very many nicely crafted Windows PowerShell functions and helper functions. One solution to the problem (in fact, the best solution) to profile bloat is to use modules; my Windows PowerShell ISE profile uses four different modules—the profile itself consists of the lines loading the modules (for more information about modules, see Chapter 7, "Creating Advanced Functions and Modules").

The following list discusses the advantages, disadvantages, and uses of the one-profile approach:

- Advantages of using one profile:
  - It requires less work.
  - It's easy to keep different profiles in sync.
  - It allows you to achieve consistency between different Windows PowerShell environments.
  - It's portable; the profile can more easily travel to different machines.
- Disadvantages:
  - It's complex to set up.
  - It requires more planning.
  - *$profile* does not point to the correct location.
- Uses:
  - Use with more complex profiles.
  - Use when your work requires multiple user accounts or multiple Windows PowerShell hosts.
  - Use if your work takes you to different computers or virtual machines.

> **Note** The approach of containing functionality for a profile inside modules and then load-ing the modules from the profile file appears in the "Create a Really Cool PowerShell ISE Profile" article on the Hey Scripting Guy! blog, at *http://www.scriptingguys.com/blog*.

## Using the All Users, All Hosts profile

One way to use a single Windows PowerShell profile is to put everything into the All Users, All Hosts profile. I know some companies that create a standard Windows PowerShell profile for everyone in the company, and they use the All Users, All Hosts profile as a means of standardizing their Windows PowerShell environment. The changes go in during the image-build process, and therefore the pro-files are available to machines built from that image.

- Advantages of using the All Users, All Hosts profile:

  - It's simple; you can use one location for everything, especially when added during the build process.

  - One file affects all Windows PowerShell users and hosts.

  - It avoids conflict between admin users and non-admin users, since both types of users use the same profile.

  - *$profile.AllUsersAllHosts* always points to the correct file.

  - It's great for central management—one file is used for all users of a machine.

- Disadvantages:

  - You must have admin rights on the current machine to make changes to the file.

  - It provides no distinction between different hosts—some commands will not work in ISE and others will not work in the Windows PowerShell console.

  - It makes no distinction between admin users and non-admin users. Non-admin users will not be able to run certain commands.

  - The files are distributed among potentially thousands of different machines. To make one change to a profile, you must copy a file to all machines using that profile (although you can use group policy to assist in this endeavor). This can be a major problem for computers such as laptops that connect only occasionally to the network. It is also a problem when attempting to use a shutdown script on a Windows 8 device (because Windows 8 devices do not perform a true shutdown).

- Uses:
  - Use for your personal profile when duties require both elevation and non-elevation of permissions across multiple Windows PowerShell hosts.
  - Use as part of a standard image build to deploy static functionality to numerous machines and users.

## Using your own file

Because the Windows PowerShell profile is a Windows PowerShell script (with the added benefit of having a special name and residing in a special location), it means that anything that can be accomplished in a Windows PowerShell script can be accomplished in a Windows PowerShell profile. A much better approach to dealing with Windows PowerShell profiles is to keep the profile itself as simple as possible, but bring in the functionality you require via other means. One way to do this is to add the profile information you require to a file. Store that file in a central location, and then dot-source it to the profile.

### Using a Central Profile Script

1. Create a Windows PowerShell script containing the profile information you require. Include aliases, variables, functions, Windows PowerShell drives, and commands to execute on Windows PowerShell startup.

2. In the Windows PowerShell profile script to host the central profile, dot-source the central profile file. The following command, placed in the *$profile* script, brings in functionality stored in a Windows PowerShell script named myprofile.ps1 that resides in a shared folder named c:\fso.

```
. c:\fso\myprofile.ps1
```

One of the advantages of using a central Windows PowerShell script to store your profile information is that only one location requires updating when you add additional functionality to your profile. In addition, if folder permissions permit, the central Windows PowerShell script becomes available to any user for any host on the local machine. If you store this central Windows PowerShell script on a network file share, you only need to update one file for the entire network.

- Advantages of using a central script for a PowerShell profile:
  - It provides one place to modify the profile, or all users and all hosts having access to the file.
  - It's easy to keep functionality synchronized among all Windows PowerShell hosts and users.
  - It makes it possible to have one profile for the entire network.

- Disadvantages:

  - It's more complicated due to multiple files.

  - It provides no access to the central file, which means you won't have a profile for machines without network access.

  - It is possible that non-role-specific commands will become available to users.

  - Filtering out specific commands for specific hosts becomes more complex.

  - One central script becomes very complicated to maintain when it grows to hundreds of lines.

- Uses:

  - Use to provide basic functionality among multiple hosts and multiple users.

  - Use for a single user who wants to duplicate capabilities between Windows PowerShell hosts.

  - Use to provide a single profile for networked computers via a file share.

# Grouping similar functionality into a module

One of the main ways to clean up your Windows PowerShell profile is to group related items into modules. For example, suppose your Windows PowerShell profile contains a few utility functions such as the following:

- A function to determine admin rights

- A function to determine if the computer is a laptop or a desktop

- A function to determine if the host is the Windows PowerShell ISE or the Windows PowerShell console

- A function to determine if the computer is 32 bit or 64 bit

- A function to write to a temporary file

All of the preceding functions relate to the central theme of being utility types of functions. They are not specific to one technology, and are in fact helper functions, useful in a wide variety of scripts and applications. It is also true that as useful as these utilities are, you might not need to use them everywhere, at all times. This is the advantage of moving the functionality into a module—you can easily load and unload them as required.

# Where to store the profile module

If you run your system as a non-elevated user, do not use the user module location for modules that require elevation of privileges. This will be an exercise in futility, because once you elevate the user account to include admin rights, your profile shifts to another location, and then you do not have access to the module you were attempting to access.

Therefore, it makes sense to store modules requiring admin rights in the system32 directory hierarchy. Keep in mind that updates to admin modules will also require elevation and therefore could add a bit of complication. Store modules that do not require admin rights in the user profile module location. When modules reside in one of the two default locations, Windows PowerShell automatically picks up on them and displays them when you use the *ListAvailable* command, as shown here:

```
Get-Module -ListAvailable
```

However, this does not mean you are limited to modules from only the default locations. If you are centralizing your Windows PowerShell profile and storing it on a shared network drive, it makes sense to likewise store the module (and module manifest) in the shared network location as well.

> **Note** Keep in mind that the Windows PowerShell profile is a script, as is a Windows PowerShell module. Therefore, your script execution policy impacts the ability to run scripts (and to load modules) from a shared network location. Even if you have a script execution policy of *Unrestricted*, if you have not added the network share to Internet Explorer's trusted sites, you will be prompted each time you open Windows PowerShell. You can use group policy to set the Internet Explorer trusted sites for your domain, or you can add them manually. You may also want to examine code signing for your scripts.

# Creating a profile: step-by-step exercises

In this exercise, you'll use the *New-Item* cmdlet to create a new Windows PowerShell profile. You'll also use the *Get-ExecutionPolicy* cmdlet to ensure script execution is enabled on your local system. You'll also create a function to edit your Windows PowerShell profile. In the next exercise, you'll add additional functionality to the profile.

### Creating a basic Windows PowerShell profile

1. Start the Windows PowerShell console.

2. Use the *Test-Path* cmdlet to determine if a Windows PowerShell console profile exists. This command appears here:

    ```
    Test-Path $PROFILE
    ```

**3.** If a profile exists, make a backup copy of the profile by using the *Copy-Item* cmdlet. The command appearing here copies the profile to the profileBackup.ps1 file in the C:\fso folder.

```
Copy-Item $profile c:\fso\profileBackUp.ps1
```

**4.** Delete the existing $profile file by using the *Remove-Item* cmdlet. The command to do this appears here:

```
Remove-Item $PROFILE
```

**5.** Use the *Test-Path* cmdlet to ensure the $profile file is properly removed. The command to do this appears here:

```
Test-Path $PROFILE
```

**6.** Use the *New-Item* cmdlet to create a new Windows PowerShell console profile. Use the *$profile* automatic variable to refer to the Windows PowerShell console profile for the current user. Use the *-force* switched parameter to avoid any prompting. Specify an *ItemType* of *file* to ensure that a Windows PowerShell file is properly created. The command to accomplish these tasks appears here:

```
New-Item $PROFILE -ItemType file -Force
```

The output from the command to create a Windows PowerShell profile for the Windows PowerShell console host and the current user appears here:

```
    Directory: C:\Users\administrator.IAMMRED\Documents\WindowsPowerShell


Mode                LastWriteTime     Length Name
----                -------------     ------ ----
-a---          5/27/2012   3:51 PM          0 Microsoft.PowerShell_profile.ps1
```

**7.** Open the Windows PowerShell console profile in the Windows PowerShell ISE. To do this, type the command appearing here:

```
Ise $profile
```

**8.** Create a function named *Set-Profile* that opens the Windows PowerShell Current User, Current Host profile for editing in the Windows PowerShell ISE. To do this, begin by using the *function* keyword, and then assign the name *Set-Profile* to the function. These commands appear here:

```
Function Set-Profile
{

} #end function set-profile
```

**9.** Add the Windows PowerShell code to the *Set-Profile* function to open the profile for editing in the Windows PowerShell ISE. The command to do this appears here:

```
ISE $profile
```

10. Save the newly modified profile and close the Windows PowerShell ISE.

11. Close the Windows PowerShell console.

12. Open the Windows PowerShell console and look for errors.

13. Test the *Set-Profile* function by typing the command that appears here into the Windows PowerShell console:

```
Set-Profile
```

The Windows PowerShell console profile for the current user should open in the Windows PowerShell ISE. The *Set-Profile* function should be the only thing in the profile file.

This concludes the exercise.

In the following exercise, you will add a variable, an alias, and a Windows PowerShell drive to your Windows PowerShell profile.

## Adding profile functionality

1. Start the Windows PowerShell console.

2. Call the *Set-Profile* function (you added this function to your Windows PowerShell console profile during the previous exercise). The command to do this appears here:

```
Set-Profile
```

3. Add comment sections at the top of the Windows PowerShell profile for the following four sections: *Variables*, *Aliases*, *PS Drives*, and *Functions*. The code to do this appears here:

```
#Variables

#Aliases

#PS drives

#Functions
```

4. Create three new variables. The first variable is *MyDocuments*, the second variable is *ConsoleProfile*, and the third variable is *ISEProfile*. Use the code appearing here to assign the proper values to these variables:

```
New-Variable -Name MyDocuments -Value ([environment]::GetFolderPath("mydocuments"))
New-Variable -Name ConsoleProfile -Value (Join-Path -Path $mydocuments -ChildPath
WindowsPowerShell\Microsoft.PowerShell_profile.ps1)
New-Variable -Name ISEProfile -Value (Join-Path -Path $mydocuments -ChildPath
WindowsPowerShell\Microsoft.PowerShellISE_profile.ps1)
```

5. Create two new aliases. One alias is named *gh* and refers to the *Get-Help* cmdlet. The second alias is named *I* and refers to the *Invoke-History* cmdlet. The code to do this appears here:

```
New-Alias -Name gh -Value get-help
New-Alias -Name i -Value Invoke-History
```

6. Create two new PS drives. The first PS drive refers to the HKEY_CLASSES_ROOT location of the registry. The second PS drive refers to the current user's *my* location. The code to create these two PS drives appears here:

```
New-PSDrive -Name HKCR -PSProvider Registry -Root hkey_classes_root
New-PSDrive -Name mycerts -PSProvider Certificate -Root Cert:\CurrentUser\My
```

7. Following the *Set-Profile* function, add another comment for commands. This code appears here:

```
#commands
```

8. Add three commands. The first command starts the transcript functionality, the second sets the working location to the root of drive C, and the last clears the Windows PowerShell console. These three commands appear here:

```
Start-Transcript
Set-Location -Path c:\
Clear-Host
```

9. Save the Windows PowerShell profile and close out the Windows PowerShell ISE. Close the Windows PowerShell console as well. Open the Windows PowerShell console and look for errors. Test each of the newly created features to ensure they work. The commands to test the profile appear here:

```
gh
$MyDocuments
$ConsoleProfile
$ISEProfile
sl hkcr:
sl mycerts:
sl c:\
Stop-Transcript
set-profile
```

This concludes the exercise.

# Chapter 9 quick reference

| To | Do this |
|---|---|
| Determine the existence of a Windows PowerShell profile | Use the *Test-Path* cmdlet and supply the *$profile* automatic variable. |
| Create a Windows PowerShell profile | Use the *New-Item* cmdlet and supply a value of *file* for the item type. Use the *-force* switch to avoid prompting. |
| Add items to a Windows PowerShell profile that all users will use | Use the All Users, All Hosts profile. |
| Obtain the path to the All Users, All Hosts profile | Use the *$profile* automatic variable and choose the *AllUsersAllHosts* property. |
| Add items to a Windows PowerShell profile that the current user will use | Use the Current User, All Hosts profile. |
| Obtain the path to the Current User, All Hosts profile | Use the *$profile* automatic variable and choose the *CurrentUserAllHosts* property. |
| Edit a specific Windows PowerShell profile | From the Windows PowerShell console, type **ISE** and specify the path to the required Windows PowerShell profile by using the *$profile* automatic variable and the appropriate property. |

# CHAPTER 10

# Using WMI

**After completing this chapter, you will be able to:**

- Understand the concept of WMI namespaces.

- Use the WMI namespaces.

- Navigate the WMI namespaces.

- Understand the use of WMI providers.

- Discover classes supplied by WMI providers.

- Use the *Get-WmiObject* cmdlet to perform simple WMI queries.

- Produce a listing of all WMI classes.

- Perform searches to find WMI classes.

The inclusion of Microsoft Windows Management Instrumentation (WMI) in virtually every operating system released by Microsoft since Windows NT 4.0 should give you an idea of the importance of this underlying technology. From a network management perspective, many useful tasks can be accomplished using just Windows PowerShell, but to begin to truly unleash the power of scripting, you need to bring in additional tools. This is where WMI comes into play. WMI provides access to many powerful ways of managing Windows systems. This section will dive into the pieces that make up WMI. It will discuss at several concepts—namespaces, providers, and classes—and show how these concepts can aid in leveraging WMI in your Windows PowerShell scripts. All the scripts mentioned in this chapter are available via the Microsoft Script Center Script Repository.

Each new version of Windows introduces improvements to WMI, including new WMI classes, as well as new capabilities for existing WMI classes. In products such as Microsoft Exchange Server, Microsoft SQL Server, and Microsoft Internet Information Services (to mention a few), support for WMI continues to grow and expand. Some of the tasks you can perform with WMI follow:

- Report on drive configuration for locally attached drives, and for mapped drives.

- Report on available memory, both physical and virtual.

- Back up the event log.

- Modify the registry.

- Schedule tasks

- Share folders

- Switch from a static to a dynamic IP address

- Enable or disable a network adapter

- Defragment a hard disk drive

# Understanding the WMI model

WMI is a *hierarchical namespace*, in which the layers build on one another, like the Lightweight Directory Access Protocol (LDAP) directory used in Active Directory, or the file system structure on your hard drive. Although it is true that WMI is a hierarchical namespace, the term by itself does not really convey the richness of WMI. The WMI model has three sections—resources, infrastructure, and consumers—with the following uses:

- **WMI resources**   Resources include anything that can be accessed by using WMI—the file system, networked components, event logs, files, folders, disks, Active Directory, and so on.

- **WMI infrastructure**   The infrastructure comprises three parts: the WMI service, the WMI repository, and the WMI providers. Of these parts, WMI providers are the most important because they provide the means for WMI to gather needed information.

- **WMI consumers**   A consumer provides a prepackaged way to process data from WMI. A consumer can be a PowerShell cmdlet, a VBScript script, an enterprise management software package, or some other tool or utility that executes WMI queries.

# Working with objects and namespaces

Let's go back to the idea of a namespace introduced earlier in this chapter. You can think of a *namespace* as a way to organize or collect data related to similar items. Visualize an old-fashioned filing cabinet. Each drawer can represent a particular namespace. Inside this drawer are hanging folders that collect information related to a subset of what the drawer actually holds. For example, at home in my filing cabinet, I have a drawer reserved for information related to my woodworking tools. Inside this particular drawer are hanging folders for my table saw, my planer, my joiner, my dust collector, and so on. In the folder for the table saw is information about the motor, the blades, and the various accessories I purchased for the saw (such as an overarm blade guard).

WMI organizes the namespaces in a similar fashion to the filing cabinets described previously. It is possible to extend the filing cabinet analogy to include the three components of WMI with which you will work. The three components are namespaces, providers, and classes. The namespaces are the file cabinets. The providers are the drawers in the file cabinet. The folders in the drawers of the file cabinet are the WMI classes. These namespaces appear in Figure 10-1.

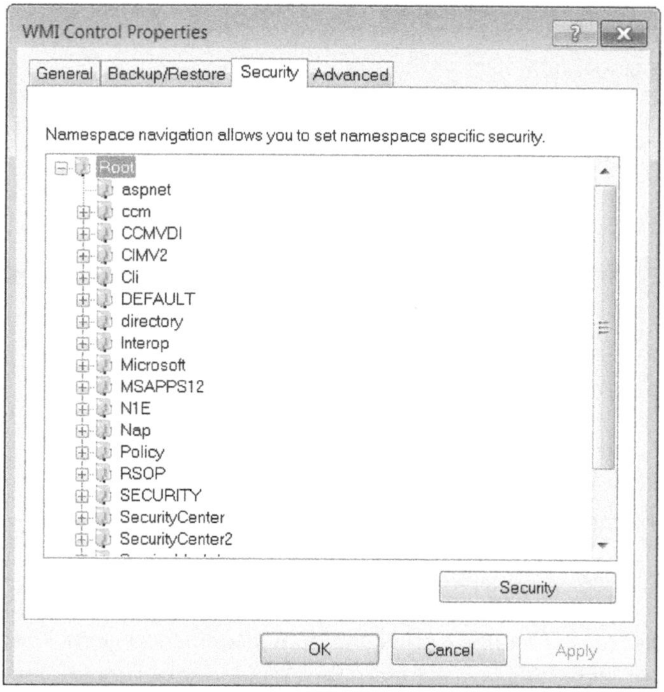

**FIGURE 10-1** WMI namespaces viewed in the WMI Control Properties dialog box.

Namespaces can contain other namespaces, as well as other objects, and these objects contain properties you can manipulate. Let's use a WMI command to illustrate the organization of the WMI namespaces. In the command that follows, the *Get-WmiObject* cmdlet is used to make the connection into WMI. The *-class* argument specifies the name of the class. In this example, the class name is __*Namespace* (the WMI class from which all WMI namespaces derive). Yes, you read that class name correctly—it is the word *namespace* preceded by two underscore characters (a double underscore is used for all WMI system classes because it makes them easy to find in sorted lists; the double underscore, when sorted, rises to the top of the list). The *-namespace* argument is *root* because it specifies the root level (the top namespace) in the WMI namespace hierarchy. The *Get-WmiObject* line of code appears here:

```
Get-WmiObject -class __Namespace -namespace root
```

The command and the associated output appear in Figure 10-2.

```
Windows PowerShell
Windows PowerShell
Copyright (C) 2011 Microsoft Corporation. All rights reserved.

PS C:\> Get-WmiObject -Class __namespace -ns root


__GENUS           : 2
__CLASS           : __NAMESPACE
__SUPERCLASS      : __SystemClass
__DYNASTY         : __SystemClass
__RELPATH         : __NAMESPACE.Name="subscription"
__PROPERTY_COUNT  : 1
__DERIVATION      : {__SystemClass}
__SERVER          : EDWILS1
__NAMESPACE       : ROOT
__PATH            : \\EDWILS1\ROOT:__NAMESPACE.Name="subscription"
Name              : subscription
PSComputerName    : EDWILS1

__GENUS           : 2
__CLASS           : __NAMESPACE
__SUPERCLASS      : __SystemClass
__DYNASTY         : __SystemClass
__RELPATH         : __NAMESPACE.Name="DEFAULT"
__PROPERTY_COUNT  : 1
__DERIVATION      : {__SystemClass}
__SERVER          : EDWILS1
__NAMESPACE       : ROOT
__PATH            : \\EDWILS1\ROOT:__NAMESPACE.Name="DEFAULT"
Name              : DEFAULT
PSComputerName    : EDWILS1

__GENUS           : 2
__CLASS           : __NAMESPACE
__SUPERCLASS      : __SystemClass
__DYNASTY         : __SystemClass
__RELPATH         : __NAMESPACE.Name="CIMV2"
__PROPERTY_COUNT  : 1
__DERIVATION      : {__SystemClass}
__SERVER          : EDWILS1
__NAMESPACE       : ROOT
__PATH            : \\EDWILS1\ROOT:__NAMESPACE.Name="CIMV2"
```

FIGURE 10-2 Namespace output obtained via the *Get-WmiObject* cmdlet.

When the *Get-WmiObject* cmdlet runs, it returns a collection of management objects. These objects contain a number of system properties, and therefore the cmdlet displays some complex output. Fixing the output requires the use of the *Select-Object* cmdlet and selection of the *name* property. Because of nesting (one namespace inside another namespace), the previous *Get-WmiObject* command returns a portion of the namespaces on the computer. To fix this situation, you must use a function. In the *Get-WmiNameSpace* function, you first create a couple of input parameters: *namespace* and *computer*. The default values of these parameters are *root* for the root of the WMI namespace, and *localhost*, which refers to the local computer. This portion of the function appears here:

```
Param(
  $nameSpace = "root",
  $computer = "localhost"
 )
```

It is possible to change the behavior of the *Get-WmiNameSpace* function by passing new values when calling the function.

**Note** When performing a WMI query against a remote computer, the user account performing the connection must be a member of the local administrators group on the remote machine. One way to accomplish this is to right-click the Windows PowerShell icon and select Run As Administrator from the menu that appears.

An example of calling the *Get-WmiNameSpace* function with alternate parameter values appears here:

```
Get-WmiNameSpace -nameSpace root\cimv2 -computer dc1
```

The *Get-WmiObject* cmdlet command looks for instances of the *__NameSpace* class on the computer and in the namespace specified when calling the function. One thing that is interesting is the use of a *custom error action*—a requirement due to a possible lack of rights on some of the namespaces. If you set the value of *erroraction* to *silentlycontinue*, any error generated, including Access Denied, does not appear, and the script ignores the error and continues to run. Without this change, the function would halt at the first Access Denied error, or by default, lots of Access Denied errors would clutter the output window and make the results difficult to read. This portion of the *Get-WmiNameSpace* function appears here:

```
Get-WmiObject -class __NameSpace -computer $computer `
 -namespace $namespace -ErrorAction "SilentlyContinue"
```

The results from the first *Get-WmiObject* command pass down the pipeline to a *Foreach-Object* cmdlet. Inside the associated *process* script block, the *Join-Path* cmdlet builds up a new namespace string using the *namespace* and *name* properties. The function skips any namespaces that contain the word *directory* to make the script run faster and to ignore any LDAP-type classes contained in the Root\Directory\LDAP WMI namespace. Once created, the new namespace name passes to the *Get-WmiObject* cmdlet, where a new query executes. This portion of the function appears here:

```
Foreach-Object `
 -Process `
   {
     $subns = Join-Path -Path $_.__namespace -ChildPath $_.name
     if($subns -notmatch 'directory') {$subns}
     $namespaces += $subns + "`r`n"
     Get-WmiNameSpace -namespace $subNS -computer $computer
   }
} #end Get-WmiNameSpace
```

The complete *Get-WmiNameSpace* function appears here:

**Get-WmiNameSpace**
```
Function Get-WmiNameSpace
{
 Param(
  $nameSpace = "root",
  $computer = "localhost"
 )
 Get-WmiObject -class __NameSpace -computer $computer `
 -namespace $namespace -ErrorAction "SilentlyContinue" |
 Foreach-Object `
 -Process `
```

```
  {
    $subns = Join-Path -Path $_.__namespace -ChildPath $_.name
    if($subns -notmatch 'directory') {$subns}
    $namespaces += $subns + "`r`n"
    Get-WmiNameSpace -namespace $subNS -computer $computer
  }
} #end Get-WmiNameSpace
```

An example of calling the *Get-WmiNameSpace* function, along with a sample of the output, appears in Figure 10-3.

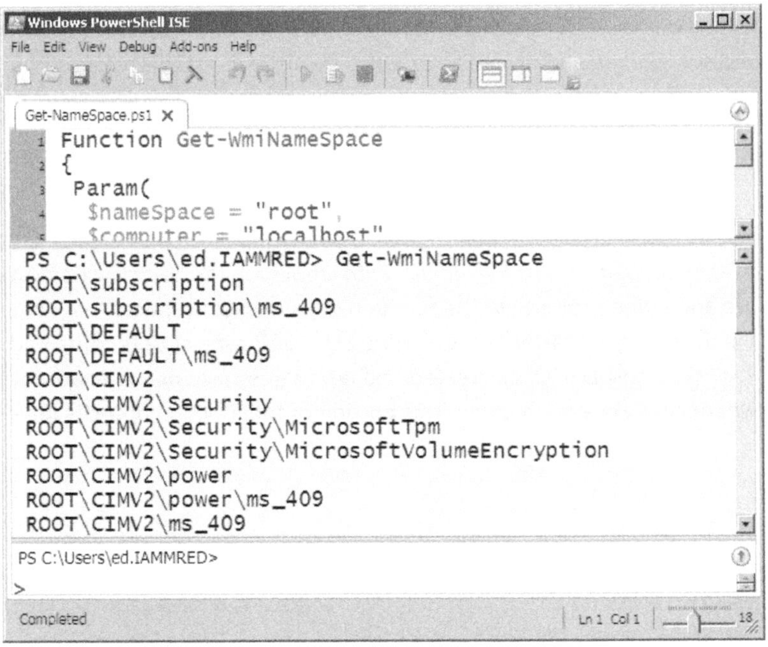

**FIGURE 10-3** WMI namespaces revealed by the *Get-WmiNameSpace* function.

So what does all this mean? It means that there are more than a dozen different WMI namespaces. Each of those WMI namespaces provides information about your computers. Understanding that the different namespaces exist is the first step to being able to navigate WMI to find the needed information. Often, students and others new to PowerShell or VBScript work on a WMI script to make the script perform a certain action, which is a great way to learn scripting. However, what they often do not know is which namespace they need to connect to so that they can accomplish their task. When I tell them which namespace to work with, they sometimes reply, "That's fine for you, but how do I know that the such-and-such namespace even exists?" By using the *Get-WmiNameSpace* function, you can easily generate a list of namespaces installed on a particular machine; and armed with that information, you can search on MSDN (*http://msdn.microsoft.com/library/default.asp*) to see what information the namespace is able to provide.

# Listing WMI providers

Understanding the namespace assists the network administrator with judiciously applying WMI scripting to his or her network duties. However, as mentioned earlier, to access information through WMI, you must have access to a WMI provider. After implementing the provider, you can gain access to the information the provider makes available.

> **Note** Keep in mind that in nearly every case, installation of providers happens in the background via operating system configuration or management application installation. For example, addition of new roles and features to server SKUs often installs new WMI providers and their attendant WMI classes.

WMI bases providers on a template class, or a system class called *__provider*. Armed with this information, you can look for instances of the *__provider* class, and you will have a list of all the providers that reside in your WMI namespace. This is exactly what the *Get-WmiProvider* function does.

The *Get-WmiProvider* function begins by assigning the string *Root\cimv2* to the *$wmiNS* variable. This value will be used with the *Get-WmiObject* cmdlet to specify where the WMI query will take place.

The *Get-WmiObject* cmdlet queries WMI. The *class* parameter limits the WMI query to the *__provider* class. The *-namespace* argument tells the *Get-WmiObject* cmdlet to look only in the Root\cimv2 WMI namespace. The array of objects returned from the *Get-WmiObject* cmdlet pipelines to the *Sort-Object* cmdlet, where the listing of objects is alphabetized based on the *name* property. After this process is completed, the reorganized objects pipeline to the *Select-Object* cmdlet, where the name of each provider is displayed. The complete *Get-WmiProvider* function appears here:

**Get-WmiProvider**

```
Function Get-WmiProvider
{
 Param(
  $nameSpace = "root\cimv2",
  $computer = "localhost"
 )
  Get-WmiObject -class __Provider -namespace $namespace |
  Sort-Object -property Name |
  Select-Object name
} #end function Get-WmiProvider
```

# Working with WMI classes

In addition to working with namespaces, the inquisitive network administrator may want to explore the concept of classes. In WMI parlance, you have core classes, common classes, and dynamic classes. *Core classes* represent managed objects that apply to all areas of management. These classes provide a basic vocabulary for analyzing and describing managed systems. Two examples of core classes are parameters and the *SystemSecurity* class. *Common classes* are extensions to the core classes and represent managed objects that apply to specific management areas. However, common classes are independent of a particular implementation or technology. The *CIM_UnitaryComputerSystem* class is an example of a common class. Network administrators do not use core and common classes because they serve as templates from which other classes derive, and as such are mainly of interest to developers of management applications. The reason IT professionals need to know about the core and common classes is to avoid confusion when it comes time to find usable WMI classes.

Many of the classes stored in Root\cimv2, therefore, are abstract classes and are of use as templates used in creating other WMI classes. However, a few classes in Root\cimv2 are dynamic classes used to hold actual information. The important aspect to remember about *dynamic classes* is that providers generate instances of a dynamic class, and therefore dynamic WMI classes are more likely to retrieve live data from the system.

To produce a simple listing of WMI classes, you can use the *Get-WmiObject* cmdlet and specify the *-list* argument. This code appears here:

```
Get-WmiObject -list
```

Partial output from the previous command is shown here:

```
Win32_TSGeneralSetting              Win32_TSPermissionsSetting
Win32_TSClientSetting               Win32_TSEnvironmentSetting
Win32_TSNetworkAdapterListSetting   Win32_TSLogonSetting
Win32_TSSessionSetting              Win32_DisplayConfiguration
Win32_COMSetting                    Win32_ClassicCOMClassSetting
Win32_DCOMApplicationSetting        Win32_MSIResource
Win32_ServiceControl                Win32_Property
```

One of the big problems with WMI is finding the WMI class needed to solve a particular problem. With literally thousands of WMI classes installed on even a basic Windows installation, searching through all the classes is difficult at best. While it is possible to search MSDN, a faster solution is to use Windows PowerShell itself. As just shown, using the *-list* switched parameter produces a listing of all the WMI classes in a particular namespace. It would be possible to combine this feature with the *Get-WmiNameSpace* function examined earlier to produce a listing of every WMI class on a computer— but that would only compound an already complicated situation.

A better solution is to stay focused on a single WMI namespace, and to use wildcard characters to assist in finding appropriate WMI classes. For example, you can use the wildcard pattern "*bios*" to find all WMI classes that contain the letters *bios* in the class name. The code that follows accomplishes this task:

```
Get-WmiObject -List "*bios*"
```

The command and associated output appear in Figure 10-4.

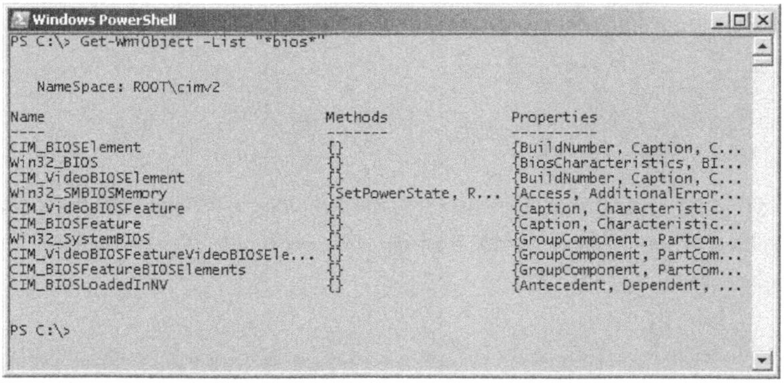

**FIGURE 10-4** Listing of WMI classes containing the pattern *bios* in the class name.

In the output shown in Figure 10-4, not all of the WMI classes will return data. In fact, you should not use all of the classes for direct query, because querying abstract classes is not supported. Nevertheless, some of the classes are useful; some of the classes solve a specific problem. "Which ones should you use?" you may ask. A simple answer—not completely accurate, but something to get you started—is to use only the WMI classes that begin with *win32*. You can easily modify the previous *Get-WMIObject* query to return only WMI classes that begin with *win32*. A regular expression pattern looks at the first position of each WMI class name to determine if the characters *win32* appear. The special character ^ tells the *match* operator to begin looking at the beginning of the string. The revised code appears here:

```
Get-WmiObject -List "*bios*" | where-object {$_.name -match '^win32'}
```

It is also possible to simplify the preceding code by taking advantage of command aliases and the simplified *Where-Object* syntax. In the code that follows, *gwmi* is an alias for the *Get-WmiObject* cmdlet. The *?* symbol is an alias for the *Where-Object* cmdlet, and the *name* property from the returned *ManagementClass* objects is examined from each instance crossing the pipeline to see if the regular expression pattern match appears. The shorter syntax appears here:

```
gwmi -list "*bios*" | ? name -match  '^win32'
```

Only a few WMI classes are returned from the preceding command. It is now time to query each WMI class to determine the WMI classes that might be useful. It is certainly possible to choose a class from the list and to query it directly. If you use the *gwmi* alias for the *Get-WmiObject* cmdlet, this doesn't require much typing. Here is the command to return BIOS information from the local computer:

```
gwmi win32_bios
```

It is also possible to pipeline the results of the query to find WMI classes to a command to query the WMI classes. The long form of the command (using complete cmdlet names) appears following. Keep in mind that this is a single-line command that appears here on two different lines for readability.

```
Get-WmiObject -List "*bios*" | Where-Object { $_.name -match '^win32'} |
ForEach-Object { Get-WmiObject -Class $_.name }
```

The short form of the command uses the alias *gwmi* for *Get-WmiObject*, *?* for the *Where-Object* cmdlet, as well as the simplified *Where-Object* syntax, and *%* for the *ForEach-Object* cmdlet. The shortened command appears here:

```
gwmi -list "*bios*" | ? name -match  '^win32' | % {gwmi $_.name}
```

## Exploring WMI objects

1.  Open the Windows PowerShell console.

2.  Use the *Get-WmiObject* cmdlet to find WMI classes that contain the string *bios* in their name. Use the alias *gwmi* for the *Get-WmiObject* cmdlet. The command appears here:

    ```
    gwmi -List "*bios*"
    ```

3.  Use the *Get-WmiObject* cmdlet to query the *Win32_Bios* WMI class. This command appears here:

    ```
    gwmi win32_bios
    ```

4.  Store the results of the previous query in a variable named *a*. Press the up arrow key to retrieve the previous command instead of retyping everything. This command appears here:

    ```
    $a = gwmi win32_bios
    ```

5.  View the contents of the *$a* variable. This command appears here:

    ```
    $a
    ```

6.  Pipeline the results stored in the *$a* variable to the *Get-Member* cmdlet. To do this, press the up arrow key to retrieve the previous command. Use the alias *gm* instead of typing the complete *Get-Member* cmdlet name. The command appears here:

    ```
    $a | gm
    ```

7.  Pipeline the results of the *Get-WmiObject* command to the *Get-Member* cmdlet. To do this, press the up arrow key twice to retrieve the previous command. Use the alias *gm* instead of typing the complete *Get-Member* cmdlet name. The command appears here:

    ```
    gwmi win32_bios | gm
    ```

8. Compare the results of the two *Get-Member* commands; the output should be the same.

9. Use the *Select-Object* cmdlet to view all of the information available from the *Win32_Bios* WMI class; choose all of the properties by using the * wildcard character. Use the alias *select* for the *Select-Object* cmdlet. The command appears here:

```
gwmi win32_bios | select *
```

10. This completes the procedure.

# Querying WMI

In most situations, when you use WMI, you are performing some sort of query. Even when you are going to set a particular property, you still need to execute a query to return a data set that enables you to perform the configuration. (A *data set* includes the data that comes back to you as the result of a query—that is, it is a set of data.) In this section, you will examine use of the *Get-WmiObject* cmdlet to query WMI.

### Using the *Get-WmiObject* cmdlet to query a specific WMI class

1. Connect to WMI by using the *Get-WmiObject* cmdlet.

2. Specify a valid WMI class name to query.

3. Specify a value for the namespace; omit the *-namespace* parameter to use the default root\ cimv2 namespace.

4. Specify a value for the *-computername* parameter; omit the *-computername* parameter to use the default value of *localhost*.

Windows PowerShell makes it easy to query WMI. In fact, at its most basic level, the only thing required is *gwmi* (the alias for the *Get-WmiObject* cmdlet) and the WMI class name, and possibly the name of the WMI namespace if using a non-default namespace. An example of this simple syntax appears here, along with the associated output:

```
PS C:\> gwmi win32_bios
SMBIOSBIOSVersion : BAP6710H.86A.0064.2011.0504.1711
Manufacturer      : Intel Corp.
Name              : BIOS Date: 05/04/11 17:11:33 Ver: 04.06.04
SerialNumber      :
Version           : INTEL  - 1072009
```

As shown in the "Exploring WMI objects" procedure in the preceding section, however, there are more properties available in the *Win32_Bios* WMI class than the five displayed in the output just shown. The command displays this limited output because a custom view of the *Win32_Bios* class defined in the Types.ps1xml file resides in the Windows PowerShell home directory on your system.

The following command uses the *Select-String* cmdlet to search the Types.ps1xml file to see if there is any reference to the WMI class *Win32_Bios*.

```
Select-String -Path $pshome\*.ps1xml -SimpleMatch "Win32_Bios"
```

In Figure 10-5, the results of several *Select-String* commands are displayed when a special format exists for a particular WMI class. The last query, for the *Win32_CurrentTime* WMI class, does not return any results, indicating that no special formatting exists for this class.

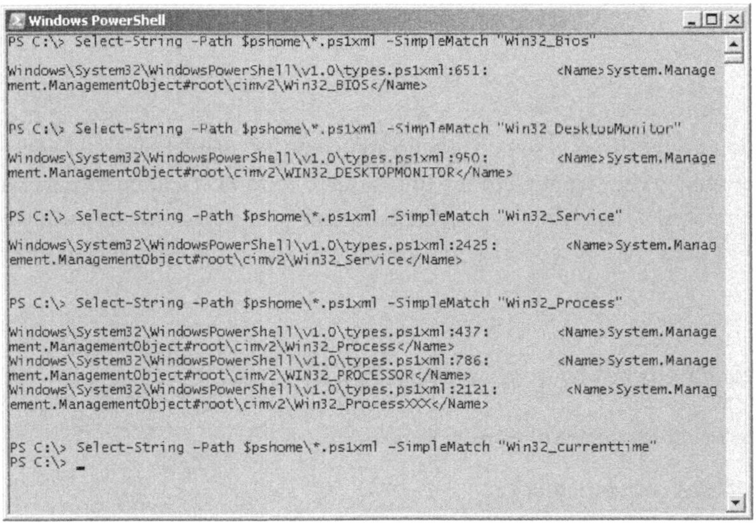

**FIGURE 10-5** The results of using *Select-String* to search the format XML files for special formatting instructions.

The previous *Select-String* queries indicate that there is special formatting for the *Win32_Bios*, *Win32_DesktopMonitor*, *Win32_Service*, *Win32_Process*, and *Win32_Processor* WMI classes. The Types.ps1xml file contains information that tells Windows PowerShell how to display a particular WMI class. When an instance of the *Win32_Bios* WMI class appears, Windows PowerShell uses the *DefaultDisplayPropertySet* configuration to display only five properties (if a *<view>* configuration is defined, it trumps the default property set). The portion of the Types.ps1xml file that details these five properties appears here:

```
<PropertySet>
    <Name>DefaultDisplayPropertySet</Name>
    <ReferencedProperties>
        <Name>SMBIOSBIOSVersion</Name>
        <Name>Manufacturer</Name>
        <Name>Name</Name>
        <Name>SerialNumber</Name>
        <Name>Version</Name>
    </ReferencedProperties>
</PropertySet>
```

The complete type definition for the *Win32_Bios* WMI class appears in Figure 10-6.

**FIGURE 10-6** The Types.ps1xml file controls which properties are displayed for specific WMI classes.

Special formatting instructions for the *Win32_Bios* WMI class indicate that there is an alternate property set available—a property set that is in addition to the *DefaultDisplayPropertySet*. This additional property set, named *PSStatus*, contains four properties. The four properties appear in the *PropertySet* description shown here:

```
<PropertySet>
    <Name>PSStatus</Name>
    <ReferencedProperties>
        <Name>Status</Name>
        <Name>Name</Name>
        <Name>Caption</Name>
        <Name>SMBIOSPresent</Name>
    </ReferencedProperties>
</PropertySet>
```

Finding the *psstatus* property set is more than a simple academic exercise, because the *psstatus* property set can be used directly with Windows PowerShell cmdlets such as *Select-Object* (*select* is an alias), *Format-List* (*fl* is an alias), and *Format-Table* (*ft* is an alias). The following commands illustrate the technique of using the *psstatus* property set to control data output:

```
gwmi win32_bios | select psstatus
gwmi win32_bios | fl psstatus
gwmi win32_bios | ft psstatus
```

Unfortunately, you cannot use the alternate property set *psstatus* to select the properties via the *property* parameter. Therefore, the command that appears here fails:

```
gwmi win32_bios -Property psstatus
```

Figure 10-7 shows the previous commands utilizing the *psstatus* property set, along with the associated output.

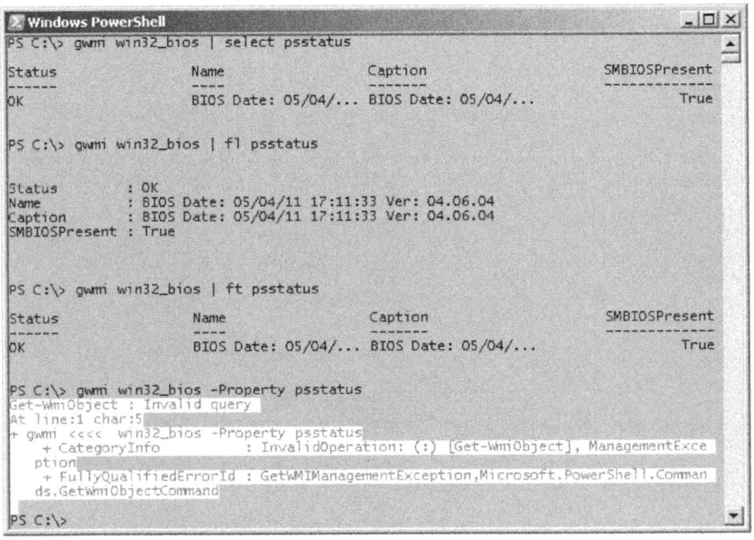

**FIGURE 10-7** Use of the *psstatus* property set, illustrated by various commands.

### Querying the *Win32_Desktop* class

1. Open the Windows PowerShell console.

2. Use the *Get-WmiObject* cmdlet to query information about desktop profiles stored on your local computer. To do this, use the *Win32_Desktop* WMI class, and use the alias *gwmi* instead of typing *Get-WmiObject*. Select only the *name* property by using the *Select-Object* cmdlet. Use the alias *select* instead of typing the *Select-Object* cmdlet name. The command appears here:

```
gwmi win32_desktop | select name
```

3. Execute the command. Your output will only contain the name of each profile stored on your machine. It will be similar to output that appears here:

```
name
----
NT AUTHORITY\SYSTEM
IAMMRED\ed
.DEFAULT
```

4. To retrieve the name of the screen saver, add the property *ScreenSaverExecutable* to the *Select-Object* command. This is shown here:

```
gwmi win32_desktop | select name, ScreenSaverExecutable
```

5. Run the command. Your output will appear something like the following:

```
name                                ScreenSaverExecutable
----                                ---------------------
NT AUTHORITY\SYSTEM
IAMMRED\ed                          C:\Windows\WLXPGSS.SCR
```

6. To identify whether the screen saver is secure, you need to query the *ScreenSaverSecure* property. This modified line of code is shown here:

```
gwmi win32_desktop | select name, ScreenSaverExecutable, ScreenSaverSecure
```

7. Run the command. Your output will appear something like the following:

```
name                ScreenSaverExecutable     ScreenSaverSecure
----                ---------------------     -----------------
NT AUTHORITY\SYSTEM
IAMMRED\ed          C:\Windows\WLXPGSS.SCR    True
.DEFAULT
```

8. To identify the screen saver timeout values, you need to query the *ScreenSaverTimeout* property. The modified command appears here:

```
gwmi win32_desktop | select name, ScreenSaverExecutable, ScreenSaverSecure,
ScreenSaverTimeout
```

9. Run the command. The output will appear something like the following:

```
name                ScreenSaverExecutable   ScreenSaverSecure   ScreenSaverTimeout
----                ---------------------   -----------------   ------------------
NT AUTHORITY\SYSTEM
IAMMRED\ed          C:\Windows\WLXPGS...    True                600
.DEFAULT
```

10. If you want to retrieve all the properties related to screen savers, you can use a wildcard asterisk screen-filter pattern. Delete the three screen saver properties and replace them with the *Screen\** wildcard pattern. The revised command appears here:

```
gwmi win32_desktop | select name, Screen*
```

11. Run the command. The output will appear similar to that shown here:

```
name                    : NT AUTHORITY\SYSTEM
ScreenSaverActive       : False
ScreenSaverExecutable   :
ScreenSaverSecure       :
ScreenSaverTimeout      :

name                    : IAMMRED\ed
ScreenSaverActive       : True
ScreenSaverExecutable   : C:\Windows\WLXPGSS.SCR
ScreenSaverSecure       : True
ScreenSaverTimeout      : 600

name                    : .DEFAULT
ScreenSaverActive       : False
ScreenSaverExecutable   :
ScreenSaverSecure       :
ScreenSaverTimeout      :
```

This concludes the procedure.

# Obtaining service information: step-by-step exercises

In this exercise, you will explore the use of the *Get-Service* cmdlet as you retrieve service information from your computer. You will sort and filter the output from the *Get-Service* cmdlet. In the second exercise, you will use WMI to retrieve similar information. You should compare the two techniques for ease of use and completeness of data.

### Obtaining Windows Service information by using the *Get-Service* cmdlet

1. Start the Windows PowerShell console.

2. From the Windows PowerShell prompt, use the *Get-Service* cmdlet to obtain a listing of all the services and their associated status. This is shown here:

   ```
   Get-Service
   ```

   A partial listing of the output from this command is shown here:

   ```
   Status   Name          DisplayName
   ------   ----          -----------
   Running  Bits          Bits
   Running  ALG           Application Layer Gateway Service
   Stopped  AppMgmt       Application Management
   Stopped  aspnet_state  ASP.NET State Service
   Running  AudioSrv      Windows Audio
   Running  BITS          Background Intelligent Transfer Ser...
   ```

3. Use the *Sort-Object* cmdlet to sort the listing of services. Specify the *status* property for *Sort-Object*. To sort the data based upon status, pipeline the results of the *Get-Service* cmdlet

into the *Sort-Object* cmdlet. Use the *sort* alias for the *Sort-Object* cmdlet to reduce the amount of typing. The results are shown here:

```
Get-Service |sort -property status
```

Partial output from this command is shown here:

```
Status   Name          DisplayName
------   ----          -----------
Stopped  RasAuto       Remote Access Auto Connection Manager
Stopped  RDSessMgr     Remote Desktop Help Session Manager
Stopped  odserv        Microsoft Office Diagnostics Service
Stopped  ose           Office Source Engine
```

4. Use the *Get-Service* cmdlet to produce a listing of services. Sort the resulting list of services alphabetically by name. To do this, use the *Sort-Object* cmdlet to sort the listing of services by the *name* property. Pipeline the object returned by the *Get-Service* cmdlet into the *Sort-Object* cmdlet. The command to do this, using the *sort* alias for *Sort-Object*, is shown here:

```
Get-Service |sort -property name
```

Partial output of this command is shown here:

```
Status   Name          DisplayName
------   ----          -----------
Running  Bits          Bits
Running  ALG           Application Layer Gateway Service
Stopped  AppMgmt       Application Management
Stopped  aspnet_state  ASP.NET State Service
Running  AudioSrv      Windows Audio
Running  BITS          Background Intelligent Transfer Ser...
```

5. Use the *Get-Service* cmdlet to produce a listing of services. Sort the objects returned by both the name and the status of the service. The command to do this is shown here:

```
Get-Service |sort status, name
```

Partial output of this command is shown here:

```
Status   Name          DisplayName
------   ----          -----------
Stopped  AppMgmt       Application Management
Stopped  aspnet_state  ASP.NET State Service
Stopped  Browser       Computer Browser
Stopped  CcmExec       SMS Agent Host
Stopped  CiSvc         Indexing Service
```

6. Use the *Get-Service* cmdlet to return an object containing service information. Pipeline the resulting object into a *Where-Object* cmdlet. Look for the word *server* in the display name. The resulting command is shown here:

```
Get-Service | where DisplayName -match "server"
```

The resulting listing is shown here:

```
Status    Name                DisplayName
------    ----                -----------
Running   DcomLaunch          DCOM Server Process Launcher
Running   InoRPC              eTrust Antivirus RPC Server
Running   InoRT               eTrust Antivirus Realtime Server
Running   InoTask             eTrust Antivirus Job Server
Stopped   lanmanserver        Server
Stopped   MSSQL$SQLEXPRESS    SQL Server (SQLEXPRESS)
Stopped   MSSQLServerADHe...  SQL Server Active Directory Helper
Stopped   SQLBrowser          SQL Server Browser
Stopped   SQLWriter           SQL Server VSS Writer
```

7. Use the *Get-Service* cmdlet to retrieve a listing of service objects. Pipeline the resulting objects to the *Where-Object* cmdlet. Use the *-equals* argument to return an object that represents the Bits service. The code that does this is shown here:

```
Get-Service | where name -eq "bits"
```

8. Press the up arrow key to retrieve the previous command that retrieves the Bits service. Store the resulting object in a variable called *$a*. This code is shown here:

```
$a=Get-Service | where name -eq "bits"
```

9. Pipeline the object contained in the *$a* variable into the *Get-Member* cmdlet. You can use the *gm* alias to simplify typing. This code is shown here:

```
$a | gm
```

10. Using the object contained in the *$a* variable, obtain the status of the Bits service. The code that does this is shown here:

```
$a.status
```

11. If the Bits service is running, then stop it. To do so, use the *Stop-Service* cmdlet. Instead of pipelining the object in the *$a* variable, you use the *-inputobject* argument from the *Stop-Service* cmdlet. The code to do this is shown here:

```
Stop-Service -InputObject $a
```

12. If the Bits service stops, then use the *Start-Service* cmdlet instead of the *Stop-Service* cmdlet. Use the *-inputobject* argument to supply the object contained in the *$a* variable to the cmdlet. This is shown here:

```
Start-Service -InputObject $a
```

**13.** Query the *status* property of the object contained in the *$a* variable to confirm that the Bits service's status has changed. This is shown here:

```
$a.status
```

> **Note** If you are working with a service that has its startup type set to Disabled, then PowerShell will not be able to start it and will return an error. If you do not have admin rights, Windows PowerShell will be unable to stop the service.

This concludes this step-by-step exercise.

In the following exercise, you will explore the use of the *Win32_Service* WMI class by using the *Get-WmiObject* cmdlet as you retrieve service information from your computer.

## Using WMI for service information

**1.** Start the Windows PowerShell console.

**2.** From the Windows PowerShell prompt, use the *Get-WmiObject* cmdlet to obtain a listing of all the services and their associated statuses. Use the *gwmi* alias instead of typing *Get-WmiObject*. The command to do this is shown here:

```
gwmi win32_sevice
```

A partial listing of the output from this command is shown here:

```
ExitCode  : 0
Name      : AdobeActiveFileMonitor6.0
ProcessId : 1676
StartMode : Auto
State     : Running
Status    : OK

ExitCode  : 0
Name      : AdobeARMservice
ProcessId : 1772
StartMode : Auto
State     : Running
Status    : OK

ExitCode  : 0
Name      : AeLookupSvc
ProcessId : 0
StartMode : Manual
State     : Stopped
Status    : OK
```

```
ExitCode   : 1077
Name       : ALG
ProcessId  : 0
StartMode  : Manual
State      : Stopped
Status     : OK
```

3. Use the *Sort-Object* cmdlet to sort the listing of services. Specify the *state* property for the *Sort-Object* cmdlet. To sort the service information based upon the *state* of the service, pipeline the results of the *Get-WmiObject* cmdlet into the *Sort-Object* cmdlet. Use the *sort* alias for the *Sort-Object* cmdlet to reduce the amount of typing. The results are shown here:

```
gwmi win32_service | sort state
```

Partial output from this command is shown here:

```
ExitCode   : 0
Name       : lmhosts
ProcessId  : 676
StartMode  : Auto
State      : Running
Status     : OK

ExitCode   : 0
Name       : TrkWks
ProcessId  : 864
StartMode  : Auto
State      : Running
Status     : OK

ExitCode   : 0
Name       : LanmanWorkstation
ProcessId  : 1316
StartMode  : Auto
State      : Running
Status     : OK
```

4. Use the *Get-WmiObject* cmdlet to produce a listing of services. Sort the resulting list of services alphabetically by *DisplayName*. To do this, use the *Sort-Object* cmdlet to sort the listing of services by the *name* property. Pipeline the object returned by the *Get-WMIObject* cmdlet into the *Sort-Object* cmdlet. The command to do this, using the *sort* alias for *Sort-Object*, is shown here:

```
gwmi win32_service | sort DisplayName
```

Notice that the output does not appear to actually be sorted by the *DisplayName* property. There are two problems at work. The first is that there is a difference between the *name* property and the *DisplayName* property. The second problem is that the *DisplayName* property is not displayed by default. Partial output of this command appears here:

```
ExitCode   : 1077
Name       : AxInstSV
ProcessId  : 0
StartMode  : Manual
State      : Stopped
Status     : OK

ExitCode   : 1077
Name       : SensrSvc
ProcessId  : 0
StartMode  : Manual
State      : Stopped
Status     : OK

ExitCode   : 0
Name       : AdobeARMservice
ProcessId  : 1772
StartMode  : Auto
State      : Running
Status     : OK
```

5. Produce a service listing that is sorted by *DisplayName*. This time, use the *Select-Object* cmdlet to display both the *state* and the *DisplayName* properties. Use the *gwmi*, *sort*, and *select* aliases to reduce typing. The command appears here:

```
gwmi win32_service | sort DisplayName | select state, DisplayName
```

Sample of the output from the previous command appears here:

```
state                              DisplayName
-----                              -----------
Stopped                            ActiveX Installer (AxInstSV)
Stopped                            Adaptive Brightness
Running                            Adobe Acrobat Update Service
Running                            Adobe Active File Monitor V6
Running                            AMD External Events Utility
Stopped                            Application Experience
```

6. Use the *Get-WmiObject* cmdlet to return an object containing service information. Pipeline the resulting object into a *Where-Object* cmdlet. Look for the word *server* in the display name. The resulting command is shown here:

```
gwmi win32_service | ? displayname -match 'server'
```

The resulting listing is shown here:

```
ExitCode   : 0
Name       : DcomLaunch
ProcessId  : 848
StartMode  : Auto
State      : Running
Status     : OK
```

```
ExitCode   : 0
Name       : LanmanServer
ProcessId  : 1028
StartMode  : Auto
State      : Running
Status     : OK

ExitCode   : 0
Name       : MSSQL$SQLEXPRESS
ProcessId  : 1952
StartMode  : Auto
State      : Running
Status     : OK
```

7.  Use the *Get-WMIObject* cmdlet to retrieve a listing of service objects. Pipeline the resulting object to *Where-Object*. Use the *-equals* argument to return an object that represents the Bits service. The code that does this is shown here:

```
gwmi win32_service | ? name -eq 'bits'
```

8.  Press the up arrow key to retrieve the command that retrieves the Bits service. Store the resulting object in a variable called *$a*. This code is shown here:

```
$a= gwmi win32_service | ? name -eq 'bits'
```

9.  Pipeline the object contained in the *$a* variable into the *Get-Member* cmdlet. You can use the *gm* alias to simplify typing. This code is shown here:

```
$a | gm
```

10. Using the object contained in the *$a* variable, obtain the status of the Bits service. The code that does this is shown here:

```
$a.state
```

11. If the Bits service is running, then stop it. To do so, use the *StopService* method. Instead of pipelining the object in the *$a* variable, you use dotted notation. The code to do this is shown here:

```
$a.StopService()
```

12. If the Bits service stops, you will see a *ReturnValue* of 0. If you see a *ReturnValue* of 2, it means that access is denied, and you will need to start the Windows PowerShell console with admin rights to stop the service. Query the *state* property of the object contained in the *$a* variable to confirm that the Bits service's status has changed. This is shown here:

```
$a.state
```

**13.** If you do not refresh the object stored in the *$a* variable, the original state is reported—regardless of whether the command has completed or not. To refresh the data stored in the *$a* variable, run the WMI query again. The code to do this appears here:

```
$a = gwmi win32_service | ? {$_.name -eq 'bits'}
$a.state
```

**14.** If the Bits service is stopped, go ahead and start it back up by using the *StartService* method. The code to do this appears here:

```
$a.StartService()
```

This concludes this step-by-step exercise.

# Chapter 10 quick reference

| To | Do this |
|---|---|
| Find the default WMI namespace on a computer | Use the Advanced tab in the WMI Control Properties dialog box. |
| Browse WMI classes on a computer | Use the *Get-WmiObject* cmdlet with the *-list* argument. Use a wildcard for the WMI class name. |
| Make a connection into WMI | Use the *Get-WmiObject* cmdlet in your script. |
| Use a shortcut name for the local computer | Use a dot (.) and assign it to the variable holding the computer name in the script. |
| Find detailed information about all WMI classes on a computer | Use the Platform SDK information found in the MSDN library (*http://msdn2.microsoft.com/en-us/library/aa394582.aspx*) |
| List all the namespaces on a computer | Query for a class named *__NameSpace*. |
| List all providers installed in a particular namespace | Query for a class named *__Win32Provider*. |
| List all the classes in a particular namespace on a computer | Use the *-list* argument for the *Get-WmiObject* cmdlet. |
| Quickly retrieve similarly named properties from a class | Use the *Select-Object* cmdlet and supply a wildcard asterisk (*) for the *-property* argument. |

# CHAPTER 11

# Querying WMI

**After completing this chapter, you will be able to:**

- Understand the different methods for querying WMI.

- Use the *Select-Object* cmdlet to create a custom object from a WMI query.

- Configure the *-filter* argument to limit information returned by WMI.

- Configure the WMI query to return selected properties.

- Use the *Where-Object* cmdlet to filter information returned from WMI.

- Leverage both hardware classes and system classes to configure machines.

After network administrators and consultants get their hands on a couple of Microsoft Windows Management Instrumentation (WMI) scripts, they begin to arrange all kinds of scenarios for use. This is both a good thing and a bad thing. The good thing is that WMI is powerful technology that can quickly solve many real problems. The bad thing is that a poorly written WMI script can adversely affect the performance of everything it touches—from client machines logging on to the network for the first time to huge infrastructure servers that provide the basis for mission-critical networked applications. This chapter will examine the fundamentals of querying WMI in an effective manner. Along the way, it will examine some of the more useful WMI classes and add to your Windows PowerShell skills.

## Alternate ways to connect to WMI

Chapter 10, "Using WMI," examined the basics of the *Get-WmiObject* cmdlet to obtain specific information. When you make a connection to WMI, it is important to realize there are default values utilized for the WMI connection.

The default values are stored in the following registry location: HKEY_LOCAL_MACHINE\ SOFTWARE\Microsoft\WBEM\Scripting. There are two keys: DEFAULT IMPERSONATION LEVEL and DEFAULT NAMESPACE. DEFAULT IMPERSONATION LEVEL is set to a value of 3, which means that WMI impersonates the logged-on user and therefore uses the logged-on user name, credentials, and rights. The default namespace is Root\cimv2, which means that for many of the tasks you will need to perform, the classes are immediately available. Use the *Get-ItemProperty* cmdlet to verify the default WMI configuration on a local computer. This command appears here:

```
get-itemproperty HKLM:\SOFTWARE\Microsoft\WBEM\Scripting
```

In Figure 11-1, the *Get-ItemProperty* cmdlet retrieves the default WMI settings on a local computer. Next, the *Invoke-Command* cmdlet retrieves the same information from a remote computer named Win8-C1. Both the commands and the output from the commands appear in the figure.

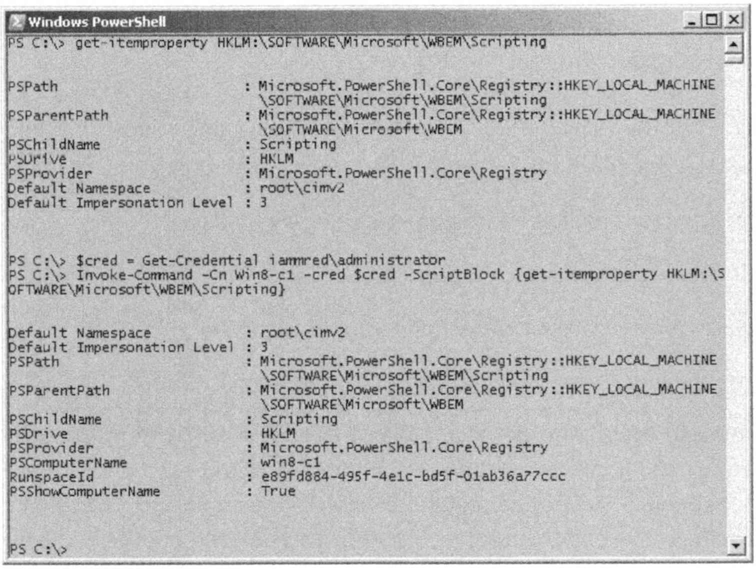

**FIGURE 11-1** Use of the *Get-ItemProperty* cmdlet to verify default WMI settings.

In reality, a default namespace of root/cimv2 and a default impersonation level of *impersonate* are good defaults. The default computer is the local machine, so you do not need to specify the computer name when you are simply running against the local machine.

> **Tip** Use default WMI values to simplify your WMI scripts. If you only want to return information from the local machine, the WMI class resides in the default namespace, and you intend to impersonate the logged-on user, then the defaults are perfect. The defaults are fine when you are logged on to a machine with an account that has permission to access the information you need. The following command illustrates obtaining BIOS information from the local computer.

**SmallBios.ps1**

```
Get-WmiObject win32_bios
```

When you use the *Get-WmiObject* cmdlet and only supply the name of the WMI class, then you are relying on the default values: default computer, default WMI namespace, and default impersonation level. The SmallBios.ps1 script produces the information shown here, which is the main information you would want to see about the BIOS: the version, name, serial number, and maker.

```
SMBIOSBIOSVersion : Version 1.40
Manufacturer      : TOSHIBA
Name              : v1.40
SerialNumber      : 55061728HU
Version           : TOSHIB - 970814
```

The amazing thing is that you can obtain such useful information by typing about 15 characters on the keyboard (using tab completion). Doing this in VBScript would require much more typing. However, if you want to retrieve different information from the *WIN32_Bios* WMI class, or if you would like to see a different kind of output, then you will need to work with the *Format* cmdlets, *Select-Object*, or *Out-GridView*. This technique appears in the procedure.

### Retrieving properties

1. Open the Windows PowerShell console.

2. Use the *Get-WmiObject* cmdlet to retrieve the default properties of the *WIN32_ComputerSystem* WMI class:

   ```
   Get-WmiObject WIN32_computersystem
   ```

   The results, with the default properties, are shown here:

   ```
   Domain              : nwtraders.com
   Manufacturer        : TOSHIBA
   Model               : TECRA M3
   Name                : MRED1
   PrimaryOwnerName    : Mred
   TotalPhysicalMemory : 2146680832
   ```

3. If you are only interested in the name and the make and model of the computer, then you will need to pipeline the results into a *Format-List* cmdlet and choose only the properties you wish. This revised command is shown here:

   ```
   Get-WmiObject WIN32_computersystem | Format-List name,model, manufacturer
   ```

   The results are shown here:

   ```
   name         : MRED1
   model        : TECRA M3
   manufacturer : TOSHIBA
   ```

4. If you are interested in all the properties from the *WIN32_ComputerSystem* class, you have several options. The first is to use the up arrow key and modify the *Format-List* cmdlet. Instead of choosing three properties, use an asterisk (*). This revised command is shown here:

   ```
   Get-WmiObject WIN32_ComputerSystem | Format-List *
   ```

**5.** The results from this command are shown following. Notice, however, that although the results seem impressive at first, they quickly degenerate into seemingly meaningless drivel. Note the number of classes that begin with double underscore, such as _CLASS. These are system properties that get attached to every WMI class when they are created. Although useful to WMI gurus, they are less exciting to normal network administrators.

```
AdminPasswordStatus          : 0
BootupState                  : Normal boot
ChassisBootupState           : 3
KeyboardPasswordStatus       : 0
PowerOnPasswordStatus        : 0
PowerSupplyState             : 3
PowerState                   : 0
FrontPanelResetStatus        : 0
ThermalState                 : 3
Status                       : OK
Name                         : MRED1
PowerManagementCapabilities  :
PowerManagementSupported     :
__GENUS                      : 2
__CLASS                      : Win32_ComputerSystem
__SUPERCLASS                 : CIM_UnitaryComputerSystem
__DYNASTY                    : CIM_ManagedSystemElement
__RELPATH                    : Win32_ComputerSystem.Name="MRED1"
__PROPERTY_COUNT             : 54
__DERIVATION                 : {CIM_UnitaryComputerSystem, CIM_ComputerSystem,
                               CIM_System, CIM_LogicalElement...}
__SERVER                     : MRED1
__NAMESPACE                  : root\cimv2
__PATH                       : \\MRED1\root\cimv2:Win32_ComputerSystem.Name=
                               "MRED1"
AutomaticResetBootOption     : True
AutomaticResetCapability     : True
BootOptionOnLimit            :
BootOptionOnWatchDog         :
BootROMSupported             : True
Caption                      : MRED1
CreationClassName            : Win32_ComputerSystem
CurrentTimeZone              : 60
DaylightInEffect             : False
Description                  : AT/AT COMPATIBLE
Domain                       : northamerica.corp.microsoft.com
DomainRole                   : 1
EnableDaylightSavingsTime    : True
InfraredSupported            : False
InitialLoadInfo              :
InstallDate                  :
LastLoadInfo                 :
Manufacturer                 : TOSHIBA
Model                        : TECRA M3
NameFormat                   :
NetworkServerModeEnabled     :
NumberOfProcessors           : 1
OEMLogoBitmap                :
OEMStringArray               : {PTM30U-0H001V59,SQ003648A83,138}
```

```
PartOfDomain                    : True
PauseAfterReset                 : -1
PrimaryOwnerContact             :
PrimaryOwnerName                : Mred
ResetCapability                 : 1
ResetCount                      : -1
ResetLimit                      : -1
Roles                           :
SupportContactDescription       :
SystemStartupDelay              : 15
SystemStartupOptions            : {"Microsoft Windows XP Professional" /noexecute=
                                  optin /fastdetect}
SystemStartupSetting            : 0
SystemType                      : X86-based PC
TotalPhysicalMemory             : 2146680832
UserName                        : NORTHAMERICA\edwils
WakeUpType                      : 6
Workgroup                       :
```

6. To remove the system properties from the list, use the up arrow key to retrieve the *Get-WmiObject win32_computersystem | Format-List \** command. Delete the asterisk in the *Format-List* command and replace it with an expression that limits the results to property names that are returned to only those that begin with the letters *a* through *z*. This command is shown here:

```
Get-WmiObject WIN32_computersystem | Format-List [a-z]*
```

7. To see a listing of properties that begin with the letter *d*, use the up arrow key to retrieve the *Get-WmiObject win32_computersystem | Format-List [a-z]\** command and change the *Format-List* cmdlet to retrieve only properties that begin with the letter *d*. To do this, substitute *d\** for *[a-z]\**. The revised command is shown here:

```
Get-WmiObject WIN32_computersystem | Format-List D*
```

8. Retrieve a listing of all the properties and their values that begin with either the letter *d* or the letter *t* from the *WIN32_computersystem* WMI class. Use the up arrow key to retrieve the previous *Get-WmiObject win32_computersystem | Format-List D\** command. Use a comma to separate the *t\** from the previous command. The revised command is shown here:

```
Get-WmiObject WIN32_computersystem | Format-List d*,t*
```

This concludes the procedure.

**Tip** After you use the *Get-WmiObject* cmdlet for a while, you may get tired of using tab completion and having to type *Get-W<tab>*. It may be easier to use the default alias of *gwmi*. This alias can be discovered by using the following command:

```
Get-Alias | where definition -eq 'Get-WmiObject'
```

## Working with disk drives

1. Open the Windows PowerShell console.

2. Use the *gwmi* alias to retrieve the default properties for each drive defined on your system. To do this, use the *WIN32_LogicalDisk* WMI class. This command is shown here:

```
gwmi win32_logicaldisk
```

The results of the *gwmi win32_logicaldisk* command are shown here:

```
DeviceID     : C:
DriveType    : 3
ProviderName :
FreeSpace    : 6164701184
Size         : 36701163520
VolumeName   : c

DeviceID     : D:
DriveType    : 3
ProviderName :
FreeSpace    : 11944701952
Size         : 23302184960
VolumeName   : d

DeviceID     : E:
DriveType    : 5
ProviderName :
FreeSpace    :
Size         :
VolumeName   :
```

3. To limit the disks returned by the WMI query to only local disk drives, you can supply a value of 3 for the *DriveType* property. Use the up arrow key to retrieve the previous command. Add the *DriveType* property to the *-filter* parameter of the *Get-WMIObject* cmdlet with a value of 3. This revised command is shown here:

```
gwmi win32_logicaldisk -filter drivetype=3
```

The resulting output from the *gwmi win32_logicaldisk -filter drivetype=3* command is shown here:

```
DeviceID     : C:
DriveType    : 3
ProviderName :
FreeSpace    : 6163599360
Size         : 36701163520
VolumeName   : c
DeviceID     : D:
DriveType    : 3
ProviderName :
FreeSpace    : 11944701952
Size         : 23302184960
VolumeName   : d
```

4. Open the Windows PowerShell ISE or some other script editor, and save the file as *<yourname>*Logical Disk.ps1.

5. Use the up arrow key in PowerShell to retrieve the *gwmi win32_logicaldisk -filter drivetype=3* command. Highlight it with your mouse and press Enter.

6. Paste the command into the *<yourname>*LogicalDisk.ps1 script.

7. Declare a variable called *$objDisk* at the top of your script. This command is shown here:

```
$objDisk
```

8. Use the *$objDisk* variable to hold the object returned by the command you copied from your PowerShell console. As you are planning on saving the script, replace the *gwmi* alias with the actual name of the cmdlet. The resulting command is shown here:

```
$objDisk=Get-WmiObject win32_logicaldisk -filter drivetype=3
```

9. Use the *Measure-Object* cmdlet to retrieve the minimum and the maximum values for the *freespace* property. To do this, pipeline the previous object into the *Measure-Object* cmdlet. Specify *freespace* for the *-property* argument, and use the *-minimum* and *-maximum* switches. Use the pipe character to break your code into two lines. This command is shown here:

```
$objDisk=Get-WmiObject win32_logicaldisk -filter drivetype=3 |
    Measure-Object -property freespace -Minimum -Maximum
```

10. Print out the resulting object that is contained in the *$objDisk* variable. This command is shown here:

```
$objDisk
```

The resulting printout on my computer is shown here:

```
Count    : 2
Average  :
Sum      :
Maximum  : 11944701952
Minimum  : 6163550208
Property : freespace
```

11. To dispose of the empty properties, pipeline the previous command into a *Select-Object* cmdlet. Select the property and the *minimum* and *maximum* properties. Use the pipe character to break your code into multiple lines The revised command is shown here:

```
$objDisk=Get-WmiObject win32_logicaldisk -filter drivetype=3 |
    Measure-Object -property freespace  -Minimum -Maximum |
    Select-Object -Property property, maximum, minimum
```

12. Save and run the script. Notice how the output is spread over the console. To tighten up the display, pipeline the resulting object into the *Format-Table* cmdlet. Use the *-autosize* switch. The revised command is shown here:

```
$objDisk=Get-WmiObject win32_logicaldisk -filter drivetype=3 |
   Measure-Object -property freespace  -Minimum -Maximum |
   Select-Object -Property property, maximum, minimum |
   Format-Table -autosize
```

**13.** Save and run the script. The output on my computer is shown here:

```
Property     Maximum     Minimum
--------     -------     -------
freespace 11944685568 6164058112
```

**Note** The *WIN32_LogicalDisk* WMI class property *DriveType* can have a value of 0 to 6 (inclusive). The most useful of these values are as follows: 3 (local disk), 4 (network drive), 5 (compact disk), and 6 (RAM disk).

## Tell me everything about everything!

When novices first write WMI scripts, they nearly all begin by asking for every property from every instance of a class. That is, the queries will essentially say, "Tell me everything about every process." (This is also referred to as the infamous *select* * query.) This approach can often return an overwhelming amount of data, particularly when you are querying a class such as installed software or processes and threads. Rarely would one need to have so much data. Typically, when looking for installed software, you're looking for information about a *particular* software package.

There are, however, several occasions when you may want to use the "Tell me everything about all instances of a particular class" query, including the following:

- During development of a script to see representative data

- When troubleshooting a more directed query—for example, when you're possibly trying to filter on a field that does not exist

- When the returned items are so few that being more precise doesn't make sense.

To return all information from all instances, perform the following steps:

1. Make a connection to WMI by using the *Get-WmiObject* cmdlet.

2. Use the *-query* argument to supply the WQL query to the *Get-WmiObject* cmdlet.

3. In the query, use the *Select* statement to choose everything:

   ```
   Select *.
   ```

4. In the query, use the *From* statement to indicate the class from which you wish to retrieve data. For example, *From Win32_Share*.

In the next script, you'll make a connection to the default namespace in WMI and return all the information about all the shares on a local machine. Reviewing the shares on your system is actually good practice, because in the past, numerous worms have propagated through unsecured shares, and you might have unused shares around. For example, a user might create a share for a friend and then forget to delete it. In the script that follows, called ListShares.ps1, all the information about shares present on the machine are reported. The information returned by ListShares.ps1 will include the properties for the *WIN32_Share* class that appear in Table 11-1.

ListShares.Ps1

```
$strComputer = "."
$wmiNS = "root\cimv2"
$wmiQuery = "Select * from win32_share"

$objWMIServices = Get-WmiObject -computer $strComputer -namespace $wmiNS `
  -query $wmiQuery
 $objWMIServices | Format-List *
```

**TABLE 11-1** *Win32_Share* properties

| Data type | Property | Meaning |
|-----------|----------|---------|
| *Boolean* | *AllowMaximum* | Allow maximum number of connections? (True or false) |
| *String* | *Caption* | Short one-line description |
| *String* | *Description* | Description |
| *Datetime* | *InstallDate* | When the share was created (optional) |
| *Uint32* | *MaximumAllowed* | Number of concurrent connections allowed (only valid when *AllowMaximum* is set to *false*) |
| *String* | *Name* | Share name |
| *String* | *Path* | Physical path to the share |
| *String* | *Status* | Current status of the share (degraded, OK, or failed) |
| *Uint32* | *Type* | Type of resource shared (disk, file, printer, etc.) |

## Quick check

Q. What is the syntax for a query that returns all properties of a given WMI object?

A. *Select * from <WMI class name>* returns all properties of a given object.

Q. What is one reason for using *Select *** instead of a more directed query?

A. In troubleshooting, *Select *** is useful because it returns any available data. In addition, *Select ** is useful for trying to characterize the data that might be returned from a query.

# Selective data from all instances

The next level of sophistication (from using *Select \**) is to return only the properties you are interested in. This is a more efficient strategy than returning everything from a class. For instance, in the previous example, you entered *Select \** and were returned a lot of data you may not necessarily have been interested in. Suppose you want to know only what shares are on each machine.

To select specific data, perform the following steps:

1. Make a connection to WMI by using the *Get-WmiObject* cmdlet.

2. Use the *-query* argument to supply the WMI query to the *Get-WmiObject* cmdlet.

3. In the query, use the *Select* statement to choose the specific property you are interested in—for example, *Select name*.

4. In the query, use the *From* statement to indicate the class from which you want to retrieve data—for example, *From Win32_Share*.

Only two small changes in the ListShares.ps1 script are required to enable garnering specific data through the WMI script. In place of the asterisk in the *Select* statement assigned at the beginning of the script, substitute the property you want. In this case, only the name of the shares is required.

The second change is to eliminate all unwanted properties from the *Output* section. The strange thing here is the way that PowerShell works. In the *Select* statement, you selected only the *name* property. However, if you were to print out the results without further refinement, you would retrieve unwanted system properties as well. By using the *Format-List* cmdlet and selecting only the property name, you eliminate the unwanted excess. Here is the modified ListNameOnlyShares.ps1 script:

**ListNameOnlyShares.Ps1**

```
$strComputer = "."
$wmiNS = "root\cimv2"
$wmiQuery = "Select name from win32_Share"

$objWMIServices = Get-WmiObject -computer $strComputer -namespace $wmiNS `
    -query $wmiQuery
$objWMIServices | Sort-Object -property name | Format-List -property name
```

# Selecting multiple properties

If you're interested in only a certain number of properties, you can use *Select* to specify that. All you have to do is separate the properties by a comma. Suppose you run the preceding script and find a number of undocumented shares on one of the servers—you might want a little bit more information, such as the path to the share and how many people are allowed to connect to it. By default, when a share is created, the "maximum allowed" bit is set, which basically says anyone who has rights to the share can connect. This can be a problem, because if too many people connect to a share, they can degrade the performance of the server. To preclude such an eventuality, I always specify a maximum number of connections to the server. The commands to list these properties are in the ListNamePathShare.ps1 script, which follows.

> **Note** I occasionally see people asking whether spaces or capitalization in the property list matter. In fact, when I first started writing scripts and they failed, I often modified spacing and capitalization in feeble attempts to make the script work. Spacing and capitalization *do not matter* for WMI properties.

ListNamePathShare.ps1

```
$strComputer = "."
$wmiNS = "root\cimv2"
$wmiQuery = "Select name,path, AllowMaximum from win32_share"

$objWMIServices = Get-WmiObject -computer $strComputer -namespace $wmiNS `
  -query $wmiQuery
$objWMIServices | Sort-Object -property name |
Format-List -property name,path,allowmaximum
```

### Working with running processes

1.  Open the Windows PowerShell console.

2.  Use the *Get-Process* cmdlet to obtain a listing of processes on your machine.

    A portion of the results from the command is shown here:

    | Handles | NPM(K) | PM(K) | WS(K) | VM(M) | CPU(s) | Id | ProcessName |
    |---------|--------|-------|-------|-------|--------|------|-------------|
    | 101 | 5 | 1132 | 3436 | 32 | 0.03 | 660 | alg |
    | 439 | 7 | 1764 | 2856 | 60 | 6.05 | 1000 | csrss |
    | 121 | 5 | 912 | 3532 | 37 | 0.22 | 1256 | ctfmon |
    | 629 | 19 | 23772 | 23868 | 135 | 134.13 | 788 | explorer |
    | 268 | 7 | 12072 | 18344 | 109 | 1.66 | 1420 | hh |

3.  To return information about the Explorer process, use the *-name* argument. This command is shown here:

    ```
    Get-Process -name explorer
    ```

    The results of this command are shown here:

    | Handles | NPM(K) | PM(K) | WS(K) | VM(M) | CPU(s) | Id | ProcessName |
    |---------|--------|-------|-------|-------|--------|------|-------------|
    | 619 | 18 | 21948 | 22800 | 115 | 134.28 | 788 | explorer |

4.  Use the *Get-WmiObject* cmdlet to retrieve information about processes on the machine. Pipe the results into the *more* function, as shown here:

    ```
    Get-WmiObject win32_process |more
    ```

5.  Notice that the results go on for page after page. The last few lines of one of those pages is shown here:

```
QuotaPagedPoolUsage          : 0
QuotaPeakNonPagedPoolUsage : 0
QuotaPeakPagedPoolUsage      : 0
ReadOperationCount           : 0
<SPACE> next page; <CR> next line; Q quit
```

6.  To retrieve information only about the Explorer.exe process, use the *-filter* argument and specify that the *name* property is equal to *Explorer.exe*. The revised command is shown here:

```
Get-WmiObject win32_process -Filter "name='explorer.exe'"
```

7.  To display a table that is similar to the one produced by *Get-Process*, use the up arrow key to retrieve the previous *Get-WmiObject* command. Copy it to the clipboard by selecting it with the mouse and then pasting it into Notepad or some other script editor. Pipeline the results into the *Format-Table* cmdlet and choose the appropriate properties, as shown following. Saving this command into a script makes it easier to work with later. It also makes it easier to write the script by breaking the lines instead of requiring you to type one long command. I called the script ExplorerProcess.ps1, and it is shown here:

```
Get-WmiObject win32_process -Filter "name='explorer.exe'" |
Format-Table handlecount,quotaNonPagedPoolUsage, PeakVirtualSize,
WorkingSetSize, VirtualSize, UserModeTime,KernelModeTime,
ProcessID, Name
```

This concludes the working with running processes procedure.

**Caution**  When using the *-filter* argument of the *Get-WmiObject* cmdlet, pay attention to the use of quotation marks. The *-filter* argument is surrounded by double quotation marks. The value being supplied for the property is surrounded by single quotes—for example, *-Filter "name='explorer.exe'"*. This can cause a lot of frustration if not followed exactly.

## Adding logging

1.  Open the Windows PowerShell console.

2.  Use the alias for the *Get-WmiObject* cmdlet and supply the *WIN32_logicalDisk* class as the argument to it. Use the redirection arrow (>) to redirect output to a file called Diskinfo.txt. Place this file in the C:\Mytest folder. This command is shown here:

```
gwmi win32_logicaldisk >c:\mytest\DiskInfo.txt
```

**3.** Use the up arrow key and retrieve the previous command. This time, change the class name to *WIN32_OperatingSystem* and call the text file OSinfo.txt. This command is shown here:

```
gwmi win32_operatingsystem >c:\mytest\OSinfo.txt
```

**4.** Use the up arrow key and retrieve the previous *gwmi WIN32_OperatingSystem* command. Change the WMI class to *WIN32_ComputerSystem* and use two redirection arrows (>>) to cause the output to append to the file. Use Notepad to open the file, but include the *Get-WmiObject* (*gwmi*) command, separated by a semicolon. This is illustrated next. (I've continued the command to the next line using the grave accent character (`) for readability.)

```
gwmi win32_ComputerSystem >>c:\mytest\OSinfo.txt; `
notepad c:\mytest\OSinfo.txt
```

This concludes the procedure.

---

## Quick check

**Q.** To select specific properties from an object, what do you need to do on the *Select* line?

**A.** You need to separate the specific properties of an object with a comma on the *Select* line of the *execQuery* method.

**Q.** To avoid error messages, what must be done when selecting individual properties on the *Select* line?

**A.** Errors can be avoided if you make sure each property used is specified on the *Select* line. For example, the WMI query is just like a paper bag that gets filled with items that are picked up using the *Select* statement. If you do not put something in the paper bag, you cannot pull anything out of it. In the same manner, if you do not select a property, you cannot later print or sort on that property. This is exactly the way that an SQL *Select* statement works.

**Q.** What can you check for in your script if it fails with an "object does not support this method or property" error?

**A.** If you are getting this type of error message, you might want to ensure you have referenced the property in your *Select* statement before to trying to work with it in an *Output* section. In addition, you may want to check to ensure that the property actually exists.

---

## Choosing specific instances

In many situations, you will want to limit the data you return to a specific instance of a particular WMI class in the data set. If you go back to your query and add a *Where* clause to the *Select* statement, you'll be able to greatly reduce the amount of information returned by the query. Notice that in the value associated with the WMI query, you added a dependency that indicated you wanted only information with share name *C$*. This value is not case sensitive, but it must be surrounded with single quotation marks, as you can see in the *WMI Query* string in the following script. These single quotation marks are important because they tell WMI that the value is a string value and not some other programmatic item. Because the addition of the *Where* statement was the only thing you really added to the ListShares.ps1 script, I won't provide a long discussion of the ListSpecificShares.ps1 script.

To limit specific data, do the following:

1. Make a connection to WMI by using the *Get-WmiObject* cmdlet.

2. Use the *Select* statement in the *WMI Query* argument to choose the specific property you are interested in—for example, *Select name*.

3. Use the *From* statement in the *WMI Query* argument to indicate the class from which you want to retrieve data—for example, *From Win32_Share*.

4. Add a *Where* clause in the *WMI Query* argument to further limit the data set that is returned. Make sure the properties specified in the *Where* clause are first mentioned in the *Select* statement—for example, *Where name*.

5. Add an evaluation operator. You can use the equal sign (=), or the less-than (<) or greater-than (>) symbols—for example, *Where name = 'C$'*.

### Eliminating the *WMI Query* argument

1. Open the Windows PowerShell ISE or the Windows PowerShell script editor.

2. Declare a variable called *$strComputer* and assign the WMI shortcut dot (.) to it. The shortcut dot means, "Connect to the WMI service on the local computer." This command is shown here:

```
$strComputer = "."
```

3. Declare another variable and call it *$wmiClass*. Assign the string *WIN32_Share* to the variable. This code is shown here:

```
$wmiClass = "win32_Share"
```

4. Declare a variable and call it *$wmiFilter*. This variable will be used to hold the string that will contain the WMI filter to be used with the *Get-WmiObject* command. The variable and the associated string value are shown here:

```
$wmifilter = "name='c$'"
```

5. Declare a variable called *objWMIServices* and assign the object that is returned from the *Get-WmiObject* cmdlet to the variable. Specify the *-computer* argument and supply the value

contained in the *$strComputer* variable to it. At the end of the line, use the grave accent character (`) to indicate line continuation. This line of code is shown here:

```
$objWMIServices = Get-WmiObject -computer $strComputer `
```

6. Use the *-class* argument to supply the class name for the WMI query to the *Get-WmiObject* cmdlet. The class name to query is contained in the *$wmiClass* variable. On the same line, use the *-filter* argument to supply the filter string contained in the *$wmiFilter* variable to the *Get-WmiObject* cmdlet. This line of code is shown here:

```
-class $wmiClass -filter $wmiFilter
```

7. On the next line, use the object contained in the *$objWMIServices* variable and pipeline it to the *Format-List* cmdlet. Use the asterisk to tell the *Format-List* cmdlet you wish to retrieve all properties. This line of code is shown here:

```
$objWMIServices | Format-List *
```

The completed script is shown here:

```
$strComputer = "."
$wmiClass = "win32_Share"
$wmiFilter = "name='c$'"
$objWMIServices = Get-WmiObject -computer $strComputer `
    -class $wmiClass -filter $wmiFilter
    $objWMIServices | Format-List *
```

Sample output is shown here:

```
Status          : OK
Type            : 2147483648
Name            : C$
__GENUS         : 2
__CLASS         : Win32_Share
__SUPERCLASS    : CIM_LogicalElement
__DYNASTY       : CIM_ManagedSystemElement
```

8. If your results are not similar, compare your script with the ShareNoQuery.ps1 script.

This completes the procedure.

## Utilizing an operator

One of the nice things you can do is use greater-than and less-than operators in your evaluation clause. What is so great about greater-than? It makes working with some alphabetic and numeric characters easy. If you work on a server that hosts home directories for users (which are often named after their user names), you can easily produce a list of all home directories from the letters *D* through *Z* by using the > D operation. Keep in mind that *D$* is greater than *D*, and if you really want shares that begin with the letter *E*, then you can specify "greater than or equal to E." This command would look like >='E'.

ListGreaterThanShares.ps1

```
$strComputer = "."
$wmiNS = "root\cimv2"
$wmiQuery = "Select name from win32_Share where name > 'd'"

$objWMIServices = Get-WmiObject -computer $strComputer `
    -namespace $wmiNS -query $wmiQuery
    $objWMIServices | Sort-Object -property name |
    Format-List -property name
```

### Identifying service accounts

1. Open Notepad or some other script editor.

2. On the first line, declare a variable called *$strComputer*. Use the dot (.) WMI shortcut to point to the local computer. This line of code is shown here:

   ```
   $strComputer = "."
   ```

3. On the next line, declare a variable called *$wmiNS*. Assign the string *Root\cimv2* to the variable. This will cause the WMI query to use the Root\cimv2 WMI namespace. This line of code is shown here:

   ```
   $wmiNS = "root\cimv2"
   ```

4. On the next line, declare a variable called *$wmiQuery*. You will select only the *startname* property and the *name* property from the *WIN32_Service* WMI class. This line of code is shown here:

   ```
   $wmiQuery = "Select startName, name from win32_service"
   ```

5. On the next line, declare the *$objWMIServices* variable. Use the *$objWMIServices* variable to hold the object that comes back from using the *Get-WmiObject* cmdlet. Use the *-computer* argument of the *Get-WmiObject* cmdlet to point the query to the local computer. To do this, use the dot (.) value that is contained in the variable *$strComputer*. Because you will continue the command on the next line, use the grave accent character (`) to tell Windows PowerShell to continue the command on the next line. The code that does this is shown here:

   ```
   $objWMIServices = Get-WmiObject -computer $strComputer `
   ```

6. Use the *-namespace* argument of the *Get-WmiObject* cmdlet to specify the WMI namespace specified in the *$wmiNS* variable. Use the *-query* argument of the *Get- WmiObject* cmdlet to specify the WMI query contained in the variable *$wmiQuery*. This code is shown here:

   ```
   -namespace $wmiNS -query $wmiQuery
   ```

7. Use the object that comes back from the *Get-WmiObject* cmdlet that is contained in the *$objWMIServices* variable and pipeline it into the *Sort-Object* cmdlet. Use the *Sort-Object*

cmdlet to sort the list first by the *startName* property and second by the *name* property. Place the pipe character at the end of the line because you will pipeline this object into another cmdlet. The code that does this is shown here:

```
$objWMIServices | Sort-Object startName, name |
```

8. Finally, you will receive the pipelined object into the *Format-List* cmdlet. You first format the list by the *name* property from *WIN32_Service* and then print out the *startName*. This code is shown here:

```
Format-List name, startName
```

The completed script is shown here:

```
$strComputer = "."
$wmiNS = "root\cimv2"
$wmiQuery = "Select startName, name from win32_service"

$objWMIServices = Get-WmiObject -computer $strComputer `
    -namespace $wmiNS -query $wmiQuery
    $objWMIServices | Sort-Object startName, name |
    Format-List name, startName
```

9. Save the script as *<yourname>*IdentifyServiceAccounts.ps1. Run the script. You should see output similar that shown here. If not, compare your script to the IdentifyServiceAccounts.ps1 script.

```
name       : BITS
startName : LocalSystem

name       : Browser
startName : LocalSystem

name       : CcmExec
startName : LocalSystem

name       : CiSvc
startName : LocalSystem
```

This completes the procedure.

## Logging service accounts

1. Open the IdentifyServiceAccounts.ps1 script in Notepad or your favorite script editor. Save the script as *<yourname>*IdentifyServiceAccountsLogged.ps1.

2. Declare a new variable called *$strFile*. This variable will be used for the *-filePath* argument of the *Out-File* cmdlet. Assign the string *C:\Mytest\ServiceAccounts.txt* to the *$strFile* variable. This code is shown here:

```
$strFile = "c:\mytest\ServiceAccounts.txt"
```

3. Under the line of code where you declared the *$strFile* variable, use the *New-Variable* cmdlet to create a constant called *constASCII*. When you assign the *constASCII* value to the *-name* argument of the *New-Variable* cmdlet, remember to leave off the dollar sign. Use the *-value* argument of the *New-Variable* cmdlet to assign a value of *ASCII* to the *constASCII* constant. Use the *-option* argument and supply *constant* as the value for the argument. The completed command is shown here:

```
New-Variable -name constASCII -value "ASCII" `
    -option constant
```

4. At the end of the *Format-List* line, place the pipe character (|). This is shown here:

```
Format-List name, startName |
```

5. On the next line, use the *Out-File* cmdlet to produce an output file containing the results of the previous command. Use the *-filepath* argument to specify the path and file name to create. Use the value contained in the *$strFile* variable. To ensure that the output file is easily read, use ASCII encoding. To do this, use the *-encoding* argument of the *Out-File* cmdlet and supply the value contained in the *$constASCII* variable. Use the grave accent character (`) to indicate the command will continue to the next line. The resulting code is shown here:

```
Out-File -filepath $strFile -encoding $constASCII `
```

6. On the next line, use two arguments of the *Out-File* cmdlet. The first argument tells *Out-File* to append to a file if it exists. The second argument tells *Out-File* not to overwrite any existing files. This code is shown here:

```
-append -noClobber
```

7. Save and run your script. You should see a file called ServiceAccounts.txt in your Mytest directory on drive C. The contents of the file will be similar to the output shown here:

```
name      : AppMgmt
startName : LocalSystem

name      : AudioSrv
startName : LocalSystem

name      : BITS
startName : LocalSystem
```

8. If you do not find output similar to this, compare your script with IdentifyServiceAccountsLogged.ps1.

This concludes the procedure.

# Where is the *where*?

To more easily modify the *Where* clause in a WMI query, substitute the *Where* clause with a variable. This configuration can be modified to include command-line input as well. This is shown in the ListSpecificWhere.ps1 script, which follows.

**ListSpecificWhere.ps1**

```
$strComputer = "."
$wmiNS = "root\cimv2"
$strWhere = "'ipc$'"
$wmiQuery = "Select * from win32_Share where name="+$strWhere

"Properties of Share named: " + $strWhere

$objWMIServices = Get-WmiObject -computer $strComputer `
  -namespace $wmiNS -query $wmiQuery
  $objWMIServices |
  Format-List -property [a-z]*
```

## Quick check

**Q.** To limit the specific data returned by a query, what WQL technique can be used?

**A.** The *Where* clause of the *WMIquery* argument is very powerful in limiting the specific data returned by a query.

**Q.** What are three possible operators that can be employed in creating powerful *Where* clauses for WMI queries?

**A.** The equal sign (=) and the greater-than and the less-than symbols (> and <) can be used to evaluate the data before returning the data set.

# Shortening the syntax

Windows PowerShell is a great tool to use interactively from the command line. The short syntax, cmdlet and function parameters, and shortcut aliases to common cmdlets all work together to create a powerful command-line environment. WMI also benefits from this optimization. Rather than typing complete WQL *select* statements and *where* clauses and storing them into a variable, and then using the *query* parameter from the *Get-WMIObject*, you can use the *-property* and *-filter* parameters from the cmdlet. Use the *-property* parameter to replace the property names normally supplied as part of the *select* clause, and the *-filter* parameter to replace the portion of code usually contained in the *where* clause of the WQL statement.

## Using the *-property* parameter

In the code that follows, the traditional WQL *select* statement retrieves the *name* and *handle* properties from the *WIN32_Process* WMI class. The *$query* variable stores the WQL query, and the *Get-WmiObject* command utilizes this query to retrieve the desired information from the WMI class.

```
$query = "Select name, handle from win32_process"
Get-WmiObject -Query $query
```

You can obtain the exact same information in a single line by using the *-class* parameter to specify the WMI class name and the *-property* parameter to specify the two properties from the *WIN32_Process* WMI class to select. The revised code appears here:

```
Get-WmiObject -Class WIN32_Process -Property name, handle
```

The difference between the two commands—the one that uses the WQL syntax and the one that supplies values directly for parameters—is not in the information returned, but rather the approach to using the *Get-WmiObject* cmdlet. For some people, the WQL syntax may be more natural, and for others, the use of direct parameters may be easier. On the back end, WMI treats both types of commands in the same manner.

It is possible to shorten the length of the WQL type of command by supplying the WQL query directly to the *query* parameter. This technique appears here:

```
Get-WmiObject -Query "Select name, handle from win32_process"
```

For short WQL queries, this technique is perfectly valid; however, for longer WQL queries that extend to multiple lines of code, it is more readable to store the query in a variable and supply the variable to the *query* parameter instead of using the query directly.

## Using the *-filter* parameter

The *-filter* parameter of the *Get-WmiObject* cmdlet replaces the *where* clause of a WQL query. For example, in the code that follows, the WQL query chooses the *name* and *handle* properties from the *WIN32_Process* WMI class, where the name of the process begins with a letter greater than *t* in the alphabet. The WQL query stored in the *$query* variable executes via the *Get-WmiObject* cmdlet, and the results pipeline to the *Format-Table* cmdlet, where the column's name and handle are automatically sized to fit the Windows PowerShell console. The commands appear here:

```
$query = "Select name, handle from win32_process where name > 't'"
Get-WmiObject -Query $query | Format-Table name, handle -autosize
```

To perform the exact same WMI query by using the parameters of the *Get-WmiObject* cmdlet instead of composing a WQL query, you simply use the property names that follow the *select* statement in the original WQL query, as well as the filter that follows the *where* clause. The resulting command appears here:

```
Get-WmiObject -Class win32_process -Filter "name > 't'"
```

To display succinct output from the previous command, pipeline the results to the *Format-Table* cmdlet and select the two properties named in the *properties* parameter, and use the *-autosize* switch to tighten up the output in the Windows PowerShell console. The revised commands, along with the associated output, appear in Figure 11-2.

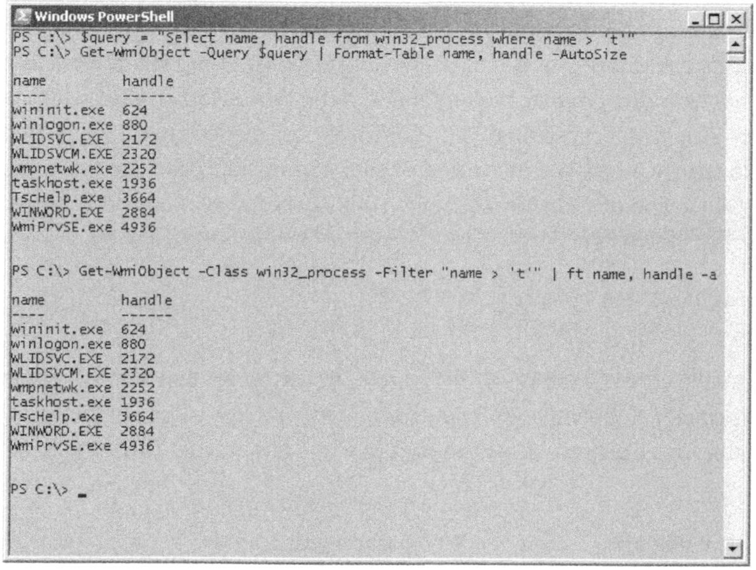

**FIGURE 11-2** WMI output derived from a WQL query and use of the *Get-WmiObject* parameters.

# Working with software: step-by-step exercises

In the first exercise, you will explore the use of *WIN32_product* and classes provided by the Windows installer provider. In the second exercise, you will work with the environment provider.

### Using WMI to find installed software

1. Open the Windows PowerShell ISE or your favorite script editor.

2. At the top of your script, declare a variable called *$strComputer*. Assign the WMI shortcut dot character (.) to indicate you want to connect to WMI on your local machine. This line of code is shown here:

   ```
   $strComputer = "."
   ```

3. On the next line, declare the variable *$wmiNS*, which will be used to hold the WMI namespace for your query. Assign the string *Root\cimv2* to the variable. This line of code is shown here:

   ```
   $wmiNS = "root\cimv2"
   ```

4. On the next line, you will use the variable *$wmiQuery* to hold your WMI query. This query will select everything from the *WIN32_product* WMI class. This code is shown here:

```
$wmiQuery = "Select * from win32_product"
```

5. Because this query can take a rather long time to complete (depending on the speed of your machine, CPU load, and number of installed applications), use the *Write-Host* cmdlet to inform the user that the script could take a while to run. As long as you're using *Write-Host*, let's have a little fun and specify the *-foregroundcolor* argument of the *Write-Host* cmdlet, which will change the color of your font. I chose blue, but you can choose any color you wish. Use the `n escape sequence to specify a new line at the end of your command. I used the grave accent character (`) to break the line of code for readability, but this certainly is not necessary for you. The completed code is shown here:

```
Write-Host "Counting Installed Products. This" `
    "may take a little while. " -foregroundColor blue `n
```

6. On the next line, use the variable *$objWMIServices* to hold the object that is returned by the *Get-WmiObject* cmdlet. Supply the *-computer* argument with the value contained in the *$strComputer* variable. Use the grave accent to continue to the next line. This code is shown here:

```
$objWMIServices = Get-WmiObject -computer $strComputer `
```

7. On the next line, use the *-namespace* argument to specify the WMI namespace for the WMI query. Use the value contained in the *$wmiNS* variable. Use the *-query* argument to supply the WMI query contained in the *$wmiQuery* variable to the *Get-WmiObject* cmdlet. This line of code is shown here:

```
-namespace $wmiNS -query $wmiQuery
```

8. Use the *for* statement to print out a progress indicator. Use the variable *$i* as the counter. Continue counting until the value of *$i* is less than or equal to the value of the *count* property of the *IwbemObjectSet* object contained in the *$objWMIServices* variable. (If you need to review the use of the *for* statement, refer to Chapter 5.) The *for* statement code is shown here:

```
for ($i=1; $i -le $objWMIServices.count;$i++)
```

9. The code that will be run as a result of the *for* statement uses the *Write-Host* cmdlet. You will write "/\" to the console. To keep the *Write-Host* cmdlet from writing everything on a new line, use the *-noNewLine* argument. To make the progress bar different from the first prompt, use the *-foregroundcolor* argument and specify an appropriate color. I chose red. This line of code is shown here:

```
{Write-Host "/\" -noNewLine -foregroundColor red}
```

**10.** Use the *Write-Host* cmdlet to print out the number of installed applications on the machine. To make the value a little easier to read, use two `n escape sequences to produce two blank lines from the progress indicator. This line of code is shown here:

```
Write-Host `n`n "There are " $objWMIServices.count `
    " products installed."
```

**11.** Save and run your script. Call it <yourname>CountInstalledApplications.ps1. You should see output similar to that shown here. If you do not, compare it with CountInstalledApplications.ps1.

```
Counting Installed Products. This may take a little while.

/\/\/\/\/\/\/\/\/\/\/\/\/\/\/\/\/\/\/\/\/\/\/\/\/\/\/\/\
/\/\/\/\/\/\/\/\/\/\/\/\/\/\/\/\/\/\/\/\/\/\/\/\/\/\/\/\
/\/\/\/\/\/\

There are 87 products installed.
```

**12.** Now you'll add a timer to your script to see how long it takes to execute. On the fourth line of your script, under the *$wmiQuery* line, declare a variable called *$dteStart* and assign the date object that is returned by the *Get-Date* cmdlet to it. This line of code is shown here:

```
$dteStart = Get-Date
```

**13.** At the end of your script, under the last *Write-Host* command, declare a variable called *$dteEnd* and assign the date object that is returned by the *Get-Date* cmdlet to it. This line of code is shown here:

```
$dteEnd = Get-Date
```

**14.** Declare a variable called *$dteDiff* and assign the date object that is returned by the *New-TimeSpan* cmdlet to it. Use the *New-TimeSpan* cmdlet to subtract the two date objects contained in the *$dteStart* and *$dteEnd* variables. The *$dteStart* variable will go first. This command is shown here:

```
$dteDiff = New-TimeSpan $dteStart $dteEnd
```

**15.** Use the *Write-Host* cmdlet to print out the total number of seconds it took for the script to run. This value is contained in the *totalSeconds* property of the date object held in the *$dteDiff* variable. This command is shown here:

```
Write-Host "It took " $dteDiff.totalSeconds " Seconds" `
    " for this script to complete"
```

**16.** Save your script as *<yourname>*CountInstalledApplicationsTimed.ps1. Run your script and compare your output with that shown here. If your results are not similar, then compare your script with the CountInstalledApplicationsTimed.ps1 script.

```
Counting Installed Products. This may take a little while.

/\/\/\/\/\/\/\/\/\/\/\/\/\/\/\/\/\/\/\/\/\/\/\/\/\/\
/\/\/\/\/\/\/\/\/\/\/\/\/\/\/\/\/\/\/\/\/\/\/\/\/\/\
/\/\/\/\/\/\

There are 87 products installed.
It took 120.3125 Seconds for this script to complete
```

This concludes the exercise.

In the following exercise, you'll explore Windows environment variables.

## Windows environment variables

**1.** Open Windows PowerShell.

**2.** Use the *Get-WmiObject* cmdlet to view the common properties of the *WIN32_Environment* WMI class. Use the *gwmi* alias to make it easier to type. This command is shown here:

```
gwmi win32_environment
```

Partial output from this command is shown here:

```
VariableValue            Name                 UserName
-------------            ----                 --------
C:\PROGRA~1\CA\SHARED~1... AVENGINE            <SYSTEM>
%SystemRoot%\system32\c... ComSpec             <SYSTEM>
NO                       FP_NO_HOST_CHECK     <SYSTEM>
```

**3.** To view all the properties of the *WIN32_Environment* class, pipeline the object returned by the *Get-WmiObject* cmdlet to the *Format-List* cmdlet while specifying the asterisk. Use the up arrow key to retrieve the previous *gwmi* command. This command is shown here:

```
gwmi win32_environment | Format-List *
```

The output from the previous command will be similar to that shown here:

```
Status          : OK
Name            : TMP
SystemVariable  : False
__GENUS         : 2
__CLASS         : Win32_Environment
__SUPERCLASS    : CIM_SystemResource
```

4. Scroll through the results returned by the previous command, and examine the properties and their associated values. *Name*, *UserName*, and *VariableValue* are the most important variables from the class. Use the up arrow key to retrieve the previous *gwmi* command and change *Format-List* to *Format-Table*. After the *Format-Table* cmdlet, type the three variables you want to retrieve: *Name*, *VariableValue*, and *Username*. This command is shown here:

```
gwmi win32_environment | Format-Table name, variableValue, userName
```

5. The results from this command will be similar to the partial results shown here:

```
name                    variableValue              userName
----                    -------------              --------
AVENGINE                C:\PROGRA~1\CA\SHARED~1...  <SYSTEM>
ComSpec                 %SystemRoot%\system32\c...  <SYSTEM>
FP_NO_HOST_CHECK        NO                          <SYSTEM>
INOCULAN                C:\PROGRA~1\CA\ETRUST~1     <SYSTEM>
```

6. Use the up arrow key to retrieve the previous *gwmi* command, and delete the variable *userName* and the trailing comma. This command is shown here:

```
gwmi win32_environment | Format-Table name, variableValue
```

The results from this command will be similar to those shown here:

```
name                    variableValue
----                    -------------
AVENGINE                C:\PROGRA~1\CA\SHARED~1\SCANEN~1
ComSpec                 %SystemRoot%\system32\cmd.exe
FP_NO_HOST_CHECK        NO
INOCULAN                C:\PROGRA~1\CA\ETRUST~1
```

7. Notice how the spacing is a little strange. To correct this, use the up arrow key to retrieve the previous command. Add the *-autosize* argument to the *Format-Table* command. You can use tab completion to finish the command by typing **-a \<tab>**. The completed command is shown here:

```
gwmi win32_environment | Format-Table name, variableValue -AutoSize
```

8. Now that you have a nicely formatted list, you'll compare the results with those produced by the environment provider. To do this, you'll use the Env PS drive. Use the *Set-Location* cmdlet to set your location to the Env PS drive. The command to do this is shown here. (You can, of course, use the *sl* alias if you prefer.)

```
Set-Location env:
```

9. Use the *Get-ChildItem* cmdlet to produce a listing of all the environment variables on the computer. The command to do this is shown here:

```
Get-ChildItem
```

Partial output from the *Get-ChildItem* cmdlet is shown here:

```
Name                            Value
----                            -----
Path                            C:\WINDOWS\system32;C:\WINDOWS;C:\WINDOWS\Sys...
TEMP                            C:\DOCUME~1\EDWILS~1.NOR\LOCALS~1\Temp
```

10. Set your location back to drive C. The command to do this is shown here:

```
Set-Location c:\
```

11. Retrieve the alias for the *Get-History* cmdlet. To do this, use the *Get-Alias* cmdlet and pipe the resulting object to the *Where-Object*. Use the special variable *$_* to indicate the current pipeline object, and look for a match to the *definition* property that is equal to the *Get-History* cmdlet. The command to do this is shown here:

```
Get-Alias | where definition -eq "Get-History"
```

The resulting output, shown here, tells you there are three aliases defined for *Get-History*:

```
CommandType     Name                                     ModuleName
-----------     ----                                     ----------
Alias           ghy -> Get-History
Alias           h -> Get-History
Alias           history -> Get-History
```

12. Use the up arrow key and retrieve the previous *Get-Alias* command. Change the definition from *Get-History* to *Invoke-History*. This command is shown here:

```
Get-Alias | where definition -eq "Invoke-History"
```

13. The resulting output, shown here, tells you there are two aliases defined for *Get-History*:

```
CommandType     Name                                     ModuleName
-----------     ----                                     ----------
Alias           ihy -> Invoke-History
Alias           r -> Invoke-History
```

14. Use the *Get-History* cmdlet to retrieve a listing of all the commands you have typed into Windows PowerShell. I prefer to use *ghy* for *Get-History* because of similarity with *ihy* (for *Invoke-History*). The *Get-History* command using *ghy* is shown here:

```
ghy
```

**15.** Examine the output from the *Get-History* cmdlet. You will see a list similar to the one shown here:

```
 1 gwmi win32_environment
 2 gwmi win32_environment | Format-List *
 3 gwmi win32_environment | Format-Table name, variableValue, userName
 4 gwmi win32_environment | Format-Table name, variableValue
 5 gwmi win32_environment | Format-Table name, variableValue -AutoSize
 6 sl env:
 7 gci
 8 sl c:\
 9 Get-Alias | where {$_.definition -eq "Get-History"}
10 Get-Alias | where {$_.definition -eq "Invoke-History"}
```

**16.** Produce the listing of environment variables by using the Environment PS drive. This time, you will do it in a single command. Use *Set-Location* to set the location to the Env PS drive. Then continue the command by using a semicolon and then *Get-ChildItem* to produce the list. Use the *sl* alias and the *gci* alias to type this command. The command is shown here:

```
sl env:;gci
```

**17.** Note that your PS drive is still set to the Env PS drive. Use the *Set-Location* cmdlet to change back to the C PS drive. This command is shown here:

```
sl c:\
```

**18.** Use the up arrow key to bring up the *sl env:;gci* command, and this time, add another semicolon and another *sl* command to change back to the C PS drive. The revised command is shown here:

```
sl env:;gci;sl c:\
```

You should now have output similar to that shown here, and you should also be back at the C PS drive.

```
Name                          Value
----                          -----
ALLUSERSPROFILE               C:\ProgramData
APPDATA                       C:\Users\ed.IAMMRED\AppData\Roaming
CommonProgramFiles            C:\Program Files\Common Files
CommonProgramFiles(x86)       C:\Program Files (x86)\Common Files
CommonProgramW6432            C:\Program Files\Common Files
COMPUTERNAME                  EDLT
ComSpec                       C:\WINDOWS\system32\cmd.exe
FP_NO_HOST_CHECK              NO
HOMEDRIVE                     C:
HOMEPATH                      \Users\ed.IAMMRED
LOCALAPPDATA                  C:\Users\ed.IAMMRED\AppData\Local
LOGONSERVER                   \\DC1
NUMBER_OF_PROCESSORS          8
```

```
OS                                Windows_NT
Path                              C:\WINDOWS\system32;C:\WINDOWS;C:\WINDOWS\System32...
PATHEXT                           .COM;.EXE;.BAT;.CMD;.VBS;.VBE;.JS;.JSE;.WSF;.WSH;....
PROCESSOR_ARCHITECTURE            AMD64
PROCESSOR_IDENTIFIER              Intel64 Family 6 Model 42 Stepping 7, GenuineIntel
PROCESSOR_LEVEL                   6
PROCESSOR_REVISION                2a07
ProgramData                       C:\ProgramData
ProgramFiles                      C:\Program Files
ProgramFiles(x86)                 C:\Program Files (x86)
ProgramW6432                      C:\Program Files
PSModulePath                      C:\Users\ed.IAMMRED\Documents\WindowsPowerShell\Mo...
PUBLIC                            C:\Users\Public
SESSIONNAME                       Console
SystemDrive                       C:
SystemRoot                        C:\WINDOWS
TEMP                              C:\Users\ED6C0B~1.IAM\AppData\Local\Temp
TMP                               C:\Users\ED6C0B~1.IAM\AppData\Local\Temp
USERDNSDOMAIN                     IAMMRED.NET
USERDOMAIN                        IAMMRED
USERDOMAIN_ROAMINGPROFILE         IAMMRED
USERNAME                          ed
USERPROFILE                       C:\Users\ed.IAMMRED
windir                            C:\WINDOWS
```

**19.** Now use the *ghy* alias to retrieve a history of your commands. Identify the command that contains your previous *gwmi* command that uses *Format-Table* with the *-autosize* argument. This command is shown here:

```
gwmi win32_environment | Format-Table name, variableValue -AutoSize
```

**20.** Use the *ihy* alias to invoke the history command that corresponds to the command identified in step 19. For me, the command is *ihy 5*, as shown here:

```
ihy 5
```

**21.** When the command runs, it prints out the value of the command you are running on the first line. After this, you obtain the results normally associated with the command. Partial output is shown here:

```
gwmi win32_environment | Format-Table name, variableValue -AutoSize

name                     variableValue
----                     -------------
FP_NO_HOST_CHECK         NO
USERNAME                 SYSTEM
Path                     %SystemRoot%\system32;%SystemRoot%;%SystemRoot%\System32\W...
ComSpec                  %SystemRoot%\system32\cmd.exe
TMP                      %SystemRoot%\TEMP
OS                       Windows_NT
windir                   %SystemRoot%
PROCESSOR_ARCHITECTURE   AMD64
TEMP                     %SystemRoot%\TEMP
```

```
PATHEXT                    .COM;.EXE;.BAT;.CMD;.VBS;.VBE;.JS;.JSE;.WSF;.WSH;.MSC
PSModulePath               %SystemRoot%\system32\WindowsPowerShell\v1.0\Modules\
NUMBER_OF_PROCESSORS       8
PROCESSOR_LEVEL            6
PROCESSOR_IDENTIFIER       Intel64 Family 6 Model 42 Stepping 7, GenuineIntel
PROCESSOR_REVISION         2a07
TMP                        %USERPROFILE%\AppData\Local\Temp
TEMP                       %USERPROFILE%\AppData\Local\Temp
TMP                        %USERPROFILE%\AppData\Local\Temp
TEMP                       %USERPROFILE%\AppData\Local\Temp
```

22. Scroll up in the Windows PowerShell console, and compare the output from the *gwmi* command you just ran with the output from the *sl env:;gci* command.

This concludes this exercise.

Commands used are stored in the OneStepFurtherWindowsEnvironment.txt file.

# Chapter 11 quick reference

| To | Do this |
|---|---|
| Simplify connecting to WMI while using default security permissions | Use the *Get-WmiObject* cmdlet. |
| Control security when making a remote connection | Specify the impersonation levels in your script. |
| Allow a script to use the credentials of the person launching the script | Use the *impersonate* impersonation level. |
| Allow a script to load a driver | Use the *loadDriver* privilege. |
| Control security when making a remote connection | Specify the impersonation levels in your script. |
| Get rid of system properties when printing out all properties of a WMI class | Use the *Format-List* cmdlet and specify that the *-property* argument must be in the range of *[a-z]\**. |
| Get the current date and time | Use the *Get-Date* cmdlet. |
| Subtract two dates | Use the *New-TimeSpan* cmdlet. Supply two date objects as arguments. |
| Retrieve a listing of all commands typed during a Windows PowerShell session | Use the *Get-History* cmdlet. |
| Run a command from the Windows PowerShell session history | Use the *Invoke-History* cmdlet. |
| Retrieve the minimum and maximum values from an object | Use the *Measure-Object* cmdlet while specifying the *-property* argument as well as the *-minimum* and *-maximum* arguments. |
| Produce paged output from a long-scrolling command | Pipeline the resulting object from the command into the *more* function. |

# Remoting WMI

**After completing this chapter, you will be able to:**

- Use native WMI remoting to connect to a remote system.

- Use Windows PowerShell remoting to run WMI commands on a remote system.

- Use the CIM cmdlets to run WMI classes on a remote system.

- Receive the results of remote WMI commands.

- Run WMI remote commands as a job.

## Using WMI against remote systems

Microsoft Windows Management Instrumentation (WMI) remoting is an essential part of Windows PowerShell. In fact, way back in Windows PowerShell 1.0, WMI remoting was one of the primary ways of making configuration changes on remote systems. Windows Server 2012 permits remote WMI by default. The Windows 8 client does not. The best way to manage the Windows 8 client is to use group policy to permit the use of WMI inbound. Keep in mind, the issue here is the Windows firewall, not WMI itself. The steps to use group policy to configure WMI appear here:

1. Open the group policy management console.

2. Expand the Computer Config | Policies | Windows Settings | Security Settings | Windows Firewall With Advanced Security | Windows Firewall With Advanced Security | Inbound Rules node.

3. Right-click in the working area and choose New Rule.

4. Choose the Predefined option, and select Windows Management Instrumentation (WMI) from the drop-down list.

5. There are a number of options here, but you should start with one: the (WMI-In) option with the Domain profile value. If you aren't sure what you need, then just remember you can come back and add the others later. Click Next.

6. Allow the connection to finish.

Until the Windows firewall permits WMI connection, attempts to connect result in a remote procedure call (RPC) error. This error appears here, where an attempt to connect to a computer named w8c504 fails due to the firewall not permitting WMI traffic to pass.

```
PS C:\> gwmi win32_bios -cn w8c504
gwmi : The RPC server is unavailable. (Exception from HRESULT: 0x800706BA)
At line:1 char:1
+ gwmi win32_bios -cn w8c504
+ ~~~~~~~~~~~~~~~~~~~~~~~~~~
    + CategoryInfo          : InvalidOperation: (:) [Get-WmiObject], COMException
    + FullyQualifiedErrorId : GetWMICOMException,Microsoft.PowerShell.Commands.
GetWmiObjectCommand
```

Additionally, the remote caller must be a member of the local administrators group on the target machine. By default, members of the Domain Admin group are placed into the local administrators group when the system joins the domain. If you attempt to make a remote WMI connection without membership in the local admin group on the target system, an Access Denied error is raised. This error appears as follows when a user attempts to connect to a remote system without permission:

```
PS C:\Users\ed.IAMMRED> gwmi win32_bios -cn w8s504
gwmi : Access is denied. (Exception from HRESULT: 0x80070005 (E_ACCESSDENIED))
At line:1 char:1
+ gwmi win32_bios -cn w8s504
+ ~~~~~~~~~~~~~~~~~~~~~~~~~~
    + CategoryInfo          : NotSpecified: (:) [Get-WmiObject],
UnauthorizedAccessException
    + FullyQualifiedErrorId : System.UnauthorizedAccessException,Microsoft.PowerShell.
Commands.GetWmiObjectCommand
```

> **Important** Pay close attention to the specific errors returned by WMI when attempting to make a remote connection. The error tells you if the problem is related to the firewall or security access. This information is vital in making remote WMI work.

## Supplying alternate credentials for the remote connection

A low-level user can make a remote WMI connection by supplying credentials that have local admin rights on the target system. The *Get-WMIObject* Windows PowerShell cmdlet accepts a credential object. There are two common ways of supplying the credential object for the remote connection. The first way is to type the domain and the user name values directly into the *credential* parameter. When the *Get-WMIObject* cmdlet runs, it prompts for the password. The syntax of this command appears here:

```
PS C:\Users\ed.IAMMRED> gwmi win32_bios -cn w8s504 -Credential iammred\administrator
```

When you run the command, a dialog box appears prompting for the password to use for the connection. Once supplied, the command continues. The dialog box appears in Figure 12-1.

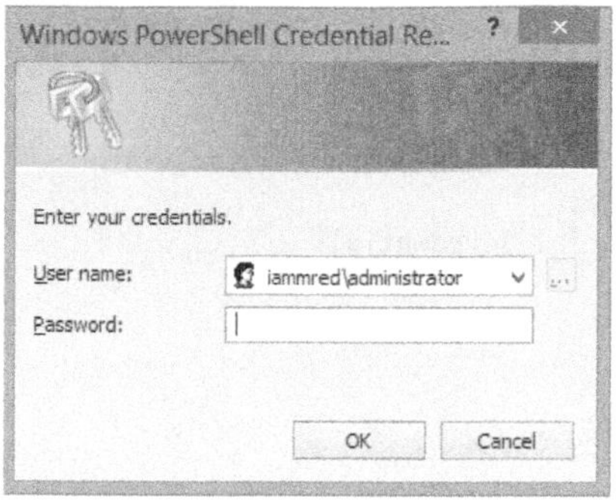

**FIGURE 12-1** When run with the *credential* parameter, the *Get-WMIObject* cmdlet prompts for the account password.

## Storing the credentials for a remote connection

There is only one problem with supplying the credential directly to the *credential* parameter for the *Get-WMIObject* cmdlet—it requires you to supply the credential each time you run the command. This requirement is enforced when you use the up arrow key to retrieve the command, as well as for any subsequent connections to the same remote system.

When opening a Windows PowerShell console session that may involve connection to numerous remote systems, or even multiple connections to the same system, it makes sense to store the credential object in a variable for the duration of the Windows PowerShell session. To store your credentials for later consumption, use the *Get-Credential* Windows PowerShell cmdlet to retrieve your credentials and store the resulting credential object in a variable. If you work with multiple systems with different passwords, it makes sense to create variables that will facilitate remembering which credentials go to which system. Remember that the Windows PowerShell console has tab expansion; therefore, it is not necessary to use short cryptic variable names just to reduce typing. The command appearing here obtains a credential object and stores the resulting object in the *$credential* variable.

```
$credential = Get-Credential -Credential iammred\administrator
```

The use of the credential object to make a remote WMI connection appears here:

```
PS C:\Users\ed.IAMMRED> $credential = Get-Credential -Credential iammred\administrator
PS C:\Users\ed.IAMMRED> gwmi win32_bios -cn w8s504 -Credential $credential


SMBIOSBIOSVersion : 090004
Manufacturer      : American Megatrends Inc.
Name              : BIOS Date: 03/19/09 22:51:32  Ver: 09.00.04
SerialNumber      : 0385-4074-3362-4641-2411-8229-09
Version           : VRTUAL - 3000919
```

When the same query must be executed against remote systems that use the same credential, the *Get-WMIObject* cmdlet makes it easy to execute the command. The following code runs the same query with the same credentials against three different systems. The remote computers are a combination of three Windows Server 2012 and Windows 2008 R2 servers. The commands and the related output appear here:

```
PS C:\Users\ed.IAMMRED> $credential = Get-Credential -Credential iammred\administrator
PS C:\Users\ed.IAMMRED> $cn = "w8s504","hyperv2","hyperv3"
PS C:\Users\ed.IAMMRED> gwmi win32_bios -cn $cn -Credential $credential


SMBIOSBIOSVersion : 090004
Manufacturer      : American Megatrends Inc.
Name              : BIOS Date: 03/19/09 22:51:32  Ver: 09.00.04
SerialNumber      : 0385-4074-3362-4641-2411-8229-09
Version           : VRTUAL - 3000919

SMBIOSBIOSVersion : A11
Manufacturer      : Dell Inc.
Name              : Phoenix ROM BIOS PLUS Version 1.10 A11
SerialNumber      : BDY91L1
Version           : DELL   - 15

SMBIOSBIOSVersion : BAP6710H.86A.0072.2011.0927.1425
Manufacturer      : Intel Corp.
Name              : BIOS Date: 09/27/11 14:25:42 Ver: 04.06.04
SerialNumber      :
Version           : INTEL  - 1072009
```

One problem with the preceding output is that it does not contain the name of the remote system. The returned WMI object contains the name of the system in the *__Server* variable, but the default display does not include this information. Therefore, a *Select-Object* cmdlet (which has an alias of *select*) is required to pick up the *__server* property. The revised command and associated output appear here:

```
PS C:\Users\ed.IAMMRED> gwmi win32_bios -cn $cn -Credential $credential | select
smbiosbiosversion, manufacturer, name, serialnumber, __server


smbiosbiosversion : 090004
manufacturer      : American Megatrends Inc.
name              : BIOS Date: 03/19/09 22:51:32  Ver: 09.00.04
serialnumber      : 0385-4074-3362-4641-2411-8229-09
__SERVER          : W8S504

smbiosbiosversion : A11
manufacturer      : Dell Inc.
name              : Phoenix ROM BIOS PLUS Version 1.10 A11
serialnumber      : BDY91L1
__SERVER          : HYPERV2

smbiosbiosversion : BAP6710H.86A.0072.2011.0927.1425
manufacturer      : Intel Corp.
name              : BIOS Date: 09/27/11 14:25:42 Ver: 04.06.04
serialnumber      :
__SERVER          : HYPERV3
```

Besides just using WMI remoting, Windows PowerShell also permits using Windows PowerShell remoting. The advantage to using Windows PowerShell remoting is that in addition to permitting WMI to connect to remote systems with elevated permissions, Windows PowerShell remoting also permits running WMI commands with alternate credentials from within the same Windows PowerShell session against the local computer. WMI does not support alternate credentials for a local connection, but Windows PowerShell remoting does. In the code that follows, the *Get-WMIObject* cmdlet queries the *WIN32_loggedonuser* WMI class. It returns only the antecedent property from this association class. The results show that the logged-on user is iammred\ed. Next, the credentials of the administrator account are retrieved via the *Get-Credential* Windows PowerShell cmdlet and stored in the *$credential* variable. The *invoke-Command* cmdlet runs the *Get-WMIObject* cmdlet and queries the *WIN32_loggedonuser* WMI class against the local machine using the administrator credentials. The results reveal all of the logged-on users, not merely the non-admin user, illustrating the different user context that was used for the query.

```
PS C:\Users\ed.IAMMRED> (gwmi win32_loggedonuser).antecedent
\\.\root\cimv2:Win32_Account.Domain="IAMMRED",Name="ed"
PS C:\Users\ed.IAMMRED> $credential = Get-Credential iammred\administrator
PS C:\Users\ed.IAMMRED> Invoke-Command -cn localhost -ScriptBlock
    {(gwmi Win32_loggedonuser).antecedent} -Credential $credential
\\.\root\cimv2:Win32_Account.Domain="W8C504",Name="SYSTEM"
\\.\root\cimv2:Win32_Account.Domain="W8C504",Name="LOCAL SERVICE"
\\.\root\cimv2:Win32_Account.Domain="W8C504",Name="NETWORK SERVICE"
\\.\root\cimv2:Win32_Account.Domain="IAMMRED",Name="ed"
\\.\root\cimv2:Win32_Account.Domain="IAMMRED",Name="ed"
\\.\root\cimv2:Win32_Account.Domain="IAMMRED",Name="Administrator"
\\.\root\cimv2:Win32_Account.Domain="IAMMRED",Name="Administrator"
\\.\root\cimv2:Win32_Account.Domain="IAMMRED",Name="Administrator"
\\.\root\cimv2:Win32_Account.Domain="IAMMRED",Name="Administrator"
\\.\root\cimv2:Win32_Account.Domain="IAMMRED",Name="Administrator"
\\.\root\cimv2:Win32_Account.Domain="W8C504",Name="ANONYMOUS LOGON"
\\.\root\cimv2:Win32_Account.Domain="W8C504",Name="DWM-1"
\\.\root\cimv2:Win32_Account.Domain="W8C504",Name="DWM-1"
\\.\root\cimv2:Win32_Account.Domain="W8C504",Name="DWM-2"
\\.\root\cimv2:Win32_Account.Domain="W8C504",Name="DWM-2"
PS C:\Users\ed.IAMMRED>
```

# Using Windows PowerShell remoting to run WMI

Use of the *Get-WMIObject* cmdlet is a requirement for using WMI to talk to down-level systems—systems that will not even run Windows PowerShell 2.0. There are several disadvantages to using native WMI remoting. These appear here:

- WMI remoting requires special firewall rules to permit access to client systems.

- WMI remoting requires opening multiple holes in the firewall.

- WMI remoting requires local administrator rights.

- WMI remoting provides no support for alternate credentials on a local connection.

- WMI remoting output does not return the name of the target system by default.

Beginning with Windows PowerShell 2.0, you can use Windows PowerShell remoting to run your WMI commands. Using Windows PowerShell remoting, you can configure different access rights for the remote endpoint that do not require admin rights on the remote system. In addition, use of *Enable-PSRemoting* simplifies configuration of the firewall and the services. In addition, Windows PowerShell remoting requires that only a single port be open, not the wide range of ports required by the WMI protocols (RPC and DCOM). In addition, Windows PowerShell remoting supports alternate credentials for a local connection. (For more information about Windows PowerShell remoting, see Chapter 4, "Using PowerShell Remoting and Jobs").

In the code appearing here, the *Get-Credential* cmdlet stores a credential object in the *$credential* variable. Next, this credential is used with the *Invoke-Command* cmdlet to run a script block containing a WMI command. The results return to the Windows PowerShell console.

```
PS C:\Users\ed.IAMMRED> $credential = Get-Credential iammred\administrator
PS C:\Users\ed.IAMMRED> Invoke-Command -cn w8s504
   -ScriptBlock {gwmi win32_bios} -Credential $credential

SMBIOSBIOSVersion : 090004
Manufacturer      : American Megatrends Inc.
Name              : BIOS Date: 03/19/09 22:51:32  Ver: 09.00.04
SerialNumber      : 0385-4074-3362-4641-2411-8229-09
Version           : VRTUAL - 3000919
PSComputerName    : w8s504
```

Use Windows PowerShell remoting to communicate to any system that runs Windows PowerShell 2.0 or Windows PowerShell 3.0. As shown here, you can run WMI commands against remote systems with a single command, and engage multiple operating systems. The nice thing is the inclusion of the *PSComputerName* property. Because the *Invoke-Command* cmdlet accepts an array of computer names, the command is very simple.

```
PS C:\Users\ed.IAMMRED> $credential = Get-Credential iammred\administrator
PS C:\Users\ed.IAMMRED> $cn = "dc1","dc3","hyperv1","W8s504"
PS C:\Users\ed.IAMMRED> Invoke-Command -cn $cn -cred $credential -ScriptBlock {gwmi win32_
operatingsystem}


SystemDirectory : C:\Windows\system32
Organization    :
BuildNumber     : 8504
RegisteredUser  : Windows User
SerialNumber    : 00184-70000-00072-AA253
Version         : 6.2.8504
PSComputerName  : W8s504

SystemDirectory : C:\Windows\system32
Organization    :
BuildNumber     : 7601
RegisteredUser  : Windows User
SerialNumber    : 55041-507-3502855-84574
Version         : 6.1.7601
PSComputerName  : hyperv1
```

```
SystemDirectory : C:\Windows\system32
Organization    :
BuildNumber     : 6002
RegisteredUser  : Windows User
SerialNumber    : 55041-222-5263084-76207
Version         : 6.0.6002
PSComputerName  : dc1

SystemDirectory : C:\Windows\system32
Organization    :
BuildNumber     : 7601
RegisteredUser  : Windows User
SerialNumber    : 55041-507-0212466-84605
Version         : 6.1.7601
PSComputerName  : dc3
```

# Using CIM classes to query WMI classes

There are several ways of using the Common Information Model (CIM) classes to perform remote WMI queries. The most basic way is to use the *Get-CimInstance* cmdlet. In fact, this generic method is required if no specific CIM implementation class exists. There are steps required to use the *Get-CimInstance* cmdlet to query a remote system. These steps appear here.

## Using CIM to query remote WMI data

Use the *New-CimSession* cmdlet to create a new CIM session. Store the returned session in a variable.

Supply the stored CIM session from the variable to the *-cimsession* parameter when querying with the *Get-CIMInstance* cmdlet.

In the code that appears here, the *New-CimSession* cmdlet creates a new CIM session with a target computer of W8s504 and a user name of Iammred\administrator. The cmdlet returns a CIM session that it stores in the *$w8s504* variable. Next, the *Get-CimInstance* cmdlet uses the CIM session to connect to the remote w8s504 system and to return the data from the *Win32_bios* WMI class. The output is displayed in the Windows PowerShell console.

```
PS C:\Users\ed.IAMMRED> $w8s504 = New-CimSession -ComputerName w8s504
-Credential iammred\administrator
PS C:\Users\ed.IAMMRED> Get-CimInstance -CimSession $w8s504 -ClassName win32_bios


SMBIOSBIOSVersion : 090004
Manufacturer      : American Megatrends Inc.
Name              : BIOS Date: 03/19/09 22:51:32  Ver: 09.00.04
SerialNumber      : 0385-4074-3362-4641-2411-8229-09
Version           : VRTUAL - 3000919
PSComputerName    : w8s504
```

Besides automatically returning the target computer name, *Get-CimInstance* automatically converts the date from a UTC string to a *datetime* type. As shown here, an extra step is required to convert the WMI UTC string to a *datetime* type:

```
PS C:\Users\ed.IAMMRED> $bios = gwmi win32_bios
PS C:\Users\ed.IAMMRED> $bios.ReleaseDate
20090319000000.000000+000
PS C:\Users\ed.IAMMRED> $bios.ConvertToDateTime($bios.ReleaseDate)

Wednesday, March 18, 2009 8:00:00 PM
```

However, if you use the *Get-CIMInstance* cmdlet, CIM automatically converts the UTC string to a *datetime* type. This appears here:

```
PS C:\Users\ed.IAMMRED> $bios = Get-CimInstance -CimSession $w8s504 -ClassName win32_bios
PS C:\Users\ed.IAMMRED> $bios.ReleaseDate

Wednesday, March 18, 2009 8:00:00 PM
PS C:\Users\ed.IAMMRED> $bios.ReleaseDate.gettype()

IsPublic IsSerial Name                                     BaseType
-------- -------- ----                                     --------
True     True     DateTime                                 System.ValueType
```

As long as the credentials work, you can create a new CIM session connection for multiple computers, and even for multiple operating systems. This works because the *-computername* parameter of the *New-CIMSession* cmdlet accepts an array of computer names. In the code appearing here, the *New-CIMSession* cmdlet creates a new CIM session with two target computers and the same credentials. It then stores the returned CIM session in the *$cn* variable. Next, the *Get-CimInstance* cmdlet queries the *Win32_OperatingSystem* WMI class from the CIM session stored in the *$cn* variable. The code and the results from the code appear here:

```
PS C:\Users\ed.IAMMRED> $cn = New-CimSession -ComputerName w8s504,w8c504
-Credential iammred\administrator
PS C:\Users\ed.IAMMRED> Get-CimInstance -CimSession $cn -ClassName win32_operatingsystem

System           Organization BuildNumber Registered   SerialNumber Version  PSComputer
Directory                                 User                               Name
-----------      ------------ ----------- -----------  ------------ -------  -----------
C:\Window...                  8504        ed           00178-101... 6.2.8504 w8c504
C:\Window...                  8504        Windows User 00184-700... 6.2.8504 w8s504
```

# Working with remote results

When working with remote systems, it may be important to consider the network bandwidth and the cost of repeatedly retrieving unfiltered data. There are basically two choices—the first choice involves gathering the information and storing it in a local variable. Using this technique, you incur the bandwidth cost once, and you can use the same data in multiple ways without incurring the bandwidth hit again. But if your data changes rapidly, this technique does not help much.

> **Important** In potentially bandwidth-constrained situations, it is a best practice to store data retrieved locally to facilitate reuse of the information at a later time. The easiest place to store the data is in a variable, but do not forget about storing the data in XML for a more persisted storage. Using the *Export-CliXML* cmdlet is extremely easy and preserves the data relationships well.

In the command appearing here, the *Get-CimInstance* cmdlet retrieves all of the process information from the remote computer session stored in the *$session* variable. The process information is stored in the *$process* variable. Next, the data is explored and the name and process IDs returned.

```
PS C:\Users\ed.IAMMRED> $process = Get-CimInstance -CimSession $session
-ClassName win32_process
PS C:\Users\ed.IAMMRED> $process | ft name, processID -AutoSize
```

```
name                 processID
----                 ---------
System Idle Process          0
System                       4
smss.exe                   268
csrss.exe                  356
csrss.exe                  408
wininit.exe                416
winlogon.exe               444
services.exe               508
lsass.exe                  516
svchost.exe                608
svchost.exe                644
svchost.exe                716
LogonUI.exe                748
dwm.exe                    764
svchost.exe                784
svchost.exe                828
svchost.exe                908
svchost.exe                284
spoolsv.exe               1092
svchost.exe               1144
svchost.exe               1484
svchost.exe               1536
msdtc.exe                 1132
csrss.exe                 1760
winlogon.exe              1848
dwm.exe                    916
taskhostex.exe             520
rdpclip.exe               2172
explorer.exe              2240
svchost.exe               1756
powershell.exe             760
conhost.exe               2276
more.com                  2468
WmiPrvSE.exe               496
```

Upon examining the data, the next command returns only processes with the name svchost.exe. Once again, the data is displayed in a table.

```
PS C:\Users\ed.IAMMRED> $process | where name -eq 'svchost.exe' | ft name, processID
-AutoSize

name         processID
----         ---------
svchost.exe        608
svchost.exe        644
svchost.exe        716
svchost.exe        784
svchost.exe        828
svchost.exe        908
svchost.exe        284
svchost.exe       1144
svchost.exe       1484
svchost.exe       1536
svchost.exe       1756
```

Now a different property needs to be added to the data—the *commandline* property, which is used to launch the process. This information provides clues as to what process runs in the particular svchost.exe process. The command appears here:

```
PS C:\Users\ed.IAMMRED> $process | where name -eq 'svchost.exe' | ft name, processID,
commandline -AutoSize

name         processID commandline
----         --------- -----------
svchost.exe        608 C:\Windows\system32\svchost.exe -k DcomLaunch
svchost.exe        644 C:\Windows\system32\svchost.exe -k RPCSS
svchost.exe        716 C:\Windows\System32\svchost.exe -k LocalServiceNetworkRestricted
svchost.exe        784 C:\Windows\system32\svchost.exe -k netsvcs
svchost.exe        828 C:\Windows\system32\svchost.exe -k LocalService
svchost.exe        908 C:\Windows\system32\svchost.exe -k NetworkService
svchost.exe        284 C:\Windows\system32\svchost.exe -k LocalServiceNoNetwork
svchost.exe       1144 C:\Windows\System32\svchost.exe -k LocalSystemNetworkRestricted
svchost.exe       1484 C:\Windows\System32\svchost.exe -k termsvcs
svchost.exe       1536 C:\Windows\System32\svchost.exe -k ICService
svchost.exe       1756 C:\Windows\system32\svchost.exe -k NetworkServiceNetworkRestricted
```

Now, home in on the data a bit more to see which of the svchost.exe processes requires the largest working set size of memory, and is using the most kernel mode time. The answer to the question of which instance uses most resources appears in the code is shown here:

```
PS C:\Users\ed.IAMMRED> $process | where name -eq 'svchost.exe' | ft processID, workingset
size, kernel* -AutoSize

processID workingsetsize KernelModeTime
--------- -------------- --------------
      608        8998912      115312500
      644        7143424        3281250
      716       15360000       31250000
```

```
784        32837632        29218750
828        11382784         8906250
908        23146496         5781250
284        10878976         1875000
1144       15548416        17968750
1484       31571968        45156250
1536        7712768        43125000
1756        4079616               0
```

The second approach involves filtering the data at the source and only returning the needed information to the local client machine. There are two ways of doing this: the first is to use the Windows PowerShell *-property* and *-filter* parameters to reduce the data returned; the second is to use a native WQL query to reduce the data.

## Reducing data via Windows PowerShell parameters

The first method to reduce data and filter it at the source involves using two Windows PowerShell parameters. The first parameter, the *-property* parameter, reduces properties returned, but it does not reduce instances. The second parameter, the *-filter* parameter, reduces the instances returned, but does not reduce the number of properties. For example, the code that follows retrieves only the name and the start mode of services on a remote server named w8s504. The command executes as the administrator from the domain.

```
$session = New-CimSession -ComputerName w8s504 -Credential iammred\administrator
Get-CimInstance -ClassName win32_service -CimSession $session -Property name, startmode
```

The command that follows uses the previously created session on the remote computer named w8s504, and this time it introduces the *-filter* parameter as well. Now the command returns the name and start mode of only the running services on the remote system. The services are sorted by start mode, and a table displays the results. The command and the associated output appear here:

```
PS C:\Users\ed.IAMMRED> Get-CimInstance -ClassName win32_service -CimSession $session
-Property name, startmode -Filter "state = 'running'" | sort startmode | ft name, startmode
-AutoSize

name                 startmode
----                 ---------
NlaSvc               Auto
MSDTC                Auto
Netlogon             Auto
Winmgmt              Auto
nsi                  Auto
Power                Auto
ProfSvc              Auto
RpcEptMapper         Auto
MpsSvc               Auto
RpcSs                Auto
Schedule             Auto
SENS                 Auto
ShellHWDetection     Auto
Spooler              Auto
```

```
Themes                  Auto
TrkWks                  Auto
UALSVC                  Auto
SamSs                   Auto
LSM                     Auto
WinRM                   Auto
LanmanWorkstation       Auto
BFE                     Auto
BrokerInfrastructure    Auto
CryptSvc                Auto
lmhosts                 Auto
Dhcp                    Auto
Dnscache                Auto
DPS                     Auto
EventLog                Auto
EventSystem             Auto
DcomLaunch              Auto
gpsvc                   Auto
IKEEXT                  Auto
iphlpsvc                Auto
FontCache               Auto
LanmanServer            Auto
PolicyAgent             Manual
W32Time                 Manual
vmicvss                 Manual
vmictimesync            Manual
vmicshutdown            Manual
vmickvpexchange         Manual
vmicheartbeat           Manual
BITS                    Manual
TermService             Manual
CertPropSvc             Manual
Netman                  Manual
SessionEnv              Manual
netprofm                Manual
PlugPlay                Manual
UmRdpService            Manual
Appinfo                 Manual
```

You can obtain the same results by using a WQL query. The easiest way to do this is to create a new variable named *$query* to hold the WQL query. In the WQL query, choose the WMI properties and the WMI class name, and limit the instances to only those that are running. Next, supply the WMI query stored in the *$query* variable to the *-query* parameter of the *Get-CimInstance* cmdlet. The parameter sets do not permit use of the *-query* parameter at the same time as the use of the *-classname* parameter or the *-property* or *-filter* parameter. Once the change is made, the sorting and formatting of the output is the same. The results, as expected, are the same as well. The code and the output associated with the code appear here:

```
PS C:\Users\ed.IAMMRED> $query = "Select name, startmode from win32_Service where state =
'running'"
PS C:\Users\ed.IAMMRED> Get-CimInstance -Query $query -CimSession $session | sort
startmode | ft name, startmode -AutoSize
```

```
name                    startmode
----                    ---------
NlaSvc                  Auto
MSDTC                   Auto
Netlogon                Auto
Winmgmt                 Auto
nsi                     Auto
Power                   Auto
ProfSvc                 Auto
RpcEptMapper            Auto
MpsSvc                  Auto
RpcSs                   Auto
Schedule                Auto
SENS                    Auto
ShellHWDetection        Auto
Spooler                 Auto
Themes                  Auto
TrkWks                  Auto
UALSVC                  Auto
SamSs                   Auto
LSM                     Auto
WinRM                   Auto
LanmanWorkstation       Auto
BFE                     Auto
BrokerInfrastructure    Auto
CryptSvc                Auto
lmhosts                 Auto
Dhcp                    Auto
Dnscache                Auto
DPS                     Auto
EventLog                Auto
EventSystem             Auto
DcomLaunch              Auto
gpsvc                   Auto
IKEEXT                  Auto
iphlpsvc                Auto
FontCache               Auto
LanmanServer            Auto
PolicyAgent             Manual
W32Time                 Manual
vmicvss                 Manual
vmictimesync            Manual
vmicshutdown            Manual
vmickvpexchange         Manual
vmicheartbeat           Manual
BITS                    Manual
TermService             Manual
CertPropSvc             Manual
Netman                  Manual
SessionEnv              Manual
netprofm                Manual
PlugPlay                Manual
UmRdpService            Manual
Appinfo                 Manual
```

# Running WMI jobs

If DCOM is not an issue and you are using the *Get-WMIObject* cmdlet to work with remote systems, it is easy to run a remote WMI job. To do this, use the *Get-WMIObject* cmdlet and specify the *-asjob* parameter. Once you do this, use the *Get-Job* cmdlet to check on the status of the job, and use *Receive-Job* to receive the job results. (For more information about Windows PowerShell remoting and jobs, see Chapter 4.) In the following code, the *Get-WMIObject* cmdlet retrieves information from the *Win32_Bios* WMI class from a machine named dc3. The *-asjob* switched parameter is used to ensure that the command runs as a job. The output is a *pswmijob* object.

```
PS C:\Users\administrator.IAMMRED> gwmi win32_bios -ComputerName dc3 -AsJob

Id   Name   PSJobTypeName   State     HasMoreData   Location
--   ----   -------------   -----     -----------   --------
2    Job2   WmiJob          Running   True          dc3
```

The *Get-Job* cmdlet is used to retrieve the status of the WMI job. From the output appearing here, it is apparent that the job with an ID of 2 has completed, and that the job has more data to deliver.

```
PS C:\Users\administrator.IAMMRED> Get-Job -id 2

Id   Name   PSJobTypeName   State       HasMoreData   Location
--   ----   -------------   -----       -----------   --------
2    Job2   WmiJob          Completed   True          dc3
```

As with any other job in Windows PowerShell, to receive the results of the WMI job, use the *Receive-Job* cmdlet. This appears here:

```
PS C:\Users\administrator.IAMMRED> Receive-Job -id 2

SMBIOSBIOSVersion : 090004
Manufacturer      : American Megatrends Inc.
Name              : BIOS Date: 03/19/09 22:51:32  Ver: 09.00.04
SerialNumber      : 8994-9999-0865-2542-2186-8044-69
Version           : VRTUAL - 3000919
```

If you do not have DCOM and RPC access to the remote system, you can use the *Invoke-Command* cmdlet to run the WMI command on the remote system as a job. To do this, use the *-asjob* parameter on the *Invoke-Command* cmdlet. This technique appears here, where first the *Get-Credential* cmdlet creates a new credential object for the remote system. The *Invoke-Command* cmdlet uses Windows PowerShell remoting to connect to the remote system and query WMI by using the *Get-WMIObject* cmdlet to ask for information from the *WIN32_Service* class. The *-asjob* parameter causes the query to occur as a job.

```
PS C:\Users\ed.IAMMRED> $credential = Get-Credential iammred\administrator
PS C:\Users\ed.IAMMRED> Invoke-Command -ComputerName w8s504 -Credential $credential
-ScrtBlock {gwmi win32_service} -AsJob

Id   Name   PSJobTypeName   State     HasMoreData   Location
--   ----   -------------   -----     -----------   --------
4    Job4   RemoteJob       Running   True          w8s504
```

The *Get-Job* cmdlet queries for the status of job 4, and as shown following, the job has completed and it has more data. Notice this time that the job is of type *remotejob*, not *wmijob*, as was created earlier. Next, the *Receive-Job* cmdlet is used to receive the results of the WMI query. The *-keep* switch tells Windows PowerShell to retain the results for further analysis.

```
PS C:\Users\ed.IAMMRED> Get-Job -Id 4

Id      Name         PSJobTypeName    State      HasMoreData   Location
--      ----         -------------    -----      -----------   --------
4       Job4         RemoteJob        Completed  True          w8s504

PS C:\Users\ed.IAMMRED> Receive-Job -id 4 -Keep

ExitCode        : 1077
Name            : AeLookupSvc
ProcessId       : 0
StartMode       : Manual
State           : Stopped
Status          : OK
PSComputerName  : w8s504

ExitCode        : 1077
Name            : ALG
ProcessId       : 0
StartMode       : Manual
State           : Stopped
Status          : OK
PSComputerName  : w8s504
<output truncated>
```

You can also use the CIM cmdlets as jobs by using the *Invoke-Command* cmdlet. The following example uses *Get-Credential* to retrieve a credential object. Next, the *Invoke-Command* cmdlet runs the *Get-CimInstance* cmdlet on a remote computer named w8s504. The command runs as a job. The *Get-Job* cmdlet checks on the status of the job, and the *Receive-Job* cmdlet retrieves the results. The code and output appear here:

```
PS C:\Users\ed.IAMMRED> $credential = Get-Credential iammred\administrator
PS C:\Users\ed.IAMMRED> Invoke-Command -ComputerName w8s504 -ScriptBlock {Get-CimInstance
win32_bios} -Credential $credential -AsJob

Id      Name         PSJobTypeName    State      HasMoreData   Location
--      ----         -------------    -----      -----------   --------
8       Job8         RemoteJob        Running    True          w8s504

PS C:\Users\ed.IAMMRED> Get-Job -Id 8

Id      Name         PSJobTypeName    State      HasMoreData   Location
--      ----         -------------    -----      -----------   --------
8       Job8         RemoteJob        Completed  True          w8s504

PS C:\Users\ed.IAMMRED> Receive-Job -Id 8
```

```
SMBIOSBIOSVersion : 090004
Manufacturer      : American Megatrends Inc.
Name              : BIOS Date: 03/19/09 22:51:32  Ver: 09.00.04
SerialNumber      : 0385-4074-3362-4641-2411-8229-09
Version           : VRTUAL - 3000919
PSComputerName    : w8s504
```

# Using Windows PowerShell remoting and WMI: Step-by-step exercises

In this exercise, you will practice using Windows PowerShell remoting to run remote commands. For the purpose of this exercise, you can use your local computer, but commands designed to fail (in the exercise) will more than likely succeed instead of creating the errors appearing here.

### Using PowerShell remoting to retrieve remote information

1. Log on to your computer with a user account that does not have administrator rights.

2. Open the Windows PowerShell console.

3. Use the *Get-CimInstance* cmdlet to retrieve process information from a remote system that has WMI remoting enabled on it. Do not supply alternate credentials. The command appears here:

   ```
   Get-CimInstance -CimSession w8s504 -ClassName win32_process
   ```

4. The command fails due to an Access Denied error. Now create a new CIM session to the remote system and connect with alternate credentials. Store the CIM session in a variable named *$session*. This command appears following. (Use a remote system accessible to you and credentials appropriate to that system.)

   ```
   $session = New-CimSession -Credential iammred\administrator -ComputerName w8s504
   ```

5. Use the stored CIM session from the *$session* variable to retrieve process information from the remote system. The command appears here:

   ```
   Get-CimInstance -CimSession $session -ClassName win32_process
   ```

6. Use the stored CIM session from the *$session* variable to retrieve the name and the status of all services on the remote system. Sort the output by state, and format a table with the name and the state. The command appears here:

   ```
   Get-CimInstance -CimSession $session -ClassName win32_service -Property name, state |
   sort state | ft name, state -AutoSize
   ```

7. Use the *Get-WMIObject* cmdlet to run a WMI command on a remote system. Use the *Win32_Bios* WMI class and target the same remote system you used earlier. Specify appropriate credentials for the connection. Here is an example:

```
$credential = Get-Credential iammred\administrator
Get-WmiObject -Class win32_bios -ComputerName w8s504 -Credential $credential
```

8. Use Windows PowerShell remoting by using the *Invoke-Command* cmdlet to run a WMI command against a remote system. Use the credentials you stored earlier. Use the *Get-CimInstance* cmdlet to retrieve BIOS information from WMI. The command appears here:

```
Invoke-Command -ComputerName w8s504 -ScriptBlock {Get-CimInstance win32_bios} -Credential
$credential
```

This concludes the exercise. Leave the Windows PowerShell console open for the next exercise.

In the following exercise, you will create and receive Windows PowerShell jobs.

## Creating and receiving WMI jobs

1. Open the Windows PowerShell console as a non-elevated user.

2. Use the *Get-WMIObject* cmdlet to retrieve BIOS information from a remote system. Use the *-asjob* parameter to run the command as a job. Use the credentials you stored in the *$credential* variable in the previous exercise.

```
Get-WmiObject win32_bios -ComputerName w8s504 -Credential $credential -AsJob
```

3. Check on the success or failure of the job by using the *Get-Job* cmdlet. Make sure you use the job ID from the previous command. A sample appears here:

```
Get-Job -Id 10
```

4. If the job was successful, receive the results of the job by using the *Receive-Job* cmdlet. Do not bother with storing the results in a variable or keeping the results because you will not need them.

5. Create a new PowerShell session object by using the *New-PSSession* cmdlet. Store the results in a variable named *$psSession*. The command appears following. (Use appropriate computer names and credentials for your network.)

```
$PSSession = New-PSSession -Credential iammred\administrator -ComputerName w8s504
```

6. Use the *Invoke-Command* cmdlet to make the *Get-WMIObject* cmdlet retrieve BIOS information from the remote system. Use the session information stored in the *$psSession* variable. Make sure you use the *-asjob* parameter with the command. The command appears here:

```
Invoke-Command -Session $PSSession -ScriptBlock {gwmi win32_bios} -AsJob
```

7. Use the *Get-Job* cmdlet with the job ID returned by the previous command to check on the status of the job. The command will be similar to the one shown here:

```
Get-Job -id 12
```

8. Use the *Receive-Job* cmdlet to retrieve the results of the WMI command. Store the returned information in a variable named *$bios*. The command appears here (ensure you use the job ID number from your system):

```
$bios = Receive-Job -id 12
```

9. Now query the BIOS version by accessing the *version* property from the *$bios* variable. This appears here:

```
$bios.Version
```

This concludes the exercise.

# Chapter 12 quick reference

| To | Do this |
| --- | --- |
| Retrieve WMI information from a remote legacy system | Use the *Get-WMIObject* cmdlet and specify credentials as needed, and the target system. |
| Retrieve WMI information from a Windows 8 system or a Windows Server 2012 system | Use the *Get-CimInstance* cmdlet and specify the target computer and WMI class. |
| Run a WMI command on multiple Windows 8 or Windows Server 2012 computers | Use the *New-CIMSession* cmdlet to create a CIM session for the multiple systems. Then specify that session for *Get-CimInstance*. |
| Filter returning WMI data | Use the *-filter* parameter with either *Get-WMIObject* or *Get-CimInstance*. |
| Reduce the number of returned properties | Use the *-property* parameter with either *Get-WMIObject* or *Get-CimInstance*. |
| Use a legacy WQL type of query | Use the *-query* parameter with either *Get-WMIObject* or *Get-CimInstance*. |
| Retrieve the WMI results with a job | Use the *Start-Job* and *Receive-Job* cmdlets with *Get-CimInstance* or the *-asjob* parameter with *Get-WmiObject*. |

# CHAPTER 13

# Calling WMI Methods on WMI Classes

**After completing this chapter, you will be able to:**

- Use WMI cmdlets to execute instance methods.

- Use WMI cmdlets to execute static methods.

## Using WMI cmdlets to execute instance methods

There are actually several ways to call Microsoft Windows Management Instrumentation (WMI) methods in Windows PowerShell. One reason for this is that some WMI methods are *instance methods*, which means they only work on an instance of a class. Other methods are *static methods*, which mean they do not operate on an instance of the class. For example, the *Terminate* method from the *WIN32_Process* class is an instance method—it will only operate against a specific instance of the *WIN32_Process* class. If you do not have a reference to a process, you cannot terminate the process—which makes sense. On the other hand, if you want to *create* a new instance of a *WIN32_Process* class, you do not grab a reference to an instance of the class. For example, you do not grab an instance of a running Calculator process to create a new instance of a Notepad process. Therefore, you need a static method that is always available.

Let's examine the first of these two approaches—using instance methods—with a short example. First, create an instance of notepad.exe. Then use the *Get-WmiObject* cmdlet to view the process. (As you may recall from earlier chapters, *gwmi* is an alias for *Get-WmiObject*). This appears here:

```
PS C:\> Start-Process notepad
PS C:\> gwmi win32_process -Filter "name = 'notepad.exe'"

__GENUS              : 2
__CLASS              : Win32_Process
__SUPERCLASS         : CIM_Process
__DYNASTY            : CIM_ManagedSystemElement
__RELPATH            : Win32_Process.Handle="1888"
__PROPERTY_COUNT     : 45
__DERIVATION         : {CIM_Process, CIM_LogicalElement, CIM_ManagedSystemElement}
__SERVER             : W8C504
```

```
__NAMESPACE                    : root\cimv2
__PATH                         : \\W8C504\root\cimv2:Win32_Process.Handle="1888"
Caption                        : notepad.exe
CommandLine                    : "C:\Windows\system32\notepad.exe"
CreationClassName              : Win32_Process
CreationDate                   : 20120707150100.342933-240
CSCreationClassName            : Win32_ComputerSystem
CSName                         : W8C504
Description                    : notepad.exe
ExecutablePath                 : C:\Windows\system32\notepad.exe
ExecutionState                 :
Handle                         : 1888
HandleCount                    : 75
InstallDate                    :
KernelModeTime                 : 156250
MaximumWorkingSetSize          : 1380
MinimumWorkingSetSize          : 200
Name                           : notepad.exe
OSCreationClassName            : Win32_OperatingSystem
OSName                         : Microsoft Windows 8
                                 Pro|C:\Windows|\Device\Harddisk0\Partition2
OtherOperationCount            : 67
OtherTransferCount             : 110
PageFaults                     : 1559
PageFileUsage                  : 1236
ParentProcessId                : 2964
PeakPageFileUsage              : 1236
PeakVirtualSize                : 91176960
PeakWorkingSetSize             : 6088
Priority                       : 8
PrivatePageCount               : 1265664
ProcessId                      : 1888
QuotaNonPagedPoolUsage         : 8
QuotaPagedPoolUsage            : 174
QuotaPeakNonPagedPoolUsage     : 8
QuotaPeakPagedPoolUsage        : 175
ReadOperationCount             : 1
ReadTransferCount              : 60
SessionId                      : 2
Status                         :
TerminationDate                :
ThreadCount                    : 1
UserModeTime                   : 156250
VirtualSize                    : 91172864
WindowsVersion                 : 6.2.8504
WorkingSetSize                 : 6234112
WriteOperationCount            : 0
WriteTransferCount             : 0
PSComputerName                 : W8C504
ProcessName                    : notepad.exe
Handles                        : 75
VM                             : 91172864
WS                             : 6234112
Path                           : C:\Windows\system32\notepad.exe
```

Once you have the instance of the Notepad process you want to terminate, there are at least four choices to stop the process:

- You can call the method directly using dotted notation (because there is only one instance of notepad).

- You can store the reference in a variable and then terminate it directly.

- You can use the *Invoke-WmiMethod* cmdlet.

- You can use the *[wmi]* type accelerator.

These techniques are described in the following sections.

## Using the *terminate* method directly

Notice that each time the method is called, a *ReturnValue* property is returned from the method call. This value is used to determine if the method completed successfully. Return codes are documented for the *terminate* method on MSDN (each method has its return codes detailed on MSDN).

Because there is only one instance of the notepad.exe process running on the system, it is possible to use the group-and-dot process. *Grouping characters* (that is, opening and closing parentheses) placed around the expression return an instance of the object. From there, you can directly call the *terminate* method by using dotted notation. An example of this syntax appears next. (This technique works in the same manner when there is more than one instance of the object.)

```
PS C:\Users\ed.IAMMRED> (gwmi win32_process -Filter "name = 'notepad.exe'").terminate()
```

```
__GENUS           : 2
__CLASS           : __PARAMETERS
__SUPERCLASS      :
__DYNASTY         : __PARAMETERS
__RELPATH         :
__PROPERTY_COUNT  : 1
__DERIVATION      : {}
__SERVER          :
__NAMESPACE       :
__PATH            :
ReturnValue       : 0
PSComputerName    :
```

The second way of calling the *terminate* method directly is to use WMI to return an instance of the object, store the returned object in a variable, and then call the method via dotted notation.

To directly call an instance method, use the *Get-WmiObject* cmdlet to return objects containing an instance method, and store the returned object in a variable. Once stored, instance methods are directly available to you.

The example that follows uses the group-and-dot dotted notation to call the method. In this example, two instances of the notepad.exe process start. The *Get-WmiObject* cmdlet returns both instances of the process and stores them in a variable. Next, dotted notation calls the *terminate* method. This technique of calling the method is new for Windows PowerShell 3.0. In Windows PowerShell 2.0, a direct call to the *terminate* method fails because the object contained in the variable is an array.

> **Note** Tab expansion does not enumerate the *terminate* method when the underlying object is an array; therefore, this is one instance where you will need to type out the entire method name.

```
PS C:\> notepad
PS C:\> notepad
PS C:\> $a = gwmi win32_process -Filter "name = 'notepad.exe'"
PS C:\> $a.terminate()


__GENUS          : 2
__CLASS          : __PARAMETERS
__SUPERCLASS     :
__DYNASTY        : __PARAMETERS
__RELPATH        :
__PROPERTY_COUNT : 1
__DERIVATION     : {}
__SERVER         :
__NAMESPACE      :
__PATH           :
ReturnValue      : 0
PSComputerName   :

__GENUS          : 2
__CLASS          : __PARAMETERS
__SUPERCLASS     :
__DYNASTY        : __PARAMETERS
__RELPATH        :
__PROPERTY_COUNT : 1
__DERIVATION     : {}
__SERVER         :
__NAMESPACE      :
__PATH           :
ReturnValue      : 0
PSComputerName   :
```

## Using the *Invoke-WmiMethod* cmdlet

If you want to use the *Invoke-WmiMethod* Windows PowerShell cmdlet to call an instance method, you must pass a path to the instance to be operated upon. The easiest way to obtain the path to the instance is to first perform a WMI query, and then to use the *__RelPath* system property. The

_RelPath_ system property contains the relative path to the instance of the class. In the example that appears here, an instance of the notepad.exe process starts. Next, the *Get-WmiObject* cmdlet retrieves an instance of the process. Next, the __*RELPATH* system property is retrieved from the object stored in the *$a* variable.

```
PS C:\> notepad
PS C:\> $a = gwmi win32_process -Filter "name = 'notepad.exe'"
PS C:\> $a.__RELPATH
Win32_Process.Handle="1872"
```

If working against a remote machine, you will want the complete path to the instance. The complete path includes the machine name and the WMI namespace, as well as the class and the key to the class. The complete path appears in the __*Path* system property as shown following. (Do not get confused; the *WIN32_Process* WMI class also contains a *path* property). The complete path to the current notepad.exe process stored in the *$a* variable appears here:

```
PS C:\> $a.__PATH
\\W8C504\root\cimv2:Win32_Process.Handle="1872"
```

If you have multiple instances of the notepad.exe process stored in the *$a* variable, you can still access the __*path* and __*relpath* properties. This appears here:

```
PS C:\> notepad
PS C:\> notepad
PS C:\> notepad
PS C:\> $a = gwmi win32_process -Filter "name = 'notepad.exe'"
PS C:\> $a.__RELPATH
Win32_Process.Handle="1644"
Win32_Process.Handle="2940"
Win32_Process.Handle="828"
PS C:\> $a.__PATH
\\W8C504\root\cimv2:Win32_Process.Handle="1644"
\\W8C504\root\cimv2:Win32_Process.Handle="2940"
\\W8C504\root\cimv2:Win32_Process.Handle="828"
```

As shown following, first create an instance of the Notepad process, use the *Get-WmiObject* cmdlet to retrieve that instance of the process, display the value of the __*RELPATH* property, and then call the *Invoke-WmiMethod* cmdlet. When calling the *Invoke-WmiMethod* cmdlet, pass the path to the instance and the name of the method to use. This appears in the following commands:

```
PS C:\> notepad
PS C:\> $a = gwmi win32_process -Filter "name = 'notepad.exe'"
PS C:\> $a.__RELPATH
Win32_Process.Handle="1264"
PS C:\> Invoke-WmiMethod -Path $a.__RELPATH -Name terminate
```

```
__GENUS            : 2
__CLASS            : __PARAMETERS
__SUPERCLASS       :
__DYNASTY          : __PARAMETERS
__RELPATH          :
__PROPERTY_COUNT   : 1
__DERIVATION       : {}
__SERVER           :
__NAMESPACE        :
__PATH             :
ReturnValue        : 0
PSComputerName     :
```

# Using the *[wmi]* type accelerator

Another way to call an instance method is to use the *[wmi]* type accelerator. The *[wmi]* type accelerator works with WMI instances. Therefore, if you pass a path to the *[wmi]* type accelerator, you can call instance methods directly. For this example, start an instance of the Notepad process. Next, use the *Get-WmiObject* cmdlet to retrieve all instances of Notepad (there is only one instance). Next, pass the value of the *__RELPATH* system property to the *[wmi]* type accelerator. This command returns the entire instance of the *WIN32_Process* class. That is, it returns all properties and methods that are available. All of the properties associated with the *WIN32_Process* WMI class (the same properties shown earlier) for the specific instance of *WIN32_Process* are available via the *__RelPath* system property (keep in mind that *__RelPath* is preceded with two underscores—a double underscore—not one). To see this object in action, select only the *name* property from the object and display it on the screen. To this point, you can retrieve a specific instance of a *WIN32_Process* WMI class via the *[wmi]* type accelerator. Therefore, it is time to call the *Terminate* method. This technique appears here, along with the associated output:

```
PS C:\> notepad
PS C:\> $a = gwmi win32_process -Filter "name = 'notepad.exe'"
PS C:\> [wmi]$a.__RELPATH | select name

name
----
notepad.exe
PS C:\> ([wmi]$a.__RELPATH).terminate()

__GENUS            : 2
__CLASS            : __PARAMETERS
__SUPERCLASS       :
__DYNASTY          : __PARAMETERS
__RELPATH          :
__PROPERTY_COUNT   : 1
__DERIVATION       : {}
__SERVER           :
__NAMESPACE        :
__PATH             :
ReturnValue        : 0
PSComputerName     :
```

# Using WMI to work with static methods

When working with WMI and Windows PowerShell, it is common to think about using the *Get-WmiObject* cmdlet. Unfortunately, when using the *Get-WmiObject* cmdlet with the *Win32_SecurityDescriptorHelper* class, nothing happens. When you attempt to pipeline the results to *Get-Member*, an error is produced. The two commands appear here (note that *gwmi* is an alias for *Get-WmiObject*, and *gm* is an alias for *Get-Member*):

```
PS C:\> gwmi win32_SecurityDescriptorHelper
PS C:\> gwmi win32_SecurityDescriptorHelper | gm
gm : No object has been specified to the Get-Member cmdlet.
At line:1 char:39
+ gwmi win32_SecurityDescriptorHelper | gm
+                                       ~~
    + CategoryInfo          : CloseError: (:) [Get-Member], InvalidOperationException
    + FullyQualifiedErrorId : NoObjectInGetMember,Microsoft.PowerShell.Commands.
GetMemberCommand
```

Look up the class in the Windows Management Instrumentation Tester (WbemTest). The WbemTest utility always exists with WMI. To find it, you can type **WbemTest** from within Windows PowerShell. From WbemTest, you can see that *Win32_SecurityDescriptorHelper* is a dynamic class, and that there are many methods available from the class. This appears in Figure 13-1.

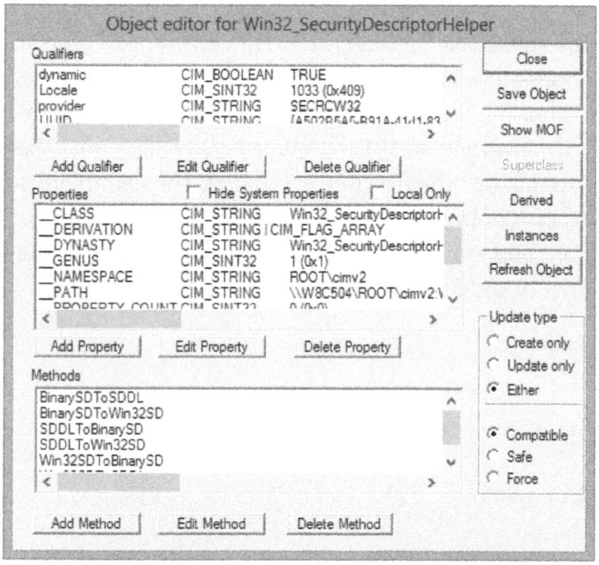

**FIGURE 13-1** The WbemTest utility shows that the *Win32_SecurityDescriptorHelper* WMI class is dynamic and contains many methods.

When you click the Instances button (the sixth button from the top on the right side), you will see that there are no instances available. Next, click the Show MOF button (the third button from the top on the right side), and you'll see that all methods are implemented. A method will only work if it is marked as "implemented." For example, the *WIN32_Processor* WMI class has two methods listed—*Reset* and *SetPowerState*—but unfortunately, neither method is implemented, and therefore neither method works (in the case of *WIN32_Processor*, the methods are defined on the abstract class *CIM_LogicalDevice* and are inherited). The MOF description for the *Win32_SecurityDescriptorHelper* WMI class appears in Figure 13-2.

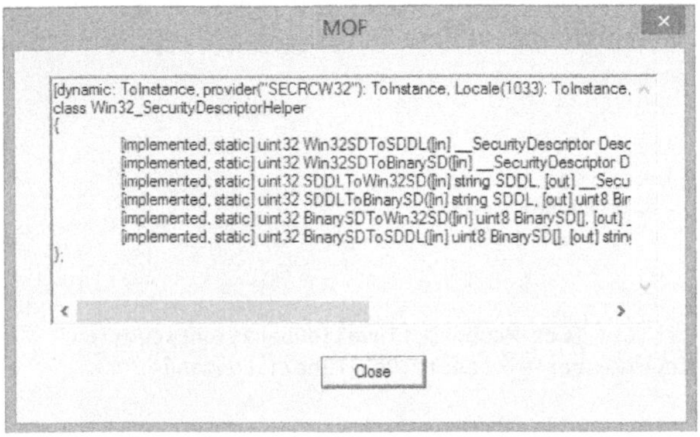

**FIGURE 13-2** The *Win32_SecurityDescriptorHelper* methods are implemented. They are also static.

Notice that each method is static. Static methods do not use an instance of the WMI class—the *Get-WmiObject* command does not work with *Win32_SecurityDescriptorHelper* because *Get-WmiObject* returns instances of the class. With this WMI class, there are no instances.

Perhaps the easiest way to work with the static WMI method is to use the *[wmiclass]* type accelerator. The *SDDLToBinarySD* method will translate a Security Descriptor Definition Language (SDDL) string into binary byte array security descriptor (binary SD) format. The best way to talk about this technique is to walk through an example of converting an SDDL string to binary SD format. First, you need to obtain an SDDL string—you can do that by using the *Get-Acl* cmdlet. The first thing to do is give the *Get-Acl* cmdlet (ACL stands for Access Control List) the path to a file on your computer. Then store the resulting object in the *$acl* variable, and examine the SDDL string associated with the file by querying the *SDDL* property. These two lines of code appear here:

```
$acl = Get-Acl C:\bootmgr
$acl.Sddl
```

The two commands and associated output appear in Figure 13-3.

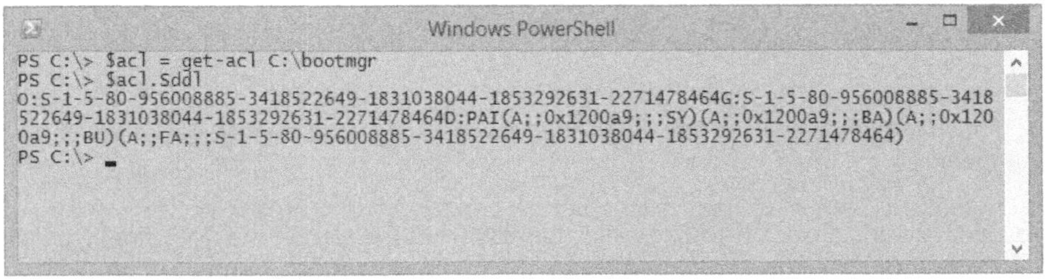

**FIGURE 13-3** Use the *Get-Acl* cmdlet to retrieve the ACL from a directory. Next, obtain the SDDL via the *sddl* property.

To convert the SDDL string to binary SD format, use the *[wmiclass]* type accelerator and call the method directly while supplying an SDDL string to the *SDDLToBinarySD* method. The syntax for the command appears here:

```
([wmiclass]"Win32_SecurityDescriptorHelper").SDDLToBinarySD($acl.Sddl)
```

One thing that is a bit confusing is that in Windows PowerShell, double colons are required to call a static method. For example, to obtain the sine of a 45 degree angle, use the *SIN* static method from the *system.math* class. This appears here:

```
[math]::sin(45)
```

But, here, in WMI, there appears to be no difference between calling a static method or calling an instance method.

All the methods return both the *returnvalue* property, which provides the status of the command, and the specific output for the converted security descriptor. To retrieve only the binary SD output, you can add that to the end of the method call. The syntax of this command appears here:

```
([wmiclass]"Win32_SecurityDescriptorHelper").SDDLToBinarySD($acl.Sddl).BinarySD
```

One of the cool things that you can do with the static methods from the *Win32_SecurityDescriptorHelper* class is convert an SDDL security descriptor into an instance of the *Win32_SecurityDescriptor* WMI class. The *Win32_SecurityDescriptor* WMI class is often used to provide security for various resources. For example, if you create a new share and want to assign security to the share, you will need to provide an instance of *Win32_SecurityDescriptor*. Using the *SDDLToWin32SD* method, you can use an SDDL string to get the *Win32_SecurityDescriptor* you need. To illustrate using the *SDDLToWin32SD* method, use the *Invoke-WmiMethod* cmdlet to perform the conversion. The following one-line command illustrates using the *Invoke-WmiMethod* cmdlet to call the *SDDLToWin32SD* method.

```
PS C:\> Invoke-WmiMethod -Class Win32_SecurityDescriptorHelper -Name SDDLToWin32SD
-ArgumentList $acl.Sddl
```

```
__GENUS          : 2
__CLASS          : __PARAMETERS
__SUPERCLASS     :
__DYNASTY        : __PARAMETERS
__RELPATH        :
__PROPERTY_COUNT : 2
__DERIVATION     : {}
__SERVER         :
__NAMESPACE      :
__PATH           :
Descriptor       : System.Management.ManagementBaseObject
ReturnValue      : 0
PSComputerName   :
```

The other WMI methods from this class behave in a similar fashion, and therefore will not be explored.

# Executing instance methods: step-by-step exercises

In this exercise, you will use the *terminate* instance method from the *WIN32_Process* WMI class. This provides practice calling WMI instance methods. In the next exercise, you will practice calling static class methods.

### Stopping several instances of a process using WMI

1.  Log on to your computer with a user account that does not have administrator rights.

2.  Open the Windows PowerShell console.

3.  Start five copies of Notepad. The command appears here:

    ```
    1..5 | % {notepad}
    ```

4.  Use the *Get-WmiObject* cmdlet to retrieve all instances of the notepad.exe process. The command appears here:

    ```
    gwmi win32_process -Filter "name = 'notepad.exe'"
    ```

5.  Now pipeline the resulting objects to the *Remove-WmiObject* cmdlet.

    ```
    gwmi win32_process -Filter "name = 'notepad.exe'" | Remove-WmiObject
    ```

6.  Start five instances of notepad. The command appears here:

    ```
    1..5 | % {notepad}
    ```

7.  Use the up arrow key to retrieve the *Get-WmiObject* command that retrieves all instances of Notepad.exe. The command appears here:

    ```
    gwmi win32_process -Filter "name = 'notepad.exe'"
    ```

8.  Store the returned WMI objects in a variable named *$process*. This command appears here:

    ```
    $process = gwmi win32_process -Filter "name = 'notepad.exe'"
    ```

9.  Call the *terminate* method from the *$process* variable. The command appears here:

    ```
    $process.terminate()
    ```

10. Start five copies of notepad back up. The command appears here:

    ```
    1..5 | % {notepad}
    ```

11. Use the up arrow key to retrieve the *Get-WmiObject* command that retrieves all instances of Notepad.exe. The command appears here:

    ```
    gwmi win32_process -Filter "name = 'notepad.exe'"
    ```

**12.** Call the *terminate* method from the above expression. Put parentheses around the expression, and use dotted notation to call the method. The command appears here:

```
(gwmi win32_process -Filter "name = 'notepad.exe'").terminate()
```

This concludes the exercise.

In the following exercise, you will use the static *create* method from the *Win32_Share* WMI class to create a new share.

## Executing static WMI methods

**1.** Open the Windows PowerShell console as a user that has admin rights on the local computer. To do this, you can right-click the Windows PowerShell console shortcut and select Run As Administrator from the menu.

**2.** Create a test folder off of the root named testshare. Here is the command using the *MD* alias for the *mkdir* function:

```
MD c:\testshare
```

**3.** Create the *Win32_Share* object and store it in a variable named *$share*. Use the *[wmiclass]* type accelerator. The code appears here:

```
$share = [wmiclass]"win32_share"
```

**4.** Call the static *create* method from the *Win32_Share* object stored in the *$share* variable. The arguments are *path, name, type, maximumallowed, description, password,* and *access*. However, you only need to supply the first three. *type* is 0, which is a disk drive share. The syntax of the command appears here:

```
$share.Create("C:\testshare","testshare",0)
```

**5.** Use the *Get-WmiObject* cmdlet and the *Win32_Share* class to verify that the share was properly created. The syntax of the command appears here:

```
gwmi win32_share
```

**6.** Now add a filter so that the *Get-WmiObject* cmdlet only returns the newly created share. The syntax appears here:

```
gwmi win32_share -Filter "name = 'testshare'"
```

**7.** Remove the newly created share by pipelining the results of the previous command to the *Remove-WmiObject* cmdlet. The syntax of the command appears here:

```
gwmi win32_share -Filter "name = 'testshare'" | Remove-WmiObject
```

8. Use the *Get-WmiObject* cmdlet and the *Win32_Share* WMI class to verify that the share was properly removed. The command appears here:

```
gwmi win32_share
```

This concludes the exercise.

# Chapter 13 quick reference

| To | Do this |
|---|---|
| Use the *terminate* method directly | Group the returning WMI object and use dotted notation to call the *terminate* method. |
| Use the *terminate* method from a variable containing the WMI object | Use dotted notation to call the *terminate* method. |
| Call a static method via the *Invoke-WMIMethod* cmdlet | Use the *-class* parameter to specify the WMI class name, and specify the name of the method via the *name* parameter. |
| Call a static WMI method without using the *Invoke-WMIMethod* cmdlet | Use the *[wmi]* type accelerator to retrieve the WMI class, store the resulting object in a variable, and use dotted notation to call the method. |
| Stop processes via WMI and not call the *terminate* method | Use the *Get-WMIObject* cmdlet to return the process objects and pipeline the results to the *Remove-WMIObject* cmdlet. |
| Find static WMI methods | Use the *[wmiclass]* type accelerator to create the WMI object and pipeline the resulting object to the *Get-Member* cmdlet. |
| Find the relative path to a particular WMI instance | Use the *Get-WMIObject* cmdlet to retrieve instances and choose the *__RELPATH* system property. |

# Using the CIM Cmdlets

**After completing this chapter, you will be able to:**

- Use the CIM cmdlets to explore WMI classes.
- Use CIM classes to obtain WMI data classes.
- Use the CIM cmdlets to create a remote session.

## Using the CIM cmdlets to explore WMI classes

In Microsoft Windows PowerShell 3.0, the Common Information Model (CIM) exposes a new application programming interface (API) for working with Windows Management Instrumentation (WMI) information. The CIM cmdlets support multiple ways of exploring WMI. They work well when working in an interactive fashion. For example, tab expansion expands the namespace when you use the CIM cmdlets, thereby permitting exploring namespaces in a simple fashion. These namespaces might not otherwise be very discoverable. You can even drill down into namespaces by using this technique of tab expansion. All CIM classes support tab expansion of the *namespace* parameter, as well as the *-class* parameter. But to explore WMI classes, you want to use the *Get-CimClass* cmdlet.

> **Note** The default WMI namespace on all operating systems after Windows NT 4.0 is Root/Cimv2. Therefore, all of the CIM cmdlets default to Root/Cimv2. The only time you need to change the default WMI namespace (via the *namespace* parameter) is when you need to use a WMI class from a nondefault WMI namespace.

## Using the *-classname* parameter

Using the *Get-CimClass* cmdlet, you can use wildcards for the *-classname* parameter to enable you to quickly identify potential WMI classes for perusal. You can also use wildcards for the *-qualifiername* parameter. In the example appearing here, the *Get-CimClass* cmdlet looks for WMI classes related to computers.

```
PS C:\> Get-CimClass -ClassName *computer*


    NameSpace: ROOT/CIMV2

CimClassName                          CimClassMethods        CimClassProperties
------------                          ---------------        ------------------
Win32_ComputerSystemEvent             {}                     {SECURITY_DESCRIPTOR, TIME_CR...
Win32_ComputerShutdownEvent           {}                     {SECURITY_DESCRIPTOR, TIME_CR...
CIM_ComputerSystem                    {}                     {Caption, Description, Instal...
CIM_UnitaryComputerSystem             {SetPowerState}        {Caption, Description, Instal...
Win32_ComputerSystem                  {SetPowerState, R...   {Caption, Description, Instal...
CIM_ComputerSystemResource            {}                     {GroupComponent, PartComponent}
CIM_ComputerSystemMappedIO            {}                     {GroupComponent, PartComponent}
CIM_ComputerSystemDMA                 {}                     {GroupComponent, PartComponent}
CIM_ComputerSystemIRQ                 {}                     {GroupComponent, PartComponent}
Win32_ComputerSystemProcessor         {}                     {GroupComponent, PartComponent}
CIM_ComputerSystemPackage             {}                     {Antecedent, Dependent}
Win32_ComputerSystemProduct           {}                     {Caption, Description, Identi...
Win32_NTLogEventComputer              {}                     {Computer, Record}
```

> **Note** If you try to use a wildcard for the *-classname* parameter of the *Get-CimInstance* cmdlet, an error returns because the parameter design does not permit wildcard characters.

# Finding WMI class methods

If you want to find WMI classes related to processes that contain a method that begins with the letters *term\**, you use a command similar to the one appearing here:

```
PS C:\> Get-CimClass -ClassName *process* -MethodName term*


    NameSpace: ROOT/cimv2

CimClassName        CimClassMethods        CimClassProperties
------------        ---------------        ------------------
Win32_Process       {Create, Terminat...   {Caption, Description, Instal...
```

To find all WMI classes related to processes that expose any methods, you would use the command appearing here:

```
PS C:\> Get-CimClass -ClassName *process* -MethodName *


    NameSpace: ROOT/cimv2

CimClassName        CimClassMethods        CimClassProperties
------------        ---------------        ------------------
Win32_Process       {Create, Terminat...   {Caption, Description, Instal...
CIM_Processor       {SetPowerState, R...   {Caption, Description, Instal...
Win32_Processor     {SetPowerState, R...   {Caption, Description, Instal...
```

To find any WMI class in the root/cimv2 WMI namespace that expose a method called *create*, use the command appearing here:

```
PS C:\> Get-CimClass -ClassName * -MethodName create


   NameSpace: ROOT/cimv2

CimClassName                CimClassMethods         CimClassProperties
------------                ---------------         ------------------
Win32_Process               {Create, Terminat...    {Caption, Description, Instal...
Win32_ScheduledJob          {Create, Delete}        {Caption, Description, Instal...
Win32_DfsNode               {Create}                {Caption, Description, Instal...
Win32_BaseService           {StartService, St...    {Caption, Description, Instal...
Win32_SystemDriver          {StartService, St...    {Caption, Description, Instal...
Win32_Service               {StartService, St...    {Caption, Description, Instal...
Win32_TerminalService       {StartService, St...    {Caption, Description, Instal...
Win32_Share                 {Create, SetShare...    {Caption, Description, Instal...
Win32_ClusterShare          {Create, SetShare...    {Caption, Description, Instal...
Win32_ShadowCopy            {Create, Revert}        {Caption, Description, Instal...
Win32_ShadowStorage         {Create}                {AllocatedSpace, DiffVolume, ...
```

## Filtering classes by qualifier

To find WMI classes that possess a particular WMI qualifier, use the *-QualifierName* parameter. For example, the following command finds WMI classes that relate to computers and have the *supportsupdate* WMI qualifier.

```
PS C:\> Get-CimClass -ClassName *computer* -QualifierName *update


   NameSpace: ROOT/cimv2

CimClassName                CimClassMethods         CimClassProperties
------------                ---------------         ------------------
Win32_ComputerSystem        {SetPowerState, R...    {Caption, Description, Instal...
```

The parameters can be combined to produce powerful searches that without using the CIM cmdlets would require rather complicated scripting. For example, the following command finds all WMI classes in the root/Cimv2 namespace that have the *singleton* qualifier and also expose a method.

```
PS C:\> Get-CimClass -ClassName * -QualifierName singleton -MethodName *


   NameSpace: ROOT/cimv2

CimClassName                CimClassMethods         CimClassProperties
------------                ---------------         ------------------
__SystemSecurity            {GetSD, GetSecuri...    {}
Win32_OperatingSystem       {Reboot, Shutdown...    {Caption, Description, Instal...
Win32_OfflineFilesCache     {Enable, RenameIt...    {Active, Enabled, Location}
```

One qualifier that is important to review is the *deprecated* qualifier. Deprecated WMI classes are not recommended for use because they are being phased out. Using the *Get-CimClass* cmdlet makes it easy to spot these WMI classes. This technique appears here:

```
PS C:\> Get-CimClass * -QualifierName deprecated


   NameSpace: ROOT/cimv2

CimClassName                        CimClassMethods      CimClassProperties
-----------                         ---------------      ------------------
Win32_PageFile                      {TakeOwnerShip, C... {Caption, Description, Instal...
Win32_DisplayConfiguration          {}                   {Caption, Description, Settin...
Win32_DisplayControllerConfigura... {}                   {Caption, Description, Settin...
Win32_VideoConfiguration            {}                   {Caption, Description, Settin...
Win32_AllocatedResource             {}                   {Antecedent, Dependent}
```

Using this technique, it is easy to find association classes. *Association classes* relate two different WMI classes. For example, the *Win32_DisplayConfiguration* WMI class relates displays and the associated configuration. The code that follows finds all of the WMI classes in the root/cimv2 WMI namespace that relate to sessions. In addition, it looks for the *association* qualifier. Luckily, you can use wildcards for the qualifier names; in keeping with this, the following code uses *assoc\** instead of the typed-out *association*.

```
PS C:\> Get-CimClass -ClassName *session* -QualifierName assoc*


   NameSpace: ROOT/cimv2

CimClassName                        CimClassMethods      CimClassProperties
-----------                         ---------------      ------------------
Win32_SubSession                    {}                   {Antecedent, Dependent}
Win32_SessionConnection             {}                   {Antecedent, Dependent}
Win32_LogonSessionMappedDisk        {}                   {Antecedent, Dependent}
Win32_SessionResource               {}                   {Antecedent, Dependent}
Win32_SessionProcess                {}                   {Antecedent, Dependent}
```

One qualifier you should definitely look for is the *dynamic* qualifier. This is because querying abstract WMI classes is unsupported. An abstract WMI class is basically a template class that is used by WMI when creating new WMI classes. Therefore, all *dynamic* WMI classes will derive from an abstract class. Therefore, when looking for WMI classes, you will want to ensure that at some point you run your list through the *dynamic* filter. In the code that follows, three WMI classes related to time are returned.

```
PS C:\> Get-CimClass -ClassName *time


   NameSpace: ROOT/cimv2
```

| CimClassName | CimClassMethods | CimClassProperties |
| --- | --- | --- |
| Win32_CurrentTime | {} | {Day, DayOfWeek, Hour, Millis... |
| Win32_LocalTime | {} | {Day, DayOfWeek, Hour, Millis... |
| Win32_UTCTime | {} | {Day, DayOfWeek, Hour, Millis... |

By adding the query for the qualifier, you identify the appropriate WMI classes. One class is abstract, and the other two are dynamic classes that could prove to be useful. In the following code, the *dynamic* qualifier is first used, and the *abstract* qualifier appears second.

PS C:\> **Get-CimClass** -ClassName *time -QualifierName dynamic


NameSpace: ROOT/cimv2

| CimClassName | CimClassMethods | CimClassProperties |
| --- | --- | --- |
| Win32_LocalTime | {} | {Day, DayOfWeek, Hour, Millis... |
| Win32_UTCTime | {} | {Day, DayOfWeek, Hour, Millis... |


PS C:\> **Get-CimClass** -ClassName *time -QualifierName abstract


NameSpace: ROOT/cimv2

| CimClassName | CimClassMethods | CimClassProperties |
| --- | --- | --- |
| Win32_CurrentTime | {} | {Day, DayOfWeek, Hour, Millis... |

# Retrieving WMI instances

To query for WMI data, use the *Get-CimInstance* cmdlet. The easiest way to use the *Get-CimInstance* cmdlet is to query for all properties and all instances of a particular WMI class on the local machine. This is extremely easy to do. The following command illustrates returning BIOS information from the local computer:

PS C:\> **Get-CimInstance** win32_bios


```
SMBIOSBIOSVersion : 090004
Manufacturer      : American Megatrends Inc.
Name              : BIOS Date: 03/19/09 22:51:32  Ver: 09.00.04
SerialNumber      : 4429-0046-2083-1237-7579-8937-43
Version           : VRTUAL - 3000919
```

The *Get-CimInstance* cmdlet returns the entire WMI object, but it honors the *.format.ps1xml files that Windows PowerShell uses to determine which properties are displayed by default for a particular WMI class. The command appearing here shows the properties available from the *Win32_Bios* WMI class:

```
PS C:\> $b = Get-CimInstance win32_bios
PS C:\> $b.CimClass.CimClassProperties | fw name -Column 3
```

```
Caption                 Description             InstallDate
Name                    Status                  BuildNumber
CodeSet                 IdentificationCode      LanguageEdition
Manufacturer            OtherTargetOS           SerialNumber
SoftwareElementID       SoftwareElementState    TargetOperatingSystem
Version                 PrimaryBIOS             BiosCharacteristics
BIOSVersion             CurrentLanguage         InstallableLanguages
ListOfLanguages         ReleaseDate             SMBIOSBIOSVersion
SMBIOSMajorVersion      SMBIOSMinorVersion      SMBIOSPresent
```

## Reducing returned properties and instances

To limit the amount of data returned from a remote connection, you can reduce the number of properties returned, as well as the number of instances. To reduce properties, use the *-property* parameter. To reduce the number of returned instances, use the *-filter* parameter. The command following uses *gcim*, which is an alias for the *Get-CimInstance* cmdlet. The command also abbreviates the *-classname* parameter and the *-filter* parameter. As shown here, the command only returns the name and the state of the *bits* service. The default output, however, shows all of the property names as well as the system properties. As shown here, however, only the two selected properties contain data.

```
PS C:\> gcim -clas win32_service -Property name, state -Fil "name = 'bits'"
```

```
Name                     : BITS
Status                   :
ExitCode                 :
DesktopInteract          :
ErrorControl             :
PathName                 :
ServiceType              :
StartMode                :
Caption                  :
Description              :
InstallDate              :
CreationClassName        :
Started                  :
SystemCreationClassName  :
SystemName               :
AcceptPause              :
AcceptStop               :
DisplayName              :
ServiceSpecificExitCode  :
StartName                :
State                    : Running
TagId                    :
CheckPoint               :
ProcessId                :
WaitHint                 :
```

```
PSComputerName            :
CimClass                  : root/cimv2:Win32_Service
CimInstanceProperties     : {Caption, Description, InstallDate, Name...}
CimSystemProperties       : Microsoft.Management.Infrastructure.CimSystemProperties
```

## Cleaning up output from the command

To produce cleaner output, send the selected data to the *Format-Table* cmdlet (you can use the *ft* alias for the *Format-Table* cmdlet to reduce typing).

```
PS C:\> gcim -clas win32_service -Property name, state -Fil "name = 'bits'" | ft name, state

name                              state
----                              -----
BITS                              Running
```

Make sure you choose properties you have already selected in the *-property* parameter, or else they will not display. In the command appearing here, the *status* property is selected in the *Format-Table* cmdlet. There is a *status* property on the *WIN32_Service* WMI class, but it was not chosen when the properties were selected.

```
PS C:\> gcim -clas win32_service -Property name, state -Fil "name = 'bits'" |
ft name, state, status

name                   state                   status
----                   -----                   ------
BITS                   Running
```

The *Get-CimInstance* cmdlet does not accept a wildcard parameter for property names (neither does the *Get-WmiObject* cmdlet, for that matter). One thing that can simplify some of your coding is to put your property selection into a variable. This permits you to use the same property names in both the *Get-CimInstance* cmdlet and the *Format-Table* cmdlet (or *Format-List* or *Select-Object*, or whatever you are using after you get your WMI data) without having to type things twice. This technique appears here:

```
PS C:\> $property = "name","state","startmode","startname"
PS C:\> gcim -clas win32_service -Pro $property -fil "name = 'bits'" | ft $property -A

name state   startmode startname
---- -----   --------- ---------
BITS Running Manual    LocalSystem
```

## Working with associations

In the old-fashioned VBScript days, working with association classes was extremely complicated. This is unfortunate, because WMI association classes are extremely powerful and useful. Earlier versions of Windows PowerShell simplified working with association classes, primarily because it simplified working with WMI data in general. However, figuring out how to utilize the Windows PowerShell advantage was still pretty much an advanced technique. Luckily, Windows PowerShell 3.0 has the CIM classes that introduce the *Get-CimAssociatedInstance* cmdlet.

The first thing to do when attempting to find a WMI association class is retrieve a CIM instance and store it in a variable. In the example that follows, instances of the *Win32_LogonSession* WMI class are retrieved and stored in the *$logon* variable. Next, the *Get-CimAssociatedInstance* cmdlet is used to retrieve instances associated with this class. To see what type of objects will return from the command, pipe the results to the *Get-Member* cmdlet. As shown here, two things are returned: the *Win32_UserAccount* class, and all processes that are related to the corresponding user account in the form of instances of the *WIN32_Process* class.

```
PS C:\> $logon = Get-CimInstance win32_logonsession
PS C:\> Get-CimAssociatedInstance $logon | Get-Member


   TypeName: Microsoft.Management.Infrastructure.CimInstance#root/cimv2/Win32_UserAccount

Name                        MemberType   Definition
----                        ----------   ----------
Clone                       Method       System.Object ICloneable.Clone()
Dispose                     Method       void Dispose(), void IDisposable.Dispose()
Equals                      Method       bool Equals(System.Object obj)
GetCimSessionComputerName   Method       string GetCimSessionComputerName()
GetCimSessionInstanceId     Method       guid GetCimSessionInstanceId()
GetHashCode                 Method       int GetHashCode()
GetObjectData               Method       void GetObjectData(System.Runtime.Serialization....
GetType                     Method       type GetType()
ToString                    Method       string ToString()
AccountType                 Property     uint32 AccountType {get;}
Caption                     Property     string Caption {get;}
Description                 Property     string Description {get;}
Disabled                    Property     bool Disabled {get;set;}
Domain                      Property     string Domain {get;}
FullName                    Property     string FullName {get;set;}
InstallDate                 Property     CimInstance#DateTime InstallDate {get;}
LocalAccount                Property     bool LocalAccount {get;set;}
Lockout                     Property     bool Lockout {get;set;}
Name                        Property     string Name {get;}
PasswordChangeable          Property     bool PasswordChangeable {get;set;}
PasswordExpires             Property     bool PasswordExpires {get;set;}
PasswordRequired            Property     bool PasswordRequired {get;set;}
PSComputerName              Property     string PSComputerName {get;}
SID                         Property     string SID {get;}
SIDType                     Property     byte SIDType {get;}
Status                      Property     string Status {get;}
PSStatus                    PropertySet  PSStatus {Status, Caption, PasswordExpires}
```

TypeName: Microsoft.Management.Infrastructure.CimInstance#root/cimv2/Win32_Process

| Name | MemberType | Definition |
| ---- | ---------- | ---------- |
| Handles | AliasProperty | Handles = Handlecount |
| ProcessName | AliasProperty | ProcessName = Name |
| VM | AliasProperty | VM = VirtualSize |
| WS | AliasProperty | WS = WorkingSetSize |
| Clone | Method | System.Object ICloneable.Clone() |
| Dispose | Method | void Dispose(), void IDisposable.Dispose() |
| Equals | Method | bool Equals(System.Object obj) |
| GetCimSessionComputerName | Method | string GetCimSessionComputerName() |
| GetCimSessionInstanceId | Method | guid GetCimSessionInstanceId() |
| GetHashCode | Method | int GetHashCode() |
| GetObjectData | Method | void GetObjectData(System.Runtime.Serializat... |
| GetType | Method | type GetType() |
| ToString | Method | string ToString() |
| Caption | Property | string Caption {get;} |
| CommandLine | Property | string CommandLine {get;} |
| CreationClassName | Property | string CreationClassName {get;} |
| CreationDate | Property | CimInstance#DateTime CreationDate {get;} |
| CSCreationClassName | Property | string CSCreationClassName {get;} |
| CSName | Property | string CSName {get;} |
| Description | Property | string Description {get;} |
| ExecutablePath | Property | string ExecutablePath {get;} |
| ExecutionState | Property | uint16 ExecutionState {get;} |
| Handle | Property | string Handle {get;} |
| HandleCount | Property | uint32 HandleCount {get;} |
| InstallDate | Property | CimInstance#DateTime InstallDate {get;} |
| KernelModeTime | Property | uint64 KernelModeTime {get;} |
| MaximumWorkingSetSize | Property | uint32 MaximumWorkingSetSize {get;} |
| MinimumWorkingSetSize | Property | uint32 MinimumWorkingSetSize {get;} |
| Name | Property | string Name {get;} |
| OSCreationClassName | Property | string OSCreationClassName {get;} |
| OSName | Property | string OSName {get;} |
| OtherOperationCount | Property | uint64 OtherOperationCount {get;} |
| OtherTransferCount | Property | uint64 OtherTransferCount {get;} |
| PageFaults | Property | uint32 PageFaults {get;} |
| PageFileUsage | Property | uint32 PageFileUsage {get;} |
| ParentProcessId | Property | uint32 ParentProcessId {get;} |
| PeakPageFileUsage | Property | uint32 PeakPageFileUsage {get;} |
| PeakVirtualSize | Property | uint64 PeakVirtualSize {get;} |
| PeakWorkingSetSize | Property | uint32 PeakWorkingSetSize {get;} |
| Priority | Property | uint32 Priority {get;} |
| PrivatePageCount | Property | uint64 PrivatePageCount {get;} |
| ProcessId | Property | uint32 ProcessId {get;} |
| PSComputerName | Property | string PSComputerName {get;} |
| QuotaNonPagedPoolUsage | Property | uint32 QuotaNonPagedPoolUsage {get;} |
| QuotaPagedPoolUsage | Property | uint32 QuotaPagedPoolUsage {get;} |
| QuotaPeakNonPagedPoolUsage | Property | uint32 QuotaPeakNonPagedPoolUsage {get;} |
| QuotaPeakPagedPoolUsage | Property | uint32 QuotaPeakPagedPoolUsage {get;} |
| ReadOperationCount | Property | uint64 ReadOperationCount {get;} |
| ReadTransferCount | Property | uint64 ReadTransferCount {get;} |
| SessionId | Property | uint32 SessionId {get;} |
| Status | Property | string Status {get;} |

```
TerminationDate          Property        CimInstance#DateTime TerminationDate {get;}
ThreadCount              Property        uint32 ThreadCount {get;}
UserModeTime             Property        uint64 UserModeTime {get;}
VirtualSize              Property        uint64 VirtualSize {get;}
WindowsVersion           Property        string WindowsVersion {get;}
WorkingSetSize           Property        uint64 WorkingSetSize {get;}
WriteOperationCount      Property        uint64 WriteOperationCount {get;}
WriteTransferCount       Property        uint64 WriteTransferCount {get;}
Path                     ScriptProperty  System.Object Path {get=$this.ExecutablePath;}
```

When the command runs without piping to the *Get-Member* object, the instance of the *Win32_UserAccount* WMI class is returned. The output shows the user name, account type, SID, domain, and caption of the user account. As shown in the output from *Get-Member*, a lot more information is available, but this is the default display. Following the user account information, the default process information displays the process ID, name, and a bit of performance information related to the processes associated with the user account.

```
PS C:\> $logon = Get-CimInstance win32_logonsession
PS C:\> Get-CimAssociatedInstance $logon

Name          Caption          AccountType      SID              Domain
----          -------          -----------      ---              ------
ed            IAMMRED\ed       512              S-1-5-21-14579... IAMMRED


ProcessId     : 2780
Name          : taskhostex.exe
HandleCount   : 215
WorkingSetSize : 8200192
VirtualSize   : 242356224


ProcessId     : 2804
Name          : rdpclip.exe
HandleCount   : 225
WorkingSetSize : 8175616
VirtualSize   : 89419776


ProcessId     : 2352
Name          : explorer.exe
HandleCount   : 1078
WorkingSetSize : 65847296
VirtualSize   : 386928640


ProcessId     : 984
Name          : powershell.exe
HandleCount   : 577
WorkingSetSize : 94527488
VirtualSize   : 690466816
```

```
ProcessId      : 296
Name           : conhost.exe
HandleCount    : 54
WorkingSetSize : 7204864
VirtualSize    : 62164992
```

If you do not want to retrieve both classes from the association query, you can specify the resulting class by name. To do this, use the *resultclassname* parameter from the *Get-CimAssociatedInstance* cmdlet. In the code that follows, only the *Win32_UserAccount* WMI class is returned from the query.

```
PS C:\> $logon = Get-CimInstance win32_logonsession
PS C:\> Get-CimAssociatedInstance $logon -ResultClassName win32_useraccount

Name      Caption        AccountType    SID               Domain
----      -------        -----------    ---               ------
ed        IAMMRED\ed     512            S-1-5-21-14579... IAMMRED
```

When working with the *Get-CimAssociatedInstance* cmdlet, the *inputobject* you supply must be a single instance. If you supply an object that contains more than one instance of the class, an error is raised. This error is shown following, where more than one disk is provided to the *inputobject* parameter:

```
PS C:\> $disk = Get-CimInstance win32_logicaldisk
PS C:\> Get-CimAssociatedInstance $disk
Get-CimAssociatedInstance : Cannot convert 'System.Object[]' to the type
'Microsoft.Management.Infrastructure.CimInstance' required by parameter 'InputObject'.
Specified method is not supported.
At line:1 char:27
+ Get-CimAssociatedInstance $disk
+                           ~~~~~
    + CategoryInfo          : InvalidArgument: (:) [Get-CimAssociatedInstance],
    ParameterBindingException
    + FullyQualifiedErrorId : CannotConvertArgument,Microsoft.Management.Infrastructure.
    CimCmdlets.GetCimAssociatedInstanceCommand
```

There are two ways to correct this particular error. The first, and the easiest, is to use *array indexing*. This technique places square brackets beside the variable holding the collection and retrieves a specific instance from the collection. This appears here, where the first disk returns associated instances:

```
PS C:\> $disk = Get-CimInstance win32_logicaldisk
PS C:\> Get-CimAssociatedInstance $disk[0]

Name      PrimaryOwner    Domain     TotalPhysical Model    Manufacturer
          Name                       Memory
----      ------------    ------     ------------- -----    ------------
W8C504    ed              iammred.net 2147012608   Virtual Ma... Microsoft ...
```

```
PS C:\> Get-CimAssociatedInstance $disk[1]
```

| Name | Hidden | Archive | Writeable | LastModified |
|------|--------|---------|-----------|--------------|
| ---- | ------ | ------- | --------- | ------------ |
| c:\  |        |         |           |              |

```
NumberOfBlocks   : 265613312
BootPartition    : False
Name             : Disk #0, Partition #1
PrimaryPartition : True
Size             : 135994015744
Index            : 1


Domain              : iammred.net
Manufacturer        : Microsoft Corporation
Model               : Virtual Machine
Name                : W8C504
PrimaryOwnerName    : ed
TotalPhysicalMemory : 2147012608
```

Using array indexing is fine when you find yourself with an object that contains an array. However, the results might be a bit inconsistent. A better approach is to ensure that you do not have an array in the first place. To do this, use the *-filter* parameter to reduce the number of instances of your WMI class that are returned. In the code appearing here, the filter returns the number of WMI instances to drive C.

```
PS C:\> $disk = Get-CimInstance win32_logicaldisk -Filter "name = 'c:'"
PS C:\> Get-CimAssociatedInstance $disk
```

| Name | Hidden | Archive | Writeable | LastModified |
|------|--------|---------|-----------|--------------|
| ---- | ------ | ------- | --------- | ------------ |
| c:\  |        |         |           |              |

```
NumberOfBlocks   : 265613312
BootPartition    : False
Name             : Disk #0, Partition #1
PrimaryPartition : True
Size             : 135994015744
Index            : 1


Domain              : iammred.net
Manufacturer        : Microsoft Corporation
Model               : Virtual Machine
Name                : W8C504
PrimaryOwnerName    : ed
TotalPhysicalMemory : 2147012608
```

An easy way to see the objects returned by the *Get-CimAssociatedInstance* cmdlet is to pipeline the returned objects to the *Get-Member* cmdlet and then select the *typename* property. Because more than one instance of the object may return and clutter the output, it is important to choose unique type names. This command appears here:

```
PS C:\> Get-CimAssociatedInstance $disk | gm | select typename -Unique
```

```
TypeName
--------
Microsoft.Management.Infrastructure.CimInstance#root/cimv2/Win32_Directory
Microsoft.Management.Infrastructure.CimInstance#root/cimv2/Win32_DiskPartition
Microsoft.Management.Infrastructure.CimInstance#root/cimv2/Win32_ComputerSystem
```

Armed with this information, it is easy to explore the returned associations. This technique appears here:

```
PS C:\> Get-CimAssociatedInstance $disk -ResultClassName win32_directory
```

| Name | Hidden | Archive | Writeable | LastModified |
|------|--------|---------|-----------|--------------|
| c:\ |  |  |  |  |

```
PS C:\> Get-CimAssociatedInstance $disk -ResultClassName win32_diskpartition
```

| Name | NumberOfBlocks | BootPartition | Primary Partition | Size | Index |
|------|---------------|---------------|-------------------|------|-------|
| Disk #0, Part... | 265613312 | False | True | 135994015744 | 1 |

```
PS C:\> Get-CimAssociatedInstance $disk -ResultClassName win32_Computersystem
```

| Name | PrimaryOwner Name | Domain | TotalPhysical Memory | Model | Manufacturer |
|------|-------------------|--------|----------------------|-------|--------------|
| W8C504 | ed | iammred.net | 2147012608 | Virtual Ma... | Microsoft ... |

Keep in mind that the entire WMI class is returned from the previous command, and is therefore ripe for further exploration by IT professionals who are interested in the disk subsystems of their computers. The easy way to do this exploring is to store the results into a variable, and then walk through the data. Once you have what interests you, you may decide to display a nicely organized table. This appears here:

```
PS C:\> $dp = Get-CimAssociatedInstance $disk -ResultClassName win32_diskpartition
PS C:\> $dp | FT deviceID, BlockSize, NumberOfBLocks, Size, StartingOffSet -AutoSize
deviceID              BlockSize NumberOfBLocks      Size StartingOffSet
--------              --------- --------------      ---- --------------
Disk #0, Partition #1       512                135994015744      368050176
```

# Retrieving WMI instances: step-by-step exercises

In these exercises, you will practice using the CIM cmdlets to find and to retrieve WMI instances. The first example uses the CIM cmdlets to explore WMI classes related to video. In the second exercise, you will examine association WMI classes.

## Exploring WMI video classes

1. Log on to your computer with a user account that does not have administrator rights.

2. Open the Windows PowerShell console.

3. Use the *Get-CimClass* cmdlet to identify WMI classes related to video. The command and associated output appear here:

```
PS C:\> Get-CimClass *video*


   NameSpace: ROOT/cimv2

CimClassName                        CimClassMethods        CimClassProperties
------------                        ---------------        ------------------
CIM_VideoBIOSElement                {}                     {Caption, Description, Instal...
CIM_VideoController                 {SetPowerState, R...   {Caption, Description, Instal...
CIM_PCVideoController               {SetPowerState, R...   {Caption, Description, Instal...
Win32_VideoController               {SetPowerState, R...   {Caption, Description, Instal...
CIM_VideoBIOSFeature                {}                     {Caption, Description, Instal...
CIM_VideoControllerResolution       {}                     {Caption, Description, Settin...
Win32_VideoConfiguration            {}                     {Caption, Description, Settin...
CIM_VideoSetting                    {}                     {Element, Setting}
Win32_VideoSettings                 {}                     {Element, Setting}
CIM_VideoBIOSFeatureVideoBIOSEle... {}                     {GroupComponent, PartComponent}
```

4. Filter the output to only return dynamic WMI classes related to video. The command and associated output appear here:

```
PS C:\> Get-CimClass *video* -QualifierName dynamic


   NameSpace: ROOT/cimv2

CimClassName                     CimClassMethods        CimClassProperties
------------                     ---------------        ------------------
Win32_VideoController            {SetPowerState, R...   {Caption, Description, Instal...
CIM_VideoControllerResolution    {}                     {Caption, Description, Settin...
Win32_VideoSettings              {}                     {Element, Setting}
```

5. Display the *cimclassname* and the *cimclassqualifiers* properties of each found WMI class. To do this, use the *Format-Table* cmdlet. The command and associated output appear here:

```
PS C:\> Get-CimClass *video* -QualifierName dynamic | ft cimclassname, cimclassqualifiers

CimClassName                     CimClassQualifiers
------------                     ------------------
Win32_VideoController            {Locale, UUID, dynamic, provider}
CIM_VideoControllerResolution    {Locale, UUID, dynamic, provider}
Win32_VideoSettings              {Association, Locale, UUID, dynamic...}
```

6. Change the *$FormatEnumerationLimit* value from the original value of 4 to 8 to permit view-
   ing of the truncated output. Remember that you can use tab expansion to keep from typing
   the entire variable name. The command appears here:

   ```
   $FormatEnumerationLimit = 8
   ```

7. Now use the up arrow key to retrieve the previous *Get-CimClass* command. Add the *autosize*
   command to the table. The command and associated output appear here:

   ```
   PS C:\> Get-CimClass *video* -QualifierName dynamic | ft cimclassname, cimclassqualifiers
   -autosize

   CimClassName                    CimClassQualifiers
   ------------                    ------------------
   Win32_VideoController           {Locale, UUID, dynamic, provider}
   CIM_VideoControllerResolution   {Locale, UUID, dynamic, provider}
   Win32_VideoSettings             {Association, Locale, UUID, dynamic, provider}
   ```

8. Query each of the three WMI classes. To do this, pipeline the result of the *Get-CimClass* command to the *ForEach-Object* command. Inside the script block, call *Get-CimInstance* and pass
   the *cimclassname* property. The command appears here:

   ```
   Get-CimClass *video* -QualifierName dynamic | % {Get-CimInstance $_.cimclassname}
   ```

   This concludes the exercise. Leave your Windows PowerShell console for the next exercise.

In the next exercise, you will create and receive associated WMI classes.

## Retrieving associated WMI classes

1. Open the Windows PowerShell console as a non-elevated user.

2. Use the *Get-CimInstance* cmdlet to retrieve the *Win32_VideoController* WMI class. The command appears following. Store the returned WMI object in the *$v* variable.

   ```
   $v = gcim Win32_VideoController
   ```

3. Use the *Get-CimAssociatedInstance* cmdlet and supply *$v* to the *inputobject* parameter. The
   command appears here:

   ```
   Get-CimAssociatedInstance -InputObject $v
   ```

4. Use the up arrow key to retrieve the previous command. Pipeline the returned WMI objects to
   the *Get-Member* cmdlet. Pipeline the results from the *Get-Member* cmdlet to the *Select-Object*
   cmdlet and use the *-unique* switched parameter to limit the amount of information returned.
   The command appears here:

   ```
   Get-CimAssociatedInstance -InputObject $v | Get-Member | select typename -Unique
   ```

5. Use the up arrow key to retrieve the previous command and change it so that it only returns instances of *Win32_PNPEntity* WMI classes. The command appears here:

```
Get-CimAssociatedInstance -InputObject $v -ResultClassName win32_PNPEntity
```

6. Display the complete information from each of the associated classes. To do this, pipeline the result from the *Get-CimAssociatedInstance* cmdlet to a *ForEach-Object* cmdlet, and inside the loop, pipeline the current object on the pipeline to the *Format-List* cmdlet. The command appears here:

```
Get-CimAssociatedInstance -InputObject $v | ForEach-Object {$input | Format-List*}
```

This concludes the exercise.

# Chapter 14 quick reference

| To | Do this |
|---|---|
| Find WMI classes related to disks | Use the *Get-CimClass* cmdlet and use a wildcard pattern such as *disk*. |
| Find WMI classes that have a method named *create* | Use the *Get-CimClass* cmdlet and a wildcard for the -*classname* parameter. Use the -*methodname* parameter to specify that you want classes that have the *create* method. |
| Find dynamic WMI classes | Use the *Get-CimClass* cmdlet and specify that you want the qualifier named *dynamic*. |
| Reduce the number of instances returned by the *Get-CimInstance* cmdlet | Use the -*filter* parameter and supply a filter that reduces the instances. |
| Reduce the number of properties returned by the *Get-CimInstance* cmdlet | Use the -*property* parameter and enumerate the required properties to return. |
| Find the types of WMI classes returned by the *Get-CimAssociatedInstance* cmdlet | Pipeline the resulting objects to the *Get-Member* cmdlet and select the *typename* property. |
| Only return a particular associated WMI class from the *Get-CimAssociatedInstance* cmdlet | Use the *resultclassname* parameter and specify the name of one of the returned objects. |

# Working with Active Directory

**After completing this chapter, you will be able to:**

- Make a connection to Active Directory.

- Understand the use of ADSI providers.

- Understand how to work with Active Directory namespaces.

- Create organizational units in Active Directory.

- Create users in Active Directory.

- Create groups in Active Directory.

- Modify both users and groups in Active Directory.

## Creating objects in Active Directory

Network management in the Microsoft Windows world begins and ends with Active Directory. This chapter will cover the user life cycle from a scripting and Active Directory perspective. You will learn how to create organizational units (OUs), users, groups, and computer accounts. The chapter will then describe how to modify the users and groups, and finally how to delete the user account. Along the way, you will pick up some more Windows PowerShell techniques.

The most fundamental object in Active Directory is the OU. One of the most frustrating problems for new network administrators is that by default, when Active Directory is installed, all users are put in the *users* container, and all computers are put in the *computers* container—and of course you cannot apply group policy to a container.

### Creating an OU

The process of creating an OU in Active Directory provides the basis for creating other objects in Active Directory because the technique is basically the same. The key to effectively using PowerShell to create objects in Active Directory is using the Active Directory Service Interfaces (ADSI) accelerator.

To create an object by using ADSI, perform the following steps:

1. Use the *[ADSI]* accelerator.

2. Use the appropriate ADSI provider.

3. Specify the path to the appropriate object in Active Directory.

4. Use the *SetInfo()* method to write the changes.

The CreateOU.ps1 script shown following illustrates each of the steps required to create an object by using ADSI. The variable *$strClass* is used to hold the class of object to create in Active Directory. For this script, you will be creating an OU. You could just as easily create a user or a computer—as you will see shortly. You use the variable *$strOUName* to hold the name of the OU you are going to create. For the CreateOU.ps1 script, you are going to create an OU called MyTestOU. Because you will pass this variable directly to the *Create* method, it is important that you use the distinguished-name form, shown here:

```
$strOUName="ou=MyTestOU"
```

The attribute that is used with the *Create* method to create an object in Active Directory is called the *relative distinguished name (RDN)*. Standard attribute types are expected by ADSI—such as *ou* for "organizational unit." The next line of code in the CreateOU.ps1 script makes the actual connection into Active Directory. To do this, it uses the *[ADSI]* accelerator. The *[ADSI]* accelerator wants to be given the exact path to your connection point in Active Directory (or some other directory, as you will see shortly) and the name of the ADSI provider. The target of the ADSI operation is called the ADsPath.

In the CreateOU.ps1 script, you are connecting to the root of the NwTraders.msft domain, and you are using the LDAP provider. The other providers you can use with ADSI are shown in Table 15-1. After you make your connection into Active Directory, you hold the *system.DirectoryServices.DirectoryEntry* object in the *$objADSI* variable.

Armed with the connection into Active Directory, you can now use the *create* method to create your new object. The *system.DirectoryServices.DirectoryEntry* object that is returned is held in the *$objOU* variable. You use this object on the last line of the script to call the *SetInfo()* method to write the new object into the Active Directory database. The entire CreateOU.ps1 script is shown here:

**CreateOU.ps1**

```
$strCLass = "organizationalUnit"
$StrOUName = "ou=MyTestOU"
$objADSI = [ADSI]"LDAP://dc=nwtraders,dc=msft"
$objOU = $objADSI.create($strCLass, $StrOUName)
$objOU.setInfo()
```

# ADSI providers

Table 15-1 lists four providers available to users of ADSI. Connecting to a Microsoft Windows NT 4 system requires using the special *WinNT* provider. During Active Directory migrations, consultants often write a script that copies users from a Windows NT 4 domain to a Microsoft Windows Server 2003 Active Directory OU or domain. In some situations (such as with customized naming schemes), writing a script is easier than using the Active Directory Migration Tool (ADMT).

**TABLE 15-1** ADSI-supported providers

| Provider | Purpose |
| --- | --- |
| WinNT | To communicate with Windows NT 4.0 primary domain controllers (PDCs) and backup domain controllers (BDCs), and with local account databases for Windows 2000 and newer workstations and servers |
| LDAP | To communicate with LDAP servers, including Exchange 5.x directories and Windows 2000 Server or Windows Server 2003 Active Directory |
| NDS | To communicate with Novell Directory Services servers |
| NWCOMPAT | To communicate with Novell NetWare 3.x servers |

The first time I tried using ADSI to connect to a machine running Windows NT, I had a very frustrating experience because of the way the provider was implemented. Type the *WinNT* provider name *exactly* as shown in Table 15-1. It cannot be typed using all lowercase letters or all uppercase letters. All other provider names must be all uppercase letters, but the *WinNT* name is Pascal cased—that is, it is partially uppercase and partially lowercase. Remembering this will save a lot of grief later. In addition, you don't get an error message telling you that your provider name is spelled or capitalized incorrectly—rather, the bind operation simply fails to connect.

> **Tip** The ADSI provider names are case sensitive. *LDAP* is all caps; *WinNT* is Pascal-cased. Keep this in mind to save a lot of time in troubleshooting.

After the ADSI provider is specified, you need to identify the path to the directory target. A little knowledge of Active Directory comes in handy here, because of the way the hierarchical naming space is structured. When connecting to an LDAP service provider, you must specify where in the LDAP database hierarchy to make the connection, because the hierarchy is a structure of the database itself—not the protocol or the provider. For instance, in the CreateOU.ps1 script, you create an OU that resides off the root of the domain, which is called MyTestOU. This can get confusing, until you realize that the MyTestOU OU is contained in a domain that is called NWTRADERS.MSFT. It is vital, therefore, that you understand the hierarchy with which you are working. One tool you can use to make sure you understand the hierarchy of your domain is ADSI Edit.

ADSI Edit is included with the feature called *AD DS and AD LDS Tools*. To install these tools on Windows 8 Server, use the *Add-WindowsFeature* cmdlet from the *ServerManager* module. To determine installation status of the AD DS tools, use the *Get-WindowsFeature* cmdlet, as illustrated here:

```
Get-WindowsFeature rsat-ad-tools
```

To determine everything that comes with AD DS and AD LDS Tools, pipe the result of the previous command to the *Format-List* cmdlet. This technique, along with the associated output from the command, appears here:

```
PS C:\> Get-WindowsFeature rsat-ad-tools | Format-List *


Name                        : RSAT-AD-Tools
DisplayName                 : AD DS and AD LDS Tools
Description                 : <a href="features.chm::/html/529acbe5-8749-4fb4-9a2a-300
                              6e9250329.htm">Active Directory Domain Services (AD DS)
                              and Active Directory Lightweight Directory Services (AD
                              LDS) Tools</a> includes snap-ins and command-line tools
                              for remotely managing AD DS and AD LDS.
Installed                   : False
InstallState                : Available
FeatureType                 : Feature
Path                        : Remote Server Administration Tools\Role Administration
                              Tools\AD DS and AD LDS Tools
Depth                       : 3
DependsOn                   : {}
Parent                      : RSAT-Role-Tools
ServerComponentDescriptor   : ServerComponent_RSAT_AD_Tools
SubFeatures                 : {RSAT-AD-PowerShell, RSAT-ADDS, RSAT-ADLDS}
SystemService               : {}
Notification                : {}
BestPracticesModelId        :
EventQuery                  :
PostConfigurationNeeded      : False
AdditionalInfo              : {MajorVersion, MinorVersion, NumericId, InstallName}
```

To install the tools, pipeline the results from the *Get-WindowsFeature* cmdlet to *Add-WindowsFeature*. This is as easy as using the up arrow key to retrieve the previous command that displayed the components of the AD DS tools and exchanging *Format-List* for *Add-WindowsFeature*. If automatic updates are not enabled, a warning message is displayed. The command and associated warning appear here:

```
PS C:\> Get-WindowsFeature rsat-ad-tools | Add-WindowsFeature

Success Restart Needed Exit Code      Feature Result
------- -------------- ---------      --------------
True    No             Success        {Remote Server Administration Tools, Activ...
WARNING: Windows automatic updating is not enabled. To ensure that your
newly-installed role or feature is automatically updated, turn on Windows Update.
```

After installing the tools (the output from the *Add-WindowsFeature* cmdlet states that no reboot is needed following this task), open a blank Microsoft Management Console (MMC) and add the ADSI Edit snap-in.

> **Note** Because I already have Windows PowerShell open due to adding Active Directory tools, I launch the MMC by typing **MMC** at the Windows PowerShell prompt. I also add additional Active Directory tools, such as Active Directory Users and Computers, Active Directory Domains and Trusts, and Active Directory Sites and Services. Save this custom MMC to your profile for quick ease of reuse.

After you install the snap-in, right-click the ADSI Edit icon, select Connect To, and specify your domain, as illustrated in Figure 15-1.

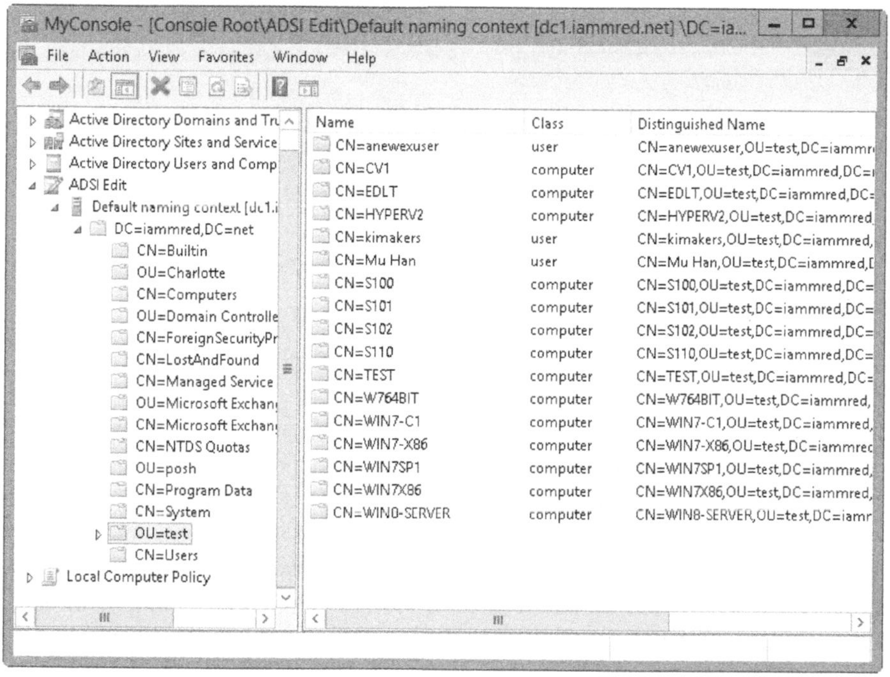

**FIGURE 15-1** Exploring the hierarchy of a forest to ensure the correct path for ADSI.

## LDAP names

When specifying the OU and the domain name, you have to use the LDAP naming convention, in which the namespace is described as a series of naming parts called RDNs (mentioned previously). The RDN will always be a name part that assigns a value by using the equal sign. When you put together all the RDNs, as well as the RDNs of each of the ancestors all the way back to the root, you end up with a single globally unique distinguished name.

The RDNs are usually made up of an attribute type, an equal sign, and a string value. Table 15-2 lists some of the attribute types you will see when working with Active Directory. An example of a distinguished name is shown in Figure 15-2.

**TABLE 15-2** Common relative distinguished name attribute types

| Attribute | Description |
|-----------|-------------|
| DC | Domain component |
| CN | Common name |
| OU | Organizational unit |
| O | Organization name |
| Street | Street address |
| C | Country name |
| UID | User ID |

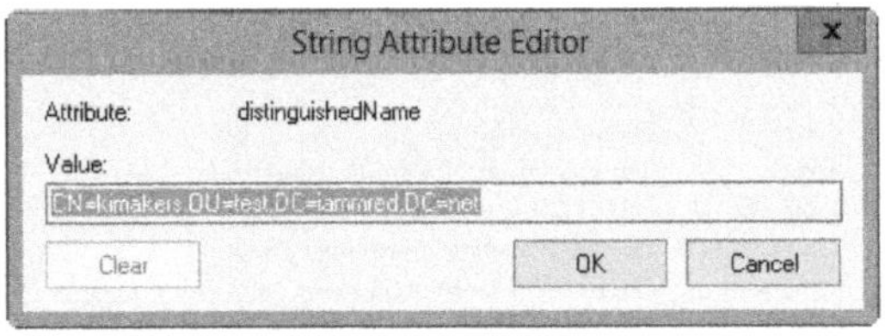

**FIGURE 15-2** Using the String Attribute Editor in ADSI Edit to quickly verify the distinguished name of a potential target for ADSI scripting.

## Binding

Whenever you want to do anything with ADSI, you must connect to an object in Active Directory—a process also known as *binding*. Think of binding as being like tying a rope around an object to enable you to work with it. Before you can do any work with an object in Active Directory, you must supply binding information. The *binding string* enables you to use various ADSI elements, including methods and properties. The target of the proposed action is specified as a computer, a domain controller, a user, or another element that resides within the directory structure. A binding string consists of four parts. These parts are illustrated in Table 15-3, which shows a binding string from a sample script.

**TABLE 15-3** Sample binding string

| Accelerator | Variable | Provider | ADsPath |
|-------------|----------|----------|---------|
| *[ADSI]* | *$objDomain* | *LDAP://* | *OU=hr, dc=a, dc=com* |

> **Note** Avoid a mistake I made early on: make sure that when you finish connecting and creating, you actually commit your changes to Active Directory. Changes to Active Directory are transactional in nature, so your change will roll back if you don't commit it. Committing the change requires you to use the *SetInfo()* method, as illustrated in the following line from the CreateOU.ps1 script:
>
> ```
> $objOU.SetInfo()
> ```
>
> Also keep in mind when calling a method such as *SetInfo()* that you must append empty parentheses to the method call.

## Working with errors

1. Open the Windows PowerShell ISE or some other Windows PowerShell script editor.

2. On the first line of your script, type a line that will generate an error by trying to create an object called *test*. Use the variable *$a* to hold this object. The code to do this is shown here:

   ```
   $a = New-Object test #creates an error
   ```

3. Print out the value of *$error.count*. The *count* property should contain a single error when the script is run. This line of code is shown here:

   ```
   $error.count
   ```

4. Save your script as *<yourname>*WorkWithErrors.ps1. Run your script; you should see it print out the number 1 to let you know there is an error on the *Error* object.

5. The most recent error will be contained on the variable *error[0]*. Use this to return the *CategoryInfo* property the error. This code is shown here:

   ```
   $error[0].CategoryInfo
   ```

6. Print out the details of the most recent error. This code to do this is shown here:

   ```
   $error[0].ErrorDetails
   ```

7. Print out the exception information. To do this, print out the value of the *Exception* property of the *$error* variable. This is shown here:

   ```
   $error[0].Exception
   ```

8. Print out the fully qualified error ID information. This is contained in the *FullyQualifiedErrorId* property of the *$error* variable. The code to do this is shown here:

   ```
   $error[0].FullyQualifiedErrorId
   ```

9. Print out the invocation information about the error. To do this, use the *InvocationInfo* property of the *$error* variable. The code to do this is shown here:

```
$error[0].InvocationInfo
```

10. The last property to query from *$error* is the *TargetObject* property. This is shown here:

```
$error[0].TargetObject
```

11. Save and run your script. Notice that you will not obtain information from all the properties.

12. The *$error* variable contains information about all errors that occur during the particular Windows PowerShell session, so it is quite likely to contain more than a single error. To introduce an additional error into your script, try to create a new object called *testB*. Assign the object that comes back to the variable *$b*. This code is shown here:

```
$b = New-Object testB
```

13. Because you now have more than a single error on the *Error* object, you need to walk through the collection of errors. To do this, you can use the *for* statement. Use a variable called *$i* as the counter variable and proceed until you reach the value of *$error.count*. Make sure you enclose the statement in parentheses and increment the value of *$i* at the end of the statement. The first line of this code is shown here:

```
for ($i = 0 ; $error.count ; $i++)
```

14. Now change each of the *error[0]* statements that print out the various properties of the *Error* object to use the counter variable *$i*. Because this will be the code block for the *for* statement, place an opening curly bracket at the beginning of the first statement and a closing one at the end of the last statement. The revised code block is shown here:

```
{$error[$i].CategoryInfo
    $error[$i].ErrorDetails
    $error[$i].Exception
    $error[$i].FullyQualifiedErrorId
    $error[$i].InvocationInfo
    $error[$i].TargetObject}
```

15. Save and run your script. You will see output similar to that shown here:

```
New-Object : Cannot find type [test]: make sure the assembly containing this
  type is loaded.
At D:\BookDocs\WindowsPowerShell\scripts\ch15\WorkWithErrors.PS1:14 char:16
 + $a = New-Object  <<<< test #creates an error
New-Object : Cannot find type [testB]: make sure the assembly containing this
  type is loaded.
At D:\BookDocs\WindowsPowerShell\scripts\ch15\WorkWithErrors.PS1:15 char:16
 + $b = New-Object  <<<< testB #creates another error

Category   : InvalidType
Activity   : New-Object
Reason     : PSArgumentException
```

16. The first error shown is a result of the Windows PowerShell command interpreter. The last error shown—with the category, activity, and reason—is a result of your error handling. To remove the first run-time error, use the *$erroractionpreference* variable and assign a value of *SilentlyContinue* to it. This code is shown here:

```
$erroractionpreference = "SilentlyContinue"
```

17. Save and run your script. Notice that the run-time error disappears from the top of your screen.

18. To find out how many errors are on the *Error* object, you can print out the value of *$error.count*. However, just having a single number at the top of the screen would be a little confusing. To take care of that, add a descriptive string, such as *"There are currently " + $error.count + "errors"*. The code to do this is shown here:

```
"There are currently " + $error.count + "errors"
```

19. Save and run your script. Notice that the string is printed out at the top of your script, as shown here:

```
There are currently 2 errors
```

20. In your Windows PowerShell window, use the *$error.clear()* method to clear the errors from the *Error* object because it continues to count errors until a new Windows PowerShell window is opened. This command is shown here:

```
$Error.clear()
```

21. Now comment out the line that creates the *testB* object. This revised line of code is shown here:

```
#$b = New-Object testB
```

22. Now save and run your script. Notice that the string at the top of your Windows PowerShell window looks a little strange because of the grammatical error. This is shown here:

```
There is currently 1 errors
```

23. To fix this problem, you need to add some logic to detect if there is one error or more than one error. To do this, you will use an *if...else* statement. The first line will evaluate whether *$error.count* is equal to 1. If it is, then you will print out *There is currently 1 error*. This code is shown here:

```
if ($error.count -eq 1)
    {"There is currently 1 error"}
```

**24.** You can simply use an *else* clause and add curly brackets around your previous error statement. This revised code is shown here:

```
else
    {"There are currently " + $error.count + "errors"}
```

**25.** Save and run the script. It should correctly detect that there is only one error.

**26.** Now remove the comment from the beginning of the line of code that creates the *testB* object and run the script. It should detect two errors.

This concludes the procedure.

## Adding error handling

**1.** Use the CreateOU.ps1 script (from earlier in this chapter) and save it as *<yourname>*CreateOUwithErrorHandler.ps1.

**2.** On the first line of the script, use the *$erroractionpreference* variable to assign the *SilentlyContinue* parameter. This will tell the script to suppress error messages and continue running the script if possible. This line of code is shown here:

```
$erroractionpreference = "SilentlyContinue"
```

**3.** To ensure there are no current errors on the *Error* object, use the *clear* method. To do this, use the *$error* variable. This line of code is shown here:

```
$error.clear()
```

**4.** At the end of the script, use an *if* statement to evaluate the error count. If an error has occurred, then the count will not be equal to 0. This line of code is shown here:

```
if ($error.count -ne 0)
```

**5.** If the condition occurs, the code block to run should return a message stating that an error has occurred. It should also print out the *categoryInfo* and *invocationinfo* properties from the current *$error* variable. The code to do this is shown here:

```
{"An error occurred during the operation. Details follow:"
    $error[0].categoryInfo
    $error[0].invocationinfo
    $error[0].tostring()}
```

**6.** Save and run your script. You should see an error generated (due to a duplicate attempt to create MyTestOU).

**7.** Change the OU name to MyTestOU1 and run the script. You should not see an error generated. The revised line of code is shown here:

```
$StrOUName = "ou=MyTestOU1"
```

This concludes the procedure. If you do not get the results you were expecting, compare your script with the CreateOUWithErrorHandler.ps1 script.

---

## Quick check

**Q.** What is the process of connecting to Active Directory called?

**A.** The process of connecting to Active Directory is called binding.

**Q.** When specifying the target of an ADSI operation, what is the target called?

**A.** The target of the ADSI operation is called the ADsPath.

**Q.** An LDAP name is made up of several parts. What do you call each part separated by a comma?

**A.** An LDAP name is made up of multiple parts that are called relative distinguished names (RDNs).

---

# Creating users

One fundamental technique you can use with ADSI is creating users. Although using the graphical user interface (GUI) to create a single user is easy, using the GUI to create a dozen or more users would certainly not be. In addition, as you'll see, because there is a lot of similarity among ADSI scripts, deleting a dozen or more users is just as simple as creating them. And because you can use the same input text file for all the scripts, ADSI makes creating temporary accounts for use in a lab or school a real snap.

To create users, do the following:

1. Use the appropriate provider for your network.

2. Connect to the container for your users.

3. Specify the domain.

4. Specify the *User* class of the object.

5. Bind to Active Directory.

6. Use the *Create* method to create the user.

7. Use the *Put* method to at least specify the *sAMAccountName* attribute.

8. Use *SetInfo()* to commit the user to Active Directory.

The CreateUser.ps1 script, which follows, is very similar to the CreateOU.ps1 script. In fact, CreateUser.ps1 was created from CreateOU.ps1, so a detailed analysis of the script is unnecessary. The only difference is that *$strClass* is equal to the *User* class instead of an *organizationalUnit* class.

> **Tip** These scripts use a Windows PowerShell trick. When using VBScript to create a user or a group, you must supply a value for the *sAMAccountName* attribute. When using Windows PowerShell on Windows 2000, this is also the case. With Windows PowerShell on Windows Server 2003 (or later), however, the *sAMAccountName* attribute will be automatically created for you. In the CreateUser.ps1 script, I have included the *$objUser.Put* command, which would be required for Windows 2000, but it is not required for Windows Server 2003 (or later). Keep in mind that the *sAMAccountName* property, when auto-generated, is not very user friendly. Here is an example of such an autogenerated name: $441000-1A0UVA0MRB0T. Any legacy application requiring the *sAMAccountName* value would therefore require users to type a value that is difficult to use at best.

**CreateUser.ps1**

```
$strCLass = "User"
$StrName = "CN=MyNewUser"
$objADSI = [ADSI]"LDAP://ou=myTestOU,dc=nwtraders,dc=msft"
$objUser = $objADSI.create($strCLass, $StrName)
$objUser.Put("sAMAccountName", "MyNewUser")
$objUser.setInfo()
```

## Quick check

**Q.** To create a user, which class must be specified?

**A.** You need to specify the *User* class to create a user.

**Q.** What is the *Put* method used for?

**A.** The *Put* method is used to write additional property data to the object that it is bound to.

### Creating groups

1. Open the CreateUser.ps1 script in Notepad and save it as *<yourname>*CreateGroup.ps1.

2. Declare a variable called *$intGroupType*. This variable will be used to control the type of group to create. Assign the number 2 to the variable. When used as the group type, a type 2 group will be a distribution group. This line of code is shown here:

   ```
   $intGroupType = 2
   ```

3. Change the value of *$strClass* from *User* to *Group*. This variable will be used to control the type of object that gets created in Active Directory. This is shown here:

```
$strGroup = "Group"
```

4. Change the name of the *$objUser* variable to *$objGroup* (it's less confusing that way). This will need to be done in two places, as shown here:

```
$objGroup = $objADSI.create($strCLass, $StrName)
$objGroup.setInfo()
```

5. Above the *$objGroup.setInfo()* line, use the *Put* method to create a distribution group. The distribution group has a group type of 2, and you can use the value held in the *$intGroupType* variable. This line of code is shown here:

```
$ObjGroup.put("GroupType",$intGroupType)
```

6. Save and run the script. It should create a group called MyNewGroup in the MyTestOU in Active Directory. If the script does not perform as expected, compare your script with the CreateGroup.ps1 script.

This concludes the procedure.

## Creating a computer account

1. Open the CreateUser.ps1 script in Notepad and save it as *<yourname>*CreateComputer.ps1.

2. Change the *$strClass* value from *user* to *computer*. The revised command is shown here:

```
$strCLass = "computer"
```

3. Change the *$strName* value from *CN=MyNewUser* to *CN=MyComputer*. This command is shown here:

```
$StrName = "CN=MyComputer"
```

The *[ADSI]* accelerator connection string is already connecting to *ou=myTestOU* and should not need modification.

4. Change the name of the *$objUser* variable used to hold the object that is returned from the *Create* method to *$objComputer*. This revised line of code is shown here:

```
$objComputer = $objADSI.create($strCLass, $StrName)
```

5. Use the *Put* method from the *DirectoryEntry* object created in the previous line to put the value *MyComputer* in the *sAMAccountName* attribute. This line of code is shown here:

```
$objComputer.put("sAMAccountName", "MyComputer")
```

6. Use the *SetInfo()* method to write the changes to Active Directory. This line of code is shown here:

```
$objComputer.setInfo()
```

7. After the *Computer* object has been created in Active Directory, you can modify the *UserAccountControl* attribute. The value 4128 in *UserAccountControl* means the workstation is a trusted account and does not need to change the password. This line of code is shown here:

```
$objComputer.put("UserAccountControl",4128)
```

8. Use the *SetInfo()* method to write the change back to Active Directory. This line of code is shown here:

```
$objComputer.setinfo()
```

9. Save and run the script. You should see a computer account appear in the Active Directory Users and Computers utility. If your script does not produce the expected results, compare it with CreateComputer.ps1.

This concludes the procedure.

## What is user account control?

*UserAccountControl* is an attribute stored in Active Directory that is used to enable or disable a user account, computer account, or other object defined in Active Directory. It is not a single string attribute; rather, it is a series of bit flags that get computed from the values listed in Table 15-4. Because of the way the *UserAccountControl* attribute is created, simply examining the numeric value is of little help, unless you can decipher the individual numbers that make up the large number. These flags, when added together, control the behavior of the user account on the system. In the script CreateComputer.ps1, you set two user account control flags: the ADS_UF_PASSWD_NOTREQD flag and the ADS_UF_WORKSTATION_TRUST_ACCOUNT flag. The password-not-required flag has a hexadecimal value of 0x20, and the trusted-workstation flag has a hexadecimal value of 0x1000. When added together and turned into a decimal value, they equal 4128, which is the value actually shown in ADSI Edit.

**TABLE 15-4** User account control values

| ADS constant | Value |
| --- | --- |
| ADS_UF_SCRIPT | 0X0001 |
| ADS_UF_ACCOUNTDISABLE | 0X0002 |
| ADS_UF_HOMEDIR_REQUIRED | 0X0008 |
| ADS_UF_LOCKOUT | 0X0010 |
| ADS_UF_PASSWD_NOTREQD | 0X0020 |
| ADS_UF_PASSWD_CANT_CHANGE | 0X0040 |
| ADS_UF_ENCRYPTED_TEXT_PASSWORD_ALLOWED | 0X0080 |
| ADS_UF_TEMP_DUPLICATE_ACCOUNT | 0X0100 |
| ADS_UF_NORMAL_ACCOUNT | 0X0200 |
| ADS_UF_INTERDOMAIN_TRUST_ACCOUNT | 0X0800 |
| ADS_UF_WORKSTATION_TRUST_ACCOUNT | 0X1000 |
| ADS_UF_SERVER_TRUST_ACCOUNT | 0X2000 |
| ADS_UF_DONT_EXPIRE_PASSWD | 0X10000 |
| ADS_UF_MNS_LOGON_ACCOUNT | 0X20000 |
| ADS_UF_SMARTCARD_REQUIRED | 0X40000 |
| ADS_UF_TRUSTED_FOR_DELEGATION | 0X80000 |
| ADS_UF_NOT_DELEGATED | 0X100000 |
| ADS_UF_USE_DES_KEY_ONLY | 0x200000 |
| ADS_UF_DONT_REQUIRE_PREAUTH | 0x400000 |
| ADS_UF_PASSWORD_EXPIRED | 0x800000 |
| ADS_UF_TRUSTED_TO_AUTHENTICATE_FOR_DELEGATION | 0x1000000 |

# Working with users

In this section, you will use ADSI to modify user properties stored in Active Directory. The following list summarizes a few of the items you can change or configure:

- Office and telephone contact information

- Mailing address information

- Department, title, manager, and direct reports (people who report to the user inside the chain of command)

User information that is stored in Active Directory can easily replace data that used to be contained in separate disparate places. For instance, you might have an internal website that contains a telephone directory; you can put phone numbers into Active Directory as attributes of the *User* object. You might also have a website containing a social roster that includes employees and their hobbies; you can put hobby information in Active Directory as a custom attribute. You can also add to Active Directory information such as an organizational chart. The problem, of course, is that during a migration, information such as a user's title is the last thing the harried mind of the network administrator thinks about. To leverage the investment in Active Directory, you need to enter this type of information because it quickly becomes instrumental in the daily lives of users. This is where ADSI and Windows PowerShell really begin to shine. You can update hundreds or even thousands of records easily and efficiently using scripting. Such a task would be unthinkable using conventional point-and-click methods.

To modify user properties in Active Directory, do the following:

1. Implement the appropriate protocol provider.

2. Perform binding to Active Directory.

3. Specify the appropriate ADsPath.

4. Use the *Put* method to write selected properties to users.

5. Use the *SetInfo()* method to commit changes to Active Directory.

## General user information

One of the more confusing issues when you use Windows PowerShell to modify information in Active Directory is that the names displayed on the property page do not correspond with the ADSI nomenclature. This was not done to make your life difficult; rather, the names you see in ADSI are derived from LDAP standard naming convention. Although this naming convention makes traditional LDAP programmers happy, it does nothing for the network administrator who is a casual scripter. This is where the following script, ModifyUserProperties.ps1, comes in handy. The LDAP properties corresponding to each field in Figure 15-3 are used in this script.

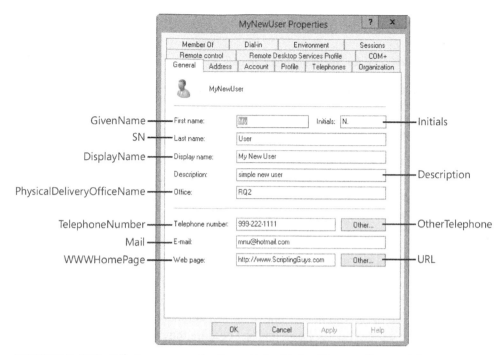

**FIGURE 15-3** ADSI attribute names on the General tab of Active Directory Users and Computers.

Some of the names make sense, but others appear to be rather obscure. Notice the series of *objUser.Put* statements. Each lines up with the corresponding field in Figure 15-3. Use the values to see which display name maps to which LDAP attribute name. Two of the attributes accept an array: *OtherTelephone* and *url*. The *url* attribute is particularly misleading—first because it is singular, and second because the *othertelephone* value uses the style *otherTelephone*. In addition, the primary webpage uses the name *wwwHomePage*. When supplying values for the *OtherTelephone* and *url* attributes, ensure the input value is accepted as an array by using the @() characters to cast the string into an array. The use of all these values is illustrated in ModifyUserProperties.ps1, shown here:

**ModifyUserProperties.ps1**

```
$objUser = [ADSI]"LDAP://cn=MyNewUser,ou=myTestOU,dc=iammred,dc=net"
$objUser.put("SamaccountName", "myNewUser")
$objUser.put("givenName", "My")
$objUser.Put("initials", "N.")
$objUser.Put("sn", "User")
$objUser.Put("DisplayName", "My New User")
$objUser.Put("description" , "simple new user")
$objUser.Put("physicalDeliveryOfficeName", "RQ2")
$objUser.Put("telephoneNumber", "999-222-1111")
$objUser.Put("OtherTelephone",@("555-555-1212","555-555-1213"))
$objUser.Put("mail", "mnu@hotmail.com")
$objUser.Put("wwwHomePage", "http://www.ScriptingGuys.com")
$objUser.Put("url",@("http://www.ScriptingGuys.Com/blog","http://www.ScriptingGuys.com/
LearnPowerShell"))
$objUser.setInfo()
```

## Quick check

Q. What is the field name for the user's first name?

A. The field for the user's first name is *GivenName*. You can find field-mapping information in the Platform SDK.

Q. Why do you need to use the *SetInfo()* command?

A. Without the *SetInfo()* command, all changes introduced during the script are lost because the changes are made to a cached set of attribute values for the object being modified. Nothing is committed to Active Directory until you call *SetInfo()*.

## Creating the address page

One of the more useful tasks you can perform with Active Directory is exposing address information. This ability is particularly important when a company has more than one location and more than a few hundred employees. I remember one of my first intranet projects was to host a centralized list of employees. Such a project quickly paid for itself because the customer no longer needed an administrative assistant to modify, copy, collate, and distribute hundreds of copies of the up-to-date employee directory—potentially a full-time job for one person. After the intranet site was in place, personnel at each location were given rights to modify the list. This was the beginning of a company-wide directory. With Active Directory, you avoid this duplication of work by keeping all information in a centralized location. The second tab in Active Directory Users and Computers is the Address tab, shown in Figure 15-4 with the appropriate Active Directory attribute names filled in.

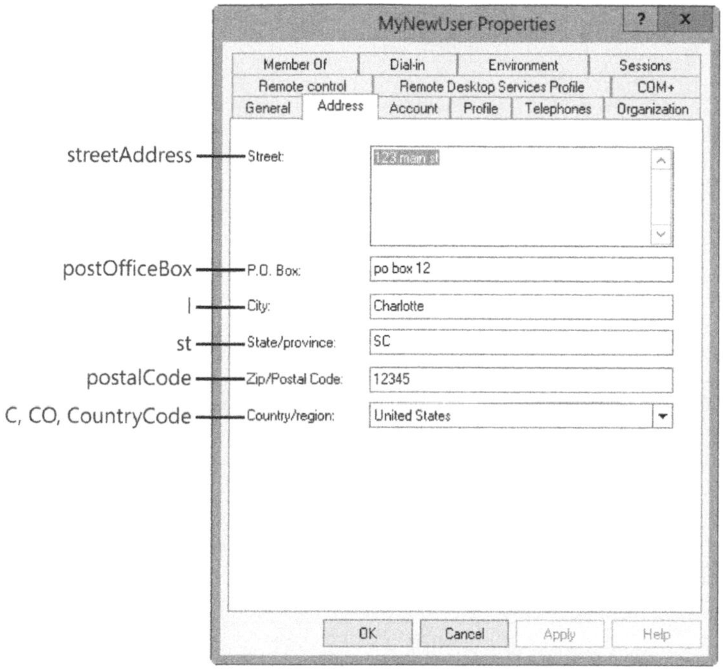

**FIGURE 15-4** Every item on the Address tab in Active Directory Users and Computers can be filled in via ADSI and Windows PowerShell.

In the ModifySecondPage.ps1 script, you use ADSI to set the *Street*, *PostOfficeBox*, *City*, *State*, *PostalCode*, *C*, *CO*, and *CountryCode* values for the *User* object. Table 15-5 lists the Active Directory attribute names and their mappings to the Active Directory Users and Computers "friendly" display names.

**TABLE 15-5** Address page mappings

| Active Directory Users and Computers label | Active Directory attribute name |
|---|---|
| Street | *streetAddress* |
| P.O. Box | *postOfficeBox* |
| City | *l* (Note that this is lowercase L.) |
| State/province | *st* |
| Zip/Postal Code | *postalCode* |
| Country/region | *C ,CO, CountryCode* |

When working with address-type information in Windows PowerShell, the hard thing is keeping track of the country codes. These values must be properly supplied. Table 15-6 illustrates some typical country codes. At times, the country codes seem to make sense; at others times, they do not. Rather than guess, you can simply make the changes in Active Directory Users and Computers and use ADSI Edit to examine the modified values, or you can look up the codes in ISO 3166-1.

ModifySecondPage.ps1

```
$objUser = [ADSI]"LDAP://cn=MyNewUser,ou=myTestOU,dc=iammred,dc=net"
$objUser.put("streetAddress", "123 main st")
$objUser.put("postOfficeBox", "po box 12")
$objUser.put("l", "Charlotte")
$objUser.put("st", "SC")
$objUser.put("postalCode" , "12345")
$objUser.put("c", "US")
$objUser.put("co", "United States")
$objUser.put("countryCode", "840")
$objUser.setInfo()
```

**TABLE 15-6** ISO 3166-1 country codes

| Country code | Country name |
| --- | --- |
| AF | AFGHANISTAN |
| AU | AUSTRALIA |
| EG | EGYPT |
| LV | LATVIA |
| ES | SPAIN |
| US | UNITED STATES |

> **Caution** The three country fields are not linked in Active Directory. You could easily have a *C* code value of US, a *CO* code value of Zimbabwe, and a *CountryCode* value of 470 (Malta). This could occur if someone uses the Active Directory Users and Computers to make a change to the *country* property. When this occurs, it updates all three fields. If someone later runs a script to only update the *CountryCode* value or the *CO* code value, then Active Directory Users and Computers will still reflect the translated value of the *C* code. This could create havoc if your enterprise resource planning (ERP) application uses the *CO* or *CountryCode* value and not the *C* attribute. Best practice is to update all three fields through your script.

## Quick check

Q. To set the country name on the address page for Active Directory Users and Computers, what is required?

A. To update the country name on the address page for Active Directory Users and Computers, you must specify the C field and feed it a two-letter code that is found in ISO publication 3166.

Q. What field name in ADSI is used to specify the city information?

A. You set the city information by assigning a value to the *l* (lowercase *L*) field after making the appropriate connection to Active Directory.

Q. If you put an inappropriate letter code in the C field, what error message is displayed?

A. None.

### Modifying the user profile settings

1. Open the ModifySecondPage.ps1 script you created earlier and save it as *<yourname>*ModifyUserProfile.ps1.

2. The user profile page in Active Directory is composed of four attributes. Delete all but four of the *$objUser.put* commands. The actual profile attributes are shown in Figure 15-5.

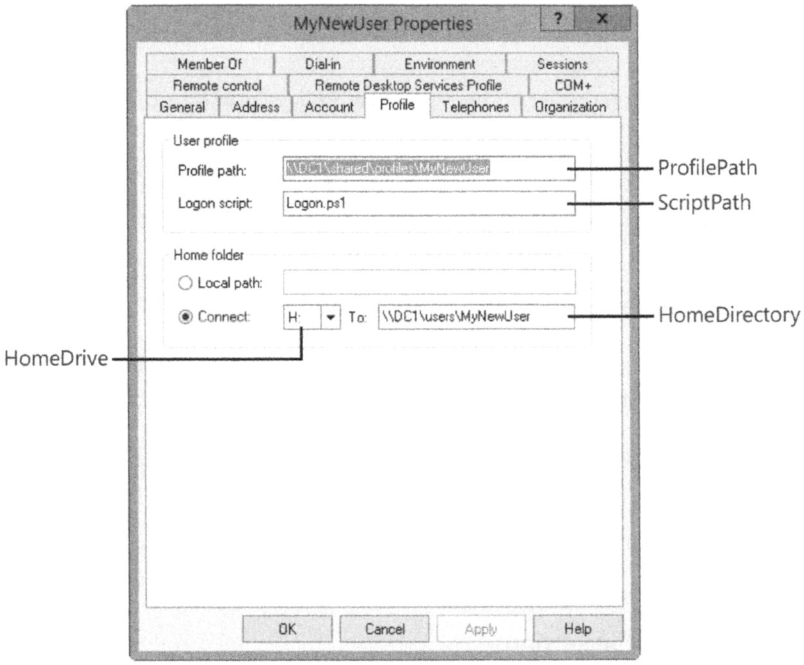

**FIGURE 15-5** ADSI attributes used to fill out the Profile tab in Active Directory.

3. The first attribute you need to supply a value for is *ProfilePath*. This controls where the user's profile will be stored. On my server, the location is \\London\Profiles in a folder named after the user, which in this case is myNewUser. Edit the first of the *$objUser.put* commands you left in your script to match your environment. The modified *$objUser.put* command is shown here:

```
$objUser.put("profilePath", "\\London\profiles\myNewUser")
```

4. The next attribute you need to supply a value for is *ScriptPath*. This controls which logon script will be run when the user logs on. Even though this attribute is called *ScriptPath*, it does not expect an actual path statement (it assumes the script is in the *sysvol* share); rather, it simply needs the name of the logon script. On my server, I use a logon script called logon.vbs. Modify the second *$objUser.put* statement in your script to point to a logon script. The modified command is shown here:

```
$objUser.put("scriptPath", "logon.vbs")
```

5. The third attribute that needs to be set for the user profile is called *HomeDirectory*, and it is used to control where the user's home directory will be stored. This attribute needs a Universal Naming Convention (UNC)–formatted path to a shared directory. On my server, each user has a home directory named after his or her logon user name. The folders are stored in a shared directory called Users. Modify the third *$objUser.put* statement in your

script to point to the appropriate home directory location for your environment. The completed command is shown here:

```
$objUser.put("homeDirectory", "\\london\users\myNewUser")
```

6. The last user profile attribute that needs to be modified is *HomeDrive*. The *HomeDrive* attribute in Active Directory is used to control the mapping of a drive letter to the user's home directory. On my server, all users' home drives are mapped to drive H (for *home*). Please note that Active Directory does not expect a trailing backslash for the *HomeDirectory* attribute. Modify the last *$objUser.put* command to map the user's home drive to the appropriate drive letter for your environment. The modified command is shown here:

```
$objUser.put("homeDrive", "H:")
```

7. Save and run your script. If it does not modify the user's profile page as expected, compare your script with the ModifyUserProfile.ps1 script shown here.

```
$objUser = [ADSI]"LDAP://cn=MyNewUser,ou=myTestOU,dc=iammred,dc=net"
$objUser.put("profilePath", "\\DC1\shared\profiles\MyNewUser")
$objUser.put("ScriptPath", "Logon.PS1")
$objUser.put("HomeDrive", "H:")
$objUser.put("HomeDirectory", "\\DC1\users\MyNewUser")
$objUser.setInfo()
```

This concludes the procedure.

## Modifying the user telephone settings

1. Open the ModifySecondPage.ps1 script you created earlier and save the file as *<yourname>*ModifyTelephone Attributes.ps1.

2. The Telephones tab in Active Directory Users and Computers for a user account is composed of six attributes. These attribute names are shown in Figure 15-6, which also illustrates the field names, as shown in Active Directory Users and Computers on the Telephones tab for the *User* object. Delete all but six of the *$objUser.put* commands from your script.

3. The first attribute you modify is the *HomePhone* attribute for the MyNewUser user account. To do this, change the value of the first *$objUser.put* command so that it is now writing to the *HomePhone* attribute in Active Directory. The phone number for the MyNewUser account is (555) 555-1222. For this example, you are leaving off the country code and enclosing the area code in parentheses. This is not required, however, for Active Directory. The modified line of code is shown here:

```
$objUser.Put("homePhone", "(555)555-1222")
```

4. The next telephone attribute in Active Directory is the *Pager* attribute. Your user account has a pager number that is (555) 555-1333. Modify the second *$objUser.put* line of your script to put this value into the *Pager* attribute. The revised line of code is shown here:

```
$objUser.Put("pager", "(555)555-1333")
```

5. The third telephone attribute you need to modify on your user account is the mobile telephone attribute. The name of this attribute in Active Directory is *Mobile*. The mobile telephone number for your user is (555) 555-1223. Edit the third *$objUser.put* command in your script so that you are writing this value into the *Mobile* attribute. The revised line of code is shown here:

```
$objUser.Put("mobile", "(555)555-1223")
```

6. The fourth telephone attribute that needs to be assigned a value is for the fax machine. The attribute in Active Directory that is used to hold the fax machine telephone number is *FacsimileTelephoneNumber*. Our user has a fax number that is (555) 555-1224. Edit the fourth *$objUser.put* command in your script to write the appropriate fax number into the *FacsimileTelephoneNumber* attribute in Active Directory. The revised code is shown here:

```
$objUser.Put("facsimileTelephoneNumber", "(555)555-1224")
```

7. The fifth telephone attribute that needs to be assigned a value for your user is for the IP address of the user's IP telephone. In Active Directory, this attribute is called *IPPhone*. The myNewUser account has an IP telephone with the IP address of 192.168.6.112. Modify the fifth *$objUser.put* command so that it will supply this information to Active Directory when the script is run. The revised command is shown here:

```
$objUser.Put("ipPhone", "192.168.6.112")
```

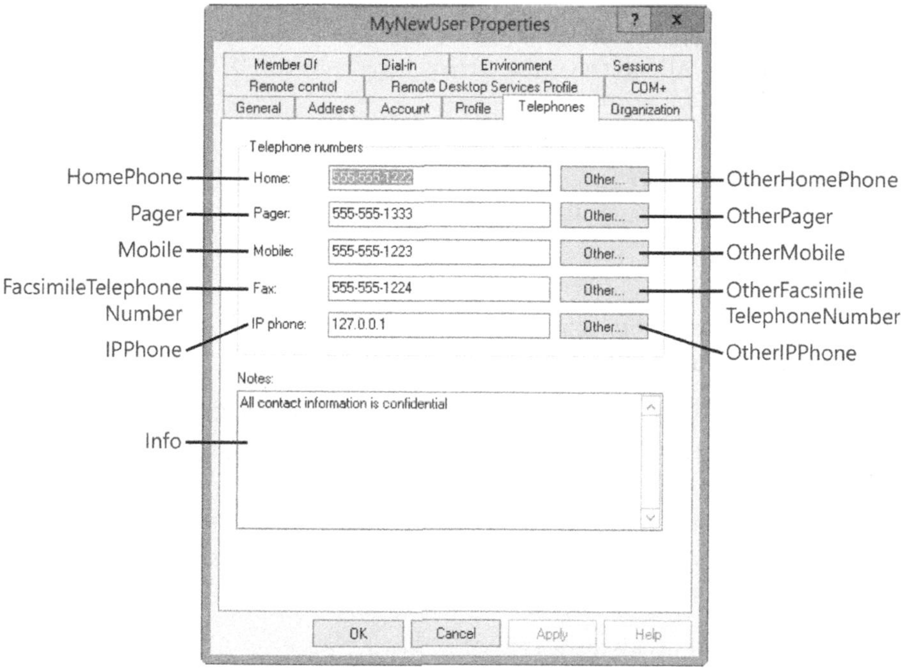

**FIGURE 15-6** Attributes on the Telephones tab in Active Directory.

8. Copy the previous telephone attributes and modify them for the *other*-type attributes. These include the following: *OtherFacsimileTelephoneNumber*, *OtherHomePhone*, *OtherPager*, *OtherMobile*, and *OtherIPPhone*.

9. Finally, the last telephone attribute is the notes. In Active Directory, this field is called the *info* attribute. Use the *put* method to add the following information to the *info* attribute.

```
$objUser.Put("info", "All contact information is confidential")
```

10. Save and run your script. You should see the all the properties on the Telephones tab filled in for the MyNewUser account. If this is not the case, you may want to compare your script with the ModifyTelephoneAttributes.ps1 script shown here.

```
$objUser = [ADSI]"LDAP://cn=MyNewUser,ou=myTestOU,dc=iammred,dc=net"
$objUser.put("homePhone", "555-555-1222")
$objUser.put("pager", "555-555-1333")
$objUser.put("mobile", "555-555-1223")
$objUser.put("facsimileTelephoneNumber", "555-555-1224")
$objUser.put("ipPhone", "127.0.0.1")
$objUser.put("otherfacsimileTelephoneNumber", "555-555-1229")
$objUser.put("otherhomePhone", "555-555-1223")
$objUser.put("otherpager", "555-555-1334")
```

```
$objUser.put("othermobile", @("555-555-1225","555-555-1226"))
$objUser.put("otheripPhone", @("127.0.0.2","127.0.0.3"))
$objUser.put("info", "All contact information is confidential")
$objUser.setInfo()
```

This concludes the procedure.

## Creating multiple users

1. Open the CreateUser.ps1 script you created earlier and save it as
   *<yourname>*CreateMultipleUsers.ps1.

2. On the second line of your script, change the name of the variable *$strName* to *$aryNames*
   because the variable will be used to hold an array of user names. On the same line, change the
   CN=MyNewUser user name to CN=MyBoss. Leave the quotation marks in place. At the end
   of the line, place a comma and type in the next user name—**CN=MyDIrect1**—ensuring you
   encase the name in quotation marks. The third user name is going to be CN=MyDirect2. The
   completed line of code is shown here:

   ```
   $aryNames = "CN=MyBoss","CN=MyDirect1","CN=MyDirect2"
   ```

3. Under the *$objADSI* line that uses the *[ADSI]* accelerator to connect into Active Directory, and
   above the *$objUser* line that creates the user account, place a *foreach* statement. Inside the
   parentheses, use the variable *$strName* as the single object and *$aryNames* as the name of
   the array. This line of code is shown here:

   ```
   foreach($StrName in $aryNames)
   ```

4. Below the *foreach* line, place an opening curly bracket to mark the beginning of the code
   block. On the line after *$objUser.setinfo()*, close the code block with a closing curly bracket.
   The entire code block is shown here:

   ```
   {
     $objUser = $objADSI.create($strCLass, $StrName)

     $objUser.setInfo()
   }
   ```

5. Save and run your script. You should see three user accounts—MyBoss, MyDirect1, and
   MyDirect2—magically appear in the MyTestOU OU. If this does not happen, compare your
   script with the CreateMultipleUsers.ps1 script shown here.

   ```
   $strCLass = "User"
   $aryNames = "CN=MyBoss","CN=MyDirect1","CN=MyDirect2"
   $objADSI = [ADSI]"LDAP://ou=myTestOU,dc=iammred,dc=net"
   foreach($StrName in $aryNames)
   ```

```
{
  $objUser = $objADSI.create($strCLass, $StrName)
  $objUser.setInfo() }
```

This concludes the procedure.

> **Note** One interesting thing about Windows PowerShell is that it can read inside a string, find a variable, and substitute the value of the variable, instead of just interpreting the variable as a string literal. This makes it easy to build up compound strings from information stored in multiple variables. Here's an example:
>
> ```
> $objUser = [ADSI]"LDAP://$strUser,$strOU,$strDomain"
> ```

## Modifying the organizational settings

1. Open the ModifySecondPage.ps1 script and save it as
   *<yourname>*ModifyOrganizationalPage.ps1.

2. In this script, you are going to modify four attributes in Active Directory, so you can delete all but four of the *$objUser.put* commands from your script. The Organization tab from Active Directory Users and Computers is shown in Figure 15-7, along with the appropriate attribute names.

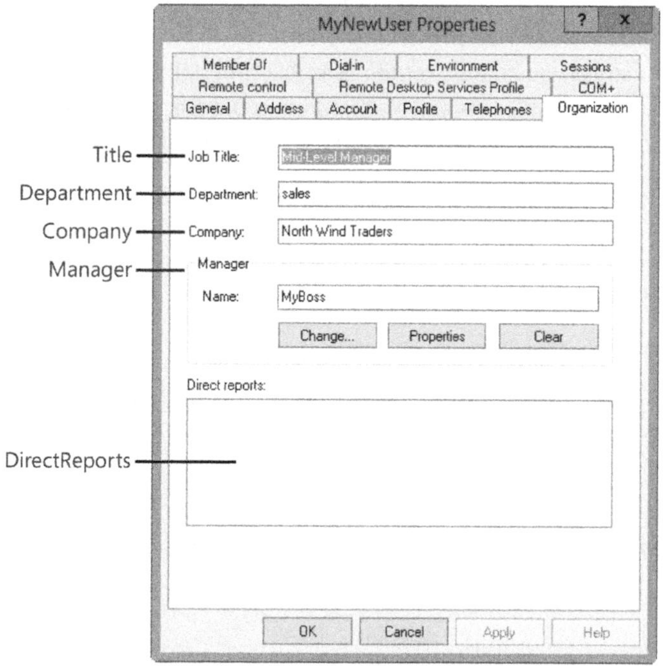

**FIGURE 15-7** Organization attributes in Active Directory.

3. To make your script more flexible, you are going to abstract much of the connection string information into variables. The first variable you will use is one to hold the domain name. Call this variable *$strDomain* and assign it a value of *dc=nwtraders,dc=msft* (assuming this is the name of your domain). This code is shown here:

```
$strDomain = "dc=nwtraders,dc=msft"
```

4. The second variable you'll declare is the one that will hold the name of the OU. In this procedure, your users reside in an OU called ou=myTestOU, so you should assign this value to the variable *$strOU*. This line of code is shown here:

```
$strOU = "ou=myTestOU"
```

5. The user name you are going to be working with is MyNewUser. Users are not domain components (referred to with *DC*), nor are they OUs; rather, they are containers (referred to with *CN*). Assign the string *cn=MyNewUser* to the variable *$strUser*. This line of code is shown here:

```
$strUser = "cn=MyNewUser"
```

6. The last variable you need to declare and assign a value to is the one that will hold MyNewUser's manager. His name is myBoss. The line of code that holds this information in the *$strManager* variable is shown here:

```
$strManager = "cn=myBoss"
```

7. So far, you have hardly used any information from the ModifySecondPage.ps1 script. Edit the *$objUser* line that holds the connection into Active Directory by using the *[ADSI]* accelerator so that it uses the variables you created for the user, OU, and domain. Windows PowerShell will read the value of the variables instead of interpreting them as strings. This makes it really easy to modify the connection string. The revised line of code is shown here:

```
$objUser = [ADSI]"LDAP://$strUser,$strOU,$strDomain"
```

8. Modify the first *$objUser.put* command so that it assigns the value *Mid-Level Manager* to the *title* attribute in Active Directory. This command is shown here:

```
$objUser.put("title", "Mid-Level Manager")
```

9. Modify the second *$objUser.put* command so that it assigns a value of *sales* to the *department* attribute in Active Directory. This command is shown here:

```
$objUser.put("department", "sales")
```

10. Modify the third *$objUser.put* command and assign the string *North Wind Traders* to the *company* attribute. This revised line of code is shown here:

```
$objUser.put("company", "North Wind Traders")
```

11. The last attribute you need to modify is the *manager* attribute. To do this, you will use the last *$objUser.put* command. The *manager* attribute needs the complete path to the object, so you will use the name stored in *$strManager*, the OU stored in *$strOU*, and the domain stored in *$strDomain*. This revised line of code is illustrated here:

```
$objUser.put("manager", "$strManager,$strou,$strDomain")
```

12. Save and run your script. You should see the Organization tab filled out in Active Directory Users and Computers. The only attribute that has not been filled out is the attribute for the MyNewUser user direct reports. However, if you open the MyBoss user, you will see MyNewUser listed as a direct report for the MyBoss user. If your script does not perform as expected, then compare your script with the ModifyOrganizationalPage.ps1 script shown here.

```
$strDomain = "dc=iammred,dc=net"
$strOU = "ou=myTestOU"
$strUser = "cn=MyNewUser"
$strManager = "cn=myBoss"

$objUser = [ADSI]"LDAP://$strUser,$strOU,$strDomain"
$objUser.put("title", "Mid-Level Manager")
$objUser.put("department", "sales")
$objUser.put("company", "North Wind Traders")
$objUser.put("manager", "$strManager,$strou,$strDomain")

$objUser.setInfo()
```

This concludes the procedure.

## Deleting users

There are times when you'll need to delete user accounts, and with ADSI, you can very easily delete large numbers of users with the single click of a mouse. Some reasons for deleting user accounts follow:

- To clean up a computer lab environment—that is, to return machines to a known state.

- To clean up accounts at the end of a school year. Many schools delete all student-related accounts and files at the end of each year. Scripting makes it easy to both create and delete the accounts.

- To clean up temporary accounts created for special projects. If the creation of accounts is scripted, their deletion can also be scripted, ensuring no temporary accounts are left lingering in the directory.

To delete users, take the following steps:

1. Perform the binding to the appropriate OU.

2. Use *[ADSI]* to make a connection.

3. Specify the appropriate provider and ADsPath.

4. Call the Delete method.

5. Specify *User* for the *object* class.

6. Specify the user to delete by the *CN* attribute value.

To delete a user, call the *Delete* method after binding to the appropriate level in the Active Directory namespace. Then specify both the *object* class, which in this case is *User*, and the *CN* attribute value of the user to be deleted. This can actually be accomplished in only two lines of code:

```
$objDomain = [ADSI]($provider + $ou + $domain)
$objDomain.Delete ($oClass, $oCn + $oUname)
```

If you modify the CreateUser.ps1 script, you can easily transform it into a DeleteUser.ps1 script, which follows. The main change is in the *Worker* section of the script. The binding string, shown here, is the same as earlier:

```
$objADSI = [ADSI]"LDAP://ou=myTestOU,dc=nwtraders,dc=msft"
```

However, in this case, you use the connection that was made in the binding string and call the *Delete* method. You specify the class of the object in the *$strClass* variable in the *Reference* section of the script. You also list the *$strName*. The syntax is *Delete(Class, target)*. The deletion takes effect immediately. No *SetInfo()* command is required. This command is shown here:

```
$objUser = $objADSI.delete($strCLass, $StrName)
```

The DeleteUser.ps1 script entailed only two real changes from the CreateUser.ps1 script. This makes user management very easy. If you need to create a large number of temporary users, you can save the script and then use it to get rid of them when they have completed their projects. The complete DeleteUser.ps1 script is shown here:

**DeleteUser.ps1**
```
$strCLass = "User"
$StrName = "CN=MyNewUser"
$objADSI = [ADSI]"LDAP://ou=myTestOU,dc=nwtraders,dc=msft"
$objUser = $objADSI.delete($strCLass, $StrName)
```

# Creating multiple organizational units: step-by-step exercises

In these exercises, you will explore the use of a text file to hold the names of multiple OUs you wish to create in Active Directory. After you create the organizational units in the first exercise, you will add users to the OU in the second exercise.

**Note** To complete these exercises, you will need access to a Windows server running AD DS. Modify the domain names listed in the exercises to match the name of your domain.

## Creating OUs from a text file

1. Open the Windows PowerShell ISE or some other script editor.

2. Create a text file called stepbystep.txt. The contents of the text file appear here:

```
ou=NorthAmerica
ou=SouthAmerica
ou=Europe
ou=Asia
ou=Africa
```

3. Make sure you have the exact path to this file. On the first line of your script, create a variable called *$aryText*. Use this variable to hold the object that is returned by the *Get-Content* cmdlet. Specify the path to the stepbystep.txt file as the value of the *-path* argument. The line of code that does this is shown here:

```
$aryText = Get-Content -Path "c:\labs\ch15\stepbystep.txt"
```

4. When the *Get-Content* cmdlet is used, it creates an array from a text file. To walk through each element of the array, you will use the *ForEach* cmdlet. Use a variable called *$aryElement* to hold the line from the *$aryText* array. This line of code is shown here:

```
forEach ($aryElement in $aryText)
```

5. Begin your script block with an opening curly bracket. This is shown here:

```
{
```

6. Use the variable *$strClass* to hold the string *organizationalUnit*, because this is the kind of object you will be creating in Active Directory. The line of code to do this is shown here:

```
$strCLass = "organizationalUnit"
```

7. The name of each OU you are going to create comes from each line of the stepbystep.txt file. In your text file, to simplify the coding task, you included *ou=* as part of each OU name. The *$strOUName* variable that will be used in the *Create* command has a straight value assignment of one variable to another. This line of code is shown here:

```
$StrOUName = $aryElement
```

8. The next line of code in your code block is the one that connects into Active Directory by using the *[ADSI]* accelerator. You are going to use the LDAP provider and connect to the NwTraders.msft domain. You assign the object that is created to the *$objADSI* variable. This line of code is shown here:

```
$objADSI = [ADSI]"LDAP://dc=nwtraders,dc=msft"
```

9. Now you are ready to actually create the OUs in Active Directory. To do this, you will use the *Create* method. You specify two properties for the *Create* method: the name of the class to

create and the name of the object to create. Here, the name of the class is stored in the variable *$strClass*. The name of the object to create is stored in the *$strOUName* variable. The object that is returned is stored in the *$objOU* variable. This line of code is shown here:

```
$objOU = $objADSI.create($strCLass, $StrOUName)
```

10. To write changes back to Active Directory, you use the *SetInfo()* method. This is shown here:

```
$objOU.setInfo()
```

11. Now you must close the code block. To do this, close it with a curly bracket, as shown here:

```
}
```

12. Save your script as *<yourname>*StepByStep.ps1. Run your script. You should see five OUs created off the root of your domain. If this is not the case, compare your script with the StepByStep.ps1 script that appears here:

```
$aryText = Get-Content -Path "c:\labs\ch15\stepbystep.txt"

forEach ($aryElement in $aryText)
{
    $strCLass = "organizationalUnit"
    $StrOUName = $aryElement
    $objADSI = [ADSI]"LDAP://dc=nwtraders,dc=msft"
    $objOU = $objADSI.create($strCLass, $StrOUName)
    $objOU.setInfo()`
}
```

This concludes the exercise.

In the following exercise, you will create nine temporary user accounts using concatenation. You'll specify values for the users from a text file and populate attributes on both the Address tab and the Telephones tab.

## Creating multivalued users

1. Open the Windows PowerShell ISE or your favorite Windows PowerShell script editor.

2. Create a text file called OneStepFurther.txt. The contents of this file appear here:

```
123 Main Street
Box 123
Atlanta
Georgia
123456
US
united states
840
1-555-345-8765
All information is confidential and is for official use only
```

3. Use the *Get-Content* cmdlet to open the OneStepFurther.txt file. Use the *-path* argument to point to the exact path to the file. Hold the array that is created in a variable called *$aryText*. This line of code is shown here:

```
$aryText = Get-Content -Path "c:\labs\ch15\OneStepFurther.txt"
```

4. Create a variable called *$strUser*. This will be used to determine the class of object to create in Active Directory. Assign the string *User* to this variable. This line of code is shown here:

```
$strCLass = "User"
```

5. Create a variable called *$intUsers*. This variable will be used to determine how many users to create. For this exercise, you will create nine users, so assign the integer 9 to the value of the variable. This code is shown here:

```
$intUsers = 9
```

6. Create a variable called *$strName*. This variable will be used to create the prefix for each user that is created. Because these will be temporary users, use the prefix *cn=tempuser*. This code is shown here:

```
$strName = "cn=tempUser"
```

7. Create a variable called *$objADSI*. This variable will be used to hold the object that is returned by using the *[ADSI]* accelerator that is used to make the connection into Active Directory. Specify the LDAP provider and connect to the MyTestOU OU that resides in the NwTraders.msft domain. This line of code is shown here:

```
$objADSI = [ADSI]"LDAP://ou=myTestOU,dc=nwtraders,dc=msft"
```

8. Use a *for* loop to count from 1 to 9. Use the *$i* variable as the counter variable. When the value of *$i* is less than or equal to the integer stored in the *$intUsers* variable, exit the loop. Use the *$i++* operator to increment the value of *$i*. This code is shown here:

```
for ($i=1; $i -le $intUsers; $i++)
```

9. Open and close your code block by using curly brackets. This is shown here:

```
{

}
```

10. Between the curly brackets, use the object contained in the *$objADSI* variable to create the class of object stored in the variable *$strClass*. The name of each object will be created by concatenating the *$strName* prefix with the number current in *$i*. Store the object returned by the *Create* method in the variable *$objUser*. This line of code is shown here:

```
$objUser = $objADSI.create($strCLass, $StrName+$i)
```

**11.** On the next line in the code block, write the new *User* object to Active Directory using the *SetInfo()* method. This line of code is shown here:

```
$objUser.setInfo()
```

**12.** Open the OneStepFurther.txt file and examine the contents. Note that each line corresponds to a property in Active Directory. The trick is to ensure that each line in the text file matches each position in the array. Beginning at *element*, use the array contained in the variable *$aryText* to write the *streetaddress*, *postofficebox*, *l*, *st*, *postalcode*, *c*, *co*, *countrycode*, *facsimiletelephonenumber*, and *info* attributes for each *User* object that is created. This section of code, shown here, is placed after the *User* object is created, and *SetInfo()* writes it to Active Directory.

```
$objUser.put("streetAddress", $aryText[0])
$objUser.put("postOfficeBox", $aryText[1])
$objUser.put("l", $aryText[2])
$objUser.put("st", $aryText[3])
$objUser.put("postalCode" , $aryText[4])
$objUser.put("c", $aryText[5])
$objUser.put("co", $aryText[6])
$objUser.put("countryCode", $aryText[7])
$objUser.Put("facsimileTelephoneNumber", $aryText[8])
$objUser.Put("info", $aryText[9])
```

**13.** Commit the changes to Active Directory by calling the *SetInfo()* method. This line of code is shown here:

```
$objUser.setInfo()
```

**14.** Save your script as *<yourname>*OneStepFurtherPt1.ps1. Run your script and examine Active Directory Users and Computers. You should find the nine users with attributes on both the Address tab and the Telephones tab. If this is not the case, then compare your script with the OneStepFurtherPt1.ps1 script shown here.

```
$aryText = Get-Content -Path "c:\labs\ch15\OneStepFurther.txt"
$strCLass = "User"
$intUsers = 9
$strName = "cn=tempUser"

$objADSI = [ADSI]"LDAP://ou=myTestOU,dc=nwtraders,dc=msft"
for ($i=1; $i -le $intUsers; $i++)
{
$objUser = $objADSI.create($strCLass, $StrName+$i)
$objUser.setInfo()
$objUser.put("streetAddress", $aryText[0])
$objUser.put("postOfficeBox", $aryText[1])
$objUser.put("l", $aryText[2])
$objUser.put("st", $aryText[3])
$objUser.put("postalCode" , $aryText[4])
$objUser.put("c", $aryText[5])
```

```
$objUser.put("co", $aryText[6])
$objUser.put("countryCode", $aryText[7])
$objUser.Put("facsimileTelephoneNumber", $aryText[8])
$objUser.Put("info", $aryText[9])
$objUser.setInfo()
```

15. After the users are created, proceed to the second part of the exercise, described in the following steps.

16. Save OneStepFurtherPt1.ps1 as *<yourname>*OneStepFurtherPt2.ps1.

17. Delete the *$aryText = Get-Content -Path "c:\labs\ch15\OneStepFurther.txt"* from the script.

18. Delete everything from inside the code block except for the line of code that creates the *User* object. This line of code is *$objUser = $objADSI.create($strCLass, $StrName+$i)*, and the code to delete is shown here:

```
$objUser.setInfo()
$objUser.put("streetAddress", $aryText[0])
$objUser.put("postOfficeBox", $aryText[1])
$objUser.put("l", $aryText[2])
$objUser.put("st", $aryText[3])
$objUser.put("postalCode" , $aryText[4])
$objUser.put("c", $aryText[5])
$objUser.put("co", $aryText[6])
$objUser.put("countryCode", $aryText[7])
$objUser.Put("facsimileTelephoneNumber", $aryText[8])
$objUser.Put("info", $aryText[9])
$objUser.setInfo()
```

19. Inside the code block, change the *Create* method in the *$objADSI Create* command to *Delete*, as shown here:

```
$objUser = $objADSI.Delete($strCLass, $StrName+$i)
```

20. Save and run your script. You should see the nine users, created earlier, disappear. If this does not happen, compare your script with the OneStepFurtherPt2.ps1 script shown here.

```
$strCLass = "User"
$intUsers = 9
$strName = "cn=tempUser"
$objADSI = [ADSI]"LDAP://ou=myTestOU,dc=nwtraders,dc=msft"
for ($i=1; $i -le $intUsers; $i++)

{
  $objUser = $objADSI.Delete($strCLass, $StrName+$i)

}
```

This concludes the exercise.

# Chapter 15 quick reference

| To | Do this |
|---|---|
| Delete users easily | Modify the script you used to create the user and change the *Create* method to *Delete*. |
| Commit changes to Active Directory when deleting a user | Do nothing—changes take place automatically when users are deleted. |
| Find country codes used in Active Directory Users and Computers | Use ISO 3166. |
| Modify a user's first name via ADSI | Add a value to the *GivenName* attribute. Use the *SetInfo()* method to write the change to Active Directory. Use the *Put* method to at least specify the *sAMAccountName* attribute if using Windows 2000 Active Directory. |
| Overwrite a field that is already populated in Active Directory | Use the *Put* method. |
| Assign a value to a terminal server profile attribute after making a connection into Active Directory | Assign the value to the property. There is no need to use the Put method. |
| Read a text file and turn it into an array | Use the *Get-Content* cmdlet and specify the path to the file by using the *-path* argument. |

# Working with the AD DS Module

**After completing this chapter, you will be able to:**

- Use the AD DS cmdlets to manage users.

- Use the AD DS cmdlets to manage organizational units.

- Use the AD DS cmdlets to manage computer objects.

- Use the AD DS cmdlets to manage groups.

## Understanding the Active Directory module

Microsoft made Active Directory Domain Services (AD DS) Microsoft Windows PowerShell cmdlets available with Windows Server 2008 R2. You can also download and install the Active Directory Management Gateway Service (ADMGS). ADMGS provides a web service interface to Active Directory domains, and to Active Directory Lightweight Directory Services. ADMGS runs on the domain controller. ADMGS can run on Windows Server 2003 with Service Pack (SP) 2, or Windows Server 2008. On Windows Server 2008 R2 and above, ADMGS installs as a role and does not require an additional download. Once you have one domain controller running Windows Server 2008 R2 (or later) in your domain, you can use the new cmdlets to manage your AD DS installation. Installing ADMGS on Windows Server 2003 or Windows Server 2008 does not make it possible to load the Active Directory module on those machines, but it does permit you to use the Active Directory module from another machine to manage those servers.

## Installing the Active Directory module

The Active Directory module is available beginning with Windows 7 on the client side and with Windows 2008 R2 on servers. To make the cmdlets available on the desktop operating system, you need to download and install the Remote Server Administration Tools (RSAT). The Active Directory cmdlets ship in a Windows PowerShell module, and you may therefore be interested in the *Get-MyModule* function from the Microsoft TechNet Script Center Script Repository. The *Get-MyModule* function is useful because it will verify the presence of an optional module prior to its use in a Windows PowerShell script. When using optional modules, scripts commonly fail because a particular module may not be available on all systems. The *Get-MyModule* function helps to detect this condition prior to actual script failure.

To install the Active Directory module on either a Windows Server 2008 R2 machine or on Windows Server 2012, you can use the *Add-WindowsFeature* cmdlet. This is because the Active Directory module is directly available to the operating system as an optional Windows feature. Therefore, installation on a server operating system does not require downloading RSAT. To install RSAT for Active Directory, use the procedure that follows.

## Installing the Active Directory module

1. Use the *Get-WindowsFeature* cmdlet to verify that the *rsat-ad-tools* feature is available to install. The command appears here:

    ```
    Get-WindowsFeature rsat-ad-tools
    ```

2. Use the up arrow key to retrieve the *Get-WindowsFeature* command and pipeline the results to the *Add-WindowsFeature* cmdlet. The command appears here:

    ```
    Get-WindowsFeature rsat-ad-tools | Add-WindowsFeature
    ```

3. Use the up arrow key twice to retrieve the first *Get-WindowsFeature* command. The command appears here:

    ```
    Get-WindowsFeature rsat-ad-tools
    ```

The use of the procedure and the associated output appear in Figure 16-1.

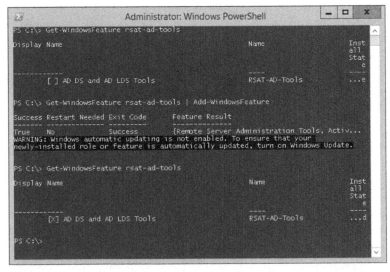

**FIGURE 16-1** Installing RSAT provides access to the Active Directory module.

# Getting started with the Active Directory module

Once you have installed RSAT, you will want to verify that the Active Directory module is present and that it loads properly. To do this, follow the next procedure.

### Verifying the Active Directory module

1. Use the *Get-Module* cmdlet with the *-ListAvailable* switch to verify that the Active Directory module is present. The command to do this appears here:

```
Get-Module -ListAvailable ActiveDirectory
```

2. Use the *Import-Module* cmdlet to import the Active Directory module. The command to do this appears following. (In Windows PowerShell 3.0, it is not required to explicitly import the Active Directory module. However, if you know you are going to use the module, it makes sense to go ahead and explicitly import it, because it is faster).

```
Import-Module ActiveDirectory
```

3. Use the *Get-Module* cmdlet to verify that the Active Directory module loaded properly. The command to do this appears here:

```
Get-Module ActiveDirectory
```

4. Once the Active Directory module loads, you can obtain a listing of the Active Directory cmdlets by using the *Get-Command* cmdlet and specifying the *-Module* parameter. This command appears here:

```
Get-Command -Module ActiveDirectory
```

# Using the Active Directory module

It is not necessary to always load the Active Directory module (or for that matter any module) because Windows PowerShell 3.0 automatically loads the module containing a referenced cmdlet. The location searched by Windows PowerShell for modules comes from environment variable *PSModulePath*. To view the value of this environment variable, prefix the variable name with the environment drive. The following command retrieves the default module locations and displays the associated paths:

```
PS C:\> $env:PSModulePath
C:\Users\ed.IAMMRED\Documents\WindowsPowerShell\Modules;C:\Windows\system32\WindowsPowerShell\
v1.0\Modules\
```

If you do not want to install the Active Directory module on your client operating systems, all you need to do is to add the *rsat-ad-tools* feature to at least one server. Once it's installed on the server, use Windows PowerShell remoting to connect to the server hosting the *rsat-ad-tools* feature from your client workstation. Once in the remote session, if the remote server is Windows 8, all you need to do is call one of the Active Directory cmdlets. The Active Directory module automatically loads, and the information returns. The following commands illustrate this technique:

```
$credential = get-credential
Enter-PSSession -ComputerName w8Server6 -Credential $credential
Get-ADDomain
```

Figure 16-2 illustrates the techniques for using Windows PowerShell remoting to connect to a server that contains the Active Directory module and for automatically loading that module while using a cmdlet from it.

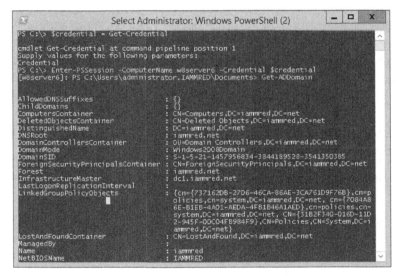

**FIGURE 16-2** Using Windows PowerShell remoting to obtain Active Directory information without first loading the module.

# Finding the FSMO role holders

To find information about domain controllers and Flexible Single Master Operation (FSMO) roles, you do not have to write a Windows PowerShell script; you can do it directly from the Windows PowerShell console or ISE using the Active Directory cmdlets. The first thing you'll need to do, more than likely, is load the Active Directory module into the current Windows PowerShell session. While it is possible to add the *Import-Module* command to your Windows PowerShell profile, in general it is not a good idea to load a bunch of modules that you may or you may not use on a regular basis. In fact, you can load all the modules at once by piping the results of the *Get-Module -listavailable* command to the *Import-Module* cmdlet. This is shown here:

```
PS C:\> Get-Module -ListAvailable | Import-Module
PS C:\> Get-Module
```

```
ModuleType  Name                      ExportedCommands
----------  ----                      ----------------
Script      BasicFunctions            {Get-ComputerInfo, Get-OptimalSize}
Script      ConversionModuleV6        {ConvertTo-Feet, ConvertTo-Miles, ConvertTo-...
Script      PowerShellPack            {New-ByteAnimationUsingKeyFrames, New-TiffBi...
Script      PSCodeGen                 {New-Enum, New-ScriptCmdlet, New-PInvoke}
Script      PSImageTools              {Add-CropFilter, Add-RotateFlipFilter, Add-O...
Script      PSRss                     {Read-Article, New-Feed, Remove-Article, Rem...
Script      PSSystemTools             {Test-32Bit, Get-USB, Get-OSVersion, Get-Mul...
Script      PSUserTools               {Start-ProcessAsAdministrator, Get-CurrentUs...
Script      TaskScheduler             {Remove-Task, Get-ScheduledTask, Stop-Task, ...
Script      WPK                       {Get-DependencyProperty, New-ModelVisual3D, ...
Manifest    ActiveDirectory           {Set-ADOrganizationalUnit, Get-ADDomainContr...
Manifest    AppLocker                 {Get-AppLockerPolicy, Get-AppLockerFileInfor...
Manifest    BitsTransfer              {Start-BitsTransfer, Remove-BitsTransfer, Re...
Manifest    FailoverClusters          {Set-ClusterParameter, Get-ClusterParameter,...
Manifest    GroupPolicy               {Get-GPStarterGPO, Get-GPOReport, Set-GPInhe...
Manifest    NetworkLoadBalancingCl... {Stop-NlbClusterNode, Remove-NlbClusterVip, ...
Script      PSDiagnostics             {Enable-PSTrace, Enable-WSManTrace, Start-Tr...
Manifest    TroubleshootingPack       {Get-TroubleshootingPack, Invoke-Troubleshoo...


PS C:\>
```

Once you have loaded the Active Directory module, you will want to use the *Get-Command* cmdlet to see the cmdlets that are exported by the module. This is shown here:

```
PS C:\> Get-Module -ListAvailable

ModuleType  Name                      ExportedCommands
----------  ----                      ----------------
Script      BasicFunctions            {}
Script      ConversionModuleV6        {}
Script      DotNet                    {}
Manifest    FileSystem                {}
Manifest    IsePack                   {}
Manifest    PowerShellPack            {}
Manifest    PSCodeGen                 {}
Manifest    PSImageTools              {}
Manifest    PSRSS                     {}
Manifest    PSSystemTools             {}
Manifest    PSUserTools               {}
Manifest    TaskScheduler             {}
Manifest    WPK                       {}
Manifest    ActiveDirectory           {}
Manifest    AppLocker                 {}
Manifest    BitsTransfer              {}
Manifest    FailoverClusters          {}
Manifest    GroupPolicy               {}
Manifest    NetworkLoadBalancingCl... {}
Manifest    PSDiagnostics             {}
Manifest    TroubleshootingPack       {}
```

```
PS C:\> Import-Module active*
PS C:\> Get-Command -Module active*

CommandType     Name                                    Definition
-----------     ----                                    ----------
Cmdlet          Add-ADComputerServiceAccount            Add-ADComputerServiceAccount [...
Cmdlet          Add-ADDomainControllerPasswordR...      Add-ADDomainControllerPassword...
Cmdlet          Add-ADFineGrainedPasswordPolicy...      Add-ADFineGrainedPasswordPolic...
Cmdlet          Add-ADGroupMember                       Add-ADGroupMember [-Identity] ...
Cmdlet          Add-ADPrincipalGroupMembership          Add-ADPrincipalGroupMembership...
Cmdlet          Clear-ADAccountExpiration               Clear-ADAccountExpiration [-Id...
Cmdlet          Disable-ADAccount                       Disable-ADAccount [-Identity] ...
Cmdlet          Disable-ADOptionalFeature               Disable-ADOptionalFeature [-Id...
Cmdlet          Enable-ADAccount                        Enable-ADAccount [-Identity] <...
Cmdlet          Enable-ADOptionalFeature                Enable-ADOptionalFeature [-Ide...
Cmdlet          Get-ADAccountAuthorizationGroup         Get-ADAccountAuthorizationGrou...
Cmdlet          Get-ADAccountResultantPasswordR...      Get-ADAccountResultantPassword...
Cmdlet          Get-ADComputer                          Get-ADComputer -Filter <String...
<output truncated>
```

To find a single domain controller, if you are not sure of one in your site, you can use the *-Discover* switch on the *Get-ADDomainController* cmdlet. One thing to keep in mind is that the *-Discover* parameter could return information from the cache. If you wish to ensure that a fresh discover command is sent, use the *-forceDiscover* switch in addition to the *-Discover* switch. These techniques appear here:

```
PS C:\> Get-ADDomainController -Discover


Domain      : NWTraders.Com
Forest      : NWTraders.Com
HostName    : {HyperV.NWTraders.Com}
IPv4Address : 192.168.1.100
IPv6Address :
Name        : HYPERV
Site        : NewBerlinSite




PS C:\> Get-ADDomainController -Discover -ForceDiscover


Domain      : NWTraders.Com
Forest      : NWTraders.Com
HostName    : {HyperV.NWTraders.Com}
IPv4Address : 192.168.1.100
IPv6Address :
Name        : HYPERV
Site        : NewBerlinSite



PS C:\>
```

When you use the *Get-ADDomainController* cmdlet, a minimal amount of information is returned. If you wish to see additional information from the domain controller you discovered, you would need to connect to it by using the *-Identity* parameter. The value of the *Identity* property can be an IP address, a globally unique identifier (GUID), a host name, or even a NetBIOS type of name. This technique appears here:

```
PS C:\> Get-ADDomainController -Identity hyperv
```

```
ComputerObjectDN               : CN=HYPERV,OU=Domain Controllers,DC=NWTraders,DC=Com
DefaultPartition               : DC=NWTraders,DC=Com
Domain                         : NWTraders.Com
Enabled                        : True
Forest                         : NWTraders.Com
HostName                       : HyperV.NWTraders.Com
InvocationId                   : 6835f51f-2c77-463f-8775-b3404f2748b2
IPv4Address                    : 192.168.1.100
IPv6Address                    :
IsGlobalCatalog                : True
IsReadOnly                     : False
LdapPort                       : 389
Name                           : HYPERV
NTDSSettingsObjectDN           : CN=NTDS Settings,CN=HYPERV,CN=Servers,CN=NewBerlinSite,
                                 CN=Sites,CN=Configuration,DC=NWTraders,DC=Com
OperatingSystem                : Windows Server 2008 R2 Standard
OperatingSystemHotfix          :
OperatingSystemServicePack     :
OperatingSystemVersion         : 6.1 (7600)
OperationMasterRoles           : {SchemaMaster, DomainNamingMaster}
Partitions                     : {DC=ForestDnsZones,DC=NWTraders,DC=Com, DC=DomainDns
                                 Zones,DC=NWTraders,DC=Com, CN=Schema,CN=Configuration,
                                 DC=NWTraders,DC=Com, CN=Configuration,DC=NWTraders,DC=
                                 Com...}
ServerObjectDN                 : CN=HYPERV,CN=Servers,CN=NewBerlinSite,CN=Sites,CN=
                                 Configuration,DC=NWTraders,DC=Com
ServerObjectGuid               : ab5e2830-a4d6-47f8-b2b4-25757153653c
Site                           : NewBerlinSite
SslPort                        : 636
```

```
PS C:\>
```

As shown in the preceding output, the server named Hyperv is a global catalog server (the *IsGlobalCatalog* property is *True*). It also holds the *SchemaMaster* and *DomainNamingMaster* FSMO roles. It is running Windows Server 2008 R2 Standard Edition. The *Get-ADDomainController* cmdlet accepts a *-filter* parameter that can be used to perform a search-and-retrieve operation. It uses a special search syntax that is discussed in the online help files. Unfortunately, it does not accept Lightweight Directory Access Protocol (LDAP) syntax.

Luckily, you do not have to learn the special filter syntax, because the *Get-ADObject* cmdlet will accept an LDAP dialect filter. You can simply pipeline the results of *the Get-ADObject* cmdlet to the *Get-ADDomainController* cmdlet. This technique appears here:

```
PS C:\> Get-ADObject -LDAPFilter "(objectclass=computer)" -searchbase "ou=domain
controllers,dc=nwtraders,dc=com" | Get-ADDomainController
```

```
ComputerObjectDN          : CN=HYPERV,OU=Domain Controllers,DC=NWTraders,DC=Com
DefaultPartition          : DC=NWTraders,DC=Com
Domain                    : NWTraders.Com
Enabled                   : True
Forest                    : NWTraders.Com
HostName                  : HyperV.NWTraders.Com
InvocationId              : 6835f51f-2c77-463f-8775-b3404f2748b2
IPv4Address               : 192.168.1.100
IPv6Address               :
IsGlobalCatalog           : True
IsReadOnly                : False
LdapPort                  : 389
Name                      : HYPERV
NTDSSettingsObjectDN      : CN=NTDS Settings,CN=HYPERV,CN=Servers,CN=NewBerlinSite,
                            CN=Sites,CN=Configuration,DC=NWTraders,DC=Com
OperatingSystem           : Windows Server 2008 R2 Standard
OperatingSystemHotfix     :
OperatingSystemServicePack :
OperatingSystemVersion    : 6.1 (7600)
OperationMasterRoles      : {SchemaMaster, DomainNamingMaster}
Partitions                : {DC=ForestDnsZones,DC=NWTraders,DC=Com, DC=DomainDns
                            Zones,DC=NWTraders,DC=Com, CN=Schema,CN=Configuration,
                            DC=NWTraders,DC=Com, CN=Configuration,DC=NWTraders,DC=
                            Com...}
ServerObjectDN            : CN=HYPERV,CN=Servers,CN=NewBerlinSite,CN=Sites,CN=
                            Configuration,DC=NWTraders,DC=Com
ServerObjectGuid          : ab5e2830-a4d6-47f8-b2b4-25757153653c
Site                      : NewBerlinSite
SslPort                   : 636

ComputerObjectDN          : CN=DC1,OU=Domain Controllers,DC=NWTraders,DC=Com
DefaultPartition          : DC=NWTraders,DC=Com
Domain                    : NWTraders.Com
Enabled                   : True
Forest                    : NWTraders.Com
HostName                  : DC1.NWTraders.Com
InvocationId              : fb324ced-bd3f-4977-ae69-d6763e7e029a
IPv4Address               : 192.168.1.101
IPv6Address               :
IsGlobalCatalog           : True
IsReadOnly                : False
LdapPort                  : 389
Name                      : DC1
NTDSSettingsObjectDN      : CN=NTDS Settings,CN=DC1,CN=Servers,CN=NewBerlinSite,CN=
                            Sites,CN=Configuration,DC=NWTraders,DC=Com
OperatingSystem           : Windows Serverr 2008 Standard without Hyper-V
OperatingSystemHotfix     :
OperatingSystemServicePack : Service Pack 2
OperatingSystemVersion    : 6.0 (6002)
OperationMasterRoles      : {PDCEmulator, RIDMaster, InfrastructureMaster}
```

```
Partitions                : {DC=ForestDnsZones,DC=NWIraders,DC=Com, DC=DomainDns
                            Zones,DC=NWTraders,DC=Com, CN=Schema,CN=Configuration,
                            DC=NWTraders,DC=Com, CN=Configuration,DC=NWTraders,
                            DC=Com...}
ServerObjectDN            : CN=DC1,CN=Servers,CN=NewBerlinSite,CN=Sites,CN=
                            Configuration,DC=NWTraders,DC=Com
ServerObjectGuid          : 80885b47-5a51-4679-9922-d6f41228f211
Site                      : NewBerlinSite
SslPort                   : 636


PS C:\>
```

If this returns too much information, note that the Active Directory cmdlets work just like any other Windows PowerShell cmdlet, and therefore permit using the pipeline to choose the information you wish to display. To obtain only the FSMO information, you really only need to use two commands. (If you want to include importing the Active Directory module in your count, you'll need three commands, and if you need to make a remote connection to a domain controller to run the commands, you'll need four). One useful thing about using Windows PowerShell remoting is that you specify the credentials you need to run the command. If your normal account is a standard user account, you only use an elevated account when you need to do things with elevated rights. If you have already started the Windows PowerShell console with elevated credentials, you can skip typing in credentials when you enter the remote Windows PowerShell session (assuming the elevated account also has rights on the remote server). The command shown here creates a remote session on a remote domain controller:

```
Enter-PSSession w8Server6
```

Once the Active Directory module loads, you type a one-line command to get the forest FSMO roles, and another one-line command to get the domain FSMO roles. These two commands appear here:

```
Get-ADForest iammred.net | Format-Table SchemaMaster,DomainNamingMaster
Get-ADDomain iammred.net | format-table PDCEmulator,RIDMaster,InfrastructureMaster
```

That is it—two or three one-line commands, depending on how you want to count. Even at worst case, this is much easier to type than the 33 lines of code that would be required if you did not have access to the Active Directory module. In addition, the Windows PowerShell code is much easier to read and understand. The commands and the associated output appear in Figure 16-3.

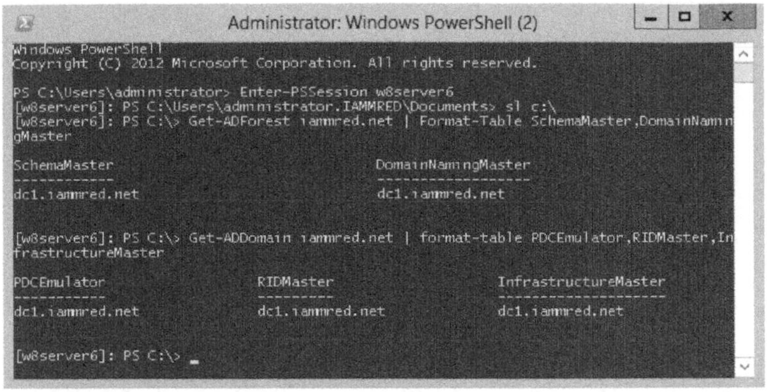

**FIGURE 16-3** Using Windows PowerShell remoting to obtain FSMO information.

## Discovering Active Directory

Using the Active Directory Windows PowerShell cmdlets and remoting, you can easily discover information about the forest and the domain. The first thing you need to do is to enter a PS session on the remote computer. To do this, you use the *Enter-PSSession* cmdlet. Next, you import the Active Directory module and set the working location to the root of drive C. The reason for setting the working location to the root of drive C is to regain valuable command-line space. These commands appear here:

```
PS C:\Users\Administrator.NWTRADERS> Enter-PSSession dc1
[dc1]: PS C:\Users\Administrator\Documents> Import-Module activedirectory
[dc1]: PS C:\Users\Administrator\Documents> Set-Location c:\
```

Once you have connected to the remote domain controller, you can use the *Get-WMIObject* cmdlet to verify your operating system on that computer. This command and the associated output appear here:

```
[dc1]: PS C:\> Get-WmiObject win32_operatingsystem
SystemDirectory : C:\Windows\system32
Organization    :
BuildNumber     : 7601
RegisteredUser  : Windows User
SerialNumber    : 55041-507-0212466-84005
Version         : 6.1.7601
```

Now you want to get information about the forest. To do this, you use the *Get-ADForest* cmdlet. The output from *Get-ADForest* includes lots of great information such as the domain-naming master, forest mode, schema master, and domain controllers. The command and associated output appear here:

```
[dc1]: PS C:\> Get-ADForest
ApplicationPartitions : {DC=DomainDnsZones,DC=nwtraders,DC=com, DC=ForestDnsZones,DC=nwtraders,
                        DC=com}
CrossForestReferences : {}
DomainNamingMaster    : DC1.nwtraders.com
Domains               : {nwtraders.com}
ForestMode            : Windows2008Forest
GlobalCatalogs        : {DC1.nwtraders.com}
Name                  : nwtraders.com
PartitionsContainer   : CN=Partitions,CN=Configuration,DC=nwtraders,DC=com
RootDomain            : nwtraders.com
SchemaMaster          : DC1.nwtraders.com
Sites                 : {Default-First-Site-Name}
SPNSuffixes           : {}
UPNSuffixes           : {}
```

Next, you'll use the *Get-ADDomain* cmdlet to obtain information about the domain. The command returns important information, such as the location of the default domain controller OU, the PDC Emulator, and the RID Master. The command and associated output appear here:

```
[dc1]: PS C:\> Get-ADDomain
AllowedDNSSuffixes                  : {}
ChildDomains                        : {}
ComputersContainer                  : CN=Computers,DC=nwtraders,DC=com
DeletedObjectsContainer             : CN=Deleted Objects,DC=nwtraders,DC=com
DistinguishedName                   : DC=nwtraders,DC=com
DNSRoot                             : nwtraders.com
DomainControllersContainer          : OU=Domain Controllers,DC=nwtraders,DC=com
DomainMode                          : Windows2008Domain
DomainSID                           : S-1-5-21-909705514-2746778377-2082649206
ForeignSecurityPrincipalsContainer  : CN=ForeignSecurityPrincipals,DC=nwtraders,DC=com
Forest                              : nwtraders.com
InfrastructureMaster                : DC1.nwtraders.com
LastLogonReplicationInterval        :
LinkedGroupPolicyObjects            : {CN={31B2F340-016D-11D2-945F-00C04FB984F9},CN=Policies,CN=
                                      System,DC=nwtraders,DC=com}
LostAndFoundContainer               : CN=LostAndFound,DC=nwtraders,DC=com
ManagedBy                           :
Name                                : nwtraders
NetBIOSName                         : NWTRADERS
ObjectClass                         : domainDNS
ObjectGUID                          : 0026d1fc-2e4d-4c35-96ce-b900e9d67e7c
ParentDomain                        :
PDCEmulator                         : DC1.nwtraders.com
QuotasContainer                     : CN=NTDS Quotas,DC=nwtraders,DC=com
ReadOnlyReplicaDirectoryServers     : {}
ReplicaDirectoryServers             : {DC1.nwtraders.com}
RIDMaster                           : DC1.nwtraders.com
SubordinateReferences               : {DC=ForestDnsZones,DC=nwtraders,DC=com, DC=DomainDnsZones,
                                      DC=nwtraders,DC=com, CN=Configuration,DC=nwtraders,DC=com}
SystemsContainer                    : CN=System,DC=nwtraders,DC=com
UsersContainer                      : CN=Users,DC=nwtraders,DC=com
```

From a security perspective, you should always check the domain password policy. To do this, use the *Get-ADDefaultDomainPasswordPolicy* cmdlet. Things you want to pay attention to are the use of complex passwords, minimum password length, password age, and password retention. Of course, you also need to check the account lockout policy too. This policy is especially important to review closely when inheriting a new network. Here is the command and associated output to do this:

```
[dc1]: PS C:\> Get-ADDefaultDomainPasswordPolicy
ComplexityEnabled            : True
DistinguishedName            : DC=nwtraders,DC=com
LockoutDuration              : 00:30:00
LockoutObservationWindow     : 00:30:00
LockoutThreshold             : 0
MaxPasswordAge               : 42.00:00:00
MinPasswordAge               : 1.00:00:00
MinPasswordLength            : 7
objectClass                  : {domainDNS}
objectGuid                   : 0026d1fc-2e4d-4c35-96ce-b900e9d67e7c
PasswordHistoryCount         : 24
ReversibleEncryptionEnabled  : False
```

Finally, you need to check the domain controllers themselves. To do this, use the *Get-ADDomainController* cmdlet. This command returns important information about domain controllers, such as whether the domain controller is read-only, is a global catalog server, or owns one of the operations master roles; it also returns operating system information. Here is the command and associated output:

```
[dc1]: PS C:\> Get-ADDomainController -Identity dc1
ComputerObjectDN          : CN=DC1,OU=Domain Controllers,DC=nwtraders,DC=com
DefaultPartition          : DC=nwtraders,DC=com
Domain                    : nwtraders.com
Enabled                   : True
Forest                    : nwtraders.com
HostName                  : DC1.nwtraders.com
InvocationId              : b51f625f-3f60-44e7-8577-8918f7396c2a
IPv4Address               : 10.0.0.1
IPv6Address               :
IsGlobalCatalog           : True
IsReadOnly                : False
LdapPort                  : 389
Name                      : DC1
NTDSSettingsObjectDN      : CN=NTDS Settings,CN=DC1,CN=Servers,CN=Default-First-Site-Name,CN=
                            Sites,CN=Configuration,DC=nwtraders,DC=com
OperatingSystem           : Windows Server 2008 R2 Enterprise
OperatingSystemHotfix     :
OperatingSystemServicePack : Service Pack 1
OperatingSystemVersion    : 6.1 (7601)
OperationMasterRoles      : {SchemaMaster, DomainNamingMaster, PDCEmulator, RIDMaster...}
Partitions                : {DC=ForestDnsZones,DC=nwtraders,DC=com, DC=DomainDnsZones,DC=
                            nwtraders,DC=com, CN=Schema,CN=Configuration,DC=nwtraders,DC=com,
                            CN=Configuration,DC=nwtraders,DC=com...}
ServerObjectDN            : CN=DC1,CN=Servers,CN=Default-First-Site-Name,CN=Sites,CN=
                            Configuration,DC=nwtraders,DC=com
ServerObjectGuid          : 5ae1fd0e-bc2f-42a7-af62-24377114e03d
Site                      : Default-First-Site-Name
SslPort                   : 636
```

Producing a report is as easy as redirecting the output to a text file. The following commands gather the information discussed earlier in this section and store the retrieved information in a file named AD_Doc.txt. The commands also illustrate that it is possible to redirect the information to a file stored in a network share.

```
Get-ADForest >> \\dc1\shared\AD_Doc.txt
Get-ADDomain >> \\dc1\shared\AD_Doc.txt
Get-ADDefaultDomainPasswordPolicy >> \\dc1\shared\AD_Doc.txt
Get-ADDomainController -Identity dc1 >>\\dc1\shared\AD_Doc.txt
```

The file as viewed in Notepad appears in Figure 16-4.

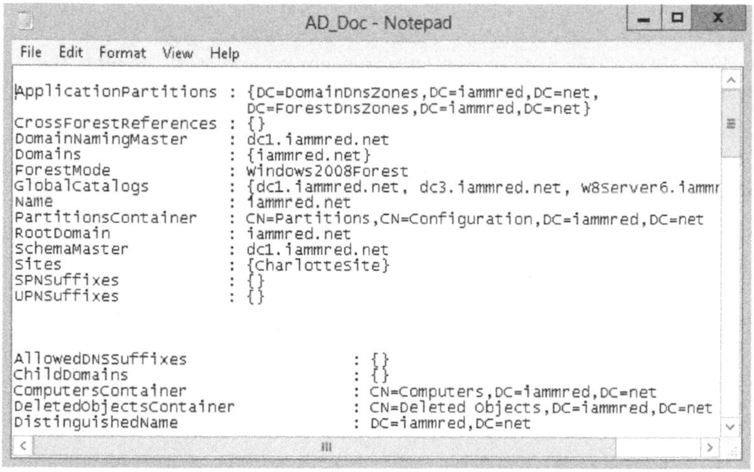

**FIGURE 16-4** Active Directory documentation displayed in Notepad.

## Renaming Active Directory sites

It is easy to rename a site. All you need to do is to right-click the site and select Rename from the action menu in the Microsoft Management Console (MMC). By default, the first site is called Default-First-Site-Name, which is not too illuminating. To work with Active Directory sites, it is necessary to understand that they are a bit strange. First, they reside in the configuration-naming context. Connecting to this context using the Active Directory module is rather simple. All you need to do is to use the *Get-ADRootDSE* cmdlet and then select the *ConfigurationNamingContext* property. First, you have to make a connection to the domain controller and import the Active Directory module (assuming that you do not have RSAT installed on your client computer). This appears here:

```
Enter-PSSession -ComputerName dc3 -Credential iammred\administrator
Import-Module activedirectory
```

Here is the code that will retrieve all of the sites. It uses the *Get-ADObject* cmdlet to search the configuration-naming context for objects that are of class *site*.

```
Get-ADObject -SearchBase (Get-ADRootDSE).ConfigurationNamingContext -filter "objectclass -eq
'site'"
```

Once you have the site you wish to work with, you first change the *DisplayName* attribute. To do this, you pipeline the *site* object to the *Set-ADOObject* cmdlet. The *Set-ADOObject* cmdlet allows you to set a variety of attributes on an object. This command appears following. (This is a single command that is broken into two pieces at the pipe character).

```
Get-ADObject -SearchBase (Get-ADRootDSE).ConfigurationNamingContext -filter "objectclass -eq
'site'" | Set-ADObject -DisplayName CharlotteSite
```

Once you have set the *-DisplayName* attribute, you can rename the object itself. To do this, you use a cmdlet called *Rename-ADObject*. Once again, to simplify things, you pipeline the *site* object to the cmdlet and assign a new name for the site. This command appears following. (This is also a one-line command broken at the pipe).

```
Get-ADObject -SearchBase (Get-ADRootDSE).ConfigurationNamingContext -filter "objectclass -eq
'site'" | Rename-ADObject -NewName CharlotteSite
```

# Managing users

To create a new organizational unit (OU), you use the *New-ADOrganizationalUnit* cmdlet, as shown here:

```
New-ADOrganizationalUnit -Name TestOU -Path "dc=nwtraders,dc=com"
```

If you wish to create a child OU, you use the *New-ADOrganizationalUnit* cmdlet, but in the path, you list the location that will serve as the parent. This is illustrated here:

```
New-ADOrganizationalUnit -Name TestOU1 -Path "ou=TestOU,dc=nwtraders,dc=com"
```

If you wish to create several child OUs in the same location, use the up arrow key to retrieve the previous command and edit the name of the child. You can use the Home key to move to the beginning of the line, the End key to move to the end of the line, and the left and right arrow keys to find your place on the line so you can edit it. A second child OU is created here:

```
New-ADOrganizationalUnit -Name TestOU2 -Path "ou=TestOU,dc=nwtraders,dc=com"
```

To create a computer account in one of the newly created child OUs, you must type the complete path to the OU that will house the new computer account. The *New-ADComputer* cmdlet is used to create new computer accounts in AD DS. In this example, the TestOU1 OU is a child of the TestOU OU, and therefore both OUs must appear in the *-Path* parameter. Keep in mind that the path that is supplied to the *-Path* parameter must be contained inside quotation marks, as shown here:

```
New-ADComputer -Name Test -Path "ou=TestOU1,ou=TestOU,dc=nwtraders,dc=com"
```

To create a user account, you use the *New-ADUser* cmdlet, as shown here:

```
New-ADUser -Name TestChild -Path "ou=TestOU1,ou=TestOU,dc=nwtraders,dc=com"
```

Because there could be a bit of typing involved that tends to become redundant, you may wish to write a script to create the OUs at the same time the computer and user accounts are created. A sample script that creates OUs, users, and computers is the UseADCmdletsToCreateOuComputerAndUser.ps1 script shown here:

**UseADCmdletsToCreateOuComputerAndUser.ps1**

```
Import-Module -Name ActiveDirectory
$Name = "ScriptTest"
$DomainName = "dc=nwtraders,dc=com"
$OUPath = "ou={0},{1}" -f $Name, $DomainName

New-ADOrganizationalUnit -Name $Name -Path $DomainName -ProtectedFromAccidentalDeletion $false

For($you = 0; $you -le 5; $you++)
{
 New-ADOrganizationalUnit -Name $Name$you -Path $OUPath -ProtectedFromAccidentalDeletion $false
}

For($you = 0 ; $you -le 5; $you++)
{
 New-ADComputer -Name  "TestComputer$you" -Path $OUPath
 New-ADUser -Name "TestUser$you" -Path $OUPath
}
```

The UseADCmdletsToCreateOuComputerAndUser.ps1 script begins by importing the Active Directory module. It then creates the first OU. When testing a script, it is important to disable the deletion protection by using the *-ProtectedFromAccidentalDeletion* parameter. This will allow you to easily delete the OU and avoid having to change the protected status on each OU in the Advanced view in Active Directory Users and Computers.

Once the ScriptTest OU is created, the other OUs and user and computer accounts can be created inside the new location. It may seem obvious that you cannot create a child OU inside the parent OU if the parent has not yet been created—but it is easy to make a logic error like this.

To create a new global security group, use the *New-ADGroup* Windows PowerShell AD DS cmdlet. The *New-ADGroup* cmdlet requires three parameters: *-Name*, for the name of the group; *-Path*, for a path inside the directory to the location where the group will be stored; and *-groupScope*, which can be *global*, *universal*, or *domainlocal*. Before running the command shown here, remember that you must import the Active Directory module into your current Windows PowerShell session.

```
New-ADGroup -Name TestGroup -Path "ou=TestOU,dc=nwtraders,dc=com" -groupScope global
```

To create a new universal group, you only need to change the *-groupScope* parameter value, as shown here:

```
New-ADGroup -Name TestGroup1 -Path "ou=TestOU,dc=nwtraders,dc=com" -groupScope universal
```

To add a user to a group using the *New-ADGroup* cmdlet, you must supply values for the *-Identity* parameter and the *-Members* parameter. The value you use for the *-Identity* parameter is the name of the group. You do not need to use the LDAP syntax of *cn=groupname*; you only need to supply the name. Use ADSI Edit to examine the requisite LDAP attributes needed for a group in ADSI Edit.

It is a bit unusual that the *-Members* parameter is named *-Members* and not *-Member*, because most Windows PowerShell cmdlet parameter names are singular, not plural. The parameter names are singular even when they accept an array of values (such as the *-computername* parameter). The command to add a new group named TestGroup1 to the UserGroupTest group is shown here:

```
Add-ADGroupMember -Identity TestGroup1 -Members UserGroupTest
```

To remove a user from a group, use the *Remove-ADGroupMember* cmdlet with the name of the user and group. The *-Identity* and the *-Members* parameters are required, but the command will not execute without confirmation, as shown here:

```
PS C:\> Remove-ADGroupMember -Identity TestGroup1 -Members UserGroupTest

Confirm
Are you sure you want to perform this action?
Performing operation "Set" on Target "CN=TestGroup1,OU=TestOU,DC=NWTraders,DC=Com".
[Y] Yes  [A] Yes to All  [N] No  [L] No to All  [S] Suspend  [?] Help (default is "Y"): y
PS C:\>
```

If you are sure you wish to remove the user from the group and you wish to suppress the query, you use the *-Confirm* parameter and assign the value *$false* to it. Note that you will need to supply a colon between the parameter and the *$false* value.

> **Note** The use of the colon after the *-Confirm* parameter is not documented, but the technique works on several different cmdlets. Unfortunately, you cannot use the *-Force* switched parameter to suppress the query.

The command is shown here:

```
Remove-ADGroupMember -Identity TestGroup1 -Members UserGroupTest -Confirm:$false
```

You need the ability to suppress the confirmation prompt to be able to use the *Remove-ADGroupMember* cmdlet in a script. The first thing the RemoveUserFromGroup.ps1 script does is load the Active Directory module. Once the module is loaded, the *Remove-ADGroupMember* cmdlet is used to remove the user from the group. To suppress the confirmation prompt, the *-Confirm:$false* command is used. The RemoveUserFromGroup.ps1 script is shown here:

**RemoveUserFromGroup.ps1**

```
import-module activedirectory
Remove-ADGroupMember -Identity TestGroup1 -Members UserGroupTest -Confirm:$false
```

# Creating a user

In this section, you'll create a new user in Active Directory with the name Ed. The command to create a new user is simple: it is *New-ADUser* and the user name. The command to create a disabled user account in the *Users* container in the default domain appears here:

```
New-ADUser -Name Ed
```

When the command that creates a new user completes, nothing is returned to the Windows PowerShell console. To check to ensure that the user is created, use the *Get-ADUser* cmdlet to retrieve the *User* object. This command appears here:

```
Get-ADUser Ed
```

Once you are certain your new user is created, you can create an OU to store the user account. The command to create a new OU off the root of the domain appears here:

```
New-ADOrganizationalUnit Scripting
```

As with the previously used *New-ADUser* cmdlet, nothing returns to the Windows PowerShell console. If you use the *Get-ADOrganizationalUnit* cmdlet, you must use a different methodology. A simple *Get-ADOrganizationalUnit* command returns an error; instead, you can use the *-LDAPFilter* parameter to find the OU, as follows:

```
Get-ADOrganizationalUnit -LDAPFilter "(name=scripting)"
```

Now that you have a new user and a new OU, you need to move the user from the *Users* container to the newly created Scripting OU. To do that, you use the *Move-ADObject* cmdlet. You first get the *distinguishedname* attribute for the Scripting OU and store it in a variable called *$oupath*. Next, you use the *Move-ADObject* cmdlet to move the Ed user to the new OU. The trick here is that whereas the *Get-ADUser* cmdlet is able to find a user with the name of Ed, the *Move-ADObject* cmdlet must have the distinguished name of the *Ed USER* object in order to move it. You could use the *Get-ADUser* cmdlet to retrieve the distinguished name in a similar manner as you did with the Scripting OU.

The next thing you need to do is to enable the user account. To do this, you need to assign a password to the user account prior to enabling the account. The password must be a secure string. To do this, you can use the *ConvertTo-SecureString* cmdlet. By default, warnings about converting text to a secure string are displayed, but you can suppress these prompts by using the *-force* parameter. Here is the command you use to create a secure string for a password:

```
$pwd = ConvertTo-SecureString -String "P@ssword1" -AsPlainText -Force
```

Now that you have created a secure string to use for a password for your user account, you call the *Set-ADAccountPassword* cmdlet to set the password. Because this is a new password, you need to use the *-NewPassword* parameter. In addition, because you do not have a previous password, you use the *-Reset* parameter. This command appears here:

```
Set-ADAccountPassword -Identity ed -NewPassword $pwd -Reset
```

Once the account has an assigned password, it is time to enable the user account. This command appears here:

```
Enable-ADAccount -Identity ed
```

As with the previous cmdlets, none of these cmdlets returns any information. To ensure you have actually enabled the Ed user account, you use the *Get-ADUser* cmdlet. In the output, you are looking for the value of the *enabled* property. The *enabled* property is a Boolean, so therefore expect the value to be *true*.

## Finding and unlocking Active Directory user accounts

When using the Active Directory cmdlets, locating locked-out users is a snap. The *Search-ADAccount* cmdlet even has a *-LockedOut* switch. Use the *Search-ADAccount* cmdlet with the *-LockedOut* parameter to find all user accounts in the domain that are locked out. This command appears here:

```
Search-ADAccount -LockedOut
```

**Note** Many network administrators who spend the majority of their time working with Active Directory import the Active Directory module via their Windows PowerShell profile. In this way, they never need to worry about the initial performance hit that occurs due to autoloading the Active Directory module.

The *Search-ADAccount* command and the associated output appear here:

```
[w8server6]: PS C:\> Search-ADAccount -LockedOut

AccountExpirationDate :
DistinguishedName     : CN=kimakers,OU=test,DC=iammred,DC=net
Enabled               : True
LastLogonDate         : 1/24/2012 8:40:29 AM
LockedOut             : True
Name                  : kimakers
ObjectClass           : user
ObjectGUID            : d907fa99-cd08-435f-97de-1e99d0eb485d
PasswordExpired       : False
PasswordNeverExpires  : False
SamAccountName        : kimakers
SID                   : S-1-5-21-1457956834-3844189528-3541350385-1608
UserPrincipalName     : kimakers@iammred.net

[w8server6]: PS C:\>
```

You can unlock the locked-out user account as well—assuming you have permission. Figure 16-5 shows an attempt to unlock the user account with an account that is for a normal user—an error arises.

> **Note** People are often worried about Windows PowerShell from a security perspective. Windows PowerShell is only an application, and therefore users are not able to do anything that they do not have rights or permission to accomplish. This is a case in point.

If your user account does not have admin rights, you need to start Windows PowerShell with an account that has the ability to unlock a user account. To do this, you right-click the Windows PowerShell icon while holding down the Shift key; this allows you to select Run As Different User from the Tasks menu.

Once you start Windows PowerShell back up with an account that has rights to unlock users, the Active Directory module needs to load once again. You then check to ensure that you can still locate the locked-out user accounts. Once you can do that, you pipeline the results of the *Search-ADAccount* cmdlet to *Unlock-ADAccount*. A quick check ensures you have unlocked all the locked-out accounts. The series of commands appears here:

```
Search-ADAccount -LockedOut
Search-ADAccount -LockedOut | Unlock-ADAccount
Search-ADAccount -LockedOut
```

The commands and associated output appear in Figure 16-5.

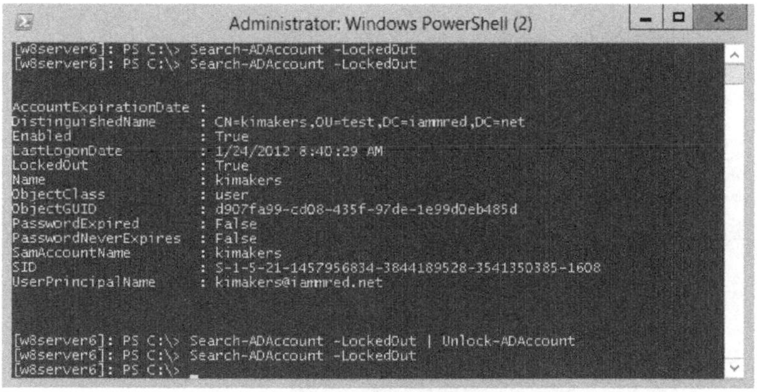

**FIGURE 16-5** Using the Active Directory module to find and to unlock user accounts.

> **Note** Keep in mind that the command *Search-ADAccount -LockedOut | Unlock-ADAccount* will unlock every account that you have permission to unlock. In most cases, you will want to investigate prior to unlocking all locked-out accounts. If you do not want to unlock all locked-out accounts, use the *-confirm* switch to be prompted prior to unlocking an account.

If you do not want to unlock all users, you use the -*confirm* parameter when calling the *Unlock-ADAccount* cmdlet. As an example, you first check to see what users are locked out by using the *Search-ADAccount* cmdlet—but you do not want to see everything, only their names. Next, you pipeline the locked-out users to the *Unlock-ADAccount* cmdlet with the -*confirm* parameter. You are then prompted for each of the three locked-out users. You choose to unlock the first and third users, but not the second user. You then use the *Search-ADAccount* cmdlet one last time to ensure that the second user is still locked out.

## Finding disabled users

Luckily, by using Windows PowerShell and the Active Directory cmdlets, you can retrieve the disabled users from your domain with a single line of code. The command appears following. (Keep in mind that running this command automatically imports the Active Directory module into the current Windows PowerShell host.)

```
Get-ADUser -Filter 'enabled -eq $false' -Server dc3
```

Not only is the command a single line of code, but it is also a single line of *readable* code. You get users from AD DS; you use a filter that looks for the *enabled* property set to *false*. You also specify that you want to query a server named dc3 (the name of one of the domain controllers on my network). The command and the associated output appear in Figure 16-6.

**FIGURE 16-6** Finding disabled user accounts.

If you want to work with a specific user, you can use the -*identity* parameter. The -*identity* parameter accepts several things: *distinguishedname*, *sid*, *guid*, and *SamAccountName*. Probably the easiest one to use is the *SamAccountName*. This command and associated output appears here:

```
PS C:\Users\ed.IAMMRED>    Get-ADUser -Server dc3 -Identity teresa
DistinguishedName : CN=Teresa Wilson,OU=Charlotte,DC=iammred,DC=net
Enabled           : True
GivenName         : Teresa
Name              : Teresa Wilson
ObjectClass       : user
ObjectGUID        : 75f12010-b952-4d16-9b22-3ada7d26eed8
SamAccountName    : Teresa
SID               : S-1-5-21-1457956834-3844189528-3541350385-1104
Surname           : Wilson
UserPrincipalName : Teresa@iammred.net
```

To use the *distinguishedname* value for the *-identity* parameter, you need to supply it inside a pair of quotation marks—either single or double. This command and associated output appear here:

```
PS C:\Users\ed.IAMMRED>    Get-ADUser -Server dc3 -Identity 'CN=Teresa Wilson,OU
=Charlotte,DC=iammred,DC=net'
DistinguishedName : CN=Teresa Wilson,OU=Charlotte,DC=iammred,DC=net
Enabled           : True
GivenName         : Teresa
Name              : Teresa Wilson
ObjectClass       : user
ObjectGUID        : 75f12010-b952-4d16-9b22-3ada7d26eed8
SamAccountName    : Teresa
SID               : S-1-5-21-1457956834-3844189528-3541350385-1104
Surname           : Wilson
UserPrincipalName : Teresa@iammred.net
```

It is not necessary to use quotation marks when using the SID for the value of the *-identity* parameter. This command and associated output appear here:

```
PS C:\Users\ed.IAMMRED>    Get-ADUser -Server dc3 -Identity S-1-5-21-1457956834-
3844189528-3541350385-1104


DistinguishedName : CN=Teresa Wilson,OU=Charlotte,DC=iammred,DC=net
Enabled           : True
GivenName         : Teresa
Name              : Teresa Wilson
ObjectClass       : user
ObjectGUID        : 75f12010-b952-4d16-9b22-3ada7d26eed8
SamAccountName    : Teresa
SID               : S-1-5-21-1457956834-3844189528-3541350385-1104
Surname           : Wilson
UserPrincipalName : Teresa@iammred.net
```

Once again, you can also use the *ObjectGUID* for the *-identity* parameter value. It does not require quotation marks either. This command and associated output appear here:

```
PS C:\Users\ed.IAMMRED>    Get-ADUser -Server dc3 -Identity 75f12010-b952-4d16-9
b22-3ada7d26eed8
DistinguishedName : CN=Teresa Wilson,OU=Charlotte,DC=iammred,DC=net
Enabled           : True
GivenName         : Teresa
Name              : Teresa Wilson
ObjectClass       : user
ObjectGUID        : 75f12010-b952-4d16-9b22-3ada7d26eed8
SamAccountName    : Teresa
SID               : S-1-5-21-1457956834-3844189528-3541350385-1104
Surname           : Wilson
UserPrincipalName : Teresa@iammred.net
```

## Finding unused user accounts

To obtain a listing of all the users in Active Directory, supply a wildcard to the *-filter* parameter of the
*Get-ADUser* cmdlet. This technique appears here:

```
Get-ADUser -Filter *
```

If you wish to change the base of the search operations, use the *-SearchBase* parameter. The
*-SearchBase* parameter accepts an LDAP style of naming. The following command changes the search
base to the TestOU OU:

```
Get-ADUser -Filter * -SearchBase "ou=TestOU,dc=nwtraders,dc=com"
```

When you use the *Get-ADUser* cmdlet, only a certain subset of user properties are displayed
(10 properties, to be exact). These properties will be displayed when you pipeline the results to
*Format-List* and use a wildcard and the *-force* parameter, as shown here:

```
PS C:\> Get-ADUser -Identity bob | format-list -Property * -Force


DistinguishedName : CN=bob,OU=TestOU,DC=NWTraders,DC=Com
Enabled           : True
GivenName         : bob
Name              : bob
ObjectClass       : user
ObjectGUID        : 5cae3acf-f194-4e07-a466-789f9ad5c84a
SamAccountName    : bob
SID               : S-1-5-21-3746122405-834892460-3960030898-3601
Surname           :
UserPrincipalName : bob@NWTraders.Com
PropertyNames     : {DistinguishedName, Enabled, GivenName, Name...}
PropertyCount     : 10



PS C:\>
```

Anyone who knows very much about AD DS knows there are certainly more than 10 properties associated with a *User* object. If you try to display a property that is not returned by the *Get-ADUser* cmdlet, such as the *whenCreated* property, an error is not returned, but the value of the *whenCreated* property is not returned either. This is shown here:

```
PS C:\> Get-ADUser -Identity bob | Format-List -Property name, whenCreated


name        : bob
whencreated :
```

The *whenCreated* property for the *User* object has a value—it just is not displayed. However, suppose you were looking for users that had never logged on to the system? Suppose you used a query such as the one shown here, and you were going to base a delete operation upon the results—the results could be disastrous.

```
PS C:\> Get-ADUser -Filter * | Format-Table -Property name, LastLogonDate

name                                    LastLogonDate
----                                    -------------
Administrator
Guest
krbtgt
testuser2
ed
SystemMailbox{1f05a927-a261-4eb4-8360-8...
SystemMailbox{e0dc1c29-89c3-4034-b678-e...
FederatedEmail.4c1f4d8b-8179-4148-93bf-...
Test
TestChild
<results truncated>
```

To retrieve a property that is not a member of the default 10 properties, you must select it by using the *-property* parameter. The reason that *Get-ADUser* does not automatically return all properties and their associated values is because of performance issues on large networks—there is no reason to return a large data set when a small data set will perfectly suffice. To display the *name* and the *whenCreated* date for the user named bob, the following command can be used:

```
PS C:\> Get-ADUser -Identity bob -Properties whencreated | Format-List -Property name
, whencreated


name        : bob
whencreated : 6/11/2010 8:19:52 AM


PS C:\>
```

To retrieve all of the properties associated with a *User* object, use the wildcard * for the *-properties* parameter value. You would use a command similar to the one shown here:

```
Get-ADUser -Identity kimakers -Properties *
```

Both the command and the results associated with the command to return all user properties appear in Figure 16-7.

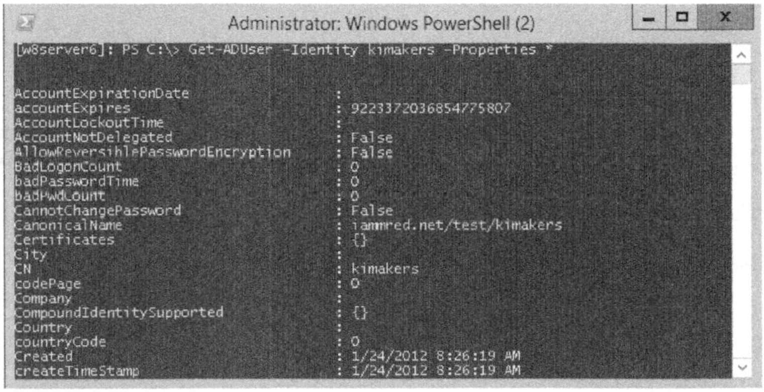

**FIGURE 16-7** Using the *Get-ADUser* cmdlet to display all user properties.

To produce a listing of all the users and their last logon date, you can use a command similar to the one shown here. This is a single command that might wrap the line depending on your screen resolution.

```
Get-ADUser -Filter * -Properties "LastLogonDate" |
sort-object -property lastlogondate -descending |
Format-Table -property name, lastlogondate -AutoSize
```

The output produces a nice table. Both the command and the output associated with the command to obtain the time a user last logged on appear in Figure 16-8.

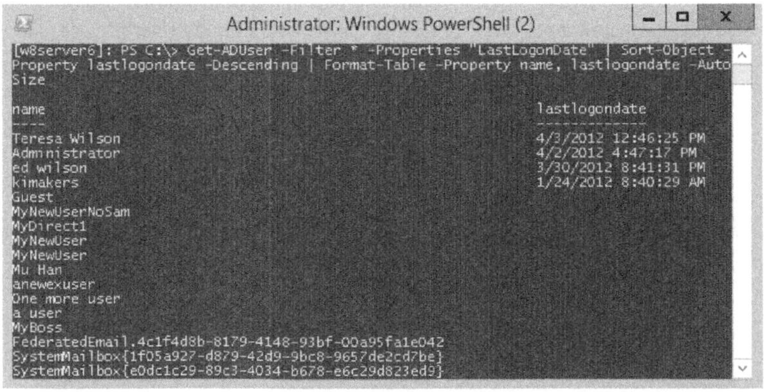

**FIGURE 16-8** Using the *Get-ADUser* cmdlet to identify the last logon times for users.

# Updating Active Directory objects: step-by-step exercises

In these exercises, you will search for users in a specific OU that do not have a *description* attribute populated. You will create a script that updates this value. In addition, you will change the password for users in Active Directory.

> **Note** To complete these exercises, you will need access to a Windows server running AD DS. Modify the domain names listed in the exercises to match the name of your domain.

### Using the Active Directory module to update Active Directory objects

1. Open the Windows PowerShell ISE or some other script editor.

2. Use the *Import-Module* cmdlet to import the Active Directory module.

   ```
   Import-Module ActiveDirectory
   ```

3. Set the *$users* and *$you* variables to *$null*.

   ```
   $users = $you = $null
   ```

4. Use the *Get-ADUser* cmdlet to retrieve users from the TestOU OU in the nwtraders.com domain. The *filter* property is required, and therefore you give it a wildcard * to tell it you want everything returned. In addition, you specify that you want the *description* property returned in the search results.

   ```
   $users = Get-ADUser -SearchBase "ou=testou,dc=nwtraders,dc=com" -filter * `
       -property description
   ```

5. Use the *ForEach* statement to walk through the collection. Inside the collection, use the static *isNullOrEmpty* method from the *system.string* .NET Framework class to check the *description* property on the *User* object. If the property is empty or null, display a string that states the script will modify the *User* object. The code to do this appears here:

   ```
   ForEach($user in $users)
     {
      if([string]::isNullOrEmpty($user.description))
       {
         "modifying $($user.name)"
   ```

6. Use the *Set-ADUser* cmdlet to modify the user. Pass the *-identity* parameter a distinguished name. Use the *-description* parameter to hold the value to add to the *description* attribute on the object. This command is shown here:

   ```
   Set-ADUser -Identity $user.distinguishedName -Description "added via script"
   ```

7. Increment the *$you* counter variable and display a summary string. This portion of the script is shown here:

```
$you++
    }
  }
  "modified $you users"
```

8. Compare your script with the one that appears here:

```
    SetADPropertyADCmdlets.ps1
Import-Module ActiveDirectory
 $users = $you = $null
 $users = Get-ADUser -SearchBase "ou=testou,dc=nwtraders,dc=com" -filter * `
  -property description
 ForEach($user in $users)
  {
    if([string]::isNullOrEmpty($user.description))
     {
       "modifying $($user.name)"
       Set-ADUser -Identity $user.distinguishedName -Description "added via script"
       $you++
     }
  }
  "modified $you users"
```

In the following exercise, you will change a user's password.

## Changing user passwords

1. Open the Windows PowerShell console with administrator rights.

2. Use the *Get-Credential* cmdlet to retrieve and store credentials that have permission on a remote domain controller. Store the credentials in a variable named *$credential*.

```
$credential = Get-Credential
```

3. Use the *Enter-PSSession* cmdlet to enter a remote Windows PowerShell session on a domain controller that contains the Active Directory module:

```
Enter-PSSession -ComputerName DC1 -Credential $credential
```

4. Use the *Get-ADUser* cmdlet to identify a user whose password you want to reset:

```
Get-ADUser ed
```

5. Use the *Set-ADAccountPassword* cmdlet to reset the password:

```
Set-ADAccountPassword -Identity ed -Reset
```

6. A warning appears stating that the remote computer is requesting to read a line securely. Type in the new password for the user:

Password

7. A second warning appears with a prompt to repeat the password. The warning itself is the same as the previous warning about reading a secure line. Type in the same password you previously typed.

8. Type **Get-History** to review the commands you typed during the remote session.

9. Type **Exit** to exit the remote session.

10. Type **Get-History** to review the commands you typed prior to entering the remote session.

This concludes the exercise.

> **Note** If you need to work with local user accounts, download the Local User Management module from the TechNet Script Center Script Repository. This module provides the ability to create, modify, and delete both local users and groups. It also permits you to change local user account passwords.

## Chapter 16 quick reference

| To | Do this |
| --- | --- |
| Find domain FSMO role holders | Use the *Get-ADDomain* cmdlet and select PDCEmulator, RIDMaster, and InfrastructureMaster. |
| Find forest FSMO role holders | Use the *Get-ADForest* cmdlet and select SchemaMaster and DomainNamingMaster. |
| Rename a site in AD DS | Use the *Get-ADObject* cmdlet to retrieve the site and the *Rename-ADObject* cmdlet to set a new name. |
| Create a new user in AD DS | Use the *New-ADUser* cmdlet. |
| Find locked-out user accounts in AD DS | Use the *Search-ADAccount* cmdlet with the *-lockedout* switch. |
| Unlock a user account in AD DS | Use the *Unlock-ADAccount* cmdlet. |
| Set a user's password in AD DS | Use the *Set-ADAccountPassword* cmdlet. |

# Deploying Active Directory with Windows Server 2012

**After completing this chapter, you will be able to:**

- Use the Active Directory module to deploy a new forest and a new domain controller.

- Use the Active Directory module to add a new domain controller to an existing domain.

- Use the Active Directory module to deploy a read-only domain controller.

## Using the Active Directory module to deploy a new forest

Deploying Microsoft Active Directory Domain Services (AD DS) is not a simple matter. There are pre-requisites that must be met and multiple items that need to be configured. One of the first things that might need to be accomplished is setting the script execution policy. Whereas the easiest way to do this is via group policy, if you are configuring the first domain controller in the first domain in a new forest, you do not have that luxury. To set the script execution policy, use the *Set-ExecutionPolicy* cmdlet and set it to something like *remotesigned*. The command appears following. (The command must execute with admin rights, but more than likely you will be logged on as an administrator any-way if you are just beginning your configuration.)

```
Set-ExecutionPolicy remotesigned -force
```

Some of the infrastructure prerequisites are listed here:

- Ensure the server has the correct name.

- Set a static Internet Protocol (IP) address configuration.

- Ensure the DNS Server Windows feature is deployed and configured.

In addition to infrastructure prerequisites, there are role-based prerequisites that need to be deployed. These role-based prerequisites appear here:

- Active Directory module for Windows PowerShell

- Active Directory Administrative Center tools

- AD DS snap-ins and command-line tools

Luckily, all of these tools are installable via the *ServerManager* module and the *Add-WindowsFeature* cmdlet. In fact, from a Windows-feature standpoint, the *rsat-ad-tools* feature group gives you everything you need here. The AddADPrereqs.ps1 script sets a static IP address by using the *New-NetIPAddress* cmdlet. To determine the interface index, the *Get-NetAdapter* cmdlet is used. This portion of the script appears here:

```
#set static IP address
$ipaddress = "192.168.0.225"
$ipprefix = "24"
$ipgw = "192.168.0.1"
$ipdns = "192.168.0.225"
$ipif = (Get-NetAdapter).ifIndex
New-NetIPAddress -IPAddress $ipaddress -PrefixLength $ipprefix `
    -InterfaceIndex $ipif -DefaultGateway $ipgw
```

Once the new IP address is assigned, the *Rename-Computer* cmdlet assigns a new name to the computer. The *Rename-Computer* cmdlet has a *-restart* parameter, but the AddADPrereqs.ps1 script holds off rebooting the script until the end, and therefore the *restart* parameter is not used. This portion of the script appears here:

```
#rename the computer
$newname = "dc8508"
Rename-Computer -NewName $newname -force
```

Now that the computer has received a new IP address and has been renamed, it is time to add the features. The first thing the script does is create a log file in a directory named *poshlog*. This log will hold details resulting from adding the features. In addition, once the configuration completes, a *Get-WindowsFeature* command runs to gather the installed features. The result is written to a log file in the *poshlog* directory. The *Add-WindowsFeature* cmdlet appears to accept an array for the features to be installed, but when attempting to add multiple features with a single call, the secondary features get trampled. Therefore, it is best to add tools one at a time. This portion of the script installs the Active Directory Domain Services (AD DS) tools that include the Active Directory Windows PowerShell module. The command appears here:

```
#install features
$featureLogPath = "c:\poshlog\featurelog.txt"
New-Item $featureLogPath -ItemType file -Force
$addsTools = "RSAT-AD-Tools"

Add-WindowsFeature $addsTools
Get-WindowsFeature | Where installed >>$featureLogPath
```

The last thing to accomplish here is restarting the computer. This is performed via a simple call to the *Restart-Computer* cmdlet. This command appears here:

```
#restart the computer
Restart-Computer
```

The complete AddAdPrereqs.ps1 script appears here:

**AddAdPrereqs.ps1**

```
#set static IP address
$ipaddress = "192.168.0.225"
$ipprefix = "24"
$ipgw = "192.168.0.1"
$ipdns = "192.168.0.225"
$ipif = (Get-NetAdapter).ifIndex
New-NetIPAddress -IPAddress $ipaddress -PrefixLength $ipprefix `
    -InterfaceIndex $ipif -DefaultGateway $ipgw

#rename the computer
$newname = "dc8508"
Rename-Computer -NewName $newname -force

#install features
$featureLogPath = "c:\poshlog\featurelog.txt"
New-Item $featureLogPath -ItemType file -Force
$addsTools = "RSAT-AD-Tools"

Add-WindowsFeature $addsTools
Get-WindowsFeature | Where installed >>$featureLogPath

#restart the computer
Restart-Computer
```

Once the computer reboots, log on and check things. Immediately, the Server Manager utility launches and provides feedback that the name change and the IP address change completed successfully. Server Manager appears in Figure 17-1.

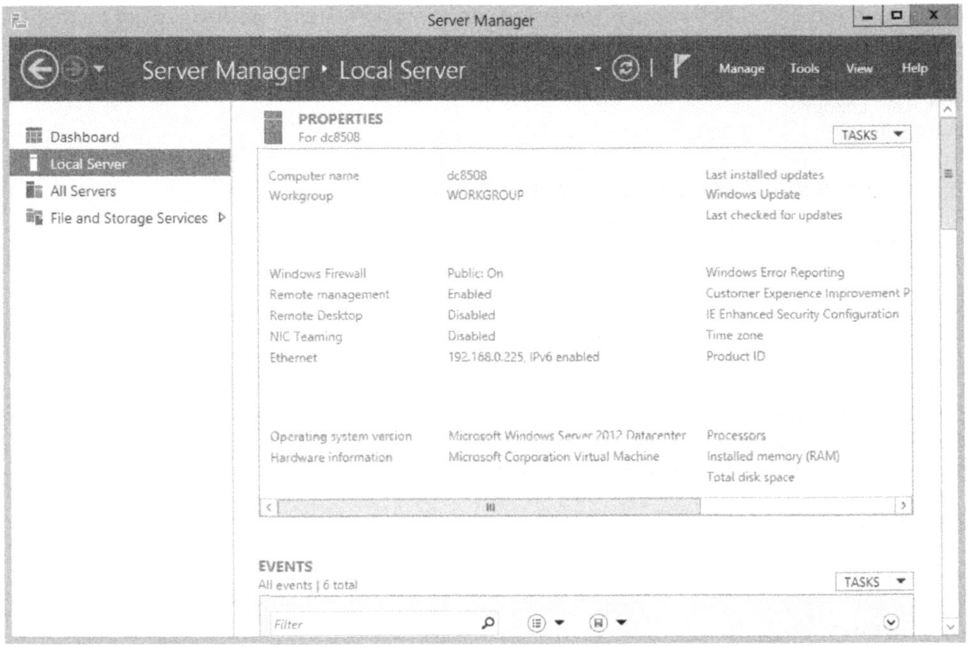


**FIGURE 17-1** After the AddAdPrereqs.ps1 script is run, Server Manager appears and confirms that the name change and the IP address assignment completed successfully.

Next, you'll verify that the roles and features have been added properly. To do this, use the FeatureLog.txt log file that was created prior to the reboot. Figure 17-2 shows what will be displayed if the features and roles have been added properly.

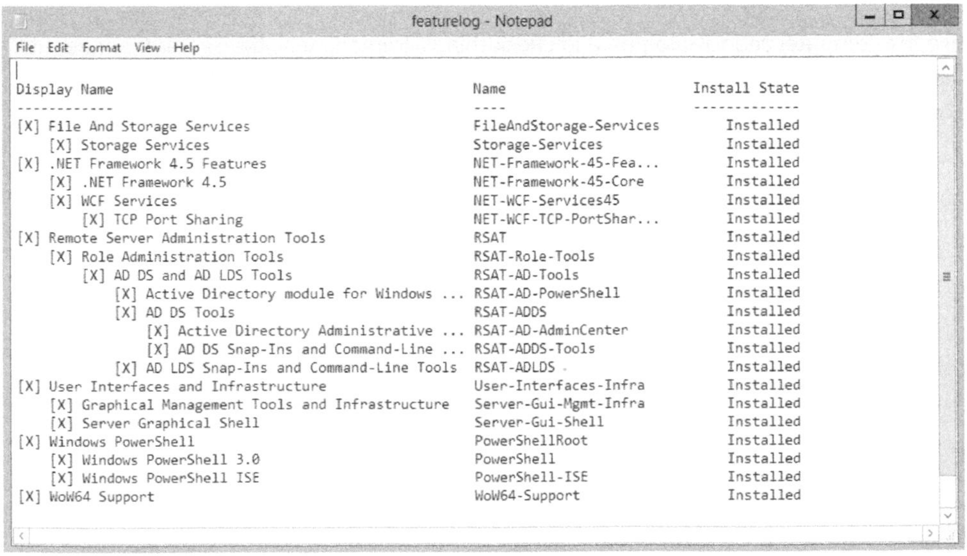


```
Display Name                                            Name                       Install State
------------                                            ----                       -------------
[X] File And Storage Services                           FileAndStorage-Services        Installed
    [X] Storage Services                                Storage-Services               Installed
[X] .NET Framework 4.5 Features                         NET-Framework-45-Fea...        Installed
    [X] .NET Framework 4.5                              NET-Framework-45-Core          Installed
    [X] WCF Services                                    NET-WCF-Services45             Installed
        [X] TCP Port Sharing                            NET-WCF-TCP-PortShar...        Installed
[X] Remote Server Administration Tools                  RSAT                           Installed
    [X] Role Administration Tools                       RSAT-Role-Tools                Installed
        [X] AD DS and AD LDS Tools                      RSAT-AD-Tools                  Installed
            [X] Active Directory module for Windows ... RSAT-AD-PowerShell             Installed
            [X] AD DS Tools                             RSAT-ADDS                      Installed
                [X] Active Directory Administrative ... RSAT-AD-AdminCenter            Installed
                [X] AD DS Snap-Ins and Command-Line ... RSAT-ADDS-Tools                Installed
            [X] AD LDS Snap-Ins and Command-Line Tools  RSAT-ADLDS                     Installed
[X] User Interfaces and Infrastructure                  User-Interfaces-Infra          Installed
    [X] Graphical Management Tools and Infrastructure   Server-Gui-Mgmt-Infra          Installed
    [X] Server Graphical Shell                          Server-Gui-Shell               Installed
[X] Windows PowerShell                                  PowerShellRoot                 Installed
    [X] Windows PowerShell 3.0                          PowerShell                     Installed
    [X] Windows PowerShell ISE                          PowerShell-ISE                 Installed
[X] WoW64 Support                                       WoW64-Support                  Installed
```

**FIGURE 17-2** The FeatureLog.txt file confirms that the roles and features have been added successfully to the computer.

Once you have your computer renamed, with a static IP address and RSAT installed, it is time to add the AD DS role, the DNS Server role, and the group policy management feature. The first thing to do is add the log path for the report at the end of the script. Once this is done, the script starts a job named *addfeature*. The use of a job allows the script to wait until the job completes prior to executing the next step of the script. Because the script adds the features in the background, no progress tests appear in the foreground. Each of the *Add-WindowsFeature* commands includes all of the subfeatures and the management tools. This is a great way to ensure you obtain the bits your specific feature needs. You can always fine-tune it at a later time. Once the job executes, the *Wait-Job* cmdlet pauses the script until the *addfeature* job completes. Then it returns the completed job object. At this time, the final command is a *Get-WindowsFeature* cmdlet call that writes all installed features to the log file. The complete Add-ADFeatures.ps1 script appears here:

**Add-ADFeatures.ps1**

```
#Install AD DS, DNS and GPMC
$featureLogPath = "c:\poshlog\featurelog.txt"
start-job -Name addFeature -ScriptBlock {
  Add-WindowsFeature -Name "ad-domain-services" -IncludeAllSubFeature -IncludeManagementTools
  Add-WindowsFeature -Name "dns" -IncludeAllSubFeature -IncludeManagementTools
  Add-WindowsFeature -Name "gpmc" -IncludeAllSubFeature -IncludeManagementTools   }
Wait-Job -Name addFeature
Get-WindowsFeature | Where installed >>$featureLogPath
```

Once the script finishes running, the featurelog text file can be examined. The log appears in Figure 17-3.

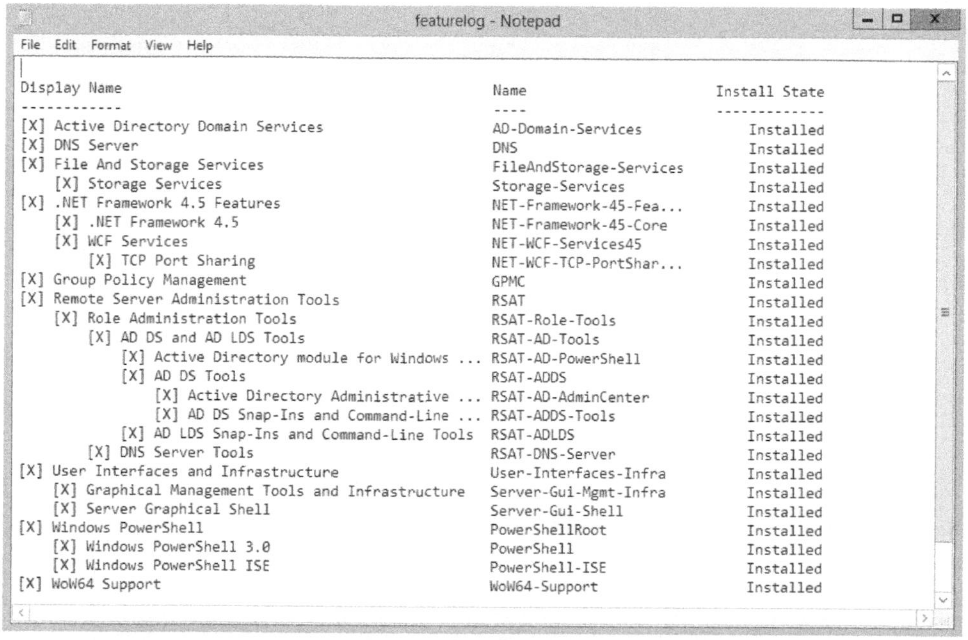

**FIGURE 17-3** The feature log details all installed features and roles on the system.

Now it is time to create the new forest, and add the server as the first domain controller in the newly created forest. The tool required is contained in the *ADDSDeployment* module. The InstallNewForest.ps1 script is essentially one cmdlet: *Install-ADDSForest*. The domain name and the NetBIOS domain name appear as variables. When the script first runs, it prompts for an Active Directory password. This password becomes the administrator password for the new domain. Following the installation, the function automatically reboots the computer to complete configuration. The complete InstallNewForest.ps1 script appears here:

**InstallNewForest.ps1**

```
# Create New Forest, add Domain Controller
$domainname = "nwtraders.msft"
$netbiosName = "NWTRADERS"

  Import-Module ADDSDeployment
  Install-ADDSForest -CreateDnsDelegation:$false `
   -DatabasePath "C:\Windows\NTDS" `
   -DomainMode "Win2012" `
   -DomainName $domainname `
   -DomainNetbiosName $netbiosName `
   -ForestMode "Win2012" `
   -InstallDns:$true `
   -LogPath "C:\Windows\NTDS" `
   -NoRebootOnCompletion:$false `
   -SysvolPath "C:\Windows\SYSVOL" `
   -Force:$true
```

While the script is running, a progress bar appears. This is shown in Figure 17-4.

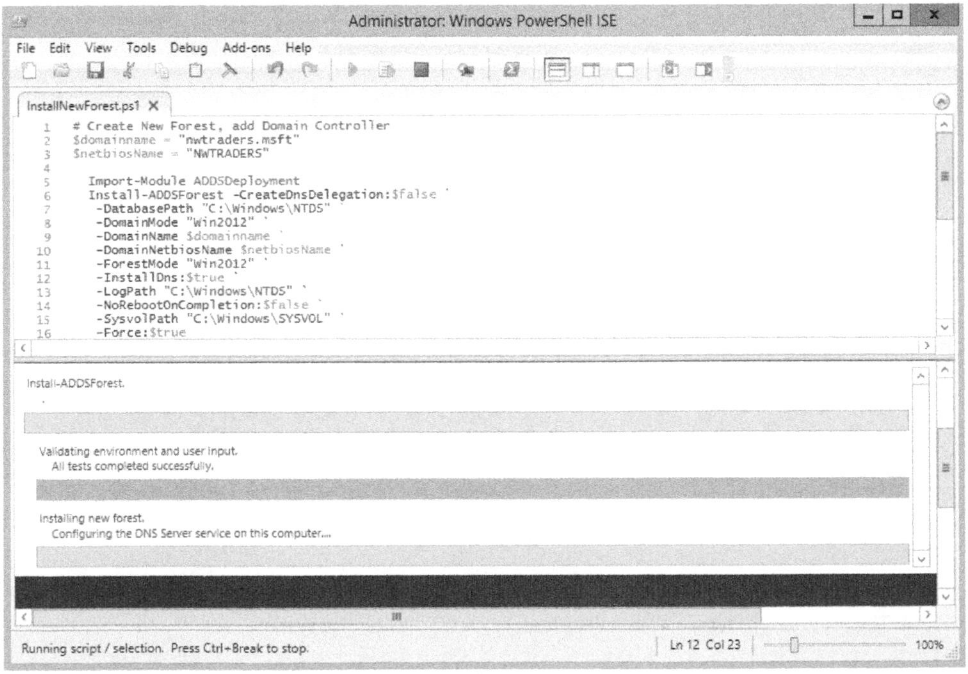

**FIGURE 17-4** A progress bar displays while the script runs. This lets you know the progress of the operations.

Once the script completes running, a quick check of the DNS Manager tool should reveal that DNS is set up properly. The nwtraders.msft forward-lookup zone should be configured properly, and an A record, NS record, and SOA record should be configured. This appears in Figure 17-5.

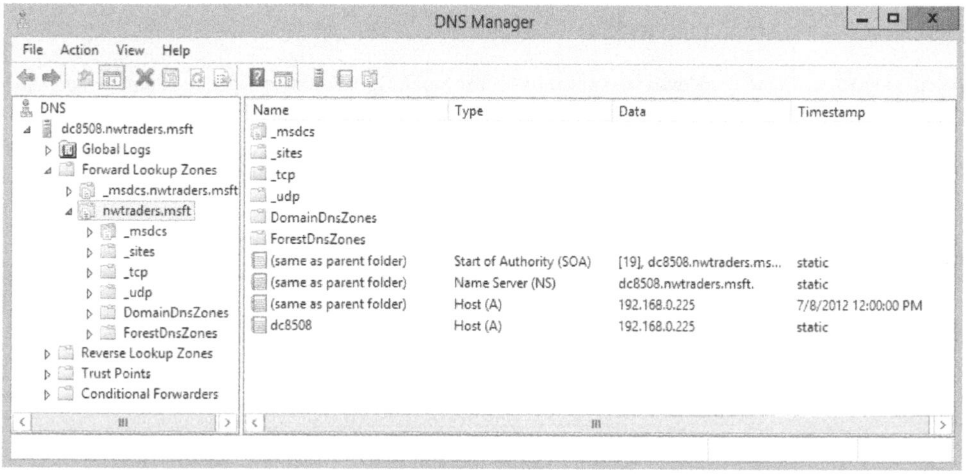

**FIGURE 17-5** Following the running of the InstallNewForest.ps1 script, DNS Manager reveals a properly set up forward-lookup zone.

# Adding a new domain controller to an existing domain

Once you install the first domain controller into your forest root, it is time to add a second domain controller to the domain. The process is similar to the steps required for configuring and installing the first domain controller. There are the usual system configuration steps that must take place, such as setting a static IP address, renaming the computer, and adding the AD DS role and tools. Because this is a second domain controller, it is not necessary to add the DNS server role if you do not want to do so. But the server requires the ability to resolve names, so you must assign a DNS server to the DNS client. To add a DNS server to the IP configuration, use the *Set-DNSClientServerAddress* cmdlet. Specify the same interface index that the *New-NetIPAddress* cmdlet uses. Finally, specify the DNS server IP address to the *-serveraddresses* parameter. This portion of the script appears here:

```
#set static IP address
$ipaddress = "192.168.0.226"
$ipprefix = "24"
$ipgw = "192.168.0.1"
$ipdns = "192.168.0.225"
$ipif = (Get-NetAdapter).ifIndex
New-NetIPAddress –IPAddress $ipaddress -PrefixLength $ipprefix -InterfaceIndex $ipif
-DefaultGateway $ipgw
Set-DnsClientServerAddress -InterfaceIndex $ipif -ServerAddresses $ipdns
```

Following the IP address configuration, it is time to rename the server. This portion of the script is exactly the same as the AddAdPrereqs.ps1 script and will not be discussed here. Note that because only the AD DS bits are required, the script goes ahead and adds the role-based portion of the installation. This reduces the need for an additional script. The portion of the script that installs the AD DS role appears here:

```
#install roles and features
$featureLogPath = "c:\poshlog\featurelog.txt"
New-Item $featureLogPath -ItemType file -Force

Add-WindowsFeature -Name "ad-domain-services" -IncludeAllSubFeature -IncludeManagementTools
Get-WindowsFeature | Where installed >>$featureLogPath
```

Finally, it is time to reboot the server. To do that, use the *Restart-Computer* cmdlet. The complete Add-DNDSPrereqsDC2.ps1 script appears here:

**Add-DNDSPrereqsDC2.ps1**

```
#set static IP address
$ipaddress = "192.168.0.226"
$ipprefix = "24"
$ipgw = "192.168.0.1"
$ipdns = "192.168.0.225"
$ipif = (Get-NetAdapter).ifIndex
New-NetIPAddress -IPAddress $ipaddress -PrefixLength $ipprefix -InterfaceIndex $ipif
-DefaultGateway $ipgw
Set-DnsClientServerAddress -InterfaceIndex $ipif -ServerAddresses $ipdns

#rename the computer
$newname = "dc28508"
Rename-Computer -NewName $newname -force

#install roles and features
$featureLogPath = "c:\poshlog\featurelog.txt"
New-Item $featureLogPath -ItemType file -Force

Add-WindowsFeature -Name "ad-domain-services" -IncludeAllSubFeature -IncludeManagementTools
Get-WindowsFeature | Where installed >>$featureLogPath

#restart the computer
Restart-Computer
```

Once the computer reboots, it is time to add the server to the domain as a domain controller. The first step is to import the *ADDSDeployment* module. Next, the *Install-ADDSDomainController* cmdlet is used to add the server as a domain controller to an existing domain. Because you did not want to install DNS, the *-installdns* parameter receives *$false*. In addition, the *-replicationsourcedc* parameter is set to the first domain controller that was built. The complete CreateAdditionalDC.ps1 script appears here:

**CreateAdditionalDC.ps1**

```
Import-Module ADDSDeployment
Install-ADDSDomainController `
-NoGlobalCatalog:$false `
-CreateDnsDelegation:$False `
-Credential (Get-Credential) `
-CriticalReplicationOnly:$false `
-DatabasePath "C:\Windows\NTDS" `
```

```
-DomainName "nwtraders.msft" `
-InstallDns:$False `
-LogPath "C:\Windows\NTDS" `
-NoRebootOnCompletion:$false `
-ReplicationSourceDC "dc8508.nwtraders.msft" `
-SiteName "Default-First-Site-Name" `
-SysvolPath "C:\Windows\SYSVOL" `
-Force:$true
```

Once the server comes out of the reboot, it is time to log on to the server using domain credentials. The server needs a little time to complete configuration. Back on the first domain controller, Active Directory Users and Computers shows both domain controllers in the Domain Controllers organizational unit (OU). This appears in Figure 17-6.

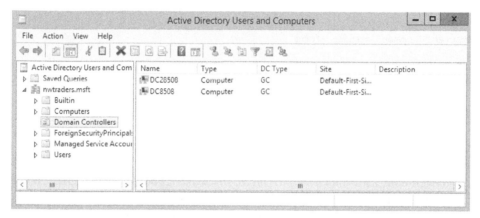

**FIGURE 17-6** Active Directory Users and Computers shows both domain controllers in the Domain Controllers OU.

# Adding a read-only domain controller

Adding a read-only domain controller to an existing domain is only slightly different from adding a full domain controller to an existing domain. The process is a two-step procedure. First, the prerequisites must be installed, and then, following the reboot, the server is configured as a read-only domain controller. The prerequisite installation script can be simplified a bit from the prerequisite script developed in the previous section. The first portion of the script creates the static IP address and sets the DNS client to point to the DNS server running on the first domain controller that was installed. This portion of the script is the same as the Add-DNDSPrereqsDC2.ps1 script in the previous section. Next, the server is renamed via the *Rename-Computer* cmdlet. This simple command is the same one that was used in the previous scripts.

The big change involves using the *Add-WindowsFeature* cmdlet to add the AD DS role as well as all associated features and management tools. This is a great shortcut that simplifies your task. The change appears here:

```
#install AD DS Role and tools
Add-WindowsFeature -Name "ad-domain-services" -IncludeAllSubFeature -IncludeManagementTools
```

The last step is to use the *Restart-Computer* cmdlet to reboot the server. The complete CreateDC3Prereqs.ps1 script appears here:

**CreateDC3Prereqs.ps1**

```
#set static IP address
$ipaddress = "192.168.0.227"
$ipprefix = "24"
$ipgw = "192.168.0.1"
$ipdns = "192.168.0.225"
$ipif = (Get-NetAdapter).ifIndex
New-NetIPAddress -IPAddress $ipaddress -PrefixLength $ipprefix -InterfaceIndex $ipif
-DefaultGateway $ipgw
Set-DnsClientServerAddress -InterfaceIndex $ipif -ServerAddresses $ipdns

#rename the computer
$newname = "dc38508"
Rename-Computer -NewName $newname -force

#install AD DS Role and tools
Add-WindowsFeature -Name "ad-domain-services" -IncludeAllSubFeature -IncludeManagementTools

#restart the computer
Restart-Computer
```

Once the server has been given IP configuration and you've loaded the prerequisites, it is time to add a read-only domain controller to the domain. The script for this first imports the *ADDSDeployment* module, and then it calls the *Install-ADDomainController* cmdlet. Because the domain controller is read-only, the *AllowPasswordReplicationAccountName* parameter must be used to specify whose passwords will be replicated. This value is an array. The credentials for contacting the domain must be supplied. To do this, you use the *Get-Credential* cmdlet and enter the domain admin credentials. Next, the Directory Restore Password prompt appears. In addition to specifying who can replicate the passwords, you must also specify who cannot replicate passwords. This array is entered on multiple lines to make it easier to read. This scenario did not call for installing and configuring DNS on this particular machine, and therefore that role is not added. The complete CreateReadOnlyDomainController.ps1 script appears here:

**CreateReadOnlyDomainController.ps1**

```
Import-Module ADDSDeployment
Install-ADDSDomainController `
-AllowPasswordReplicationAccountName @("NWTRADERS\Allowed RODC Password Replication Group") `
-NoGlobalCatalog:$false `
-Credential (Get-Credential -Credential nwtraders\administrator) `
-CriticalReplicationOnly:$false `
-DatabasePath "C:\Windows\NTDS" `
-DenyPasswordReplicationAccountName @("BUILTIN\Administrators",
  "BUILTIN\Server Operators", "BUILTIN\Backup Operators",
  "BUILTIN\Account Operators",
  "NWTRADERS\Denied RODC Password Replication Group") `
-DomainName "nwtraders.msft" `
-InstallDns:$false `
```

```
-LogPath "C:\Windows\NTDS" `
-NoRebootOnCompletion:$false `
-ReadOnlyReplica:$true `
-SiteName "Default-First-Site-Name" `
-SysvolPath "C:\Windows\SYSVOL" `
-Force:$true
```

When the script runs, Active Directory Users and Computers on the first domain controller refreshes to include the new read-only domain controller. This appears in Figure 17-7.

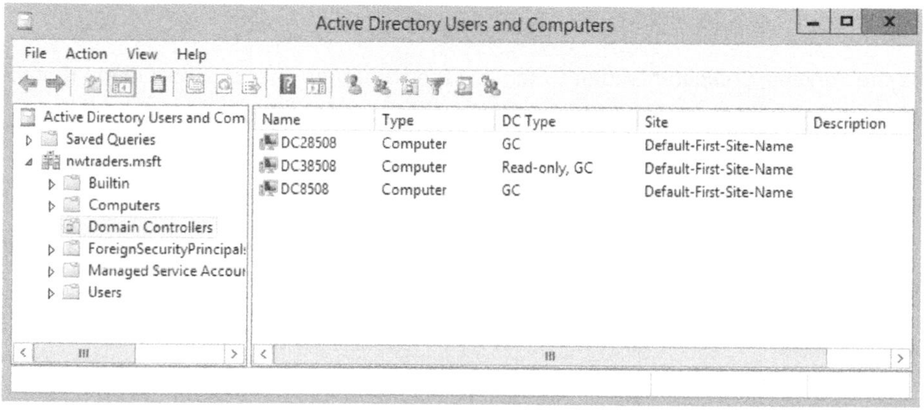

**FIGURE 17-7** Active Directory Users and Computers shows the newly added read-only domain controller.

# Domain controller prerequisites: step-by-step exercises

In the first exercise, you will install the base requirements for a domain controller on a fresh installation of Windows Server 2012. This exercise will assign a static IP address, rename the server, and install the AD DS admin tools. In the subsequent exercise, you will add a new domain controller to a new forest.

## Installing domain controller prerequisites

1. Log on to your server with the administrator account.

2. Open the Windows PowerShell ISE.

3. Set the script execution policy to *remotesigned*. The command appears here:

   ```
   Set-ExecutionPolicy remotesigned -force
   ```

4. Use the *Get-NetAdapter* cmdlet to determine the interface index number of the active network adapter. The command appears here:

   ```
   $ipif = (Get-NetAdapter).ifIndex
   ```

5. Use the *New-NetIPAddress* cmdlet to assign a static IP address to the active network adapter. Specify the *ipaddress, prefixlength, interfaceindex, and defaultgateway* values that are appropriate for your network. Sample values appear here:

```
$ipaddress = "192.168.0.225"
$ipprefix = "24"
$ipgw = "192.168.0.1"
$ipdns = "192.168.0.225"
$ipif = (Get-NetAdapter).ifIndex
New-NetIPAddress -ipaddress $ipaddress -prefixlength $ipprefix `
    -interfaceindex $ipif -defaultgateway $ipgw
```

6. Use the *Rename-Computer* cmdlet to rename the computer. Specify a new name that follows your naming convention. The command appears here with a sample name:

```
$newname = "dc8508"
Rename-Computer -NewName $newname -force
```

7. Add the AD DS, DNS, and GPMC features and roles, including all subfeatures and tools, by using the *Add-WindowsFeature* cmdlet. The command appears here:

```
Add-WindowsFeature -Name "ad-domain-services" -IncludeAllSubFeature
-IncludeManagementTools
Add-WindowsFeature -Name "dns" -IncludeAllSubFeature -IncludeManagementTools
Add-WindowsFeature -Name "gpmc" -IncludeAllSubFeature -IncludeManagementTools
```

8. Restart the computer by using the *Restart-Computer* cmdlet. This command appears here:

```
Restart-Computer -force
```

This concludes the exercise.

In the following exercise, you will add the server configured in the preceding exercise to a new forest.

### Adding a domain controller to a new forest

1. Log on to the freshly rebooted server as the administrator.

2. Open the Windows PowerShell ISE.

3. Create a variable for your fully qualified domain name. An example appears here:

```
$domainname = "nwtraders.msft"
```

4. Create a variable to hold your NetBIOS name. Normally, the NetBIOS name is the same as your domain name without the extension. An example appears here:

```
$netbiosName = "NWTRADERS"
```

5. Import the *ADDSDeployment* module. The command appears here:

```
Import-Module ADDSDeployment
```

6. Add the *Install-ADDSForest* cmdlet to your script. Use tab expansion to simplify typing. Add the *-CreateDnsDelegation* parameter and set it to *false*. Add the line-continuation character at the end of the line. This appears here:

```
Install-ADDSForest -CreateDnsDelegation:$false `
```

7. Specify the *-DatabasePath*, *-DomainMode*, *-DomainName*, and *-DomainNetbiosName* parameters. Use the domain name and NetBIOS name stored in the variables created earlier. Make sure you have line continuation at the end of each line. This portion of the command appears here:

```
-DatabasePath "C:\Windows\NTDS" `
-DomainMode "Win2012" `
-DomainName $domainname `
-DomainNetbiosName $netbiosName
```

8. Specify the *-ForestMode*, *-LogPath*, and *-SysVolpath* parameters. In addition, you will need to supply options for the *-installDNS* and *-rebootoncompletion* parameters. Use the *-Force* parameter. This portion of the script appears here:

```
-ForestMode "Win2012" `
-InstallDns:$true `
-LogPath "C:\Windows\NTDS" `
-NoRebootOnCompletion:$false `
-SysvolPath "C:\Windows\SYSVOL" `
-Force:$true
```

9. Run the script. You will be prompted for a directory-restore password, and you'll have to type it twice. Your server will also reboot once the configuration is completed. To log on to the server, use your directory-restore password.

This concludes the exercise.

# Chapter 17 quick reference

| To | Do this |
| --- | --- |
| Assign a static IP address | Use the *New-NetIPAddress* cmdlet. |
| Install a new Windows feature or role | Use the *Add-WindowsFeature* cmdlet from the *ServerManager* module. |
| Restart a computer | Use the *Restart-Computer* cmdlet. |
| Find the index number of the active network adapter | Use *Get-NetAdapter* cmdlet and select the *IfIndex* property. |
| See what features or roles are installed on a server | Use the *Get-WindowsFeature* cmdlet, pipe the results to the *Where-Object* cmdlet, and filter on the installed property. |
| Add a Windows role as well as the associated management tools | Use the *Add-WindowsFeature* cmdlet and specify the *-includemanagementtools* parameter. |
| Create a new forest | Use the *Install-ADDSForest* cmdlet from the *ADDSDeployment* module. |

# Debugging Scripts

**After completing this chapter, you will be able to:**

- Use the *Write-Debug* cmdlet to provide detailed information from a script.

- Use the *Set-StrictMode* cmdlet to prevent errors during development.

- Understand how to work with the Windows PowerShell debugger.

## Understanding debugging in Windows PowerShell

No one enjoys debugging scripts. In fact, the best debugging is no debugging. It is also true that well-written, well-formatted, well-documented, and clearly constructed Microsoft Windows PowerShell code requires less effort to debug than poorly formatted, undocumented spaghetti code. It is fair to say that debugging begins when you first open the Windows PowerShell ISE. Therefore, you might want to review Chapter 5, "Using PowerShell Scripts," Chapter 6, "Working with Functions," and Chapter 7, "Creating Advanced Functions and Modules," before you dive too deep into this chapter.

If you can read and understand your Windows PowerShell code, chances are you will need to do very little debugging. But what if you do need to do some debugging? Well, just as excellent golfers spend many hours practicing chipping out of the sand trap in hopes that they will never need to use the skill, so too must competent Windows PowerShell scripters practice debugging skills in hopes that they will never need to apply the knowledge. Understanding the color coding of the Windows PowerShell ISE, detecting when closing quotation marks are missing, and knowing which pair of braces corresponds to which command can greatly reduce the debugging that may be needed later.

## Understanding three different types of errors

Debugging is a skill used to track down and eliminate errors from a Windows PowerShell script. There are three different types of errors that coders make: syntax errors, run-time errors, and logic errors.

### Working with syntax errors

Syntax errors are the easiest to spot, and you usually correct them at design time—that is, while you have the Windows PowerShell ISE open and you are writing your script. Syntax errors generally get corrected at design time because the language parser runs in the background of the Windows PowerShell ISE, and when it detects a syntax error, it marks it with a squiggly line (thus indicating that the command requires additional parameters, decoration, or other attention). Seasoned scripters don't usually even view this process as error correction, but as simply completing commands so that scripts run properly. (Learning to use IntelliSense inside the Windows PowerShell ISE is a good way to reduce these errors.) The most seasoned scripters learn to pay attention to the syntax parser and fix errors indicated by the red squiggly lines prior to actually running the code. When syntax errors aren't corrected, the error messages generated often provide good guidance toward correcting the offending command. Figure 18-1 illustrates a syntax error.

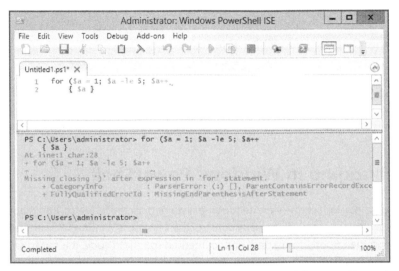

**FIGURE 18-1** The Windows PowerShell ISE highlights potential errors with a red squiggly line. The error message states the offending command, and often provides clarification for required changes.

## Working with run-time errors

The syntax parser often does not detect run-time errors. Rather, run-time errors are problems that manifest themselves only when a script runs. Examples of these types of errors include an unavailable resource (such as a drive or a file), permission problems (such as a non-elevated user not having the rights to perform an operation), misspelled words, and code dependencies that are not met (such as access to a required module). The good thing is that many of these run-time errors are detectible from within the Windows PowerShell ISE due to the robust tab expansion mechanism in Windows PowerShell 3.0. For example, it is possible to eliminate the "Resource not available" run-time error if you use tab expansion. This is possible because tab expansion works even across Universal Naming Convention (UNC) shares. Figure 18-2 shows an example of employing this feature when attempting to use the *Get-Content* cmdlet to read the contents of the AD_Doc.txt file from the data share on a server named hyperv1.

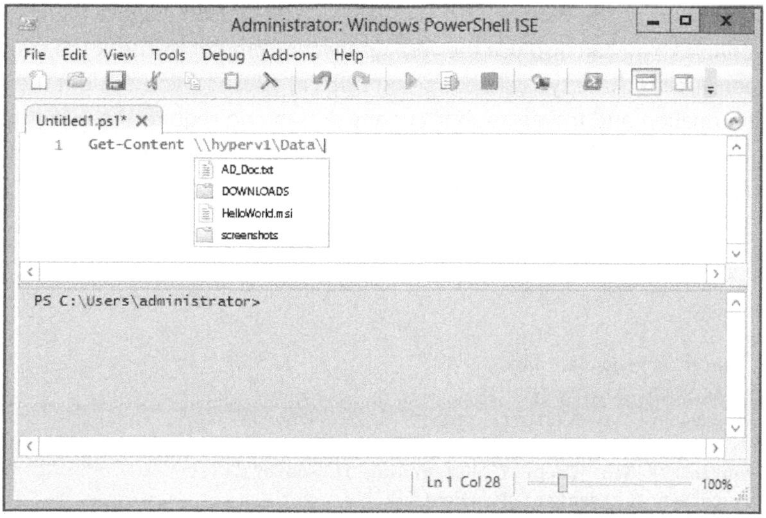

**FIGURE 18-2** Improved tab expansion makes it possible to avoid certain run-time errors.

Unfortunately, tab expansion does not help when it comes to dealing with permission issues. Paying attention to the returned error message, however, helps to identify that you are dealing with a permission issue. In these cases, you usually receive an "Access is denied" error message. Such an error message appears here when bogususer attempts to access the DC1 server to perform a Windows Management Instrumentation (WMI) query.

```
PS C:\> Get-WmiObject win32_bios -cn dc1 -Credential iammred\bogususer
Get-WmiObject : Access is denied. (Exception from HRESULT: 0x80070005
(E_ACCESSDENIED))
At line:1 char:1
+ Get-WmiObject win32_bios -cn dc1 -Credential iammred\bogususer
+ ~~~~~~~~~~~~~~~~~~~~~~~~~~~~~~~~~~~~~~~~~~~~~~~~~~~~~~~~~~~~~~~~~
    + CategoryInfo          : NotSpecified: (:) [Get-WmiObject],
    UnauthorizedAccessException
    + FullyQualifiedErrorId : System.UnauthorizedAccessException,
    Microsoft.PowerShell.Commands.GetWmiObjectCommand
```

One way to detect run-time errors is to use the *Write-Debug* cmdlet to display the contents of variables that are most likely to contain erroneous data. By moving from a one-line command to a simple script containing variables and a variety of *Write-Debug* commands, you are automatically set up to perform the most common troubleshooting techniques on your script. For example, in the script that appears here, there are two main sources of run-time errors: the availability of the target computer and the credentials used to perform the connection.

**RemoteWMISessionNoDebug.ps1**

```
$credential = Get-Credential
$cn = Read-Host -Prompt "enter a computer name"
Get-WmiObject win32_bios -cn $cn -Credential $credential
```

By using the immediate window in the Windows PowerShell ISE, you can interrogate the value of the *$cn* and *$credential* variables. You can also use the *Test-Connection* cmdlet to check the status of the *$cn* computer. By performing these typical debugging steps in advance, you can get the script to display the pertinent information and therefore shortcut any debugging required to make the script properly work. The DebugRemoteWMISession.ps1 script that appears here illustrates using the *Write-Debug* cmdlet to provide debugging information.

**DebugRemoteWMISession.ps1**

```
$oldDebugPreference = $DebugPreference
$DebugPreference = "continue"
$credential = Get-Credential
$cn = Read-Host -Prompt "enter a computer name"
Write-Debug "user name: $($credential.UserName)"
Write-Debug "password: $($credential.GetNetworkCredential().Password)"
Write-Debug "$cn is up:
  $(Test-Connection -Computername $cn -Count 1 -BufferSize 16 -quiet)"
Get-WmiObject win32_bios -cn $cn -Credential $credential
$DebugPreference = $oldDebugPreference
```

Figure 18-3 illustrates running the DebugRemoteWMISession.ps1 script inside the Windows PowerShell ISE to determine why the script fails. According to the output, the remote server, DC1, is available, but the user Bogus User with the password of BogusPassowrd is receiving "Access is denied." It might be that the user does not have an account or access rights, or that the password is not really BogusPassowrd. The detailed debugging information should help to clarify the situation.

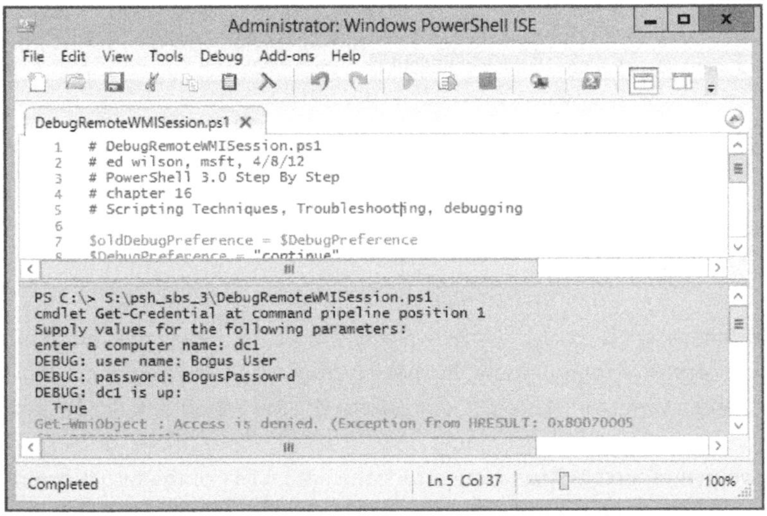

**FIGURE 18-3** Detailed debugging makes solving run-time errors more manageable.

A better way to use the *Write-Debug* cmdlet is to combine it with the *[CmdletBinding()]* attribute at the beginning of the script (or function). Getting the *[CmdletBinding()]* attribute to work requires a couple of things. First, the script or function must use at least one parameter. This means that the *param* keyword will be present in the script. Second, the *[CmdletBinding()]* attribute must appear prior to the *param* keyword. Once implemented, this change permits use of the common *-debug* parameter. When calling the script or function, use of the *-debug* switched parameter causes the debug stream from the *Write-Debug* cmdlet in the code to appear in the output. This simple change also means that your code no longer needs to change the value of the *$DebugPreference* variable. It also means that you do not need to create your own switched *-debug* parameter and include code such as the following at the beginning of your script:

```
Param([switch]$debug)
If($debug) {$DebugPreference = "continue"}
```

The revised and simplified DebugRemoteWMISession.ps1 script appears following, as Switch_DebugRemoteWMISession.ps1. The changes to the script include the addition of the *[CmdletBinding()]* attribute, the creation of a parameter named *cn*, and the setting of the default value to the name of the local computer. The other changes involve removing the toggling of the *$DebugPreference* variable. The complete script appears here:

**Switch_DebugRemoteWMISession.ps1**

```
[CmdletBinding()]
Param($cn = $env:computername)
$credential = Get-Credential
Write-Debug "user name: $($credential.UserName)"
Write-Debug "password: $($credential.GetNetworkCredential().Password)"
Write-Debug "$cn is up:
  $(Test-Connection -Computername $cn -Count 1 -BufferSize 16 -quiet)"
Get-WmiObject win32_bios -cn $cn -Credential $credential
```

When the Switch_DebugRemoteWMISession.ps1 script runs with the *-debug* switch from the Windows PowerShell console, in addition to displaying the debug stream, it also prompts to continue the script. This permits halting execution upon reaching an unexpected value. Figure 18-4 illustrates this technique, in which a user named Bogus User, who wishes to connect to a remote server named DC1, unexpectedly discovers that he is connecting to a workstation named W8Client6.

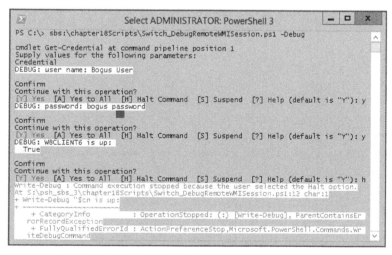

**FIGURE 18-4** Using the *-debug* switched parameter to step through potential problems in a script.

## Working with logic errors

Logic errors can be very difficult to detect because they may be present even when your script appears to be working correctly. But when things go wrong, they can be difficult to fix. Most of the time, just examining the values of variables does not solve the problem, because the code itself works fine. The problem often lies in what are called the *business rules* of the script. These are decisions the code makes that have nothing to do with the correct operation of, for example, a *switch* statement. At times, it may appear that the *switch* statement is not working correctly, because the wrong value is displayed at the end of the code, but quite often, the business rules themselves are causing the problem.

For a simple example of a logic error, consider the function called *my-function* that appears here:

**My-Function.ps1**

```
Function my-function
{
 Param(
  [int]$a,
  [int]$b)
  "$a plus $b equals four"
}
```

The *my-function* function accepts two command-line parameters: *a* and *b*. It then combines the two values and outputs a string stating the value is *four*. The tester performs four different tests, and each time the function performs as expected. These tests and the associated output appear here:

```
PS C:\> S:\psh_sbs_3\chapter18Scripts\my-function.ps1

PS C:\> my-function -a 2 -b 2
2 plus 2 equals four

PS C:\> my-function -a 1 -b 3
1 plus 3 equals four

PS C:\> my-function -a 0 -b 4
0 plus 4 equals four

PS C:\> my-function -a 3 -b 1
3 plus 1 equals four
```

Once the function goes into production, however, users begin to complain. Most of the time, the function displays incorrect output. However, the users also report that no errors are generated when the function runs. What is the best way to solve the logic problem? Simply adding a couple of *Write-Debug* commands to display the values of the variables *a* and *b* will more than likely not lead to the correct solution. A better way is to step through the code one line at a time and examine the associated output. The easy way to do this is to use the *Set-PSDebug* cmdlet—the topic of the next section in this chapter.

# Using the *Set-PSDebug* cmdlet

The *Set-PSDebug* cmdlet was available in Windows PowerShell 1.0, it did not change in Windows PowerShell 2.0, and it remains the same in Windows PowerShell 3.0. This does not mean it is a neglected feature, but rather that it does what it needs to do. For performing basic debugging quickly and easily, you cannot beat the combination of features that are available. There are three things you can do with the *Set-PSDebug* cmdlet: you can trace script execution in an automated fashion, step through the script interactively, and enable *strict mode* to force good Windows PowerShell coding practices. Each of these features will be examined in this section. The *Set-PSDebug* cmdlet is not designed to do heavy debugging; it is a lightweight tool that is useful when you want to produce a quick trace or rapidly step through a script.

## Tracing the script

One of the simplest ways to debug a script is to turn on script-level tracing. When you turn on script-level tracing, each command that is executed is displayed to the Windows PowerShell console. By watching the commands as they are displayed to the Windows PowerShell console, you can determine if a line of code in your script executes, or if it is being skipped. To enable script tracing, you use the *Set-PSDebug* cmdlet and specify one of three levels for the *-trace* parameter. The three levels of tracing are shown in Table 18-1.

**TABLE 18-1** *Set-PSDebug* trace levels

| Trace level | Meaning |
| --- | --- |
| 0 | Turns script tracing off. |
| 1 | Traces each line of the script as it is executed. Lines in the script that are not executed are not traced. Does not display variable assignments, function calls, or external scripts. |
| 2 | Traces each line of the script as it is executed. Displays variable assignments, function calls, and external scripts. Lines in the script that are not executed are not traced. |

To understand the process of tracing a script and the differences between the different trace levels, examine the CreateRegistryKey.ps1 script. It contains a single function called *Add-RegistryValue*. In the *Add-RegistryValue* function, the *Test-Path* cmdlet is used to determine if the registry key exists. If the registry key exists, a property value is set. If the registry key does not exist, the registry key is created and a property value is set. *The Add-RegistryValue* function is called when the script executes. The complete CreateRegistryKey.ps1 script is shown here:

**CreateRegistryKey.ps1**

```
Function Add-RegistryValue($key,$value)
{
 $scriptRoot = "HKCU:\software\ForScripting"
 if(-not (Test-Path -path $scriptRoot))
   {
    New-Item -Path HKCU:\Software\ForScripting | Out-null
    New-ItemProperty -Path $scriptRoot -Name $key -Value $value `
    -PropertyType String | Out-Null
   }
```

```
  Else
  {
   Set-ItemProperty -Path $scriptRoot -Name $key -Value $value | `
   Out-Null
  }

} #end function Add-RegistryValue

# *** Entry Point to Script ***
Add-RegistryValue -key forscripting -value test
```

## Working with trace level 1

When the trace level is set to 1, each line in the script that executes is displayed to the Windows PowerShell console. To set the trace level to 1, you use the *Set-PSDebug* cmdlet and assign a value of 1 to the *-trace* parameter.

Once the trace level has been set, it applies to everything that is typed in the Windows PowerShell console. If you run an interactive command, run a cmdlet, or execute a script, it will be traced. When the CreateRegistryKey.ps1 script is run and there is no registry key present, the first command-debug line displays the path to the script that is being executed. Because Windows PowerShell parses from the top down, the next line that is executed is the line that creates the *Add-RegistryValue* function. This command is on line 7 of the script because the actual script that executed contains 6 lines that are commented out. When you add the status bar to Notepad (via View | Status Bar), the status bar at the lower-right corner of Notepad will display the line number. By default, Notepad does not display line and column numbers. This is shown in Figure 18-5.

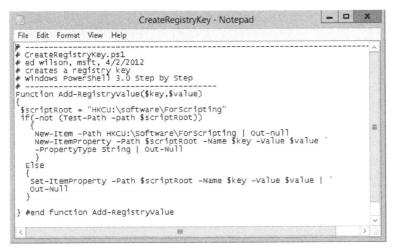

**FIGURE 18-5**  By default, Notepad does not display line numbers.

After the function is created, the next line of the script that executes is line 25. Line 25 of the CreateRegistryKey.ps1 script follows the comment that points to the entry point to the script (this last line is shown in Figure 18-5), and calls the *Add-RegistryValue* function by passing two values for the *-key* and *-value* parameters. This appears here:

```
PS C:\> y:\CreateRegistryKey.ps1
DEBUG:    1+  <<<< y:\CreateRegistryKey.ps1
DEBUG:    7+ Function Add-RegistryValue <<<< ($key,$value)
DEBUG:   25+  <<<< Add-RegistryValue -key forscripting -value test
```

Once control of script execution is inside the *Add-RegistryValue* function, the *HKCU:\software\ForScripting* string is assigned to the *$scriptRoot* variable. This is shown here:

```
DEBUG:    9+ $scriptRoot = <<<<  "HKCU:\software\ForScripting"
```

The *if* statement is now evaluated. If the *Test-Path* cmdlet is unable to find the *$scriptRoot* location in the registry, then the *if* statement is entered and the commands inside the associated script block will be executed. In this example, *$scriptRoot* is located and the commands inside the script block are not executed. This is shown here:

```
DEBUG:   10+  if <<<< (-not (Test-Path -path $scriptRoot))
```

The *Set-ItemProperty* cmdlet is called on line 18 of the CreateRegistryKey.ps1 script. This is shown here:

```
DEBUG:   18+     <<<< Set-ItemProperty -Path $scriptRoot -Name $key -Value
$value | `
```

Once the *Set-ItemProperty* cmdlet has executed, the script ends. The Windows PowerShell console parser now enters, with the same three lines of feedback shown when the tracing was first enabled. This is shown here:

```
DEBUG:    2+        $foundSuggestion = <<<<  $false
DEBUG:    4+        if <<<< ($lastError -and
DEBUG:   15+        $foundSuggestion <<<<
PS C:\>
```

When you set the debug trace level to 1, a basic outline of the execution plan of the script is produced. This technique is good for quickly determining the outcome of branching statements (such as the *if* statement) to see if a script block is being entered. This appears in Figure 18-6.

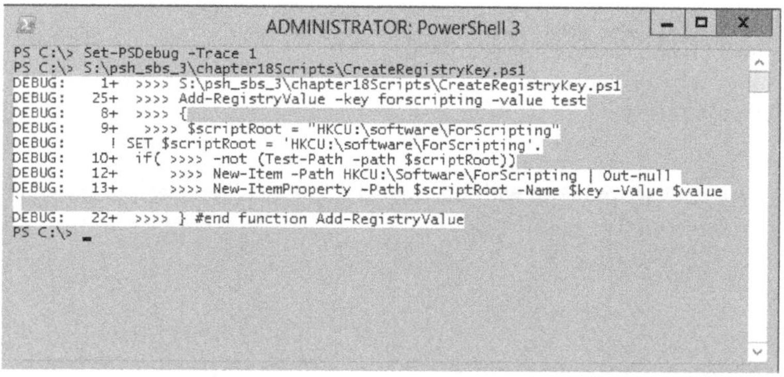

**FIGURE 18-6** Script-level 1 tracing displays each executing line of the script.

## Working with trace level 2

When the trace level is set to 2, each line in the script that executes is displayed to the Windows PowerShell console. In addition, each variable assignment, function call, and outside script call is displayed. These additional tracing details are all prefixed with an exclamation mark to make them easier to spot. When the *Set-PSDebug -trace* parameter is set to 2, an extra line is displayed, indicating a variable assignment. This is shown here:

```
PS C:\> Set-PSDebug -Trace 2
DEBUG:    1+  <<<< Set-PSDebug -Trace 2
DEBUG:    2+          $foundSuggestion = <<<<  $false
DEBUG:    ! SET $foundSuggestion = 'False'.
DEBUG:    4+          if <<<< ($lastError -and
DEBUG:   15+          $foundSuggestion <<<<
```

When the CreateRegistryKey.ps1 script is run, the function trace points first to the script, stating it is calling a function called CreateRegistryKey.ps1. Calls to functions are prefixed with *! CALL*, making them easy to spot. Windows PowerShell treats scripts as functions. The next function that is called is the *Add-RegistryValue* function. The trace also states where the function is defined by indicating the path to the file. This is shown here:

```
PS C:\> y:\CreateRegistryKey.ps1
DEBUG:    1+  <<<< y:\CreateRegistryKey.ps1
DEBUG:    ! CALL function 'CreateRegistryKey.ps1'  (defined in file
'y:\CreateRegistryKey.ps1')
DEBUG:    7+ Function Add-RegistryValue <<<< ($key,$value)
DEBUG:   25+  <<<< Add-RegistryValue -key forscripting -value test
DEBUG:    ! CALL function 'Add-RegistryValue'  (defined in file
'y:\CreateRegistryKey.ps1')
```

The *! SET* keyword is used to preface variable assignments. The first variable that is assigned is the *$scriptRoot* variable. This is shown here:

```
DEBUG:    9+  $scriptRoot = <<<<  "HKCU:\software\ForScripting"
DEBUG:    ! SET $scriptRoot = 'HKCU:\software\ForScripting'.
DEBUG:   10+  if <<<< (-not (Test-Path -path $scriptRoot))
DEBUG:   18+      <<<< Set-ItemProperty -Path $scriptRoot -Name $key -Value $value | `
DEBUG:    2+          $foundSuggestion = <<<<  $false
DEBUG:    ! SET $foundSuggestion = 'False'.
DEBUG:    4+          if <<<< ($lastError -and
DEBUG:   15+          $foundSuggestion <<<<
PS C:\>
```

When the CreateRegistryKey.ps1 script is run with trace level 2, the detailed tracing shown in Figure 18-7 is displayed.

**FIGURE 18-7** Script-level 2 tracing adds variable assignments, function calls, and external script calls.

# Stepping through the script

Watching the script trace the execution of the lines of code in the script can often provide useful insight that can lead to a solution to a misbehaving script. If a script is more complicated and is composed of several functions, a simple trace might not be a workable solution. For the occasions when your script is more complex and comprises multiple functions, you will want the ability to step through the script. When you step through a script, you are prompted before each line of the script runs. An example of a script that you might want to step through is the BadScript.ps1 script shown here:

**BadScript.ps1**

```
Function AddOne([int]$num)
{
 $num+1
} #end function AddOne

Function AddTwo([int]$num)
{
 $num+2
} #end function AddTwo

Function SubOne([int]$num)
{
 $num-1
} #end function SubOne

Function TimesOne([int]$num)
{
   $num*2
} #end function TimesOne

Function TimesTwo([int]$num)
{
 $num*2
} #end function TimesTwo
```

```
Function DivideNum([int]$num)
{
 12/$num
} #end function DivideNum

# *** Entry Point to Script ***

$num = 0
SubOne($num) | DivideNum($num)
AddOne($num) | AddTwo($num)
```

The BadScript.ps1 script contains a number of functions that are used to add numbers, subtract numbers, multiply numbers, and divide numbers. There are some problems with the way the script runs, because it contains several errors. It would be possible for you to set the trace level to 2 and examine the trace of the script. But with the large number of functions and the types of errors contained in the script, it might be difficult to spot the problems with the script. By default, the trace level is set to level 1 when stepping is enabled, and in nearly all cases this is the best trace level for this type of solution.

You might prefer to be able to step through the script as each line executes. There are two benefits to using the -*step* parameter from the *Set-PSDebug* cmdlet. The first benefit is that you are able to watch what happens when each line of the script executes. This allows you to very carefully walk through the script. With the trace feature of *Set-PSDebug*, it is possible to miss important clues that would help solve problems because everything is displayed on the Windows PowerShell console. With the prompt feature, you are asked to choose a response before each line in the script executes. The default choice is *Y* for yes (continue the operation), but you have other choices. When you respond with *Y*, the debug line is displayed to the Windows PowerShell console. This is the same debug statement shown in the trace output, and it is governed by your debug-trace-level settings. The step prompting is shown here:

```
PS C:\> Set-PSDebug -Step
DEBUG:    1+  >>>> Set-PSDebug -Step
DEBUG:     ! CALL function '<ScriptBlock>'
PS C:\> S:\psh_sbs_3\chapter18Scripts\BadScript.ps1

Continue with this operation?
   1+  >>>> S:\psh_sbs_3\chapter18Scripts\BadScript.ps1
[Y] Yes  [A] Yes to All  [N] No  [L] No to All  [S] Suspend  [?] Help
(default is "Y"):y
DEBUG:    1+  >>>> S:\psh_sbs_3\chapter18Scripts\BadScript.ps1
y
Continue with this operation?
  48+  >>>> $num = 0
[Y] Yes  [A] Yes to All  [N] No  [L] No to All  [S] Suspend  [?] Help
(default is "Y"):y
DEBUG:   48+  >>>> $num = 0

Continue with this operation?
  49+  >>>> SubOne($num) | DivideNum($num)
[Y] Yes  [A] Yes to All  [N] No  [L] No to All  [S] Suspend  [?] Help
(default is "Y"):y
DEBUG:   49+  >>>> SubOne($num) | DivideNum($num)
```

```
Continue with this operation?
   27+  >>>> {
[Y] Yes  [A] Yes to All  [N] No  [L] No to All  [S] Suspend  [?] Help
(default is "Y"):y
DEBUG:   27+  >>>> {


Continue with this operation?
   28+  >>>> $num-1
[Y] Yes  [A] Yes to All  [N] No  [L] No to All  [S] Suspend  [?] Help
(default is "Y"):y
DEBUG:   28+  >>>> $num-1


Continue with this operation?
   29+  >>>> } #end function SubOne
[Y] Yes  [A] Yes to All  [N] No  [L] No to All  [S] Suspend  [?] Help
(default is "Y"):y
DEBUG:   29+  >>>> } #end function SubOne


Continue with this operation?
   42+  >>>> {
[Y] Yes  [A] Yes to All  [N] No  [L] No to All  [S] Suspend  [?] Help
(default is "Y"):y
DEBUG:   42+  >>>> {


Continue with this operation?
   43+  >>>> 12/$num
[Y] Yes  [A] Yes to All  [N] No  [L] No to All  [S] Suspend  [?] Help
(default is "Y"):y
DEBUG:   43+  >>>> 12/$num


Continue with this operation?
   19+                              if ( &  >>>> { Set-StrictMode -Version
 1; $_.PSMessageDetails } ) {
[Y] Yes  [A] Yes to All  [N] No  [L] No to All  [S] Suspend  [?] Help
(default is "Y"):y
DEBUG:   19+                              if ( &  >>>> { Set-StrictMode
-Version 1; $_.PSMessageDetails } ) {


Continue with this operation?
   19+                              if ( & {  >>>> Set-StrictMode -Version
 1; $_.PSMessageDetails } ) {
[Y] Yes  [A] Yes to All  [N] No  [L] No to All  [S] Suspend  [?] Help
(default is "Y"):y
DEBUG:   19+                              if ( & {  >>>> Set-StrictMode
-Version 1; $_.PSMessageDetails } ) {


Continue with this operation?
   19+                              if ( & { Set-StrictMode -Version 1;
 >>>> $_.PSMessageDetails } ) {
[Y] Yes  [A] Yes to All  [N] No  [L] No to All  [S] Suspend  [?] Help
(default is "Y"):y
DEBUG:   19+                              if ( & { Set-StrictMode
-Version 1;  >>>> $_.PSMessageDetails } ) {
```

```
Continue with this operation?
   1+ &  >>>> { Set-StrictMode -Version 1;
$this.Exception.InnerException.PSMessageDetails }
[Y] Yes  [A] Yes to All  [N] No  [L] No to All  [S] Suspend  [?] Help
(default is "Y"):y
DEBUG:    1+ &  >>>> { Set-StrictMode -Version 1;
$this.Exception.InnerException.PSMessageDetails }

Continue with this operation?
   1+ & {  >>>> Set-StrictMode -Version 1;
$this.Exception.InnerException.PSMessageDetails }
[Y] Yes  [A] Yes to All  [N] No  [L] No to All  [S] Suspend  [?] Help
(default is "Y"):y
DEBUG:    1+ & {  >>>> Set-StrictMode -Version 1;
$this.Exception.InnerException.PSMessageDetails }

Continue with this operation?
   1+ & { Set-StrictMode -Version 1;  >>>>
$this.Exception.InnerException.PSMessageDetails }
[Y] Yes  [A] Yes to All  [N] No  [L] No to All  [S] Suspend  [?] Help
(default is "Y"):y
DEBUG:    1+ & { Set-StrictMode -Version 1;  >>>>
$this.Exception.InnerException.PSMessageDetails }

Continue with this operation?
   1+ & { Set-StrictMode -Version 1; $this.Exception.InnerException.PSMessageDetails
   >>>> }
[Y] Yes  [A] Yes to All  [N] No  [L] No to All  [S] Suspend  [?] Help
(default is "Y"):y
DEBUG:    1+ & { Set-StrictMode -Version 1;
$this.Exception.InnerException.PSMessageDetails  >>>> }

Continue with this operation?
   19+                              if ( & { Set-StrictMode -Version 1;
$_.PSMessageDetails  >>>> } ) {
[Y] Yes  [A] Yes to All  [N] No  [L] No to All  [S] Suspend  [?] Help
(default is "Y"):y
DEBUG:   19+                                    if ( & { Set-StrictMode
-Version 1; $_.PSMessageDetails  >>>> } ) {

Continue with this operation?
   26+                                  $errorCategoryMsg = &  >>>> {
Set-StrictMode -Version 1; $_.ErrorCategory_Message }
[Y] Yes  [A] Yes to All  [N] No  [L] No to All  [S] Suspend  [?] Help
(default is "Y"):y
DEBUG:   26+                                    $errorCategoryMsg = &  >>>> {
Set-StrictMode -Version 1; $_.ErrorCategory_Message }

Continue with this operation?
   26+                                  $errorCategoryMsg = & {  >>>>
Set-StrictMode -Version 1; $_.ErrorCategory_Message }
[Y] Yes  [A] Yes to All  [N] No  [L] No to All  [S] Suspend  [?] Help
(default is "Y"):y
DEBUG:   26+                                    $errorCategoryMsg = & {  >>>>
Set-StrictMode -Version 1; $_.ErrorCategory_Message }
```

```
Continue with this operation?
  26+                                        $errorCategoryMsg = & { Set-StrictMode
  -Version 1;  >>>> $_.ErrorCategory_Message }
[Y] Yes  [A] Yes to All  [N] No  [L] No to All  [S] Suspend  [?] Help
(default is "Y"):y
DEBUG:  26+                                        $errorCategoryMsg = & {
Set-StrictMode -Version 1;  >>>> $_.ErrorCategory_Message }

Continue with this operation?
  26+                                        $errorCategoryMsg = & { Set-StrictMode
  -Version 1; $_.ErrorCategory_Message  >>>> }
[Y] Yes  [A] Yes to All  [N] No  [L] No to All  [S] Suspend  [?] Help
(default is "Y"):y
DEBUG:  26+                                        $errorCategoryMsg = & {
Set-StrictMode -Version 1; $_.ErrorCategory_Message  >>>> }

Continue with this operation?
  42+                                        $originInfo = &  >>>> { Set-StrictMode
  -Version 1; $_.OriginInfo }
[Y] Yes  [A] Yes to All  [N] No  [L] No to All  [S] Suspend  [?] Help
(default is "Y"):y
DEBUG:  42+                                        $originInfo = &  >>>> {
Set-StrictMode -Version 1; $_.OriginInfo }

Continue with this operation?
  42+                                        $originInfo = & {  >>>> Set-StrictMode
  -Version 1; $_.OriginInfo }
[Y] Yes  [A] Yes to All  [N] No  [L] No to All  [S] Suspend  [?] Help
(default is "Y"):y
DEBUG:  42+                                        $originInfo = & {  >>>>
Set-StrictMode -Version 1; $_.OriginInfo }

Continue with this operation?
  42+                                        $originInfo = & { Set-StrictMode
-Version 1;  >>>> $_.OriginInfo }
[Y] Yes  [A] Yes to All  [N] No  [L] No to All  [S] Suspend  [?] Help
(default is "Y"):y
DEBUG:  42+                                        $originInfo = & {
Set-StrictMode -Version 1;  >>>> $_.OriginInfo }

Continue with this operation?
  42+                                        $originInfo = & { Set-StrictMode
-Version 1; $_.OriginInfo  >>>> }
[Y] Yes  [A] Yes to All  [N] No  [L] No to All  [S] Suspend  [?] Help
(default is "Y"):y
DEBUG:  42+                                        $originInfo = & {
Set-StrictMode -Version 1; $_.OriginInfo  >>>> }
Attempted to divide by zero.
At S:\psh_sbs_3\chapter18Scripts\BadScript.ps1:43 char:2
+  12/$num
+  ~~~~~~~
    + CategoryInfo          : NotSpecified: (:) [], RuntimeException
    + FullyQualifiedErrorId : RuntimeException
```

```
Continue with this operation?
  44+  >>>> } #end function DivideNum
[Y] Yes  [A] Yes to All  [N] No  [L] No to All  [S] Suspend  [?] Help
(default is "Y"):y
DEBUG:   44+  >>>> } #end function DivideNum

Continue with this operation?
  50+  >>>> AddOne($num) | AddTwo($num)
[Y] Yes  [A] Yes to All  [N] No  [L] No to All  [S] Suspend  [?] Help
(default is "Y"):y
DEBUG:   50+  >>>> AddOne($num) | AddTwo($num)

Continue with this operation?
  17+  >>>> {
[Y] Yes  [A] Yes to All  [N] No  [L] No to All  [S] Suspend  [?] Help
(default is "Y"):y
DEBUG:   17+  >>>> {

Continue with this operation?
  18+   >>>> $num+1
[Y] Yes  [A] Yes to All  [N] No  [L] No to All  [S] Suspend  [?] Help
(default is "Y"):y
DEBUG:   18+   >>>> $num+1

Continue with this operation?
  19+  >>>> } #end function AddOne
[Y] Yes  [A] Yes to All  [N] No  [L] No to All  [S] Suspend  [?] Help
(default is "Y"):y
DEBUG:   19+  >>>> } #end function AddOne

Continue with this operation?
  22+  >>>> {
[Y] Yes  [A] Yes to All  [N] No  [L] No to All  [S] Suspend  [?] Help
(default is "Y"):y
DEBUG:   22+  >>>> {

Continue with this operation?
  23+   >>>> $num+2
[Y] Yes  [A] Yes to All  [N] No  [L] No to All  [S] Suspend  [?] Help
(default is "Y"):y
DEBUG:   23+   >>>> $num+2
2

Continue with this operation?
  24+  >>>> } #end function AddTwo
[Y] Yes  [A] Yes to All  [N] No  [L] No to All  [S] Suspend  [?] Help
(default is "Y"):y
DEBUG:   24+  >>>> } #end function AddTwo
PS C:\>
```

The second benefit to using the *-step* parameter with the *Set-PSDebug* cmdlet is the ability to suspend script execution, run additional Windows PowerShell commands, and then return to the script execution. The ability to return the value of a variable from within the Windows PowerShell console can offer important clues to the problem of what the script is doing. You choose *S* (for suspend) at the prompt and you are dropped into a nested Windows PowerShell prompt. From there, you retrieve the variable value the same way you do when working at a regular Windows PowerShell console—by typing the name of the variable (tab expansion even works). When you are finished retrieving the value of the variable, you type **exit** to return to the stepping trace. This is shown here:

```
Continue with this operation?
  48+  >>>> $num = 0
[Y] Yes  [A] Yes to All  [N] No  [L] No to All  [S] Suspend  [?] Help
(default is "Y"):y
DEBUG:    48+  >>>> $num = 0
Continue with this operation?
  49+  >>>> SubOne($num) | DivideNum($num)
[Y] Yes  [A] Yes to All  [N] No  [L] No to All  [S] Suspend  [?] Help
(default is "Y"):s
PS C:\>> $num
0
PS C:\>> exit
```

If you decide that you would like to see what happens if you run continuously from the point you just inspected, you can choose *A* (for "yes to all"), and the script will run to completion without further prompting. If this is the case, you have found the problem. It is also possible that you may see an error such as the one shown here, where the script attempts to divide by zero.

```
Continue with this operation?
  50+  >>>> AddOne($num) | AddTwo($num)
[Y] Yes  [A] Yes to All  [N] No  [L] No to All  [S] Suspend  [?] Help
(default is "Y"):A
DEBUG:    50+  >>>> AddOne($num) | AddTwo($num)
2
PS C:\>
```

Once you have found a specific error, you may want to change the value of a variable from within the suspended Windows PowerShell console to see if it corrects the remaining logic. To do this, you run the script again and choose *S* (for suspend) at the line that caused the error. This is where some careful reading of the error messages comes into play. When you chose *A* (yes to all) in the previous example, the script ran until it came to line 43. The line number indicator follows a colon after the script name. The plus sign (+) indicates the command, which is *12/ $num*. The four left-facing arrows indicate that it is the value of the *$num* variable that is causing the problem. This is shown here:

```
Attempted to divide by zero.
At Y:\BadScript.ps1:43 char:5
+   12/ <<<< $num
```

You will need to step through the code until you come to the prompt for line 43. This will be shown as *43+ 12/ <<<< $num*, which means you are at line 43, and the operation will be to divide 12 by the value of the number contained in the *$num* variable. At this point, you will want to type **S** (for suspend) to drop into a nested Windows PowerShell prompt. Inside there, you can query the value contained in the *$num* variable and change it to a number such as 2. You exit the nested Windows PowerShell prompt and are returned to the stepping. At this point, you should continue to step through the code to see if any other problems arise. If they do not, you know you have located the source of the problem. This is shown here:

```
Continue with this operation?
   28+ $num- <<<< 1
[Y] Yes  [A] Yes to All  [N] No  [L] No to All  [S] Suspend  [?] Help
(default is "Y"):y
DEBUG:    28+   $num- <<<< 1

Continue with this operation?
   43+  12/ <<<< $num
[Y] Yes  [A] Yes to All  [N] No  [L] No to All  [S] Suspend  [?] Help
(default is "Y"):s
PS C:\>>> $num
0
PS C:\>>> $num = 2
PS C:\>>> exit

Continue with this operation?
   43+  12/ <<<< $num
[Y] Yes  [A] Yes to All  [N] No  [L] No to All  [S] Suspend  [?] Help
(default is "Y"):y
DEBUG:    43+   12/ <<<< $num
6

Continue with this operation?
   50+ <<<< AddOne($num) | AddTwo($num)
[Y] Yes  [A] Yes to All  [N] No  [L] No to All  [S] Suspend  [?] Help
(default is "Y"):
```

Of course, locating the source of the problem is not the same as solving the problem, but the previous example points to a problem with the value of *$num*. Your next step would be to look at how *$num* is being assigned its values.

There are a couple of annoyances when working with the *Set-PSDebug* tracing features. The first problem is stepping through the extra lines of output created by the debugging features. The prompts and output will use half of the Windows PowerShell console window. If you use *Clear-Host* to attempt to clear the host window, you will spend several minutes attempting to step through all the commands used by *Clear-Host*. This is also true if you attempt to change the debug tracing level midstream. By default, the trace level is set to 1 by the *Set-PSDebug -step* parameter. The second problem with the *Set-PSDebug -step* parameter occurs when you attempt to bypass a command in the script. You are not allowed to step over a command. Instead, the stepping session ends with an error displayed to the Windows PowerShell console. This is shown in Figure 18-8.

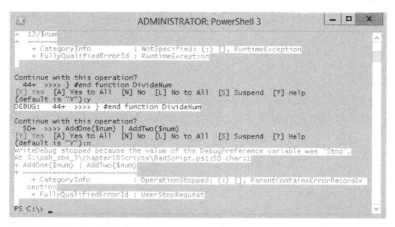

FIGURE 18-8  *Set-PSDebug -step* does not allow you to step over functions or commands.

To turn off stepping, you use the *-off* parameter. You will be prompted to step through this command as well. This is shown here:

```
PS C:\> Set-PSDebug -Off
Continue with this operation?
   1+ Set-PSDebug -Off
[Y] Yes  [A] Yes to All  [N] No  [L] No to All  [S] Suspend  [?] Help
(default is "Y"):y
DEBUG:    1+ Set-PSDebug -Off
PS C:\>
```

# Enabling strict mode

One easily correctable problem that can cause debugging nightmares in a script involves variables. Variables are often used incorrectly, are nonexistent, or are initialized improperly. An easy mistake to make when using variables is a simple typing error. Simple typing errors can also cause problems when contained in a large complex script. Enabling strict mode causes Windows PowerShell to display an error if a variable is not declared. This helps you to avoid the problem of nonexistent or improperly initialized variables.

## Using *Set-PSDebug -Strict*

An example of a simple typing error in a script is shown in the SimpleTypingError.ps1 script.

SimpleTypingError.ps1

```
$a = 2
$b = 5
$d = $a + $b
'The value of $c is: ' + $c
```

When the SimpleTypingError.ps1 script is run, the following output is shown:

```
PS C:\> y:\SimpleTypingError.ps1
The value of $c is:
PS C:\>
```

As you can see, the value of the *$c* variable is not displayed. If you use the *-Strict* parameter from the *Set-PSDebug* cmdlet, an error is generated. The error tells you that the value of *$c* has not been set. This is shown here:

```
PS C:\> Set-PSDebug -Strict
PS C:\> y:\SimpleTypingError.ps1
The variable $c cannot be retrieved because it has not been set yet.
At y:\SimpleTypingError.ps1:4 char:27
+ 'The value of $c is: ' + $c <<<<
PS C:\>
```

When you go back to the SimpleTypingError.ps1 script and examine it, you will see that the sum of *$a* and *$b* was assigned to *$d*, not *$c*. The way to correct the problem is to assign the sum of *$a* and *$b* to *$c* instead of *$d* (which was probably the original intention). It is possible to include the *Set-PSDebug -Strict* command in your scripts to provide a quick check for uninitialized variables while you are actually writing the script, and you can therefore avoid the error completely.

If you routinely use an expanding string to display the value of your variables, you need to be aware that an uninitialized variable is not reported as an error. The SimpleTypingErrorNotReported.ps1 script uses an expanding string to display the value of the *$c* variable. The first instance of the *$c* variable is escaped by the use of the backtick character. This causes the variable name to be displayed, and does not expand its value. The second occurrence of the *$c* variable is expanded. The actual line of code that does this is shown here:

```
"The value of `$c is: $c"
```

When the SimpleTypingErrorNotReported.ps1 script is run, the following is displayed:

```
PS C:\> Set-PSDebug -Strict
PS C:\> y:\SimpleTypingErrorNotReported.ps1
The value of $c is:
PS C:\>
```

The complete SimpleTypingErrorNotReported.ps1 script is shown here:

**SimpleTypingErrorNotReported.ps1**

```
$a = 2
$b = 5
$d = $a + $b
"The value of `$c is: $c"
```

To disable strict mode, you use the *Set-PSDebug -off* command.

# Using the *Set-StrictMode* cmdlet

The *Set-StrictMode* cmdlet can also be used to enable strict mode. It has the advantage of being scope aware. Whereas the *Set-PSDebug* cmdlet applies globally, if the *Set-StrictMode* cmdlet is used inside a function, it enables strict mode for only the function. There are two modes of operation that can be defined when using the *Set-StrictMode* cmdlet. The first is version 1, which behaves the same as the *Set-PSDebug -Strict* command (except that scope awareness is enforced). This is shown here:

```
PS C:\> Set-StrictMode -Version 1
PS C:\> y:\SimpleTypingError.ps1
The variable '$c' cannot be retrieved because it has not been set.
At y:\SimpleTypingError.ps1:4 char:28
+ 'The value of $c is: ' + $c <<<<
    + CategoryInfo          : InvalidOperation: (c:Token) [], RuntimeException
    + FullyQualifiedErrorId : VariableIsUndefined
PS C:\>
```

The *Set-StrictMode* cmdlet is not able to detect the uninitialized variable contained in the expanding string that is shown in the SimpleTypingErrorNotDetected.ps1 script.

When version 2 is enacted, the technique of calling a function like a method is stopped. The AddTwoError.ps1 script passes two values to the *add-two* function via method notation. Because method notation is allowed when calling functions, no error is normally generated. But method notation of passing parameters for functions only works when there is a single value to pass to the function. To pass multiple parameters, function notation must be used, as shown here:

```
add-two 1 2
```

Another way to call the *add-two* function correctly is to use the parameter names when passing the values. This is shown here:

```
add-two -a 1 -b 2
```

Either of the two syntaxes would produce the correct result. The method notation of calling the function displays incorrect information but does not generate an error. An incorrect value being returned from a function with no error being generated can take a significant amount of time to debug. The method notation of calling the *add-two* function is used in the AddTwoError.ps1 script, and is shown here:

```
add-two(1,2)
```

When the script is run and the *Set-StrictMode -Version 2* command has not been enabled, no error is generated. The output seems to be confusing because the result of adding the two variables $a and $b is not displayed. This is shown here:

```
PS C:\> y:\AddTwoError.ps1
1
2
PS C:\>
```

Once the *Set-StrictMode -Version 2* command has been entered and the AddTwoError.ps1 script is run, an error is generated. The error that is generated states that the function was called as if it were a method. The error points to the exact line where the error occurred and shows the function call that caused the error. The function call is preceded with a + sign followed by the name of the function, followed by four arrows that indicate what was passed to the function. The error message is shown here:

```
PS C:\> Set-StrictMode -Version 2
PS C:\> y:\AddTwoError.ps1
The function or command was called as if it were a method. Parameters should be
 separated by spaces. For information about parameters, see the about_Parameters Help topic.
At Y:\AddTwoError.ps1:7 char:8
+ add-two <<<< (1,2)
    + CategoryInfo          : InvalidOperation: (:) [], RuntimeException
    + FullyQualifiedErrorId : StrictModeFunctionCallWithParens
PS C:\>
```

The complete AddTwoError.ps1 script is shown here:

*AddTwoError.ps1*

```
Function add-two ($a,$b)
{
 $a + $b
}

add-two(1,2)
```

When you specify *Set-StrictMode* for version 2.0, it checks the following items:

- References to uninitialized variables, both directly and from within expanded strings

- References to nonexistent properties of an object

- Functions that are called like methods

- Variables without a name

If you set strict mode for version 1.0, it only checks for references to uninitialized variables.

If you are not sure whether you want to use strict mode for PowerShell version 2 or 3 (there are no changes), an easy way to solve the problem is to use the value *latest*. By using *latest* for the value of the *-version* parameter, you always ensure that your script will use the latest strict mode rules. This technique appears here:

```
Set-StrictMode -version latest
```

One issue that can arise with using *latest* is that you do not know what the latest changes might do to your script. Therefore, it is generally safer to use version 1 or version 2 when looking for specific types of protection.

# Debugging the script

The debugging features of Windows PowerShell 3.0 make the use of the *Set-PSDebug* cmdlet seem rudimentary or even cumbersome. Once you are more familiar with the debugging features of Windows PowerShell 3.0, you may decide to look no longer at the *Set-PSDebug* cmdlet. Several cmdlets enable debugging from the Windows PowerShell console and from the Windows PowerShell ISE.

The debugging cmdlets appear in Table 18-2.

**TABLE 18-2** Windows PowerShell debugging cmdlets

| Cmdlet name | Cmdlet function |
| --- | --- |
| *Set-PSBreakpoint* | Sets breakpoints on lines, variables, and commands |
| *Get-PSBreakpoint* | Gets breakpoints in the current session |
| *Disable-PSBreakpoint* | Turns off breakpoints in the current session |
| *Enable-PSBreakpoint* | Reenables breakpoints in the current session |
| *Remove-PSBreakpoint* | Deletes breakpoints from the current session |
| *Get-PSCallStack* | Displays the current call stack |

## Setting breakpoints

The debugging features in Windows PowerShell use breakpoints. A breakpoint is something that is very familiar to developers who have used products such as Microsoft Visual Studio in the past. But for many IT professionals without a programming background, the concept of a breakpoint is somewhat foreign. A breakpoint is a spot in the script where you would like the execution of the script to pause. Because the script pauses, it is like the stepping functionality shown earlier. But because you control where the breakpoint will occur, instead of halting on each line of the script, the stepping experience is much faster. In addition, because many different methods for setting breakpoints are available, you can tailor your breakpoints to reveal precisely the information you are looking for.

## Setting a breakpoint on a line number

To set a breakpoint, you use the *Set-PSBreakpoint* cmdlet. The easiest way to set a breakpoint is to set it on line 1 of the script. To set a breakpoint on the first line of the script, you use the *line* parameter and the *script* parameter. When you set a breakpoint, an instance of the *System.Management.Automation.LineBreak* .NET Framework class is returned. It lists the *ID*, *Script*, and *Line* properties that were assigned when the breakpoint was created. This is shown here:

```
PS C:\> Set-PSBreakpoint -line 1 -script Y:\BadScript.ps1
  ID Script            Line Command            Variable         Action
  -- ------            ---- -------            --------         ------
   0 BadScript.ps1        1
```

This will cause the script to break immediately. You can then step through the function in the same way you did using the *Set-PSDebug* cmdlet with the *-step* parameter. When you run the script, it stops at the breakpoint that was set on the first line of the script, and Windows PowerShell enters the script debugger, permitting you to use the debugging features of Windows PowerShell. Windows PowerShell will enter the debugger every time the BadScript.ps1 script is run from the Y drive. When Windows PowerShell enters the debugger, the Windows PowerShell prompt changes to *[DBG]: PS C:\>>>* to visually alert you that you are inside the Windows PowerShell debugger. To step to the next line in the script, you type **s**. To quit the debugging session, you type **q**. (The debugging commands are not case sensitive.) This is shown here:

```
PS C:\> Y:\BadScript.ps1
Hit Line breakpoint on 'Y:\BadScript.ps1:1'

BadScript.ps1:1   #
-----------------------------------------------------------------------
[DBG]: PS C:\>>> s
BadScript.ps1:16  Function AddOne([int]$num)
[DBG]: PS C:\>>> s
BadScript.ps1:21  Function AddTwo([int]$num)
[DBG]: PS C:\>>> s
BadScript.ps1:26  Function SubOne([int]$num)
[DBG]: PS C:\>>> s
BadScript.ps1:31  Function TimesOne([int]$num)
[DBG]: PS C:\>>> s
BadScript.ps1:36  Function TimesTwo([int]$num)
[DBG]: PS C:\>>> s
BadScript.ps1:41  Function DivideNum([int]$num)
[DBG]: PS C:\>>> s
BadScript.ps1:48  $num = 0
[DBG]: PS C:\>>> s
BadScript.ps1:49  SubOne($num) | DivideNum($num)
[DBG]: PS C:\>>> s
BadScript.ps1:28    $num-1
[DBG]: PS C:\>>> s
BadScript.ps1:43    12/$num
[DBG]: PS C:\>>> s
                              if ($_.FullyQualifiedErrorId -ne
"NativeCommandErrorMessage" -and $ErrorView -ne "CategoryView") {
[DBG]: PS C:\>>> q
PS C:\>
```

**Note** Keep in mind that breakpoints are dependent upon the location of the specific script when you specify a breakpoint on a script. When you create a breakpoint for a script, you specify the location to the script on which you want to set a breakpoint. Often, I have several copies of a script that I keep in different locations (for version control). At times, I get confused in a long debug session, and may open up the wrong version of the script to debug it. This will not work. If the script is identical to another in all respects except for the path to the script, it will not break. If you want to use a single breakpoint that could apply to a specific script that is stored in multiple locations, you can set the breakpoint for the condition inside the Windows PowerShell console, and not use the *-script* parameter.

## Setting a breakpoint on a variable

Setting a breakpoint on line 1 of the script is useful for easily entering a debug session, but setting a breakpoint on a variable can often make a problem with a script easy to detect. This is, of course, especially true when you have already determined that the problem is with a variable that is either getting assigned a value or being ignored. There are three modes that can be used when the breakpoint is specified for a variable. You specify these modes by using the *-mode* parameter. The three modes of operation are listed in Table 18-3.

**TABLE 18-3** Variable breakpoint access modes

| Access mode | Meaning |
| --- | --- |
| Write | Stops execution immediately before a new value is written to the variable. |
| Read | Stops execution when the variable is read—that is, when its value is accessed, either to be assigned, displayed, or used. In read mode, execution does not stop when the value of the variable changes. |
| ReadWrite | Stops execution when the variable is read or written. |

To see when the BadScript.ps1 script writes to the *$num* variable, you will use write mode. When you specify the value for the *-variable* parameter, do not include the dollar sign in front of the variable name. To set a breakpoint on a variable, you only need to supply the path to the script, the name of the variable, and the access mode. When a variable breakpoint is set, the *System.Management.Automation.LineBreak* .NET Framework class object that is returned does not include the access mode value. This is true even if you use the *Get-PSBreakpoint* cmdlet to directly access the breakpoint. If you pipe the *System.Management.Automation.LineBreak* .NET Framework class object to the *Format-List* cmdlet, you will be able to see that the access mode property is available. In this example, you set a breakpoint when the *$num* variable is written to in the y:\BadScript.ps1 script:

```
PS C:\> Set-PSBreakpoint -Variable num -Mode write -Script Y:\BadScript.ps1
 ID Script            Line Command        Variable        Action
 -- ------            ---- -------        --------        ------
  3 BadScript.ps1                          num
```

```
PS C:\> Get-PSBreakpoint
  ID Script           Line Command       Variable        Action
  -- ------           ---- -------       --------        ------
   3 BadScript.ps1                        num

PS C:\> Get-PSBreakpoint  | Format-List * -Force
AccessMode : Write
Variable   : num
Action     :
Enabled    : True
HitCount   : 0
Id         : 3
Script     : Y:\BadScript.ps1
```

After setting the breakpoint, when you run the script (if the other breakpoints have been removed or deactivated, which will be discussed later), the script enters the Windows PowerShell debugger when the breakpoint is hit (that is, when the value of the *$num* variable is written to). If you step through the script by using the *s* command, you will be able to follow the sequence of operations. Only one breakpoint is hit when the script is run. This is on line 48 when the value is set to 0 (if you are following along with this chapter, your line numbers may be different than mine). This is shown is shown here:

```
PS C:\> Y:\BadScript.ps1
Hit Variable breakpoint on 'Y:\BadScript.ps1:$num' (Write access)

BadScript.ps1:48  $num = 0
[DBG]: PS C:\>>> $num
[DBG]: PS C:\>>> Write-Host $num

[DBG]: PS C:\>>> s
BadScript.ps1:49  SubOne($num) | DivideNum($num)
[DBG]: PS C:\>>> $num
0
```

To set a breakpoint on a read operation for the variable, you specify the *-variable* parameter and name of the variable, the *-script* parameter with the path to the script, and *read* as the value for the *-mode* parameter. This is shown here:

```
PS C:\> Set-PSBreakpoint -Variable num -Script Y:\BadScript.ps1 -Mode read

  ID Script           Line Command       Variable        Action
  -- ------           ---- -------       --------        ------
   4 BadScript.ps1                        num
```

When you run the script, a breakpoint will be displayed each time you hit a read operation on the variable. Each breakpoint will be displayed in the Windows PowerShell console as *Hit Variable breakpoint*, followed by the path to the script and the access mode of the variable. In the BadScript. ps1 script, the value of the *$num* variable is read several times. The truncated output is shown here:

```
PS C:\> Y:\BadScript.ps1
Hit Variable breakpoint on 'Y:\BadScript.ps1:$num' (Read access)
```

```
BadScript.ps1:49  SubOne($num) | DivideNum($num)
[DBG]: PS C:\>>> s
Hit Variable breakpoint on 'Y:\BadScript.ps1:$num' (Read access)

BadScript.ps1:49  SubOne($num) | DivideNum($num)
[DBG]: PS C:\>>> s
BadScript.ps1:28    $num-1
[DBG]: PS C:\>>> s
Hit Variable breakpoint on 'Y:\BadScript.ps1:$num' (Read access)

BadScript.ps1:28    $num-1
[DBG]: PS C:\>>> s
```

If you set the readwrite access mode for the *-mode* parameter for the variable *$num* for the BadScript.ps1 script, you receive the feedback shown here:

```
PS C:\> Set-PSBreakpoint -Variable num -Mode readwrite -Script Y:\BadScript.ps1

  ID Script            Line Command        Variable      Action
  -- ------            ---- -------        --------      ------
   6 BadScript.ps1                         num
```

When you run the script (assuming you have disabled the other breakpoints), you will hit a breakpoint each time the *$num* variable is read to or written to. If you get tired of typing *s* and pressing Enter while you are in the debugging session, you can press Enter, and it will repeat your previous *s* command as you continue to step through the breakpoints. When the script has stepped through the code and arrives at the error in the BadScript.ps1 script, type **q** to exit the debugger. This is shown here:

```
PS C:\> Y:\BadScript.ps1
Hit Variable breakpoint on 'Y:\BadScript.ps1:$num' (ReadWrite access)

BadScript.ps1:48  $num = 0
[DBG]: PS C:\>>> s
BadScript.ps1:49  SubOne($num) | DivideNum($num)
[DBG]: PS C:\>>>
Hit Variable breakpoint on 'Y:\BadScript.ps1:$num' (ReadWrite access)

BadScript.ps1:49  SubOne($num) | DivideNum($num)
[DBG]: PS C:\>>>
Hit Variable breakpoint on 'Y:\BadScript.ps1:$num' (ReadWrite access)

BadScript.ps1:49  SubOne($num) | DivideNum($num)
[DBG]: PS C:\>>>
BadScript.ps1:28    $num-1
[DBG]: PS C:\>>>
Hit Variable breakpoint on 'Y:\BadScript.ps1:$num' (ReadWrite access)

BadScript.ps1:28    $num-1
[DBG]: PS C:\>>>
BadScript.ps1:43    12/$num
[DBG]: PS C:\>>>
Hit Variable breakpoint on 'Y:\BadScript.ps1:$num' (ReadWrite access)
```

```
BadScript.ps1:43    12/$num
[DBG]: PS C:\>>>
                                        if ($_.FullyQualifiedErrorId -ne
"NativeCommandErrorMessage" -and $ErrorView -ne "CategoryView") {
[DBG]: PS C:\>>> q
PS C:\>
```

When you use the readwrite access mode of the *-mode* parameter for breaking on variables, the breakpoint does not tell you if the operation is a read operation or a write operation. You have to look at the code that is being executed to determine if the value of the variable is being written or read.

By specifying a value for the *-action* parameter, you can include regular Windows PowerShell code that will execute when the breakpoint is hit. If, for example, you are trying to follow the value of a variable within the script and you wish to display the value of the variable each time the breakpoint is hit, you might want to specify an action that uses the *Write-Host* cmdlet to display the value of the variable. By using the *Write-Host* cmdlet, you can also include a string that indicates that the value of the variable is being displayed. This is crucial for picking up variables that never initialize and therefore is easier to spot than a blank line that would be displayed if you attempted to display the value of an empty variable. The technique of using the *Write-Host* cmdlet in an *-action* parameter is shown here:

```
PS C:\> Set-PSBreakpoint -Variable num -Action { write-host "num = $num" ;
Break } -Mode readwrite -script Y:\BadScript.ps1

   ID Script            Line Command        Variable       Action
   -- ------            ---- -------        --------       ------
    5 BadScript.ps1                         num            write-host "...
```

When you run the Y:\BadScript.ps1 with the breakpoint set, you receive the following output inside the Windows PowerShell debugger:

```
PS C:\> Y:\BadScript.ps1
num =
Hit Variable breakpoint on 'Y:\BadScript.ps1:$num' (ReadWrite access)

BadScript.ps1:48    $num = 0
[DBG]: PS C:\>>> s
BadScript.ps1:49    SubOne($num) | DivideNum($num)
[DBG]: PS C:\>>> s
Set-PSBreakpoint -Variable num -Action { write-host "num = $num" ; break }
-Mode readwrite -script Y:\BadScript.ps1
[DBG]: PS C:\>>> s
num = 0
Set-PSBreakpoint -Variable num -Action { write-host "num = $num" ; break }
-Mode readwrite -script Y:\BadScript.ps1
[DBG]: PS C:\>>> c
Hit Variable breakpoint on 'Y:\BadScript.ps1:$num' (ReadWrite access)

BadScript.ps1:49    SubOne($num) | DivideNum($num)
[DBG]: PS C:\>>>
```

# Setting a breakpoint on a command

To set the breakpoint on a command, you use the *-command* parameter. You can break on a call to a Windows PowerShell cmdlet, function, or external script. You can use aliases when setting breakpoints. When you create a breakpoint on an alias for a cmdlet, the debugger will only stop on the use of the alias—not the actual command name. In addition, you do not have to specify a script for the debugger to break. If you do not type a path to a script, the debugger will be active for everything within the Windows PowerShell console session. Every occurrence of the *foreach* command will cause the debugger to break. Because *foreach* is a language statement as well as an alias for the *Foreach-Object* cmdlet, you might wonder whether the Windows PowerShell debugger will break on both the language statement and the use of the alias for the cmdlet—and the answer is no. You can set breakpoints on language statements, but the debugger will not break on a language statement. As shown here, the debugger breaks on the use of the *Foreach* alias, but not on the use of the *Foreach-Object* cmdlet.

```
PS C:\> Set-PSBreakpoint -Command foreach

 ID Script            Line Command        Variable         Action
 -- ------            ---- -------        --------         ------
 10                        foreach


PS C:\> 1..3 | ForEach-Object { $_}
1
2
3
PS C:\> 1..3 | foreach { $_ }
Hit Command breakpoint on 'foreach'

1..3 | foreach { $_ }
[DBG]: PS C:\>>> c
1
Hit Command breakpoint on 'foreach'

1..3 | foreach { $_ }
[DBG]: PS C:\>>> c
2
Hit Command breakpoint on 'foreach'

1..3 | foreach { $_ }
[DBG]: PS C:\>>> c
3
```

> **Note** You can use the shortcut technique of creating the breakpoint for the Windows PowerShell session and not specifically for the script. By leaving out the *-script* parameter when creating a breakpoint, you cause the debugger to break into any running script that uses the named function. This allows you to use the same breakpoints when debugging scripts that use the same function.

When creating a breakpoint for the *DivideNum* function used by the Y:\BadScript.ps1 script, you can leave off the path to the script, because only this script uses the *DivideNum* function. This makes the command easier to type, but could become confusing if you're looking through a collection of breakpoints. If you are debugging multiple scripts in a single Windows PowerShell console session, it could become confusing if you do not specify the script to which the breakpoint applies—unless of course you are specifically debugging the function as it is used in multiple scripts. Creating a command breakpoint for the *DivideNum* function is shown here:

```
PS C:\> Set-PSBreakpoint -Command DivideNum

  ID Script            Line Command       Variable        Action
  -- ------            ---- -------       --------        ------
   7                        DivideNum
```

When you run the script, it hits a breakpoint when the *DivideNum* function is called. When BadScript.ps1 hits the *DivideNum* function, the value of *$num* is 0. As you step through the *DivideNum* function, you assign a value of 2 to the *$num* variable, a result of 6 is displayed, and then the *12/$num* operation is carried out. Next, the *AddOne* function is called and the value of *$num* once again becomes 0. When the *AddTwo* function is called, the value of *$num* also becomes 0. This is shown here:

```
PS C:\> Y:\BadScript.ps1
Hit Command breakpoint on 'DivideNum'

BadScript.ps1:49  SubOne($num) | DivideNum($num)
[DBG]: PS C:\>>> s
BadScript.ps1:43    12/$num
[DBG]: PS C:\>>> $num
0
[DBG]: PS C:\>>> $num =2
[DBG]: PS C:\>>> s
6
BadScript.ps1:50  AddOne($num) | AddTwo($num)
[DBG]: PS C:\>>> s
BadScript.ps1:18    $num+1
[DBG]: PS C:\>>> $num
0
[DBG]: PS C:\>>> s
BadScript.ps1:23    $num+2
[DBG]: PS C:\>>> $num
0
[DBG]: PS C:\>>> s
2
PS C:\>
```

## Responding to breakpoints

When the script reaches a breakpoint, control of the Windows PowerShell console is turned over to you. Inside the debugger, you can type any legal Windows PowerShell command, and even run cmdlets such as *Get-Process* or *Get-Service*. In addition, there are several new debugging commands that can be typed into the Windows PowerShell console when a breakpoint has been reached. The available debug commands are shown in Table 18-4.

**TABLE 18-4** Windows PowerShell debugging commands

| Keyboard shortcut | Command name | Command meaning |
|---|---|---|
| S | *Step-Into* | Executes the next statement and then stops. |
| V | *Step-Over* | Executes the next statement, but skips functions and invocations. The skipped statements are executed, but not stepped through. |
| O | *Step-Out* | Steps out of the current function up one level if nested. If in the main body, it continues to the end or the next breakpoint. The skipped statements are executed, but not stepped through. |
| C | *Continue* | Continues to run until the script is complete or until the next breakpoint is reached. The skipped statements are executed, but not stepped through. |
| L | *List* | Displays the part of the script that is executing. By default, it displays the current line, 5 previous lines, and 10 subsequent lines. To continue listing the script, press Enter. |
| L <M> | *List* | Displays 16 lines of the script, beginning with the line number specified by M. |
| L <M> <N> | *List* | Displays the number of lines of the script specified by N, beginning with the line number specified by M. |
| Q | *Stop* | Stops executing the script and exits the debugger. |
| K | *Get-PsCallStack* | Displays the current call stack. |
| Enter | *Repeat* | Repeats the last command if it was *Step-Into*, *Step-Over*, or *List*. Otherwise, represents a submit action. |
| H or ? | *Help* | Displays the debugger command help. |

When the BadScript.ps1 script is run using the *DivideNum* function as a breakpoint, the script breaks on line 49 when the *DivideNum* function is called. The s debugging command is used to step into the next statement and stop the script before the command is actually executed. The *l* debugging command is used to list the 5 previous lines of code from the BadScript.ps1 script and the 10 lines of code that follow the current line in the script. This is shown here:

```
PS C:\> Y:\BadScript.ps1
Hit Command breakpoint on 'Y:\BadScript.ps1:dividenum'

BadScript.ps1:49  SubOne($num) | DivideNum($num)
[DBG]: PS C:\>>> s
BadScript.ps1:43    12/$num
[DBG]: PS C:\>>> l

   38:    $num*2
   39:  } #end function TimesTwo
   40:
   41:  Function DivideNum([int]$num)
   42:  {
   43:*  12/$num
   44:  } #end function DivideNum
   45:
```

```
46:   # *** Entry Point to Script ***
47:
48:   $num = 0
49:   SubOne($num) | DivideNum($num)
50:   AddOne($num) | AddTwo($num)
51:
```

After reviewing the code, the *o* debugging command is used to step out of the *DivideNum* function. The remaining code in the *DivideNum* function is still executed, and therefore the divide-by-zero error is displayed. There are no more prompts until the next line of executing code is met. The *v* debugging statement is used to step over the remaining functions in the script. The remaining functions are still executed, and the results are displayed at the Windows PowerShell console. This is shown here:

```
[DBG]: PS C:\>>> o
Attempted to divide by zero.
At Y:\BadScript.ps1:43 char:5
+  12/ <<<< $num
    + CategoryInfo          : NotSpecified: (:) [], RuntimeException
    + FullyQualifiedErrorId : RuntimeException

BadScript.ps1:50  AddOne($num) | AddTwo($num)
[DBG]: PS C:\>>> v
2
PS C:\>
```

# Listing breakpoints

Once you have set several breakpoints, you might wish to know where they were created. One thing to keep in mind is the breakpoints are stored in the Windows PowerShell environment, not in the individual script. Using the debugging features does not involve editing of the script or modifying your source code. This enables you to debug any script without worry of corrupting the code. But because you may have set several breakpoints in the Windows PowerShell environment during a typical debugging session, you may wish to know what breakpoints have been defined. To do this, you use the *Get-PSBreakpoint* cmdlet. This is shown here:

```
PS C:\> Get-PSBreakpoint
  ID Script             Line Command      Variable      Action
  -- ------             ---- -------      --------      ------
  11 BadScript.ps1           dividenum
  13 BadScript.ps1           if
   3 BadScript.ps1                        num
   5 BadScript.ps1                        num
   6 BadScript.ps1                        num
   7                         DivideNum
   8                         foreach
   9                         gps
  10                         foreach
PS C:\>
```

If you are interested in which breakpoints are currently enabled, you need to use the *Where-Object* cmdlet and pipeline the results from the *Get-PSBreakpoint* cmdlet. This is shown here:

```
PS C:\> Get-PSBreakpoint | where { $_.enabled }

  ID Script              Line Command       Variable      Action
  -- ------              ---- -------       --------      ------
  11 BadScript.ps1            dividenum


PS C:\>
```

You could also pipeline the results of the *Get-PSBreakpoint* to the *Format-Table* cmdlet, as shown here:

```
PS C:\> Get-PSBreakpoint |
Format-Table -Property id, script, command, variable, enabled -AutoSize

Id Script           Command     variable Enabled
-- ------           -------     -------- -------
11 Y:\BadScript.ps1 dividenum            True
13 Y:\BadScript.ps1 if                   False
 3 Y:\BadScript.ps1             num       False
 5 Y:\BadScript.ps1             num       False
 6 Y:\BadScript.ps1             num       False
 7                  DivideNum            False
 8                  foreach              False
 9                  gps                  False
10                  foreach              False
```

Because the creation of the custom-formatted breakpoint table requires a little bit of typing, and because the display is extremely helpful, you might consider placing the code in a function that could be included in your profile, or in a custom debugging module. The function shown here is stored in the Get-EnabledBreakpointsFunction.ps1 script.

**Get-EnabledBreakpointsFunction.ps1**

```
Function Get-EnabledBreakpoints
{
  Get-PSBreakpoint |
  Format-Table -Property id, script, command, variable, enabled -AutoSize
}

# *** Entry Point to Script ***

Get-EnabledBreakpoints
```

# Enabling and disabling breakpoints

While you are debugging a script, you might need to disable a particular breakpoint to see how the script runs. To do this, you use the *Disable-PSBreakpoint* cmdlet. This is shown here:

```
Disable-PSBreakpoint -id 0
```

On the other hand, you may also need to enable a breakpoint. To do this, you use the *Enable-PSBreakpoint* cmdlet, as shown here:

```
Enable-PSBreakpoint -id 1
```

As a best practice, while in a debugging session I will selectively enable and disable breakpoints to see how the script is running in an attempt to troubleshoot the script. To keep track of the status of breakpoints, I use the *Get-PSBreakpoint* cmdlet as illustrated in the previous section.

# Deleting breakpoints

When you are finished debugging the script, you will want to remove all of the breakpoints that were created during the Windows PowerShell session. There are two ways to do this. The first is to close the Windows PowerShell console. While this is a good way to clean up the environment, you may not want to do this if you have remote Windows PowerShell sessions defined, or variables that are populated with the results of certain queries. To delete all of the breakpoints, you can use the *Remove-PSBreakpoint* cmdlet. Unfortunately, there is no *all* switch for the *Remove-PSBreakpoint* cmdlet. When you're deleting a breakpoint, the *Remove-PSBreakpoint* cmdlet requires a breakpoint ID number. To remove a single breakpoint, you specify the ID number for the *-id* parameter. This is shown here:

```
Remove-PSBreakpoint -id 3
```

If you want to remove all of the breakpoints, pipeline the results from *Get-PSBreakpoint* to *Remove-PSBreakpoint*, as shown here:

```
Get-PSBreakpoint | Remove-PSBreakpoint
```

If you want to only remove the breakpoints from a specific script, you can pipeline the results through the *Where* object, as shown here:

```
(Get-PSBreakpoint | Where ScriptName - eq "C:\Scripts\Test.ps1") |
Removeakpoint
```

# Debugging a function: step-by-step exercises

In this exercise, you will explore the use of the debugger in the Windows PowerShell ISE. (Note that if you have defined your own custom Windows PowerShell prompt, you may not see the *[DBG]* prompt portion of the Windows PowerShell prompt.) Once you have completed debugging a function, in the subsequent exercise you will debug a script.

## Using the PowerShell debugger to debug a function

1. Open the Windows PowerShell ISE.

2. Create a function called *My-Function*. The contents of the function appear following. Save the function to a file named my-function.ps1. (If you do not save the file, you are not running a script, and you will not enter the debugger.)

```
Function my-function
{
 Param(
  [int]$a,
  [int]$b)
  "$a plus $b equals four"
}
```

3. Select the line of code that states that *$a* plus *$b* equals four. This line of code appears here:

```
"$a plus $b equals four"
```

4. Choose Toggle Breakpoint from the Debug menu. The line of code should change colors, indicating that a breakpoint is now set on that line.

5. Run the My-Function script to load the function into memory.

6. In the bottom pane of the Windows PowerShell ISE (the command pane), type the function name so that you execute the function. (You can use tab expansion to avoid typing the complete *My-Function* name.) This appears here:

```
My-Function
```

7. In the output pane of the Windows PowerShell ISE, you will see that you have now hit a breakpoint. Examine the output and determine which line the breakpoint is defined upon. The line number in the output pane corresponds with the line number in the script pane (the upper pane). Sample output appears here:

```
PS C:\> my-function
Hit Line breakpoint on 'S:\psh_sbs_3\chapter18Scripts\my-function.ps1:6'
```

8. Examine the prompt in the Windows PowerShell ISE command pane. It should be prefixed by *[DBG]*. This tells you that you are in a debug prompt. This prompt appears here:

```
[DBG]: PS C:\>>
```

9. At the debug prompt in the Windows PowerShell ISE command pane, examine the value of the *$a* variable.

```
[DBG]: PS C:\>> $a
0
```

**10.** Now examine the value of the *$b* variable.

```
[DBG]: PS C:\>> $b
0
```

**11.** Now assign a value of 2 to both *$a* and *$b*.

```
[DBG]: PS C:\>> $a = $b = 2
```

**12.** Now choose Step Out from the Debug menu to permit the script to continue execution and to run the line upon which the breakpoint was set. Notice that the function now uses the new value of *$a* and *$b*. The output appears here:

```
[DBG]: PS C:\>>
2 plus 2 equals four
```

**13.** Select Remove All Breakpoints from the Debug menu. Examine the script pane. The high-lighted line of code should now appear normally.

**14.** In the command pane of the Windows PowerShell ISE, call *My-Function* once again. This time you will notice that the function still exhibits the problem. The output appears here:

```
PS C:\> my-function
0 plus 0 equals four
```

**15.** You should now fix the function. To do this, change the output line so that it does not have the hard-coded word *four* in it. This change appears following. Save the revised function as my-function1.ps1.

```
"$a plus $b equals $($a+$b)"
```

This concludes the exercise.

In the next exercise, you will set breakpoints that will be used when debugging a script.

## Debugging a script

**1.** Open the Windows PowerShell console.

**2.** Use the *Set-PSBreakPoint* cmdlet to set a breakpoint on the *my-function* function inside the script my-function.ps1. Remember that you will need to use the full path to the script when you do this. The command will look something like the following:

```
Set-PSBreakpoint -Script sbs:\chapter18Scripts\my-function.ps1 -Command my-function
```

**3.** Run the my-function.ps1 scrip inside the Windows PowerShell console by typing its complete path. The command will look something like the following. (Notice that the command does not break).

```
sbs:\chapter18Scripts> .\my-function.ps1
```

4.  Dot-source the function, and then call the function directly from memory and watch to see if the command breaks. The two commands will look something like the following:

```
.  .\my-function.ps1
my-function
```

5.  Use the *Get-PSBreakPoint cmdlet* to display the breakpoint. The command and associated output appear here:

```
PS C:\> Get-PSBreakpoint


  ID Script              Line Command        Variable        Action
  -- ------              ---- -------        --------        ------
   0 my-function.ps1          my-function
```

6.  Remove the breakpoint for the *my-function* command by using the *Remove-PSBreakPoint* cmdlet. It should have an ID of 0. The command appears here:

```
Remove-PSBreakpoint -Id 0
```

7.  Set a breakpoint for the *my-function* command without specifying a script. The command appears here:

```
Set-PSBreakpoint -Command my-function
```

8.  Call *my-function*. When you do, the Windows PowerShell console will enter debug mode. The command and debug mode appear here:

```
PS C:\> my-function
Entering debug mode. Use h or ? for help.

Hit Command breakpoint on 'my-function'

At S:\psh_sbs_3\chapter18Scripts\my-function.ps1:2 char:1
+ {
+ ~
```

9.  Inside debug mode, display the value of the *$a* variable and the *$b* variable. The command and output appear here:

```
[DBG]: PS C:\>> $a
0
[DBG]: PS C:\>> $b
0
```

10. Exit debug mode by typing the command *exit*. The Windows PowerShell console exits debug mode and continues running the function, as shown here:

```
[DBG]: PS C:\>> exit
0 plus 0 equals four
```

11. Dot-source the my-function1.ps1 script. The command will be similar to the one that appears here:

```
. sbs:\chapter18Scripts\my-function1.ps1
```

12. Run the *my-function* function and supply the value 12 for the *a* parameter and the value 14 for the *b* parameter. The command follows. Note that once again the Windows PowerShell console enters debug mode.

```
PS C:\> my-function -a 12 -b 14
Hit Command breakpoint on 'my-function'

At S:\psh_sbs_3\chapter18Scripts\my-function1.ps1:2 char:1
+ {
+ ~
```

13. Query for the value of *$a* and *$b*. The command and associated values appear here:

```
[DBG]: PS C:\>> $a
12
[DBG]: PS C:\>> $b
14
```

14. Change the value of *$b* to be equal to 0 and exit debug mode. The commands appear here:

```
[DBG]: PS C:\>> $b = 0
[DBG]: PS C:\>> exit
```

15. When the console exits debug mode, the new value for the *b* parameter is used. The output appears here:

```
12 plus 0 equals 12
```

16. Use the *Get-PSBreakPoint* cmdlet to retrieve all breakpoints, and pipeline them to the *Remove-PSBreakPoint* cmdlet. This command appears here:

```
Get-PSBreakpoint | Remove-PSBreakpoint
```

17. Use the *Get-PSBreakPoint* cmdlet to ensure that the breakpoint is removed. This command appears here:

```
Get-PSBreakpoint
```

This concludes the exercise.

# Chapter 18 quick reference

| To | Do this |
|---|---|
| Step through a script or a function | Use the *Set-PSDebug* cmdlet and specify the *-step* switch. |
| Follow code execution into and out of functions in a script | Use the *Set-PSDebug* cmdlet and specify a value of 2 for the *-trace* parameter. |
| Set a breakpoint for a particular line number in a script | Use the *Set-PSBreakPoint* cmdlet and specify the line number to the *-line* parameter. Also specify the script by using the *-script* parameter. |
| Set a breakpoint on a script when a particular variable is written to | Use the *Set-PSBreakPoint* cmdlet, specify the variable name (leave off the $ sign when specifying the variable name) to the *-variable* parameter, and specify the script to the *-name* parameter. |
| Set a breakpoint when a particular command is run from any script | Use the *Set-PSBreakPoint* cmdlet and the *-command* parameter to specify the command to watch, and do not set a script name. |
| List all breakpoints currently defined in the session | Use the *Get-PSBreakpoint* cmdlet. |
| Delete all breakpoints currently defined in the session | Use the *Get-PSBreakpoint* cmdlet and pipeline the results to the *Remove-PSBreakpoint* cmdlet. |

# CHAPTER 19

# Handling Errors

### After completing this chapter, you will be able to:

- Handle missing parameters in scripts.

- Limit the choices available to users of your scripts.

- Handle missing rights and permissions in scripts.

- Handle missing WMI providers in scripts.

- Use *Try...Catch...Finally* to catch single and multiple errors in scripts.

When it comes to handling run-time errors in your script, you need to have an understanding of the intended use of the script. For example, just because a script runs once does not mean it will run a second time. Disks fail, networks fail, computers fail, and things are constantly in flux. The way that a script will be used is sometimes called the *use-case scenario*, and it describes how the user will interact with the script. If the use-case scenario is simple, the user may not need to do anything more than type the name of the script inside the Microsoft Windows PowerShell console. A script such as Get-Bios.ps1, shown following, could get by without much need for any error handling. This is because there are no inputs to the script. The script is called, it runs, and it displays information that should always be readily available, because the *Win32_Bios* Windows Management Instrumentation (WMI) class is present in all versions of Windows since Windows 2000 (however, even a simple script like Get-Bios.ps1 could fail because it relies on a WMI service that might be broken, or because the COM interface is corrupt).

**Get-Bios.ps1**

```
Get-WmiObject -class Win32_Bios
```

## Handling missing parameters

When you examine the Get-Bios.ps1 script, you can see that it does not receive any input from the command line. This is a good way to avoid user errors in your script, but it is not always practical. When your script accepts command-line input, you are opening the door for all kinds of potential problems. Depending on how you accept command-line input, you may need to test the input data to ensure that it corresponds to the type of input the script is expecting. The Get-Bios.ps1 script does not accept command-line input; therefore, it avoids most potential sources of errors (of course, the Get-Bios.ps1 script is also extremely limited in scope—so you win some and you lose some).

# Creating a default value for a parameter

There are two ways to assign default values for a command-line parameter. You can assign the default value in the *param* declaration statement, or you can assign the value in the script itself. Given a choice between the two, it is a best practice to assign the default value in the *param* statement. This is because it makes the script easier to read, which in turn makes the script easier to modify and troubleshoot. For more information on troubleshooting scripts, see Chapter 18, "Debugging Scripts."

## Detecting a missing value and assigning it in the script

In the Get-BiosInformation.ps1 script, which follows, a command-line parameter, *computerName*, allows the script to target both local and remote computers. If the script runs without a value for the *computerName* parameter, the *Get-WMIObject* cmdlet fails because it requires a value for the *computername* parameter. To solve the problem of the missing parameter, the Get-BiosInformation.ps1 script checks for the presence of the *$computerName* variable. If this variable is missing, it means it was not created via the command-line parameter, and the script therefore assigns a value to the *$computerName* variable. Here is the line of code that populates the value of the *$computerName* variable:

```
If(-not($computerName)) { $computerName = $env:computerName }
```

The completed Get-BiosInformation.ps1 script is shown here:

**Get-BiosInformation.ps1**

```
Param(
  [string]$computerName
) #end param

Function Get-BiosInformation($computerName)
{
 Get-WmiObject -class Win32_Bios -computerName $computername
} #end function Get-BiosName

# *** Entry Point To Script ***
If(-not($computerName)) { $computerName = $env:computerName }
Get-BiosInformation -computerName $computername
```

## Assigning a value in the *param* statement

To assign a default value in the *param* statement, you use the equality operator following the parameter name and assign the value to the parameter. This technique appears here:

```
Param(
  [string]$computerName = $env:computername
) #end param
```

An advantage of assigning the default value for the parameter in the *param* statement is that it makes the script is easier to read. Because the parameter declaration and the default parameter are in the same place, you can see immediately which parameters have default values and which do not. The second advantage that arises from assigning a default value in the *param* statement is that the script is easier to write. Notice that there is no *if* statement to check the existence of the *$computerName* variable. The Get-BiosInformationDefaultParam.ps1 script illustrates using the *param* statement to assign a default value for a script. The complete script is shown here:

**Get-BiosInformationDefaultParam.ps1**

```
Param(
  [string]$computerName = $env:computername
) #end param

Function Get-BiosInformation($computerName)
{
 Get-WmiObject -class Win32_Bios -computername $computername
} #end function Get-BiosName

# *** Entry Point To Script ***

Get-BiosInformation -computerName $computername
```

## Making the parameter mandatory

The best way to handle an error is to ensure the error does not occur in the first place. In Windows PowerShell 3.0, you can mark a parameter as mandatory (for the scripts as well as for functions). The advantage of marking a parameter as mandatory is that it requires the user of the script to supply a value for the parameter. If you do not want the user of the script to be able to run the script without making a particular selection, you will want to make the parameter mandatory. To make a parameter mandatory, you use the *mandatory* parameter attribute. This technique appears here:

```
Param(
    [Parameter(Mandatory=$true)]
    [string]$drive,
    [string]$computerName = $env:computerName
) #end param
```

The complete MandatoryParameter.ps1 script appears here:

**MandatoryParameter.ps1**

```
#Requires -version 3.0
Param(
    [Parameter(Mandatory=$true)]
    [string]$drive,
    [string]$computerName = $env:computerName
) #end param
```

```
Function Get-DiskInformation($computerName,$drive)
{
 Get-WmiObject -class Win32_volume -computername $computername `
-filter "DriveLetter = '$drive'"
} #end function Get-BiosName

# *** Entry Point To Script ***

 Get-DiskInformation -computername $computerName -drive $drive
```

When a script with a *mandatory* parameter runs without supplying a value for the parameter, an error is not generated. Instead, Windows PowerShell prompts for the required parameter value. This behavior appears here:

```
PS C:\bp> .\MandatoryParameter.ps1

cmdlet MandatoryParameter.ps1 at command pipeline position 1
Supply values for the following parameters:
drive:
```

# Limiting choices

Depending on the design of the script, several scripting techniques can ease error-checking requirements. If you have a limited number of choices you wish to display to your user, you can use the *PromptForChoice* method. If you want to limit the selection to computers that are currently running, you can the *Test-Connection* cmdlet prior to attempting to connect to a remote computer. If you would like to limit the choice to a specific subset of computers or properties, you can parse a text file and use the *-contains* operator. In this section, you will examine each of these techniques for limiting the permissible input values from the command line.

## Using *PromptForChoice* to limit selections

For example, if you use the *PromptForChoice* method of soliciting input from the user, your user has a limited number of options from which to choose. You eliminate the problem of bad input because the user only has specific options available to supply to your script. The user prompt from the *PromptForChoice* method is shown in Figure 19-1.

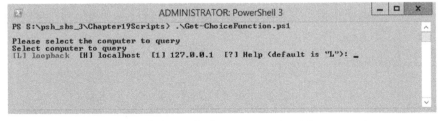

**FIGURE 19-1** The *PromptForChoice* method presents a selectable menu to the user.

The use of the *PromptForChoice* method appears in the Get-ChoiceFunction.ps1 script, which follows. In the *Get-Choice* function, the *$caption* variable and the *$message* variable hold the caption and the message that is used by the *PromptForChoice* method. The choices are an array of instances of the *ChoiceDescription* .NET Framework class. When you create the *ChoiceDescription* class, you also supply an array with the choices that will appear. This is shown here:

```
$choices = [System.Management.Automation.Host.ChoiceDescription[]] `
 @("&loopback", "local&host", "&127.0.0.1")
```

You next need to select a number that will be used to represent which choice will be the default choice. When you begin counting, keep in mind that *ChoiceDescription* is an array, and the first option is numbered 0. Next, you call the *PromptForChoice* method and display the options. This is shown here:

```
[int]$defaultChoice = 0
$choiceRTN = $host.ui.PromptForChoice($caption,$message, $choices,$defaultChoice)
```

Because the *PromptForChoice* method returns an integer, you could use the *if* statement to evaluate the value of the *$choiceRTN* variable. The syntax of the *switch* statement is more compact and is actually a better choice for this application. The *switch* statement from the *Get-Choice* function is shown here:

```
switch($choiceRTN)
 {
  0    { "loopback"  }
  1    { "localhost"  }
  2    { "127.0.0.1"  }
 }
```

When you call the *Get-Choice* function, it returns the computer that was identified by the *PromptForChoice* method. You place the method call in a set of parentheses to force it to be evaluated before the rest of the command. This is shown here:

```
Get-WmiObject -class win32_bios -computername (Get-Choice)
```

This solution to the problem of bad input works well when you have help desk personnel who will be working with a limited number of computers. One caveat to this approach is that you do not want to have to change the choices on a regular basis, so you would want a stable list of computers to avoid creating a maintenance nightmare for yourself. The complete Get-ChoiceFunction.ps1 script is shown here:

**Get-ChoiceFunction.ps1**

```
Function Get-Choice
{
 $caption = "Please select the computer to query"
 $message = "Select computer to query"
 $choices = [System.Management.Automation.Host.ChoiceDescription[]] `
 @("&loopback", "local&host", "&127.0.0.1")
 [int]$defaultChoice = 0
 $choiceRTN = $host.ui.PromptForChoice($caption,$message, $choices,$defaultChoice)
```

```
switch($choiceRTN)
{
  0    { "loopback"  }
  1    { "localhost" }
  2    { "127.0.0.1" }
}
} #end Get-Choice function

Get-WmiObject -class win32_bios -computername (Get-Choice)
```

# Using *Test-Connection* to identify computer connectivity

If you have more than a few computers that need to be accessible, or if you do not have a stable list
of computers that you will be working with, then one solution to the problem of trying to connect to
nonexistent computers is to ping a computer prior to attempting to make the WMI connection.

You can use the *Win32_PingStatus* WMI class to send a ping to a computer. This establishes computer connectivity, and it also verifies that name resolution works properly. The best way to use the
*Win32_PingStatus* WMI class is to use the *Test-Connection* cmdlet because it wraps the WMI class
into an easy-to-use package. An example of using the *Test-Connection* cmdlet with default values
appears here:

```
PS C:\> Test-Connection -ComputerName dc1

Source       Destination    IPV4Address        IPV6Address
------       -----------    -----------        -----------
W8CLIENT6    dc1            192.168.0.101
W8CLIENT6    dc1            192.168.0.101
W8CLIENT6    dc1            192.168.0.101
W8CLIENT6    dc1            192.168.0.101
```

If you are only interested in whether the target computer is up or not, use the *-quiet* parameter.
The *-quiet* parameter returns a Boolean value (*true* if the computer is up; *false* if the computer is
down). This appears here:

```
PS C:\> Test-Connection -ComputerName dc1 -Quiet
True
```

When you use the *Test-Connection* cmdlet, it has a tendency to be slower than the traditional ping
utility. It has a lot more capabilities, and even returns an object, but it is slower. A few seconds can
make a huge difference when attempting run a single script to manage thousands of computers. To
increase performance in these types of fan-out scenarios, use the *-count* parameter to reduce the
default number of pings from four to one. In addition, reduce the default buffer size from 32 to 16.

Because *Test-Connection -quiet* returns a Boolean value, there is no need to evaluate a number of
possible return values. In fact, the logic is simple: either the command returns a value or it does not.
If it does return, add the action to take in the *if* statement. If it does not return, add the action to take
in the *else* statement. If you do not wish to log failed connections, on the other hand, you would only
have the action in the *if* statement with which to contend. The Test-ComputerPath.ps1 script illustrates

using the *Test-Connection* cmdlet to determine if a computer is up prior to attempting a remote connection. The complete Test-ComputerPath.ps1 script appears here:

**Test-ComputerPath.ps1**

```
Param([string]$computer = $env:COMPUTERNAME)
if(Test-Connection -computer $computer -BufferSize 16 -Count 1 -Quiet)
 { Get-WmiObject -class Win32_Bios -computer $computer }
Else
 { "Unable to reach $computer computer"}
```

# Using the *-contains* operator to examine contents of an array

To verify input that is received from the command line, you can use the *-contains* operator to examine the contents of an array of possible values. This technique is illustrated here, where an array of three values is created and stored in the variable *$noun*. The *-contains* operator is then used to see if the array contains *hairy-nosed wombat*. Because the *$noun* variable does not have an array element that is equal to the string *hairy-nosed wombat*, the *-contains* operator returns *false*.

```
PS C:\> $noun = "cat","dog","rabbit"
PS C:\> $noun -contains "hairy-nosed wombat"
False
PS C:\>
```

If an array contains a match, the *-contains* operator returns *true*. This is shown here:

```
PS C:\> $noun = "cat","dog","rabbit"
PS C:\> $noun -contains "rabbit"
True
PS C:\>
```

The *-contains* operator returns *true* only when there is an exact match. Partial matches return *false*. This is shown here:

```
PS C:\> $noun = "cat","dog","rabbit"
PS C:\> $noun -contains "bit"
False
PS C:\>
```

The *-contains* operator is a case insensitive operator. (But there is also the *-icontains* operator, which is case insensitive, as well as *-ccontains*, which is case sensitive). Therefore, it will return *true* when matched, regardless of case. This is shown here:

```
PS C:\> $noun = "cat","dog","rabbit"
PS C:\> $noun -contains "Rabbit"
True
PS C:\>
```

If you need to perform a case-sensitive match, you can use the case-sensitive version of the *-contains* operator, *-ccontains*. As shown here, it will return *true* only if the case of the string matches the value contained in the array.

```
PS C:\> $noun = "cat","dog","rabbit"
PS C:\> $noun -ccontains "Rabbit"
False
PS C:\> $noun -ccontains "rabbit"
True
PS C:\>
```

In the Get-AllowedComputers.ps1 script, which follows, a single command-line parameter is created that is used to hold the name of the target computer for the WMI query. The *computer* parameter is a string, and it receives the default value from the environment drive. This is a good technique because it ensures that the script will have the name of the local computer, which could then be used in producing a report of the results. If you set the value of the *computer* parameter to *localhost*, you never know what computer the results belong to. This is shown here:

```
Param([string]$computer = $env:computername)
```

The *Get-AllowedComputer* function is used to create an array of permitted computer names and to check the value of the *$computer* variable to see if it is present. If the value of the *$computer* variable is present in the array, the *Get-AllowedComputer* function returns *true*. If the value is missing from the array, the *Get-AllowedComputer* function returns *false*. The array of computer names is created by the use of the *Get-Content* cmdlet to read a text file that contains a listing of computer names. The text file, servers.txt, is a plain ASCII text file that has a list of computer names on individual lines, as shown in Figure 19-2.

**FIGURE 19-2** Using a text file with computer names and addresses is an easy way to work with allowed computers.

A text file of computer names is easier to maintain than a hard-coded array that is embedded into the script. In addition, the text file can be placed on a central share and can be used by many different scripts. The *Get-AllowedComputer* function is shown here:

```
Function Get-AllowedComputer([string]$computer)
{
 $servers = Get-Content -path c:\fso\servers.txt
 $servers -contains $computer
} #end Get-AllowedComputer function
```

Because the *Get-AllowedComputer* function returns a Boolean value (*true* or *false*), it can be used directly in an *if* statement to determine whether the value that is supplied for the *$computer* variable is on the list of permitted computers. If the *Get-AllowedComputer* function returns *true*, the *Get-WMIObject* cmdlet is used to query for BIOS information from the target computer. This is shown here:

```
if(Get-AllowedComputer -computer $computer)
 {
   Get-WmiObject -class Win32_Bios -Computer $computer
 }
```

On the other hand, if the value of the *$computer* variable is not found in the *$servers* array, a string that states that the computer is not an allowed computer is displayed. This is shown here:

```
Else
 {
  "$computer is not an allowed computer"
 }
```

The complete Get-AllowedComputer.ps1 script is shown here:

**Get-AllowedComputer.ps1**

```
Param([string]$computer = $env:computername)

Function Get-AllowedComputer([string]$computer)
{
 $servers = Get-Content -path c:\fso\servers.txt
 $servers -contains $computer
} #end Get-AllowedComputer function

# *** Entry point to Script ***

if(Get-AllowedComputer -computer $computer)
 {
   Get-WmiObject -class Win32_Bios -Computer $computer
 }
Else
 {
  "$computer is not an allowed computer"
 }
```

# Using the *-contains* operator to test for properties

You are not limited to only testing for specified computer names in the *Get-AllowedComputer* function. All you need to do is add additional information to the text file in order to check for WMI property names or other information. This is shown in Figure 19-3.

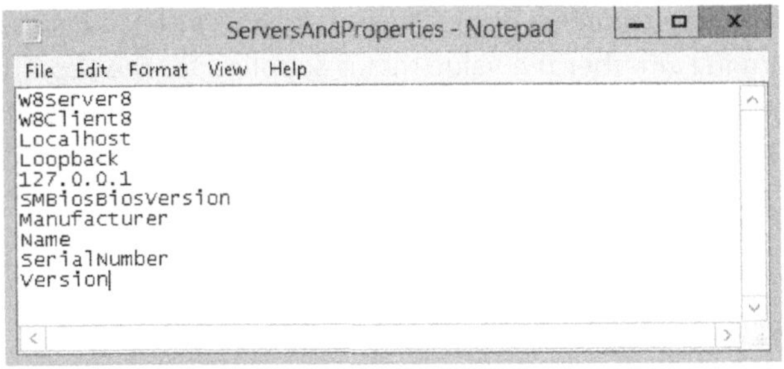

**FIGURE 19-3** A text file with server names and properties adds flexibility to the script.

You only need to make a couple of modifications to the Get-AllowedComputer.ps1 script to turn it into the Get-AllowedComputerAndProperty.ps1 script. The first is to add an additional command line parameter to allow the user to choose which property to display. This is shown here:

```
Param([string]$computer = $env:computername,[string]$property="name")
```

Next, you change the signature to the *Get-AllowedComputer* function to permit passing of the property name. Instead of directly returning the results of the *-contains* operator, you store the returned values in variables. The *Get-AllowedComputer* function first checks to see if the *$servers* array contains the computer name. It then checks to see if the *$servers* array contains the property name. Each of the resulting values is stored in variables. The two variables are then *anded*, and the result is returned to the calling code. When two Boolean values are anded, only the *$true -and $true* case is equal to *true*; all other combinations return *false*. This is shown here:

```
PS C:\> $true -and $false
False
PS C:\> $true -and $true
True
PS C:\> $false -and $false
False
PS C:\>
```

The revised *Get-AllowedComputer* function is shown here:

```
Function Get-AllowedComputer([string]$computer, [string]$property)
{
 $servers = Get-Content -path c:\fso\serversAndProperties.txt
 $s = $servers -contains $computer
 $p = $servers -contains $property
 Return $s -and $p
} #end Get-AllowedComputer function
```

The *if* statement is used to determine if both the computer value and the property value are on the list of allowed servers and properties. If the *Get-AllowedComputer* function returns *true*, the *Get-WMIObject* cmdlet is used to display the chosen property value from the selected computer. This is shown here:

```
if(Get-AllowedComputer -computer $computer -property $property)
  {
    Get-WmiObject -class Win32_Bios -Computer $computer |
    Select-Object -property $property
  }
```

If the computer value and the property value are not on the list, the Get-AllowedComputerAnd Property.ps1 script displays a message stating that there is a nonpermitted value. This is shown here:

```
Else
  {
   "Either $computer is not an allowed computer, `r`nor $property is not an allowed property"
  }
```

The complete Get-AllowedComputerAndProperty.ps1 script is shown here:

**Get-AllowedComputerAndProperty.ps1**

```
Param([string]$computer = $env:computername,[string]$property="name")

Function Get-AllowedComputer([string]$computer, [string]$property)
{
 $servers = Get-Content -path c:\fso\serversAndProperties.txt
 $s = $servers -contains $computer
 $p = $servers -contains $property
 Return $s -and $p
} #end Get-AllowedComputer function

# *** Entry point to Script ***

if(Get-AllowedComputer -computer $computer -property $property)
  {
    Get-WmiObject -class Win32_Bios -Computer $computer |
    Select-Object -property $property
  }
Else
  {
   "Either $computer is not an allowed computer, `r`nor $property is not an allowed property"
  }
```

### Quick check

Q. What is an easy way to handle a missing *-computername* parameter?

A. Assign *$env:ComputerName* as the default value.

Q. What is a good way to ensure a script does not run with missing parameters?

A. Make the parameters required parameters by using the *[Parameter(Mandatory=$true)]* parameter attribute.

Q. What is a good way to limit potential choices for a parameter value?

A. Use the *PromptForChoice* method.

# Handling missing rights

Another source of potential errors in a script is missing rights. When a script requires elevated permissions to work correctly and those rights or permissions do not exist, an error results. Windows 8 makes handling much easier to run and allows the user to work without requiring constant access to administrative rights. As a result, more and more users and even network administrators are no longer running their computers with a user account that is a member of the local administrators group. The User Account Control (UAC) feature makes it easy to provide elevated rights for interactive programs, but Windows PowerShell 3.0 and other scripting languages are not UAC aware, and do not therefore prompt when elevated rights are required to perform a specific activity. It is therefore incumbent upon the script writer to take rights into account when writing scripts. The Get-Bios.ps1 script (shown earlier in the chapter), however, does not use a WMI class that requires elevated rights. As the script is currently written, anyone who is a member of the local users group—and that includes everyone who is logged on interactively—has permission to run the Get-Bios.ps1 script. So, testing for rights and permissions prior to making an attempt to obtain information from the WMI class *Win32_Bios* is not required.

## Attempt and fail

One way to handle missing rights is to attempt the action, and then fail. This will generate an error. Windows PowerShell has two types of errors: terminating and nonterminating. *Terminating errors*, as the name implies, will stop a script dead in its tracks. *Nonterminating errors* will be output to the screen, and the script will continue. Terminating errors are generally more serious than nonterminating errors. Normally, you get a terminating error when you try to use .NET or COM from within PowerShell and you try to use a command that doesn't exist, or when you do not provide all of the required parameters to a command, method, or cmdlet. A good script will handle the errors it expects and will report unexpected errors to the user. Since any good scripting language has to provide decent error handling, PowerShell has a few ways to approach the problem. The old way is to use the *trap* statement, which can sometimes be problematic. The new way (for PowerShell) is to use *Try...Catch...Finally*.

## Checking for rights and exiting gracefully

The best way to handle insufficient rights is to check for the rights and then exit gracefully. What are some of the things that could go wrong with a simple script, such as the Get-Bios.ps1 script examined earlier in the chapter? The Get-Bios.ps1 script will fail, for example, if the Windows PowerShell script execution policy is set to *restricted*. When the script execution policy is set to *restricted*, Windows PowerShell scripts will not run. The problem with a *restricted* execution policy is that because Windows PowerShell scripts do not run, you cannot write code to detect the *restricted* script execution policy. Because the script execution policy is stored in the registry, you could write a VBScript script that would query and set the policy prior to launching the Windows PowerShell script, but that would not be the best way to manage the problem. The best way to manage the script execution policy is to use group policy to set it to the appropriate level for your network. On a stand-alone computer, you can set the execution policy by opening Windows PowerShell as an administrator and using the *Set-ExecutionPolicy* cmdlet. In most cases, the *remotesigned* setting is appropriate. The command would therefore be the one shown here:

```
PS C:\> Set-ExecutionPolicy remotesigned
PS C:\>
```

The script execution policy is generally dealt with once, and there are no more problems associated with it. In addition, the error message that is associated with the script execution policy is relatively clear in that it will tell you that script execution is disabled on the system. It also refers you to a help article that explains the various settings. This is shown here:

```
File C:\Documents and Settings\ed\Local Settings\Temp\tmp2A7.tmp.ps1 cannot be
loaded because the execution of scripts is disabled on this system. Please see
"get-help about_signing" for more details.
At line:1 char:66
+ C:\Documents` and` Settings\ed\Local` Settings\Temp\tmp2A7.tmp.ps1 <<<<
```

## Handling missing WMI providers

About the only thing that could actually go wrong with the original Get-Bios.ps1 script introduced at the beginning of this chapter is related to WMI itself. If the WMI provider that supplies the *Win32_Bios* WMI class information is corrupted or missing, the script will not work. To check for the existence of the appropriate WMI provider, you will need to know the name of the provider for the WMI class. You can use the WMI Tester (WbemTest), which is included as part of the WMI installation. If a computer has WMI installed on it, it has WbemTest. Because WbemTest resides in the system folders, you can launch it directly from within the Windows PowerShell console by typing the name of the executable. This is shown here:

```
PS C:\> wbemtest
PS C:\>
```

Once WbemTest appears, the first thing you will need to do is connect to the appropriate WMI namespace. To do this, you click the Connect button. In most cases, this namespace will be Root\Cimv2. On Windows Vista and above, Root\Cimv2 is the default WMI namespace for WbemTest. On earlier versions of Windows, the default WbemTest namespace is Root\Default. Change or accept the namespace as appropriate, and click Connect. The display changes to a series of buttons, many of which appear to have cryptic names and functionality. To obtain information about the provider for a WMI class, you will need to open the class. Click the Open Class button and type in the name of the WMI class in the dialog box that appears. You are looking for the provider name for the *Win32_Bios* WMI class, so that is the name that is entered here. Click the OK button once you have entered the class name. The Object Editor for the *Win32_Bios* WMI class now appears. This is shown in Figure 19-4. The first box in the Object Editor lists the qualifiers; *provider* is one of the qualifiers. WbemTest tells you that the provider for *Win32_Bios* is CIMWin32.

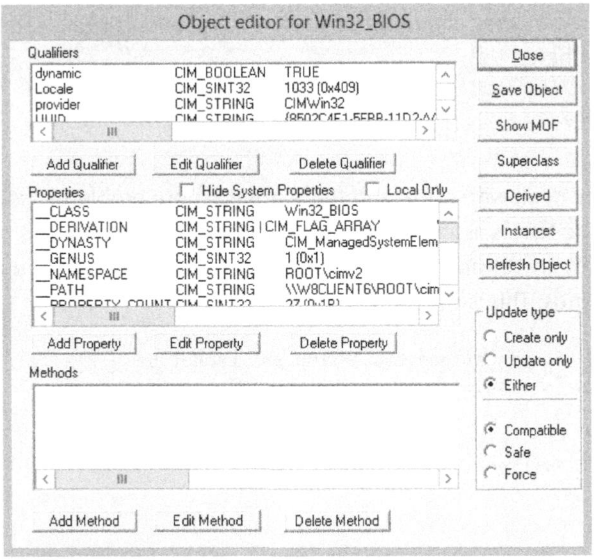

**FIGURE 19-4** The WMI Tester displays WMI class provider information.

Armed with the name of the WMI provider, you can use the *Get-WMIObject* cmdlet to determine if the provider is installed on the computer. To do this, you will query for instances of the *__provider* WMI class. All WMI classes that begin with a double underscore are system classes. The *__provider* WMI class is the class from which all WMI providers are derived. By limiting the query to providers with the name of CIMWin32, you can determine if the provider is installed on the system. This is shown here:

```
PS C:\> Get-WmiObject -Class __Provider -Filter "name = 'cimwin32'"
```

```
__GENUS                         : 2
__CLASS                         : __Win32Provider
__SUPERCLASS                    : __Provider
__DYNASTY                       : __SystemClass
__RELPATH                       : __Win32Provider.Name="CIMWin32"
__PROPERTY_COUNT                : 24
__DERIVATION                    : {__Provider, __SystemClass}
__SERVER                        : W8CLIENT6
__NAMESPACE                     : ROOT\cimv2
__PATH                          : \\W8CLIENT6\ROOT\cimv2:__Win32Provider.Name="CIMWin32"
ClientLoadableCLSID             :
CLSID                           : {d63a5850-8f16-11cf-9f47-00aa00bf345c}
Concurrency                     :
DefaultMachineName              :
Enabled                         :
HostingModel                    : NetworkServiceHost
ImpersonationLevel              : 1
InitializationReentrancy        : 0
InitializationTimeoutInterval   :
InitializeAsAdminFirst          :
Name                            : CIMWin32
OperationTimeoutInterval        :
PerLocaleInitialization         : False
PerUserInitialization           : False
Pure                            : True
SecurityDescriptor              :
SupportsExplicitShutdown        :
SupportsExtendedStatus          :
SupportsQuotas                  :
SupportsSendStatus              :
SupportsShutdown                :
SupportsThrottling              :
UnloadTimeout                   :
Version                         :
PSComputerName                  : W8CLIENT6
```

For the purposes of determining if the provider exists, you do not need all the information to be returned to the script. It is easier to treat the query as if it returned a Boolean value by using the *If* statement. If the provider exists, then you will perform the query. This is shown here:

```
If(Get-WmiObject -Class __provider -filter "name = 'cimwin32'")
 {
  Get-WmiObject -class Win32_bios
 }
```

If the CIMWin32WMI provider does not exist, then you display a message that states the provider is missing. This is shown here:

```
Else
 {
  "Unable to query Win32_Bios because the provider is missing"
 }
```

The completed CheckProviderThenQuery.ps1 script is shown here:

**CheckProviderThenQuery.ps1**
```
If(Get-WmiObject -Class __provider -filter "name = 'cimwin32'")
 {
  Get-WmiObject -class Win32_bios
 }
Else
 {
  "Unable to query Win32_Bios because the provider is missing"
 }
```

A better approach for finding out if a WMI class is available is to check for the existence of the provider. In the case of the *WIN32_product* WMI class, the MSIPROV WMI provider supplies that class. In this section, you create a function, the *Get-WmiProvider* function, which can be used to detect the presence of any WMI provider that is installed on the system.

The *Get-WmiProvider* function contains two parameters. The first parameter is the name of the provider, and the second one is a switched parameter named *-verbose*. When the *Get-WmiProvider* function is called with the *-verbose* switched parameter, detailed status information is displayed to the console. The *-verbose* information provides the user of the script information that could be useful from a troubleshooting perspective.

```
Function Get-WmiProvider([string]$providerName, [switch]$verbose)
```

After the function has been declared, the current value of the *$VerbosePreference* is stored. This is because it could be set to one of four potential values. The possible enumeration values are *SilentlyContinue*, *Stop*, *Continue*, and *Inquire*. By default, the value of the *$VerbosePreference* automatic variable is set to *SilentlyContinue*.

When the function finishes running, you will want to set the value of the *$VerbosePreference* variable back to its original value. To enable reverting to the original value of the *$VerbosePreference* variable, store the original value in the *$oldVerbosePreference* variable.

It is time to determine if the function was called with the *-verbose* switch. If the function was called with the *-verbose* switch, a variable named *$verbose* will be present on the variable drive. If the *$verbose* variable exists, the value of the *$VerbosePreference* automatic variable is set to *Continue*.

```
{
 $oldVerbosePreference = $VerbosePreference
 if($verbose) { $VerbosePreference = "continue" }
```

Next, you need to look for the WMI provider. To do this, you use the *Get-WMIObject* cmdlet to query for all instances of the *__provider* WMI system class. As mentioned previously, all WMI classes that begin with a double underscore are system classes. In most cases, they are not of much interest to IT professionals; however, familiarity with them can often provide powerful tools to the scripter who takes the time to examine them. All WMI providers are derived from the *__provider* WMI class. This is similar to the way that all WMI namespaces are derived from the *__namespace* WMI class. The properties of the *__provider* class are shown in Table 19-1.

**TABLE 19-1** Properties of the *__Provider* WMI class

| Property name | Property type |
|---|---|
| ClientLoadableCLSID | System.String |
| CLSID | System.String |
| Concurrency | System.Int32 |
| DefaultMachineName | System.String |
| Enabled | System.Boolean |
| HostingModel | System.String |
| ImpersonationLevel | System.Int32 |
| InitializationReentrancy | System.Int32 |
| InitializationTimeoutInterval | System.String |
| InitializeAsAdminFirst | System.Boolean |
| Name | System.String |
| OperationTimeoutInterval | System.String |
| PerLocaleInitialization | System.Boolean |
| PerUserInitialization | System.Boolean |
| Pure | System.Boolean |
| SecurityDescriptor | System.String |
| SupportsExplicitShutdown | System.Boolean |
| SupportsExtendedStatus | System.Boolean |
| SupportsQuotas | System.Boolean |
| SupportsSendStatus | System.Boolean |
| SupportsShutdown | System.Boolean |
| SupportsThrottling | System.Boolean |
| UnloadTimeout | System.String |
| Version | System.UInt32 |
| __CLASS | System.String |
| __DERIVATION | System.String[] |
| __DYNASTY | System.String |
| __GENUS | System.Int32 |
| __NAMESPACE | System.String |
| __PATH | System.String |

| Property name | Property type |
|---|---|
| __PROPERTY_COUNT | System.Int32 |
| __RELPATH | System.String |
| __SERVER | System.String |
| __SUPERCLASS | System.String |

The *-filter* parameter of the *Get-WMIObject* cmdlet is used to return the provider that is specified in the *$providername* variable. If you do not know the name of the appropriate WMI provider, you will need to search for it by using the WMI Tester. You can start this program by typing the name of the executable inside your Windows PowerShell console. This is shown here:

```
PS C:\> wbemtest
PS C:\>
```

Once the WMI Tester appears, open the *WIN32_Product* WMI class. The Object Editor for the *Win32_Product* WMI class appears in Figure 19-5. The first box of the Object Editor lists the qualifiers; *provider* is one of the qualifiers. WbemTest tells you that the provider for *WIN32_Product* is MSIProv.

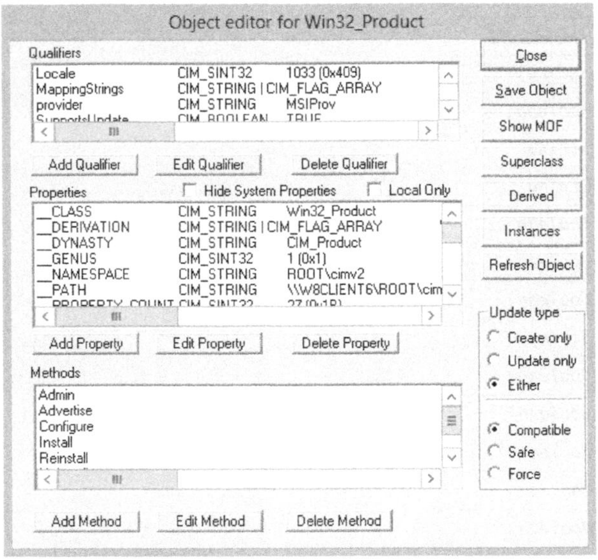

**FIGURE 19-5** The Object Editor for *WIN32_Product* displays qualifiers and methods.

You assign the name of the WMI provider to the *$providername* variable, as shown here:

```
$providerName = "MSIProv"
```

The resulting object is stored in the *$provider* variable. This is shown here:

```
$provider = Get-WmiObject -Class __provider -filter "name = '$providerName'"
```

If the provider was not found, there will be no value in the *$provider* variable. You can therefore see if the *$provider* variable is *null*. If the *$provider* variable is not equal to *null*, then the class ID of the provider is retrieved. The class ID of the WMI provider is stored in the *clsID* property. This is shown here:

```
If($provider -ne $null)
    {
     $clsID = $provider.clsID
```

If the function was run with the *-verbose* parameter, then the *$VerbosePreference* variable is set to *Continue*. When the value of *$VerbosePreference* is equal to *Continue*, the *Write-Verbose* cmdlet will display information to the console. If, on the other hand, the value of the *$VerbosePreference* variable is equal to *SilentlyContinue*, the *Write-Verbose* cmdlet does not emit anything. This makes it easy to implement tracing features in a function without needing to create extensive test conditions. When the function is called with the *-verbose* parameter, the class ID of the provider is displayed. This is shown here:

```
   Write-Verbose "$providerName WMI provider found. ClsID is $($clsID)"
   }
```

If the WMI provider is not found, the function returns *false* to the calling code. This is shown here:

```
Else
    {
     Return $false
    }
```

The next thing the function does is check the registry to ensure the WMI provider has been properly registered with DCOM. Once again, the *Write-Verbose* cmdlet is used to provide feedback on the status of the provider check. This is shown here:

```
Write-Verbose "Checking for proper registry registration ..."
```

To search the registry for the WMI provider registration, you use the Windows PowerShell registry provider. By default, there is no PowerShell drive for the HKEY_CLASSES_ROOT registry hive. However, you cannot take it for granted that one would not have created such a drive in their Windows PowerShell profile. To avoid a potential error that might arise when creating a PowerShell drive for the HKEY_CLASSES_ROOT hive, you use the *Test-Path* cmdlet to check whether an HKCR drive exists. If the HKCR drive does exist, it will be used, and the *Write-Verbose* cmdlet will be used to print out a status message that states the HKCR drive was found and the search is commencing for the class ID of the WMI provider. This is shown here:

```
If(Test-Path -path HKCR:)
    {
        Write-Verbose "HKCR: drive found. Testing for $clsID"
```

To detect if the WMI provider is registered with DCOM, you only need to see if the class ID of the WMI provider is present in the CLSID section of HKEY_CLASSES_ROOT. The best way to check for the presence of the registry key is to use the *Test-Path* cmdlet. This is shown here:

```
Test-path -path (Join-Path -path HKCR:\CLSID -childpath $clsID)
    }
```

On the other hand, if there is no HKCR drive on the computer, you can go ahead and create one. You can search for the existence of a drive that is rooted in HKEY_CLASSES_ROOT, and if you find it, you can then use the PS drive in your query. To find if there are any PS drives rooted in HKEY_CLASSES_ROOT, you can use the *Get-PSDrive* cmdlet, as shown here:

```
Get-PSDrive | Where-Object { $_.root -match "classes" } |
Select-Object name
```

This, however, may be more trouble than it is worth. There is nothing wrong with having multiple PS drives mapped to the same resource. Therefore, if there is no HKCR drive, the *Write-Verbose* cmdlet is used to print a message that the drive does not exist and will be created. This is shown here:

```
Else
    {
    Write-Verbose "HKCR: drive not found. Creating same."
```

To create a new Windows PowerShell drive, you use the *New-PSDrive* cmdlet to specify the name for the PS drive and the root location of the drive. Because this is going to be a registry drive, you will use the registry provider. When a PS drive is created, it displays feedback back to the Windows PowerShell console. This feedback is shown here:

```
PS C:\AutoDoc> New-PSDrive -Name HKCR -PSProvider registry -Root Hkey_Classes_Root

Name       Provider      Root                          CurrentLocation
----       --------      ----                          ---------------
HKCR       Registry      Hkey_Classes_Root
```

The feedback from creating the registry drive can be distracting. To get rid of the feedback, you can pipeline the results to the *Out-Null* cmdlet. This is shown here:

```
New-PSDrive -Name HKCR -PSProvider registry -Root Hkey_Classes_Root | Out-Null
```

Once the Windows PowerShell registry drive has been created, it is time to look for the existence of the WMI provider class ID. Before that is done, the *Write-Verbose* cmdlet is used to provide feedback about this step of the operation. This is shown here:

```
Write-Verbose "Testing for $clsID"
```

The *Test-Path* cmdlet is used to check for the existence of the WMI provider class ID. To build the path to the registry key, you use *Join-Path* cmdlet. The parent path is the HKCR registry drive CLSID hive, and the child path is the WMI provider class ID that is stored in the *$clsID* variable. This is shown here:

```
Test-path -path (Join-Path -path HKCR:\CLSID -childpath $clsID)
```

Once the *Test-Path* cmdlet has been used to check for the existence of the WMI provider class ID, the *Write-Verbose* cmdlet is used to display a message stating that the test is complete. This is shown here:

```
Write-Verbose "Test complete."
```

It is a best practice to avoid making permanent modifications to the Windows PowerShell environment in a script. Therefore, you will want to remove the Windows PowerShell drive if it was created in the script. The *Write-Verbose* cmdlet is employed to provide a status update, and the *Remove-PSDrive* cmdlet is used to remove the HKCR registry drive. To avoid cluttering the Windows PowerShell console, you pipeline the result of removing the HKCR registry drive to the *Out-Null* cmdlet. This is shown here:

```
Write-Verbose "Removing HKCR: drive."
Remove-PSDrive -Name HKCR | Out-Null
 }
```

Finally, you need to set *$VerbosePreference* back to the value that was stored in *$oldVerbosePreference*. This line of code is executed even if no change to *$VerbosePreference* is made. This is shown here:

```
$VerbosePreference = $oldVerbosePreference
} #end Get-WmiProvider function
```

The entry point to the script assigns a value to the *$providername* variable. This is shown here:

```
$providername = "msiprov"
```

The *Get-WmiProvider* function is called, and it passes both the WMI provider name that is stored in the *$providername* variable and the *-verbose* switched parameter. The *if* statement is used because *Get-WmiProvider* returns a Boolean value: *true* or *false*. This is shown here:

```
if(Get-WmiProvider -providerName $providerName  -verbose )
```

If the *Get-WmiProvider* function returns *true*, the WMI class supported by the WMI provider is queried via the *Get-WMIObject* cmdlet. This is shown here:

```
{

  Get-WmiObject -class win32_product

}
```

If the WMI provider is not found, a message stating this is displayed to the console. This is shown here:

```
else
  {
```

```
    "$providerName provider not found"
  }
```

The complete Get-WmiProviderFunction.ps1 script is shown here:

**Get-WmiProviderFunction.ps1**
```
Function Get-WmiProvider([string]$providerName, [switch]$verbose)
{
 $oldVerbosePreference = $VerbosePreference
 if($verbose) { $VerbosePreference = "continue" }
 $provider = Get-WmiObject -Class __provider -filter "name = '$providerName'"
 If($provider -ne $null)
   {
    $clsID = $provider.clsID
    Write-Verbose "$providerName WMT provider found. ClsID is $($clsID)"
   }
 Else
   {
     Return $false
   }
   Write-Verbose "Checking for proper registry registration ..."
   If(Test-Path -path HKCR:)
      {
        Write-Verbose "HKCR: drive found. Testing for $clsID"
        Test-path -path (Join-Path -path HKCR:\CLSID -childpath $clsID)
      }
   Else
     {
      Write-Verbose "HKCR: drive not found. Creating same."
      New-PSDrive -Name HKCR -PSProvider registry -Root Hkey_Classes_Root | Out-Null
      Write-Verbose "Testing for $clsID"
      Test-path -path (Join-Path -path HKCR:\CLSID -childpath $clsID)
      Write-Verbose "Test complete."
      Write-Verbose "Removing HKCR: drive."
      Remove-PSDrive -Name HKCR | Out-Null
     }
  $VerbosePreference = $oldVerbosePreference
} #end Get-WmiProvider function

# *** Entry Point to Script ***
$providerName = "msiprov"
 if(Get-WmiProvider -providerName $providerName  -verbose )
  {
    Get-WmiObject -class win32_product
  }
else
  {
    "$providerName provider not found"
  }
```

# Incorrect data types

There are two approaches to ensuring that your users only enter allowed values for the script parameters. The first is to offer only a limited number of values. The second approach allows the user to enter any value for the parameter. It is then determined if the value is valid before it is passed along to the remainder of the script. In the Get-ValidWmiClassFunction.ps1 script, which follows, a function named *Get-ValidWmiClass* is used to determine if the value that is supplied to the script is a legitimate WMI class name. In particular, the *Get-ValidWmiClass* function is used to determine if the string that is passed via the -*class* parameter can be cast to a valid instance of the *System.Management.ManagementClass* .NET Framework class. The purpose of using the *[wmiclass]* type accelerator is to convert a string to an instance of the *System.Management.ManagementClass* class. As shown here, when you assign a string value to a variable, the variable becomes an instance of the *System.String* class. The *GetType* method is used to get the type of a variable. An array variable is an array, yet it can contain integers and other data types. This is a very important concept.

```
PS C:\> $class = "win32_bio"
PS C:\> $class.GetType()

IsPublic IsSerial Name                                  BaseType
-------- -------- ----                                  --------
True     True     String                                System.Object
```

To convert the string to a WMI class, you can use the *[wmiclass]* type accelerator. The string value must contain the name of a legitimate WMI class. If the WMI class you are trying to create on the computer does not exist, an error is displayed. This is shown here:

```
PS C:\> $class = "win32_bio"
PS C:\> [wmiclass]$class
Cannot convert value "win32_bio" to type "System.Management.ManagementClass".
Error: "Not found "
At line:1 char:16
+ [wmiclass]$class <<<<
```

The Get-ValidWmiClassFunction.ps1 script begins by creating two command-line parameters. The first is the *computer* parameter, which is used to allow the script to run on a local or remote computer. The second parameter is the -*class* parameter, and is used to provide the name of the WMI class that will be queried by the script. A third parameter is used to allow the script to inspect other WMI namespaces. All three parameters are strings. Because the third parameter has a default value assigned, it can be left out when working with the default WMI namespace. This is shown here:

```
Param (
    [string]$computer = $env:computername,
    [string]$class,
    [string]$namespace = "root\cimv2"
) #end param
```

The *Get-ValidWmiClass* function is used to determine if the value supplied for the -*class* parameter is a valid WMI class on the particular computer. This is important because certain versions of the operating system contain unique WMI classes. For example, Windows XP contains a WMI class named *netdiagnostics* that does not exist on any other version of Windows. Windows XP does not contain the WMI class *Win32_Volume*, but Windows Server 2003 and above do. So, checking for the existence of a WMI class on a remote computer is a good practice to ensure that the script will run in an expeditious manner.

The first thing the *Get-ValidWMiClass* function does is retrieve the current value for the *$ErrorActionPreference* variable. There are four possible values for this variable. The possible enumeration values are *SilentlyContinue*, *Stop*, *Continue*, and *Inquire*. The error-handling behavior of Windows PowerShell is governed by these enumeration values. If the value of *$ErrorActionPreference* is set to *SilentlyContinue*, any error that occurs will be skipped, and the script will attempt to execute the next line of code in the script. The behavior is similar to using the VBScript setting *On Error Resume Next*. Normally, you do not want to use this setting because it can make troubleshooting scripts very difficult. It can also make the behavior of a script unpredictable and even lead to devastating consequences. Consider the case in which you write a script that first creates a new directory on a remote server. Next, it copies all of the files from a directory on your local computer to the remote server. Last, it deletes the directory and all the files from the local computer. Now you enable *$ErrorActionPreference* = "*SilentlyContinue*" and run the script. The first command fails because the remote server is not available. The second command fails because it could not copy the files—but the third command completes successfully, and you have just deleted all the files you wished to back up, instead of actually backing up the files. Hopefully, in such a case, you have a recent backup of your critical data. If you set *$ErrorActionPreference* to *SilentlyContinue*, you must handle errors that arise during the course of running the script.

In the *Get_ValidWmiClass* function, the old *$ErrorActionPreference* setting is retrieved and stored in the *$oldErrorActionPreference* variable. Next, the *$ErrorActionPreference* variable is set to *SilentlyContinue*. This is done because it is entirely possible that in the process of checking for a valid WMI class name, errors will be generated. Next, the error stack is cleared of errors. Here are the three lines of code that do this:

```
$oldErrorActionPreference = $errorActionPreference
$errorActionPreference = "silentlyContinue"
$Error.Clear()
```

The value stored in the *$class* variable is used with the *[wmiclass]* type accelerator to attempt to create a *System.Management.ManagementClass* object from the string. Because you will need to run this script on a remote computer as well as a local computer, the value in the *$computer* variable is used to provide a complete path to the potential management object. When the variables to make the path to the WMI class are concatenated, a trailing colon causes problems with the *$namespace* variable. To work around this, you use a subexpression to force evaluation of the variable before attempting to concatenate the remainder of the string. The subexpression consists of a leading dollar sign and a pair of parentheses. This is shown here:

```
[wmiclass]"\\$computer\$($namespace):$class" | out-null
```

To determine if the conversion from string to *ManagementClass* was successful, you check the error record. Because the error record was cleared earlier, any error indicates that the command failed. If an error exists, the *Get-ValidWmiClass* function returns *$false* to the calling code. If no error exists, the *Get-ValidWmiClass* function returns *true*. This is shown here:

```
If($error.count) { Return $false } Else { Return $true }
```

The last thing to do in the *Get-ValidWmiClass* function is to clean up. First, the error record is cleared, and then the value of the *$ErrorActionPreference* variable is set back to the original value. This is shown here:

```
$Error.Clear()
$ErrorActionPreference =  $oldErrorActionPreference
```

The next function in the Get-ValidWmiClassFunction.ps1 script is the *Get-WmiInformation* function. This function accepts the values from the *$computer*, *$class*, and *$namespace* variables, and passes them to the *Get-WMIObject* cmdlet. The resulting *ManagementObject* is pipelined to the *Format-List* cmdlet, and all properties that begin with the letters *a* through *z* are displayed. This is shown here:

```
Function Get-WmiInformation ([string]$computer, [string]$class, [string]$namespace)
{
  Get-WmiObject -class $class -computername $computer -namespace $namespace|
  Format-List -property [a-z]*
} # end Get-WmiInformation function
```

The entry point to the script calls the *Get-ValidWmiClass* function, and if it returns *true*, it next calls the *Get-WmiInformation* function. If, on the other hand, the *Get-ValidWmiClass* function returns *false*, a message is displayed that details the class name, namespace, and computer name. This information could be used for troubleshooting problems with obtaining the WMI information. This is shown here:

```
If(Get-ValidWmiClass -computer $computer -class $class -namespace $namespace)
  {
    Get-WmiInformation -computer $computer -class $class -namespace $namespace
  }
Else
 {
   "$class is not a valid wmi class in the $namespace namespace on $computer"
 }
```

The complete Get-ValidWmiClassFunction.ps1 script is shown here:

**Get-ValidWmiClassFunction.ps1**
```
Param (
   [string]$computer = $env:computername,
   [Parameter(Mandatory=$true)]
   [string]$class,
   [string]$namespace = "root\cimv2"
) #end param
```

```
Function Get-ValidWmiClass([string]$computer, [string]$class, [string]$namespace)
{
 $oldErrorActionPreference = $errorActionPreference
 $errorActionPreference = "silentlyContinue"
 $Error.Clear()
 [wmiclass]"\\$computer\$($namespace):$class" | out-null
 If($error.count) { Return $false } Else { Return $true }
 $Error.Clear()
 $ErrorActionPreference =  $oldErrorActionPreference
} # end Get-ValidWmiClass function

Function Get-WmiInformation ([string]$computer, [string]$class, [string]$namespace)
{
  Get-WmiObject -class $class -computername $computer -namespace $namespace|
  Format-List -property [a-z]*
} # end Get-WmiInformation function

# *** Entry point to script ***

If(Get-ValidWmiClass -computer $computer -class $class -namespace $namespace)
  {
    Get-WmiInformation -computer $computer -class $class -namespace $namespace
  }
Else
  {
    "$class is not a valid wmi class in the $namespace namespace on $computer"
  }
```

# Out-of-bounds errors

When receiving input from a user, an allowed value for a script parameter is limited to a specified range of values. If the allowable range is small, it may be best to present the user with a prompt that allows selection from a few choices. This was shown earlier in this chapter, in the "Limiting choices" section.

When the allowable range of values is great, however, limiting the choices through a menu-type system is not practical. This is where boundary checking come into play.

## Using a boundary-checking function

One technique is to use a function that will determine if the supplied value is permissible. One way to create a boundary-checking function is to have the script create a hash table of permissible values. The *Check-AllowedValue* function is used to gather a hash table of volumes that reside on the target computer. This hash table is then used to verify that the volume requested from the *drive* command-line parameter is actually present on the computer. The *Check-AllowedValue* function returns a Boolean *true* or *false* to the calling code in the main body of the script. The complete *Check-AllowedValue* function is shown here:

```
Function Check-AllowedValue($drive, $computerName)
{
 $drives = $null
 Get-WmiObject -class Win32_Volume -computername $computerName |
 Where-Object { $_.DriveLetter } |
 ForEach-Object { $drives += @{ $_.DriveLetter = $_.DriveLetter } }
 $drives.contains($drive)
} #end function Check-AllowedValue
```

Because the *Check-AllowedValue* function returns a Boolean value, an *if* statement is used to determine if the value supplied to the *drive* parameter is permissible. If the drive letter is found in the *$drives* hash table that is created in the *Check-AllowedValue* function, the *Get-DiskInformation* function is called. If the *drive* parameter value is not found in the hash table, a warning message is displayed to the Windows PowerShell console, and the script exits. The complete GetDrivesCheckAllowedValue.ps1 script is shown here:

**GetDrivesCheckAllowedValue.ps1**

```
Param(
    [Parameter(Mandatory=$true)]
    [string]$drive,
    [string]$computerName = $env:computerName
) #end param

Function Check-AllowedValue($drive, $computerName)
{
 $drives = $null
 Get-WmiObject -class Win32_Volume -computername $computerName |
 Where-Object { $_.DriveLetter } |
 ForEach-Object { $drives += @{ $_.DriveLetter = $_.DriveLetter } }
 $drives.contains($drive)
} #end function Check-AllowedValue

Function Get-DiskInformation($computerName,$drive)
{
 Get-WmiObject -class Win32_volume -computername $computername -filter "DriveLetter = '$drive'"
} #end function Get-BiosName

# *** Entry Point To Script ***

if(Check-AllowedValue -drive $drive -computername $computerName)
  {
   Get-DiskInformation -computername $computerName -drive $drive
  }
else
 {
  Write-Host -foregroundcolor blue "$drive is not an allowed value:"
 }
```

# Placing limits on the parameter

In Windows PowerShell 3.0, you can place limits directly on the parameter in the *param* section of the script. This technique works well when you are working with a limited set of allowable values. The *ValidateRange* parameter attribute will create a numeric range of allowable values, but it is also able to create a range of letters as well. Using this technique, you can greatly simplify the GetDrivesCheckAllowedValue.ps1 script by creating an allowable range of drive letters. The param statement is shown here:

```
Param(
    [Parameter(Mandatory=$true)]
    [ValidateRange("c","f")]
    [string]$drive,
    [string]$computerName = $env:computerName
) #end param
```

Because you are able to control the permissible drive letters from the command line, you increase the simplicity and readability of the script by not having the requirement to create a separate function to validate the allowed values. In the GetDrivesValidRange.ps1 script, which follows, one additional change is required, and that is to concatenate a colon to the end of the drive letter. In the GetDrivesCheckAllowedValue.ps1 script, you were able to include the drive letter and the colon from the command line. But with the *ValidateRange* attribute, this technique will not work. The trick to concatenating the colon to the drive letter is that it needs to be escaped, as shown here:

```
-filter "DriveLetter = '$drive`:'"
```

The complete GetDrivesValidRange.ps1 script is shown here:

**GetDrivesValidRange.ps1**

```
Param(
    [Parameter(Mandatory=$true)]
    [ValidateRange("c","d")]
    [string]$drive,
    [string]$computerName = $env:computerName
) #end param

Function Get-DiskInformation($computerName,$drive)
{
 Get-WmiObject -class Win32_volume -computername $computername `
 -filter "DriveLetter = '$drive`:'"
} #end function Get-BiosName

# *** Entry Point To Script ***

Get-DiskInformation -computername $computerName -drive $drive
```

# Using *Try...Catch...Finally*

When using a *Try...Catch...Finally* block, the command you wish to execute is placed in the *Try* block. If an error occurs when the command executes, the error will be written to the *$error* variable, and script execution moves to the *Catch* block. The TestTryCatchFinally.ps1 script, which follows, uses the *Try* command to attempt to create an object. A string states that the script is attempting to create a new object. The object to create is stored in the *$obj1* variable. The *New-Object* cmdlet creates the object. Once the object has been created and stored in the *$a* variable, the members of the object are displayed via the *Get-Member* cmdlet. This code illustrates the technique:

```
Try
 {
  "Attempting to create new object $obj1"
   $a = new-object $obj1
   "Members of the $obj1"
   "New object $obj1 created"
   $a | Get-Member
 }
```

You use the *Catch* block to capture errors that occurred during the *Try* block. You can specify the type of error to catch, as well as the action you wish to perform when the error occurs. The TestTryCatchFinally.ps1 script monitors for *System.Exception* errors. The *System.Exception* .NET Framework class is the base class from which all other exceptions derive. This means a *System.Exception* error is as generic as you can get—in essence, it will capture all predefined, common system run-time exceptions. Upon catching the error, you can then specify what code you would like to execute. In this example, a single string states that the script caught a system exception. The *Catch* block is shown here:

```
Catch [system.exception]
 {
  "caught a system exception"
 }
```

The *Finally* block of a *Try...Catch...Finally* sequence always runs—regardless of whether an error is generated. This means that any code cleanup you wish to do, such as explicitly releasing COM objects, should be placed in a *Finally* block. In the TestTryCatchFinally.ps1 script, the *Finally* block displays a string that states the script has ended. This appears here:

```
Finally
 {
  "end of script"
 }
```

The complete TestTryCatchFinally.ps1 script is shown here:

**TestTryCatchFinally.ps1**

```
$obj1 = "Bad.Object"
"Begin test"
Try
 {
  "`tAttempting to create new object $obj1"
   $a = new-object $obj1
   "Members of the $obj1"
   "New object $obj1 created"
   $a | Get-Member
 }
Catch [system.exception]
 {
  "`tcaught a system exception"
 }
Finally
 {
  "end of script"
 }
```

When the TestTryCatchFinally.ps1 script runs and the value of $obj1 is equal to *Bad.Object*, an error occurs, because there is no object named *BadObject* that can be created via the *New-Object* cmdlet. Figure 19-6 displays the output from the script.

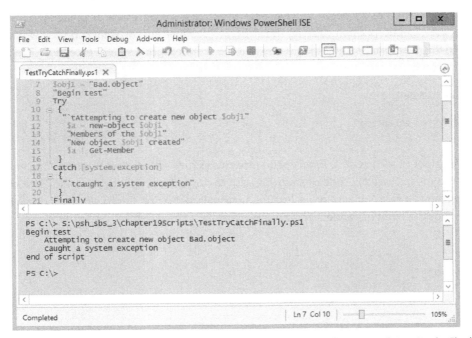

**FIGURE 19-6** Attempt to create an invalid object caught in the *Catch* portion of *Try...Catch...Finally*.

As shown in Figure 19-6, the *Begin test* string is displayed because it is outside the *Try...Catch...Finally* loop. Inside the *Try* block, the string *Attempting to create new object Bad.object* is displayed because it comes before the *New-Object* command. This illustrates that the *Try* block is always attempted. The members of the *BadObject* object are not displayed, nor is the string *new object Bad.Object created*. This indicates that once the error is generated, the script moves to the next block.

The *Catch* block catches and displays the *System.Exception* error. The string *caught a system exception* is also displayed in the ISE. Next, the script moves to the *Finally* block, and the *end of script* string appears.

If the script runs with the value of *$obj1* equal to *system.object* (which is a valid object), then the *Try* block completes successfully. As shown in Figure 19-7, the members of *System.Object* display, and the string that states the object was successfully created also appears in the output. Because no errors are generated in the script, the script execution does not enter the *Catch* block. But the *end of script* string from the *Finally* block is displayed because the *Finally* block always executes regardless of the error condition.

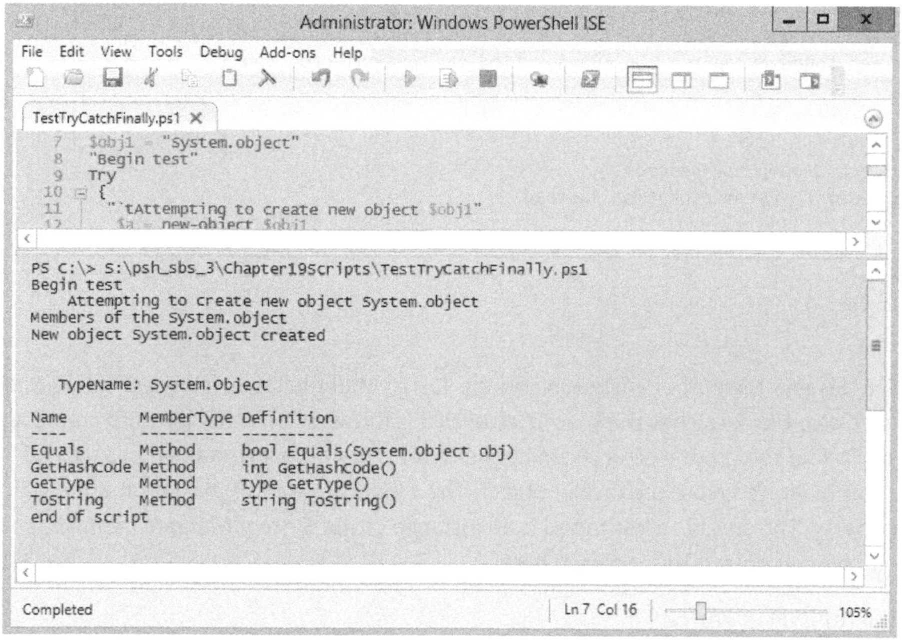

**FIGURE 19-7** The *Catch* portion of *Try...Catch...Finally* permits creation of a valid object. The *Finally* portion always runs.

# Catching multiple errors

You can have multiple *Catch* blocks in a *Try...Catch...Finally* block. The thing to keep in mind is that when an exception occurs, Windows PowerShell leaves the *Try* block and searches for the *Catch* block. The first *Catch* block that matches the exception that was generated will be used. Therefore, you want to use the most specific exception first, and then move to the more generic exceptions. This is shown in TestTryMultipleCatchFinally.ps1.

**TestTryMultipleCatchFinally.ps1**

```
$obj1 = "BadObject"
"Begin test ..."
$ErrorActionPreference = "stop"
Try
 {
  "`tAttempting to create new object $obj1 ..."
   $a = new-object $obj1
   "Members of the $obj1"
   "New object $obj1 created"
   $a | Get-Member
 }
Catch [System.Management.Automation.PSArgumentException]
 {
  "`tObject not found exception. `n`tCannot find the assembly for $obj1"
 }
Catch [system.exception]
 {
  "Did not catch argument exception."
  "Caught a generic system exception instead"
 }
Finally
 {
  "end of script"
 }
```

Figure 19-8 displays the output when running the TestTryMultipleCatchFinally.ps1 script. In this script, the first *Catch* block catches the specific error that is raised when attempting to create an invalid object. To find the specific error, examine the *ErrorRecord* object contained in *$error[0]* after running the command to create the invalid object. The exact category of exception appears in the *Exception* property. The specific error raised is an instance of the *System.Management.Automation .PSArgumentException* object. This is shown here:

```
PS C:\> $Error[0] | fl * -Force


PSMessageDetails       :
Exception              : System.Management.Automation.PSArgumentException:
                         Cannot find type [BadObject]: make sure the assembly
                         containing this type is loaded.
                             at System.Management.Automation.MshCommandRuntime.
                         ThrowTerminatingError(ErrorRecord errorRecord)
```

```
TargetObject              :
CategoryInfo              : InvalidType: (:) [New-Object], PSArgumentException
FullyQualifiedErrorId     : TypeNotFound,Microsoft.PowerShell.Commands.
                            NewObjectCommand
ErrorDetails              :
InvocationInfo            : System.Management.Automation.InvocationInfo
ScriptStackTrace          : at <ScriptBlock>, <No file>: line 7
PipelineIterationInfo     : {}
```

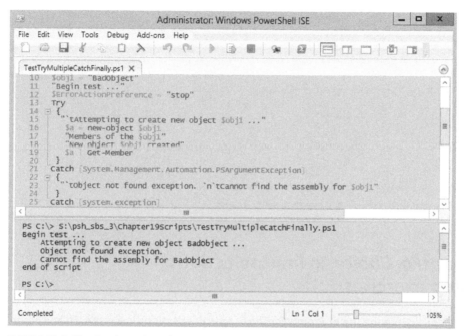

**FIGURE 19-8** The *Catch* portion of *Try...Catch...Finally* catches specific errors in the order derived.

If a script has multiple errors, and the error-action preference is set to *Stop*, the first error will cause the script to fail. If you remove the comments from the *$ErrorActionPreference* line and the *Get-Content* line, the first error to be generated will be caught by the *System.Exception Catch* block, and the script execution will therefore skip the argument exception. This is shown in Figure 19-9.

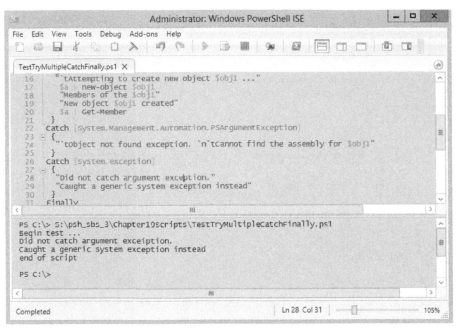

**FIGURE 19-9** The first error raised is the one that will be caught.

# Using *PromptForChoice* to limit selections: Step-by-step exercises

This exercise will explore the use of *PromptForChoice* to limit selections in a script. Following this exercise, you will explore using *Try...Catch...Finally* to detect and to catch errors.

### Exploring the *PromptForChoice* construction

1. Open the Windows PowerShell ISE.

2. Create a new script called PromptForChoiceExercise.ps1.

3. Create a variable to be used for the caption. Name the variable *caption* and assign a string value of *This is the caption* to the variable. The code to do this appears here:

   ```
   $caption = "This is the caption"
   ```

4. Create another variable to be used for the message. Name the variable *message* and assign a string value of *This is the message* to the variable. The code to do this appears here:

```
$message = "This is the message"
```

5. Create a variable named *choices* that will hold the *ChoiceDescription* object. Create an array of three choices—*choice1*, *choice2*, and *choice3*—for the *ChoiceDescription* object. Make the default letter for *choice1 c*, the default letter for *choice2 h*, and the default letter for *choice3 o*. The code to do this appears here:

```
$choices = [System.Management.Automation.Host.ChoiceDescription[]] `
  @("&choice1", "c&hoice2", "ch&oice3")
```

6. Create an integer variable named *defaultChoice* and assign the value 2 to it. The code to do this appears here:

```
[int]$DefaultChoice = 2
```

7. Call the *PromptForChoice* method and assign the return value to the *ChoiceRTN* variable. Provide *PromptForChoice* with the *caption, message, choices*, and *defaultChoice* variables as arguments to the method. The code to do this appears here:

```
$choiceRTN = $host.ui.PromptForChoice($caption,$message, $choices,$defaultChoice)
```

8. Create a *switch* statement to evaluate the return value contained in the *choiceRTN* variable. The cases are 0, 1, and 2. For case 0, display a string that states *choice1*. For case 1, display a string that states *choice2*, and for case 2, display a string that states *choice3*. The *switch* statement to do this appears here:

```
switch($choiceRTN)
  {
   0    { "choice1" }
   1    { "choice2" }
   2    { "choice3" }
  }
```

9. Save and run the script. Test each of the three options to ensure they work properly. This will require you to run the script three times and select each option in sequence.

   This concludes the exercise.

In the following exercise, you will use *Try...Catch...Finally* in a script to catch specific errors.

## Using *Try...Catch...Finally*

1. Open the Windows PowerShell ISE.

2. Create a new script called TryCatchFinallyExercise.

3. Create a parameter named *object*. Make the variable a mandatory variable, but do not assign a default value to it. The code to do this appears here:

```
Param(
  [Parameter(Mandatory=$true)]
  $object)
```

4. Display a string that states the script is beginning the test. This code appears here:

```
"Beginning test ..."
```

5. Open the *Try* portion of the *Try...Catch...Finally* block. This appears here:

```
Try
{
```

6. Display a tabbed string that states the script is attempting to create the object stored in the *object* variable. This code appears here:

```
"`tAttempting to create object $object"
```

7. Now call the *New-Object* cmdlet and attempt to create the object stored in the *object* variable. This code appears here:

```
New-Object $object }
```

8. Add the *Catch* statement and have it catch a *[system.exception]* object. This part of the code appears here:

```
Catch [system.exception]
```

9. Add a script block for the *Catch* statement that tabs over one tab and displays a string that says the script was unable to create the object. This code appears here:

```
{ "`tUnable to create $object" }
```

10. Add a *Finally* statement that states the script reached the end. This code appears here:

```
Finally
 { "Reached the end of the Script" }
```

11. Save the script.

12. Run the script, and at the prompt for an object, type the letters *sample*. You should see the following output:

```
Beginning sample ...
    Attempting to create object sample
    Unable to create sample
Reached the end of the Script
```

13. Now run the script again. This time, at the object prompt, type the letters *psobject*. You should see the following output:

```
Beginning test ...
    Attempting to create object psobject

Reached the end of the Script
```

This concludes the exercise.

## Chapter 19 quick reference

| To | Do this |
|---|---|
| Handle a potential error arising from a missing value of a computername parameter | Use the *param* statement and assign a default value of $env:computername to the *computername* parameter. |
| Make a parameter mandatory | Use the *[Parameter(Mandatory=$true)]* parameter attribute. |
| Cause the *Test-Connection* cmdlet to return a Boolean value | Use the *-quiet* switched parameter. |
| Ensure a remote computer is up prior to making a remote connection | Use the *Test-Connection* cmdlet. |
| Ensure that only valid data types are entered | Write a function to test the data prior to executing the remaining portion of the script. |
| Ensure that code will always run, regardless of whether an error is raised | Place the code in the Finally block of a Try...Catch...Finally structure. |
| Gracefully exit a script when a portion of code may cause an error | Use Try...Catch...Finally to attempt to execute the code, catch any specific errors, and clean up the environment. |

# CHAPTER 20

# Managing Exchange Server

**After completing this chapter, you will be able to:**

- Understand the providers included with Exchange Server 2010.

- Use *Get-ExCommand* to obtain a listing of Exchange Server 2010 cmdlets.

- Configure Exchange Server 2010 recipient settings.

- Configure Exchange Server 2010 storage settings.

- Query, configure, and audit policy.

The decision by the Microsoft Exchange Server team to base their management tools on Microsoft Windows PowerShell is a win for customers who desire to apply the flexibility and configurability of scripting to the management of complex mission-critical networked applications. What this means for Windows PowerShell scripters is that everything that can be done using the graphical user interface (GUI) can also be done from Windows PowerShell. In some cases, the only way to perform a certain task is through Windows PowerShell. This is the first time that the design of a major application began with the scripting interface in mind; in the past, scripting support has always been added after the product was completed.

## Exploring the Exchange 2010 cmdlets

When trying to figure out what you can do with a Windows PowerShell–enabled application, first examine the cmdlets that come with the application. You can take several approaches to this task. The easiest is to use the function *Get-ExCommand*. When you use the *Get-ExCommand* function, you will notice a listing of more than 600 functions for managing Exchange Server 2010. These functions allow you to update, uninstall, test, start, stop, suspend, set, add, and remove objects on your Exchange server. The only thing you cannot do using the Exchange Server 2010 cmdlets is create a user or group. You can create a new user in Active Directory at the same time you create the mailbox by using the *New-Mailbox* cmdlet, but you cannot create a user account without creating the mailbox. For scripts that can create Active Directory users and groups, refer to Chapter 15, "Working with Active Directory."

**Note** The Exchange Management Shell Quick Reference for Exchange 2010, which lists the common cmdlets, is available at the following URL: *http://www.microsoft.com/downloads*.

The good thing about the *Get-ExCommand* command is that you can pipeline it to other cmdlets to assist you in searching for exactly the correct cmdlet for a particular job. One thing that is different from Exchange 2007 is that Exchange Server 2010 creates proxy functions for all the commands; therefore, the object that returns from the command is a *FunctionInfo* object, not a *CmdletInfo* object. The difference is that a *FunctionInfo* object does not contain the command definition in a way that exposes the command parameters. Instead, a *FunctionInfo* object *definition* property contains the actual text of the function itself. To maintain a better representation of the function capabilities, pipe the *name* property to the *Get-Help* cmdlet. For example, if you were looking for commands related to statistics, you could use the command that follows to retrieve this information.

```
Get-ExCommand | Where-Object { $_.name -match 'statistics'} |
Foreach-Object { get-help $_.name | select-object -expandProperty syntax}
```

When this command runs, you receive a list of commands that provide information related to statistics. Sample output from the previous command appears following. Notice that when you use *Select-Object* to format the command output, the syntax of the command is not truncated, as it is in the default output format.

```
Get-ActiveSyncDeviceStatistics -Identity <ActiveSyncDeviceIdParameter> [-DomainController
<Fqdn>] [-GetMailboxLog
<SwitchParameter>] [-NotificationEmailAddresses <MultiValuedProperty>] [-ShowRecoveryPassword
<SwitchParameter>]
[<CommonParameters>]
Get-ActiveSyncDeviceStatistics -Mailbox <MailboxIdParameter> [-DomainController <Fqdn>]
[-GetMailboxLog
<SwitchParameter>] [-NotificationEmailAddresses <MultiValuedProperty>] [-ShowRecoveryPassword
<SwitchParameter>]
[<CommonParameters>]
```

## Working with remote Exchange servers

You might expect that when using Windows PowerShell 3.0, all you need to do is use *Enter-PSSession* to connect to the remote Exchange 2010 server, import the Exchange module, and be able to work—after all, this is pretty much the way things work with the Active Directory cmdlets. However, that is not the way the Exchange commands work.

The first thing to know is that there is a difference between implicit remoting and explicit remoting. In *explicit remoting*, you create a remote session and enter a remote session, and you are then presented with a Windows PowerShell console prompt. The Windows PowerShell prompt you see is *remote*—that is, it resides on the remote computer. Typing *dir* at the prompt displays the file system structure of the remote computer.

In *implicit remoting*, the cmdlets from the remote session come to the local computer and are locally defined as functions. Therefore, the Windows PowerShell prompt that appears is local; it remains on your computer. Typing *dir* at the prompt displays the file system structure of the local computer.

When you make a remote connection to an Exchange 2010 server and add the three Exchange Management snap-ins, Windows PowerShell displays no errors. However, if you attempt to run a common Exchange command, such as *Get-ExchangeServer*, an error appears. The commands and associated errors appear in Figure 20-1.

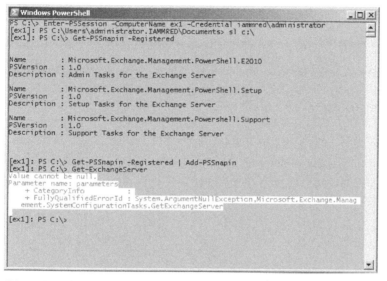

**FIGURE 20-1** Errors occur when attempting to make a standard remote connection to Exchange.

The secret to using Windows PowerShell remoting to manage an Exchange 2010 server remotely is to use implicit remoting instead of explicitly connecting to a remote Windows PowerShell session on the Exchange 2010 server. Here are the steps required to create an implicit remote Windows PowerShell session.

1.  Use the *Get-Credential* cmdlet to obtain credentials for the Exchange server (unless the current user already has rights). Store the returned credential object in a variable.

2.  Use the *New-PSSession* cmdlet to create a new session on the Exchange server. Specify the *ConnectionUri* in the form of *http://servername/powershell* and supply the credential object from step 1 to the *credential* parameter. Store the returned session object in a variable.

3.  Use the *Import-PSSession* cmdlet to connect to the session created in step 2.

The code that follows illustrates a connection to a remote Exchange server named EX1 being made by the administrator from the contoso domain.

```
PS C:\> $cred = Get-Credential contoso\administrator
PS C:\> $session = New-PSSession -ConfigurationName Microsoft.Exchange -ConnectionUri
 http://ex1/powershell -Credential $cred
PS C:\> Import-PSSession $session
```

When the *Import-PSSession* command runs, a warning appears that states some of the imported commands use unapproved verbs. This is a normal warning for the Exchange commands and can be safely ignored.

> **Note** To avoid confusing users with the warning message about nonapproved verbs, you should always use approved verbs. You can display approved verbs by using the *Get-Verb* cmdlet.

Once the connection is made, the Exchange cmdlets appear in the local Windows PowerShell console, and they work as if locally installed. To obtain information about Exchange servers, use the *Get-ExchangeServer* cmdlet. This command appears here:

```
Get-ExchangeServer
```

To avoid having to perform the several different steps involved in making an implicit remoting connection to a remote Exchange 2010 server, you can use a function instead. Here is the complete *New-ExchangeSession* function, which creates an implicit remoting connection to an Exchange server:

```
Function New-ExchangeSession
{
  <#
   .Synopsis
    This function creates an implicit remoting connection to an Exchange server
   .Description
    This function creates an implicit remoting session to a remote Exchange
    server. It has been tested on Exchange 2010. The Exchange commands are
    brought into the local PowerShell environment. This works in both the
    Windows PowerShell console as well as the Windows PowerShell ISE. It requires
    two parameters: the computername and the user name with rights on the remote
    Exchange server.
   .Example
    New-ExchangeSession -computername ex1 -user iammred\administrator
    Makes an implicit remoting connection to a remote Exchange 2010 server
    named ex1 using the administrator account from the iammred domain. The user
    is prompted for the administrator password.
   .Parameter ComputerName
    The name of the remote Exchange server
   .Parameter User
    The user account with rights on the remote Exchange server. The user
    account is specified as domain\username
   .Notes
    NAME:  New-ExchangeSession
    AUTHOR: ed wilson, msft
    LASTEDIT: 01/13/2012 17:05:32
    KEYWORDS: Messaging & Communication, Microsoft Exchange 2010, Remoting
   .Link
     Http://www.ScriptingGuys.com
```

```
#Requires -Version 2.0
#>
Param(
 [Parameter(Mandatory=$true,Position=0)]
 [String]
 $computername,
 [Parameter(Mandatory=$true,Position=1)]
 [String]
 $user
 )
 $cred = Get-Credential -Credential $user
 $session = New-PSSession -ConfigurationName Microsoft.Exchange `
   -ConnectionUri http://$computername/powershell -Credential $cred
 Import-PSSession $session
} #end function New-ExchangeSession
```

To gain access to the *New-ExchangeSession* function, you can dot-source the script containing the *New-ExchangeSession* function into your current Windows PowerShell session. When you run the function, the credential dialog box shown in Figure 20-2 appears.

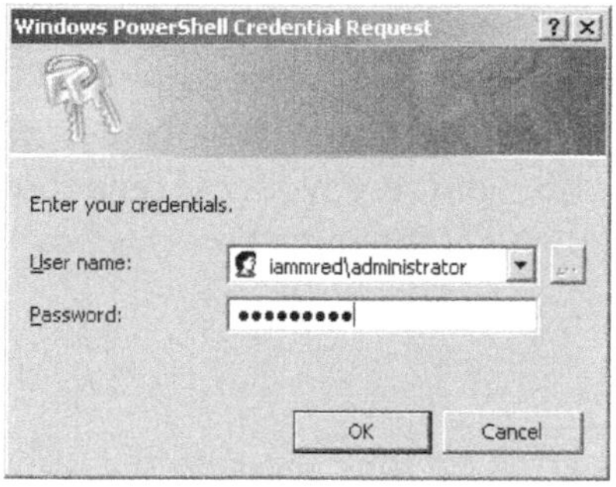

**FIGURE 20-2** When using implicit remoting to connect to Exchange, specify appropriate credentials for the connection to use.

Once you enter the credentials, the implicit remoting session starts, and you can use Exchange cmdlets as if they were installed on the local computer. The following command retrieves information about Microsoft Exchange mailbox databases:

```
PS C:\> Get-MailboxDatabase

Name                         Server       Recovery    ReplicationType
----                         ------       --------    ---------------
Mailbox Database 1301642447  EX1          False       None
```

One command that is not available is *Get-ExCommand*, which displays all of the available Exchange commands.

# Configuring recipient settings

The most basic aspect of administering any messaging-and-collaboration system is configuring the vast and varied settings that relate to recipients. First, the user account must be *mailbox enabled*, which means you need to create a mailbox on the mailbox database for the user account. To do this, you need to use the *Enable-Mailbox* cmdlet. This command appears here:

```
Enable-Mailbox -Identity nwtraders\MyNewUser -Database "mailbox database"
```

When this command runs, you will get a prompt back that appears as follows. It tells you the name of the user account, the alias assigned, the server name on which the mailbox database resides, and any quota restrictions applied to the account.

```
Name          Alias        ServerName    ProhibitSendQuota
----          -----        ----------    -----------------
MyNewUser     myNewUser    smbex01       unlimited
```

> **Tip** You cannot mailbox-enable a user account that is disabled. Although this may seem to make sense, keep in mind that often network administrators will create a group of user accounts, and then leave them all disabled for security reasons. Then, when the user creates a support ticket, the help desk enables the accounts. For these types of scenarios, use a single script that logon-enables the user account and at the same time mailbox-enables the user.

## Creating the user and the mailbox

If you want to create the user and the mailbox at the same time, then you can use the *New-Mailbox* cmdlet. This cmdlet, as you might expect, has a large number of parameters owing to the need to supply values for first name, last name, display name, mailbox name, user principal name (UPN), and many other optional parameters. An example of using this cmdlet to create a user named MyTestUser2 appears here:

```
New-Mailbox -Alias myTestUser2 -Database "mailbox database" `
-Name MyTestUser2 -OrganizationalUnit myTestOU -FirstName My `
-LastName TestUser2 -DisplayName "My TestUser2" `
-UserPrincipalName MyTestUser2@nwtraders.com
```

After you run the cmdlet, notice that it prompts for the password. It does this because the *password* parameter must be a *secureString* data type. If you try to force the password in the command by hard-coding the password as an argument, such as *-password "P@ssword1"*, you will get an error that says, "Cannot convert type string to type secureString." This error appears in Figure 20-3.

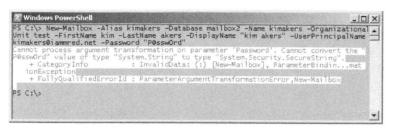

**FIGURE 20-3** An error is returned when a password is supplied directly.

One solution to this error is not to supply the *-password* argument, in which case, the command will pause, and Windows PowerShell will prompt for the password for the user account. When using implicit remoting, a warning message appears stating that the remote Exchange server is sending a prompt request. You should only type in credentials if you trust the remote computer and the script or application generating the request. If you trust the remote computer (which will be pretty obvious if you are the one who created the remoting session with the Exchange server in the first place), type in the password for the new user account (and for the associated mailbox). Figure 20-4 illustrates this behavior.

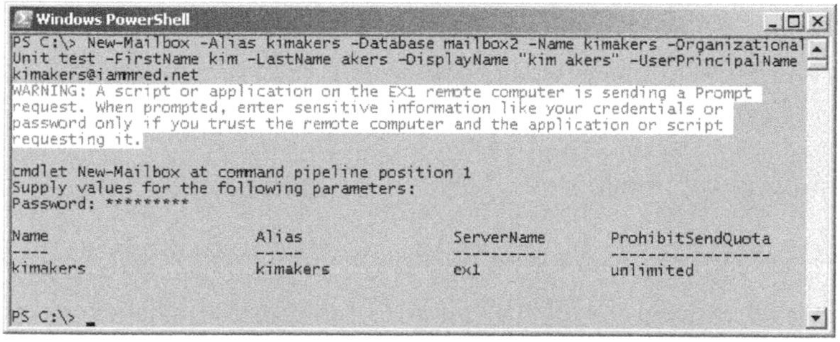

![Windows PowerShell screenshot showing the New-Mailbox cmdlet prompting for the password]

**FIGURE 20-4** The *New-Mailbox* cmdlet prompts for the password.

If you put the command to create a new mailbox in a script, then it will be easier to create the user, the mailbox, and the password. To do this, you use the *ConvertTo-SecureString* cmdlet to convert a plain text string into an encrypted password that will be acceptable to Exchange 2010. *ConvertTo-SecureString* has two arguments that enable you to do this. The first argument is the *-asplaintext* argument. This tells the *ConvertTo-SecureString* cmdlet that you are supplying a plain text string for it to convert. Because this is not a normal operation, you must also supply the *-force* argument. After you have a secure string for the password, you can supply it to the *-password* argument. This appears in the NewMailboxAndUser.ps1 script.

**NewMailboxAndUser.ps1**

```
$password = ConvertTo-SecureString "P@ssW0rD!" -asplaintext -force

New-Mailbox -Alias myTestUser2 -Database "mailbox database" `
-Name MyTestUser2 -OrganizationalUnit myTestOU -FirstName My `
-LastName TestUser2 -DisplayName "My TestUser2" `
-UserPrincipalName MyTestUser2@nwtraders.com -password $password
```

Perhaps a more interesting, and definitely more secure, method of creating a new mailbox and user is not to store the password as plain text in the script, but rather to supply it interactively when running the command. One easy way to do this is to use the *Read-Host* cmdlet. This technique appears in the code that follows. (This is a single logical line of code and no line continuation marks are included.)

```
New-Mailbox -Alias muhan -Name "Mu Han" -OrganizationalUnit test -FirstName Mu -LastName Han
-UserPrincipalName MuHan@Iammred.Net -Password (Read-host "password"-AsSecureString)
```

Once the command runs, the prompt specified in the *Read-Host* command appears. Characters entered at the prompt appear as a mask. The use of this technique to create a new user named Mu Han appears in Figure 20-5.

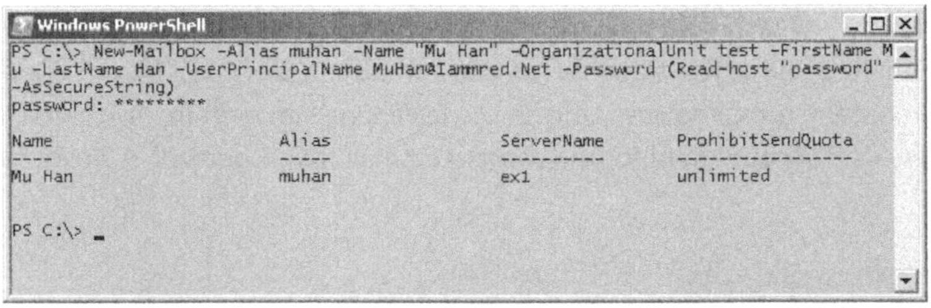

**FIGURE 20-5** Using the *Read-Host* cmdlet to accept a secure string when creating a new mailbox.

## Creating multiple new users and mailboxes

1. Open the Windows PowerShell ISE or your favorite Windows PowerShell script editor.

2. Create a variable called *$password* and use the *ConvertTo-SecureString* cmdlet to create a secure string from the plain text string *P@ssw0rd1*. To ensure this command completes properly, use the *-force* parameter. The code to do this is shown here:

   ```
   $password = ConvertTo-SecureString "P@ssW0rD!" -asplaintext -force
   ```

3. Create a variable called *$strDatabase*. This variable will be used to hold a string that is used to tell the *New-Mailbox* cmdlet on which database to create the new mailbox-enabled user account. This line of code is shown here:

   ```
   $strDatabase = "Mailbox Database"
   ```

4. On the next line, create a variable called *$strOU*. This variable is used to hold the name of the organizational unit (OU) that will hold the new user account. This line of code is shown here:

   ```
   $strOU = "myTestOU"
   ```

5. Create a new variable called *$strDomain*. This variable will hold a string that will be used for the domain portion of the user name to be created. This line of code is shown here:

   ```
   $strDomain = "Nwtraders.msft"
   ```

6. Create a variable called *$strFname*, which will be used to hold the user's first name. This line of code is shown here:

```
$strFname = "My"
```

7. Create a variable called *$strLname*, which will be used to hold the user's last name. This line of code is shown here:

```
$strLname = "TestUser"
```

8. Use a *for* statement to create a loop that will increment 11 times. Use the variable *$i* as the counter variable. Start the loop from 0 and continue until it is less than or equal to 10. Use the double plus sign operator (++) to automatically increment the variable *$i*. This code is shown here:

```
for($i=0;$i -le 10;$i++)
```

9. Type the opening and closing curly brackets as shown here:

```
{
}
```

10. Between the two curly brackets, use the *New-Mailbox* cmdlet. Use the *$strFname, $strLname,* and *$i* variables to create the user's alias. Use the *$strDatabase* variable to supply the name for the *-database* argument. Use the *$strFname, $strLname,* and *$i* variables to create the name of the account. Use the *$strOU* variable to supply the value for the *-organizationalunit* argument. Use the *$strFname* variable to supply the value for the *-firstname* argument. Use the *$strLname* variable to supply the value for the *-lastname* argument. Use the *$strFname, $strLname,* and *$i* variables to create the value for the *-displayname* argument. To create the *-userprincipalname* argument, use *$strFname, $strLname,* and *$i,* and supply the commercial-at sign in parentheses (@), and the *$strdomain* variable. The last argument that should be supplied is the password contained in the *$password* variable. This line of code is shown following. Note that you can use the grave accent character (`) to break up the line of code for readability purposes, as is done here.

```
New-Mailbox -Alias $strFname$strLname$i  -Database $strDatabase `
-Name $strFname$strLname$i -OrganizationalUnit $strOU -FirstName `
$strFname -LastName $strLname -DisplayName $strFname$strLname$i `
-UserPrincipalName $strFname$strLname$i"@"$strDomain `
-password $password
```

11. Save your script as *<yourname>*CreateMultipleUsersAndMailboxes.ps1. Run your script. Go to the Exchange Management Console and click the Mailbox node. Select Refresh from the Action menu. The new users should appear within a minute or so.

This concludes the procedure.

# Reporting user settings

After creating users in Exchange Server 2010, the next step in the user life cycle is to report on their mailbox configuration settings. To do this, you can use the *Get-Mailbox* cmdlet. This command appears here:

```
Get-Mailbox
```

Once this command runs, it produces a table of output that lists the user name, alias, server name, and other information. A sample of this output appears here:

```
Name               Alias          ServerName   ProhibitSendQuota
----               -----          ----------   -----------------
Administrator      Administrator  smbex01      unlimited
Claire O'Donnell   claire         smbex01      unlimited
Frank Miller       frank          smbex01      unlimited
Holly Holt         holly          smbex01      unlimited
```

If you are interested more detailed information, or different information, then you will need to modify the default output from the *Get-Mailbox* command. If you already know the server, and you are only interested in the alias and when the *ProhibitSendQuota* kicks in, you can use the following command:

```
Get-Mailbox | Format-Table alias, prohibitsendquota -AutoSize
```

This command uses the *Get-Mailbox* cmdlet and pipelines the resulting object into the *Format-Table* cmdlet. It then chooses the Alias column and the ProhibitSendQuota column, and uses the *-autosize* argument to format the output. A sample of the resulting output appears here:

```
Alias         ProhibitSendQuota
-----         -----------------
Administrator unlimited
claire        unlimited
frank         unlimited
holly         unlimited
```

If you use the *Get-Mailbox* cmdlet and supply the alias for a specific user, the same four default columns you obtained earlier will be returned. This command is shown here:

```
Get-Mailbox mytestuser1
```

In reality, you are supplying the string *mytestuser1* as the value for the *-identity* argument of the *Get-Mailbox* cmdlet. The command shown here produces the same result:

```
Get-Mailbox -identity mytestuser1
```

Why is it important to know you are supplying a value for the *-identity* argument of the *Get-Mailbox* cmdlet? There are two reasons: the first is that when you see the *-identity* argument of this cmdlet, you will know what it does, and the second is that there is actually confusion in

Exchange Server 2010 about what the -*identity* attribute is and when to use it. For example, technically, the identity of a *User* object in Exchange Server 2010 would look something like this:

```
nwtraders.com/MyTestOU/MyTestUser1
```

What is interesting is the way I obtained the identity value. Take a look at the syntax of the *Get-Mailbox* cmdlet:

```
Get-Mailbox -identity mytestuser1 | Format-List identity
```

Remember, this command returned the -*identity* attribute of the *User* object, so there is confusion between the -*identity* argument of the *Get-Mailbox* cmdlet and the -*identity* attribute used by Exchange Server 2010. But it gets even stranger. Supply the value for the -*identity* argument to retrieve the specific mailbox. Pipeline the results to the *Format-List* cmdlet and retrieve both the alias and the identity. The command to obtain the mailbox user alias from the identity is shown here:

```
Get-Mailbox -identity mytestuser1 | Format-List alias, identity
```

The data returned from this command is shown here:

```
Alias    : MyTestUser1
Identity : nwtraders.com/MyTestOU/MyTestUser1
```

You could move the commands around a little bit and create a script that would be very useful from an audit perspective. The FindUnrestrictedMailboxes.ps1 script uses the *Get-Mailbox* cmdlet to retrieve a listing of all user mailboxes. It then uses the *Where-Object* cmdlet to filter out the amount of returned data. It looks for objects that have the *ProhibitSendQuota* property set to *unlimited*. It then pipelines the resulting objects to return only the alias of each *User* object.

**FindUnrestrictedMailboxes.ps1**

```
"Retrieving users with unrestricted mailbox limits "
"This may take a few minutes ..."
$a = get-mailbox|
    where-object {$_.prohibitSendQuota -eq "unlimited"}

"There are " + $a.length + " users without restrictions."
"They are listed below. `r"

$a | Format-List alias
```

If you were interested in the status of all the quota settings on the Exchange server, you could revise the script to use the following command:

```
Get-Mailbox | Format-Table alias, *quota
```

Obviously, in a large environment with multiple Exchange servers, hard-coding the specific server name into a script is problematic. When working with user mailboxes, mailbox servers are the target. To avoid having to type in an array of mailbox server names, use the *Get-MailboxServer* cmdlet to retrieve all the mailbox servers. Unfortunately, the Exchange cmdlets do not accept pipelined input. If they did accept pipelined input, the command would be simple. Instead, pipeline the results from the *Get-MailboxServer* cmdlet to a *Foreach-Object* cmdlet and choose the *name* property from the piped object. The syntax of this command appears here:

```
Get-MailboxServer | Foreach { Get-Mailbox -Server $_.name }
```

# Managing storage settings

It is an Exchange administrator's truism that the user's need for storage expands to meet the total amount of available storage plus 10 percent. Without management of storage demands, you will never have enough disk space. Unfortunately, estimates of storage requirements are often haphazard at best. It is very easy to go from "We have plenty of storage" to "Where did all the disk space go?" Everything from attachments to deleted item retention to bulging inboxes demand storage space. Fortunately, you can employ Windows PowerShell to bring some sanity to the situation.

The first step in working with the storage groups is to find out how many database objects the server contains, along with names associated with the location of the database. Exchange Server 2010 no longer uses storage groups (which were used in Exchange 2007). Instead, the storage groups have moved up in the hierarchy and are on the same level as servers; the storage groups themselves having been deemed basically redundant and therefore do not exist.

## Examining the mailbox database

What most administrators think about when it comes to Exchange Server is the mailbox database itself. To retrieve information about the mailbox databases on your server, use the *Get-MailboxDatabase* cmdlet with no arguments. This is shown here:

```
Get-MailboxDatabase
```

The results from this command, shown here, are useful for helping identify the name and location of the Exchange Server mailbox database:

```
Name              Server    StorageGroup          Recovery
----              ------    ------------          --------
Mailbox Database  SMBEX01   First Storage Group   False
```

After you have decided which mailbox database to work with, you can pipeline the object returned by the *Get-MailboxDatabase* cmdlet to the *Format-List* cmdlet. This command appears here:

```
Get-MailboxDatabase | Format-List *
```

This command will return all the properties associated with the mailbox database and the associated values. A sampling of the returned data is shown here:

```
JournalRecipient            :
MailboxRetention            : 30 days
OfflineAddressBook          :
OriginalDatabase            :
```

If, however, you are only interested in storage quota limits, you can modify the command, as shown here:

```
Get-MailboxDatabase | Format-list *quota
```

The results of this command are nice, neat, and succinct, as shown here:

```
ProhibitSendReceiveQuota : 2355MB
ProhibitSendQuota        : 2GB
IssueWarningQuota        : 1945MB
```

## Managing the mailbox database

To create a new mailbox database, use the *New-MailboxDatabase* function. The Exchange server requires access to the disk that will house the new database. Also, the folder containing the database must exist. Even in you have a small Exchange 2010 installation that contains a single Exchange server, the *-server* parameter is mandatory. The minimum required parameters for using the *New-MailboxDatabase* command are the *-name*, *-server*, and *-edbFilePath* parameters. The use of this command to create a new mailbox database named *Mailbox2* on a server named *ex1* in the *mbdb2* folder on the E drive appears here:

```
New-MailboxDatabase -Name Mailbox2 -EdbFilePath e:\MbDb2\mailbox2.edb -Server ex1
```

Once the command to create the new Exchange mailbox database completes, it is a good idea to use the *Get-MailboxDatabase* command to verify that the mailbox database has been created properly. The command to create a new mailbox database (along with the use of the *Get-MailboxDatabase* command to verify the creation of the new data set, and the accompanying output from these commands) appears in Figure 20-6.

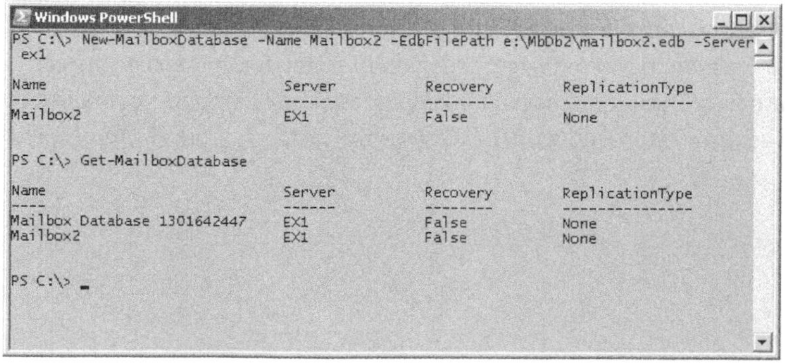

FIGURE 20-6 Creating a new mailbox database via the *New-MailboxDatabase* command.

Once created via the *New-MailBoxDatabase* command, the new mailbox database is available for use when creating new users. However, new users will not be able to log on to their new mailboxes. This is because the new mailbox database appears only in the schema, not as a physical database file residing on disk. The physical database file residing on disk does not appear until the database is mounted. By default, the database mounts at the startup of Exchange—but that does not mean you must restart the Exchange server to mount the database. One reason for waiting is to permit staging of new mailbox databases, with actual physical file creation occurring during periods of low system utilization. It is, however, unfortunate there is no *mount* parameter on the *New-MailBoxDatabase* cmdlet. Due to the need to replicate the mailbox database information for Active Directory, you can't write a script that creates the new mailbox database and then mounts it, because it will not work consistently. It is possible to add a *sleep* command to pause execution, but due to differences in replication times, this technique would be hit or miss. A better approach would be to create a background job that monitors for a new object-creation event in Active Directory. Once the new-object-creation event is triggered, then the script continues and mounts the database. To mount the mailbox database, use the *Mount-Database* function and specify the name of the database to mount. When the *Mount-Database* command runs, no feedback is returned to the command line. Here is an example of using the *Mount-Database* cmdlet to mount a mailbox database named mb4:

```
Mount-Database mb4
```

To remove a mailbox database, use the *Remove-MailboxDatabase* cmdlet. As with the *Mount-Database* cmdlet, the name of the database must uniquely identify the database as reflected in Active Directory. If, for example, you wish to remove a mailbox database named mb5, and there is only one mb5 mailbox database in the organization, you can use the command syntax indicated here:

```
Remove-MailboxDatabase mb5
```

If, on the other hand, the name mb5 is not unique, you will need to determine the full value of the identity name. To do this, use the command that appears here:

```
Get-MailboxDatabase | Select identity
```

The *Remove-MailboxDatabase* cmdlet does not have a *-force* switched parameter, which means that when using the command to remove a mailbox database, you must answer a prompt that requests confirmation of the action. Upon removing the mailbox database, it is still necessary to remove the actual database files. This is one reason for keeping mailbox databases contained in their own folders—it simplifies removal later. Figure 20-7 illustrates the process of removing a mailbox database.

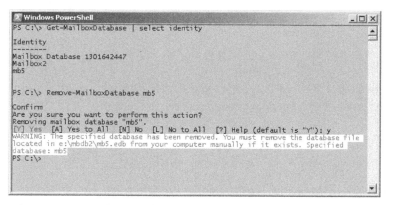

**FIGURE 20-7** Removing a mailbox database requires answering a confirmation message.

# Managing Exchange logging

A fundamental aspect of maintenance and troubleshooting involves the configuration and modification of logging settings on Exchange Server 2010. There are 210 different logs that can be configured using Windows PowerShell. In the old days, merely finding a listing of the Exchange server log files was a rather specialized and difficult task. When a problem arose on the Exchange server, you had to call a Microsoft support professional, who would simply walk you through the task of configuring logging, reproducing the problem, and then reading the appropriate log file. After reading the error message in the log file, more often than not, the situation became rather transparent.

In Exchange Server 2010, troubleshooting still consists of configuring the appropriate log file, but now you can easily do that yourself. For instance, to obtain a listing of all the event logs on your server, you use the *Get-EventLogLevel* cmdlet, as shown here:

```
Get-EventLogLevel
```

When this command is run, output similar to that shown following appears. Notice the format of the *Identity* property, because that is the required parameter to configure the logging level on any particular Exchange log.

```
Identity                             EventLevel
--------                             --------
MSExchange ActiveSync\Requests       Lowest
MSExchange ActiveSync\Configuration  Lowest
MSExchange Antispam\General          Lowest
MSExchange Assistants\Assistants     Lowest
MSExchange Autodiscover\Core         Lowest
```

You can use the name of a specific Exchange log file with *Get-EventLogLevel* to retrieve information about a specific log file. This is shown here, where you obtain the logging level of the routing log:

```
Get-EventLogLevel routing
```

If you try to use the *Set-EventLogLevel* cmdlet to change the logging level to medium, as shown here, an error occurs:

```
Set-EventLogLevel routing -Level medium
```

This is rather frustrating because the error that occurs says a specific error log must be supplied. However, you confirmed that the routing log only referred to a single event log.

```
Set-EventLogLevel : Cannot set the EventLog level on more than one category. You must specify a
unique EventSource\Category.
At line:1 char:18 + Set-EventLogLevel  <<<< routing -Level medium
```

To try to identify what Windows PowerShell is expecting for the command, you can look at all the properties of the routing event log. To obtain these properties, you pipe the object returned by the *Get-EventLogLevel* cmdlet to the *Format-List* cmdlet, as shown here:

```
Get-EventLogLevel routing | Format-List *
```

When you examine the properties of the routing event log, you see that it is not very complicated. When you use *Get-Help* on *Set-EventLoglevel,* you see that it wants the *Identity* property of the log file. As shown here, this would require a lot of typing:

```
Identity     : MSExchangeTransport\routing
IsValid      : True
ObjectState  : Unchanged
Name         : Routing
Number       : 4
EventLevel   : Lowest
```

As discussed earlier in this section, the *Get-EventLogLevel* routing command only returns a single instance of an Exchange event log. You can use this fact to avoid typing. If you store the results of the *Get-EventLogLevel* routing command in a variable, as shown here, you can reuse that variable later:

```
$a = Get-EventLogLevel routing
```

Because the *$a* variable holds only the routing event log, you can now use the *Identity* property of the routing event log object to refer to that specific log file. As shown here, you can use this reference to the routing event log when you use the *Set-EventLogLevel* cmdlet.

```
Set-EventLogLevel -Identity $a.Identity -Level medium
```

## Reporting transport-logging levels

1. Open the Windows PowerShell ISE or your favorite Windows PowerShell script editor.

2. Create a variable called *$aryLog* and use it to hold the object that is returned by using the *Get-EventLogLevel* cmdlet. At the end of the line, use the pipe character (|) both to pass the object to another object and to break the line for readability. This line of code is shown here:

   ```
   $aryLog = Get-EventLogLevel |
   ```

3. On the next line, use the *Where-Object* cmdlet to filter the current pipeline object on the *Identity* property and do a regular-expression match on the word *transport*. The line of code that does this is shown here:

```
where-object {$_.identity -match "transport"}
```

4. On the next line, use the *foreach* command to walk through the array of Exchange transport logs contained in the *$aryLog* variable. Use the variable *$strLog* as the individual instance of the event log from inside the array. This line of code is shown here:

```
foreach ($strLog in $aryLog)
```

5. On the next line, open the code block with an opening curly bracket. Skip a couple of lines, and then close the code block with a closing curly bracket. These two lines of code are shown here:

```
{


}
```

6. Inside the newly created code block, create a variable called *$strLogIdent* and use it to hold the object that is returned by querying the *Identity* property of the *$strLog* variable. This line of code is shown here:

```
$strLogIdent = $strLog.identity
```

7. On the next line, use the *Get-EventLogLevel* cmdlet. Pass the identity string stored in the *$strLogIdent* variable to the *-identity* argument of the *Get-EventLogLevel* cmdlet. The line of code that does this is shown here:

```
Get-EventLogLevel -identity $strLogIdent
```

8. Save your script as *<yourname>*ReportTransportLogging.ps1 and run it. You should see a list of 26 transport logs. If this is not the case, compare your script with the ReportTransportLogging.ps1 script.

This concludes the procedure.

## Configuring transport-logging levels

1. Open the Windows PowerShell ISE or your favorite Windows PowerShell script editor.

2. On the first line of your script, declare a variable called *$strLevel* and assign the value *medium* to it. This line of code is shown here:

```
$strLevel = "medium"
```

3. On the next line in your script, use the *Get-EventLogLevel* cmdlet to get a collection of event log objects. At the end of the line, use the pipe character (|) to pass the object to the next line. At the beginning of the line, use the variable *$aryLog* to hold the resulting object. This line of code is shown here:

```
$aryLog = Get-EventLogLevel |
```

4. On the next line, use the *Where-Object* cmdlet to filter the current pipeline object on the *Identity* property and to perform a regular-expression match on the word *transport*. The line of code that does this is shown here:

```
where-object {$_.identity -match "transport"}
```

5. On the next line, use the *ForEach* command to walk through the array of Exchange transport logs contained in the *$aryLog* variable. Use the variable *$strLog* as the individual instance of the event log from inside the array. This line of code is shown here:

```
foreach ($strLog in $aryLog)
```

6. On the next line, open the code block with an opening curly bracket. Skip a couple of lines, and then close the code block with a closing curly bracket. These two lines of code are shown here:

```
{


}
```

7. Inside the newly created script block, create a variable called *$strLogIdent* and use it to hold the object that is returned by querying the *Identity* property of the *$strLog* variable. This line of code is shown here:

```
$strLogIdent = $strLog.identity
```

8. On the next line in your script, use the *Set-EventLogLevel* cmdlet to set the logging level of the transport logs. Use the string contained in the *$strLogIdent* variable to supply the specific log identity to the *-identity* argument of the cmdlet. Use the string in the *$strLevel* variable to supply the logging level to the *-level* argument of the *Set-EventLogLevel* cmdlet. This code is shown here:

```
Set-EventLogLevel -identity $strLogIdent -level $strLevel
```

9. Save your script as *<yourname>*ConfigureTransportLogging.ps1. Run your script. After a few seconds, you will see the prompt return, but no output.

**10.** Run the ReportTransportLogging.ps1 script. You should now see a listing of all the transport logs and see that their logging level has been changed to *medium*.

**11.** If you do not see the logging level changed, open the ConfigureTransportLogging.ps1 script and it compare it with yours.

This concludes the procedure.

# Managing auditing

If your Exchange administrators use their own user accounts to do their work, and they are not using a generic login account, it is very possible that changes made to your Exchange 2010 server are logged. This is because Exchange 2010 has a feature called Administrator Audit Logging. The good news is that new installations of Exchange 2010 Service Pack (SP) 1 enable this logging by default. This feature logs when a user or an administrator makes a change to the Exchange organization. This permits the ability to trace changes back to a specific user for auditing purposes. In addition, the detailed logging provides a history of changes to the organization that are useful from a regulatory compliance perspective, or as a troubleshooting tool. By default, Microsoft Exchange Server 2010 SP1 enables audit logging on new installations. To determine the status of Administrator Audit Logging, use the *Get-AdminAuditLogConfig* command. The use of this command and associated output from the command appear in Figure 20-8.

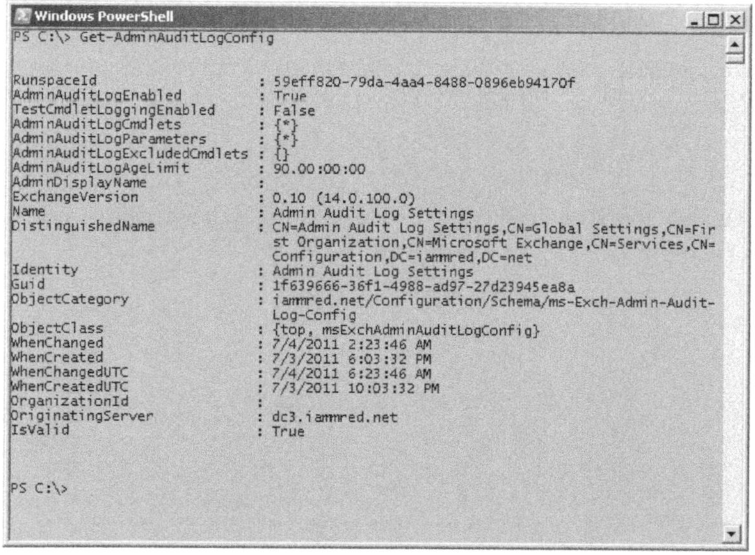

**FIGURE 20-8** The *Get-AdminAuditLogConfig* cmdlet returns valuable information about audit settings.

In a large network, it might be preferable to specify a specific domain controller from which to retrieve the Administrative Audit Logging configuration. To do this, use the *-domaincontroller* parameter. On most networks, you can use either the host name or the fully qualified domain name. These two commands appear here:

```
Get-AdminAuditLogConfig -DomainController dc1
Get-AdminAuditLogConfig -DomainController dc1.contoso.net
```

Prior to SP1, when enabled, the Administrator Audit Logging feature sent emails to a specific mailbox-audit-log mailbox configured via the *Set-AdminAuditLogConfig* cmdlet and examined via an email client. Since Exchange Server 2010 SP1, the audit entries reside in a hidden mailbox, and the *Search-AdminAuditLog* cmdlet retrieves the entries. The mailbox appears in the *Users* container in the Active Directory Users and Computers tool, and it is possible to obtain statistics about this mailbox by using the *Get-MailboxStatistics* cmdlet. This command appears here:

```
Get-MailboxStatistics "SystemMailbox{e0dc1c29-89c3-4034-b678-e6c29d823ed9}"
```

When the *Search-AdminAuditLog* cmdlet runs without any parameters, the *Search-AdminAuditLog* cmdlet returns all records. By default, the retention period for mailbox statistics is 90 days (on a fresh Exchange 2010 SP1 or later installation). Configure the retention period by using the *Set-AdminAuditLog* cmdlet. When making a change to the admin audit logging, keep in mind that changes rely upon Active Directory replication to take place, and therefore could take up to an hour to replicate through the domain. Also keep in mind that changes to auditing apply to the entire Exchange organization—there is no granularity. The following command sets the retention period to 120 days:

```
Set-AdminAuditLogConfig -AdminAuditLogAgeLimit 120
```

To retrieve all of the admin audit logs, use the *Search-AdminAuditLog* cmdlet without any parameters. This command appears here:

```
Search-AdminAuditLog
```

The command to retrieve all of the admin audit logs, as well as the output associated with that command, appears in Figure 20-9.

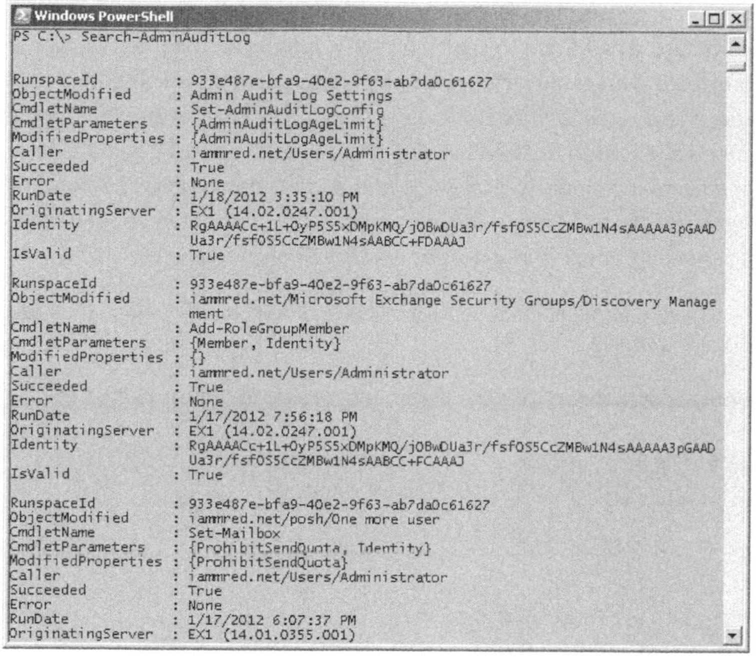

**FIGURE 20-9** Use the *Search-AdminAuditLog* cmdlet to view Exchange audit information.

It is certainly possible to pipeline the results from the *Search-AdminAuditLog* cmdlet to a *Where-Object* cmdlet, but it is better to use the parameters when possible. For example, to see only changes from the Administrator user account, use the *-userids* parameter, as appears here:

```
Search-AdminAuditLog -userids administrator
```

To see audit log entries that occurred prior to a specific date, use the *-enddate* parameter. The following commands retrieve audit entries from events that were created by the Administrator user account and occurred prior to January 18, 2012.

```
Search-AdminAuditLog -UserIds administrator -EndDate 1/18/12
```

```
Search-AdminAuditLog -UserIds administrator -EndDate "january 18, 2012"
```

To review only the audit entries generated by a specific cmdlet, use the *-cmdlets* parameter. The following example only retrieves audit entries generated by the *Enable-Mailbox* cmdlet:

```
Search-AdminAuditLog -Cmdlets Enable-Mailbox
```

The *-cmdlets* parameter accepts an array of cmdlet names. To find audit events generated by either the *Enable-Mailbox* or the *Set-Mailbox* cmdlet, use the command shown here:

```
Search-AdminAuditLog -Cmdlets Enable-Mailbox, Set-Mailbox
```

One powerful feature of the admin auditing framework is the ability to use the *New-AdminAuditLogSearch* cmdlet. In addition to searching the admin audit logs, this cmdlet also emails the report when completed. The email includes an XML attachment containing the results from the search. The *-startdate* and *-enddate* parameters are mandatory parameters that limit the size of the returned report. Reports are limited to 10 MB in size, and can take up to 15 minutes to arrive in the inbox. The following command is a single logical line command (containing no line-continuation characters) that creates a new report of all *Enable-Mailbox* commands used between January 1, 2012 and January 18, 2012. The command emails the report to *edwilson@iammred.net*.

```
New-AdminAuditLogSearch -cmdlets enable-Mailbox -StatusMailRecipients edwilson@iammred.net
-StartDate 1/1/2012 -EndDate 1/18/2012
```

The command and the output associated with the command appear in Figure 20-10.

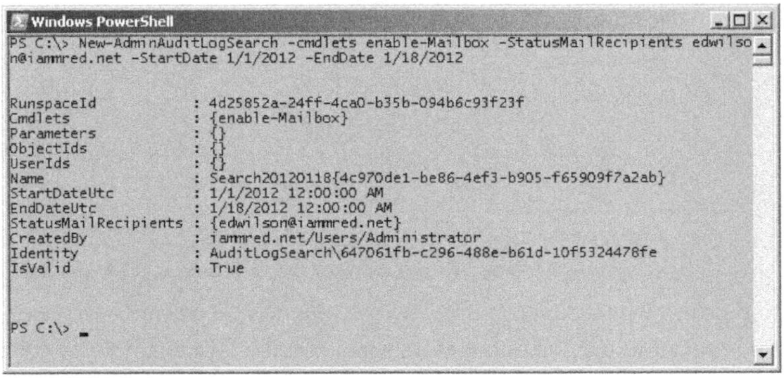

**FIGURE 20-10** The *New-AdminAuditLogSearch* cmdlet emails reports to the specified email address.

Figure 20-11 shows the email returning the search results from the previous query.

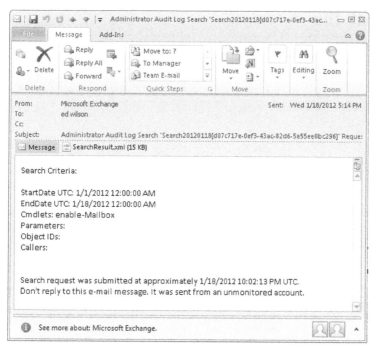

**FIGURE 20-11** Autogenerated email with attached search results.

The XML attachment appears in Figure 20-12.

```xml
<?xml version="1.0" encoding="UTF-8"?>
<SearchResults>
  <Event OriginatingServer="EX1 (14.01.0355.001)" Error="None"
  Succeeded="true" RunDate="2012-01-17T18:04:16-05:00"
  ObjectModified="iammred.net/posh/One more user" Cmdlet="Enable-Mailbox"
  Caller="iammred.net/Users/Administrator">
    <CmdletParameters>
      <Parameter Value="one more user" Name="Identity"/>
    </CmdletParameters>
    <ModifiedProperties>
      <Property Name="Extensions" NewValue="" OldValue=""/>
      <Property Name="PoliciesIncluded" NewValue="{26491cfc-9e50-4857-
        861b-0cb8df22b5d7};60f3165f-02f7-4877-9cd2-c247d3944c8d"
        OldValue=""/>
      <Property Name="EmailAddressPolicyEnabled" NewValue="True"
        OldValue="False"/>
      <Property Name="PoliciesExcluded" NewValue="" OldValue=""/>
      <Property Name="RecipientTypeDetails" NewValue="UserMailbox"
        OldValue="User"/>
      <Property Name="RejectMessagesFrom" NewValue="" OldValue=""/>
      <Property Name="RecipientTypeDetailsValue" NewValue="UserMailbox"
        OldValue="None"/>
      <Property Name="AcceptMessagesOnlyFromDLMembers" NewValue=""
        OldValue=""/>
      <Property Name="ArchiveName" NewValue="" OldValue=""/>
      <Property Name="UseDatabaseQuotaDefaults" NewValue="True"
```

**FIGURE 20-12** The SearchResult.xml file displayed in Internet Explorer.

# Parsing the audit XML file

The XML file that is generated from the *New-AdminAuditLogSearch* cmdlet is a standard formatted file, and appears in XML Notepad in Figure 20-13.

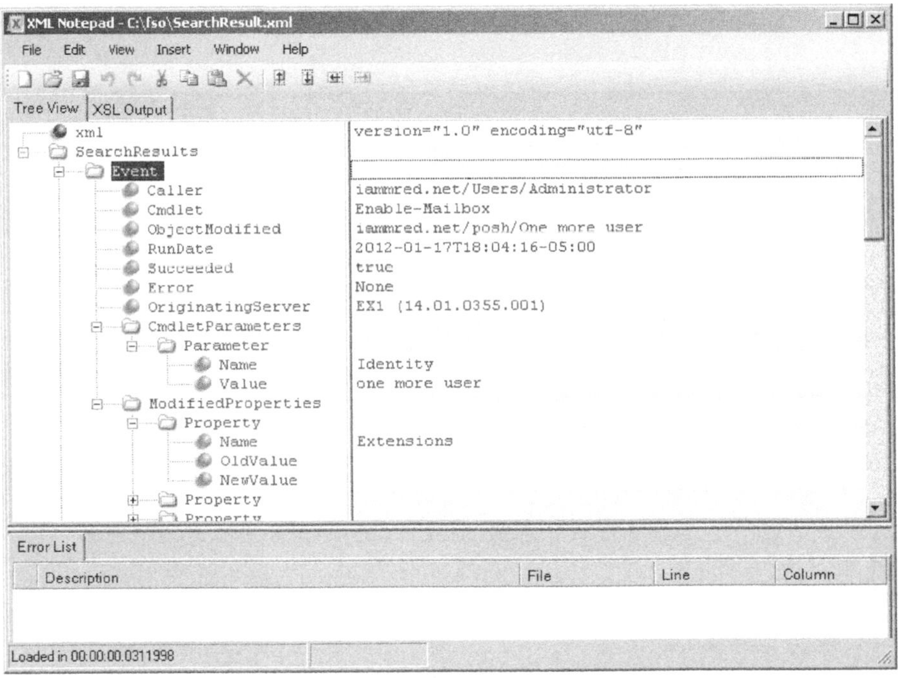

**FIGURE 20-13** XML Notepad clearly displays the structure of the SearchResult.xml file.

In Figure 20-13, the properties of the first event appear. The string properties appear here:

```
Caller
Cmdlet
Error
ObjectModified
OriginatingServer
RunDate
Succeeded
```

Two of the properties contain not simple strings but other objects. These two properties show up as additional XML elements and appear here:

```
CmdletParameters
ModifiedProperties
```

One thing that is often confusing is that the Windows PowerShell *Import-CliXML* cmdlet does not import just any old XML file; it imports only specially formatted XML that is generated from the *Export-CliXML* cmdlet. This is why efforts to import the SearchResult.xml file via *Import-CliXML* do not work.

You can use the *Get-Content* cmdlet to easily read the contents of the SearchResult.xml file and cast the resulting text to a *System.Xml.XmlDocument* type by using the *[xml]* type accelerator. This is much easier to accomplish than it sounds.

In the following example, the SearchResult.xml file, saved from Outlook, resides in the C:\fso folder. The *[xml]* type accelerator converts the text, derived via the *Get-Content* cmdlet, into an XML document.

```
[xml]$xml = Get-Content C:\fso\SearchResult.xml
```

When viewed, the *searchresults* XML element—the contents of the *$xml* variable—appears as illustrated here:

```
PS C:\> $xml

xml                                   SearchResults
---                                   -------------
version="1.0" encoding="utf-8"        SearchResults
```

To view the objects stored in the *searchresults* XML element, use dotted notation to access the *searchresults* property. This technique appears here:

```
PS C:\> $xml.SearchResults

Event
-----
{Event, Event, Event}
```

In this example, the *searchresults* element contains three objects, each named *event*. To view the objects, use dotted notation to access the *event* property, as appears here:

```
$xml.SearchResults.Event
```

As shown in Figure 20-14, the *event* property contains the audit information an Exchange administrator seeks.

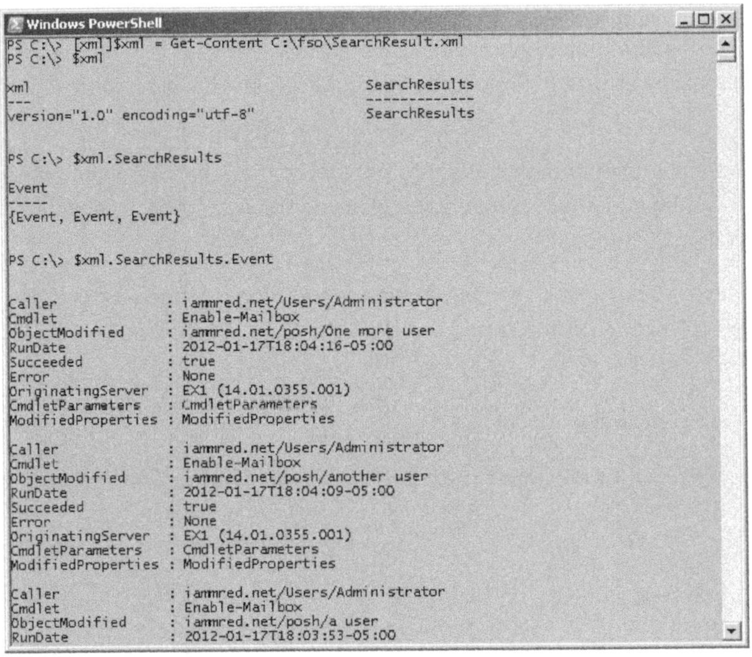

**FIGURE 20-14** Use the *[xml]* type accelerator to gain access to search-result events.

Now use standard Windows PowerShell techniques to analyze the data. For example, if you're only interested in the caller and cmdlet run during the period of the report, use the *Select-Object* cmdlet, as appears here:

```
PS C:\> $xml.SearchResults.Event | select caller, cmdlet

Caller                                   Cmdlet
------                                   ------
iammred.net/Users/Administrator          Enable-Mailbox
iammred.net/Users/Administrator          Enable-Mailbox
iammred.net/Users/Administrator          Enable-Mailbox
```

Output the results to a table by using the *Format-Table* cmdlet. The following command selects the *rundate, caller,* and *cmdlet,* and outputs the results to an automatically sized table:

```
PS C:\> $xml.SearchResults.Event | Format-Table rundate, caller, cmdlet -AutoSize

RunDate                   Caller                           Cmdlet
-------                   ------                           ------
2012-01-17T18:04:16-05:00 iammred.net/Users/Administrator Enable-Mailbox
2012-01-17T18:04:09-05:00 iammred.net/Users/Administrator Enable-Mailbox
2012-01-17T18:03:53-05:00 iammred.net/Users/Administrator Enable-Mailbox
```

The results, stored in the *$xml* variable, are addressable via array index notation. To view the run date of the first event, use the *[0]* notation to retrieve the first element. This technique appears here:

```
PS C:\> $xml.SearchResults.Event[0].rundate
2012-01-17T18:04:16-05:00
```

One cool way to parse the data is to select the appropriate properties and pipeline the results to the *Out-GridView* cmdlet. It is necessary to use the *Select-Object* cmdlet to choose the properties because *Out-GridView* does not accept a complex object; therefore, a direct pipeline fails. This technique appears here:

```
$xml.SearchResults.Event | select caller, rundate, cmdlet | Out-GridView
```

The resulting grid appears in Figure 20-15.

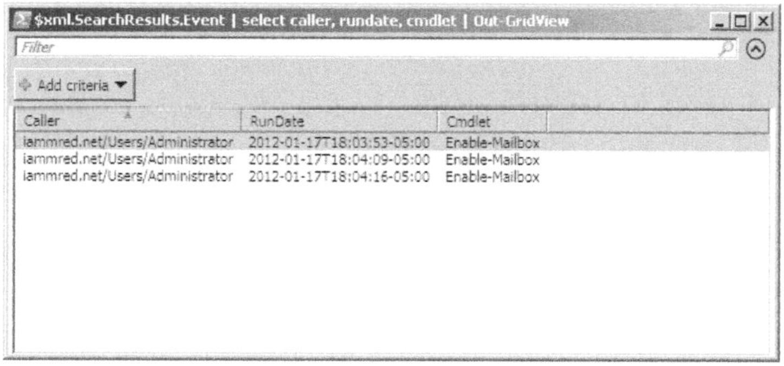

**FIGURE 20-15** The *Out-GridView* cmdlet provides an easy way to navigate audit entries.

# Creating user accounts: step-by-step exercises

In this exercise, you will explore the use of Windows PowerShell to create several users whose names are contained in a text file. Once these user accounts are created, you will use Windows PowerShell to enable message tracking on an Exchange server.

## Parsing a text file and creating Exchange user accounts

1. Open the Windows PowerShell ISE or some other Windows PowerShell script editor.

2. Create a UserNames.txt file, and ensure you have access to the path to this file. The file contains a listing of users' first and last names. A sample format for this file is shown here:

```
Chuck,Adams
Alice,Jones
Bob,Dentworth
```

3. On the first line of your script, create a variable called *$aryUsers* to hold the array of text that is returned by using the *Get-Content* cmdlet to read a text file that contains various user first and last names. Make sure you edit the string that gets supplied to the *-path* argument of the *Get-Content* cmdlet as required for your computer. This line of code is shown here:

```
$aryUsers = Get-Content -path "c:\ch9\UserNames.txt"
```

4. On the next line of your script, declare a variable called *$password* that will contain the password to use for all your users. For this example, the password is Password01. This line of code is shown here:

```
$password = "Password01"
```

5. On the next line of your script, declare a variable called *$strOU* to hold the OU to place the newly created users. For this example, place the users in the MyTestOU OU, which was created in Chapter 15, "Working with Active Directory." This line of code is shown here:

```
$strOU = "myTestOU"
```

6. On the next line, declare a variable called *$strDomain*. This variable will be used to hold the domain name of the organization. This will become part of the user's email address. For this example, use nwtraders.msft, as shown here:

```
$strDomain = "nwtraders.msft"
```

7. Now declare a variable called *$strDatabase*. This variable will hold the name of the database where the users' mailboxes will reside. On this system, the database is called Mailbox Database. This line of code is shown here:

```
$strDatabase = "Mailbox Database"
```

8. Use the *ConvertTo-SecureString* cmdlet to convert the string contained in the variable *$password* into a secure string that can be used for the *-password* argument of the *New-Mailbox* cmdlet. To convert a string to a secure string, you need to specify the *-asplaintext* argument for the string contained in the *$password* variable, and use the *-force* argument to force the conversion. Reuse the *$password* variable to hold the newly created secure string. This line of code is shown here:

```
$password = ConvertTo-SecureString $password -asplaintext -force
```

9. Use the *foreach* statement to walk through the array of text that was created by using the *Get-Content* cmdlet to read the text file. Use the variable *$i* as an individual counter. The variable that holds the array of text from the *Get-Content* cmdlet is *$aryUsers*. This line of code is shown here:

```
foreach ($i in $aryUsers)
```

10. Open and close the code block by using the opening and closing curly brackets, as shown here. You will need space for at least 9 or 10 lines of code, but that can always be added later.

```
{

}
```

11. On the first line inside your code block, use the variable $newAry to hold a new array you will create out of one line of text from the $aryUsers variable by using the *Split* method. When you call the *Split* method, supply a comma to it because the default value of the *Split* method is a blank space. The variable $i holds the current line of text from the $aryUsers variable. This line of code is shown here:

```
$newAry = $i.split(',')
```

12. The first name is held in the first column in your text file. After this line of text is turned into an array, the first column is addressed as element 0. To retrieve it, you use the name of the new array and enclose the element number in square brackets. Hold the first name in the variable *$strFname*, as shown here:

```
$strFname = $newAry[0]
```

13. The last name is in the second column of the text file and is addressed as element 1 in the new array contained in the *$newAry* variable. Retrieve the value stored in *$newAry[1]* and store it in the variable *$strLname*, as shown here:

```
$strLname = $newAry[1]
```

14. Now you need to use the *New-Mailbox* cmdlet. Supply the values for each of the parameters you have hard-coded in the script. Use the first and last name values stored in the text file to create the user name. The goal is to not have any of the arguments of the *New-Mailbox* cmdlet be hard coded. This will greatly facilitate changing the script to run in different domains and OUs, and with additional parameters.

15. On a new line, call the *New-Mailbox* cmdlet. For the *-alias* argument, create the user's alias by concatenating the first name contained in the *$strFname* variable with the last name contained in the *$strLname* variable. The database that will hold the user's mailbox is the one supplied in the *$strDatabase* variable. Because the command will stretch for several lines, use the line-continuation command (the grave accent character [`]) at the end of the line. This line of code is shown here:

```
New-Mailbox -alias $strFname$strLname -Database $strDatabase `
```

16. The next line of your *New-Mailbox* command creates the user name attribute. To create it, concatenate the first name and last name. The OU name is stored in the *$strOU* variable. Continue the command to the next line. This line of code is shown here:

```
-Name $strFname$strLname -OrganizationalUnit $strOU `
```

17. The next line is easy. The value for the *-firstname* argument is stored in *$strFname*, and the value for the *-lastname* argument is stored in the *$strLname* variable. Use line continuation to continue the command to the next line. This code is shown here:

```
-FirstName $strFname -LastName $strLname `
```

18. The display name for these users will be the first name and the last name concatenated. To concatenate them, use the first name stored in *$strFname* and the last name stored in *$strLname*. Continue the command to the next line, as shown here:

```
-DisplayName $strFname$strLname `
```

19. The *userprincipalname* value is composed of the first name concatenated with the last name, followed by the @ symbol and then the domain name stored in the *$strDomain* variable. It looks like an email address, but it is not the same thing. The code to create this is shown here:

```
-UserPrincipalName $strFname$strLname"@"$strDomain `
```

20. The value for the *-password* argument is stored in the *$password* variable. This is the last parameter you need to supply for this command.

```
-password $password
```

21. Save your script as *<yourname>*CreateUsersFromTxt.ps1. Run your script.

This concludes this step-by-step exercise.

In the next exercise, you will examine the use of Windows PowerShell to configure message tracking on an Exchange 2010 server.

## Configuring message tracking

1. Open Windows PowerShell ISE or another Windows PowerShell script editor.

2. Declare a variable called *$dteMaxAge* and use the *[timespan]* accelerator to convert a string type into a *timespan* data type. Set the time span to be equal to 30 days, 0 hours, 0 minutes, and 0 seconds. The line of code that does this is shown here:

```
$dteMaxAge = [timespan]"30.00:00:00"
```

3. On the next line, create a variable called *$intSize* and use it to hold the value *50MB*. The *Set-MailboxServer* cmdlet expects a value with both the number and suffix to indicate whether the number is in megabytes or kilobytes or some other unit. To do this, use the following code:

```
$intSize = 50MB
```

**4.** On the next line, use the variable *$strLogPath* to hold the string representing the path for storing the message-tracking logs. This needs to be a path that is local to the actual Exchange server. To do this, you use the following code:

```
$strLogPath = "c:\x2kLogs"
```

**5.** Use the variable *$aryServer* to hold a collection of Exchange mailbox servers obtained by using the *Get-MailboxServer* cmdlet. This line of code is shown here:

```
$aryServer = Get-MailboxServer
```

**6.** Use the *foreach* statement to walk through the collection of Exchange servers held in the *$aryServer* variable. Use the variable *$strServer* as the counter variable while you go through the array. This line of code is shown here:

```
foreach ($strServer in $aryServer)
```

**7.** Open and close the code block by typing an opening curly bracket and a closing curly bracket, as shown here:

```
{
}
```

**8.** Use the variable *$strServer* to hold the *Identity* property that is returned by querying the *Identity* property from the object contained in the *$strServer* variable. This line of code is shown here:

```
$strServer = $strServer.identity
```

**9.** On the next line, use the *Set-MailboxServer* cmdlet and supply the value for the *-identity* argument with the string contained in the *$strServer* variable. Use the grave accent character (`) to continue the command to the next line. The code that does this is shown here:

```
Set-MailboxServer -identity $strServer`
```

**10.** On the next line, use the *MessageTrackingLogEnabled* argument to turn on message tracking. To do this, use the value *$true* for the *MessageTrackingLogEnabled* argument. The line of code that does this is shown following. Make sure you include the grave accent character at the end of the line to continue the command to the next line.

```
-MessageTrackingLogEnabled $true`
```

**11.** On the next line, use the *MessageTrackingLogMaxAge* argument to set the maximum age of the message-tracking logs. Use the *timespan* data type to supply the value to the *MessageTrackingLogMaxAge* argument. To do this, use the value stored in the *$dteMaxAge* variable. This line of code is shown following. At the end of the line, use the grave accent character to continue the code to the next line.

```
-MessageTrackingLogMaxAge $dteMaxAge`
```

12. Now you need to configure the size of the logging directory. To do this, use the *MessageTrackingLogMaxDirectorySize* argument of the *Set-MailboxServer* cmdlet. When you specify a value for the directory size, you can tell it you want *MB* for megabytes, *GB* for gigabytes, *KB* for kilobytes, and even *B* for bytes and *TB* for terabytes. To make it easy to change later, you store the max directory size value in a variable called *$intSize*. The code that sets this argument is shown here:

```
-MessageTrackingLogMaxDirectorySize $intSize
```

13. The last parameter you need to configure for message tracking is the path for log storage. This needs to be a local path on the Exchange server. You use the following line of code to configure the *-MessageTrackingLogPath* argument:

```
-MessageTrackingLogPath $strLogPath
```

14. Save your script as *<yourname>*EnableMessageTracking.ps1, and run it.

This concludes the exercise.

# Chapter 20 quick reference

| To | Do this |
|---|---|
| Create a new user in both Windows and Exchange | Use the *New-Mailbox* cmdlet. |
| Find mailboxes that do not have quota limits applied to them | Use the *Get-Mailbox* cmdlet. |
| Disable a mailbox | Use the *Disable-Mailbox* cmdlet. |
| Enable a mailbox for an existing user | Use the *Enable-Mailbox* cmdlet. |
| Produce information about the Exchange mailbox database | Use the *Get-MailboxDatabase* cmdlet. |
| Produce a listing of all Exchange 2010–specific cmdlets | Use the *Get-ExCommand* cmdlet. |
| Produce a listing of the logging level of all Exchange event logs | Use the *Get-EventLogLevel* cmdlet. |

# Windows PowerShell Core Cmdlets

There are 208 core Microsoft Windows PowerShell 3.0 cmdlets that are contained in two modules. The two modules are the Microsoft.PowerShell.Management module and the Microsoft.PowerShell.Utility module. These cmdlets and their descriptions appear in Table A.

**TABLE A** Windows PowerShell 3.0 cmdlets

| Name | Description |
| --- | --- |
| Add-Computer | Adds the local computer to a domain or workgroup. |
| Add-Content | Appends content, such as words or data, to a file. |
| Add-Member | Adds custom properties and methods to an instance of a Windows PowerShell object. |
| Add-Printer | Adds a printer to the specified computer. |
| Add-PrinterDriver | Installs a printer driver on the specified computer. |
| Add-PrinterPort | Installs a printer port on the specified computer. |
| Add-Type | Adds a Microsoft .NET Framework type (a class) to a Windows PowerShell session. |
| Checkpoint-Computer | Creates a system restore point on the local computer. |
| Clear-Content | Deletes the contents of a file, but does not delete the file. |
| Clear-EventLog | Deletes all entries from specified event logs on the local or remote computers. |
| Clear-Item | Deletes the contents of an item, but does not delete the item. |
| Clear-ItemProperty | Deletes the value of a property but does not delete the property. |
| Clear-Variable | Deletes the value of a variable. |
| Compare-Object | Compares two sets of objects. |
| Complete-Transaction | Commits the active transaction. |
| Connect-WSMan | Connects to the WinRM service on a remote computer. |
| ConvertFrom-Csv | Converts object properties in comma-separated value (CSV) format into CSV versions of the original objects. |
| ConvertFrom-Json | Converts a JSON-formatted string to a custom object. |
| ConvertFrom-StringData | Converts a string containing one or more key/value pairs to a hash table. |
| Convert-Path | Converts a path from a Windows PowerShell path to a Windows PowerShell provider path. |

| Name | Description |
|------|-------------|
| ConvertTo-Csv | Converts objects into a series of variable-length CSV strings. |
| ConvertTo-Html | Converts .NET Framework objects into HTML that can be displayed in a web browser. |
| ConvertTo-Json | Converts an object to a JSON-formatted string. |
| ConvertTo-Xml | Creates an XML-based representation of an object. |
| Copy-Item | Copies an item from one location to another within a namespace. |
| Copy-ItemProperty | Copies an item property and value from a specified item to another item. |
| Debug-Process | Debugs one or more processes running on the local computer. |
| Disable-ComputerRestore | Disables the System Restore feature on the specified file system drive. |
| Disable-PSBreakpoint | Disables the breakpoints in the current console. |
| Disable-WSManCredSSP | Disables Credential Security Support Provider (CredSSP) authentication on a client computer. |
| Disconnect-WSMan | Disconnects the client from the WinRM service on a remote computer. |
| Enable-ComputerRestore | Enables the System Restore feature on the specified file system drive. |
| Enable-PSBreakpoint | Enables the breakpoints in the current console. |
| Enable-WSManCredSSP | Enables CredSSP authentication on a client or on a server computer. |
| Export-Alias | Exports information about currently defined aliases to a file. |
| Export-Clixml | Creates an XML-based representation of an object or objects and stores it in a file. |
| Export-Csv | Converts objects into a series of CSV strings and saves the strings in a CSV file. |
| Export-FormatData | Saves formatting data from the current session in a formatting file. |
| Export-PSSession | Imports commands from another session and saves them in a Windows PowerShell module. |
| Format-Custom | Uses a customized view to format the output. |
| Format-List | Formats the output as a list of properties in which each property appears on a new line. |
| Format-Table | Formats the output as a table. |
| Format-Wide | Formats objects as a wide table that displays only one property of each object. |
| Get-Alias | Gets the aliases for the current session. |
| Get-ChildItem | Gets the files and folders in a file system drive. |
| Get-ComputerRestorePoint | Gets the restore points on the local computer. |
| Get-Content | Gets the contents of a file. |
| Get-ControlPanelItem | Gets control panel items. |
| Get-Culture | Gets the current culture set in the operating system. |
| Get-Date | Gets the current date and time. |
| Get-Event | Gets the events in the event queue. |

| Name | Description |
|---|---|
| Get-EventLog | Gets the events in an event log, or a list of the event logs, on the local or remote computers. |
| Get-EventSubscriber | Gets the event subscribers in the current session. |
| Get-FormatData | Gets the formatting data in the current session. |
| Get-Host | Gets an object that represents the current host program. |
| Get-HotFix | Gets the hotfixes that have been applied to the local and remote computers. |
| Get-Item | Gets the item at the specified location. |
| Get-ItemProperty | Gets the properties of a specified item. |
| Get-Location | Gets information about the current working location or a location stack. |
| Get-Member | Gets the properties and methods of objects. |
| Get-PrintConfiguration | Gets the configuration information of a printer. |
| Get-Printer | Retrieves a list of printers installed on a computer. |
| Get-PrinterDriver | Retrieves the list of printer drivers installed on the specified computer. |
| Get-PrinterPort | Retrieves a list of printer ports installed on the specified computer. |
| Get-PrinterProperty | Retrieves printer properties for the specified printer. |
| Get-PrintJob | Retrieves a list of print jobs in the specified printer. |
| Get-Process | Gets the processes that are running on the local computer or a remote computer. |
| Get-PSBreakpoint | Gets the breakpoints that are set in the current session. |
| Get-PSCallStack | Displays the current call stack. |
| Get-PSDrive | Gets drives in the current session. |
| Get-PSProvider | Gets information about the specified Windows PowerShell provider. |
| Get-Random | Gets a random number, or selects objects randomly from a collection. |
| Get-Service | Gets the services on a local or remote computer. |
| Get-TraceSource | Gets the Windows PowerShell components that are instrumented for tracing. |
| Get-Transaction | Gets the current (active) transaction. |
| Get-TypeData | Gets the extended type data in the current session. |
| Get-UICulture | Gets the current user interface (UI) culture settings in the operating system. |
| Get-Unique | Returns unique items from a sorted list. |
| Get-Variable | Gets the variables in the current console. |
| Get-WmiObject | Gets instances of Windows Management Instrumentation (WMI) classes or information about the available classes. |
| Get-WSManCredSSP | Gets the CredSSP-related configuration for the client. |
| Get-WSManInstance | Displays management information for a resource instance specified by a resource URI. |
| Group-Object | Groups objects that contain the same value for specified properties. |

| Name | Description |
|------|-------------|
| Import-Alias | Imports an alias list from a file. |
| Import-Clixml | Imports a CLIXML file and creates corresponding objects within Windows PowerShell. |
| Import-Csv | Creates table-like custom objects from the items in a CSV file. |
| Import-LocalizedData | Imports language-specific data into scripts and functions based on the UI culture that is selected for the operating system. |
| Import-PSSession | Imports commands from another session into the current session. |
| Invoke-AsWorkflow | Runs a command or expression as a Windows PowerShell workflow. |
| Invoke-Expression | Runs commands or expressions on the local computer. |
| Invoke-Item | Performs the default action on the specified item. |
| Invoke-RestMethod | Sends an HTTP or HTTPS request to a REST-compliant web service. |
| Invoke-WebRequest | Sends an HTTP or HTTPS request to a web service. |
| Invoke-WmiMethod | Calls WMI methods. |
| Invoke-WSManAction | Invokes an action on the object that is specified by the resource URI and by the selectors. |
| Join-Path | Combines a path and a child path into a single path. The provider supplies the path delimiters. |
| Limit-EventLog | Sets the event log properties that limit the size of the event log and the age of its entries. |
| Measure-Command | Measures the time it takes to run script blocks and cmdlets. |
| Measure-Object | Calculates the numeric properties of objects, and the characters, words, and lines in string objects, such as files of text. |
| Move-Item | Moves an item from one location to another. |
| Move-ItemProperty | Moves a property from one location to another. |
| New-Alias | Creates a new alias. |
| New-Event | Creates a new event. |
| New-EventLog | Creates a new event log and a new event source on a local or remote computer. |
| New-Item | Creates a new item. |
| New-ItemProperty | Creates a new property for an item and sets its value. For example, you can use *New-ItemProperty* to create and change registry values and data, which are properties of a registry key. |
| New-Object | Creates an instance of a.NET Framework or COM object. |
| New-PSDrive | Creates temporary and persistent mapped network drives. |
| New-Service | Creates a new Windows service. |
| New-TimeSpan | Creates a *TimeSpan* object. |
| New-Variable | Creates a new variable. |
| New-WebServiceProxy | Creates a web service proxy object that lets you use and manage the web service in Windows PowerShell. |

| Name | Description |
|------|-------------|
| *New-WSManInstance* | Creates a new instance of a management resource. |
| *New-WSManSessionOption* | Creates a WS-Management session option hash table to use as input parameters to the following WS-Management cmdlets: *Get-WSManInstance*, *Set-WSManInstance*, *Invoke-WSManAction*, and *Connect-WSMan*. |
| *Out-File* | Sends output to a file. |
| *Out-GridView* | Sends output to an interactive table in a separate window. |
| *Out-Printer* | Sends output to a printer. |
| *Out-String* | Sends objects to the host as a series of strings. |
| *Pop-Location* | Changes the current location to the location most recently pushed onto the stack. You can pop the location from the default stack or from a stack that you create by using the *Push-Location* cmdlet. |
| *Push-Location* | Adds the current location to the top of a location stack. |
| *Read-Host* | Reads a line of input from the console. |
| *Register-EngineEvent* | Subscribes to events that are generated by the Windows PowerShell engine and by the *New-Event* cmdlet. |
| *Register-ObjectEvent* | Subscribes to events that are generated by a.NET Framework object. |
| *Register-WmiEvent* | Subscribes to a WMI event. |
| *Remove-Computer* | Removes the local computer from its domain. |
| *Remove-Event* | Deletes events from the event queue. |
| *Remove-EventLog* | Deletes an event log or unregisters an event source. |
| *Remove-Item* | Deletes the specified items. |
| *Remove-ItemProperty* | Deletes the property and its value from an item. |
| *Remove-Printer* | Removes a printer from the specified computer. |
| *Remove-PrinterDriver* | Deletes the printer driver from the specified computer. |
| *Remove-PrinterPort* | Removes the specified printer port from the specified computer. |
| *Remove-PrintJob* | Removes a print job on the specified printer. |
| *Remove-PSBreakpoint* | Deletes breakpoints from the current console. |
| *Remove-PSDrive* | Deletes temporary Windows PowerShell drives and disconnects mapped network drives. |
| *Remove-TypeData* | Deletes extended types from the current session |
| *Remove-Variable* | Deletes a variable and its value. |
| *Remove-WmiObject* | Deletes an instance of an existing WMI class. |
| *Remove-WSManInstance* | Deletes a management resource instance. |
| *Rename-Computer* | Renames a computer. |
| *Rename-Item* | Renames an item in a Windows PowerShell provider namespace. |
| *Rename-ItemProperty* | Renames a property of an item. |
| *Rename-Printer* | Renames the specified printer. |

| Name | Description |
| --- | --- |
| Reset-ComputerMachinePassword | Resets the machine account password for the computer. |
| Resolve-Path | Resolves the wildcard characters in a path and displays the path contents. |
| Restart-Computer | Restarts (reboots) the operating system on local and remote computers. |
| Restart-PrintJob | Restarts a print job on the specified printer. |
| Restart-Service | Stops and then starts one or more services. |
| Restore-Computer | Starts a system restore on the local computer. |
| Resume-PrintJob | Resumes a suspended print job. |
| Resume-Service | Resumes one or more suspended (paused) services. |
| Select-Object | Selects objects or object properties. |
| Select-String | Finds text in strings and files. |
| Select-Xml | Finds text in an XML string or document. |
| Send-MailMessage | Sends an email message. |
| Set-Alias | Creates or changes an alias (alternate name) for a cmdlet or other command element in the current Windows PowerShell session. |
| Set-Content | Replaces the contents of a file with contents that you specify. |
| Set-Date | Changes the system time on the computer to a time that you specify. |
| Set-Item | Changes the value of an item to the value specified in the command. |
| Set-ItemProperty | Creates or changes the value of a property of an item. |
| Set-Location | Sets the current working location to a specified location. |
| Set-PrintConfiguration | Sets the configuration information for the specified printer. |
| Set-Printer | Updates the configuration of an existing printer. |
| Set-PrinterProperty | Modifies the printer properties for the specified printer. |
| Set-PSBreakpoint | Sets a breakpoint on a line, command, or variable. |
| Set-Service | Starts, stops, and suspends a service, and changes its properties. |
| Set-TraceSource | Configures, starts, and stops a trace of Windows PowerShell components. |
| Set-Variable | Sets the value of a variable. It creates the variable if one with the requested name does not exist. |
| Set-WmiInstance | Creates or updates an instance of an existing WMI class. |
| Set-WSManInstance | Modifies the management information that is related to a resource. |
| Set-WSManQuickConfig | Configures the local computer for remote management. |
| Show-Command | Creates Windows PowerShell commands in a graphical command window. |
| Show-ControlPanelItem | Opens control panel items. |
| Show-EventLog | Displays the event logs of the local or a remote computer in the Event Viewer utility. |
| Sort-Object | Sorts objects by property values. |
| Split-Path | Returns the specified part of a path. |

| Name | Description |
|---|---|
| Start-Process | Starts one or more processes on the local computer. |
| Start-Service | Starts one or more stopped services. |
| Start-Sleep | Suspends the activity in a script or session for the specified period of time. |
| Start-Transaction | Starts a transaction. |
| Stop-Computer | Stops (shuts down) local and remote computers. |
| Stop-Process | Stops one or more running processes. |
| Stop-Service | Stops one or more running services. |
| Suspend-PrintJob | Suspends a print job on the specified printer. |
| Suspend-Service | Suspends (pauses) one or more running services. |
| Tee-Object | Saves command output in a file or variable and also sends it down the pipeline. |
| Test-ComputerSecureChannel | Tests and repairs the secure channel between the local computer and its domain. |
| Test-Connection | Sends ICMP echo request packets (pings) to one or more computers. |
| Test-Path | Determines whether all elements of a file or directory path exist. |
| Test-WSMan | Tests whether the WinRM service is running on a local or remote computer. |
| Trace-Command | Configures and starts a trace of the specified expression or command. |
| Unblock-File | Unblocks files that were downloaded from the Internet. |
| Undo-Transaction | Rolls back the active transaction. |
| Unregister-Event | Cancels an event subscription. |
| Update-FormatData | Updates the formatting data in the current session. |
| Update-List | Adds items to and removes items from a property value that contains a collection of objects. |
| Update-TypeData | Updates the extended type data in the session. |
| Use-Transaction | Adds the script block to the active transaction. |
| Wait-Event | Waits until a particular event is raised before continuing to run. |
| Wait-Process | Waits for the processes to be stopped before accepting more input. |
| Write-Debug | Writes a debug message to the console. |
| Write-Error | Writes an object to the error stream. |
| Write-EventLog | Writes an event to an event log. |
| Write-Host | Writes customized output to a host. |
| Write-Output | Sends the specified objects to the next command in the pipeline. If the command is the last command in the pipeline, the objects are displayed in the console. |
| Write-Progress | Displays a progress bar within a Windows PowerShell command window. |
| Write-Verbose | Writes text to the verbose message stream. |
| Write-Warning | Writes a warning message. |

# Windows PowerShell Module Coverage

Microsoft Windows PowerShell 3.0 represents a major advance over Windows PowerShell 2.0. Especially on Windows 8 and Windows Server 2012, the amount of cmdlet coverage vastly increases. But many of the cmdlets are specialized, and the actual number of cmdlets varies depending on what roles and features the configuration enables. In addition, to get a fuller picture of coverage, it is necessary to include functions—because the Common Information Model (CIM) provider wraps Windows Management Instrumentation (WMI) classes and exposes the result as a function, not a cmdlet—as well as cmdlets. On a default install of Windows Server 2012 with only the File and Storage Services role configured, there are 1,162 cmdlets and features. To get an idea of the cmdlet coverage, load all of the modules, and then use the *Get-Command* cmdlet to examine the cmdlets. The result is a list that details what modules exist and the number of cmdlets and functions exposed. Table B shows this list. The command used to find this information appears here:

```
PS C:\> Get-Module -ListAvailable | Import-Module
PS C:\> Get-Command -CommandType cmdlet, function | Group-Object module -NoElement |
Sort-Object count -Descending | Format-Table -Property count, name -AutoSize -Wrap
```

**TABLE B** Count of cmdlets and functions from modules on Windows Server 2012

| Count | Name |
|-------|------|
| 135 | ActiveDirectory |
| 92 | Microsoft.PowerShell.Utility |
| 84 | NetSecurity |
| 83 | Storage |
| 82 | Microsoft.PowerShell.Management |
| 73 | RemoteDesktop |
| 64 | NetAdapter |
| 42 | NFS |
| 41 | MsDtc |
| 34 | NetworkTransition |
| 32 | BranchCache |

| Count | Name |
| --- | --- |
| 31 | NetTCPIP |
| 28 | SmbShare |
| 23 | IscsiTarget |
| 22 | ServerManagerTasks |
| 22 | Dism |
| 20 | PrintManagement |
| 19 | ScheduledTasks |
| 18 | International |
| 17 | PKI |
| 17 | DnsClient |
| 16 | PSScheduledJob |
| 14 | UserAccessLogging |
| 13 | Microsoft.WSMan.Management |
| 13 | iSCSI |
| 13 | NetLbfo |
| 12 | CimCmdlets |
| 12 | Wdac |
| 11 | DirectAccessClientComponents |
| 10 | PSDiagnostics |
| 10 | Microsoft.PowerShell.Security |
| 9 | TrustedPlatformModule |
| 8 | BitsTransfer |
| 7 | NetSwitchTeam |
| 6 | Appx |
| 6 | Kds |
| 6 | VpnClient |
| 5 | AppLocker |
| 5 | Microsoft.PowerShell.Diagnostics |
| 5 | ServerManager |
| 5 | SecureBoot |
| 4 | MMAgent |
| 4 | NetworkConnectivityStatus |
| 4 | NetQos |
| 4 | BestPractices |

| Count | Name |
|---|---|
| 3 | ISE |
| 3 | WindowsDeveloperLicense |
| 3 | WindowsErrorReporting |
| 2 | PSWorkflow |
| 2 | SmbWitness |
| 2 | NetConnection |
| 2 | TroubleshootingPack |
| 2 | Whea |
| 2 | ServerCore |
| 2 | Microsoft.PowerShell.Host |

# Windows PowerShell Cmdlet Naming

The cmdlets installed with Microsoft Windows PowerShell all follow a standard naming convention. Windows PowerShell cmdlets use a verb-noun pair. For example, there are four commands that start with the verb *Add*: *Add-Content, Add-History, Add-Member,* and *Add-PSSnapin.* When creating cmdlets, you should endeavor to follow the same kind of naming convention. The recognition of this naming convention is helpful in learning the cmdlets that come with Windows PowerShell. Table C shows the number of Windows PowerShell cmdlets associated with each of the verbs. In addition, it shows sample Windows PowerShell cmdlet names.

**TABLE C** Cmdlet naming

| Count | Name | Sample use |
|-------|------|------------|
| 88 | Get | Get-Acl, Get-Alias, Get-AppLockerFileInformation |
| 40 | Set | Set-Acl, Set-Alias, Set-AppLockerPolicy |
| 34 | New | New-Alias, New-AppLockerPolicy, New-CertificateNotificationTask |
| 25 | Remove | Remove-AppxPackage, Remove-AppxProvisionedPackage |
| 14 | Add | Add-AppxPackage, Add-AppxProvisionedPackage, Add-BitsFile |
| 10 | Invoke | Invoke-CimMethod, Invoke-Command, Invoke-Expression |
| 10 | Import | Import-Alias, Import-Certificate, Import-Clixml |
| 10 | Export | Export-Alias, Export-Certificate, Export-Clixml |
| 10 | Enable | Enable-ComputerRestore, Enable-JobTrigger, Enable-PSBreakpoint |
| 10 | Disable | Disable-ComputerRestore, Disable-JobTrigger, Disable-PSBreakpoint |
| 9 | Test | Test-AppLockerPolicy, Test-Certificate, Test-ComputerSecureChannel |
| 9 | Clear | Clear-Content, Clear-EventLog, Clear-History |
| 8 | Start | Start-BitsTransfer, Start-DtcDiagnosticResourceManager, Start-Job |
| 8 | Write | Write-Debug, Write-Error, Write-EventLog |
| 7 | Out | Out-Default, Out-File, Out-GridView |
| 6 | Register | Register-CimIndicationEvent, Register-EngineEvent |

| Count | Name | Sample use |
|---|---|---|
| 6 | Stop | Stop-Computer, Stop-DtcDiagnosticResourceManager, Stop-Job |
| 6 | ConvertTo | ConvertTo-Csv, ConvertTo-Html, ConvertTo-Json |
| 5 | Format | Format-Custom, Format-List, Format-SecureBootUEFI |
| 4 | ConvertFrom | ConvertFrom-Csv, ConvertFrom-Json, ConvertFrom-SecureString |
| 4 | Show | Show-Command, Show-ControlPanelItem, Show-EventLog |
| 4 | Update | Update-FormatData, Update-Help, Update-List |
| 4 | Unregister | Unregister-Event, Unregister-PSSessionConfiguration |
| 3 | Select | Select-Object, Select-String, Select-Xml |
| 3 | Resume | Resume-BitsTransfer, Resume-Job, Resume-Service |
| 3 | Rename | Rename-Computer, Rename-Item, Rename-ItemProperty |
| 3 | Wait | Wait-Event, Wait-Job, Wait-Process |
| 3 | Complete | Complete-BitsTransfer, Complete-DtcDiagnosticTransaction |
| 3 | Receive | Receive-DtcDiagnosticTransaction, Receive-Job, Receive-PSSession |
| 3 | Suspend | Suspend-BitsTransfer, Suspend-Job, Suspend-Service |
| 2 | Copy | Copy-Item, Copy-ItemProperty |
| 2 | Send | Send-DtcDiagnosticTransaction, Send-MailMessage |
| 2 | Save | Save-Help, Save-WindowsImage |
| 2 | Restart | Restart-Computer, Restart-Service |
| 2 | Resolve | Resolve-DnsName, Resolve-Path |
| 2 | Disconnect | Disconnect-PSSession, Disconnect-WSMan |
| 2 | Use | Use-Transaction, Use-WindowsUnattend |
| 2 | Connect | Connect-PSSession, Connect-WSMan |
| 2 | Move | Move-Item, Move-ItemProperty |
| 2 | Measure | Measure-Command, Measure-Object |
| 2 | Join | Join-DtcDiagnosticResourceManager, Join-Path |
| 2 | Unblock | Unblock-File, Unblock-Tpm |
| 2 | Undo | Undo-DtcDiagnosticTransaction, Undo-Transaction |
| 1 | Compare | Compare-Object |
| 1 | Tee | Tee-Object |
| 1 | Split | Split-Path |
| 1 | Checkpoint | Checkpoint-Computer |
| 1 | Sort | Sort-Object |
| 1 | Trace | Trace-Command |
| 1 | Switch | Switch-Certificate |

| Count | Name | Sample use |
|-------|------|------------|
| 1 | *Dismount* | *Dismount-WindowsImage* |
| 1 | *Repair* | *Repair-WindowsImage* |
| 1 | *Reset* | *Reset-ComputerMachinePassword* |
| 1 | *Confirm* | *Confirm-SecureBootUEFI* |
| 1 | *Read* | *Read-Host* |
| 1 | *Push* | *Push-Location* |
| 1 | *Where* | *Where-Object* |
| 1 | *Mount* | *Mount-WindowsImage* |
| 1 | *Limit* | *Limit-EventLog* |
| 1 | *Initialize* | *Initialize-Tpm* |
| 1 | *Convert* | *Convert-Path* |
| 1 | *Group* | *Group-Object* |
| 1 | *ForEach* | *ForEach-Object* |
| 1 | *Exit* | *Exit-PSSession* |
| 1 | *Enter* | *Enter-PSSession* |
| 1 | *Debug* | *Debug-Process* |
| 1 | *Restore* | *Restore-Computer* |
| 1 | *Pop* | *Pop-Location* |

# Windows PowerShell FAQ

This appendix answers many questions that come up when I teach Windows PowerShell classes and when making Windows PowerShell presentations at various events.

**Q.** How many cmdlets are available on a default Windows PowerShell 3.0 installation?

**A.** 403

**Q.** How do you find out how many cmdlets are available on a default Windows PowerShell installation?

**A.** Use the following:

```
Get-Module -ListAvailable | Import-Module ; gcm -co cmdlet | measure
```

**Q.** What is the difference between a read-only variable and a constant?

**A.** A read-only variable is one whose content is read-only. You can, however, modify it by using the *Set-Variable* cmdlet with the *-force* parameter. You can also delete it by using *Remove-Variable -force*. A constant variable however, cannot be deleted, nor can it be modified, even when using *-force*.

**Q.** What are the three most important cmdlets?

**A.** The three most important cmdlets are *Get-Command*, *Get-Help*, and *Get-Member*.

**Q.** Which cmdlets can I use to work with event logs?

**A.** To work with event logs, use the *Get-EventLog* cmdlet or the *Get-WinEvent* cmdlet.

**Q.** How did you find that cmdlet?

**A.** Use the following:

```
Get-Command -Noun *event*
```

**Q.** What .NET Framework class is leveraged by the *Get-EventLog* cmdlet?

**A.** The following class is used by the *Get-EventLog* cmdlet:

```
System.Diagnostics.EventLogEntry
```

**Q.** How would I find the above information?

**A.** Use the following:

```
get-eventlog application | get-member
```

**Q.** What is the most powerful command in PowerShell?

**A.** *Switch* is the most powerful command.

**Q.** What is `t used for?

**A.** `t is used for a tab.

**Q.** How would I use the `t in a script to produce a tab?

**A.** You can do so as follows:

```
"`thi"
```

**Q.** That syntax above is ugly. What happens if I put a space in it, like this: "`t hi"?

**A.** If you include a space in the line, then you will tab over one tab stop and one additional space.

**Q.** Is the `t command case sensitive?

**A.** Yes. It is one of the few things that is case sensitive in Windows PowerShell. If you use the `t as shown here, then you will produce *Thi* on the line:

```
"`Thi"
```

**Q.** How do I run a script with a space in the path?

**A.** Use the following:

```
PS > c:\my`folder\myscript.ps1
PS> &("c:\my  folder\myscript.ps1")
```

**Q.** What is the easiest way to create an array?

**A.** Use the following:

```
$array = "1","2","3","4"
$array = 1..4
```

**Q.** How do I display a calculated value (for example, megabytes instead of bytes) from a WMI query when pipelining data into a *Format-Table* cmdlet?

**A.** Create a hash table in the position where you wish to display the data and perform the calculation inside curly brackets. Assign the results to the *expression* parameter. This is shown here:

```
gwmi win32_logicaldisk -Filter "drivetype=3" | ft -Property name, @{ Label="freespace";
expression={$_.freespace/1MB}}
```

**Q.** Which parameter of the *Get-WMIObject* cmdlet takes the place of a WQL *Where* clause?

**A.** The *-filter* parameter takes its place, as shown here:

```
Get-WMIObject win32_logicaldisk -filter "drivetype = 3"
```

**Q.** Which command, when typed at the beginning of a script, will cause Windows PowerShell to ignore errors and continue executing the code?

**A.** The following command does this:

```
$erroractionpreference=SilentlyContinue
```

**Q.** How can I display only the current year?

**A.** Use the following:

```
get-date -Format yyyy
get-date -f yyyy
(Get-Date).year
```

**Q.** What is Windows PowerShell, in 30 words or less?

**A.** Windows PowerShell is the next-generation CMD prompt and scripting language from Microsoft. It can be a replacement for VBScript and for the CMD prompt in most circumstances.

**Q.** How can you be sure that was 30 words or less?

**A.** Use the following code:

```
$a = "Windows PowerShell is the next-generation CMD prompt and scripting language
from Microsoft. It can be a replacement for VBScript and for the CMD prompt in most
circumstances."
Measure-Object -InputObject $a -Word
```

**Q.** What are three ways of querying Active Directory from within Windows PowerShell?

**A.** You can use ADO and perform an LDAP dialect query, or you can use ADO and perform an SQL dialect query. You can also use the *Get-ADOObject* cmdlet from the Active Directory module.

**Q.** How can I print out the amount of free space on a fixed disk in megabytes with two decimal places?

**A.** Use a format specifier, as shown here:

```
"{0:n2}"-f ((gwmi win32_logicaldisk -Filter "drivetype='3'").freespace/1MB)
```

**Q.** I need to replace the *2* with *12* in the following *$array* variable: *$array = "1","2","3","4"*. How can I do this?

**A.** Use the following:

```
$array=[regex]::replace($array,"2","12")
```

**Q.** I have the following *Switch* statement and I want to prevent the line *Write-Host "switched"* from being executed. How can I do this?

```
$a = 3
switch ($a) {
  1 { "one detected" }
  2 { "two detected" }
}
Write-Host "switched"
```

**A.** Add an *exit* statement to the default switch, as shown here:

```
$a = 3
switch ($a) {
1 { "one detected" }
2 { "two detected"}
DEFAULT { exit}
}
Write-Host "switched
```

**Q.** How can I supply alternate credentials for a remote WMI call when using the *Get-WmiObject* cmdlet?

**A.** Use the *-credential* parameter, as shown here:

```
Get-WmiObject Win32_BIOS -ComputerName Server01  -credential (get-credential
` Domain01@User01)
```

or as shown here:

```
$c = Get-Credential
Get-WmiObject Win32_DiskDrive -ComputerName Server01 -credential $c
```

Once you have created the credential object, create a CIM session to the remote system by using *New-CimSession*. You can also use the credential object to create a PS session to the remote system by using *New-PSSession*.

**Q.** How can I generate a random number?

**A.** Use the *Get-Random* cmdlet, or use the *System.Random* .NET Framework class, and call the *next()* method, as shown here:

```
([random]5).next()
```

**Q.** How can I generate a random number between the values of 1 and 10?

**A.** Use the *System.Random* .NET Framework class and call the *next()* method, as shown here:

```
([random]5).next("1","10")
```

You can also use the *Get-Random* cmdlet, as shown here:

```
Get-Random -Maximum 10 -Minimum 1
```

**Q.** Which of the commands support regular expressions?

**A.** *Where-Object* supports regular expressions, as shown here using *-match*:

```
get-process | where-object { $_.ProcessName -match "^p.*" }
```

In addition, the *Switch* statement uses regular expressions, as shown here:

```
switch -regex ("Hi there") { "hi" { "found" } }
```

**Q.** How can I create an audit file of all commands typed during a PowerShell session?

**A.** Use the *Start-Transcript* command, as shown here:

```
Start-transcript
```

**Q.** How can I see how many seconds it takes to retrieve objects from the application log?

**A.** Use the following:

```
(Measure-Command { Get-EventLog application }).totalseconds
```

**Q.** I want to get a list of all the modules installed with Windows PowerShell on my machine. How can I do this?

**A.** Inside a PowerShell console, type the following command:

```
Get-Module -ListAvailable
```

**Q.** I want to create an ASCII text file to hold the results of the *Get-Process* cmdlet. How can this be done?

**A.** You can pipeline the results to the *Out-File* cmdlet and use the *-encoding* parameter to specify ASCII. You can also use redirection, like this:

```
Get-Process >>c:\fso\myprocess.txt
```

**Q.** Someone told me the *Write-Host* cmdlet can use color for output. Can you give me some samples of acceptable syntax?

**A.** The following are some examples:

```
write-host -ForegroundColor 12 "hi"
write-host -ForegroundColor 12 "hi" -BackgroundColor white
write-host -ForegroundColor blue -BackgroundColor white
write-host -ForegroundColor 2 hi
write-host -backgroundcolor 2 hi
write-host -backgroundcolor ("{0:X}" -f 2) hi
for($i=0 ; $i -le 15 ; $i++) { write-host -foregroundcolor $i "hi" }
```

**Q.** How can I tell if a command has completed successfully?

**A.** Query the *$error* automatic variable. If *$error[0]* reports no information, then no errors have occurred. You can also query the *$?* automatic variable. If *$?* Is equal to *true*, then the command completed successfully.

**Q.** How can I split the string shown in the following *$a* variable?

```
$a = "atl-ws-01,atl-ws-02,atl-ws-03,atl-ws-04"
```

**A.** Use the *split* method, as follows:

```
$b = $a.split(",")
```

**Q.** How do I join an array such as the one in the $a variable shown here?

```
$a = "h","e","l","l","o"
```

**A.** Use the *join* static method from the *String* class:

```
$b = [string]::join("", $a)
```

**Q.** I need to build up a path to the Windows\system32 directory. How can I do this?

**A.** Use the following:

```
Join-Path -path (get-item env:\windir).value -ChildPath system32
```

**Q.** How can I print out the value of %systemroot%?

**A.** Use the following:

```
(get-item Env:\systemroot).value
$env:systemroot
```

**Q.** I need to display process output at the PowerShell prompt and write that same output to a text file. How can I do this?

**A.** Use the following:

```
Get-process | Tee-Object -FilePath c:\fso\proc.txt
```

**Q.** I would like to display the ASCII character associated with the ASCII value 56. How can I do this?

**A.** Use the following:

```
[char]56
```

**Q.** I want to create a strongly typed array of system diagnostics processes and store it in a variable called $a. How can I do this?

**A.** Use the following:

```
[diagnostics.process[]]$a=get-process
```

**Q.** I want to display the number 1234 in hexadecimal. How can I do this?

**A.** Use the following:

```
"{0:x}" -f 1234
```

**Q.** I want to display the decimal value of the hexadecimal number 0x4d2. How can I do this?

**A.** Use the following:

```
0x4d2
```

**Q.** I want to find out if a string contains the letter *m*. The string is stored in the variable *$a*, as shown following. How can I do this?

**A.** Use the *contains* operator, as illustrated here:

```
$a="northern hairy-nosed wombat"
[string]$a.contains("m")
$a.contains("m")
[regex]::match($a,"m")
([regex]::match($a,"m")).success
```

**Q.** How can I solicit input from the user?

**A.** Use the *Read-Host* cmdlet as shown here:

```
$in = Read-Host "enter the data"
```

**Q.** Can I use a variable named *$input* to hold input from the *Read-Host* cmdlet?

**A.** *$input* is an automatic variable that is used for script blocks in the middle of a pipeline. As such, it would be a very poor choice. Call the variable *$userInput* or something similar if you wish, but don't call it *$input*.

**Q.** How can I cause the script to generate an error if a variable has not been declared?

**A.** Place *Set-PSDebug -strict* anywhere in the script. Any nondeclared variable will generate an error when accessed. You can also use *Set-StrictMode -version latest*.

**Q.** How can I increase the number of entries stored by the *Get-History* buffer?

**A.** Assign the desired value to the *$MaximumHistoryCount* automatic variable, as shown here:

```
$MaximumHistoryCount = 65
```

**Q.** How can I specify the number 1 as a 16-bit integer array?

**A.** Use the following:

```
$a=[int16[]][int16]1
```

**Q.** I have the string *"this`"is a string"* and I want to replace the quotation mark with nothing—no space, just nothing. Effectively, I want to remove the quotation mark from the string. The backtick(`) is here used to escape the quotation mark. How can I use the *Replace* method to replace the quotation mark with nothing, if the string is held in a variable *$arr*? I want the results to look like this:

```
thisis a string
```

**A.** Use the *Replace* method from the *System.String* .NET Framework class, as shown here:

```
$arr.Replace("`"","")
```

You can also use the ASCII value of the quotation mark, and use the *Replace* method from the *System.String* .NET Framework class, as shown here:

```
$arr.Replace([char]34,"")
```

**Q.** How can I use *Invoke-Expression* to run a script inside PowerShell when the path has spaces in it?

**A.** Escape the spaces with a backtick (grave) character (`) and surround the string containing the path with single quotes, as shown here:

```
Invoke-Expression ('h:\LABS\extras\Run` With` Spaces.ps1')
```

**Q.** How can I create an array of byte values that contain hexadecimal values?

**A.** Use the *[byte]* type constraint, but include the *[]* array character such that the type constraint now looks like *[byte[]]*. To specify a hexadecimal number, use 0x format. The resulting line of code is shown here:

```
[byte[]]$mac = 0x00,0x19,0xD2,0x72,0x0E,0x2A
```

**Q.** I need to count backward. How can I do this?

**A.** Use a *for* statement. In the second position (the condition), ensure that you use greater-than-or-equal-to for the condition. In the third position (the repeat), use the decrement-and-assign character, which is a double minus (--). When you put it all together, it will look like this:

```
for($i=30;$i -ge 20 ; $i --){$i}
```

# Useful WMI Classes

With more than 2,000 WMI classes installed on a modern Microsoft Windows operating system, the question is not what you can use in a script, but what you should script. Some WMI classes return a lot of information, but for all practical purposes this information is basically useless. It makes sense to home in on the WMI classes that produce the most valuable information. This appendix doesn't provide a complete list—rather, it offers a list of WMI classes that I have found myself using again and again over the last few years. Tables E-1 through E-32 list WMI class names, as well as their associated properties, methods, and descriptions. The tables are organized by hardware components, software components, and finally by performance counter classes.

**TABLE E-1** Cooling device classes

| Class | Properties | Methods | Description |
|---|---|---|---|
| Win32_Fan | 22 | 3 | Represents the properties of a fan device in the computer system. |
| Win32_HeatPipe | 20 | 2 | Represents the properties of a heat pipe cooling device. |
| Win32_Refrigeration | 20 | 2 | Represents the properties of a refrigeration device. |
| Win32_TemperatureProbe | 35 | 2 | Represents the properties of a temperature sensor (electronic thermometer). |

**TABLE E-2** Input device classes

| Class | Properties | Methods | Description |
|---|---|---|---|
| Win32_Keyboard | 23 | 2 | Represents a keyboard installed on a Windows system. |
| Win32_PointingDevice | 33 | 2 | Represents an input device used to point to and select regions on the display of a Windows computer system. |

**TABLE E-3** Mass storage classes

| Class | Properties | Methods | Description |
|---|---|---|---|
| Win32_AutochkSetting | 4 | 0 | Represents the settings for the autocheck operation of a disk. |
| Win32_CDROMDrive | 48 | 2 | Represents a CD-ROM drive on a Windows computer system. |
| Win32_DiskDrive | 49 | 2 | Represents a physical disk drive as shown by a computer running the Windows operating system. |
| Win32_FloppyDrive | 30 | 2 | Manages the capabilities of a floppy disk drive. |
| Win32_PhysicalMedia | 23 | 0 | Represents any type of documentation or storage medium. |
| Win32_TapeDrive | 40 | 2 | Represents a tape drive on a Windows computer. |

**TABLE E-4** Motherboard, controller, and port classes

| Class | Properties | Methods | Description |
|---|---|---|---|
| Win32_1394Controller | 23 | 2 | Represents the capabilities and management of a 1394 controller. |
| Win32_1394ControllerDevice | 7 | 0 | Relates the high-speed serial bus (IEEE 1394 FireWire) controller and the Win32_LogonSession instance connected to it. |
| Win32_AllocatedResource | 2 | 0 | Relates a logical device to a system resource. |
| Win32_AssociatedProcessorMemory | 3 | 0 | Relates a processor and its cache memory. |
| Win32_BaseBoard | 29 | 1 | Represents a baseboard (also known as a motherboard or system board). |
| Win32_BIOS | 27 | 0 | Represents the attributes of the computer system's basic input/output services (BIOS) that are installed on the computer. |
| Win32_Bus | 21 | 2 | Represents a physical bus as shown by a Windows operating system. |
| Win32_CacheMemory | 53 | 2 | Represents cache memory (internal and external) on a computer system. |
| Win32_ControllerHasHub | 7 | 0 | Represents the hubs downstream from the universal serial bus (USB) controller. |
| Win32_DeviceBus | 2 | 0 | Relates a system bus and a logical device using the bus. |
| Win32_DeviceMemoryAddress | 11 | 0 | Represents a device memory address on a Windows system. |
| Win32_DeviceSettings | 2 | 0 | Relates a logical device and a setting that can be applied to it. |
| Win32_DMAChannel | 19 | 0 | Represents a direct memory access (DMA) channel on a Windows computer system. |
| Win32_FloppyController | 23 | 2 | Represents the capabilities and management capacity of a floppy disk drive controller. |

| Class | Properties | Methods | Description |
|---|---|---|---|
| Win32_IDEController | 23 | 2 | Represents the capabilities of an Integrated Drive Electronics (IDE) controller device. |
| Win32_IDEControllerDevice | 7 | 0 | Association class that relates an IDE controller and the logical device. |
| Win32_InfraredDevice | 23 | 2 | Represents the capabilities and management of an infrared device. |
| Win32_IRQResource | 15 | 0 | Represents an interrupt request line (IRQ) number on a Windows computer system. |
| Win32_MemoryArray | 39 | 2 | Represents the properties of the computer system memory array and mapped addresses. |
| Win32_MemoryArrayLocation | 2 | 0 | Relates a logical memory array and the physical memory array upon which it exists. |
| Win32_MemoryDevice | 39 | 2 | Represents the properties of a computer system's memory device along with its associated mapped addresses. |
| Win32_MemoryDeviceArray | 2 | 0 | Relates a memory device and the memory array in which it resides. |
| Win32_MemoryDeviceLocation | 2 | 0 | Association class that relates a memory device and the physical memory on which it exists. |
| Win32_MotherboardDevice | 22 | 2 | Represents a device that contains the central components of the Windows computer system. |
| Win32_OnBoardDevice | 20 | 0 | Represents common adapter devices built into the motherboard (system board). |
| Win32_ParallelPort | 26 | 2 | Represents the properties of a parallel port on a Windows computer system. |
| Win32_PCMCIAController | 23 | 2 | Manages the capabilities of a Personal Computer Memory Card Interface Adapter (PCMCIA) controller device. |
| Win32_PhysicalMemory | 30 | 0 | Represents a physical memory device located on a computer as available to the operating system. |
| Win32_PhysicalMemoryArray | 27 | 1 | Represents details about the computer system's physical memory. |
| Win32_PhysicalMemoryLocation | 3 | 0 | Relates an array of physical memory and its physical memory. |
| Win32_PNPAllocatedResource | 2 | 0 | Represents an association between logical devices and system resources. |
| Win32_PNPDevice | 2 | 0 | Relates a device (known to Configuration Manager as a PNPEntity) to the function it performs. |
| Win32_PNPEntity | 22 | 2 | Represents the properties of a plug-and-play device. |
| Win32_PortConnector | 20 | 0 | Represents physical connection ports, such as DD-25 pin male, Centronics, and PS/2. |

| Class | Properties | Methods | Description |
| --- | --- | --- | --- |
| Win32_PortResource | 11 | 0 | Represents an I/O port on a Windows computer system. |
| Win32_Processor | 44 | 2 | Represents a device capable of interpreting a sequence of machine instructions on a Windows computer system. |
| Win32_SCSIController | 31 | 2 | Represents a small computer system interface (SCSI) controller on a Windows system. |
| Win32_SCSIControllerDevice | 7 | 0 | Relates a SCSI controller and the logical device (disk drive) connected to it. |
| Win32_SerialPort | 47 | 2 | Represents a serial port on a Windows system. |
| Win32_SerialPortConfiguration | 29 | 0 | Represents the settings for data transmission on a Windows serial port. |
| Win32_SerialPortSetting | 2 | 0 | Relates a serial port and its configuration settings. |
| Win32_SMBIOSMemory | 38 | 2 | Represents the capabilities and management of memory-related logical devices. |
| Win32_SoundDevice | 23 | 2 | Represents the properties of a sound device on a Windows computer system. |
| Win32_SystemBIOS | 2 | 0 | Relates a computer system (including data such as startup properties, time zones, boot configurations, or administrative passwords) to a system BIOS (services, languages, system management properties). |
| Win32_SystemDriverPNPEntity | 2 | 0 | Relates a plug-and-play device on the Windows computer system to the driver that supports the plug-and-play device. |
| Win32_SystemEnclosure | 37 | 1 | Represents the properties associated with a physical system enclosure. |
| Win32_SystemMemoryResource | 10 | 0 | Represents a system memory resource on a Windows system. |
| Win32_SystemSlot | 31 | 0 | Represents physical connection points including ports, motherboard slots and peripherals, and proprietary connections points. |
| Win32_USBController | 23 | 2 | Manages the capabilities of a universal serial bus (USB) controller. |
| Win32_USBControllerDevice | 7 | 0 | Relates a USB controller and the Win32_LogonSession instances connected to it. |
| Win32_USBHub | 28 | 3 | Represents the management characteristics of a USB hub. |

**TABLE E-5** Network device classes

| Class | Properties | Methods | Description |
|---|---|---|---|
| Win32_NetworkAdapter | 36 | 2 | Represents a network adapter on a Windows system. |
| Win32_NetworkAdapterConfiguration | 60 | 41 | Represents the attributes and behaviors of a network adapter. This class is not guaranteed to be supported after the ratification of the Distributed Management Task Force (DMTF) CIM network specification. |
| Win32_NetworkAdapterSetting | 2 | 0 | Relates a network adapter to its configuration settings. |

**TABLE E-6** Power classes

| Class | Properties | Methods | Description |
|---|---|---|---|
| Win32_AssociatedBattery | 2 | 0 | Relates a logical device to the battery it is using. |
| Win32_Battery | 33 | 2 | Represents a battery connected to the computer system. |
| Win32_CurrentProbe | 35 | 2 | Represents the properties of a current monitoring sensor (ammeter). |
| Win32_PortableBattery | 36 | 2 | Represents the properties of a portable battery, such as one used for a notebook computer. |
| Win32_PowerManagementEvent | 4 | 0 | Represents power management events resulting from power state changes. |
| Win32_UninterruptiblePowerSupply | 43 | 2 | Represents the capabilities and management capacity of an uninterruptible power supply. |
| Win32_VoltageProbe | 35 | 2 | Represents the properties of a voltage sensor (electronic voltmeter). |

**TABLE E-7** Printing classes

| Class | Properties | Methods | Description |
|---|---|---|---|
| Win32_DriverForDevice | 2 | 0 | Relates a printer to a printer driver. |
| Win32_Printer | 86 | 9 | Represents a device connected to a Windows computer system that is capable of reproducing a visual image on a medium. |
| Win32_PrinterConfiguration | 33 | 0 | Defines the configuration for a printer device. |
| Win32_PrinterController | 7 | 0 | Relates a printer and the local device to which the printer is connected. |
| Win32_PrinterDriver | 22 | 3 | Represents the drivers for a Win32_Printer instance. |
| Win32_PrinterDriverDll | 2 | 0 | Relates a local printer to its driver file (not the driver itself). |

| Class | Properties | Methods | Description |
|---|---|---|---|
| Win32_PrinterSetting | 2 | 0 | Relates a printer to its configuration settings. |
| Win32_PrintJob | 24 | 2 | Represents a print job generated by a Windows application. |
| Win32_TCPIPPrinterPort | 17 | 0 | Represents a TCP/IP service access point. |

**TABLE E-8** Telephony classes

| Class | Properties | Methods | Description |
|---|---|---|---|
| Win32_POTSModem | 79 | 2 | Represents the services and characteristics of a plain-old telephone service (POTS) modem on a Windows system. |
| Win32_POTSModemToSerialPort | 7 | 0 | Relates a modem to the serial port the modem uses. |

**TABLE E-9** Video and monitor classes

| Class | Properties | Methods | Description |
|---|---|---|---|
| Win32_DesktopMonitor | 28 | 2 | Represents the type of monitor or display device attached to the computer system. |
| Win32_DisplayConfiguration | 15 | 0 | Represents configuration information for the display device on a Windows system. This class is obsolete. In place of this class, use the properties in the *Win32_VideoController*, *Win32_DesktopMonitor*, and *CIM_VideoControllerResolution* classes. |
| Win32_DisplayControllerConfiguration | 14 | 0 | Represents the video adapter configuration information of a Windows system. This class is obsolete. In place of this class, use the properties in the *Win32_VideoController*, *Win32_DesktopMonitor*, and *CIM_VideoControllerResolution* classes. |
| Win32_VideoConfiguration | 30 | 0 | This class has been eliminated from Windows XP and later operating systems; attempts to use it generate a fatal error. In place of this class, use the properties contained in the *Win32_VideoController*, *Win32_DesktopMonitor*, and *CIM_VideoControllerResolution* classes. |
| Win32_VideoController | 59 | 2 | Represents the capabilities and management capacity of the video controller on a Windows computer system. |
| Win32_VideoSettings | 2 | 0 | Relates a video controller to video settings that can be applied to it. |

**TABLE E-10** COM classes

| Class | Properties | Methods | Description |
|---|---|---|---|
| Win32_ClassicCOMApplicationClasses | 2 | 0 | Association class. Relates a DCOM application to a COM component grouped under it. |
| Win32_ClassicCOMClass | 6 | 0 | Instance class. Represents the properties of a COM component. |
| Win32_ClassicCOMClassSettings | 2 | 0 | Association class. Relates a COM class to the settings used to configure instances of the COM class. |
| Win32_ClientApplicationSetting | 2 | 0 | Association class. Relates an executable to a DCOM application that contains the DCOM configuration options for the executable file. |
| Win32_COMApplication | 5 | 0 | Instance class. Represents a COM application. |
| Win32_COMApplicationClasses | 2 | 0 | Association class. Relates a COM component to the COM application where it resides. |
| Win32_COMApplicationSettings | 2 | 0 | Association class. Relates a DCOM application to its configuration settings. |
| Win32_COMClass | 5 | 0 | Instance class. Represents the properties of a COM component. |
| Win32_COMClassAutoEmulator | 2 | 0 | Association class. Relates a COM class to another COM class that it automatically emulates. |
| Win32_COMClassEmulator | 2 | 0 | Association class. Relates two versions of a COM class. |
| Win32_ComponentCategory | 6 | 0 | Instance class. Represents a component category. |
| Win32_COMSetting | 3 | 0 | Instance class. Represents the settings associated with a COM component or COM application. |
| Win32_DCOMApplication | 6 | 0 | Instance class. Represents the properties of a DCOM application. |
| Win32_DCOMApplicationAccessAllowedSetting | 2 | 0 | Association class. Relates the Win32_DCOMApplication instance to the user security identifications (SID) that can access it. |

| Class | Properties | Methods | Description |
|---|---|---|---|
| Win32_DCOMApplicationLaunchAllowedSetting | 2 | 0 | Association class. Relates the *Win32_DCOMApplication* instance to the user SIDs that can launch it. |
| Win32_DCOMApplicationSetting | 12 | 0 | Instance class. Represents the settings of a DCOM application. |
| Win32_ImplementedCategory | 2 | 0 | Association class. Relates a component category to the COM class using its interfaces. |

**TABLE E-11** Desktop classes

| Class | Properties | Methods | Description |
|---|---|---|---|
| Win32_Desktop | 21 | 0 | Instance class. Represents the common characteristics of a user's desktop. |
| Win32_Environment | 8 | 0 | Instance class. Represents an environment or system environment setting on a Windows computer system. |
| Win32_TimeZone | 24 | 0 | Instance class. Represents the time zone information for a Windows system. |
| Win32_UserDesktop | 2 | 0 | Association class. Relates a user account to desktop settings that are specific to it. |

**TABLE E-12** Driver classes

| Class | Properties | Methods | Description |
|---|---|---|---|
| Win32_DriverVXD | 21 | 0 | Instance class. Represents a virtual device driver on a Windows computer system. |
| Win32_SystemDriver | 22 | 10 | Instance class. Represents the system driver for a base service. |

**TABLE E-13** File system classes

| Class | Properties | Methods | Description |
|---|---|---|---|
| Win32_CIMLogicalDeviceCIMDataFile | 4 | 0 | Association class. Relates logical devices and data files, indicating the driver files used by the device. |
| Win32_Directory | 31 | 14 | Represents a directory entry on a Windows computer system. |
| Win32_DirectorySpecification | 13 | 1 | Instance class. Represents the directory layout for the product. |
| Win32_DiskDriveToDiskPartition | 2 | 0 | Association class. Relates a disk drive to a partition existing on it. |
| Win32_DiskPartition | 34 | 2 | Instance class. Represents the capabilities and management capacity of a partitioned area of a physical disk on a Windows system. |
| Win32_DiskQuota | 6 | 0 | Association class. Tracks disk space usage for NTFS file system volumes. |

| Class | Properties | Methods | Description |
|---|---|---|---|
| Win32_LogicalDisk | 40 | 5 | Represents a data source that resolves to an actual local storage device on a Windows system. |
| Win32_LogicalDiskRootDirectory | 2 | 0 | Association class. Relates a logical disk to its directory structure. |
| Win32_LogicalDiskToPartition | 4 | 0 | Association class. Relates a logical disk drive to the disk partition it resides on. |
| Win32_MappedLogicalDisk | 38 | 2 | Represents network storage devices that are mapped as logical disks on the computer system. |
| Win32_OperatingSystemAutochkSetting | 2 | 0 | Association class. Represents the association between a *CIM_ManagedSystemElement* instance and the settings defined for it. |
| Win32_QuotaSetting | 9 | 0 | Instance class. Contains settings information for disk quotas on a volume. |
| Win32_ShortcutFile | 34 | 14 | Represents files that are shortcuts to other files, directories, and commands. |
| Win32_SubDirectory | 2 | 0 | Association class. Relates a directory (folder) and one of its subdirectories (subfolders). |
| Win32_SystemPartitions | 2 | 0 | Association class. Relates a computer system to a disk partition on that system. |
| Win32_Volume | 2 | 0 | Instance class. Represents an area of storage on a hard disk. |
| Win32_VolumeQuota | 2 | 0 | Association class. Relates a volume to the per-volume quota settings. |
| Win32_VolumeQuotaSetting | 2 | 0 | Association class. Relates disk quota settings with a specific disk volume. |
| Win32_VolumeUserQuota | 2 | 0 | Association class. Relates per-user quotas to quota-enabled volumes. |

**TABLE E-14** Job object classes

| Class | Properties | Methods | Description |
|---|---|---|---|
| Win32_CollectionStatistics | 2 | 0 | Association class. Relates a managed system element collection and the class representing statistical information about the collection. |
| Win32_LUID | 2 | 0 | Instance class. Represents a locally unique identifier (LUID). |
| Win32_LUIDandAttributes | 2 | 0 | Instance class. Represents a LUID and its attributes. |
| Win32_NamedJobObject | 4 | 0 | Instance class. Represents a kernel object that is used to group processes for the sake of controlling the life and resources of the processes within the job object. |

| Class | Properties | Methods | Description |
|---|---|---|---|
| Win32_NamedJobObjectActgInfo | 19 | 0 | Instance class. Represents the I/O accounting information for a job object. |
| Win32_NamedJobObjectLimit | 2 | 0 | Instance class. Represents an association between a job object and the job object limit settings. |
| Win32_NamedJobObjectLimitSetting | 14 | 0 | Instance class. Represents the limit settings for a job object. |
| Win32_NamedJobObjectProcess | 2 | 0 | Instance class. Relates a job object to the process contained in the job object. |
| Win32_NamedJobObjectSecLimit | 2 | 0 | Instance class. Relates a job object to the job object security limit settings. |
| Win32_NamedJobObjectSecLimitSetting | 7 | 0 | Instance class. Represents the security limit settings for a job object. |
| Win32_NamedJobObjectStatistics | 2 | 0 | Instance class. Represents an association between a job object and the job object I/O accounting information class. |
| Win32_SIDandAttributes | 2 | 0 | Instance class. Represents a security identifier (SID) and its attributes. |
| Win32_TokenGroups | 2 | 0 | Event class. Represents information about the group SIDs in an access token. |
| Win32_TokenPrivileges | 2 | 0 | Event class. Represents information about a set of privileges for an access token. |

**TABLE E-15** Memory and page file classes

| Class | Properties | Methods | Description |
|---|---|---|---|
| Win32_LogicalMemoryConfiguration | 8 | 0 | Instance class. This class is obsolete and has been replaced by the Win32_OperatingSystem class. |
| Win32_PageFile | 36 | 14 | Instance class. Represents the file used for handling virtual memory file swapping on a Windows system. |
| Win32_PageFileElementSetting | 2 | 0 | Association class. Relates the initial settings of a page file and the state of those setting during normal use. |
| Win32_PageFileSetting | 6 | 0 | Instance class. Represents the settings of a page file. |
| Win32_PageFileUsage | 9 | 0 | Instance class. Represents the file used for handling virtual memory file swapping on a Windows system. |
| Win32_SystemLogicalMemoryConfiguration | 2 | 0 | Association class. This class is obsolete because the properties existing in the Win32_LogicalMemoryConfiguration class are now a part of the Win32_OperatingSystem class. |

**TABLE E-16** Media and audio class

| Class | Properties | Methods | Description |
|-------|-----------|---------|-------------|
| Win32_CodecFile | 34 | 14 | Instance class. Represents the audio or video codec installed on the computer system. |

**TABLE E-17** Networking classes

| Class | Properties | Methods | Description |
|-------|-----------|---------|-------------|
| Win32_ActiveRoute | 2 | 0 | Association class. Relates the current IP4 route to the persisted IP route table. |
| Win32_IP4PersistedRouteTable | 9 | 0 | Instance class. Represents persisted IP routes. |
| Win32_IP4RouteTable | 18 | 0 | Instance class. Represents information that governs the routing of network data packets. |
| Win32_IP4RouteTableEvent | 2 | 0 | Event class. Represents IP route change events. |
| Win32_NetworkClient | 6 | 0 | Instance class. Represents a network client on a Windows system. |
| Win32_NetworkConnection | 17 | 0 | Instance class. Represents an active network connection in a Windows environment. |
| Win32_NetworkProtocol | 23 | 0 | Instance class. Represents a protocol and its network characteristics on a Windows computer system. |
| Win32_NTDomain | 27 | 0 | Instance class. Represents a Windows NT domain. |
| Win32_PingStatus | 24 | 0 | Instance class. Represents the values returned by the standard ping command. |
| Win32_ProtocolBinding | 3 | 0 | Association class. Relates a system-level driver, network protocol, and network adapter. |

**TABLE E-18** Operating system event classes

| Class | Properties | Methods | Description |
|-------|-----------|---------|-------------|
| Win32_ComputerShutdownEvent | 4 | 0 | Represents computer shutdown events. |
| Win32_ComputerSystemEvent | 3 | 0 | Represents events related to a computer system. |
| Win32_DeviceChangeEvent | 3 | 0 | Represents device-change events resulting from the addition, removal, or modification of devices on the computer system. |
| Win32_ModuleLoadTrace | 6 | 0 | Indicates that a process has loaded a new module. |
| Win32_ModuleTrace | 2 | 0 | Base event for module events. |
| Win32_ProcessStartTrace | 8 | 0 | Indicates that a new process has started. |
| Win32_ProcessStopTrace | 8 | 0 | Indicates that a process has terminated. |
| Win32_ProcessTrace | 8 | 0 | Base event for process events. |

| Class | Properties | Methods | Description |
|---|---|---|---|
| Win32_SystemConfigurationChangeEvent | 3 | 0 | Indicates that the device list on the system has been refreshed (a device has been added or removed, or the configuration has changed). |
| Win32_SystemTrace | 2 | 0 | Base class for all system trace events, including module, process, and thread traces. |
| Win32_ThreadStartTrace | 11 | 0 | Indicates that a new thread has started. |
| Win32_ThreadStopTrace | 4 | 0 | Indicates that a thread has stopped. |
| Win32_ThreadTrace | 4 | 0 | Base event class for thread events. |
| Win32_VolumeChangeEvent | 4 | 0 | Represents a network-mapped drive event resulting from the addition of a network drive letter or mounted drive on the computer system. |

**TABLE E-19** Operating system settings classes

| Class | Properties | Methods | Description |
|---|---|---|---|
| Win32_BootConfiguration | 9 | 0 | Instance class. Represents the boot configuration of a Windows system. |
| Win32_ComputerSystem | 54 | 4 | Instance class. Represents a computer system operating in a Windows environment. |
| Win32_ComputerSystemProcessor | 2 | 0 | Association class. Relates a computer system to a processor running on that system. |
| Win32_ComputerSystemProduct | 8 | 0 | Instance class. Represents a product. |
| Win32_DependentService | 3 | 0 | Association class. Relates two interdependent base services. |
| Win32_LoadOrderGroup | 7 | 0 | Instance class. Represents a group of system services that define execution dependencies. |
| Win32_LoadOrderGroupServiceDependencies | 2 | 0 | Instance class. Represents an association between a base service and a load order group that the service depends on to start running. |
| Win32_LoadOrderGroupServiceMembers | 2 | 0 | Association class. Relates a load order group and a base service. |
| Win32_OperatingSystem | 61 | 4 | Instance class. Represents an operating system installed on a Windows computer system. |
| Win32_OperatingSystemQFE | 2 | 0 | Association class. Relates an operating system to product updates applied, as represented in Win32_QuickFixEngineering. |

| Class | Properties | Methods | Description |
|---|---|---|---|
| Win32_OSRecoveryConfiguration | 15 | 0 | Instance class. Represents the types of information that will be gathered from memory when the operating system fails. |
| Win32_QuickFixEngineering | 11 | 0 | Instance class. Represents system-wide Quick Fix Engineering (QFE) or updates that have been applied to the current operating system. |
| Win32_StartupCommand | 7 | 0 | Instance class. Represents a command that runs automatically when a user logs on to the computer system. |
| Win32_SystemBootConfiguration | 2 | 0 | Association class. Relates a computer system to its boot configuration. |
| Win32_SystemDesktop | 2 | 0 | Association class. Relates a computer system to its desktop configuration. |
| Win32_SystemDevices | 2 | 0 | Association class. Relates a computer system to a logical device installed on that system. |
| Win32_SystemLoadOrderGroups | 2 | 0 | Association class. Relates a computer system to a load order group. |
| Win32_SystemNetworkConnections | 2 | 0 | Association class. Relates a network connection to the computer system on which it resides. |
| Win32_SystemOperatingSystem | 3 | 0 | Association class. Relates a computer system to its operating system. |
| Win32_SystemProcesses | 2 | 0 | Association class. Relates a computer system to a process running on that system. |
| Win32_SystemProgramGroups | 2 | 0 | Association class. Relates a computer system to a logical program group. |
| Win32_SystemResources | 2 | 0 | Association class. Relates a system resource to the computer system it resides on. |
| Win32_SystemServices | 2 | 0 | Association class. Relates a computer system to a service program that exists on the system. |
| Win32_SystemSetting | 2 | 0 | Association class. Relates a computer system to a general setting on that system. |

| Class | Properties | Methods | Description |
|---|---|---|---|
| Win32_SystemSystemDriver | 2 | 0 | Association class. Relates a computer system to a system driver running on that computer system. |
| Win32_SystemTimeZone | 2 | 0 | Association class. Relates a computer system to a time zone. |
| Win32_SystemUsers | 2 | 0 | Association class. Relates a computer system to a user account on that system. |

**TABLE E-20** Process classes

| Class | Properties | Methods | Description |
|---|---|---|---|
| Win32_Process | 45 | 6 | Instance class. Represents a sequence of events on a Windows system. |
| Win32_ProcessStartup | 14 | 0 | Instance class. Represents the startup configuration of a Windows process. |
| Win32_Thread | 22 | 0 | Instance class. Represents a thread of execution. |

**TABLE E-21** Registry class

| Class | Properties | Methods | Description |
|---|---|---|---|
| Win32_Registry | 8 | 0 | Instance class. Represents the system registry on a Windows computer system. |

**TABLE E-22** Scheduler job classes

| Class | Properties | Methods | Description |
|---|---|---|---|
| Win32_LocalTime | 10 | 0 | Instance class. Represents an instance in time as component seconds, minutes, day of the week, and so on. |
| Win32_ScheduledJob | 19 | 2 | Instance class. Represents a job scheduled using the Windows NT schedule service. |

**TABLE E-23** Security classes

| Class | Properties | Methods | Description |
|---|---|---|---|
| Win32_AccountSID | 2 | 0 | Association class. Relates a security account instance with a security descriptor instance. |
| Win32_ACE | 6 | 0 | Instance class. Represents an access control entry (ACE). |

| Class | Properties | Methods | Description |
|---|---|---|---|
| Win32_LogicalFileAccess | 7 | 0 | Association class. Relates the security settings of a file or directory to one member of its discretionary access control list (DACL). |
| Win32_LogicalFileAuditing | 7 | 0 | Association class. Relates the security settings of a file or directory to one member of its system access control list (SACL). |
| Win32_LogicalFileGroup | 2 | 0 | Association class. Relates the security settings of a file or directory to its group. |
| Win32_LogicalFileOwner | 2 | 0 | Association class. Relates the security settings of a file or directory to its owner. |
| Win32_LogicalFileSecuritySetting | 6 | 2 | Instance class. Represents the security settings for a logical file. |
| Win32_LogicalShareAccess | 7 | 0 | Association class. Relates the security settings of a share to one member of its DACL. |
| Win32_LogicalShareAuditing | 7 | 0 | Association class. Relates the security settings of a share to one member of its SACL. |
| Win32_LogicalShareSecuritySetting | 5 | 2 | Instance class. Represents the security settings for a logical share. |
| Win32_PrivilegesStatus | 7 | 0 | Instance class. Represents information about privileges required to complete an operation. |
| Win32_SecurityDescriptor | 5 | 0 | Instance class. Represents a structural representation of a SECURITY_ DESCRIPTOR. |
| Win32_SecuritySetting | 4 | 2 | Instance class. Represents the security settings for a managed element. |
| Win32_SecuritySettingAccess | 7 | 0 | Instance class. Represents the rights granted and denied to a trustee for a given object. |
| Win32_SecuritySettingAuditing | 7 | 0 | Instance class. Represents the auditing for a given trustee on a given object. |
| Win32_SecuritySettingGroup | 2 | 0 | Association class. Relates the security of an object to its group. |
| Win32_SecuritySettingOfLogicalFile | 2 | 0 | Instance class. Represents the security settings of a file or directory object. |
| Win32_SecuritySettingOfLogicalShare | 2 | 0 | Instance class. Represents the security settings of a share object. |
| Win32_SecuritySettingOfObject | 2 | 0 | Association class. Relates an object to its security settings. |
| Win32_SecuritySettingOwner | 2 | 0 | Association class. Relates the security settings of an object to its owner. |
| Win32_SID | 5 | 0 | Instance class. Represents an arbitrary SID. |
| Win32_Trustee | 5 | 0 | Instance class. Represents a trustee. |

**TABLE E-24** Service classes

| Class | Properties | Methods | Description |
|---|---|---|---|
| Win32_BaseService | 22 | 10 | Instance class. Represents executable objects that are installed in a registry database maintained by the Service Control Manager. |
| Win32_Service | 25 | 10 | Instance class. Represents a service on a Windows computer system. |

**TABLE E-25** Share classes

| Class | Properties | Methods | Description |
|---|---|---|---|
| Win32_DFSNode | 25 | 10 | Association class. Represents a root or junction node of a domain-based or stand-alone distributed file system (DFS). |
| Win32_DFSNodeTarget | 25 | 10 | Association class. Represents the relationship of a DFS node to one of its targets. |
| Win32_DFSTarget | 25 | 10 | Association class. Represents the target of a DFS node. |
| Win32_ServerConnection | 12 | 0 | Instance class. Represents the connections made from a remote computer to a shared resource on the local computer. |
| Win32_ServerSession | 13 | 0 | Instance class. Represents the sessions that are established with the local computer by users on a remote computer. |
| Win32_ConnectionShare | 2 | 0 | Association class. Relates a shared resource on the computer and the connection made to the shared resource. |
| Win32_PrinterShare | 2 | 0 | Association class. Relates a local printer and the share that represents it as it is viewed over a network. |
| Win32_SessionConnection | 2 | 0 | Association class. Represents an association between a session established with the local server by a user on a remote machine and the connections that depend on the session. |
| Win32_SessionProcess | 2 | 0 | Association class. Represents an association between a logon session and the processes associated with that session. |
| Win32_ShareToDirectory | 2 | 0 | Association class. Relates a shared resource on the computer system and the directory to which it is mapped. |
| Win32_Share | 10 | 4 | Instance class. Represents a shared resource on a Windows system. |

**TABLE E-26** Start menu classes

| Class | Properties | Methods | Description |
|---|---|---|---|
| Win32_LogicalProgramGroup | 7 | 0 | Instance class. Represents a program group in a Windows system. |
| Win32_LogicalProgramGroupDirectory | 2 | 0 | Association class. Relates logical program groups (groupings in the Start menu) to the file directories in which they are stored. |

| Class | Properties | Methods | Description |
|---|---|---|---|
| Win32_LogicalProgramGroupItem | 5 | 0 | Instance class. Represents an element contained by a *Win32_ProgramGroup* instance that is not itself another *Win32_ProgramGroup* instance. |
| Win32_LogicalProgramGroupItemDataFile | 2 | 0 | Association class. Relates the program group items of the Start menu to the files in which they are stored. |
| Win32_ProgramGroup | 6 | 0 | Instance class. Deprecated. Represents a program group in a Windows computer system. Use the *Win32_LogicalProgramGroup* class instead. |
| Win32_ProgramGroupContents | 2 | 0 | Association class. Relates a program group order to an individual program group or item contained in it. |
| Win32_ProgramGroupOrItem | 5 | 0 | Instance class. Represents a logical grouping of programs on the user's Start \| Programs menu. |

**TABLE E-27** Storage classes

| Class | Properties | Methods | Description |
|---|---|---|---|
| Win32_ShadowBy | 5 | 0 | Association class. Represents the association between a shadow copy and the provider that creates the shadow copy. |
| Win32_ShadowContext | 5 | 0 | Association class. Specifies how a shadow copy is to be created, queried, or deleted. |
| Win32_ShadowCopy | 5 | 0 | Instance class. Represents a duplicate copy of the original volume at a previous time. |
| Win32_ShadowDiffVolumeSupport | 5 | 0 | Association class. Represents an association between a shadow copy provider and a storage volume. |
| Win32_ShadowFor | 5 | 0 | Association class. Represents an association between a shadow copy and the volume for which the shadow copy is created. |
| Win32_ShadowOn | 5 | 0 | Association class. Represents an association between a shadow copy and where the differential data is written. |
| Win32_ShadowProvider | 5 | 0 | Association class. Represents a component that creates and represents volume shadow copies. |
| Win32_ShadowStorage | 5 | 0 | Association class. Represents an association between a shadow copy and where the differential data is written. |

| Class | Properties | Methods | Description |
|---|---|---|---|
| Win32_ShadowVolumeSupport | 5 | 0 | Association class. Represents an association between a shadow copy provider and a supported volume. |
| Win32_Volume | 42 | 9 | Instance class. Represents an area of storage on a hard disk. |
| Win32_VolumeUserQuota | 6 | 0 | Association class. Represents a volume to the per-volume quota settings. |

**TABLE E-28** User classes

| Class | Properties | Methods | Description |
|---|---|---|---|
| Win32_Account | 9 | 0 | Instance class. Represents information about user accounts and group accounts known to the Windows system. |
| Win32_Group | 9 | 1 | Instance class. Represents data about a group account. |
| Win32_GroupInDomain | 2 | 0 | Association class. Identifies the group accounts associated with a Windows NT domain. |
| Win32_GroupUser | 2 | 0 | Association class. Relates a group to an account that is a member of that group. |
| Win32_LogonSession | 9 | 0 | Instance class. Describes the logon session or sessions associated with a user. |
| Win32_LogonSessionMappedDisk | 2 | 0 | Association class. Represents the mapped logical disks associated with the session. |
| Win32_NetworkLoginProfile | 32 | 0 | Instance class. Represents the network login information of a specific user on a Windows system. |
| Win32_SystemAccount | 9 | 0 | Instance class. Represents a system account. |
| Win32_UserAccount | 16 | 1 | Instance class. Represents information about a user account on a Windows system. |
| Win32_UserInDomain | 2 | 0 | Association class. Relates a user account and a Windows domain. |

**TABLE E-29** Event log classes

| Class | Properties | Methods | Description |
|---|---|---|---|
| Win32_NTEventlogFile | 39 | 16 | Instance class. Represents data stored in a Windows log file. |
| Win32_NTLogEvent | 16 | 0 | Instance class. Represents Windows NT/Windows 2000 events. |
| Win32_NTLogEventComputer | 2 | 0 | Association class. Relates instances of Win32_NTLogEvent to Win32_ComputerSystem. |
| Win32_NTLogEventLog | 2 | 0 | Association class. Relates instances of Win32_NTLogEvent to Win32_NTEventLogFile classes. |
| Win32_NTLogEventUser | 2 | 0 | Association class. Relates instances of Win32_NTLogEvent to Win32_UserAccount. |

**TABLE E-30** Windows product-activation classes

| Class | Properties | Methods | Description |
|---|---|---|---|
| Win32_ComputerSystemWindows ProductActivationSetting | 2 | 0 | Association class. Relates instances of Win32_ComputerSystem to Win32_WindowsProductActivation. |
| Win32_Proxy | 6 | 1 | Instance class. Contains properties and methods to query and configure an Internet connection related to WPA. |
| Win32_WindowsProductActivation | 9 | 5 | Instance class. Contains properties and methods related to WPA. |

**TABLE E-31** Formatted-data classes

| Class | Properties | Methods | Description |
|---|---|---|---|
| Win32_PerfFormattedData | 9 | 0 | Abstract base class for the formatted-data classes. |
| Win32_PerfFormattedData_ASP_ ActiveServerPages | 9 | 0 | Represents performance counters for the Active Server Pages (ASP) device on the computer system. |
| Win32_PerfFormattedData_ContentFilter_ IndexingServiceFilter | 12 | 0 | Represents performance information about an Indexing Service filter. |
| Win32_PerfFormattedData_ContentIndex_ IndexingService | 20 | 0 | Represents performance data about the state of the Indexing Service. |
| Win32_PerfFormattedData_InetInfo_ InternetInformationServicesGlobal | 20 | 0 | Represents counters that monitor Internet Information Services (IIS) (the web service and the FTP service) as a whole. |
| Win32_PerfFormattedData_ISAPISearch_ HttpIndexingService | 17 | 0 | Represents performance data from the HTTP Indexing Service. |
| Win32_PerfFormattedData_MSDTC_ DistributedTransactionCoordinator | 22 | 0 | Represents Microsoft Distributed Transaction Coordinator (DTC) performance counters. |
| Win32_PerfFormattedData_NTFSDRV_ SMTPNTFSStoreDriver | 22 | 0 | Represents global counters for the Exchange NTFS store driver. |
| Win32_PerfFormattedData_PerfDisk_ LogicalDisk | 32 | 0 | Represents counters that monitor logical partitions of a hard or fixed disk drive. |
| Win32_PerfFormattedData_PerfDisk_ PhysicalDisk | 30 | 0 | Represents counters that monitor hard or fixed disk drives on a computer. |
| Win32_PerfFormattedData_PerfNet_Browser | 29 | 0 | Represents counters that measure the rates of announcements, enumerations, and other browser transmissions. |
| Win32_PerfFormattedData_PerfNet_ Redirector | 46 | 0 | Represents counters that monitor network connections originating at the local computer. |

| Class | Properties | Methods | Description |
|---|---|---|---|
| Win32_PerfFormattedData_PerfNet_Server | 35 | 0 | Represents counters that monitor communications using the WINS Server service. |
| Win32_PerfFormattedData_PerfNet_ServerWorkQueues | 26 | 0 | Represents counters that monitor the length of the queues and objects in the queues. |
| Win32_PerfFormattedData_PerfOS_Cache | 26 | 0 | Represents counters that monitor the file system cache, an area of physical memory that stores recently used data as long as possible to permit access to the data without having to read from the disk. |
| Win32_PerfFormattedData_PerfOS_Memory | 26 | 0 | Represents counters that describe the behavior of physical and virtual memory on the computer. |
| Win32_PerfFormattedData_PerfOS_Objects | 26 | 0 | Represents counts of the objects contained by the operating system (for example, events, mutexes, processes, sections, semaphores, and threads). |
| Win32_PerfFormattedData_PerfOS_PagingFile | 26 | 0 | Represents counters that monitor the paging files on the computer. |
| Win32_PerfFormattedData_PerfOS_Processor | 26 | 0 | Represents counters that measure aspects of processor activity. |
| Win32_PerfFormattedData_PerfOS_System | 26 | 0 | Represents counters that apply to more than one instance of a component processor on the computer. |
| Win32_PerfFormattedData_PerfProc_FullImage_Costly | 17 | 0 | Represents counters that monitor the virtual address usage of images executed by processes on the computer. |
| Win32_PerfFormattedData_PerfProc_Image_Costly | 17 | 0 | Represents counters that monitor the virtual address usage of images executed by processes on the computer. |
| Win32_PerfFormattedData_PerfProc_JobObject | 22 | 0 | Represents the accounting and processor usage data collected by each active named job object. |
| Win32_PerfFormattedData_PerfProc_JobObjectDetails | 36 | 0 | Represents detailed performance information about the active processes that make up a job object. |
| Win32_PerfFormattedData_PerfProc_Process | 36 | 0 | Represents counters that monitor running application program and system processes. |
| Win32_PerfFormattedData_PerfProc_ProcessAddressSpace_Costly | 46 | 0 | Represent counters that monitor memory allocation and use for a selected process. |

| Class | Properties | Methods | Description |
|---|---|---|---|
| Win32_PerfFormattedData_PerfProc_Thread | 21 | 0 | Represents counters that measure aspects of thread behavior. |
| Win32_PerfFormattedData_PerfProc_ThreadDetails_Costly | 10 | 0 | Represents counters that measure aspects of thread behavior that are difficult or time-consuming to collect. |
| Win32_PerfFormattedData_PSched_PSchedFlow | 10 | 0 | Represents flow statistics from the packet scheduler. |
| Win32_PerfFormattedData_PSched_PSchedPipe | 10 | 0 | Represents pipe statistics from the packet scheduler. |
| Win32_PerfFormattedData_RemoteAccess_RASPort | 10 | 0 | Represents counters that monitor individual Remote Access Service (RAS) ports of the RAS device on the computer. |
| Win32_PerfFormattedData_RemoteAccess_RASTotal | 10 | 0 | Represents counters that combine values for all ports of the RAS device on the computer. |
| Win32_PerfFormattedData_RSVP_ACSRSVPInterfaces | 10 | 0 | Represents the number of local network interfaces visible to and used by the RSVP service. |
| Win32_PerfFormattedData_RSVP_ACSRSVPService | 10 | 0 | Represents RSVP or ACS service performance counters. |
| Win32_PerfFormattedData_SMTPSVC_SMTPServer | 10 | 0 | Represents counters specific to the SMTP server. |
| Win32_PerfFormattedData_Spooler_PrintQueue | 22 | 0 | Represents performance statistics about a print queue. |
| Win32_PerfFormattedData_TapiSrv_Telephony | 18 | 0 | Represents the telephony system. |
| Win32_PerfFormattedData_Tcpip_ICMP | 18 | 0 | Consists of counters that measure the rates at which messages are sent and received by using ICMP protocols. |
| Win32_PerfFormattedData_Tcpip_IP | 18 | 0 | Represents counters that measure the rates at which IP datagrams are sent and received by using IP protocols. |
| Win32_PerfFormattedData_Tcpip_NBTConnection | 18 | 0 | Represents counters that measure the rates at which bytes are sent and received over the NBT connection between the local computer and a remote computer. |
| Win32_PerfFormattedData_Tcpip_NetworkInterface | 18 | 0 | Represents counters that measure the rates at which bytes and packets are sent and received over a TCP/IP network connection. |
| Win32_PerfFormattedData_Tcpip_TCP | 18 | 0 | Represents counters that measure the rates at which TCP segments are sent and received by using the TCP protocol. |

| Class | Properties | Methods | Description |
|---|---|---|---|
| Win32_PerfFormattedData_Tcpip_UDP | 18 | 0 | Represents counters that measure the rates at which UDP datagrams are sent and received by using the UDP protocol. |
| Win32_PerfFormattedData_TermService_TerminalServices | 12 | 0 | Represents terminal services summary information. |
| Win32_PerfFormattedData_TermService_TerminalServicesSession | 84 | 0 | Represents terminal services per-session resource monitoring. |
| Win32_PerfFormattedData_W3SVC_WebService | 84 | 0 | Represents counters specific to the World Wide Web Publishing Service. |

**TABLE E-32** Raw performance monitor classes

| Class | Properties | Methods | Description |
|---|---|---|---|
| Win32_PerfRawData | 9 | 0 | Abstract base class for all concrete raw performance counter classes. |
| Win32_PerfRawData_ASP_ActiveServerPages | 9 | 0 | Represents the ASP device on the computer system. |
| Win32_PerfRawData_ContentFilter_IndexingServiceFilter | 12 | 0 | Represents performance information about an Indexing Service filter. |
| Win32_PerfRawData_ContentIndex_IndexingService | 20 | 0 | Represents performance data about the state of the Indexing Service. |
| Win32_PerfRawData_InetInfo_InternetInformationServicesGlobal | 20 | 0 | Represents counters that monitor IIS (the web service and the FTP service) as a whole. |
| Win32_PerfRawData_ISAPISearch_HttpIndexingService | 19 | 0 | Represents performance data from the HTTP Indexing Service. |
| Win32_PerfRawData_MSDTC_DistributedTransactionCoordinator | 22 | 0 | Represents Microsoft DTC performance counters. |
| Win32_PerfRawData_NTFSDRV_SMTPNTFSStoreDriver | 22 | 0 | Represents global counters for the Exchange NTFS store driver. |
| Win32_PerfRawData_PerfDisk_LogicalDisk | 43 | 0 | Represents counters that monitor logical partitions of a hard or fixed disk drive. |
| Win32_PerfRawData_PerfDisk_PhysicalDisk | 40 | 0 | Represents counters that monitor hard or fixed disk drives on a computer. |
| Win32_PerfRawData_PerfNet_Browser | 29 | 0 | Represents counters that measure the rates of announcements, enumerations, and other browser transmissions. |
| Win32_PerfRawData_PerfNet_Redirector | 46 | 0 | Represents counters that monitor network connections originating at the local computer. |

| Class | Properties | Methods | Description |
|---|---|---|---|
| Win32_PerfRawData_PerfNet_Server | 35 | 0 | Represents counters that monitor communications using the WINS Server service. |
| Win32_PerfRawData_PerfNet_ServerWorkQueues | 26 | 0 | Represents counters that monitor the length of the queues and objects in the queues. |
| Win32_PerfRawData_PerfOS_Cache | 26 | 0 | Represents counters that monitor the file system cache. |
| Win32_PerfRawData_PerfOS_Memory | 26 | 0 | Represents counters that describe the behavior of physical and virtual memory on the computer. |
| Win32_PerfRawData_PerfOS_Objects | 26 | 0 | Represents counts of the objects contained by the operating system (for example, events, mutexes, processes, sections, semaphores, and threads). |
| Win32_PerfRawData_PerfOS_PagingFile | 26 | 0 | Represents counters that monitor the paging files on the computer. |
| Win32_PerfRawData_PerfOS_Processor | 26 | 0 | Represents counters that measure aspects of processor activity. |
| Win32_PerfRawData_PerfOS_System | 26 | 0 | Represents counters that apply to more than one instance of a component processor on the computer. |
| Win32_PerfRawData_PerfProc_FullImage_Costly | 17 | 0 | Represents counters that monitor the virtual address usage of images executed by processes on the computer. |
| Win32_PerfRawData_PerfProc_Image_Costly | 17 | 0 | Represents counters that monitor the virtual address usage of images executed by processes on the computer. |
| Win32_PerfRawData_PerfProc_JobObject | 22 | 0 | Represents the accounting and processor usage data collected by each active named job object. |
| Win32_PerfRawData_PerfProc_JobObjectDetails | 36 | 0 | Represents detailed performance information about the active processes that make up a job object. |
| Win32_PerfRawData_PerfProc_Process | 36 | 0 | Represents counters that monitor running application program and system processes. |
| Win32_PerfRawData_PerfProc_ProcessAddressSpace_Costly | 46 | 0 | Represents counters that monitor memory allocation and use for a selected process. |
| Win32_PerfRawData_PerfProc_Thread | 21 | 0 | Represents counters that measure aspects of thread behavior. |
| Win32_PerfRawData_PerfProc_ThreadDetails_Costly | 10 | 0 | Represents counters that measure aspects of thread behavior that are difficult or time-consuming to collect. |

| Class | Properties | Methods | Description |
|---|---|---|---|
| Win32_PerfRawData_PSched_PSchedFlow | 10 | 0 | Represents flow statistics from the packet scheduler. |
| Win32_PerfRawData_PSched_PSchedPipe | 10 | 0 | Represents pipe statistics from the packet scheduler. |
| Win32_PerfRawData_RemoteAccess_RASPort | 10 | 0 | Represents counters that monitor individual RAS ports of the RAS device on the computer. |
| Win32_PerfRawData_RemoteAccess_RASTotal | 10 | 0 | Represents counters that combine values for all ports of the RAS device on the computer. |
| Win32_PerfRawData_RSVP_ACSRSVPInterfaces | 10 | 0 | Represents the number of local network interfaces visible to and used by the RSVP service. |
| Win32_PerfRawData_RSVP_ACSRSVPService | 10 | 0 | Represents RSVP or ACS service performance counters. |
| Win32_PerfRawData_SMTPSVC_SMTPServer | 10 | 0 | Represents the counters specific to the SMTP server. |
| Win32_PerfRawData_Spooler_PrintQueue | 22 | 0 | Represents performance statistics about a print queue. |
| Win32_PerfRawData_TapiSrv_Telephony | 18 | 0 | Represents the telephony system. |
| Win32_PerfRawData_Tcpip_ICMP | 18 | 0 | Represents counters that measure the rates at which messages are sent and received by using ICMP protocols. |
| Win32_PerfRawData_Tcpip_IP | 18 | 0 | Represents counters that measure the rates at which IP datagrams are sent and received by using IP protocols. |
| Win32_PerfRawData_Tcpip_NBTConnection | 18 | 0 | Represents counters that measure the rates at which bytes are sent and received over the NBT connection between the local computer and a remote computer. |
| Win32_PerfRawData_Tcpip_NetworkInterface | 18 | 0 | Represents counters that measure the rates at which bytes and packets are sent and received over a TCP/IP network connection. |
| Win32_PerfRawData_Tcpip_TCP | 18 | 0 | Represents counters that measure the rates at which TCP segments are sent and received by using the TCP protocol. |
| Win32_PerfRawData_Tcpip_UDP | 18 | 0 | Represents counters that measure the rates at which UDP datagrams are sent and received by using the UDP protocol. |
| Win32_PerfRawData_TermService_TerminalServices | 12 | 0 | Represents terminal services summary information. |
| Win32_PerfRawData_TermService_TerminalServicesSession | 84 | 0 | Represents terminal services per-session resource monitoring. |
| Win32_PerfRawData_W3SVC_WebService | 84 | 0 | Represents counters specific to the World Wide Web Publishing Service. |

# Basic Troubleshooting Tips

This appendix contains a collection of general troubleshooting tips. They are not necessarily in any particular order of importance.

- Remember, spelling counts. Always look for misspelled cmdlet names, property names, method calls, and so on. In Windows PowerShell, if you do not spell a property name correctly, when you try to run the script, it will not generate an error. When the following code is typed inside the shell, there is no output—nothing to indicate that you choose a bad property of the *WIN32_Service* WMI class.

```
PS C:\> $wmi = Get-WmiObject -Class win32_service
PS C:\> $wmi.badproperty
PS C:\>
```

- Do not break the pipeline. This one is particularly easy to do. For example, say you start off with a command you typed at the Windows PowerShell console. You then decide to add something else to it, so you press the up arrow key and add a pipe character. Next, you decide you like the results so much, you want to create a script. Finally, you decide to clean it up and add a column header to the top of the printout—which means that you break your pipeline. The following code illustrates this. In the *Get-WMIObject* statement, you end the line with a pipe character. But you then call a function that prints out the name of the computer. The problem is that this breaks the pipeline, and the script will end with only the line *Service Dependencies on localhost*. Since you called a function, the code does not generate an error.

```
Param($computer = "localhost")

function funline ($strIN)
{
 $num = $strIN.length
 for($i=1 ; $i -le $num ; $i++)
  { $funline = $funline + "=" }
    Write-Host -ForegroundColor yellow $strIN
    Write-Host -ForegroundColor darkYellow $funline
}
```

```
Get-WmiObject -Class Win32_DependentService -computername $computer |
funline("Service Dependencies on $($computer)")
Foreach-object `
 {
  [wmi]$_.Antecedent
  [wmi]$_.Dependent
 }
```

On the other hand, if you do not call the function, then an error will be generated. This is shown in the following code. Note that just as in the preceding code sample, after the *Get-WMIObject* command, you end the line with a pipe character. You then break the pipeline by printing out the string *Dependent services on the local computer*.

```
Get-WmiObject -Class Win32_DependentService |
 "Dependent services on the local computer"
Foreach-object `
 {
  [wmi]$_.Antecedent
  [wmi]$_.Dependent
 }
```

When this code is run, an error will be generated. The error, shown here, explains that you are not allowed to use an expression in the middle of a pipeline, which of course is true.

```
Expressions are only permitted as the first element of a pipeline.
At C:\Users\EDWILS~1.NOR\AppData\Local\Temp\temp.ps1:4 char:44
+  "Dependent services on the local computer" <<<<
```

- Use debug statements when trying to see what is going on with your script. If a script is producing some strange results, then print out the value of the variable. I always try to include a debug statement behind the variable so I will know it is safe to delete the variable when I am done testing my script. In the following script, you are trying to add two numbers. However, you want to make sure the results that are printed out are correct. To do this, you use debug statements to confirm the answer is actually correct. Once you have fixed the script or verified that it is working properly, you will delete the lines containing the debug statements. If you always make your debug statements the same, then it will be easy to search for them. You could clean the script up by using the Find and Replace feature of Notepad. The code is shown here:

```
$a = 5
$b = 4
'$a is ' + $a # debug
'$b is ' +$b  # debug
$c = $a + $b
"The answer to `$a + `$b is $c"
```

- Use the *Test-Path* cmdlet to verify that a file or other object actually exists when trying to work with the object. Of course, make sure that you use a # debug statement following the command if it is not an essential part of your script. An example of using the *Test-Path* technique is shown in the following code:

```
$script = "c:\fso\mydebugscript.ps1"
Test-Path $script # debug
$debug = "# debug"

switch -regex -file $script
{
 "debug" { $switch.current }
}
```

- Initialize variables and set their value to *$null* or 0, as appropriate. When using variables to count the number of items, if you remain inside the same Windows PowerShell console session, then the values of the variables can produce unexpected results if they are not properly initialized. An example of doing this is shown in the ParseAppLog.ps1 script from the Extras folder. This script is shown here:

**ParseAppLog.ps1**

```
$tcp=$udp=$dns=$icmp=$PdnsServer=$SdnsServer=$web=$ssl=$null

$fwlog = get-content "C:\Windows\system32\LogFiles\Firewall\firewall.log"
switch -regex ($fwlog)
 {
  "65.53.192.15" { $PdnsServer+=1 }
  "65.53.192.14" { $SdnsServer+=1 }
  "tcp" { $tcp+=1 }
  "udp" { $udp+=1 }
  "icmp" { $icmp+=1 }
  "\s53"    { $dns+=1 }
  "\s80"    { $web+=1 }
  "\s443"    { $ssl+=1 ; $switch.current}
 }

"`$PdnsServer $Pdnsserver"
"`$SdnsServer $SdnsServer"
"`$tcp $tcp"
"`$udp $udp"
"`$icmp $icmp"
"`$dns $dns"
"`$web $web"
"`$ssl $ssl"
```

- *$ErrorActionPreference* specifies the action to take when data is written using *Write-Error* in a script, or *WriteError* in a cmdlet or provider. In scripts, check for *$ErrorActionPreference = "SilentlyContinue"*. By default, Windows PowerShell issues an error message the moment an error occurs. If you prefer that processing continue without an error message being displayed, then set the value of the Windows PowerShell automatic variable to *$ErrorActionPreference* to *SilentlyContinue*.

- The *$error* variable contains objects for which an error occurred while being processed in a cmdlet. The following example illustrates working with error objects contained in the *$error* variable.

```
$erroractionpreference = "SilentlyContinue"
$a = New-Object test #creates an error
$b = New-Object testB #creates another error
 if ($error.count -eq 1)
    {"There is currently 1 error"}
    else
    {"There are currently " + $error.count + " errors"}
for ($i = 0 ; $error.count ; $i++)
   {$error[$i].CategoryInfo
   $error[$i].ErrorDetails
   $error[$i].Exception
   $error[$i].FullyQualifiedErrorId
   $error[$i].InvocationInfo
   $error[$i].TargetObject}
```

- You can use *Set-PSDebug* to enable debugging features in your script. It can turn script debugging features on and off, set the trace level, and toggle strict mode. Here's an example:

```
C:\PS>set-psdebug -step; foreach ($i in 1..3) {$i}
```

This command turns on stepping and then runs a script that displays the numbers 1, 2, and 3.

```
DEBUG:1+ Set-PsDebug -step; foreach ($i in 1..3) {$i}
Continue with this operation?
  1+ Set-PsDebug -step; foreach ($i in 1..3) {$i}
[Y] Yes  [A] Yes to All  [N] No  [L] No to All  [S] Suspend  [?] Help
(default is "Y"):a
DEBUG:1+ Set-PsDebug -step; foreach ($i in 1..3) {$i}
1
2
3
```

Not all objects are created equal. Just because that old COM object had a method called *create()* does not mean it exists in Windows PowerShell.

# General PowerShell Scripting Guidelines

This appendix details Microsoft Windows PowerShell scripting guidelines. These scripting guidelines have been collected from more than a dozen different script writers from around the world. Most of these are Microsoft employees actively involved in the world of Windows PowerShell. Some are non-Microsoft employees such as network administrators and consultants who use Windows PowerShell on a daily basis to improve their work/life balance. Not every script will adhere to all of these guidelines; however, you will find that the closer you adhere to these guidelines, the easier your scripts will be to understand and to maintain. They will not necessarily be easier to write, but they will be easier to manage, and you will find that your total cost of ownership on the scripts should be lowered significantly. In the end, I only have three requirements for a script: that it is easy to read, easy to understand, and easy to maintain.

## General script construction

This section will look at some general considerations for the overall construction of scripts. This includes the use of functions, a related module, and other considerations.

### Include functions in the script that uses the function

While it is possible to use an include file or dot-source a function within Windows PowerShell, it can become a support nightmare. If you know which function you want to use, but don't know which script provides it, you have to go looking (unless the function resides in a module stored in a known location). If a script provides the function you want but has other elements that you don't want, it's hard to pick and choose from the script file. Additionally, you must be very careful when it comes to variable-naming conventions because you could end up with conflicting variable names. When you use an include file, you no longer have a portable script. It must always travel with the function library.

I use functions in my scripts because it makes them easier to read and maintain. If I were to store these functions in separate files and then dot-source them, then neither of my two personal objectives of function use would really be met.

There is one other consideration: when a script references an external script containing functions, there now exists a relationship that must not be disturbed. If, for instance, you decide you would like to update the function, you may not remember how many external scripts are calling this function and how it will affect their performance and operation. If there is only one script calling the function, then the maintenance is easy. However, for only one script, just copy the silly thing into the script file itself and be done with the whole business. The best way to deal with these situations is to store the functions in modules.

# Use full cmdlet names and full parameter names

There are several advantages to spelling out cmdlet names and avoiding the use of aliases in scripts. First of all, this makes your scripts nearly self-documenting and therefore much easier to read. Secondly, it makes the scripts resilient to alias changes by the user and more compatible with future versions of Windows PowerShell. This is easy to do using the IntelliSense feature of the Windows PowerShell 3.0 ISE.

## Understanding the use of aliases

There are three kinds of aliases in Windows PowerShell: compatibility aliases, canonical aliases, and user-defined aliases.

You can identify the compatibility aliases by using this command:

```
Get-childitem alias: |
where-object {$_.options -notmatch "Readonly" }
```

The compatibility aliases are present in Windows PowerShell to provide an easier transition from using older command shells. You can remove the compatibility aliases by deleting aliases that are not ReadOnly. To do this every time you start Windows PowerShell, add the following command to your Windows PowerShell profile):

```
Get-childitem alias: |
where-object {$_.options -notmatch "Readonly" } |
remove-item
```

The canonical aliases were created specifically to make the Windows PowerShell cmdlets easier to use from within the Windows PowerShell console. Shortness of length and ease of typing were the primary driving factors in their creation. To find the canonical aliases, use this command:

```
Get-childitem alias: |
where-object {$_.options -match "Readonly" }
```

## If you must use an alias, only use canonical aliases in a script

You are reasonably safe in using the canonical aliases in a script; however, they make the script much harder to read. Also, because there are often several aliases for the same cmdlet, different users of Windows PowerShell may have their own personal favorite aliases. Additionally, because the canonical aliases are only read-only, even a canonical alias can be removed. But worse than deleting an alias is changing its meaning.

### Always use the *description* property when creating an alias

When adding aliases to your profile, you may wish to specify the *read-only* or *constant* options. You should always include the *description* property for your personal aliases and make the description something that is relatively constant. Here is an example from my personal Windows PowerShell profile:

```
New-Alias -Name gh -Value Get-Help -Description "mred alias"
New-Alias -Name ga -Value get-alias -Description "mred alias"
```

## Use *Get-Item* to convert path strings to rich types

This is actually a pretty cool trick. When working with a listing of files, if you use the *Get-Content* cmdlet, you can only read each line and have it as a path to work with. If, however, you use *Get-Item*, then you have an object with a corresponding number of both properties and methods to work with. Here's an example that illustrates this:

```
$files = Get-Content "filelist.txt" |
Get-Item $files |
Foreach-object { $_.Fullname }
```

# General script readability

The following are points to keep in mind to promote the readability of your script:

- When creating an alias, include the *-description* parameter, and use it when searching for your personal aliases. An example of this is shown here (a better approach is to load the aliases from a private module. This way, the *modulepath* parameter also loads).

```
Get-Alias |
where-object { $_.description -match 'mred' } |
Format-Table -Property "    ",name, definition -autosize `
            -hideTableHeaders
```

- Scripts should provide help. Use comment-based help to do this.

- All procedures should begin with a brief comment describing what they do. This description should not describe the implementation details (how the procedure works) because these often change over time, resulting in unnecessary comment-maintenance work, or worse, erroneous comments. Place comments on individual lines—do not use inline comments.

- Arguments passed to a function should be described when their purpose is not obvious and when the function expects the arguments to be in a specific range.

- Return values for variables that are changed by a function should also be described at the beginning of each function.

- Every important variable declaration should include an inline comment describing the use of the variable if the name of the variable is not obvious.

- Variables and functions should be named clearly to ensure that inline comments are only needed for complex functions.

- When creating a complex function with multiple code blocks, place an inline comment for each closing curly bracket at the end of the closing brace.

- At the beginning of your script, you should include an overview that describes the script, significant objects and cmdlets, and any unique requirements for the script.

- When naming functions, use the verb-noun construction used by cmdlet names.

- Scripts should use named parameters if they accept more than one argument. If a script only accepts a single argument, then it is okay to use an unnamed (positional) argument.

- Always assume that the users will copy your script and modify it to meet their needs. Place comments in the code to facilitate this process.

- Never assume the current path. Always use the full path, either via an environment variable or an explicitly named path.

## Formatting your code

Screen space should be conserved as much as possible while still allowing code formatting to reflect logical structure and nesting. Here are a few suggestions:

- Indent standard nested blocks by at least two spaces.

- Block overview comments for a function by using the Windows PowerShell multiline comment feature.

- Block the highest-level statements, with each nested block indented an additional two spaces.

- You should align the begin and end script block brackets. This will make it easier to follow the code flow.

- Avoid single-line statements. In addition to making it easier to follow the flow of the code, this also makes it easier when you end up searching for a missing curly bracket.

- Break each pipelined object at the pipe. Leave all pipes on the right. Do this unless it is a very short, simple pipe statement.

- Avoid line continuation—the backtick character (`). The exception here is when not using line continuation would cause the user to have to scroll to read the code or the output—generally around 90 characters. One way to avoid extremely long command lines for cmdlets with a large number of parameters is through the use of hash tables and splatting of parameters to Windows PowerShell cmdlets.

- Scripts should follow Pascal-case guidelines for long variable names—the same as Windows PowerShell parameters.

- Scripts should use the *Write-Progress* cmdlet if they take more than 1 or 2 seconds to run.

- Consider supporting the *-whatif* and *-confirm* parameters in your functions as well as in your scripts, especially if they will change system state. Following is an example using the *-whatif* parameter:

```
param(
      [switch]$whatif
     )

function funwhatif()
 {
   "what if: Perform operation xxxx"
 }

if($whatif)
   {
    funwhatif #calls the funwhatif() function
   }
```

- If your script does not accept a variable set of arguments, you should check the value of *$args.count* and call the *help* function if the number is incorrect. Here is an example:

```
if($args.count -ge 0)
   {
    "wrong number of arguments"
    Funhelp  #calls the funhelp() function
   }
```

- If your script does not accept any arguments, you should use code such as the following:

```
If($args -ge 0) { funhelp }
```

## Working with functions

The following are points to keep in mind when working with your functions. It will make your code easier to read and understand.

- Functions should handle mandatory parameter checking. To make this possible, use parameter property attributes.

- Utility or shared functions should be placed in a module.

- If you are writing a function library script, consider using feature and parameter variable names that incorporate a unique name to minimize the chances of conflict with other variables in the scripts that call them. It is best to store these function libraries in modules to facilitate sharing and use.

- Consider supporting standard parameters when it makes sense for your script. The easiest way to do this is to implement cmdlet binding.

## Creating template files

The following are points to keep in mind when creating template files. Create templates that can be used for different types of scripts. Some examples might be WMI scripts, ADSI scripts, and ADO scripts. You can then add these templates to the Windows PowerShell ISE as snippets by using the *New-ISESnippet* cmdlet. When you are creating your templates, consider the following:

- Add in common functions that you would use on a regular basis.

- Do not hard-code specific values that the connection strings might require: server names, input file paths, output file paths, and so on. Instead, contain these values in variables.

- Do not hard-code version information into the template.

- Make sure you include comments where the template will require modification to be made functional.

- You may want to turn your templates into code snippets to facilitate their usage.

## Functions

When writing your own functions, there are some things you may want to consider:

- Create highly specialized functions. Good functions do one thing well.

- Make the function completely self-contained. Good functions should be portable.

- Alphabetize the functions in your script if possible. This promotes readability and maintainability.

- Give your functions descriptive names and follow verb-noun naming convention. Nouns should be singular. If the function name becomes too long, create an alias for the function and store the alias in the same module as the function.

- Every function should have a single output point (this does not include the error, verbose, or debug streams).

- Every function should have a single entry point.

- Use parameters to avoid problems with local and global variable scopes.

- Implement the common parameters *-verbose*, *-debug*, *-whatif*, and *-confirm* where appropriate to promote reusability.

# Variables, constants, and naming

When creating variables and constants, and when naming, there are some things to consider.

- Avoid hard-coded numbers. When calling methods or functions, avoid hard-coding numeric literals. Instead, create a constant that is descriptive enough that someone reading the code would be able to figure out what it is supposed to do. In the ServiceDependencies.ps1 script, a portion of which follows, you use a number to offset the printout. This number is determined by the position of a certain character in the output. Rather than just writing "+14," you create a constant with a descriptive name. Refer to Chapter 12, "Remoting WMI," for more information on this script. The applicable portion of the code is shown here:

```
New-Variable -Name c_padline -value 14 -option constant
Get-WmiObject -Class Win32_DependentService -computername $computer |
Foreach-object `
  {
   "=" * ((([wmi]$_.dependent).pathname).length + $c_padline)
```

- Do not recycle variables. Recycled variables are referred to as *unfocused variables*. Variables should serve a single purpose, and those that do are called *focused variables*.

- Give variables descriptive names. Remember that you can use tab completion to simplify typing.

- Minimize variable scope. If you are only going to use a variable in a function, then declare it in the function.

- When a constant is needed, use a read-only variable instead. Remember that constants cannot be deleted, nor can their value change.

- Avoid hard-coding values into method calls or in the worker section of the script. Instead, place values into variables.

- When possible, group your variables into a single section of each level of the script.

- Avoid using Hungarian Notation, in which you embed type names into the variable names. Remember that everything in PowerShell is basically an object, so there is no value in naming a variable *$objWMI*.

- There are times when it makes sense to use the following: *bln, int, dbl, err, dte,* and *str*. This is due to the fact that Windows PowerShell is a strongly typed language. It just acts like it is not.

- Scripts should avoid populating the global variable space. Instead, consider passing values to a function by reference *[ref]*.

# Index

## Symbols

# S

## V

# X

# About the Author

 **ED WILSON** is a well-known scripting expert who delivers popular scripting workshops to Microsoft customers and employees worldwide. He's written several books on Windows scripting, including *Windows PowerShell™ 2.0 Best Practices*, *Microsoft® Windows PowerShell™ Step By Step*, and *Microsoft® VBScript Step by Step*. Ed is a senior consultant at Microsoft Corporation and writes Hey, Scripting Guy!, one of the most popular TechNet blogs.

# How To Download Your eBook

Thank you for purchasing this Microsoft Press® title. Your companion PDF eBook is ready to download from O'Reilly Media, official distributor of Microsoft Press titles.

**To download your eBook, go to**
**http://go.microsoft.com/FWLink/?Linkid=224345**
and follow the instructions.

Please note: You will be asked to create a free online account and enter the access code below.

Your access code:

> QWJQDHL

Windows PowerShell™ 3.0 Step by Step

**Your PDF eBook allows you to:**

- Search the full text
- Print
- Copy and paste

Best yet, you will be notified about free updates to your eBook.

If you ever lose your eBook file, you can download it again just by logging in to your account.

Need help? Please contact:
**mspbooksupport@oreilly.com**
or call 800-889-8969.

**Please note**: This access code is non-transferable and is void if altered or revised in any way. It may not be sold or redeemed for cash, credit, or refund.

# What do you think of this book?

We want to hear from you!
To participate in a brief online survey, please visit:

**microsoft.com/learning/booksurvey**

Tell us how well this book meets your needs—what works effectively, and what we can do better. Your feedback will help us continually improve our books and learning resources for you.

Thank you in advance for your input!

CPSIA information can be obtained at www.ICGtesting.com
Printed in the USA
BVOW10s1514200713

325839BV00009B/9/P